CRICK

ALSO BY MATTHEW COBB

The Genetic Age: Our Perilous Quest to Edit Life

The Idea of the Brain: A History

Life's Greatest Secret: The Race to Crack the Genetic Code

*The Egg and Sperm Race: The Seventeenth-Century Scientists
Who Unravelled the Secrets of Sex, Life and Growth*

Smell: A Very Short Introduction

The Resistance: The French Fight Against the Nazis

Eleven Days in August: The Liberation of Paris in 1944

CRICK

A MIND IN MOTION –
FROM DNA TO THE BRAIN

Matthew Cobb

Profile Books

First published in Great Britain in 2025 by
PROFILE BOOKS LTD
29 Cloth Fair
London EC1A 7JQ

www.profilebooks.com

Michal McClure: 'Peyote Poem' first appeared in *Hymns to St Geryon*
(SF: Auerhahn Press, 1959); 'Moiré', was originally published in
The Paris Review, Winter 1971; 'Double Moire', was published by
Old City Publishing, and later reproduced in *Mysteriosus and Other
Poems* (NY: New Directions Publishing Corporation, 2010).

1 3 5 7 9 10 8 6 4 2

Typeset in Palatino by MacGuru Ltd
Printed and bound in Great Britain by
CPI Group (UK) Ltd, Croydon CR0 4YY

A CIP catalogue record for this book is available from the British Library.

Our product safety representative in the EU is Authorised
Rep Compliance Ltd., Ground Floor, 71 Lower Baggot Street,
Dublin, D02 P593, Ireland. www.arccompliance.com

ISBN 978 1 80081 105 8
eISBN 978 1 80081 106 5
Audio ISBN 978 1 80522 637 6

For Thomas Purcell and Clive Boothman.

CONTENTS

The whole of anything is never told.

Henry James

PROLOGUE

In July 1959, Francis Crick, the co-discoverer of the DNA double helix, took a psychedelic trip on peyote. Not directly – his experiences with hallucinogens lay in the future – but through the power of poetry.

Famous among scientists, if little known to the public, Crick, aged forty-three, was winding down after an intensive eight-month academic visit to the USA. He was now relaxing in Berkeley, just over the bay from San Francisco, with his second wife, Odile, their two young daughters, Gabrielle and Jacqueline, and the girls' French governess.[1] Their California vacation was exactly what they had hoped for, as he explained to a colleague: 'We have a very pleasant house, in just the style Odile likes – a wonderful view; a patio, full of fuchsias, lemons, hummingbirds, etc, where they can sunbathe in the nude; also a grand piano (my left hand is awful), etc.'[2]

On weekends, the Cricks would drive over to the lively North Beach area of San Francisco; on one of those outings, Francis walked into the City Lights bookstore on the edge of Chinatown. Before the Hippies, there was the Beat Generation – a cultural movement that rebelled against the social norms of post-war America and included the novelist Jack Kerouac and the poet Allen Ginsberg – and City Lights was its epicentre. Curious, Crick went down into the basement where his attention was caught by a brown paper envelope that contained a long, thin, folded broadsheet, upon which was printed a work entitled 'Peyote Poem'.[3]

Around a hundred lines of centred text, the poem described the mind-bending effects of chewing the bitter crown of the peyote cactus. It shouted capital letters, was repeatedly scored with horizontal lines, and was signed 'Mike McClure'. Although the twenty-six-year-old McClure was renowned among the Beats, Crick had never heard of him and did not even know what peyote was.* Nevertheless, he was fascinated by what he later called the poem's radiant quality:

> *There is no Time. I am visited by a man*
> *who is the god of foxes*
> *there is dirt under the nails of his paw*
> *fresh from his den.*
> *We smile at one another in recognition.*

Francis was particularly taken by the following stanza:

THIS IS THE POWERFUL KNOWLEDGE
we smile with it.

These words described his feelings exactly, he said.

On impulse, Crick bought McClure's poem and on his return to England a few weeks later pinned it up in the hallway of his Cambridge home. It would remain there for several years, eventually joined by a copy of one of his towering achievements, the genetic code. He kept the poem for the rest of his life.[4]

Francis later explained his interest in McClure's work, and in poetry in general:

---

* He would have heard of its active ingredient, mescaline, the effects of which Aldous Huxley had described a few years earlier in his influential book *The Doors of Perception*.

I hope nobody still thinks that scientists are dull, unimagina-
tive people, forever measuring things in cold blood. Every
profession has its dullies but good scientists are, if anything,
romantically attached to their subject and often passionately
involved in its pursuit. It is almost true that science itself is
poetry enough for them. But there is no effective substitute
for the subtle interplay of words and from time to time one
becomes wearied by the exact formulations of science and
longs for a poetry which speaks to one's bones.[5]

As his fascination with 'Peyote Poem' shows, Francis Crick was anything but dull. When he later experimented with various recreational
drugs, he came to appreciate how McClure's poem not only spoke
to his bones but was also a pretty accurate description of the psychedelic experience.

In the 1970s, Crick became a good friend of McClure, whose
poetry he admired for what he described as its fury and imagery.
McClure even dedicated a poem – 'Moiré' – to him, which made
Francis feel very flattered.[6] McClure's fusion of science and emotion
resonated within Crick in ways that older poetry did not. Although
he appreciated the poems of, say, Yeats and Eliot, he dismissed their
mystical and religious ideas as 'patently ridiculous to someone who
lives every day of his life among atoms and molecules, pondering on
the evolution of the Universe, the origin of life and trying to explain
the almost inexplicable oddity of biological organisms'. In McClure's
writings Francis found something thrilling that echoed his own view
of the Universe and our place within it:

The worlds in which I myself live, the private world of personal
reactions, the biological world (animals and plants and even
bacteria chase each other through the poems), the world of the
atom and molecule, the stars and the galaxies, are all there;
and in between, above and below, stands man, the howling
mammal, contrived out of 'meat' by chance and necessity.[7]

*

Francis Crick was one of the most significant scientists of the twentieth century. In 1947, aged thirty-one and with his research career in physics derailed by the Second World War, Crick decided to make an abrupt change and focus on two fundamental biological problems: life and the brain.[8] Remarkably, that is exactly what he did – over the following half century he made decisive contributions to both these fields, becoming one of the most significant figures of the period, his ideas influencing generations of scientists. His aim was not just to make discoveries about two of the major riddles of science, he was also driven by his desire to enable us to understand our true place in the Universe, shorn of superstition and religion, while remaining open to the flux of perception and emotion that he found in the poetry of McClure and others.

Over the years, he cultivated an ability to see the broad implications of a particular finding and then develop a theoretical understanding of that bigger picture. His insights into the nature of the genetic code and how genes work, and the implications for evolution, remain with us today, while in his second career in neuroscience, his drive and brilliance enabled him to exert a major influence in areas as diverse as neuroanatomy and computer models of behaviour, as well as sparking global interest in the physical basis of consciousness. For all this work he is rightly considered to be one of the most influential biologists who ever lived, his name ranking with Darwin and Mendel.

But although this is the story of the mind of a great scientist, it is above all a story of collaboration, of how Crick adopted a way of thinking and working that involved asking fundamental questions and pursuing them through intense encounters with others.

The key opportunity that transformed his world and brought his character and intellect into focus began in October 1951, when, as a mature PhD student at Cambridge, he met the young American Jim Watson, nearly twelve years his junior. Watson wanted to study viruses, while Crick was working on proteins; they eventually began thinking about something completely different – the structure of DNA. This relatively simple molecule is bound up with proteins in all cells in all organisms, and at the time it was widely assumed that this protein–DNA complex was somehow implicated in heredity, although the evidence was patchy.

After an initial attempt to crack the structure of DNA in autumn 1951 led to embarrassing failure, the pair returned to the problem at the beginning of 1953 and finally succeeded after five weeks of intensive work. They were able to make their discovery in part because they were given access to key results from Rosalind Franklin, a researcher at King's College London, who later became a close friend of the Cricks. Despite what many people believe, they did not steal Franklin's data; as you will see, the research for this book has revealed the breakthrough to have been far more collaborative than anyone realised.

The discovery of the structure of DNA was of immense significance for both science and society, indelibly linking the surnames of Watson and Crick in the global imagination. Without Watson, Crick would never have discovered the structure of DNA; indeed, he would probably never have worked on the molecule. But the encounter with Watson was not just a chance meeting: Crick had been looking for someone like the young American. Francis was at his best when collaborating with others, developing his ideas by constant discussions, usually with one interlocutor. Although there were many such figures in his life, a handful of them were especially significant.

First there was Georg Kreisel, a brilliant Austrian-born mathematician and logician. They met during the war and remained close for the rest of their lives, exchanging letters that, on Kreisel's part, were often bizarre and sexually explicit. In 1996, Crick said because of their 'frankness' Kreisel's letters were unlikely to be published in their lifetimes, 'but they should make for amusing reading for posterity'.[9] Despite his unkempt appearance and odd behaviour, Kreisel had an astonishing range of friends and acquaintances, from the writer Iris Murdoch to the singer Yves Montand, from the actor Alastair Sim to the mathematician Kurt Gödel, from Wittgenstein to the Aga Khan. As one of Crick's friends, Clover Southwell, wrote while on a visit to America in 1970:

I've met a whole host of people, almost all totally nice. But far the nicest and most exciting is Kreisel. ... I had inordinate curiosity to meet him, but I never expected to actually enjoy it! I don't think I've ever before met such an awake person, or someone who gave me such a feeling of not missing a thing.[10]

On Kreisel's seventieth birthday, Francis remarked: 'I have known him now for about fifty years. Over that time I have been immensely influenced by his powerful intellect. … If I had never met him my life would have been very different.'[11] Without Kreisel, Crick would not have been Crick.

Then there was Watson, with his confidence, ambition and enthusiasm. Their close working relationship was remarkably brief, focused on those few weeks in early 1953, followed two years later by another, less dramatic, few months. Although they remained friends, even that connection was torn to breaking point in the 1960s when Crick became enraged by the proposed publication of Watson's fictionalised account of the discovery of the structure of DNA, *The Double Helix*. They did not speak for nearly three years.

Crick next drew inspiration from the energy and experimental skill of the South African biologist Sydney Brenner. For nearly two decades their scientific lives were intimately bound up as they relentlessly argued virtually every day in Cambridge, resolving some of the main issues facing molecular biology, making fundamental discoveries and charting the way towards new approaches to studying the nervous system.

Finally, from the late 1980s until the end of his life, Crick worked with the German-American neuroscientist Christof Koch. Despite their differences in age and outlook – Koch was forty years younger than Crick, and a Catholic; he was also a rock-climber, revelling in physical effort and danger, neither of which appealed to Francis – together they revitalised the scientific study of consciousness, a subject that was widely considered to be moribund.

With each one of these thinkers – all men, all younger than him – Crick was able to find an intellectual foil or sounding-board, someone with whom he could argue, debate, and develop ideas. Those interactions enabled him to hone his thinking even further, reinforcing his reputation and influence. Whatever his undoubted intellectual ability, his greatest insights emerged through interactions with others.

*

The key other person, for over half a century, was his wife, Odile. Vivacious, talented and tolerant, she shared his enjoyment of art and poetry. Furthermore, they not only reciprocated love and affection, they both had a taste for racy parties and bohemian fun and games. An artist who excelled in portraiture, Odile sometimes feigned ignorance of all things scientific, but she famously drew the figure of the double helix that appeared in Watson and Crick's 1953 *Nature* paper describing the structure of DNA; indeed, she made illustrations for several of his scientific articles, the last appearing only a year before his death. She clearly grasped his unique way of thinking, as she explained to Kreisel in 1971:

> Although I may not have the intellectual equipment to appreciate all Francis's intellectual activities, I am nonetheless capable of recognising his genius for selecting the most vital and essential problem out of a number of interesting and tempting ones, and to illuminate it in such a way as to make it intelligible and convincing at a number of levels.[12]

Odile's interests in writers such as Simone de Beauvoir, Solzhenitsyn, Proust and Norbert Wiener, the founder of cybernetics, show that she was an intellectual in her own right. However, as May Brenner – Sydney's wife – recalled after Crick's death, this was a time when women were often relegated to a supporting role:

> How much were we part of the scene, of the scenario? How much were we in the play; the play of the great scientific discoveries, the great energy of working and trying and dreaming and getting? In that play we were the little maid who came with the tray and said, 'Tea, Master', and walked out again. That was our role. We weren't in the story of the play at all. No, I think Odile would agree with me.[13]

As well as pursuing her artistic interests, Odile ran their household, keeping track of the bills and raising their daughters, and was a

supportive stepmother to Michael, Crick's son from his first marriage. She was also the enthusiastic organiser of their Cambridge parties, which involved dancing, drinking, fancy dress and sometimes more. For example, in May 1956, while Francis was visiting the USA, Odile organised a party full of arty Cambridge friends – potters, photographers, painters – as well as scientists, including Watson, who was briefly visiting Cambridge at the time, and Rosalind Franklin, who came up with her research group from London. The party went on until four in the morning; at another party that same evening Odile did a toreador dance with Don Caspar, one of Franklin's research team.[14]

Just as Crick would not have achieved what he did without his co-thinkers, he could only be the man he was because of Odile, whom he loved deeply and unquestioningly. Despite the ups and downs, they both flourished in this relationship, which lasted for over fifty-five years. Towards the end of her life, she reflected on their marriage: 'When I married him I knew that he was a very unusual person and that sort of attracted me, because in fact he was the one person I'd ever met with whom I would never be bored. I would get irritated, or maddened, but not bored!'[15]

The Cricks' marriage was the scene of deep and long-lasting friendships with scores of people including some of the most influential scientists and thinkers of the second half of the twentieth century;

they were also relatively relaxed about sexual encounters with other people. In 1971 Odile explained to Kreisel that the very presence of an attractive, intelligent woman 'brings out in Francis a show of verbal fireworks and the compulsion to make an impression takes over completely. Anything which gets in the way is either brushed aside or totally ignored.'[16] She knew of Crick's many brief affairs, and her letters to him suggest that she was either amused or interested by them and that she also sometimes profited from their arrangement. No doubt there was sometimes pain or jealousy, but that was the way they lived their lives. Crick's sexual appetite presumably shared a psychological root with his need for intense intellectual interaction and appears to have been as much part of his character as his interest in psychedelic drugs and poetry.

None of Crick's affairs involved students and virtually none were with scientists or anyone over whom he exercised professional influence. In general, the affairs appear to have been conducted with mutual discretion and enthusiasm. In 1963, two of his old flames met up in Paris and spent a happy afternoon sharing stories, which they described in a letter to him: 'We talked a lot about you (in French): *Francis est merveilleux, unique* etc. ... We have been talking so much of you that it is like you are there with us.'[17] There are very few reproaches in the correspondence from his lovers and not one of the women involved has gone public or published any of his letters.

Not all his approaches were well received. I have found three examples; there may have been others. After a Cambridge dinner party in the 1960s, one woman complained that Crick 'took quite a fancy to me which I did not regard pleasantly'; a decade later a Cambridge tutor told Francis that his behaviour had distressed her but insisted she wanted to be friends and invited him, and Odile, for drinks at her college. The example of Nancy Hopkins, who became a leading advocate for women scientists, reveals how complex and contradictory attitudes at the time can now appear. Hopkins has described how, in 1965, Crick visited Watson's Harvard laboratory where she was a PhD student; he approached her while she was hard at work at the microscope and shockingly put his hands on her breasts. She recalled that she had not felt at all harassed but instead was 'very embarrassed, but for him'.[18]

Nevertheless, this is a biography focusing on Crick's mind and his scientific work and unlike, say, Picasso or the thriller writer John le Carré, for whom the work and the affairs were completely intertwined, Crick's affairs shed no light on the different phases of his thinking.[19] Furthermore, although his personal archive contains many letters from his lovers, his side of the correspondence is lacking. Given that these affairs do not provide any direct insight into Crick's thinking, the names and the details are simply not our business. Only a few affairs are alluded to here, anonymised and in the vaguest of terms, out of respect for the privacy of the women and their families, and of the Crick family.

*

Crick was tall – over six foot – with bright eyes that, according to his passports, were grey in his youth and blue in later life.[20] His sandy hair soon thinned and eventually turned white, while his sideburns and eyebrows grew lush. In his prime, Crick resembled the 1940s film star George Sanders, including his slightly louche air, but with shyness replacing Sanders' hint of menace. But far more than his appearance, it was his charisma and brilliant mind that made him so attractive to both sexes.

Many readers' first encounter with Francis will have been when they read 'I have never seen Francis Crick in a modest mood' – the striking opening sentence of Jim Watson's *The Double Helix*, a book that reveals Watson's deep affection for his friend. I want to show the reader why so many people fell under Crick's spell. I sensed that pull, twice, although I never met him. First, in writing my 2015 book *Life's Greatest Secret*, which describes the cracking of the genetic code after the discovery of the structure of DNA, I was amazed by Crick's brilliance and insight. Then, while working on *The Idea of the Brain* (2020), I found to my surprise that Crick repeatedly muscled his way to the forefront of the chapters dealing with modern neuroscience, shaping the field in the most profound ways. Before beginning my research, my vague impression had been that his work on the brain and on consciousness was inconsequential. I was completely wrong. The challenge of understanding how someone could have such a sustained and varied intellectual output spanning more than half a century spurred me to write this book.

There are already two biographies of Crick, each aimed at different audiences and with different objectives. In 2006 Matt Ridley published a terrific brief introduction to Crick's life, *Francis Crick: Discoverer of the Genetic Code*; three years later, the veteran historian of science Robert Olby, who had tracked Crick's life and work for four decades, produced *Francis Crick: Hunter of Life's Secrets*.[21] Olby's work is primarily an academic biography, while Ridley's shorter and more polished account gives a clearer overview of Crick's character and activities. There is also an academic summary of Crick's life, written by two friends and colleagues, Mark Bretscher and Graeme Mitchison, which captures both Crick the scientist and their warm feelings for Crick the man.[22] All are highly recommended.

This book will navigate a middle path, providing the reader with an understanding of Crick's brilliance and influence, while exploring his character, interests and personal life, including his flaws. It also emphasises his contribution to neuroscience to a greater degree than previous studies. Crick's scientific writings and ideas are described in a way that should be easy for the general reader to understand, but if you find yourself struggling, follow Crick's advice to the readers of his own books and skip the hard bits.

The vision of Crick presented here draws on his vast correspondence, which spans over fifty years and reveals not only his scientific interests, but also his generosity.[23] While occasionally impatient with cranks, he responded kindly to those in distress who sought solutions he could not provide, and he encouraged teachers and students, often responding in detail to requests for information or explanation.[24] In California, he regularly gave talks to school students; his archive is full of grateful letters from children who he inspired. One high school student wrote in 1990: 'I cannot describe to you *how wonderful* it was. Your presence brought up such emotions as inspiration, confidence and hope for the future. I also enjoyed seeing and understanding that you are a real person just like me!'[25]

With colleagues, he could be laconic. In 1992, as there was excitement about the forthcoming fortieth anniversary of the discovery of the double helix, he initially declined to be involved, explaining that he could not understand the obsession with scientific anniversaries, before closing his argument with a phrase that revealed the influence of his years in California: 'Let me remind you of the words of the Tao Te Ching: "Practice not-doing, and everything will fall into place."'[26]

Crick would undoubtedly have been dismayed at any interest in his personal life – an intensely private man, his slim memoir *What Mad Pursuit* contains more about X-ray crystallography than it does about his family. He initially deplored *The Double Helix* for its gossipy tone, which he considered intrusive: for decades he was shy of publicity and reluctant to allow his portrait to be reproduced. In 1964, *Life* magazine requested permission to print a charming photograph of him dancing with his daughter Gabrielle at the Nobel Prize ball two years earlier; Crick scrawled his response to a secretary 'Tell him "not a hope".'[27]

Although Crick's surviving children, Michael and Gabrielle, have been kind enough to talk to me, to read the manuscript and to correct my errors, this is not an authorised biography, nor are they responsible for my view of their father. Francis himself might not have liked the idea of this book being written, but I like to think he would have enjoyed reading it, had it been about someone else.[28]

*

The most interesting parts of someone's life are surely those where they differed from the ideas, attitudes and mores of their world. In Crick's case, these moments relate to his science, as he produced brilliant insights that have since guided the work of hundreds of thousands of scientists. In other respects, his outlook and attitudes reflected the times he lived in, rather than shaping them.

There were very few points where political and social events intruded on Crick's life; those that did occur were generally related to culture rather than politics. I have read thousands of his letters, but have found only one which made even a passing reference to current affairs (the 1990–91 Gulf War); in their decades of close friendship Christof Koch could recall only one discussion of contemporary events, on 9/11.[29] This shows that apart from his research, Francis was *of* his time but not always entirely *in* it – his inner world and his interactions with his loved ones, colleagues and friends seem to have been enough for him.

Growing up, his worldview was formed by his well-to-do family, as England emerged from the First World War still marked by Edwardian values. The Second World War later shook up many staid attitudes, but by that time Crick's social and political outlook was more or less fixed in the form it had taken in childhood. Although he was profoundly radical in his scientific thinking and in his views on religion, when it came to political and social issues he generally accepted the established views of his time. As May Brenner recalled: 'Francis was a very conservative gentleman politically and leant to the right in all political issues. (…) He was very, very anti-religion. But he was still conservative.'[30]

Crick was not interested in politics, he did not possess a radio or a television until the 1980s, he did not read newspapers* and claimed never to have voted.[31] When it came to the interaction between science and society, his vision was equally narrow. Overall, his approach was distinctly Edwardian – applying current scientific ideas to complex societal questions was, it appeared to Francis at the time, obvious and straightforward. Thus, for the first part of his life he held eugenicist views that were focused on class – a typical early twentieth-century English obsession. When controversies over the link between genetics, race and IQ blew up at the beginning of the 1970s, he prudently limited his public involvement, but in his private letters he expressed his belief in such a link, even though many scientists recognised that the underlying data were unreliable. From the mid-1970s onwards, his attitude became more circumspect; he recognised that these issues were more complex than he had previously imagined, but his solution was simply to avoid engaging with them.

In a way, this turned into a virtue. Many Nobel Prize winners pronounce on all sorts of questions that are outside their area of expertise, often encouraged by the media. Francis generally avoided

---

*In the 1950s he read the *Observer*, a British Sunday newspaper; when he lived in California he subscribed to *The Economist*.

such temptations. Even when the Secretary-General of the United Nations, Kofi Annan, asked for his advice (along with that of other Nobelists), Crick's reply was appropriately modest: 'I am flattered that you should want to ask me for advice and ideas, but I am afraid I am quite the wrong person to help you. I try to avoid both administration and politics, and have little knowledge of either.'[32]

That Crick's penetrating mind did not exercise its critical faculties on political issues highlights what should be obvious – he was not a saint or a hero and, no matter what graffiti in Cambridge might have proclaimed in the 1960s, nor was he a candidate for the post of God.[33] He was, instead, an extraordinarily clever man with limits to his interests and perception.

One of the tasks of a biographer – and of a reader – is to understand why people in the past thought the way they did. Some readers may be shocked by some of Crick's ideas and behaviour but they were not unusual at the time. This is not to excuse his personal views but rather to explain them. More interestingly, other readers will be disappointed by these aspects of his life. This highlights the fact that Crick's ideas in molecular biology and neuroscience not only seem modern, they created our modernity. Because of this influence, and the affection felt for his ideas by many scientists, it seems logical to assume that his social positions were equally up to date. But we must remember he was born in 1916; you would not necessarily expect your grandparent or great-grandparent to agree with you on today's cultural and social questions. That it nevertheless feels as though Crick should be modern in every respect shows quite how influential his scientific thinking has been.

*

Few of us live a linear life that proceeds from birth to death with only one love, one interest, one job, one home, and yet many of us have the impression of continuity and consistency. Similarly, the lives of Francis Crick were multiple, with complex braids, but they nevertheless formed a whole. Some of his attitudes changed from the 1970s onwards, through a combination of mellowing with age, moving to California and beginning to study neuroscience – he recognised he was an absolute beginner in this new field and adopted a degree of reserve as the Edwardian confidence of his Cambridge years gave way to a more relaxed West Coast seventies vibe.

Throughout this slow change, these two phases of his life, there was a continuity: endless curiosity, striking generosity and an appetite for life in all its aspects. There was also a tremendous sense of fun – one of the positive words he would use to describe a person, an encounter or an event. Another word he used was 'electrified', to describe those flashes of enlightenment that accompanied discovery – as he put it in 1961, the quiet moment when, out of the whole world, only he and maybe one close colleague knew the solution to a major riddle. That sensation, so rare for most of us, Francis felt many times as he perceived meaning in the fog of confusion and grasped the shape of reality beneath the veil of sometimes contradictory experimental data.

Crick's whole life can be seen as an attempt to chase the intellectual high produced by such realisation, that flash of insight that Michael McClure called THE POWERFUL KNOWLEDGE. The aim of this biography is to show how Francis was able to produce such extraordinary results in such a wide range of topics. It is the life of a great scientist, one of the most significant thinkers of the post-war world, whose influence will be felt throughout this century, and beyond.

This book is therefore for anyone who wonders how DNA came to be such a significant molecule and metaphor in our modern world, why there is such scientific interest in consciousness, or who, like me, wants to understand how someone can have arrived at such penetrating and influential ideas. It provides answers to these questions by exploring Crick's inner world, his enthusiasms and his astonishing capacity to relentlessly focus his thinking. It takes us into his mind.

Manchester, July 2025

BECOMING
CRICK

AVERAGELY BRIGHT

Childhood can reveal the outline of future fame, but in Crick's case there was nothing unusual about his early years, although according to family stories, there were portents. When Francis was born on 8 June 1916, his mother Annie was ambitious for her son and asked her sister Ethel to take the newborn child to the highest point of the house so that, as an adult, he would rise to the top, while a few years later an itinerant phrenologist told Annie that the bumps on the young Francis's skull were supposedly very striking.[1] Crick had a better explanation of his later success when he said that the course of his life, and the extraordinary global influence he eventually enjoyed, were both partly a matter of luck.[2]

That luck began from birth. His parents were a loving, encouraging pair, moderately wealthy and reasonably well-educated, although no one in either family had been to university. His father Harry ('Poppa') ran the family shoe- and boot-making company, while Annie ('Momma') had been a primary school teacher before their marriage – her family owned a string of shops.[3] Francis's childhood was shaped by the Edwardian twilight of early twentieth-century England – the Cricks lived in a comfortable house in the village of Weston Favell on the rural edge of Northampton, where the streets were lit by gas and Francis would join in the harvest, pitch-forking

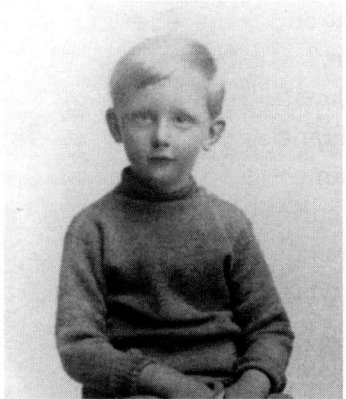

Francis as a young boy.

hay onto a horse-drawn cart. From his bedroom, he could see across the fields to the distant River Nene. The Cricks had a telephone – a rare luxury – and employed both a nanny and a housekeeper. In the evening the family would sing along as Annie played the piano (throughout his life, Francis enjoyed singing and had a fine voice; he also enjoyed playing the piano) or they would go to the local theatre – Harry and Annie also held play-readings at home. Harry loved playing bridge and as a young man had been a talented tennis player; as Francis grew older, he and his brother Anthony ('Tony'),* two years his junior, took up the sport and even watched the tennis at Wimbledon, where Harry had once played.[4]

All in all, the Cricks' family life – typical of the provincial middle class at the time – seems like something out of the pages of Richmal Crompton's *Just William* books, or a Noël Coward play. Harry and Annie Crick were members of the local Congregational Church but without strong beliefs. When, aged twelve, Francis told his beloved Momma he no longer wished to go to church, Annie was upset, but there was no great opposition from his family.[5] This decision was not prompted by any flash of insight or intellectual turmoil; instead, Francis gradually realised that religion held no emotional or explanatory power for him. Strictly speaking, he was not an atheist; as he

---

*Tony qualified as a physician in 1941. After his war service, he moved to New Zealand in 1948.

explained towards the end of his life, 'I am an agnostic, with a strong inclination to atheism.'[6]

Part of the explanation for this break with religion was that Francis – full name Francis Harry Compton Crick (as a young man he often signed his name 'Compton Crick'*) – had become fascinated by science. His deep curiosity about the world supposedly led to his family nickname, 'Craxie', although the link is not clear; at school he was more straightforwardly known as 'Crackers'.[7] Crick's interest in science was reinforced by sharing his uncle Walter's hobby of chemistry, which for Francis mainly seems to have been an opportunity to experiment with explosives – a near-miss in the family's garage led to a firm rule: bottles could be blown up only if they were immersed in a pail of water. There was also a family connection to Victorian science – Crick's paternal grandfather was an amateur geologist and biologist who corresponded with Darwin; extracts from one of his letters were included in Darwin's last published work, in *Nature*.[8]

A much greater influence on the young Francis than his uncle's tinkering or his grandfather's brush with scientific fame were the volumes of *The Children's Encyclopædia* that sat on a bookshelf at home. This wildly successful publication originally appeared in 1908 as a fortnightly magazine covering all aspects of culture, from science to mythology, geography to literature. The Cricks had the 1910 eight-volume bound edition and Francis found it engrossing:

> I read it all avidly, but it was the science that appealed to me most. What was the Universe like? What were atoms? How did things grow? I absorbed great chunks of explanation, revelling in the unexpectedness of it all, judged by the everyday world I saw around me. How marvellous to have discovered such things![9]

The kind of scientific questions covered in the *Encyclopædia* included basic chemistry, maths problems, physics, and many issues relating to anatomy and physiology, all based on the latest thinking.

---

* 'Compton' came from his mother's side of the family. Her maiden name was Wilkins – no relation to the DNA scientist Maurice Wilkins.

For example, the article 'Where Do Thoughts Come From?' told the young Crick: 'We know certainly that thoughts depend on the brain (…) we must regard the brain as the place where the real self lives.'[10] The range of subjects covered was so broad, and the scientific explanations so apparently cogent, that Francis began to worry that by the time he grew up there would be nothing left to discover. When he confided his concern to his mother, Annie laughed: 'Don't worry, Ducky! There will be plenty left for you to find out.'[11]

Much later, the precise language and simple but accurate explanations found in the pages of the *Encyclopædia* came to characterise Crick's writing and his public speaking; its influence was lifelong – not only did he hold on to the eight volumes until his death,* in 1993 he called it 'the book that most influenced me'.[12] There is no single key to understanding how Crick became the man he eventually was, but this book shaped his scientific outlook and interests in profound and varied ways.

Those volumes may have left other traces, too. The *Encyclopædia* was steeped in the politics of the British Empire, and many of its scientific articles were written by a leading eugenicist, Caleb Saleeby. Although there was nothing in the 1910 edition about reproduction, heredity, or the newly named gene, the eugenicist and racist views that dominated contemporary thinking ran through its pages. For example, the article on Australia dismissed the Aborigines as 'the ugliest and most uncivilised of all the native races. It is slow and difficult work to try and improve the blacks, who seem to be slowly dying out as a race; they have never been numerous nor of much account.'[13] There was also an illustration of three human skulls, from 'the Australian native, the lowest kind of man', to 'a European, the highest type of man', with a 'negro' in the middle.[14]

The Edwardian tenor of the *Encyclopædia*, from its lack of political curiosity, through its casual assumption of the superiority of the Empire, to its brash confidence in the power of science to change the world, found echoes in some of Crick's later views. These ideas were

---

*His son Michael now has them. In June 2023 Michael told me: 'Francis was a very good boy and (sadly) never made any marks or notes in the book. You can see from the ruffled pages that it has been heavily used.'

widespread in British culture throughout the twentieth century, and many persist to this day; it is striking that, when an adult, this cleverest of men did not seriously question them.

*

Francis went to school at the local grammar and then, from 1930, attended Mill Hill School on the northern outskirts of London, a boys' boarding school where his father and three uncles had also been pupils. By this point the Cricks were not quite so well off – the family firm had struggled after the stock market crash of 1929 and the footwear factory was eventually sold in 1932.[15] Harry now managed the company's shoe shops in London, so the family moved to Mill Hill, near to Francis's school (on a scholarship, he continued to be a boarder).[16]

School life was enjoyable, and although in many respects Mill Hill was traditional – there were daily religious services that bored him, and a compulsory cadet force – there were no beatings. Francis played in the school tennis team and, like his parents, enjoyed amateur theatrics, playing one of the ladies in the school's production of Gilbert and Sullivan's The Mikado.[17]

In the sixth form, he studied mathematics, physics and chemistry – biology was taught only to boys who were going to study medicine – and although he won a school chemistry prize and was undoubtedly clever (in his final year he gave a talk on how Niels Bohr's interpretation of the atom explained the periodic table), he was not superlative in any sense – he later described himself as an averagely bright child.[18] He mastered German and French, but his difficulties with Latin ('I was hopeless') may have contributed to his failure to get a scholarship at Oxford or Cambridge. Instead, in the autumn of 1935 he went to University College London (UCL), where he studied physics with mathematics.

Crick later said that the experimentally focused physics he learned at UCL was 'competent but a shade old-fashioned' – quantum mechanics, which was transforming physics at the time, was barely mentioned and the mathematics he was taught 'was what a previous generation of physicists had found useful'.[19] Again, he did not excel, gaining a respectable upper second degree. This was sufficient for UCL to accept him as a PhD student, studying what Francis later described as the dullest problem imaginable – how the viscosity of water, under pressure, changes with temperature. This project involved building equipment which Crick enjoyed but was not very good at (he was never very practical).

Financially supported by his uncle Arthur, who had made money as a pharmacist producing stomach powder, Francis moved into a flat on Coptic Street, next to the British Museum, which he shared with his friend Raoul Colinvaux, who later became a leading authority on insurance law. He soon began courting Doreen Dodd, whom he had first met at UCL when she was an English Literature student – she was now a civil servant.[20] Doreen was three years older than Francis; she was quite highly strung and found the stress of university life so great that she twice withdrew from her studies. Tall and glamorous, with an appetite for crossword puzzles, friends considered that she and Francis were a good match.[21]

*

While all this is useful background, it does not reveal any sign of what later made Crick unique. Hundreds of thousands of middle-class Edwardian children read *The Children's Encyclopædia* and played with chemistry sets, thousands of them subsequently studied science at university, hundreds went on to do scientific research, but only one of them turned into Francis Crick. At this point, nobody would have predicted that this otherwise unexceptional young man would become one of the greatest scientists of the twentieth century.

The transformation of Crick's ambitions, outlook and ability began with the outbreak of war in September 1939. UCL's physics department was evacuated to North Wales and Crick's research was halted as he waited to be conscripted. The call-up came at the beginning of 1940, but not from the armed forces; instead, Francis was appointed as a Temporary Experimental Officer and assigned to the Admiralty Research Laboratory at Bushy Park, Teddington. This was Crick's first job, and his new financial security enabled Francis and Doreen to get married; nine months and one week later, their son Michael was born.

In 1941, Francis and his small family moved to the town of Havant, on the south coast near Portsmouth, where he was assigned to the Mine Design Department under the Australian theoretical physicist Harrie Massey. Crick later said that in many ways this was the most decisive step in his career, because of the people he met and the ways that he learned to think.[22]

Traditional mines exploded on contact with a vessel; the Havant group was designing two kinds of device that would detonate at close distance – mines that exploded when a magnetic field was disrupted by a metal hull and others that responded to the sound of a ship. However, both types could be harmlessly set off at a distance by enemy minesweepers; Crick's task was to develop electrical circuits that would prevent the mine from exploding when it was swept, while allowing it to detonate when it was close to an enemy ship. Each time the Germans captured a mine containing this kind of apparatus, they altered their sweeping technique, so the Royal Navy had to repeatedly change its devices to keep one step ahead. Francis later said that he had a splendid time leading this work – 'We were, in effect, running a private little war of our own against enemy shipping.' The need for quick results appealed to Crick – Massey said he had 'an originality of approach on almost anything'.[23] In 1943, Massey left to work on the Manhattan Project in the USA and was replaced by Edward Collingwood, a mathematician. Although Collingwood was sixteen years older than Francis, the pair became good friends and Collingwood later acted as Crick's mentor.

One evening, Crick was working late and went to the small canteen in the country house that had been requisitioned for the Mine Design Department: 'I found myself at dinner with a physical chemist and a young man I had not noticed before. The physical chemist was holding forth and gradually I sensed that both the young man and I did not think much of what he was saying. This was the beginning of my long friendship with Kreisel.'[24]

Georg Kreisel – his friends only ever called him by his surname – was a twenty-year-old mathematician who had recently received his degree from Cambridge, after only two years' study. With a receding hairline and thick glasses, he often appeared scruffy and could be odd in his manner, but he nevertheless made a powerfully positive impression. Born into a non-observant Jewish family in the Austrian city of Graz (his father was a snail monger), Kreisel was arrested by the Nazis on *Kristallnacht*, narrowly avoided being sent to Dachau, and then escaped to Britain on a *Kindertransport* in January 1939.[25] After two years at Dudley Grammar School in the West Midlands, Kreisel won a mathematics scholarship to Trinity College, Cambridge, which was soon supplemented by a gift from a generous donor, making him financially independent.[26]

At Cambridge he was taught by Wittgenstein, who said that Kreisel was the most able philosopher he had ever met who was also a mathematician.[27] While at Havant he wrote a report proposing to mine the Baltic Sea using Wittgenstein's ideas, but he eventually turned against his teacher, claiming that their discussions had made it more difficult for him to understand philosophy.[28]

Kreisel's sharp mind, persistent questioning and occasionally unusual interests all struck a chord in Crick.* Subsequent decades saw an immense correspondence between the two men (throughout his life Kreisel wrote bizarre letters to his many friends, some of whom were also his lovers, including the novelist Iris Murdoch), as well as many dinner parties and drinking sessions.[29] Whenever they met, there was talking, discussing, arguing – things that Crick enjoyed immensely. He later described how those early meetings with Kreisel changed him:

> Kreisel was not the only person I knew with considerable intellectual powers, but he was the only one I could talk to at length about many subjects. When I met him I was a rather sloppy thinker with a taste for wit and paradoxes in the style of Oscar Wilde.† Kreisel would tactfully but sternly rebuke me for any

---

* Kreisel told Iris Murdoch that he was interested only in money, sex and mathematics. Horner, A. and Rowe, A. (eds.), (2015), *Living on Paper: Letters from Iris Murdoch, 1934–1995* (Princeton: Princeton University Press), p. 340. Murdoch dedicated her 1971 novel, *An Accidental Man*, to Kreisel, and apparently based the character of Julius in *A Fairly Honourable Defeat* (1970) on him.
† Kreisel's later impression was different: 'I don't remember you as a sloppy thinker at all,' he said. Kreisel to Crick, 3 January 1989, MSS 660, Box 5, Folder 5.

careless thinking so that under his influence my ideas became more logical and better organised.[30]

*

In February 1945, as the war in Europe approached its end, Collingwood and Crick were sent to Leningrad, to inspect a German homing torpedo that had been captured by the Soviet navy.[31] Getting there involved a series of short-hop flights; there was a refuelling stop in Marseilles, where it was so cold that the edges of the sea were frozen, then they flew on to Cairo where they had an unforgettable view of the pyramids. After a brief stopover they travelled to Damascus and then flew to Tehran, where they dined with the British Ambassador. Then they went on to Baku, before eventually landing in Moscow, where they were met by a British Navy liaison officer and interpreter called Robert Dougall (before the war, this thirty-one-year-old had been a BBC radio announcer; he would eventually become a famous TV newsreader). Dougall later recalled meeting these 'high-powered Admiralty scientists': 'One was a tall, thin, sandy-haired young man, who walked with a slight stoop. He obviously had an immense sense of fun, which frequently burst out into a high-pitched laugh more like a bray. I liked him immediately and he seemed amused by me. (...) The young physicist said his name was Francis Crick.'

While the formalities of the onward trip to Leningrad were sorted, Crick and Dougall lodged in the British officers' Moscow mess, housed in a large mansion. In the evenings they went to the opera or the ballet, which Crick described as spectacular. In Leningrad they spent two weeks in the Peter and Paul Fortress, poring over the Soviet analysis of the torpedo. They also had time to visit the city, as Dougall recalled: 'Everywhere there were women muffled in scarves clearing the snow with long wooden shovels and tiny children cocooned against the cold, as they were drawn along on mini-toboggans.' Back in Moscow, they spent a further fortnight writing a report before Crick and Collingwood returned to England. Within a couple of months, the Nazis were defeated and the war in Europe was over.

Crick continued his work at Havant, but his personal life was a mess. His relationship with Doreen had gradually deteriorated and she eventually fell in love with a Canadian soldier. Although they remained on amicable terms, Francis moved into lodgings in nearby Chichester, while Michael was sent to Northampton to live with his grandparents – they had moved back from Mill Hill at the outbreak of the war. At the beginning of 1946, Crick was transferred to Navy Intelligence at the Admiralty in London, working in a windowless bomb-proof bunker on the edge of Horse Guards Parade, known as The Citadel (now a Grade II listed building, it is still used by the Ministry of Defence). As Rear Admiral Dickson, Chief of Naval Information, explained on the BBC in 1945, the building was a hub for encoding and deciphering naval messages: 'If you went down there at this moment you'd find eighty girls working teleprinters to all the naval headquarters in Britain and the Continent. You'd see the admiralty private telephone exchange and you'd find naval ratings manning fifteen or twenty lines of direct high-speed transmission to naval Wireless stations all over the world.'[32] Burrowing away in what Dickson described as a maze of machinery and conveyor belts, Crick became a Scientific Civil Servant. The civil service panel that interviewed him for the post had not been impressed, but a second panel, headed by the Cambridge physicist-turned-novelist C. P. Snow, had ensured he got the job.

It is not clear what Crick did in Naval Intelligence, but he later recalled that he read reports on Soviet scientists, including the great geneticist Timofeeff-Ressovsky.[33] He was also involved in high-level politicking about the post-war role of the intelligence services, writing a three-page memorandum (undated, and for unknown eyes), stamped TOP SECRET, which urged the intelligence chiefs to offer jobs to German technicians working for the Russians, to encourage them to defect.[34] He later argued for the creation of a single scientific intelligence organisation, lobbying various admirals, Cabinet Office officials and the founder of British scientific intelligence, R. V. Jones.[35]

When his new job began, Francis moved into a two-bedroom flat in St George's Square, a rather run-down part of Pimlico. Francis initially shared the flat with Kreisel, who had been transferred to the oddly titled Department of Miscellaneous Weapons Development; for a short while Doreen lived there, too, even though the pair had agreed that they would get a divorce, which obliged Francis and Kreisel to share a room. When Kreisel and Doreen left, Crick asked Bob Dougall if he would like to move in. Dougall, who was living with his parents, leapt at the chance. The flatmates would discuss all sorts of things, from religion to world affairs, with Francis delighting in the fact that they often disagreed. Dougall recalled that Crick 'seemed determined to shake off any trace of stodginess in his make-up'; the pair had a cleaner and cook, Mrs Thomas, who came in every morning to make them breakfast and remained impassive whenever she found women staying in the flat.[36]

One woman soon became a regular visitor – a dark-haired twenty-five-year-old with hazel eyes whom Francis had met the previous year. In early 1945 he was visiting the Department of Torpedoes and Mining on business when he passed a Wren* junior officer at the entrance to the building. She was carrying a bag of sprouts. She later described the scene:

> The bottom fell out of the bag at that moment, spilling the sprouts all over the floor, whereupon Francis gallantly gathered them up and said, 'Come out to dinner'. You might think I would jump at the chance, but being rather cautious I declined, thinking what a very forward and brash young man he was. However, he soon found out where I worked and on his next visit to London, he had the good sense to ask me out to lunch, which I thought would be perfectly safe![37]

He dutifully wrote down her name and rank in his diary: '3rd off. Odile Speed', adding her changing addresses and work telephone numbers as the year went on.[38] Apart from the evident mutual physical attraction, Francis was soon beguiled by someone who in many respects was very different to him, although his attempts at courtship seem rather clumsy, as Odile recalled:

> In those days, Francis wasn't very good at small talk and thought that conversation existed solely for the purpose of

---

*A member of the Women's Royal Navy Service.

exchanging precise information. This seemed very strange to me at first, having been used to forms of polite and rather vague conversation, but I did find it rather intriguing.

For one of our first outings, I had prepared a delicious picnic basket complete with wine which we took to Kew Gardens (…) Sitting on the grass and enjoying our picnic, Francis asked me, out of the blue, how far up I thought gravity went and without any hesitation I replied 'Oh about five miles!' At this he laughed and proceeded to give me a long lecture on gravity which I thought was not very romantic under the circumstances.[39]

Odile Speed came from a devout Catholic family in King's Lynn – her mother was French while her English father owned a jewellers' business. Before the war she had spent two years in Vienna, learning German and studying figure drawing. When the Nazis annexed Austria in 1938, she left for Paris where she studied at art school and enjoyed the patronage of a woman artist who took her to exhibitions and taught her about fashion illustration. In the summer of 1939, she returned home for a brief holiday, expecting to go back to France. But the war intervened and she eventually joined the Navy, first listening to intercepted radio messages from German ships and then, as she put it, translating boring German documents for the Department of Torpedoes and Mining. A few months after meeting Francis, Odile left the Admiralty and went to study fashion illustration at St Martin's School of Art on Charing Cross Road. Crick soon introduced her to Kreisel, whom she found amusing – she even used his name as a verb to describe how she would quiz her brother Philippe.[40]

Once Francis had moved up to London, the pair saw each other regularly – his appointment diary for the first few months of 1946 is full of brief mentions of her: 'Lunch Odile … Odile Tea Dinner … Party at Harrow with O … O all day … O stayed … See Lady from the Sea* with O … O rang unexpectedly … O came and cooked supper and stayed … Raoul's party with Odile' (this last was followed the next day by 'In house with hangover').[41]

---

* A play by Ibsen.

As well as having fun with Odile, Francis continued to cast his roving eye on other women. A flavour of his views at the time comes from a piece of light-hearted doggerel he scribbled in his diary, entitled 'Lines to a Lady Discovered in a Third Class Railway Carriage (between Northampton and London, on a Monday, to be Precise), from a Total Stranger':

There is a law (or should be) to restrain
Excessive beauty in a railway train,
And by such means preserve the peace of mind
Of all those neither impotent nor blind.
It may be proper conduct to aspire
To set the hearts of all young men on fire,
But is it right to scatter such temptations
So casually in between the stations?
So, I beseech you (lest some maddened Brute
Should devastate your lovely form) dilute
That look of brimming love, and, when you roam,
Travel by air or road – or stay at home,
And if you must explore the world by rail
Please travel First and wear a heavy veil![42]

Tongue-in-cheek, private, and written as a distraction, this poem nevertheless points to something deeper. It reads like something that George Bernard Shaw might have put into the mouth of Henry Higgins in his 1913 play *Pygmalion* – there is no sense of the new independence of women produced by the war; even the jokey 'heavy veil' harks back to decades-old fashion. In his search for amusement, Crick was using a poetic style and humour that were prevalent before he was born.

*

In 1946, Francis realised that, as he later put it, his interests did not lie in making weapons.[43] According to Robert Dougall, the dropping of the atomic bombs on Hiroshima and Nagasaki changed Crick's ideas about using science for destructive ends, but Francis never stated it so clearly.[44] Among the career options he briefly considered were scientific journalism and working in industry, but as the year wore on he became convinced that he wanted to go back to pure research. The Admiralty had given him time off to study theoretical physics at UCL, but there was no question of returning to complete his PhD – not only was the subject incredibly dull, but 'by good fortune a land mine had blown up the apparatus I had so laboriously constructed'.[45] Furthermore, he did not feel that he was intellectually equipped to be a theoretical physicist and he was not interested in a more experimental approach. Something else would have to be found.

The answer to Crick's quest, the answer that would shape the rest of his life, came from two sources, written by two of the most important scientists of the twentieth century.[46] Kreisel and Dougall both recalled that while Francis was living in St George's Square he read *What Is Life?* by Erwin Schrödinger.[47] In this short book, Schrödinger, pioneer of quantum mechanics and inventor of an imaginary cat, outlined a physicist's view of life and its ability to temporarily defy the second law of thermodynamics. On the basis of the latest ideas in genetics, in particular the work of Max Delbrück, Schrödinger suggested genes were formed of what he described as an aperiodic crystal – a molecule (probably a protein) with a non-repetitive structure. The implication was that this molecule – and the others that gave life its mysterious properties – could be studied using the techniques of physics and chemistry, an approach that became known as biophysics.

Schrödinger's account suggested that profound explanations of life at the molecular level were on the horizon. Indeed, he went further, erroneously predicting that such investigations would lead to the development of new laws of physics. Over the next decade or two, this prospect excited some scientists, who explored the molecular basis of life in the hope of finding some kind of paradox that would require new physical laws. Crick's view was the opposite: 'my aim has always been to explain biology in terms of known physics and chemistry at least until such a position becomes demonstrably untenable,' he wrote later.[48] Nevertheless, understanding the molecular basis of life seemed to be the most challenging frontier of science.

Crick's second inspiration was a short article in *Chemical and*

Engineering News, in which the chemist Linus Pauling described recent progress in structural chemistry and looked to the future.[49] Crick's knowledge of chemistry was based on what he had learned at school, which was a decade or two out of date at the time, so Pauling's account was an eye-opener. Chemists could now precisely measure the distances between atoms in a molecule and work out the exact angles of chemical bonds, using techniques such as X-ray diffraction. The most exciting application of this technique, said Pauling, was the research on the structure of biological molecules being performed in the UK, such as J. D. Bernal's work on vitamin D2 or the investigation of penicillin by Dorothy Hodgkin and Barbara Rogers-Low.

Pauling closed his article by predicting that 'the specific physiological properties' of biological molecules would turn out to be determined by weak intramolecular forces, such as the bonds between hydrogen atoms and nitrogen or oxygen atoms, known as hydrogen bonds.[50] The inspiring vision Pauling held out was that 'knowledge of the structure not only of simple molecules but also of proteins and other complex constituents of organisms' would explain physiological effects, guiding biological and medical research, ultimately contributing to curing cancer and other diseases.

Crick was struck by Schrödinger and Pauling's ideas and found himself talking about them to his colleagues. He realised that the things that most fascinated him were the topics he loved discussing (he later called this the gossip test). There were two such questions, which he would describe as 'the borderline between the living and the non-living, and the workings of the brain'.[51] These problems had something in common: both seemed incomprehensible, so people tended to favour religious or mystical interpretations. For the rest of his life, Francis sought to discover scientific explanations of these mysterious phenomena. Decades later, Kreisel recalled in a letter to Crick how that choice had been made: 'You knew from experience that you had an exceptional gift for *learning much in a short time* (…) Now, you argued, this gift would allow you to make exceptional contributions to a topic on the *borderline of two or more disciplines,* and so biology was a prime candidate.'[52]

One of Kreisel's young physicist colleagues at the Department of Miscellaneous Weapons Development, Freeman Dyson, criticised

Crick's new interest, because physics would continue to dominate science for the next twenty years: 'If you switch to biology now, you will be too old to do the exciting stuff when biology finally takes off,' he told Crick. As Dyson ruefully remarked much later, 'It only took him seven years to prove me wrong.'[53]

*

After some reflection, Francis decided that understanding the molecular basis of life would be more tractable than understanding consciousness; in April 1947 he sought advice about how to proceed from his wartime boss Harrie Massey, who was Professor of Physics at UCL.[54] Massey put Crick in contact with UCL's Nobel Prize winning physiologist, A. V. Hill, who told Francis that he needed to learn some biology and that Cambridge was the place to do this – he even helped Crick get a job studying colour vision there. Although tempted, Francis decided not to accept the offer because the project was not focused on what he wanted to study – the biophysics of the cell.[55]

Massey therefore suggested Crick talk to one of his subordinates on the Manhattan Project, a young New Zealander called Maurice Wilkins who was working with a physicist, John Randall, in the Biophysics Research group at King's College London, funded by the Medical Research Council (MRC).* Wilkins had been seduced by the ideas of *What Is Life?* while in California and was now trying to induce mutations using ultrasound, in the hope of revealing something about the nature and structure of the gene. When Wilkins talked to Crick in the King's building on the Strand in the summer of 1947, he was immediately impressed and urged Randall to offer Francis a job. Randall felt that Crick was too boisterous and garrulous and vetoed the idea.[56]

Meanwhile, A. V. Hill was generously working behind the scenes to try and sort out Crick's future, putting him in touch with Edward

---

*Although biophysical research was not biomedical, the MRC had become the sole funder for such work, following its victory in a turf war between the three UK research councils and the Royal Society.

Mellanby, the head of the MRC. Mellanby warmed to Francis when they met ('I was very much attracted to this man,' he noted) and suggested he apply for a grant to develop his skills.[57] There was some urgency – the current round of MRC grants was about to be awarded – so with Hill's help Crick hurriedly put together a CV and an outline of his interests, in which he explained his project in remarkably clear-sighted terms:

> The particular field which excites my interest is the division between the living and the non-living, as typified by, say, proteins, virus, bacteria and the structure of chromosomes. The eventual goal, which is somewhat remote, is the description of these activities in terms of their structure, i.e., the spatial distribution of their constituent atoms, in so far as this may prove possible. This might be called the chemical physics of biology.[58]

To carry out this ambitious programme, Crick considered he needed to master two fundamental approaches:

> a) A general knowledge of these related sciences (biochemistry, bacteriology, genetics, etc.) sufficient to enable one to appreciate the advantages and limitations of their methods, and the significance of current work.
> b) A thorough grounding in at least one science. In my case this would of course be physics; but I realise that this would have to be extended in the direction of physical chemistry.

Crick's ultimate aim was to use physical methods to understand virus structure and function. He was impressed by the work of Bernal, who at the beginning of the decade had used X-ray diffraction to measure the size and shape of Tobacco Mosaic Virus (TMV), so he asked to work with him at Birkbeck College, London.[59] This could have been significant – Norwegian crystallographer Sven Furberg was just beginning his doctoral work with Bernal on X-ray diffraction analysis of nucleic acids – but Bernal was on holiday when Francis went to visit, and he got the brush-off from Miss Rimel, an 'amiable dragon' who was Bernal's secretary. Everyone wanted to work with Bernal, she pointed out. Why should he take Crick on?[60] More significantly, the MRC, like Hill, considered that Francis needed to learn some biology, which the physicist Bernal could not provide.

Just before Crick went on his summer holiday, the MRC awarded him a studentship 'for training in research methods', subject to finding a suitable supervisor.[61] Mellanby suggested he work with Honor Fell at the Strangeways Laboratory on the outskirts of Cambridge. Fell, in her late forties, was part of an MRC-funded group studying cell biology; when she interviewed Francis she not only proposed a project – studying the movement of particles in cellular fluids under a magnetic field, with the aim of gaining insight into the structure of the cytoplasm, the liquid contents of the cell – but also suggested a set of books he should read and the kind of biological lectures he should attend at the university.

Crick was not desperately interested in the research topic, but it built on both his abandoned PhD on viscosity and his work on magnetic mines, and it was a step towards his desired field of research – the study of fundamental biological processes using physical methods. For her part, Fell felt good about Crick: 'We were very favourably impressed by him – he seems intelligent and enterprising and has ideas,' she told Mellanby.[62] Although Crick had a studentship from the MRC, he would not be registered for a doctorate or a masters – instead, he would simply be provided with some basic training in biological research. As Fell put it astutely: 'It has been our experience that physicists in particular are very apt to over-simplify the interpretation of biological phenomena when they first begin work in this field.'

A few weeks later, Crick resigned from the Admiralty and moved to Cambridge.[63]

CAMBRIDGE

At this point, Francis was not associated with the university – the Strangeways Laboratory was an independent institution funded by the MRC. Nor was he working in the medieval centre – the Strangeways was an Edwardian building in what was then the rural south-east of town.[1] Nevertheless, his old boss from Havant, Edward Collingwood, sent him a well-meaning letter about managing college fees and the kinds of people he should avoid (it read like the passage in *Brideshead Revisited* where Charles Ryder is told by his strait-laced cousin Jasper how to behave at Oxford).[2] Collingwood also issued a stern injunction: 'As a matter of history and everyday experience it is quite certain that success comes to the student who keeps to his attic and not to the intellectual butterfly who flits from salon to salon to party in search of relaxation or "stimulus".'[3]

Although Collingwood knew Crick, he did not understand him: Francis inevitably ignored the advice and continued being an intellectual butterfly. He could not have stopped even if he had tried. He repeatedly observed, and even participated in, Kreisel's jousts with Wittgenstein, making a lasting impression on the philosopher – a few years later, Kreisel reported that Wittgenstein asked after him ('Do you still see Crick?').[4] He joined the Hardy Club – an informal Cambridge scientific discussion circle – and he went to scores of lectures given by the departments of Zoology, Chemistry, Physiology and Physical Chemistry.[5] He evidently enjoyed his gossipy new world, as Odile noted in one of her letters: 'Cambridge appears to be a hotbed of intrigue which you regard with the air of a lofty amused spectator.'[6]

Crick's work at the Strangeways, however, was neither intriguing nor amusing. His supervisor, Arthur Hughes, used 16mm cine film to record cell activity; Francis had to film the responses of chick cells to magnetic fields, projecting each frame onto a piece of paper and tracing the movement of iron particles that the cells had ingested. This was boring and frustrating – both the subject matter and the approach were far from the kind of fundamental investigation of molecular processes that interested him. However, it did bring home the complexity of living matter, which was the whole point. Honor Fell reported almost gleefully that Crick's project had 'considerable educational value for a physicist, as it involves many hours of close microscopic study of living cells of different types.'[7] Crick was less positive. As he later recalled, cell culture – the technique he was using – involved 'too much sort of green fingers (…) The system seemed too complicated and I didn't really feel equal to tackling it.'[8] On the other hand, he had fond memories of Fell, who 'was always very nice to me, especially as I then knew so little about biology.'[9]

His research eventually produced two papers, both published in 1950. The first, jointly written with Hughes, was a brute – forty-three pages of dense detail entitled 'The Physical Properties of Cytoplasm, Part 1'. Appearing in the first issue of a new specialist journal, *Experimental Cell Research*, the article had little impact, although it continues to be cited, partly because of Crick's subsequent reputation but also because of recent interest in nanotechnology – this was one of the first attempts to affect the internal activity of a cell using artificial particles. In some passages you can hear the emphatic cadences of Crick's sharp voice, for example when he criticised a similar experiment by a researcher called Heilbronn:

It appears to us, if we have understood the description of the experimental technique correctly, that whatever else was being measured, it was certainly not the viscosity. To measure viscosity it is necessary to measure a *rate* of movement, whereas Heilbronn found the field that would just move the particle.[10]

Or again, when the article used a striking domestic analogy as a way of describing the structure of the cytoplasm: 'If we were compelled to suggest a model we would propose Mother's Work Basket – a jumble of beads and buttons of all shapes and sizes, with pins and threads for good measure, all jostling about and held together by colloidal forces.' As to the outcome of the study, Crick and Hughes concluded that the cytoplasm was a thixotropic gel*, but accepted there was little new in this.

A second paper, authored solely by Crick (with 'many helpful and characteristic suggestions' from Kreisel), followed a few months later in the same journal, providing theoretical explanations of the movement of particles under different magnetic stresses.[11] It is not clear what Crick thought of this paper, but it is not found in his own collection of his publications.[12] Other researchers were certainly unimpressed – only two papers cited it in the following fifteen years. Although Crick's research had little consequence, his wide reading and informal attendance at lectures had a decisive impact – he later said, 'a lot of my ideas formed in that time.'[13]

As well as working with Hughes, Francis also contributed to the social life of the laboratory, persuading his colleagues to replace their usual coffee-time chit-chat with informal discussions of scientific issues (he later admitted he had to bully the staff into joining in, sometimes saying outrageous things to provoke them).[14] A cartoon by one of his colleagues, Frederick Spear, portrayed Francis as a 'dencritic cell'† trying to span physics and biology in order to grasp the riddle of the universe while also reaching out to pretty much anything (*Twenty Questions* was a popular radio quiz show).[15]

At one point Francis was invited to give a talk to the members of the laboratory and chose DNA as his subject. No trace remains of the lecture and Crick was never able to recall the content precisely,

---

* Thixotropic materials become more fluid (so less viscous) when they are put under stress.
† This is a play on the dendritic cell, a component of the immune system.

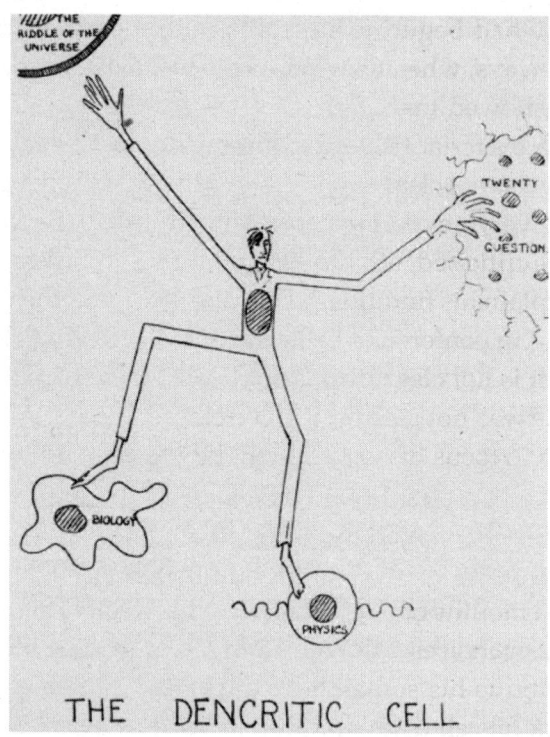

THE   DENCRITIC   CELL

apart from the fact that he did not know much.[16] Despite having no biological training, he had identified a global hot topic – between 1947 and 1949 nearly two hundred papers were published on DNA, and the Strangeways had recently recruited a biochemist to study nucleic acids in cell division.

At the time, the role of DNA was unclear. It was found in chromosomes, mixed up with proteins, and although chromosomes were known to carry genes, DNA was seen as a boring molecule. Composed simply of phosphate-sugar molecules and four other kinds of compound called bases (adenine, cytosine, guanine and thymine, generally known by their initials), it was hard to imagine how that chemical tedium could give rise to the incredibly varied functions of genes. On the other hand, proteins could be incredibly varied in size and structure. It therefore seemed logical either that genes were made of proteins, while DNA was just the scaffolding of chromosomes, or that the combination of DNA and proteins – 'nucleoproteins' – was the thing.

This view had begun to shift three years before Crick arrived at the Strangeways, when Oswald Avery of the Rockefeller Institute in New York showed that DNA appeared to be the genetic material in pneumonia bacteria. However, his research focused on only one species, and it was not clear that bacteria had genes at all. Furthermore, the results of Avery's experiments on what he called the transforming principle were criticised, because tiny amounts of protein contamination might explain his findings.[17] This dispute about the role of DNA was unfolding in conference halls and the pages of a few academic journals, but it is not clear how much Crick knew of this. Whatever he thought, he was not sufficiently convinced of the possible significance of DNA to focus his experimental work upon it.[18]

*

After eighteen months of magnets and cell culture, Francis was faced with three career choices, all of which involved staying in Cambridge. He could continue his somewhat dead-end research with Hughes, he could work on cell division (mitosis) with Michael Swann in the Zoology Department, or he could try to join the new MRC biophysics unit in the university's Cavendish Laboratory of Physics.[19] More magnets at the Strangeways was not an attractive option; working on the mechanisms of mitosis was more interesting, but it was the possibility of moving to the Cavendish that really excited him.[20]

The MRC Unit for the Study of the Molecular Structure of Biological Systems had been created two years earlier, in October 1947.[21] Although the head of the Cavendish was Sir Lawrence Bragg, the co-inventor of X-ray crystallography, the unit was led by Max Perutz, a slight, balding Austrian-born crystallographer only two years older than Crick. Before the war, Perutz had trained with Bernal and then came under Bragg's wing, studying the structure of haemoglobin until he was interned as an enemy alien at the outbreak of the war (he was eventually released and set to work doing war research on glaciers).[22] After Perutz returned to Cambridge in 1945, Bragg encouraged him to apply for MRC funding to study protein structure by X-ray crystallography, with the aim of understanding the biological functions of molecules.

Crick's name had been mentioned to Perutz by Kreisel, and Francis soon met Perutz at his tiny attic flat known as the Green Door, on Thompsons Lane, close to St John's College, where he lived with his wife Gisela and their toddler. Herbert 'Freddie' Gutfreund described the scene to Perutz's biographer, Georgina Ferry: 'Francis suggested to Max that they should go out to dinner together (…) I was babysitting and they came back to the Green Door and had a discussion about Francis coming to the lab. The idea of doing structural work appealed to him, and there wasn't any other place to go.'[23]

This marked the beginning of another significant friendship in Crick's life – Francis would work in Perutz's laboratory for nearly thirty years, and they remained friends until Perutz died in 2002. Perutz, an extremely kind man, was always supportive of Crick and admired his quicksilver mind, very different from his own. As Crick put it in 2004, 'Max wasn't a particularly quick thinker. He was a plodder, but a very persistent plodder, and he had considerable insight as a result of his plodding. It didn't come out in flashes.'[24] The aspect of Perutz's character that Crick came to most appreciate was his quiet leadership: 'Max's great talent was that he got everybody happily working together … Max made a major contribution by the tactful way he administered,' Francis recalled.

The Cambridge MRC unit was much smaller than its King's College London counterpart and was based in the Austin Wing of the Cavendish, which had been built in a courtyard during the war – a typical mid-century laboratory building, with broad corridors, high ceilings and bare brick walls. The unit was initially composed only of Perutz, John Kendrew (almost exactly the same age as Crick and also still to finish his PhD) and a research assistant. Like Crick, Kendrew's PhD research had been interrupted by the war, during which time he served as a research officer in the RAF and was stationed in South-East Asia. During the war he worked with Bernal, and while they were using an elephant to lay land-mines in Sri Lanka, Bernal convinced him of the importance of studying protein structure.[25] In 1946 Kendrew registered for a PhD under Perutz, and the pair were soon joined by PhD student Hugh Huxley and then by a skilled technician, Tony Broad, who built a powerful X-ray source that gave the Cavendish the best equipment in the world.

X-ray crystallography was developed at the beginning of the twentieth century, with key contributions from Lawrence Bragg and his father, William – the pair won the Nobel Prize in 1915 for their work, with Lawrence becoming the youngest ever scientific Nobel Prize winner at just twenty-five. When a crystal or a semi-crystalline fibre is bombarded with X-rays, the rays are diffracted by the atoms within and the resultant diffraction pattern can be captured by placing a piece of photographic film behind the crystal. By rotating the sample and taking a series of images of the diffraction patterns produced at different angles, a three-dimensional data set can be obtained.

The challenge for crystallographers is turning those data into a three-dimensional structure; for complex biological molecules such as proteins, this can be incredibly difficult, and researchers had turned to some complicated mathematics in an attempt to resolve the problem. In the 1940s, the only available calculating devices were either mechanical calculators or slide rules, so these techniques were time-consuming and extremely challenging. Part of the problem is that a given diffraction image can be produced by more than one kind of structure; because of the limited information that is present, you often cannot determine the underlying form without chemically modifying the molecule, which may not be possible.*

The potential of this approach was precisely what Crick had grasped when he read Pauling's 1946 article in *Chemical and Engineering News*: based in physics and mathematics, it could be used in the service of chemistry and biology. There would be many subsequent chance events that shaped precisely what Crick did, but once he decided to work with Perutz, the outline of his future scientific success began to take shape. It seems likely that had he not ended

---

*For the technically minded, here is the explanation that Crick gave in 1973: 'given a model, one can calculate the whole X-ray diffraction pattern yet, given the diffraction pattern, there is no simple way to arrive at the model because the X-ray pattern contains *only half the information needed*. That is, it gives the amplitude but not the phases of the reflections.' Crick, Less general remarks, undated [1973], PP/CRI/H/4/13. The amplitude is given by the intensity of the spots on the diffraction image; to calculate the phase requires experimentally replacing atoms at certain positions within the molecule.

up working on DNA, he would probably have made a substantial contribution to the work on the structure of myoglobin and haemoglobin which led to Perutz and Kendrew winning the Nobel Prize in 1962, the same year that Crick, Watson and Wilkins won their prize for the structure of DNA.

*

While all this was going on, the country, the continent and indeed the whole planet were changing dramatically. The Labour government had launched a programme of nationalisation and had created the National Health Service, the London Olympics in 1948 captured the imagination of the British public while, more seriously, Europe was being divided into two blocs, heralding a growing Cold War. Francis and Odile were naturally aware of these events, but their memoirs and letters reveal no traces of their views.

Instead, Odile's side of their correspondence (which is all that has survived) focused on their emotional and social lives. From September 1947 they lived in different cities, which inevitably led to yearning and frustration – 'Darling, I miss you' began one of Odile's letters to Francis shortly after he moved to Cambridge, while one of her cards to him read, 'There is such a beautiful sunshine today. I feel ... Well, this is a postcard. I'll tell you all about it on Saturday.'[26] Even at this stage, their relationship was not traditional, as Odile jokingly hinted: 'Won't you be grand with a whole house to play in. Eccentric Englishman sets up Harem in English University Town.'[27] Similarly, Odile's 1948 new year wishes for Francis included lots of 'entanglements du coeur' (affairs of the heart) while she later wrote 'Cambridge must be full of temptations round every corner! I haven't even time to look for any just now. Unless of course ...'[28]

Odile's scientific curiosity was encouraged by Francis; they both read *The Small Back Room* by Nigel Balchin, a novel about wartime defence scientists and later went to see the Powell and Pressburger film adaptation. Crick also gave Odile a book about science, which she read on a train journey and found 'quite interesting', although she noted it was full of 'queer diagrams of hemispheres hanging in mid-air and air pumps etc'.*[29] And in April 1949 they went to hear Bragg talk about giant molecules at the Royal Institution in London.[30]

Maurice Wilkins had now become a good friend and would invite the couple to dinner at his London flat.[31] During these meals Crick and Wilkins chatted about their work – by this stage Wilkins was beginning to focus on DNA, although he was using microscopes to infer the organisation of nucleic acids in the cell and had not yet turned to X-ray crystallography. And, as always, there was Kreisel – it is not clear if his conversation with Odile was as coarse as his correspondence with Francis, but she was amused by him.

After Francis's divorce from Doreen in May 1947, Francis had sole legal responsibility for Michael, who continued to live with his grandparents, Annie and Harry, with Francis visiting every other weekend.[32] Odile began to take on the role of stepmother, visiting Michael and acting as an emergency contact – for example, when Michael got mumps, Annie phoned Odile.[33]

In contrast, Odile's family were completely in the dark about Francis – Odile's mother was a devout Catholic and would not accept that her daughter was stepping out with a divorced man. Francis was therefore hidden from her family, and at times their lives threatened to turn into a French farce. When one of Odile's relatives unexpectedly visited her flat in Earl's Court, Francis would be told to make himself scarce or instructed to telephone only at certain times. Odile's letters are full of annoyance that various family members were descending on her, putting the kibosh on their plans. The Speeds seemed so omnipresent and invasive that Francis and Odile referred to them collectively as 'the Octopus'. Every now and again, however, there were tidings of joy, such as when Mrs Speed changed her mind about visiting and Odile immediately sent a telegram to Francis – 'COME IF NOT OTHERWISE OCCUPIED'.[34] Francis found the tensions bewildering and frustrating; Odile could only sympathise: 'How my aunts and other relations haunt you! An

---

* Twitter helped me decipher Odile's handwriting and work out that this was James B. Conant's 1947 book of lectures for the general public, *On Understanding Science: An Historical Approach* (Yale University Press).

absolute nightmare. – Yes, I was quite fond of <u>her</u> but she had RELA-TIONS you know!'[35]

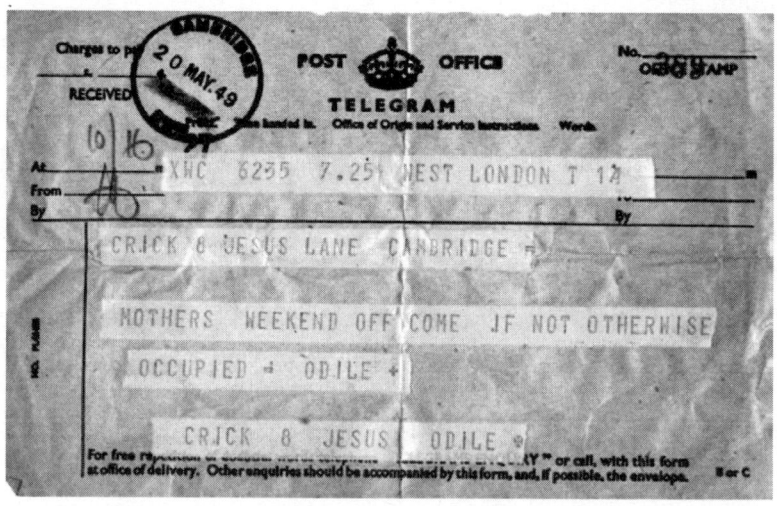

*

At the beginning of February 1948, Francis's Poppa suddenly passed away. Harry Crick, who had already had one heart attack, died at his club 'of the excitement brought on by making a grand slam at bridge', as Francis later put it.[36] Odile immediately sent a heartfelt letter of commiseration, followed the next day by Maurice Wilkins, who also sought to provide some distraction:

> Dear Crick,
> Very sorry to hear about your father – I felt pretty bad when mine died not long ago. And I hope it doesn't upset your finances. (…) If you would like to bring your girl friend to my place I should be very pleased and would do my best with the help of the Concise Encyclopaedia of Gastronomy and a few titbits from Soho.[37]

The end of the year was marked by a happier moment: in December Francis and Odile decided to get married. Odile described the reaction of her mother and father: 'I broke the news to [my] parents yesterday. Mother still rather prejudiced but it doesn't take much to bring her round and that's really up to you when you meet her. (…) Papa seemed pleased about the news and not a bit surprised.'[38]

It would be nearly two months before Mr and Mrs Speed finally met their prospective son-in-law; although they accepted him, some frostiness remained, and for the rest of their lives he rarely visited their home in King's Lynn.[39] Annie Crick wished the couple well in a letter to Francis, but bluntly expressed her concerns about their finances: 'Your profession is so badly paid that there are great risks as to the financial position you may find yourself in (…) you would be wise to budget your finance for the years to come, on a firm basis (…) In your type of work you won't succeed if you have domestic worries, and believe me, they will be many on a small income.'[40]

One of Crick's old flames had similar misgivings: 'I only see the marriage going where the last one went unless your future wife (lucky thing) is prepared to wait on you hand and foot, be patient with your incessant reading and deal carefully with your finances (…) I have never yet met a man as frivolous as you were.'[41]

They were all quite right to be worried about the couple's finances. Francis's poorly paid studentship would soon end and Odile was now studying in the School of Fashion Design at the Royal College of Art – neither of them had clear prospects. Although Odile's studies brought her into contact with well-heeled ladies who wanted dresses made – this enabled her to be almost self-supporting, as she put it – she could not make a living and began to look for teaching work, as well as searching for jobs with fashion houses and *Vogue* magazine.[42] However, nothing solid came of this and money remained a problem. Like many in such circumstances, Odile longed for a magic solution: 'If only someone would give me £1000 or so just to keep going life would be wonderful.'[43] Instead there were repeated visits to pawn shops to raise money on their two most precious objects, Odile's accordion and Francis's typewriter, which they would redeem when money was less tight.[44] These financial strains inevitably caused tensions between them, for example in the summer of 1948, when a planned boating holiday with friends went awry and Odile wrote in exasperation to Francis: 'It's time we stopped fooling around getting involved in more and more expense. (…) For the sake of not having to organise anything yourself you let yourself be pushed around and involved in bankruptcy.'[45] After they became engaged, Odile joked: 'I must be dreadfully romantic to be marrying an impecunious man like you!'[46]

Crick's finances soon began to look more secure as his move to the Cavendish MRC unit took shape. In February 1949 he had a meeting with Perutz and Bragg to finalise things, and then met Mellanby at the end of the month to get official approval.[47] Shortly afterwards, Francis explained his decision to his sponsor, A. V. Hill:

> After much thought I've decided, in spite of your advice to me, to try to join Perutz's group. However much I looked at other possible lines of work I always returned to this one. The problem really does fascinate me, and I feel that having given up my Civil Service job in order to do work in which I was really interested, it would be better for me to do this, even if the work is difficult. (…) It will be interesting to see how far we have got in, say, five years time.[48]

Hill replied with equanimity: 'I expect you are quite right. If the X-ray diffraction studies of protein are what interest you most, in spite of any deterrent I may have exerted, you can be reasonably sure that your decision is the best one.'[49]

Bragg and Perutz now asked the MRC to approve Crick's transfer to the Cavendish.[50] Bragg's support sounded half-hearted – 'I am leaving it to Perutz and Crick to consult you about the transfer; this is merely to say that as far as I am concerned I should welcome the arrangement.'[51] Perutz was effusive, nailing Crick's character in a sentence: 'I had many conversations with him and he has always struck me as an exceptionally intelligent person, with a lively interest, a remarkably clear analytical mind and a capacity for quickly grasping the essence of any problem.'[52] Perutz also raised the question of Crick's salary, pointing out that his war work meant that he was much older than someone in his position would normally be, and that he had a family. The outcome was that the MRC decided to employ him on a more stable three-year contract, beginning in June

1949. By 1950, his pay had reached £740,* with another boost the following year, all of which made Francis and Odile's life much easier.[53]

Odile followed the negotiations, which were clearly stressful for both of them: 'So glad that you are feeling better and that your interviews etc are satisfactory so far. Very glad to hear A. V. Hill is reconciled and sends his blessing, it looks as though all will be settled fairly soon now' (15 March); 'Write and tell me what you've been doing and whether you've heard anything from MRC' (24 April); with a final conclusion on 5 May: 'So glad you've heard at last … Let's do something really exciting on Sunday. Any ideas?'[54]

The couple still had three important things to do: get married, organise a honeymoon and find somewhere to live in Cambridge (Francis's lodgings on Jesus Lane would never do). And exactly as Crick's ex had predicted, it was Odile who had to arrange everything, reminding Francis to get his suit cleaned before he met her parents, ordering little boxes for the wedding cake, getting engraved cufflinks for Francis, and even sourcing her own wedding ring and urging him not to lose it: 'Darling do give a little concentrated thought to all these matters.'[55] She did the same with the honeymoon, booking the hotel and getting hold of the foreign currency (a tricky affair given she would be changing her name and needed a new passport – there were still strict currency controls).[56] And she had to remind Francis to visit the local estate agents regularly to be sure he heard of any flats to let.[57]

Francis did find them somewhere to live, but it was not really his doing. Max and Gisela Perutz were expecting a second baby and were leaving the Green Door attic flat, with its tiny space and the bath in the kitchen. With the agreement of the landlord, Perutz offered the tenancy to Francis and Odile. Odile was keen – it would mean they had somewhere to live when they returned from their honeymoon – but sent Francis an immensely practical letter, full of questions that had to be answered before she could agree.[58]

First, there was storage ('or rather lack of same') – 'imagine both our untidy selves wading knee-deep in garments and junk!' The flat

---

*The average UK salary at the time was around £520, while the average house price was about £1,900.

was cramped – just a bedroom, a living room and a small room for when Michael came to stay – and they needed space for their clothes, household linen, some of Michael's clothes and toys, Odile's artist's materials, their books and for the carpet sweeper and her accordion. Odile was not fazed by the lack of a bathroom – 'I don't object to the bath in the kitchen, you can wallow in the bath while I cook breakfast!' – but there was a more fundamental problem: 'Where is the WC?' (It was halfway up the enclosed outside staircase that led to the front door.) How was the place heated? If by coal, how would they get the fuel up to the attic flat? (There was a gas fire.) Would there be enough light for her to paint? Did the flat have electricity? Even when these questions were answered, Odile worried about how they would be able to pay the Perutzes £20 for a bookcase they were leaving behind ('one can't really keep them waiting for it as it's a private friendly arrangement,' she wrote).[59]

Eventually all these problems were overcome and Francis even wangled the installation of a telephone ('how nice to think you are put on the same level as a Doctor for priority!' wrote Odile), while she was able to save most of the money needed to buy a refrigerator.[60] Crick then had to schmooze his prospective in-laws yet again when the Speeds came to visit Cambridge, which he did with aplomb. Odile was appreciative: 'My Darling, Tomorrow week we shall be married – won't that be fun. You behaved beautifully yesterday, Maman and Dad were charmed with their day in Cambridge.'[61]

Odile and Francis were married on 13 August 1949, two days after Odile's twenty-ninth birthday, at Marylebone Registry Office in London. There were nearly fifty guests, including Raoul Colinvaux, Maurice Wilkins and various wartime friends; there was also the inevitable Kreisel – 'I've warned my friends that there will be a very queer specimen at the wedding!' wrote Odile.[62] The bride wore a stylish calf-length dress and broad-brimmed white hat, both of which she had made herself, while the groom looked neat in his dark suit with a carnation in the lapel and his hair slicked down. After a riverside reception in Chelsea the newly-weds were off on a ten-day honeymoon in Italy.*

---

* From this point onwards the correspondence from Odile to Francis becomes

When they returned, the pair began their new life in the Green Door, which Francis recalled with evident fondness: 'Odile luxuriated in her newly found leisure, read French novels in front of the small gas fire, and attended, informally, a few lectures on French literature, while I revelled in the romance of doing real scientific research and in the fascination of my new subject.'[63]

They developed a circle of friends, including many people outside of the world of science, from the aristocratic Greek artist Count Nicholas Egon, who specialised in war paintings and portraits of glamorous socialites, to the Iranian economist, Eprime Eshag, who became a lifelong friend.[64] Odile was able to get some teaching hours at the Cambridge School of Art, which helped bring in much-needed extra cash. She also drew pictures of Francis, including a portrait* of him lounging on a sofa reading what looks like an academic journal, or maybe *Vogue*, and another large sketch of Francis in his dressing gown, working at his desk. They were in love, and life was good.

*

When Crick joined Perutz's unit in June 1949, he wanted to study the structure of proteins using X-ray crystallography. There was one snag – he did not know much about the technique, so he had to learn it by reading and by talking to Perutz and Kendrew. Francis also needed something to study; at a time before bioscience companies sold synthesised molecules, he had to isolate his own proteins.[65] This proved easier said than done, and for eighteen months he struggled to crystallise anything in sufficient quantity and purity. Often working on the weekend and in the evening (the Green Door was a short walk from the Cavendish), occasionally helped by Odile, Francis transported his samples to two nearby laboratories which had the necessary freezers and centrifuges.

While Crick's domestic life was going well, his notebooks were

---

sparse, inevitably sent only when they were apart, reducing what can be known about their lives. Presumably the relaxed and amusing interactions of their letters continued in their conversations. Only a handful of letters from Francis to Odile survive from the nearly sixty years they spent together.
*This was sold for $17,500 at Christie's in 2013.

full of reports of leaking equipment, spillages of precious samples, refrigerators that either broke down or froze everything, lamps that burned out, film that was not properly loaded, misaligned and lost sample holders, or pumps that ran dry.[66] All this was accompanied by glum descriptions of dashed hopes ('closer examination showed crystal had dried out'), misinterpretation ('seemed like salt'), ignorance ('had no idea how much acetate buffer to add'), error ('should clearly have done this on the *filtered* solution'), perplexity ('not really clear why phosphate is so much darker'), wishful thinking ('decided to risk it') and bemusement ('of course might be salt'). There were occasional moments of cheer ('Found a precipitate!'), such as when he glanced at the dried-up remains of an experiment abandoned five months earlier ('was astonished to see large crystals'), and ultimately of relief ('This is really very satisfactory').

He finally succeeded in crystallising a number of proteins, such as trypsin, trypsin inhibitor and chymotrypsin, and colleagues gave him samples of haemoglobin and insulin to study. Francis was becoming focused on interpreting the results from his own X-ray experiments and from those of colleagues in the unit, rather than collecting new data, discovering that his logical mind, coupled with his visual intuition, helped him solve the algebraic problems involved in crystallography. As he recalled: 'I soon found I could see the answer to many of these mathematical problems by a combination of imagery and logic, without first having to slog through the mathematics.'[67]

Once the MRC agreed to pay his PhD registration fees, he became a postgraduate student with Perutz as his supervisor. He even ended up in a college – Gonville and Caius – although he paid little attention to what he saw as the pointless traditions of college life and for many years did not even possess a gown.[68]

Crick's approach to resolving molecular structures was transformed in spring 1951, when there was a dramatic challenge to the work done at the Cavendish on a protein called keratin – the material that makes up hair and teeth. For over a decade, researchers had been trying to understand this molecule. The University of Leeds crystallographer Bill Astbury had found that there were two forms of keratin, known as α (alpha) and β (beta) but their structures remained unknown, although it was generally agreed that at least part of the molecule contained a kind of folded chain with a repeated component.

In 1950, Bragg, Kendrew and Perutz published what they claimed were the possible structures of this repeated part of the α version of keratin, although none of their proposals fitted the X-ray crystallographic data perfectly.[69] Less than a year later, the Cavendish was rocked by the news that Linus Pauling and two of his colleagues at Caltech had proposed a radically different, spiral structure for the α version of keratin, which they called the α-helix. A month later, *seven* further papers from Pauling's laboratory described other structural features of proteins.[70]

Pauling had first realised that α-keratin might have a helical structure in 1948; he now not only showed that Bragg and the others had missed two likely structures, but also went on to use chemical logic – not X-ray diffraction – to show that *none* of the Bragg group's proposed structures corresponded to the known features of the molecule. Chemistry told Pauling that the orientation of the bonds between the amino acids in Bragg's models was wrong and that, in contrast, the α-helix was correct. Bragg said this was his biggest scientific mistake, while Perutz was 'thunderstruck'.[71] The Cavendish crew had not only been scooped, they were humiliated.

Pauling was able to succeed partly because he disregarded a significant piece of data known as the 5.1 Ångstrom reflection (a blob at a point on the X-ray diffraction image). The Cambridge team had worked hard to make their models include this data point, but the Caltech group discovered that this reflection was not produced by a synthetic keratin molecule and correctly realised that whatever caused it was not fundamental to what they suspected was a spiral structure. They then put the bonds between atoms in their correct orientation and produced a helical structure.

When Pauling's first paper appeared, Crick was wide-eyed. The Caltech wizard described a strikingly novel way of arriving at a molecular structure – he had used his profound chemical knowledge, and occasional leaps of intuition, to ignore a data point that made no sense and build a model that could be tested against existing data. The Cambridge approach of relying solely on the crystallographic data appeared leaden-footed in comparison. Although Pauling had a specific reason to ignore the 5.1Å blob, Crick began to turn this approach to unruly data points – he later called it the 'don't worry method' – into a principle that he would apply for the rest of his career.

Crick was hugely respectful of Bragg – like everyone else, he called the pioneer of X-ray crystallography 'Professor' – but Pauling's approach, with its panache and elegance, was electrifying.[72] Crick spent some time drawing out the implications for his own work, and that of Perutz and Bragg. This eventually shaped his approach to the structure of DNA, but first it led to a series of increasingly acrimonious clashes with Bragg.

*

Since the beginning of 1951, Francis had been working on Perutz and Bragg's proposed structure of haemoglobin, a model they called the hatbox, because it looked like a squat cylinder made of parallel rods. Studying Perutz's results, Crick began to suspect a problem. The model was based on a complex mathematical procedure known as the Patterson analysis, which worked well for simple molecules, but which Crick thought could not reveal the structure of a complex biological molecule.

In early July 1951, Francis gave a brief research seminar at the Cavendish, pretentiously titled 'What Mad Pursuit', after a poem by Keats, in which he used some clever reverse engineering to show that the hatbox could not possibly be correct.[73] Bragg and Perutz had used Patterson analysis to conclude that it was principally composed of uniform parallel rods. Francis now calculated the Patterson that would be expected if this model were correct and showed that the data recorded by Perutz should have been much more intense. The implication was crushing – the haemoglobin molecule must be more complex than Bragg and Perutz imagined. Crick even used a prop – a little wooden ball, painted by Odile – to underline his point.[74]

Things got worse as Francis explained that this was not simply an error of calculation: the methods used by the Bragg group would never produce a correct structure. They could only have 'some prospect of success' if used in conjunction with the isomorphous replacement method – swapping one kind of atom in the molecule for another and using the difference between the diffraction images produced by the two forms as an indicator of the inner structure.[75] Crick had previously discussed these problems with Perutz, but they were news to Bragg, who was livid.[76] Not only had Crick proved him wrong, he had done so in public. As Crick recalled:

> Here was this newcomer telling experienced X-ray crystallographers, including Bragg himself, who had founded the subject and been in the forefront of it for almost forty years, that what they were doing was most unlikely to lead to any useful result. The fact that I clearly understood the theory of the subject and indeed was apt to be unduly loquacious about it did not help.[77]

A few weeks later, when Francis muttered some disparaging remarks about someone else's talk, Bragg turned round and hissed, 'Crick, you're rocking the boat.' Crick's relationship with Bragg, never warm, was cooling by the minute.

If Crick realised that this was a problem, he had little time to dwell on it, for the following week, on 15 July, Francis and Odile's first child, Gabrielle, was born. Shortly afterwards, Odile took the baby to stay at her parents' house for a few weeks, leaving Francis to his own devices.[78] Kreisel came on a brief visit, so they punted on the Cam and drank in the Blue Boar Hotel on Trinity Street. In a rare surviving letter, Francis told Odile that without her, his usual watering-holes seemed 'really rather dull' and the flat felt empty.

On the other hand, this was an opportunity to spend time with Michael, who was now a boarder at Bedales School in Hampshire. Michael was staying with his grandmother Annie, who had moved to Cambridge, but the boy was 'at a bit of a loose end' during the long school holidays. All three of Crick's children – Michael and his half-sisters Gabrielle and Jacqueline* – have said that their father was not a hands-on parent, but this time Francis rose to the occasion.[79]

---

*Jacqueline died in February 2011.

He took Michael to Heffers bookshop and bought his son a weather atlas; they also went to the Cavendish where Michael played about with litmus paper and acids and alkalis. One evening, Francis told Odile, they went punting on the Cam where Michael 'had a wonderful time splashing me'.

Once Odile and Gabrielle returned to Cambridge, their life settled into a new normal, punctuated by letters and visits from Kreisel, who soon sent Crick one of his typical letters from his holiday in Devon. This freewheeling eighteen-pager opened with a reference to Odile's recent erotic dream about a youthful mutual friend, the mathematician Gabriel Dirac,* before proceeding with obscenities about the hotel maids.[80] Kreisel then reopened old arguments about Wittgenstein's ideas (these would continue on and off for the next five decades) and launched complex new criticisms of Bertrand Russell's theory of classes, before promising Crick a 'bachelors' dinner' in Cambridge and signing off in his usual enigmatic style, 'Your saviour'.

Meanwhile, relations with Bragg were becoming increasingly strained. Crick's place in the MRC unit depended upon Bragg's approval, and his support would be needed when it came to finding a permanent job. Not only had Francis humiliated Bragg over the haemoglobin model, the very presence of this late-starting postgraduate seemed to irritate the knighted Nobel laureate. Twice, Crick's forgetfulness during an experiment led to a sink overflowing, cascading water into the corridor outside Bragg's office. And then there was the incessant loud talking – Bragg later said that Crick's voice made his ears buzz.[81]

All this annoyance would be compounded by events in December 1951, which led to an inter-university row and humiliation for Crick. That was the direct consequence of the arrival in October that year of a tall, thin, bug-eyed American called Jim Watson.

---

*The adopted son of Paul Dirac the mathematician.

WATSON

Neither Watson nor Crick could remember the exact day they met, but both recalled the immediate impact they had on each other. Watson, aged only twenty-three, was a post-doctoral researcher who had been working in Copenhagen on DNA biochemistry using viruses that attack bacteria. In May 1951 he had gone to a conference in Naples, where Maurice Wilkins had shown some of his new X-ray diffraction images of DNA. According to Watson's novelised account of events, *The Double Helix*, the young American immediately decided he wanted to study the structure of DNA with Wilkins, but unable to 'snare' Wilkins' attention, he 'proceeded to forget Maurice'.[1] Whether this is true or not, Watson made no attempt to contact the King's College group, nor Bill Astbury's team in Leeds, nor Bernal's laboratory at Birkbeck, all of which studied DNA using biophysical techniques.[2] Instead, Watson ignored the wishes of his funders, who wanted him to stay in Copenhagen, and joined the Cambridge MRC unit, intending to learn the basics of X-ray crystallography and apply them to the structure of viruses.

On the early October day when Watson arrived in Cambridge, he was shown around town by Max Perutz; by chance they bumped into Odile, who was pushing Gabrielle in a pram. When Francis came home that evening, Odile told him that she had met Perutz 'with a young American he wanted you to meet and – you know what – he had no hair!'[3] (Watson's crew cut soon grew out and his hair eventually became daringly long for the time.) Half a century later, Odile recalled her first impressions: Watson was 'awkward', 'a very gawky, sort of skinny young man'.[4]

The next day, or perhaps a few days later, Watson and Crick met for the first time, at the Cavendish. The effect was instantaneous, as Crick recalled: 'Jim and I hit it off immediately, partly because our interests were astonishingly similar and partly, I suspect, because a certain youthful arrogance, a ruthlessness, and an impatience with sloppy thinking came naturally to both of us.'[5]

This style, which Crick had honed with Kreisel, fitted Watson perfectly. Watson was an amazingly smart young man. He had enrolled at the University of Chicago at just fifteen years old, with the intention of becoming a zoologist (throughout his life he was fascinated by birds) but then, like Crick and so many others, he read Schrödinger's *What Is Life?* and decided to study the physical basis of genetics. This led him to a doctorate with Salvador Luria, a member of what is now called the Phage Group – a loose set of scientists who studied bacteriophages, viruses that attack bacteria – obtaining his PhD at the age of twenty-two.

In *The Double Helix*, Watson claimed that from the moment he arrived in Cambridge, both he and Crick wanted to uncover the physical nature of the gene, which they thought was made of DNA. Crick's memory was more nuanced, as he explained to Watson in 1966: 'I cannot now remember what I thought at the time about the relative importance of proteins and DNA but I don't think it was quite as clear in my mind as you make out.'[6]

Through his friendship with Maurice Wilkins, Crick had plenty of opportunities to poke his nose into DNA structure long before Watson came on the scene, but he appears not to have been interested. Given that neither man sought to focus his research on DNA, we can conclude that Watson and Crick, like Wilkins and most other scientists, thought that the nucleoproteins that make up chromosomes had a genetic function, but did not consider that DNA was the sole genetic material.

In the middle of 1951, shortly after the row with Bragg over the haemoglobin hatbox, there was a small scientific meeting at the Cavendish where Wilkins presented X-ray diffraction images of DNA from four different organisms, three of which gave a characteristic X-shape. The previous year, Wilkins had been given some remarkably pure DNA samples by the Swiss chemist Rudolf Signer, which he first studied with microscopes before Ray Gosling, his PhD student, suggested they use a new X-ray source to investigate Signer's delicate, snot-like fibres.[7] This approach rapidly yielded some striking results – much better than existing X-ray images of DNA, which had been published by Bill Astbury and Florence Bell in 1938.[8] To interpret the photographs, Wilkins enlisted the help of a colleague, the theoretician Alec Stokes. At the Cavendish meeting, he presented the initial conclusions of their work and stated that DNA was helical.[9] This claim apparently made little impression on Crick, who later could not remember anything about the talk – Wilkins suggested that this forgetfulness indicated that his friend was not 'really interested at that stage' in uncovering the structure of DNA.[10] Francis may have been somewhat distracted – not only was he focused on working out the structure of the proteins he was studying for his PhD, he was about to become a father for the second time.

*

When Watson arrived in Cambridge, Crick, Perutz and Kendrew were sharing an office in the Cavendish. Watson joined them and the atmosphere soon became polluted by the incessant chatter between Watson and Crick, prompting Perutz to put the garrulous duo into Room 103 of the Austin Wing, where they could talk as much as they wanted. The chatter went on outside the laboratory too, with Crick soon inviting the new boy round for dinner, explaining the social niceties of the Cavendish over a meal cooked by Odile.[11]

Watson settled into Cambridge life, dissecting horse hearts to obtain the muscle protein he was studying, while also desperately trying to meet young women and going on weekend birdwatching trips.[12] Francis, meanwhile, was thinking about helical motifs in X-ray diffraction images of biological molecules.[13] Following Pauling's breakthrough with the α-helix earlier in the year, Crick, like many other people, was convinced that helices would turn out to be widespread in all sorts of molecules. The idea of the helix, he said later, was 'very much in the air'.[14]

Crick soon had another clash with Bragg, who had found a new way of tackling the structure of haemoglobin, the blood protein that was the focus of much of the laboratory's work. When Bragg, pleased as Punch, came into the Cavendish to announce his discovery, Crick said something like 'I must go away and check whether you are right' – at which Bragg, as he later put it, blew his top off.[15] As he explained, 'a growing irritation made me lose my temper but it was perhaps a very understandable reaction.' Crick was once again inadvertently stoking Bragg's animosity.

Even when things went right between Crick and Bragg, they went wrong. At the end of October 1951, Bragg asked Bill Cochran, a recently appointed physics lecturer, to look at a draft paper from Vladimir Vand of the University of Glasgow.[16] Vand's manuscript described a theory of X-ray diffraction by helical structures; Bragg wanted Cochran to tell him if it was correct. Somewhere along the way, Crick also saw the manuscript and agreed with Cochran that Vand's argument was not quite right.[17]

Francis then went home early, sat in front of the gas fire and idly began working on Vand's problem, eventually coming to a 'very clumsy' solution.[18] He then put down his pen and went to a wine tasting at nearby Matthew & Son, a grocers on Trinity Street.* Most of the wines on offer (nineteen Hocks and Moselles) were unimpressive – 'thin', 'a bit thin', 'a sharp aftertaste' were among his tasting notes – but as he got to the end of the list, perhaps because of the amount of wine he had drunk (he later admitted that he did not spit any out after tasting it), or perhaps because these tended to be the more expensive wines, his views mellowed: 'excellent', 'good', 'very good'.[19] With the evening turning rather dull, Francis took his leave and weaved his way past the ornate gates of Trinity and of St John's to the covered stairway that led to the Green Door.[20]

The next day, Cochran and Crick found they had made an identical correction to Vand's theory, but Cochran's version was more

---

* Heffers bookshop now occupies the premises.

thorough.[21] For once, Bragg was pleased with Crick's work, but he could not resist putting the upstart in his place. As he later wrote, ruefully: 'I was perhaps rather unfair to Crick in stressing how strongly I thought Cochran's was the solution they ought to publish as being the more elegant.'[22]

To test their theory, Crick and Cochran used some X-ray diffraction data from a synthetic polypeptide and found a perfect fit: the synthetic molecule was a helix.[23] Over the next six weeks the pair worked on a short article for *Nature*, which was submitted in December 1951.[24]

This was Crick's first publication from the Cavendish, and the beginning of a half-century association with *Nature* – he published around thirty articles in the journal, the last in 2001, at the age of eighty-five. For Cochran, their brief paper constituted 'the first fairly conclusive experimental evidence for the existence of a helical structure at the molecular level' (Pauling's model of the α-helix was a hypothesis, not a proof).[25] That would seem to be pretty significant, but at the time Cochran was underwhelmed and wrote in his diary: 'this is the most uninspiring term I've ever had in Cambridge as far as research is concerned.'[26] For Crick, the paper was the first published example of what was to become a systematic method in his research – looking at the work of other scientists and seeing how it could be improved. Crick was an intellectual magpie, attracted by other people's bright things, particularly if he perceived potential where they did not.

He was also working on two further articles related to helices. In early November he submitted a paper to the specialist journal *Acta Crystallographica*, in which he interpreted X-ray crystallographic data from haemoglobin, using Perutz's unpublished material and including a toned-down version of his Cavendish critique of the hatbox model.[27] And he was collaborating with Cochran and Vand on a fleshed-out version of Vand's theory, showing the mathematics that underpinned the paper in *Nature* and arguing that evidence from a variety of proteins suggested that many of them had a common structure – a helix.

*

Over the weekend of 10–11 November, Wilkins came to Cambridge to visit the Cricks. Watson was invited to dinner too, and Wilkins explained the state of his DNA research while baby Gabrielle grizzled. Shortly after his July talk at the Cavendish, Wilkins had asked Alec Stokes to see if it was possible to *prove* that the X-shaped diffraction pattern he obtained from DNA was produced by a helical structure. Stokes found a theoretical explanation linking the pattern and a helix, but he was reluctant to say that this constituted a proof – after all, other structures might equally produce that shape. Because of this inherent uncertainty, Stokes and Wilkins did not publish their hypothesis about the structure of the molecule.[28] As Crick later admitted, 'Maurice and Stokes were the first people to realise that DNA might be a helix', but, like Stokes, he recognised there was a fundamental problem: 'theory is not enough to prove that a given picture represents a helix'.[29]

Wilkins' description of his situation at King's excited both Crick's taste for gossip and Watson's curiosity. At the beginning of the year, the King's MRC unit had been joined by Rosalind Franklin, a Cambridge-trained physical chemist who had learned X-ray crystallography in Paris as part of her post-doctoral research on the molecular structure of coal.[30] Franklin came from a well-to-do British Jewish family where debate and argument were an essential part of life – one reason she had enjoyed Paris, where intellectuals would argue about anything. She had obtained a fellowship to return to the UK to study the structure of proteins in solution at King's, but after discussing with Wilkins, the head of the unit, John Randall, suggested she work instead on the structure of DNA. Franklin accepted the change to her research project, saying that she had no strong feelings about the idea, but emphasised that 'I am very ignorant about all such work.'[31] What turned out to be the key point in Randall's letter was that he told Franklin she would be the only person working on DNA. When she arrived at King's, as far as she was concerned, it was her project and hers alone.

Wilkins did not learn of this part of the letter for decades, although to his shock he soon discovered one consequence when he returned from his holiday to find that Gosling, who had been his student, had been transferred to Franklin without consultation. This was the first in a series of events that rapidly poisoned the working relationship between Wilkins and Franklin. Even if these problems had not intervened, it would have been hard going. He was introverted and generally diffident; she was outgoing and intellectually combative. He took her vivacity as a form of aggression; she viewed his reserve as a sign of mediocrity. He was alarmed by her; she was scornful of him. And, thanks to Randall, he believed she was working for him while she thought she was completely independent. As a result of their utterly different personalities and outlooks, compounded by Randall's lack of frankness, they were soon barely on speaking terms.* Indeed, although no one at King's knew it, Franklin was so appalled by the rows with Wilkins that in September 1951, only a few months after joining King's, she seriously considered leaving.[32]

Watson and Crick lapped up Wilkins' sad tale, accepting his side of the story without question. They had never met Franklin, but Wilkins' descriptions gave them a clearly negative impression. Laddish solidarity laced with sexism, as well as Crick's friendship with Wilkins, shaped their views. Franklin had no idea about any of this.

Apart from moaning about Franklin, Wilkins told Watson and Crick that his laboratory was holding an informal DNA colloquium on 21 November, at which Stokes, Wilkins and Franklin would all be speaking; Watson and Crick would be welcome to attend. Crick was otherwise engaged in London that evening so could not go; he also had an appointment in Oxford the following day to talk to the crystallographer Dorothy Hodgkin about his work on helices. Watson was keen to see Oxford, so it was agreed that he would go to the symposium and then travel with Crick from London to Oxford.

Watson's description in *The Double Helix* of his behaviour at

---

*Some indication of Wilkins' later attitude to Franklin and her work on DNA can be gained from an embittered letter he wrote to a friend in 1957: 'the silly bitch botched the whole business so effectively that I don't think she should be mentioned too often but she did make very useful contributions (as well as sabotage)'. Wilkins to Hamilton, 21 May [1957]. This letter was sold by Christie's in February 2023 and is archived at: http://tinyurl.com/MW-LH-21-May-1957

King's has become notorious, although it is impossible to tell how accurate it is. According to his own account, despite struggling with crystallographic jargon, Watson followed his usual practice and did not take notes during any of the three talks. While Franklin was presenting her data, he claimed he became distracted, musing about what she might look like if she 'took off her glasses and did something novel with her hair'.*[33] When Watson and Crick met at Paddington Station the next morning to get the Oxford train, Francis was in a buoyant mood. Taken together with the drily discreet comment by Crick's biographer, Robert Olby, that 'Crick had other business', it seems probable that he had been seeing a lover the previous evening.[34] Had he gone to the colloquium, subsequent events might have been very different.

On the train to Oxford, Watson struggled to recall what Franklin had said the night before – with no notes, he had to rely on his memory. Crick was simultaneously gripped by the challenge of working out what appeared to be a relatively simple structure and irritated by his friend's failure to remember important bits of detail.[35] Seizing on one fact that Watson recalled from Franklin's presentation – the water content of crystalline DNA – Crick became eager to work out the chemical implications, so as soon as they got to Oxford they went to Blackwell's bookshop where they studied a copy of Pauling's book *The Nature of the Chemical Bond* and decided that magnesium ions might play a key role.[36]

After Francis had talked to Dorothy Hodgkin about his method for studying helical motifs (helices were not found in the molecules she studied, so their meeting was of little consequence), Watson and Crick dined in Oxford with Kreisel, who was by now a lecturer at nearby Reading University. Kreisel's coarse language and freewheeling conversation and interests shocked Watson – he later complained of Kreisel's unwashed appearance and idiom.† Repelled by Kreisel's

---

*The focus on Franklin is part of Watson's novelisation of events in *The Double Helix*. The colloquium was not simply about Franklin – Wilkins presented his results, while Stokes described his helical theory, but none of that is mentioned by Watson. Stokes to Randall, 19 October 1972, GBR/0014/RNDL/3/1/6.
†The dislike was mutual and long-lasting. Over forty years later, Kreisel told Crick: 'I cannot stand Watson's unrelenting breeziness, and his OBVIOUS

oddness and perhaps jealous at meeting someone who was personally closer to Francis than he was, Watson was briefly able to see Crick
as others sometimes saw him: 'Francis greeted [Kreisel's] arrival
with great gusto, and the sound of Francis' laughter and Kreisel's
Austrian accent dominated the spiffy atmosphere of the restaurant,'
he wrote in *The Double Helix*.[37] Unhappy with the course the evening
was taking, Watson made his excuses and left Crick and Kreisel to it.

When they got back to Cambridge, Watson and Crick decided
they would attempt to work out the structure of DNA – Crick stopped
work on his thesis for the next month to concentrate on the task.[38]
They had no data of their own, only the things Wilkins had told them
and Watson's dim recollections of Franklin's presentation and an
immense dollop of confidence – or over-confidence as it turned out.
DNA, they reasoned, was clearly a lot simpler than any of the proteins that Crick was working on, so it should be amenable to a purely
intellectual attack. They were guided by two principles, which Crick
later described as the power of the helix and a strategy for solving
structures.[39] That strategy was outlined in a somewhat pretentious
document they drew up (mainly written by Crick), in which they
insisted on the apparently counter-intuitive principle of incorporating
'the *minimum* number of experimental facts' into their theory.[40] Their
justification was that 'the right model may be rejected because of some
difficulty which will sort itself out at a later stage' – a lesson of Pauling's successful solution of the α-helix. This approach sounds very
clever, but it hinges on correctly distinguishing those difficulties that
will eventually evaporate, and so can be ignored, and those which are
truly significant. That distinction may not be immediately obvious.

For a couple of weeks, they worked through the problem and
explored various possible structures, discussing them with Kendrew
and Perutz along the way, finally building a physical model of the
molecule using small metal parts made by the Cavendish workshop. Under pressure from Kendrew and others to tell the King's
group what they were up to, they decided to unveil their answer.[41]

---

assumption that he is – not merely the centre of, but – the whole universe.'
Kreisel, untitled [fictitious dialogue with Crick], undated [1994],
PP/CRI/J/1/4/10.

Wilkins and four colleagues – Franklin, researcher Bill Seeds and PhD students Ray Gosling and Bruce Fraser – soon took the train to Cambridge.[42] This was the first time that Crick met Franklin; it did not go well. She took one look at the structure – it had three intertwined helices, with the bases on the outside – and dismissed it.

Everyone, including Watson and Crick, realised that she was correct. Not only was it inside out (Franklin had clearly stated in her talk that the bases were on the inside of the molecule), but it turned out that Watson – distracted, over-confident or both – had either misunderstood or misremembered the amount of water in the crystal. As a result, the Cambridge duo had vastly underestimated the significance of water molecules in the chemical interactions that hold the DNA molecule in shape. This in turn forced them to include some entirely spurious magnesium ions to stabilise their weird structure. Nothing about their model was correct. As Crick recalled: 'It was not only that Watson made the mistake but that I did not notice it, which is equally valid. So it was a complete waste of time.' More frankly, he later called the whole thing a fiasco.[43]

This attempt to scoop the King's College MRC researchers soon threatened Crick's future. On hearing of the incident, Randall was so furious that he threatened to write an official letter of complaint to Bragg – only Wilkins' intervention stopped the whole thing turning very bad indeed. When Bragg learned of the affair, he was livid. Two nobodies in his laboratory had caused a row with another MRC unit based in a different university. How embarrassing, and how annoying.

Although there was no nasty letter from Randall – or worse, from the MRC – Crick soon received two letters from Wilkins, both written on 11 December.[44] The first letter was typewritten and somewhat stern, giving the official response from King's (Wilkins was the deputy head of the MRC unit, after all), and was copied to Randall. Wilkins pointed out that 'your ideas are made directly from statements made in the colloquium' and that while discussions between MRC units were useful, he had begun to have 'very slight uneasy feelings' about Crick's attitude. To preserve inter-laboratory relations, Wilkins wanted the Cambridge pair to cease working on nucleic acids. This had Bragg's approval and he made it clear that

Crick and Watson should get on with the work they were supposed to be doing and stop interfering with other people's research. This was not a formal ban on working on DNA, but it amounted to the same thing.

Wilkins' second letter to Crick was handwritten, and much more personal (the two men were still friends, despite everything): 'This is just to say how bloody browned off I am entirely and how rotten I feel about it all and how entirely friendly I am (...) We are really between forces which may grind us into little pieces.' There were occasional hints of Wilkins' real feelings – as well as shedding 'a crocodile tear' for 'poor Jim', he gave Francis some friendly advice: 'As far as your security with Bragg is concerned, it is probably much more important to pipe down and build up the idea of a quiet steady worker who never creates "situations" than to collect all the credit for your excellent ideas at the expense of goodwill.'

Whether or not that was good advice, there was never any chance of Crick piping down. He drafted a reply to Wilkins to be jointly signed by Watson, in which he gave a glimmer of recognition of what they had done: 'It is extremely probable that in a short space of time you and your unit will have solved decisively one of the key problems in biomolecular structure. Cheer up and take it from us that even if we kicked you in the pants it was between friends. We hope our burglary will at least produce a united front in your group!'[45]

There is no evidence this letter was sent. Even if it had been, it seems unlikely that Crick's well-meaning suggestion that everyone at King's should pull together would have been heeded. To console Watson, Crick bought his friend a copy of Pauling's *The Nature of the Chemical Bond* as a Christmas present.[46]

The day after drafting his letter to Wilkins, Francis opened his laboratory notebook, wrote the heading 'D. N. A. Chain Building' in pencil and continued trying to make the triple helix work. He accepted that the model was 'not pretty', but he thought he could understand how the chains might connect with each other. On the other hand, he considered that '2 chain model topologically possible but not possible to join'. There was just one page of this – thereafter he appears to have accepted Bragg's instruction and returned to his thesis work.[47] In a final attempt to keep open the lines of communication to King's, on 17 December he responded to a request from Stokes for a draft of the paper he had just submitted to *Nature*.[48] Helical theorists could still talk to each other, even if building models of DNA was no longer possible. In one of the few practical consequences of the whole affair, Bragg insisted that all the metal DNA components be sent to King's, where they might be useful. When the parts arrived in London, they remained in their box.

Bragg was not done with Crick. On 18 January he sent a handwritten letter to A. V. Hill, asking for advice about what to do with the wayward student:

> My worry is that it is almost impossible to get him to settle down to any steady job and I doubt whether he has got enough material for his PhD which should be taken this year. Yet he is determined to do nothing but research and is very keen to hang on here. With a wife and family he ought to be looking out for a job. I think that he overrates his research ability, and that he ought not to count on getting a job with no other commitments. Are you interested in his career enough to wish to discuss it? I should like some help in deciding what line to take with him.[49]

Bragg also wrote to the head of the MRC, expressing concerns about Crick's behaviour.[50] Even Perutz pitched in, suggesting the MRC should give Crick a shock by withholding his upcoming salary increase until he finished his PhD; the MRC turned down Perutz's unusually disciplinarian approach. Crick knew nothing of all this, but it indicates that his situation was not at all secure.

Some external perspective on his problems was soon provided by the arrival of a letter from Kreisel, who was travelling through the north African desert from Algiers to Tunis. 'Dear Prick', he began, 'I HAVE *GIVEN* THE CLAP TO A NORTH AFRICAN WHORE ZOHARA!' The letter was signed 'PURITY'.[51]

*

As far as Bragg and the people at King's were concerned, the inside-out triple helix fiasco marked the end of Crick's meddling with DNA. He turned obediently to his thesis work; his laboratory notebooks for 1952 are full of attempts to analyse X-ray diffraction images of the various proteins that he had either crystallised himself, or which had been given to him.[52] But DNA kept on pushing itself into his field of view.

In the early weeks of 1952, Wilkins wrote to Crick with the results of a recent experiment on squid sperm DNA that showed a series of 'helical layer lines'.[53] He sketched this diffraction image, which showed the distinctive X shape that would be expected from a helical molecule. Each arm of the X showed three separate bands – layer lines – revealing the presence of repetitive elements, together with two more distant reflections above and below, with the most distant being the strongest, suggesting it was formed by a reflection of a full turn of the helix.

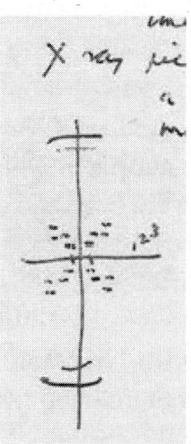

This confirmed what both Crick and Wilkins already felt – DNA was probably composed of some number of helices. Wilkins said he was fairly certain that the phosphates were on the outside of the mol-ecule and the bases were on the inside, just as Franklin had explained a few weeks earlier, and optimistically promised that 'if helices are right we might hit on the explanation soon', promising to discuss his future results with Crick. But there were no more discussions of Wilkins' results on DNA in 1952, because the only X-ray studies he made that year were on nucleoproteins – complexes of proteins and nucleic acids.[54]

A less genteel pair of letters soon arrived from Kreisel, who was now travelling around Europe, stopping off at a conference in St Moritz. He included a message for Odile – 'Please thank your gracious lady for having borne with me (with unusual grace) last time I was in Cambridge' – but followed this with descriptions of his attempts at picking up women (a year earlier he had told Crick that his approach involved 'obscene or no talk, immediate fucking etc'*[55]) and a moment of self-perception: 'This letter is a mirror of my soul – or rather of its backside.'[56]

*

In April, the biological significance of DNA began to come into clearer focus when Watson received news of an experiment on bacteriophage viruses by Al Hershey and Martha Chase at Cold Spring Harbor Laboratory on Long Island. Their results suggested, but did not prove, that DNA was the genetic material not only in bacteria, as Avery had found, but also in viruses. As Crick later explained, the result 'provided a second example of DNA apparently acting alone. This made it less likely that the first case was a freak.'[57]

Shortly afterwards, Crick had a flash of insight, through one of those brain-storming sessions that were so important to his thinking. The Cambridge astronomer Tommy Gold, one of his drinking pals, had co-authored a paper with Hermann Bondi and Fred Hoyle on the nature of the universe that invoked what Gold called 'the perfect cosmological principle'. At the end of April, Gold gave a talk at the Cambridge mathematical society, the $\nabla^2 v$ Club[†], and Crick, Watson and a host of other people from the Cavendish went along.[58] After the talk, Crick got chatting in the Bun Shop pub with John Griffith, a

---

* According to Matt Ridley, Crick's typical chat-up line was more in keeping with the times: 'He was apt to say to women at parties, "I know you are very happily married, but everybody needs a little excitement".' Ridley, M. (2006), *Francis Crick: Discoverer of the Genetic Code* (London: Harper), p. 136.
† Delta (or 'Del') Squared V – this referred to $\nabla^2 v$, the Laplace operator of a vector.

mathematically gifted fellow student. Inspired by Gold's cosmological notion, Francis mused that some kind of 'perfect principle' might also exist in biology, such as pairing.[59] He then leapt from this idea to the structure of DNA: perhaps the bases attracted each other, like with like, along the length of the DNA molecule.[60] Working out if this was possible in terms of quantum physics was beyond Crick's skills, but it was right up Griffith's street.[61] A few days later, Griffith reported that like-with-like attraction was unlikely, but that perhaps adenine attracted thymine and guanine attracted cytosine.* Crick replied that this would mean that replication of the molecule would involve complementarity – each base would be attracted to a counterpart. But his thinking stopped there; he put Griffith's answer to the back of his mind and rapidly forgot the chemical details, including the names of the four bases.[62]

A month later, biochemist Erwin Chargaff passed through Cambridge on the first leg of a scientific tour around Europe and Israel.[63] Chargaff had been an early and vociferous supporter of Avery's claim that DNA was the genetic material; since 1947 he had published twenty-eight papers on the chemical composition of nucleic acids, focusing on the proportions of the four bases in DNA from different organisms. He found that the amounts of adenine and thymine were always roughly equal, as were the amounts of guanine and cytosine. Neither Chargaff nor anyone else was sure what this meant, nor even if it was real.

Kendrew arranged for Watson and Crick to meet Chargaff at his college, Peterhouse.[64] Chargaff, who was only forty-six but affected the airs of a Grand Old Man of science, took an immediate dislike to the younger men. His impression was still vivid and precise a quarter of a century later: 'One, thirty-five years old; the looks of a fading racing tout, something out of Hogarth ("The Rake's Progress") ...

---

*Griffith was right, but for the wrong reasons. Crick had asked him to calculate the effect of electrostatic forces between bases stacked on top of each other, rather than the hydrogen bonds that in fact attract the bases to each other across the chains; his correct answer was therefore a fluke. Griffith did not know it at the time, but in the 1920s his uncle Fred had discovered the transformation of pneumonia bacteria that Avery had later shown was based on DNA.

an incessant falsetto, with occasional nuggets glittering in the turbid stream of prattle. The other, quite undeveloped at twenty-three, a grin, more sly than sheepish; saying little, nothing of consequence …'[65] And Watson's hair was shockingly long.

Things got worse as the pair immediately wounded Chargaff's pride by showing they knew nothing of his work. As Chargaff recalled, bitterly: 'It was clear to me that I was faced with a novelty: enormous ambition and aggressiveness, coupled with an almost complete ignorance of, and a contempt for, chemistry, that most real of exact sciences (…) they did not seem to know much about anything.'[66]

Indeed, as Crick remembered it, when Chargaff referred to the 1:1 ratios he had found between the pairs of bases, Crick had to ask him to explain.[67] When he did, Crick recalled that the effect was electric: 'I suddenly thought, "Why, my God, if you have complementary pairing, you are bound to get a one to one ratio." By this time, I had forgotten what Griffith had told me. I did not remember the names of the bases.'

Crick's lack of chemical nous only reinforced Chargaff's impression that he was dealing with a couple of chancers; the meeting ended on the same sour note with which it had begun.[68]

Frustrated because he could not remember any of the detail from his discussions with Griffith, the next day Crick went to find his colleague in Trinity College. Griffith had a girl in his room, but Francis interrupted proceedings, asking him to repeat the patterns of attraction he thought might exist, writing them down before making a hurried exit. As Crick told it, that still did not help: 'I had forgotten what Chargaff had told me, so I had to go back and look at the literature. And to my astonishment the pairs that Griffith said were the pairs that Chargaff said.'[69]

In retrospect this insight might seem incredibly significant, but at the time it was not. What are now often called Chargaff's rules – the amounts of A and T in DNA are equal, as are the amounts of G and C – were anything but rules at the time. Even if the ratios were correct, they might be explained by some metabolic process, not by the structure of the DNA molecule. In fact, there was no evidence that the bases paired up at all. Francis tried to find chemical proof of links between them, but the experiments did not work, and he returned to his thesis.[70]

A few weeks later, the research students at the Cavendish – over one hundred of them – were lined up in front of the Austin Wing for the annual laboratory photograph, with Bragg in the centre. Watson and Crick were there together, looking slightly uncomfortable. Photos of Crick at this time are rare, but he generally wore spectacles; as the photograph shows, at some point in the early 1950s he stopped wearing glasses.

Shortly after the photograph was taken, Watson disappeared on a three-month trip around Europe; in August he wrote a five-page letter to Francis and Odile, but there was not a word about nucleic acids. As for Wilkins, he went to a conference in France and then spent the summer teaching for a month in Brazil before visiting La Paz and Lima. He sent Crick a postcard from Rio de Janeiro telling him that the 'scenery, architecture, weather and women are exceedingly beautiful'.[71] At this point, the only people working on DNA structure were Franklin and her student, Gosling, and that would not last long – exhausted by the rows with Wilkins and frustrated by the atmosphere in the laboratory, Franklin asked Randall and her funders to allow her to move to Birkbeck from 1 January 1953 (she eventually left in the middle of March).[72]

At the beginning of August, Franklin went to a Cambridge meeting on 'The Physical Chemistry of Proteins'.[73] Crick bumped into her in the coffee queue; this was the first time they had met since the inside-out triple helix embarrassment the previous December – as Crick put it later, he had 'very little real impression of Rosalind' at the time.[74] Her impression of him was probably somewhat stronger, and presumably negative. Crick had been kept informed about the situation in the King's group through regular letters and visits from Wilkins. He knew that Franklin had been able to gain exquisite control over two different states of the DNA molecule, known as A and B, each of which appeared at specific levels of humidity, an effect that had first been observed by Wilkins.[75] The A form, which appeared at around 70 per cent humidity, was Franklin's focus – to try and overcome the differences between Wilkins and Franklin, Randall had divided the DNA work between them. Franklin concentrated on the crystalline A form and Wilkins on the paracrystalline B form, which appeared at higher humidity.

Franklin's aim was to establish the crystal structure of DNA.* The A form was not only crystalline, it had also given one very precise but complex X-ray diffraction image. Although the blurrier images of the B form that both she and Wilkins had obtained clearly suggested a helical structure – 'Big helix with several chains, phosphates on outside, phosphate-phosphate interhelical bonds, disrupted by water,' she wrote in her notes – the exciting A form image did not lend itself to a helical explanation.[76] Franklin and Gosling became convinced that the A form had some other shape – they even sent a facetious handwritten 'death notice' to Stokes, the King's theoretician of helices, announcing the demise of the helical structure for the A form.[77] Stokes later recalled that Franklin's argument seemed so convincing that he scaled down his work on a general theory of diffraction by helical structures.[78] Franklin considered that the helical B form appeared as the crystalline form lost order and dissolved – 'the stuff ultimately dissolves, i.e. chains are separated from one another by water,' she wrote – while the A form was some

---

*The insights into Franklin's thinking that follow emerged in a memorable day-long exchange with the historian Nathaniel Comfort, which took place as we engaged in a close reading of her notes in the archives of Churchill College, Cambridge.

non-helical structure, the true shape of the molecule. This apparently rigorous approach, which ignored the wet reality of the cell, was entirely understandable given Franklin's training in chemistry.

When Franklin described her data to Crick and explained why she concluded that the crystalline structure was not helical, he responded, 'You know, I think it's misleading'.[79] He suspected that, like the Cavendish researchers with the α-helix, Franklin was being misled by details in the data. Francis later recognised that whatever the validity of his argument, his behaviour had been counter-productive, making it less likely that Franklin would accept his views: 'I'm afraid we always used to adopt – let's say a patronising attitude towards her. When she told us DNA couldn't be a helix, we said "Nonsense." And when she said but her measurements showed it couldn't, we said "Well they're wrong." You see, that was our sort of attitude.'[80]

Crick's criticisms may have had an effect. Less than a week after the Cambridge meeting, Franklin began taking X-ray photos for the first time since Easter, trying to repeat the image that had convinced her that the A structure of DNA was not helical. None of the attempts was successful.[81]

*

A few weeks after meeting Franklin, Crick's PhD research brought him into conflict with Linus Pauling. Crick had found an explanation for the 5.1Å blob in X-ray images of the α-helix that had beguiled the Cavendish group; this reflection appeared because the protein samples formed what he called a coiled coil, in which multiple helices were crammed close together. As the X-rays bounced off these structures, they produced that weird spot. When Pauling visited Cambridge in September 1952, Crick explained his idea and, a month or so later, sent a paper on his theory to *Nature*, which appeared in November.[82] However, a week *before* Crick's submission, the journal received a longer manuscript on a similar topic from Pauling. This did not appear until January 1953.[83]

Both men were immediately suspicious: when Pauling saw that Crick's paper had appeared in print before his own, he was furious at being scooped, even claiming that Perutz had written to the editor of *Nature* asking for Crick's paper to be fast-tracked. In turn, Francis considered that Pauling had either lacked candour by not revealing that he was working on a similar approach, or perhaps he had been inspired by their conversation and had moved rapidly to outflank a junior rival.[84] Letters flew between Pasadena and Cambridge before both sides calmed down. The spat revealed the underlying tension between the Cavendish group and Pauling; it also showed that Crick was making a name for himself, not always in a good way.

A few weeks later Francis submitted another article to *Acta Crystallographica*, describing the structure of four proteins he had been able to successfully crystallise and interpret through X-ray diffraction images.[85] He noted that in two cases – trypsin and trypsin inhibitor – the unit cell (the basic repeated structure of the crystal) showed what was called face-centred monoclinic symmetry. Whatever Bragg's frustrations about Crick's character, he was producing papers and confirming his status as a skilled member of the small circle of crystallographers studying biological molecules.

Life was equally busy domestically. The Green Door had become far too small for the family – Gabrielle was by now a toddler, and when Michael came to visit in the school holidays things were decidedly cramped. They had been happy there, but the time had come to find somewhere new to live.

Francis initially planned to build a house, an eccentric idea at the time. He set about constructing models, trying to find the right disposition of rooms for his fantasy self-build, even enlisting the help of an architect.[86] In spring 1952 he obtained a provisional building licence from the town council and asked various Cambridge colleges if they would sell him some land. None of them could help, and he eventually realised that buying a house would be easier than building one. In July 1952 the Cricks bought a four-storey townhouse at 19 Portugal Place – a passage off Bridge Street, a stone's throw from the Green Door and next to the Maypole pub. The house cost £2,000; his annual salary was now £915, but even with a child supplement for Michael and Gabrielle on top, he needed financial help from his family to complete the purchase.[87] After months of legal paperwork, the Cricks moved house in October 1952. A few years later they bought next door, too, forming a single dwelling. This would be the Cricks' home for the next twenty-five years; in recognition of the importance of the helix in biological molecules, and in Francis's own research, in 1961 they named their house The Golden Helix.* The Cavendish workshop made a large brass golden helix which was hung over the door of number 20; it is still there today.

Despite the purchase of the house on Portugal Place, the Cricks' immediate future lay far away from Cambridge. With Francis's thesis due to be completed the following year and with his position at the Cavendish threatened by the rows with Bragg, at the end of 1952 he accepted an offer from David Harker to study proteins for a year at the Brooklyn Polytechnic Institute in New York beginning in September 1953.[88] Applying for visas, getting permission from the Divorce Court to take Michael abroad and finding accommodation all caused the Cricks some concern.[89] Although there was a real intellectual excitement associated with Harker's laboratory – he had obtained $1 million (a colossal sum at the time) to describe the first full structure of a protein – neither Francis nor Odile was enthusiastic about moving to the USA.[90] To cheer Francis up, Kreisel sent him a list of US slang sex words that might come in handy.[91]

All this gives little sense that Crick was on the cusp of a scientific breakthrough that would change the world. Although in October he had been irritated to learn over dinner with Wilkins that the King's group had made no progress on the structure of DNA, it was really not his problem. Even according to Watson's nucleic acid-focused account in *The Double Helix*, during these months their regular lunches at the Eagle pub frequently went by without a mention of DNA.[92] All that changed at the beginning of 1953, when Pauling inadvertently led Crick and Watson to attack the structure of DNA once more, this time with Bragg's enthusiastic approval.

---

*Note the singular helix – this is not a reference to the double helix of DNA.

THE DOUBLE HELIX

On Thursday 19 March 1953, Francis wrote to Michael, who was in a sick bed at boarding school. Despite his illness, Michael read his father's letter repeatedly.[1] That night he had vivid dreams about some immense secret; when he awoke, his fever had broken and the dream had evaporated but the letter – and the secret – remained.* The letter described the double helix structure of DNA, using language that would have fitted perfectly in *The Children's Encyclopædia*:

> My Dear Michael,
> Jim Watson and I have probably made a most important discovery. We have built a model of the structure of des-oxy-ribose-nucleic-acid (read it carefully), called DNA for short. (…) Our structure is very beautiful.

Francis went on to explain how the structure appeared to solve two fundamental mysteries – how genes had such a wide range of

---

*Michael auctioned the letter in 2013. It was sold for $6 million; half of the proceeds went to the Salk Institute in La Jolla, San Diego, where Crick worked for the last decades of his life.

functions and how they were able to copy themselves. DNA was made of two helical chains, connected by the bases:

> Now on one chain, as far as we can see, one can have the bases in any order, but if the order is *fixed*, then the order on the other chain is also fixed. (…) It is like a code. If you are given one set of letters you can write down the others. Now we believe DNA *is* a code. That is, the order of the bases (the letters) makes one gene different from another gene.

Several years earlier, scientists had speculated that, if DNA was indeed the genetic material, the order of the bases might explain how genes could have such a variety of functions.[2] The double helix structure strongly suggested this was the case. Furthermore, if the molecule were unwound and the strands separated, two new identical daughter molecules could be created, as Francis explained to his son:

> Now the exciting thing is that while there are 4 different bases, we find we can only put certain pairs of them together. The bases have names. They are Adenine, Guanine, Thymine and Cytosine. I will call them A, G, T and C. Now we find that the pairs we can make – which have one base from one chain joined to one base from another – are only A with T and G with C. (…) In other words we think we have found the basic copying mechanism by which life, comes from life. The beauty of our model is that the shape of it is such that *only* these pairs can go together (…) You can understand that we are very excited. We have to have a letter off to *Nature* in a day or so. Read this carefully so that you understand it. When you come home we will show you the model. Lots of love

> Daddy

The discovery of the double helix eventually revolutionised our understanding of life, utterly transformed science and medicine, and slowly and ineluctably altered Crick's life forever. But it was not just one of the most significant moments in the history of science – it is now widely seen as one of the most controversial. Watson and Crick were able to confirm their breakthrough only because they were given access to some key data from Rosalind Franklin, without her explicit agreement. This has increasingly shifted attention to Watson and Crick's apparently underhand behaviour, transforming perceptions of the discovery.[3] The truth is rather different.*

*

Crick and Watson found themselves in the astonishing position of making one of the greatest discoveries in history only because Linus Pauling made a mistake. In December 1952, Pauling wrote to his son, Peter, saying that he had completed a structure for DNA, based on the pre-war data from Astbury and Bell. Peter had recently become a research student at the Cavendish and was sharing Watson and Crick's office; he immediately showed them his father's letter. The news was alarming, if not surprising, but all they could do was wait. A month later, another letter announced that Linus had submitted an article describing the structure; Peter quickly replied, asking his father for a copy of the manuscript: 'You know how children are threatened "You had better be good or the bad ogre will come get you." Well, for more than a year, Francis and others have been saying to the nucleic acid people at King's, "You had better work hard or Pauling will get interested in nucleic acids."'[4]

Crick's warning had come true, but strictly speaking this was none of his business. However, shortly before Pauling's manuscript arrived, Crick received a note from Pauline Cowan, a PhD student at King's who he had befriended. Scribbled in coloured pencil, Cowan's letter, dated 19 January, mainly described problems with her data analysis and asked for his advice. But then she added that 'you may like to know' that a farewell colloquium on DNA would be given by 'Rosalind and Raymond' at King's on 28 January, shortly before

---

*Much of the analysis that follows was developed jointly with Nathaniel Comfort: Cobb, M. and Comfort, N. (2023), What Watson and Crick really took from Franklin. *Nature* 616:657–60.

Franklin's departure for Birkbeck. Crick immediately responded saying he would be there for Franklin's talk, but within a couple of days, Cowan wrote again, saying she had put her foot in it: 'the colloquium is supposed to be internal – outside visitors are not being asked,' she said. Soon afterwards, Wilkins confirmed that there had been a 'silly muddle', and that Cowan should not have invited him. Wilkins' letter gave a flavour of the situation at King's: 'I think that as the intention was to have it as a private fight it would be best to keep it entirely so. (…) Let's have some talks afterwards when the air is a little clearer. I hope the smoke of witchcraft will soon be getting out of our eyes.'[5] A postscript read: 'Tell Jim the answer to his question "When did you last speak to her" is *this morning*. The entire conversation consisted of one word from me.' Private fight, witchcraft, one-word conversations – things in London had gone horribly wrong.[6]

A few days later, Pauling's manuscript arrived, describing a DNA structure that resembled the ill-fated inside-out triple helix that Watson and Crick had concocted a year earlier.[7] To Watson's eyes, Pauling's version was even worse – according to *The Double Helix*, a series of basic errors meant that the structure was not actually an acid. Whatever the truth of this claim, the structure was so unstable that, as one of Pauling's colleagues put it, 'it would explode!'*[8] Watson excitedly told Bragg that as soon as Pauling realised that he had made some simple mistakes, he would inevitably find the correct structure. There would therefore be a brief period during which the Cavendish (in other words, Crick and Watson) might be able to resolve the structure before Pauling. Despite his distaste for anything to do with Crick, Bragg was attracted by the idea of getting revenge for the α-helix debacle, so he agreed to allow Crick and Watson to try and

---

* Pauling insisted to Watson that these claims were incorrect and were 'based upon on a mistake that you have made, a deficiency in your knowledge of acid strengths, that of DNA in particular'. Pauling to Watson, 20 October 1966, JDW/2/2/1384/14. Much later, Crick stated that Pauling had indeed made a mistake, but not the one Watson accused him of: 'He put a hydrogen on the phosphate group and used it to hold the structure together. This only happens under very acidic conditions (pH = 1).' Crick to Gerard, 19 June 1998, PP/CRI/J/2/18/1.

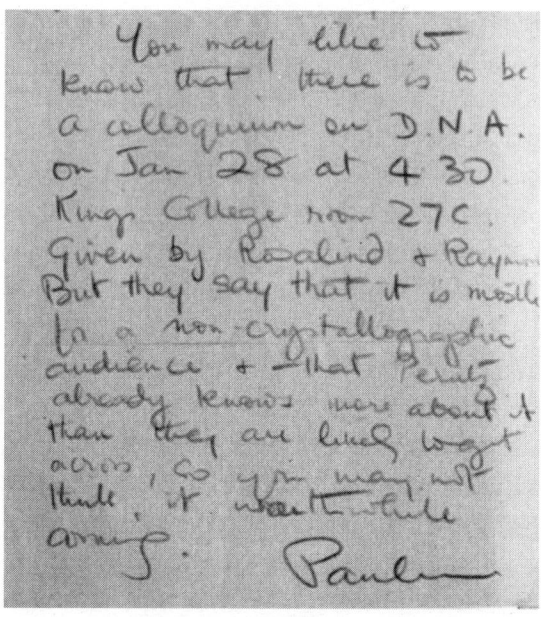

discover the structure, without informing King's. No one outside of the Cavendish knew, but now there was a race – with Linus Pauling – to find the structure of DNA.

This is where the ethics of the affair begin to get murky. Six weeks earlier, Perutz, together with other members of an MRC committee, had visited the King's unit to discuss its work.[9] This was part of an MRC initiative to increase inter-unit communication – each member of the King's group had presented their research and the committee members were given an informal laboratory report.[10] Through this visit and the accompanying report, Perutz knew all about the DNA work at King's. He may have told Crick about the visit at the time, but Francis would certainly have noticed a striking remark from Franklin and Gosling at the end of Cowan's ill-fated invitation of the previous week: 'You may like to know that there is to be a colloquium on DNA on Jan 28 at 4:30. King's College room 27C. Given by Rosalind and Raymond. But they say that it is mostly for a non-crystallographic audience and that Perutz already knows more about it than they are likely to get across so you may not think it worthwhile coming.'[11] The implication was that if Crick was interested, he should talk to Perutz about their results.

Whatever the case, at some point in January, Crick and Watson saw Franklin's and Wilkins' written summaries of their research. Franklin's casual comment suggests this would not have surprised or shocked her – as Crick later pointed out, she would equally have realised he and Watson knew about her findings, through Wilkins.*[12]

The story about Franklin's data that people are familiar with comes solely from the pages of The Double Helix and involves Watson glimpsing an X-ray diffraction image of the B form supposedly taken by Franklin (in fact by Gosling) in May 1952, known as Photograph 51.[13] Although Franklin and Gosling were supposed to be studying the A form, changes in humidity sometimes caused samples to spontaneously alter during exposure, unexpectedly producing a B form picture, such as this one, which Franklin had simply put in a drawer.[14] This image, which Wilkins casually showed Watson at King's in early February (with Franklin's imminent departure for Birkbeck, Gosling had been handed back to Wilkins, along with his data), displayed a similar set of reflections to those sketched by Wilkins in his letter to Crick nearly a year earlier.†

According to Watson's account, the image proved that DNA must be helical. But that was what everyone at King's – including Franklin – thought with regards to the B form, what Crick expected and what Wilkins and Stokes had concluded twenty months earlier.[15] Watson was clearly excited by the photograph, and perhaps also at the idea of stealing a march on Franklin – over forty years later, Kreisel recalled 'a memorable luncheon in Rose Crescent', a narrow Cambridge street full of cafés, where Watson told Crick that 'he had important information and that Franklin was unaware of this'.[16] But Crick did not see the photo until weeks after they had discovered

---

*Ray Gosling, who was Wilkins' (and Franklin's) PhD student, later wrote that the double helix was 'an accident arising out of Maurice's relationship with Crick'. Gosling, Some recollections of DNA studies in the Biophysics Laboratories of King's College, (undated [1976]), K/PP178/5/24.

† In his 2003 autobiography, Wilkins superimposed his sketch from March 1952 over Photograph 51. The sketch matches the lower reflections perfectly, but not the strong outer reflection, because it was not drawn to scale; it also lacks some of the intermediary reflections. Photograph 51 is clearer and more intense than the photograph Wilkins used to make his sketch, but virtually all the key parts of the B form image had already been revealed by Wilkins and shared with Crick a year earlier.

the structure, nor did it provide Watson with any new information beyond a very rough idea of the intensity distribution.*

This image and its supposed role has now passed into popular culture – *Photograph 51* was the title of a play on the London stage that starred Nicole Kidman as Franklin; it also appears on a UK fifty-pence piece issued to commemorate the centenary of Franklin's birth in 2020.[17] But despite this notoriety, in the real unfolding of events Photograph 51 played no part in the discovery of the double helix.[18]

*

On Thursday 5 February 1953, Wilkins wrote to Francis accepting an invitation to visit the Cricks and thanking him for his 'shoal of daily letters' (infuriatingly, these have all been lost; their frequency indicates Crick's intense interest).[19] Crick had promised to share Pauling's manuscript with his friend; in return Wilkins now offered to tell him 'all I can remember and scribble down from Rosie'.

Wilkins arrived at Portugal Place looking forward to a 'jolly, light-hearted weekend of sociability' after the tensions of the previous week.[20] That was not to be. He found himself having Sunday lunch not only with Francis and Odile but also with Watson and Peter Pauling – and he was the main course.[21] After a few social niceties, he was bombarded with questions about DNA. Appearing to be good sports, Watson and Crick urged him to start building a structure, but Wilkins insisted that would have to wait until Franklin left King's and stopped working on DNA, as she had agreed with Randall.[22] Unable to budge his friend, Crick asked the decisive question: in the meantime, would Wilkins agree to the Cavendish duo reviving their attempt to find the structure? Eeyore-ish, Wilkins agreed. He did not even have the wit to say that he needed to consult Randall. The moment stuck in Crick's mind, as he recalled in 1966: 'I must say the sort of agreement was given slightly reluctantly, there was

---

*By making a great fuss of this moment in his book, Watson put himself at the centre of the story and made matters easier for those who could not follow more detailed arguments (he later said he 'under-described the science' in order not to 'kill the book for the general reader'). Perutz, M., Wilkins, M. and Watson, J. (1969), DNA helix. *Science* 164:1537–9, p. 1539.

no doubt about that (...) I remember the scene because we were somewhat edgy about it.'[23] A downcast Wilkins returned to London, having agreed to a one-sided pact engineered by a man he considered a friend.

Crick's cruel question was intended to save that friendship, but it was completely hypocritical. Bragg had already given the go-ahead for Watson and Crick to focus on DNA structure, ordering the Cavendish workshop to make new metal components for them to use in a model. Crucially, Crick and Watson did not accord Franklin the same courtesy they had just extended to Wilkins. Perhaps they were encouraged by her brief comment to Pauline Cowan, but nevertheless they – or Perutz or Bragg – should have asked Franklin, and Randall, for permission to use her data. Ambition, or thoughtlessness, stayed their hand.

*

Resolving the structure took five weeks of hard work. For Watson, this was interspersed with games of tennis, visits to the cinema and more attempts to find a girlfriend. Francis had his thesis to finish and was writing up two mathematical explorations of his coiled-coil idea that were so complex he needed Kreisel's help, so his only break from work came with domesticity.[24] Even then, there was little respite and Odile recalled that at home he was more preoccupied than usual: 'There was a sort of suppressed excitement, great sorts of goings on, the whole time they were thinking about it, all the time. (...) Francis was think think think.'[25]

Francis was also worried by money problems and again requested Kreisel's aid – this time with a loan – only to be met with a bizarre reference to his friend's stock market speculation: 'Do you mind waiting a week for the money?' Kreisel wrote, 'I am most excited about Stalin's impending death, I am convinced it'll rock the market.'*[26]

Although the method Watson and Crick adopted to solve the structure is generally called model-building, in their full description

---

*Kreisel signed his note 'HE WHO GAMBLES WITH DEATH'.

of the double helix, published in 1954, they more correctly described it as 'the classical method of trial and error'.[27] This meant they stumbled towards the final answer through a series of mistakes, which were revealed and resolved through intense discussion and attempts to test each step against known chemical principles. As Francis recalled: 'Most of the time we were engaged in complicated discussions concerning points in crystallography and biochemistry. The major motivation was to understand. (...) The most important requirements in theoretical work are a combination of accurate thinking and imaginative ideas.'[28]

All this took the form of one long, free-flowing argument, a perpetual mutual questioning and probing. Much of this discussion took place in the Cavendish, but it flowed over as the pair ate meals together at Portugal Place and made many visits to the Eagle, which soon became the stuff of scientific legend.[29] In 1965, seventeen-year-old Bunty Bains from British Columbia wrote to Crick in disbelief, having heard at a local science fair that the double helix structure 'was formulated with Dr J. D. Watson in a pub'. Shocked, she demanded to know if this was true. Crick replied, somewhat sheepishly: 'Jim Watson and I did a lot of our talking in a pub, but that is a long story'.[30]

Their starting point was that there were a number of helices in the molecule (most likely one, two or three), and that the bases were 3.4Å apart, which had first been reported by Astbury and Bell in 1938.[31] They also knew from Franklin's part of the MRC report (and probably also from conversations with Wilkins) that the two forms of DNA molecules, A and B, had different dimensions – the B form repeated every 34 Å, suggesting ten or twenty bases per turn, whereas the crystalline A form was somewhat squatter, at 28 Å.[32] Franklin's report also included the dimensions of the unit cell and the molecule's symmetry, but neither of these pieces of information were used in building the model. The possibility that there was complementary pairing of the bases, which had briefly excited Crick the previous year, was not raised until the end of the process, something that Crick later admitted might seem incredible but was nonetheless true.[33]

After deciding that two chains were more likely than three, they put the bases on the outside of the molecule, just as they had in 1951, despite the common view of everyone at King's that they were on the inside. Watson – who was doing most of the work – persisted with this approach for some time, until Crick broached the problem with him at the end of a meal in the basement dining room at Portugal Place: 'Why not put them on the inside?' he asked. 'That would be too easy!' came the reply. As Watson climbed the stairs, Francis called out after him, 'Then why don't you do it?'[34] So he did.

That only raised another problem – the bases had to fit into the space between the two strands. Watson was convinced that the phosphate chains were parallel, running in the same direction. Structural considerations required that such a helix would have an angle of eighteen degrees between each base and twenty bases per full turn. This meant jettisoning the ten bases per turn suggested by Wilkins' and Franklin's X-ray data; it also pushed the sugars in the sugar-phosphate backbones too close together.[35] Crick recalled: 'Watson was always trying to build it with the sugars too close. He went away one day and said, "You try it," and while he was playing tennis I didn't try his scheme; I was convinced it was wrong, [so] I built one with a thirty-six degree of rotation.'[36] Once he had completed the small single-stranded model, which implied ten bases per complete turn of the helix, he left a note on it to Watson, 'This is it – thirty-six degrees rotation', and went off to lunch.[37]

*

The final phase of Watson and Crick's work revealed that despite having at the forefront of their minds Bragg and Perutz's failure to discover the α-helix because they focused on a feature that was not in fact significant, they had similarly made a fundamental assumption that was profoundly misleading.[38] It all related to the bases and how they might pair up. Watson and Crick had assumed that the precise molecular structure of the bases was not constant – previous research had suggested that the position of a hydrogen atom in the bases could vary, producing slightly different versions of each molecule, called tautomers. A mixture of tautomers implied that hydrogen bonds – weak bonds between hydrogen and nitrogen or oxygen atoms, which held the α-helix together – could not be involved in joining the bases in DNA because the hydrogen atoms would not always be in the same place.[39]

At some point, Watson found figures in a thesis that suggested the position of the hydrogen atoms in each base was constant; hydrogen bonds could therefore exist between bases. Crick described the next step in the argument, which involved the expertise of Jerry Donohue, a US chemist who had worked with Pauling and was now sharing Watson and Crick's office:

> I remember this very clearly, Jerry and Jim were by the blackboard and I was by my desk, and we suddenly thought, 'Well perhaps we could explain 1:1 ratios by pairing the bases.' It seemed too good to be true. So at that point all three of us were in possession of the idea we should put the bases together and do the hydrogen bonding.[40]

So, Watson tried a model in which each base would link via hydrogen bonds with another base of the same kind. Crick pointed out that this did not explain Chargaff's ratios, but this was not a decisive argument – no one was sure they were real or that they were related to the structure of the molecule.

A bigger problem emerged when Donohue told Watson that three of the four base structures he had found were wrong and that in the correct form (called keto) the hydrogen atoms were located elsewhere.[41] After carefully checking that Donohue was correct, Watson had to admit that his like-with-like scheme would not work with the keto forms, either. Another impasse.

On the morning of Saturday 28 February, Watson was in room 103, idly fiddling with the flat cardboard outlines of the bases, turning them over, when Donohue came in. Suddenly, wrote Watson, 'I became aware that an adenine-thymine pair held together by two hydrogen bonds was identical in shape to a guanine-cytosine pair held together by at least two hydrogen bonds.'[42] Donohue could see no problem with Watson's scheme, and neither could Crick when he rolled in a short while later.

This was the decisive moment. Not only did the A–T and G–C pairings explain Chargaff's ratios, the whole thing fitted a piece of

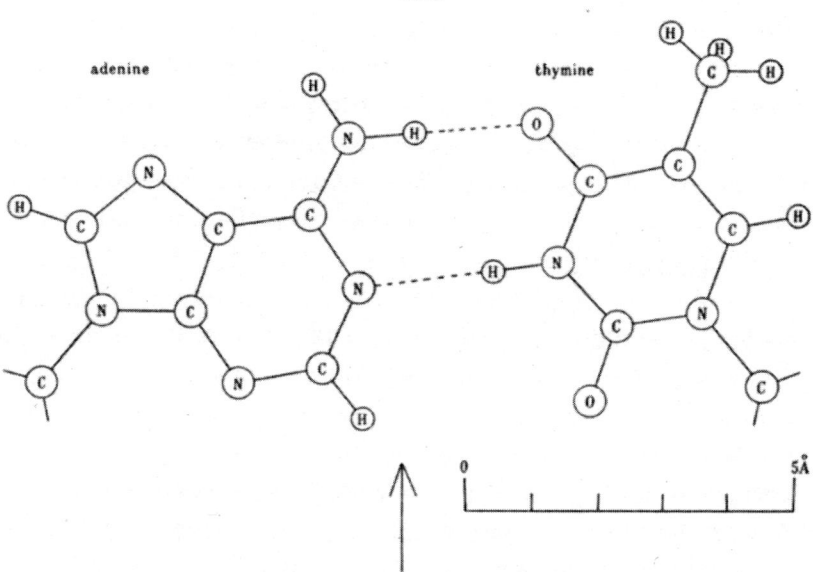

FIGURE 3. The pairing of adenine and thymine. Hydrogen bonds are shown dotted. One carbon atom of each sugar is shown. The arrow represents the crystallographic diad.

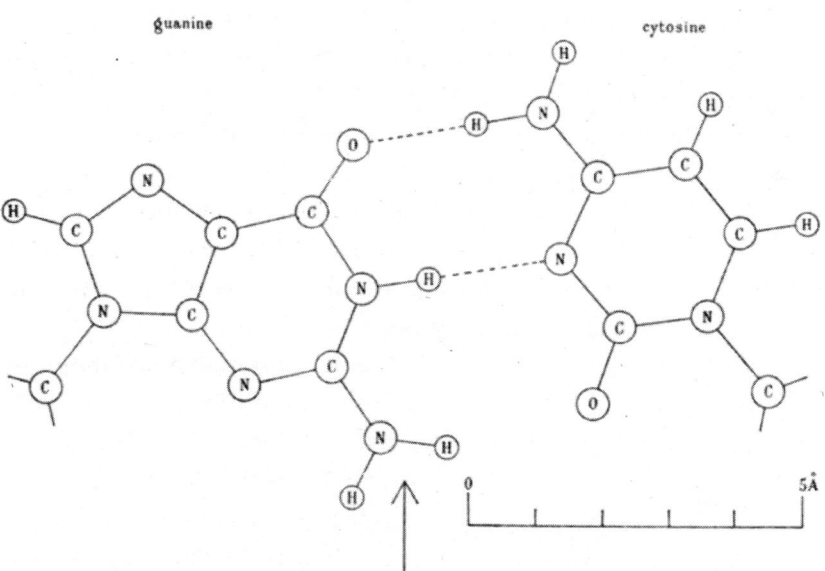

FIGURE 4. The pairing of guanine and cytosine. Hydrogen bonds are shown dotted. One carbon atom of each sugar is shown. The arrow represents the crystallographic diad.

Figures from Crick and Watson's 1954 paper. There are in fact three hydrogen bonds in the guanine–cytosine pair.

crystallographic jargon that Franklin had used to describe the A form in her MRC summary: 'It was apparent that the crystalline form was based on a face-centred monoclinic unit cell with the C-axis parallel to the fibre axis.'[43] This implied that in the A form the space group – how the crystal could be rotated in three dimensions – was what was called C2. Having by chance studied monoclinic symmetry in trypsin and trypsin inhibitor over the previous couple of years, Crick realised that it implied that the bases must lie perpendicular to the strands; if there were two strands, they would be oriented in opposite directions. As he recalled: 'As soon as I saw Watson's base pairing I said, "Look, it's got the right symmetry."' He later said that although this was not a watertight argument, it was one of the important things contained in Franklin's summary.[44]

Watson, however, had resisted this idea whenever Crick raised it. As Francis later put it, somewhat acidly, 'Jim never liked this argument, I don't think he could quite follow it'.[*][45] This was even more true than Crick realised. Franklin's outline of her talk at the November 1951 colloquium in King's – the one at which Watson had not taken notes – shows that she described the C2 space group at that early stage.[46] Had Watson paid more attention or simply transcribed her words, or had Crick attended her talk, the implications for the structure would surely have become evident much earlier.[47]

As well as this satisfying fit with Franklin's data, there was also the instant, intuitive confirmation that the structure revealed two of the molecule's essential functions: replication could occur by reciprocal base-pairing, and the variability of the sequences of the bases could specify variable gene function. Many molecular structures tell us little about function – for example, in terms of its biological

---

*As a result, Watson and Crick saw the process by which the double helix was constructed in different ways. *The Double Helix* contains no mention of this symmetry question and skips over the MRC report in half a sentence. In 2003, Crick told Mark Bretscher: 'Jim failed to grasp the implication of the C2 symmetry (and did not trust Chargaff's rules) so his account does not agree with mine.' Crick to Bretscher, 13 May 2003, GBR/0014/BRTS 42/73. By 2016, however, Watson agreed with Bretscher about the 'prime importance' of C2 symmetry in formulating the structure. Watson to Bretscher, 16 September 2016, courtesy of Mark Bretscher.

function the α-helix was mute, as Watson's mentor Max Delbrück put it.[48] DNA is different: with only a brief explanation anyone can see how it works, because of how the bases pair up. Watson had found the key not by logic but serendipity.[49]

At this point they went to the pub for lunch. Watson later claimed that 'Francis winged into the Eagle to tell everyone within hearing distance that we had found the secret of life.'[50] This is now so widely believed that it is even referred to on a plaque outside the pub, but although this phrase captured Watson and Crick's elated mood, things did not happen that way. Francis always denied he said anything of the sort and in 2016, at a celebration of the centenary of Crick's birth, Watson publicly admitted that he had made it up for dramatic effect (a few years earlier, he had confessed as much to Kindra Crick, Francis's granddaughter).[51]

The days after the breakthrough saw a flurry of activity at the Cavendish as the metal components arrived, with Francis doing most of the work building a physical model, which they then checked using compasses and plumb lines, tightening the clamps and bosses that held the precise metal components.[52] The physicists on the floor above later said that there was so much noise and excitement in the MRC unit that steam seemed to be rising through the building.[53] At first, the physical model consisted of just a single base and its attached phosphate-sugar molecule, not the tall double-stranded model that everyone is familiar with. In fact, they were not sure how the atoms might fit together, so they built two, slightly different models.[54] After deciding which version seemed more correct, Crick then devised a mathematical way of being certain that the complementary base would fit, without having to build a complete physical model at this stage.[55] The structure was then approved by Bragg, who inspected it once he had got over a nasty bout of flu, and by Alexander Todd, the head of chemistry at Cambridge.[56] All that now remained was the delicate problem of telling the King's researchers.

The trickiness of that soon became clear. With the structure complete except for some final tweaks, Crick received a letter from Wilkins, dated Saturday 7 March, in which he referred to Franklin's imminent departure to Birkbeck and promised a collaborative attack on the structure of DNA: 'I think you will be interested to know that our dark lady leaves us next week and much of the 3-dimensional data is already in our hands. (…) At last the decks are clear and we can put all hands to the pumps! It won't be long now.'[57] Francis recalled his mixed feelings at receiving the letter: 'was it more a question of laughing or – well – you know, sadness almost. You see, there was the model.'[58]

When he told Odile that they seemed to have made a big discovery, she did not pay much attention: 'You were always coming home and saying things like that, so naturally I thought nothing of it,' she recalled.[59] Much later, Crick gave a pithy summary of the whole affair: 'It's true that by blundering about we stumbled on gold, but the fact remains that we were looking for gold.'[60]

*

Unknown to Watson, Crick, Wilkins or anyone else until the late 1960s, Franklin was hot on their heels – though she would not have perceived it this way, having no idea that Bragg had unleashed Watson and Crick.[61] If she had thought she was in a race, it would have been with Pauling. Working hard to finish up before leaving for Birkbeck, Franklin was applying the complex Patterson analysis to her data, hoping that the structure would emerge. This was an approach that Crick had counselled her against the previous summer, because of his doubts about its appropriateness for DNA, and because he feared it would mislead her. For over a month the A form resisted her attempts to interpret it, so she eventually turned her attention to the simpler, clearly helical B form and began to explore what kinds of structure might account for the data – her version of model-building.

By late February she had accepted that both the B form and the A form were probably helical, with two strands, and she had also realised that the bases could occur in any order along a strand, with a major implication for function. As she noted: 'an infinite variety of nucleotide sequences would be possible to explain the biological specificity of DNA', showing she now considered that DNA was the genetic material.[62] However, there were two structural points she did not grasp: the existence of complementary base-pairing and the fact that the two strands were oriented in different directions – one of the main implications of C2 symmetry.

These errors are easy to explain. Firstly, like Crick and Watson until the final stages, Franklin was using the wrong structures of the bases, so she would not have been able to work out base pairing had she tried. Second, there are over two hundred space groups and unlike Crick, Franklin was not familiar with C2 (she apparently had to be guided to the final identification by Dorothy Hodgkin).[63] Nonetheless, she later apparently said she could kick herself for having failed to realise the structural implications of this piece of her data.[64]

Both Watson and Aaron Klug – who became Franklin's close collaborator – argued that her failure to discover the structure revealed that she lacked a certain conceptual boldness.[65] Crick later said she was too focused on following the systematic approach she considered to be correct, and wanted to avoid 'short cuts'.[66] Even Franklin's sympathetic biographer, Brenda Maddox, agreed: 'An outrageous leap of the imagination would have been as out of character as running up an overdraft or wearing a strapless red dress.'[67] A more measured estimation of the difference between Franklin's approach and that of Watson and Crick is that she was working on her own, without anyone with whom she could discuss.[68] There seems little doubt that, left to her own devices, she would eventually have found the correct structure. But she did not. In the third week of March, Franklin left King's for the happier, more cosmopolitan environment of Birkbeck, her mind already moving away from DNA.*

*

The earliest account of the discovery of the double helix can be found in Crick's notes for a 1961 lecture, 'The Gene: History of the DNA Model', which he gave in Cambridge in January and then in Oxford in May.[69] As well as acknowledging the importance of the MRC report and of Franklin's work, Crick also highlighted some general lessons.[70]

---

*In an end-of-year letter to her friend Anne Sayre, summing up all her activities of 1953, Franklin described her move to Birkbeck, her new work on viruses and her continuing interest in coal, but did not mention DNA. The 'only interesting thing that has happened' in the last year, she said, was a wonderful summer holiday in Israel. Franklin to Anne and David Sayre, 17 December 1953, ASMB.

First, he argued that 'scientific discovery is tortuous'. The twists and turns revealed science not as an inevitable progression of logical steps, but as something unpredictable and exciting, with no guarantee of success. However, as both Watson and Crick subsequently explained, had they not found the structure, then Wilkins, or Franklin, or Pauling, or someone else, would soon have done so. Watson and Crick discovered it because they were smart and somewhat unscrupulous and because Watson was determined to make the breakthrough. They were also very lucky.

Francis also emphasised the advantages of collaboration. Without Watson, he would never have even begun working on the problem, while Watson would have been unable to find the solution on his own. Without the starting point of the King's data – an odd form of 'collaboration' – they would have found it much harder to succeed. This also relates to another of Crick's conclusions: the importance of 'personal matters' in science. The King's unit was hampered because the researchers involved were unable to cooperate. As Watson has said several times, had that barrier not existed, we would undoubtedly speak of the Franklin–Wilkins structure. In contrast, Crick's relationship with Watson, and the ease with which he and Odile welcomed the young American into their social circle, were all part of the magic that made the collaboration so effective. Had Crick not enjoyed Watson's company, not only in room 103 but also in the Eagle, walking the Backs and at the dinner table, events would have turned out differently.

Finally, Crick highlighted the importance of three factors: 'preconceived ideas, plus informed thinking, plus adventurousness'. These corresponded to his confidence that the structure must be helical, the importance of general knowledge of the topic and a readiness to explore even unorthodox solutions.

Making such leaps is easier if you have a collaborator to say that you have jumped too far, or to encourage you in the right direction if something seems intuitively correct. That style of working eventually enabled Crick to think further and deeper than most of his contemporaries. The double helix not only made Crick's reputation, it gave him a key that would unlock the string of major discoveries and insights that shaped his whole career.

WATSON AND CRICK

The five months that separated March 1953, when Francis co-discovered the double helix, and August, when he and his family boarded a transatlantic liner bound for New York, were the most transformational, intense and stressful of his whole life.

He made a scientific revolution by writing four articles with Watson, exploring different aspects of the structure of DNA. These articles marked their place in history, down to the order by which their names are known.

He completed his PhD thesis, got it typed up and submitted and, days before embarking for America, passed his viva examination.

He dealt with press interest in the discovery and its implications from around the world, made his first foray into broadcasting, and repeatedly presented the structure to colleagues (Wilkins, Franklin, Randall, Hodgkin, Pauling …) and to the public.

He made his presence felt on the national scientific scene, through his interventions at a conference at King's and an ingenious invited lecture about the double helix at the University of Edinburgh.

He negotiated – not entirely successfully – the deep tensions provoked by the discovery and by his desire to communicate it, which affected his relations with friends, colleagues and superiors.

He struck up a mutually respectful and collegial relationship with Franklin, discussing with her repeatedly and giving her detailed feedback on her draft articles on DNA, forming a friendship that would last the rest of her short life.

He worried over money, struggled with the MRC over his future, and was finally able to ensure his employment when he eventually returned to the UK.

He fulfilled all the tedious obligations for entering the USA – visas, medicals, finances – he found tenants for Portugal Place and made domestic arrangements for his family in New York, including finding a school for Michael.

He also went with Odile to the usual round of parties and at some point in June she fell pregnant again.

*

The most significant part of all this busy-ness began in early March. Even before the precise detail of their DNA structure was complete, Crick started writing a short scientific article outlining the discovery.[1] This paper, which heralded a profound change in our understanding of the world, was signed Watson and Crick, which is why their names are known in that order. It was that way from the first draft – the words were mainly Crick's, but Watson had done most of the actual work in those decisive weeks in February and so came first. The deal was that Crick would be first author on a subsequent paper, describing the structure in more detail.[2]

As the metal model gradually grew out of the bench in room 103, Kendrew volunteered to break the bad news to King's; he telephoned Wilkins, inviting him to come and see the model (Franklin and Randall came separately, a few weeks later).[3] Wilkins rushed to Cambridge and was silently impressed – 'rather stunned' was the phrase he used in his memoirs. Watson recalled that the King's man was remarkably unresentful; for his part, Wilkins remembered feeling some inner turmoil and a slight tetchiness, but the atmosphere remained amicable.[4] Trying to be generous, Watson suggested that Wilkins be a co-signatory on the article he and Crick were writing, but Wilkins declined the offer.[5]

With the model needing only a few final adjustments, Watson

left for a week-long work trip to Paris, leaving Crick to deal with the King's situation and to explain the structure to the growing number of curious visitors.[6] On Saturday 14 March, once all the coordinates and angles had been calculated, the model was truly complete. Crick's diary entry for that day reads: 'Finally refined structure.'[7] He was so tired he went straight to bed.[8] A few days later, Francis wrote to a colleague expressing his glee at what they had just achieved: 'You will have no doubt surmised that not having heard from me I have been doing other things. How right you are! (…) Jim and I have produced a structure for DNA (if you remember what that is) which is so beautiful that we swoon every time we think of it.'[9]

While Watson was away, Francis sent Wilkins a draft of the *Nature* article; his friend responded with a mixture of resignation, self-aggrandisement and a stiff upper lip:

> I think you're a couple of old rogues but you may well have something. I like the idea. Thanks for the MSS. I was a bit peeved because I was convinced the 1:1 ratio was significant & had a planar group sketched and was going to look into it & as I was back again on helical schemes I might, given a little time, have got it. But there is *no good grousing* – I think it's a very exciting notion & who the hell got it isn't what matters.[10]

Randall was apparently less equanimous. Bill Seeds recalled that his boss was 'like a scalded rat' on hearing the news, while two of his colleagues said that 'Randall was furious, his nose out of joint.'[11] Once the venting was over, the King's researchers rightly decided that the best response was to ensure that their experimental data appeared in *Nature* alongside the Watson and Crick paper. Initially this just involved Wilkins' group, but to his irritation, Franklin understandably decided she, too, should be involved (Wilkins described her article as 'a new entrant in the rat race').[12]

The second half of March saw a terrific rush as the three articles (signed Watson and Crick, Wilkins, Stokes and their colleague Wilson, and Franklin and Gosling) were hurriedly completed. Odile got roped in, turning Crick's rough pencil sketch of a half turn of the double helix into an elegant image that would be published alongside her husband's prose.[13] Wilkins told Crick the situation at King's was a 'madhouse' and 'frantic chaos'; Francis, meanwhile, had to deal with the Cambridge end of things without Watson.[14] He sent the latest draft of their paper to Wilkins ('Jim has gone to Paris, the lucky dog'), asking for his friend's comments on various points. Wilkins' reply included a strangely self-effacing suggestion. Watson and Crick's original acknowledgements read: 'We have also been stimulated by the very beautiful experimental work of Dr. M. F. Wilkins and his co-workers at Kings College, London.' That would not do, said Wilkins: 'delete very beautiful and say we have been stimulated by the work of the group at Kings or something,' he told Crick.[15] Bemused, Francis did as he asked, but added Franklin's name.

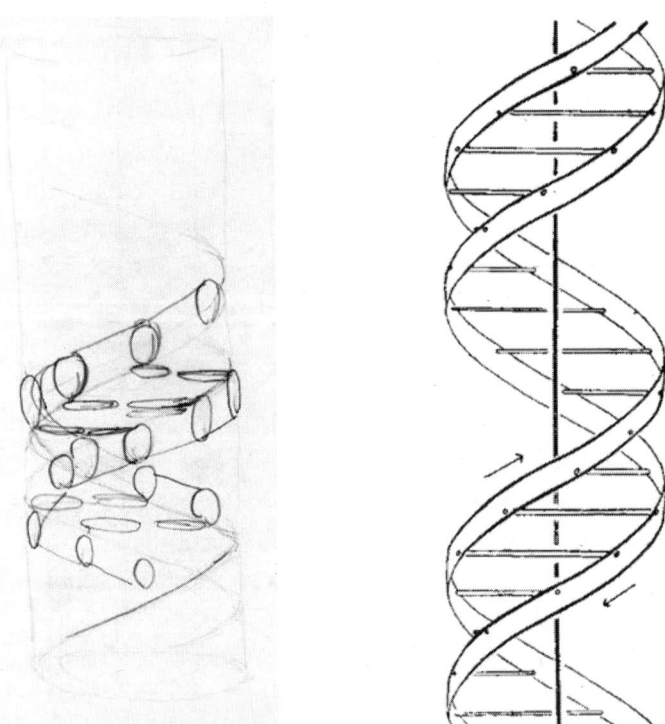

Francis's sketch of the double helix (*left*) and Odile's schematic drawing for *Nature* (*right*).

Crick also had views about Wilkins' draft.[16] Disappointed by Wilkins' focus on technical detail, Crick told his friend the paper should begin by highlighting the three important points it contained:

1. the helical nature of the structure
2. the qualitative agreement with our model
3. the biological occurrence of the structure*

Wilkins did not take Crick's advice, and his paper was all the duller for it.

In the same letter, Crick argued that all three groups should see each other's papers before submitting them – 'We think it essential that the whole position should be brought into the open and cleared up as soon as possible,' he wrote. To further pressure Wilkins, Crick warned him that Franklin might hand over her data to Pauling, who was coming to England shortly – if this happened, it might be Pauling who confirmed the structure, rather than Wilkins (none of the three papers contained decisive proof of the double helix). Frustrated by having to wait to submit his article with Watson, Crick urged Wilkins to cooperate with Franklin:

> For this reason, therefore, and also because the present position is embarrassing to us, we have written a short note to Randall to suggest a meeting on Wednesday. (...) As we shall have held up our letter for 10 days we feel that we should see Rosy's letter before ours is submitted and that she should see ours. (...) Would you ring us up and tell us how you feel about all this.

In an undated draft letter to Randall, Francis attempted to find the right words to navigate a difficult situation, insisting he wanted to discuss 'the question of Miss Franklin' although what this involved is unclear. They did all eventually get sight of each other's papers, but there is no evidence that a meeting took place.[17] Wilkins was certainly hostile to the suggestion – 'I don't see why we have to have a *meeting*,' he complained to Crick.[18]

---

*Crick was urging Wilkins to emphasise that he had found the same result in several sources of DNA from across the kingdom of life, including squid sperm, bacteriophages and Avery's transforming principle in bacteria. Wilkins ignored this suggestion and these significant findings, which linked the structural studies with the ground-breaking genetic work on DNA by Avery and by Hershey and Chase, were hidden away at the end of Wilkins' article where they are rarely noticed.

The explanation for Wilkins' truculence was that underneath his apparently calm exterior, he was raging – that 'couple of old rogues' business was an act. On 19 March he wrote bitterly to his friend, the chemist Leonard Hamilton:

> Francis and Jim Watson have a helical model with a clever notion in it and our exp. evidence & their model all appear in Nature in about a month.
>
> But it is an absolute *Rat Race*. Francis is being by no means ethical about it all, using all the data & ideas he & Jim got from here & then maintaining he has done it all by pure reason. But keep that to yourself. I am very fond of Francis but he is rather bad on these things. (…)
>
> This may sound very mean & anti-scientific but people *just aren't playing the game* in this business. Pauling pinches ideas & Francis pinches data & doesn't acknowledge.[19]

Crick knew nothing of this, and he soon worsened his reputation at King's. At the end of March, Randall hosted a one-day conference on collagen – a relatively simple molecule which is the most common protein in the human body. Crick strolled down to the meeting, where he was so impressed by Pauline Cowan's X-ray diffraction images of collagen that he could not resist the temptation to get up and speak. Inevitably, this was more of a comment than a question, as he explained to his friend and her colleagues what they had found, using that 'beautiful' word again:

> I did not intend to say anything, but having seen that extremely beautiful photograph which the workers here have produced I do not think that the occasion should pass without one who is in crystallography commenting upon it … it really is quite overwhelming … it has the two characteristics of a helix; absence of a lot of the spots, which means the structure is defined by a few parameters, and an open space in the centre without reflections.[20]

As he sat down, he predicted that the structure of the molecule would be discovered 'in a short period'. This attitude – which seemed arrogant but was in fact a blithe product of confidence in the data and Crickian enthusiasm – must have ramped up Randall's irritation. It undoubtedly reinforced the impression that, as Bragg put it, Crick was the sort of chap who was always doing someone else's crossword.[21] Wilkins would have used much stronger terms, in private at least. To Francis, he limited himself to a sarcastic comment a few days later: 'Have you a structure for collagen yet?'[22]

On 2 April, all three papers were simultaneously submitted to *Nature*, in a coordinated move intended to give equal priority to all three groups.[23] The three papers appeared together, under the collective title 'Molecular structure of nucleic acids,' without having gone through peer review (typical for the time) and in slightly under four weeks (the usual publication time in *Nature* was four to five months).[24] The cover of the journal gave no indication of the significance of what lay within – like *The Times*, in this period *Nature* had advertisements on its front page.

The papers from Wilkins and Franklin were both full of data relating to the B form – Wilkins showed that DNA had a similar structure in a range of organisms and samples, while Franklin and Gosling focused on a detailed analysis of Photograph 51, concluding 'our general ideas are not inconsistent with the model proposed by Watson and Crick' (they also thanked Crick, Stokes and Wilkins for discussion; Watson was not mentioned). In contrast, the paper by Watson and Crick, which appeared first, was shorter – crammed into less than a page of text – and was data-free. As Crick later admitted, 'The structure is produced like a rabbit out of a hat, with no indication as to how we arrived at it.'[25]

The simple opening paragraph, which was added in the final version of the article, set out their stall: 'We wish to suggest a structure for the salt of deoxyribose nucleic acid (D.N.A.). This structure has novel features which are of considerable biological interest.' A striking element of the article was Odile's uncredited drawing – much later, Francis remarked, 'It is ironical that this, her most widely reproduced drawing, should be in a style totally unlike her normal one.'[26] There was just one mention of the function of DNA, written by Crick and found towards the end, in a stand-alone paragraph: 'It has not escaped our notice that the specific pairing we have postulated immediately suggests a possible copying mechanism for the genetic material.' This coy phrase, which is known to all students of molecular biology, was written by Crick as a claim of priority – because base pairing was complementary, if the DNA molecule was somehow untwisted, two identical molecules could be produced, each by synthesising a complementary strand.[27] But this striking fact was not the only point being made in that sentence. Those final three words, 'the genetic material', signalled a decisive shift in our understanding of the role of DNA, which was now identified with the gene. This change was impelled not by new experimental evidence but by the implications of the structure, with complementary base pairing allowing for replication and the infinitely variable sequence of bases hinting at how genes might function.

While all this earth-shaking stuff was going on, Francis and Odile were worrying about their impending move to the USA, which was posing severe financial problems. In the middle of March, Kreisel promised to lend them more cash and Crick wrote him two IOUs for £200 (he also borrowed a substantial sum from his mother).[28] But six weeks later, Kreisel's money had still not arrived; he sent Crick another letter ('Dear Prick'), promising to bring him the loan, followed by some sordid details of a recent encounter with a Soho prostitute, before praising the recent *Nature* article as 'very plausible/convincing' (he was more impressed by the experimental detail in the articles from Wilkins and Franklin), although he did not like 'it has not escaped our notice ...' – 'God what a filthy style', he wrote.[29]

*

One of the earliest visitors to see the structure was Linus Pauling, who arrived in Cambridge on his way to a conference in Brussels that Bragg was also attending. Although Pauling reserved final judgement until he had seen all the data in the papers from King's, he had to admit it looked right. That evening, Linus and his wife dined at the Cricks' along with their son Peter; they were joined by Pauline Cowan and by Watson and his sister, Betty.[30] Despite the Burgundy, the conversation was slow – Crick was unusually subdued and the Paulings were jet-lagged – so the party finished at midnight. The next day, Watson went off to Paris yet again, this time with Betty, to celebrate his twenty-fifth birthday and to mark her impending marriage.

When Pauling got to Belgium there was yet more Watson and Crick. No doubt already uncomfortable that he was scheduled to present his moribund triple helix model, Pauling found that Bragg was presenting the double helix structure at the meeting, reading a brief paper by Watson and Crick that summarised the structure and some of the underlying evidence. Pauling had no alternative but to admit defeat and say in public 'the Watson-Crick structure is essentially correct.'[31] Bragg's hostility to Crick must have softened, even if only for a moment.

In their unpublished account presented by Bragg, Watson and Crick cautiously suggested only that 'DNA is the carrier of at least part of the genetic specificity of chromosomes', leaving open the possibility that proteins might also play a genetic role.[32] This was more conservative than the identification of DNA as 'the genetic material' in their *Nature* paper, or Watson's bold claim in a letter to his parents that 'we have solved the structure of the gene'. It also did not fit with the impression of others in the scientific community, who were enthusiastically accepting the structure and its implications for genetics. For example, a week before the *Nature* articles appeared, Max Delbrück, who had been kept abreast of developments through regular letters from Watson, wrote to the organisers of the upcoming Cold Spring Harbor meeting on viruses, highlighting the 'exceedingly important implications' of the structure and urging them to invite Watson to speak. Delbrück told Pauling: 'I am very much excited about the biological implications of the WATSON-CRICK structure, every day we seem to discover new ones. We are eagerly awaiting your return to talk these over with you.'[33] Pauling replied that he was 'very deeply impressed by the Watson-Crick structure. (…) It has very important implications, as you mention. I think that it is the most significant step forward that has been taken for a very long time.'[34]

*

While Watson was swanning around Paris, Francis began work on an article that would explore these important implications – how the double helix might explain gene replication and function. Watson was deeply opposed to this venture; it was one thing to speculate about such things in private but quite another to put them into print.[35] As Crick recalled, Watson experienced 'periodic fears that the structure might be wrong and that he had made an ass of himself' – making grandiose claims based on a mistake would inevitably attract ridicule. Confident as ever, Crick brushed away such doubts and Watson eventually allowed the article to be sent to *Nature*, to preserve peace.[36]

The paper – 'Genetical Implications of the Structure of Deoxyribonucleic Acid' – was submitted by Bragg on 8 May 1953, with a covering note claiming a strong case for early publication.[37] Convinced either by the content or by Bragg's support, or both, the editor duly fast-tracked the article and it appeared a little over three weeks later, on 30 May. Despite Watson's reluctance to see the article published, it was again signed Watson and Crick – they tossed a coin to determine author order, and Crick lost.[38]

About twice as long as their first *Nature* paper, this article included four figures – Odile's DNA drawing again, together with three schematic outlines, two of which gave the chemical formula of a DNA chain in single- and double-chain conformations, and a fourth that showed the proposed location of the hydrogen bonds in the base pairs (they mistakenly suggested that the G–C pair was held together by two hydrogen bonds; in fact it has three).

The most significant part of the paper explored the implications of the structure and the way it allowed the bases to occur in any sequence. This not only suggested how mutations could occur – altering one base could change the structure of the gene – it also led Crick to put forward a radically new conception. In one half-sentence, he proposed a powerful new way of looking at the world of genes: 'it therefore seems likely that the precise sequence of the bases is the code which carries the genetical information.'[39] That phrase, or something like it, is now said every day in classrooms and university lecture theatres all over the world. It has become self-evident, and yet at the time it was completely novel. For me, this phrase is the most revolutionary insight made by Crick.*[40]

Each of these ideas – sequence, code, information – was already in the zeitgeist: a few years earlier, John Masson Gulland, André Boivin and others had suggested that the sequence of the bases might determine gene function, while Schrödinger's *What Is Life?* included the idea that genes contained a 'code-script'. In 1948, 'information' had been given a mathematical definition by Claude Shannon, and the use of information as a vague metaphor soon became widespread – in one of the 1950 Reith Lectures on BBC radio, the term 'information' was used ten times in the first five minutes of a talk on the brain.[41] Without a wireless, it is unlikely that Crick heard that broadcast, but he may have read the lecture in the BBC's magazine *The Listener*, or simply picked up on the term from Cavendish coffee-queue chatter.[42]

----

*I am so convinced of the significance of these words that in 2015 I wrote a whole book about them and their implications: *Life's Greatest Secret*.

Whatever the exact sources of this unique synthesis, Crick's idea soon swept through the scientific community. The gene was now seen to contain information in the sequence of the bases – a code that instructed the cell to make a particular kind of protein. The modern informational view of the gene and ultimately of life itself was born in that brief half-phrase coined by Crick.

Despite this overwhelming influence, the second Watson and Crick *Nature* paper is less renowned than its predecessor. But citations do not necessarily correlate with enthusiasm or understanding – or even reading. The French geneticist François Jacob recalled that the first article had not even caused a ripple among his colleagues – this was the kind of response that led Crick to suspect that few people understood the implications of the double helix and that they needed to have things spelled out for them.[43] However, some researchers, including Wilkins, found the whole thing rather distasteful and felt that the second article 'went over the top'.[44] Resentment and hostility to Crick's claims were beginning to brew.

The two other papers that the pair wrote in early summer made less of a splash, but nonetheless contained novel features of considerable biological interest. Having been suddenly invited to talk at the Cold Spring Harbor symposium in June, Watson had to quickly prepare a lecture that could be published in the symposium proceedings. Again signed Watson and Crick, this article, largely written by Watson, was basically a summary of the structure and the evidence that underpinned it, including figures from the *Nature* papers as well as photographs of the A and B forms from Wilkins and Franklin.[45] However, Watson's wariness at being wrong can be seen peeking through, for example in the final sentence, when he reminded the audience that it was still not certain that gene function was due to DNA alone.[46] The whole business might yet turn out to be mistaken.

Few people in the audience at Cold Spring Harbor shared those doubts, as Watson, in shorts and unlaced sneakers with his shirt hanging out, rapidly ran through the structure and the evidence, generously and repeatedly emphasising Crick's role in the discovery.*[47]

---

*All three *Nature* articles from April were given to each of the attendees at the meeting. Delbrück to Watson, 1 May 1953, Delbrück papers, Box 23, Folder 22.

François Jacob was entranced – 'this could not be false', he recalled thinking – and the audience were beguiled. The structure was so perfect that even those who did not understand the chemistry felt that the functional implications meant it must be true.[48]

The final paper, written in a rush after Watson's return to Cambridge, is the least cited of the four, but was nonetheless essential, because it provided a detailed atomic description of the structure – something completely lacking in the first *Nature* paper. With Francis caught in the headlights of his rapidly approaching thesis deadline, most of the writing was again done by Watson, but under their initial agreement, Crick's name came first. Entitled 'The Complementary Structure of Deoxyribonucleic Acid', the article was submitted to the *Proceedings of the Royal Society* on 21 August – the day before Crick left for New York. Bragg's covering letter expressed the hope that the article might be published quickly, but it was afflicted by the glacial pace of most scientific publishing and did not appear until well into the following year.[49]

In the article, Crick and Watson not only provided the kind of detailed evidence that was necessary to convince the chemically minded reader that the structure was correct, they also showed how the model was supported by various studies by Wilkins, Franklin and others that had appeared since the first *Nature* paper. The one piece of supporting evidence that was not mentioned was $C2$ monoclinic symmetry, even though this had been reported by Franklin and Gosling in a *Nature* paper in July, which Crick and Watson cited.[50] Watson did not include this fact because he did not understand it (in 2016 he admitted 'I had not mastered its unambiguous implications'); much later, Crick expressed his surprise that this evidence was not included in the paper – as Watson suggested in 2016, Francis seems to have been too busy with his thesis and with preparing for the USA to notice.[51]

All four articles contained attempts by Watson and Crick to explain exactly how they had come up with the model, trying to give credit to Franklin and Wilkins without encouraging the whispering voices that, even then, were suggesting they had pirated the results from King's.[52] That whisper has since grown to a clamour and it is now widely believed that Watson and Crick stole Franklin's data (Wilkins is never mentioned) and did not acknowledge her contribution.[53] But Franklin and Wilkins were both credited repeatedly in all four papers and the final article clearly outlined exactly what had happened, explicitly referring to the December 1952 MRC report. Crick and Watson declared:

> As far as we can tell our structure is compatible with the X-ray evidence of Wilkins and Franklin and their co-workers (…). In a preliminary report on their work, they have independently suggested that the basic structure of the paracrystalline form is helical and contains two intertwined chains. They also suggest that the sugar-phosphate backbone forms the outside of the helix and that each chain repeats itself after one revolution in 34 Å.[54]

Together with Franklin and Gosling's comment to Pauline Cowan in January, this clear acknowledgement of the source of the information they used to frame and then confirm the model explains one of the lasting enigmas of the affair – why Franklin never complained about how Watson and Crick discovered the structure. She read the 1954 paper, so she knew the answer.[55]

None of this means that Watson and Crick acted correctly throughout. Once they were given the MRC report, they should have requested permission to use the data it contained and then made clear exactly what had happened from the outset, first to those whose data they were using and then to the rest of the world. They did not.

Many years later, on the fortieth anniversary of the publication of the three *Nature* articles, Francis wrote a little article entitled 'DNA: A Cooperative Discovery', which began 'First and foremost I should remind you of Rosalind Franklin, whose contributions have not been sufficiently acknowledged'.[56] An ageing Maurice Wilkins wrote to Crick, saying how much he agreed with the sentiment expressed in the title and asking Francis why he had changed his mind. Crick replied that he was not conscious of any shift in attitude, but admitted he had 'mellowed a little' – 'when I was younger I was rather brasher and so I may not always have said what I should.'[57]

Scientists' use of other researchers' ideas and data is a powerful part of the process of discovery. But it requires transparency, fairness and honesty for everyone to benefit.

*

From April onwards scientists began what now looks like a pilgrim-
age to see the model in the Cavendish. Franklin came in the middle of
the month and immediately said that it looked basically correct (she
and Wilkins soon showed that it contained some minor errors). She
also surprised Watson and Crick by being agreeable, highlighting
the extent to which their view of her had been distorted by Wilkins'
malicious gossip.

This new cordial relationship probably also reveals that they
were now being particularly agreeable with her. Some insight into
her feelings can be seen in a brief note she sent to Crick: 'Would it be
all right to come and see you and Watson to talk about your model
and about viruses next Tuesday?' [58] Had she been cross about being
scooped, she would surely not have talked about her new work with
them, for fear of the same thing happening again. Francis soon struck
up a friendship with Franklin, visiting her in her Birkbeck office to
discuss her refinements of the structure and sending ultra-polite
letters ('Dear Miss Franklin'*) about her draft articles on the structure
that she had shared with him. [59]

Dorothy Hodgkin was another early visitor to see the model and
was suitably impressed and convinced the structure was correct. [60]
Later on, some of her colleagues – a delegation of Oxford students
and researchers – also made the journey over. They included two
young men who were to play major roles in Crick's life – the Briton
Leslie Orgel and the South African Sydney Brenner, both aged
twenty-six (they were born a day apart). Brenner recalled the scene
and its impact upon him:

> We entered a brick-walled room in the Austin wing of the Cav-
> endish Laboratories and there stood the model; connected with
> tall laboratory retort stands and clamps, the bases represented

---

*The failure to use her academic title of Doctor was not condescension, it was
the polite way of referring to a woman scientist at the time. See for example
the obituary of Franklin written by her friend and colleague J. D. Bernal, in
which he referred to her repeatedly as 'Miss Franklin'. Bernal, J. D. (1958),
Dr. Rosalind E. Franklin, *Nature* 182:154.

with shiny metal plates that had been specially machined to
scale. (...) Standing there and looking at the DNA structure I
felt as if a curtain had been lifted in my mind, in the sense that
I knew that this was a fundamental breakthrough in biology
and that we could now find out how genes worked. On that
day I knew exactly what I wanted to do. I wanted to work on
genes and their function.[61]

An American visitor from the Rockefeller Foundation described
in his diary how Watson and Crick presented the model together:
'Both young men are somewhat mad hatters who bubble over about
their new structure in characteristically Cambridge style (...) [they]
are certainly not lacking, however, in either enthusiasm or ability.'[62]
But as the days wore on, it was increasingly Francis who did most
of the talking, repeatedly explaining the model and its significance.
By the time Brenner got there, it was all Crick: 'He couldn't stop
talking about the model and its implications and it was enormously
interesting to listen to him prattle away in his loud voice.'[63]

The first time you heard him it must have been enormously
interesting, but Crick's prattle gradually grated on the Cavendish
researchers who were subjected to his grandiose claims over and
over again, and they hatched a plot to get their revenge. Francis soon
received a letter from Pauling, who was organising a meeting in Pasadena that Crick was planning to attend in September. Pauling not only
invited him to stay on for a few weeks as an honorary professor, he also
requested that Crick 'speak as much as possible during the meeting.'[64]
Francis was initially over the moon, but eventually twigged that the
whole thing was a hoax. It had been dreamed up by Watson, Kendrew
and a young visiting US chemist, Sid Bernhard with the decisive help
of Peter Pauling, who obtained some suitable headed notepaper and
imitated his father's signature (Pauling senior was not amused and
docked his son's allowance to the tune of £5; Peter passed the fine on
to Watson, with additional 'costs' of seven shillings).*[65]

---

*As to Crick's behaviour at the meeting, Kendrew reported to Pauling junior
'while he may have talked less than usual he did talk continuously'. Peter
Pauling to Linus Pauling, 16 October 1953, LP Science, Box 9.001, 1.42.

Watson's response to Crick's chatter was positively kind-hearted compared to the secret feelings of Wilkins, who seethed in a letter to Hamilton:

> Take the Watson Crick model with a pinch of salt. Francis is quite certain he has solved all the problems of the universe by pure thought and his lack of tact has lost him many friends temporarily until he recovers from DNA hysteria. I am very fond of Francis but he can be a bit much at times & he can be a ruthless careerist when he thinks it suits him.[66]

*

As Wilkins' letter indicates, Crick was irritating not only because of the annoying sound of his brassy voice, but also because of *what* he was saying – his claims about the significance of the discovery. Wilkins' view that this was DNA hysteria was widely held; it did not matter if these claims were correct, for many people at Cambridge he was behaving in an unseemly fashion. This feeling grew when the press eventually got hold of the story a few weeks later.

On 15 May, Bragg gave a talk on the double helix at Guy's Medical School in London. This was accompanied by the first public announcement of the discovery – a brief article on the front page of the UK daily, the *News Chronicle*, that same morning.[67] Written by Bragg's friend, the science journalist Ritchie Calder, the article put the spotlight on Bragg's talk and briefly described the structure, base-pairing, replication and how the arrangement of the bases would eventually explain 'all the characters which are passed from one generation to the next', although understanding this would 'keep the scientists busy for the next 50 years'. Using terms that recall Crick's Cavendish monologues, Calder described the finding as 'the biological equivalent of crashing the sound barrier' and predicted that it would 'open up a vast new field of investigations into the secret of life'. Although the article mentioned Watson and Crick as well as Wilkins and Randall, there was no name-check for Franklin. Nevertheless, she was the only one of the group to keep a copy of the article.

Two days later, *The New York Times* picked up the story, quoting Bragg's talk.[68] Less than a month later, shortly after the Cold Spring Harbor symposium, the newspaper returned at length to the topic, quoting Francis as saying that he might have to leave the country to pursue research on DNA structure and function.[69] The article also contained what appears to have been the first use of the phrase that is now synonymous with the discovery – 'a double helix'. Crick obviously cherished this piece – he kept a copy of it in his passport.[70]

A few days later, the *Sunday Times* hailed the discovery, using the same phrase – a version of this article also appeared on the front page of the *Birmingham Post* – and there was a second long feature by Calder in the *News Chronicle*. The news finally spanned the globe, with the *South China Sunday Post* repeating a line from the *Sunday Times* – probably originally from Crick – about the discovery being a 'biochemical Mount Everest'.*[71]

Following the *Sunday Times* article, Crick and then Watson wrote to the newspaper correcting some minor inaccuracies and also flattering Todd and Wilkins, trying to ensure that feathers were not further ruffled.[72] Neither Watson nor Crick highlighted the role of Franklin, who was ignored by the press. One notable exception was an article that was never actually published. In late May, Joan Bruce, a journalist working in London for Time-Life, produced an article on the breakthrough, which she had worked on with Franklin.[73] The piece – which contained some striking scientific howlers – framed the discovery as the 'combined work of the two teams' from King's and Cambridge, and emphasised Franklin's ability to switch DNA between the A and B forms. Had the article been scientifically corrected and published, it might have reinforced perceptions of the

---

*Edmund Hillary and Tenzing Norgay climbed Everest on 29 May 1953; news reached the UK on 2 June, the day of the coronation of Queen Elizabeth II. Because the expedition was British, the conquest of Everest instantly became a symbol of national pride, even though Hillary was a New Zealander and Norgay was Nepalese. The expedition had been tracked excitedly in the press – immediately below Ritchie Calder's article about the double helix that appeared on the front page of the 15 May 1953 edition of the *News Chronicle* was the weather forecast for Everest.

discovery as a cooperative achievement rather than that later view that this was a race that had been won by Watson and Crick.

This collaborative interpretation was very much in the air. When *Nature* produced reprints of the three DNA articles these included a single multi-page booklet reprinting all three articles, bound together.[74] Then, at the end of June, the double helix featured in one of that year's Royal Society Conversaziones – a kind of science fair for leading researchers, now rebranded as the Summer Exhibition. At the June Conversazione, Stand 19 presented 'A Proposed Structure for DNA'. This was the first public presentation of the model, and the authors were, in alphabetical order, grouped by institution, Franklin, Gosling, Stokes, Wilson, Wilkins, Crick and Watson – all those who had signed the three *Nature* articles two months earlier.

> **19** *Dr R. E. Franklin, Mr R. G. Gosling, Dr A. R. Stokes, Dr H. R. Wilson, King's College, London, Dr M. H. F. Wilkins, Medical Research Council Unit, King's College, Mr F. H. C. Crick, Dr J. D. Watson, Cavendish Laboratory, Cambridge*
>
> A PROPOSED STRUCTURE FOR DNA
>
> DNA (desoxyribonucleic acid) is a very long thin molecule, which is believed to carry at least part of the genetic specificity of the chromosomes in living cells. The structure has been derived from X-ray data and from stereochemical consideration. It suggests a possible way in which the DNA molecule might duplicate itself.

Extract from the programme of the June 1953
Royal Society Conversazione.

Franklin's position as lead author in the Conversazione programme may suggest that she was responsible for explaining to the public the model to which she had contributed so much.[75] How, or if, Crick, Watson or Wilkins were involved is not known, although Crick wrote a draft of the abstract and noted the event in his diary. In July, on Gabrielle's birthday, he gave a similar presentation of the structure at the annual Cavendish Laboratory Open Day.[76]

Shortly before the Joan Bruce article was due to appear, the London Time-Life office commissioned Antony Barrington Brown, a recent Cambridge graduate, to photograph Watson and Crick for the article. He took eight pictures, but they followed Bruce's piece into oblivion until two of them appeared in *The Double Helix* fifteen years later. One of those photos portrays Watson and Crick at their desks,

Francis cradling a mug while Watson holds a saucer-less teacup; the other has them in front of the model, a dramatic two-metre-high construction held together by clamps and bosses. Crick stands on a chair pointing with a slide rule, while Watson looks up, apparently awed by the structure, or Francis, or both. Pinned to the bare brick wall behind them is a large copy of Odile's diagram. The two men look relaxed and happy – Francis is beaming in all eight photos, even though Barrington Brown wanted him to look portentous.[77]

Crick's appetite for publicity eventually dismayed his colleagues and friends. Bragg was happy at the scientific impact made by the structure but felt that the press attention 'has not been quite so desirable'.[78] Wilkins complained that since the journalists got hold of what he called the DNA story, life was hell, while Watson eventually became so annoyed by the media excitement, largely fostered by Francis, that he threatened to break off their friendship.[79] It happened like this. In May, BBC journalists from the Third Programme and the European Service separately invited Bragg to talk on the radio about the discovery.[80] Bragg declined and suggested they contact Watson and Crick. Watson was not interested, but Crick most certainly was, and he soon wrote and recorded a twenty-minute radio talk entitled 'A Molecular Shape that May Explain Reproduction – Cell Duplication'. This was broadcast on the BBC European Service on 7 August in the *Science Review* slot (the transcript has been lost; Crick later recalled 'it was not a gossipy account. It was a perfectly straightforward account of the structure').[81] A few weeks later, when the Third Programme, which broadcast to the UK, asked to repeat the talk for a British audience, Watson immediately vetoed the suggestion, arguing that the structure might be wrong and that he did not want the talk to be heard by people he knew. Crick was annoyed (the BBC paid well – £35 for the rebroadcast, on top of 15 guineas from the European Service, and he needed the cash); the BBC was disappointed.[82]

The issue re-emerged dramatically in October, when both Crick and Watson were in the USA. Francis wrote to Watson asking if he had changed his mind, pointing out that he was still very short of money and claiming that criticism over their behaviour had 'cooled down a bit'. Watson scornfully commented on Francis's appetite for self-publicity, dismissed his financial concerns and priggishly warned Crick he would cut all relations should the broadcast go ahead:

> I still think a talk on the 3rd would be in bad taste. There are still those who think we pirated data (...) My main concern is not to be dragged into it as I'm afraid I was in Cambridge. If you need the money that much, go ahead. Needless to say I shall not think any higher of you and shall have good reason to avoid any further collaboration with you.[83]

Two months later, Watson tersely repeated his view: 'I'm still opposed to the BBC.'[84] The broadcast never happened.

*

On 15 May – the same day that Bragg gave the talk at Guy's that sparked the media excitement – Francis took the long train journey to Edinburgh, where he gave his first invited talk on any topic.[85] At the beginning of the year, he had been asked to speak about proteins by Michael Swann, of the university's Department of Zoology, who had recently moved to Scotland from Cambridge.[86] However, the discovery of the double helix changed everything and the event was now advertised on specially printed posters proclaiming that Francis Crick, Esq., M.A.* would talk at an informal colloquium on 'Molecular Biophysics and the Structure of Nucleic Acid'.[87]

In his lecture, Francis gave an ingenious demonstration of the reality of the 1:1 base ratios, which he had worked out with Watson.[88] Collating data from around forty papers, he showed that although only a minority of studies gave the precise ratio of 1:1 for A:T and G:C, the values clearly clustered around 1:1. The convincing comparison came from the flat distribution of the ratios of A:G – these ranged from 1:0.4 to 1:1.9. It would be hard to look at that figure and not be completely convinced that the A:T and G:C ratios were both

---

*Someone must have thought Crick was a graduate of Cambridge, where a BA can automatically become an MA.

really 1:1 and the observed slight variation was simply due to measurement error.

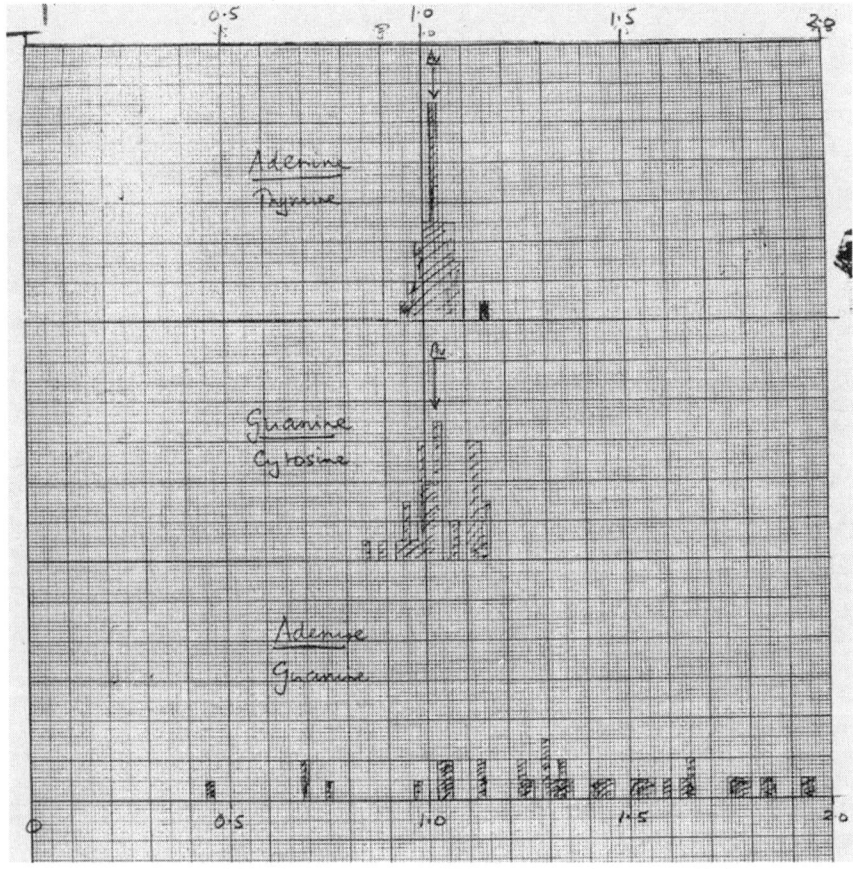

Francis also carried to Edinburgh a small model of the double
helix, which he had made out of copper wire and bits of paper and
cardboard.[89] It is not clear if he showed it in his talk, but he gave it to
his host Michael Swann; it is now on display at the National Museum
of Scotland. This appears to have been the first public 3-D representation of the double helix. Like Odile's drawing, on which it was clearly
based, it is not anatomically correct – the base pairs are presented as
single shapes, while the intervals between the bases are irregular –
nevertheless, it gives a striking representation of the molecule.

DEPARTMENT OF ZOOLOGY

FRANCIS CRICK, Esq., M.A.
of the Cavendish Laboratory, Cambridge

WILL GIVE A TALK ON

" **Molecular Biophysics and the
Structure of Nucleic Acid** "

At an INFORMAL COLLOQUIUM to be held in the

DEPARTMENT OF ZOOLOGY
(WEST MAINS ROAD)

On FRIDAY, 15th MAY, at 4.30 p.m.

Tea will be served in the Library at 4 p.m.

*

Crick's financial worries were growing worse, leading to a series
of negotiations with the MRC. First, there was the question of his
college fees, which 'in the hustle and bustle of the scientific life' he
had forgotten to pay – the bill amounted to a hefty £41/13/0, which
he needed the MRC to settle.[90] Then he had to deal with what would
happen after he returned from the USA. In June he wrote to the head
of the MRC, explaining his imminent departure for New York and
emphasising Perutz's desire that he should return to the Cavendish
after his year abroad.[91] Francis admitted he could get a job as a university lecturer, but found this unattractive; at the advanced age of
thirty-seven and with no academic experience, he would have to
start at the bottom. He continued:

> Employment by the MRC, on the other hand, would allow me
> to devote all my effort to research, at a time when my thoughts
> and energies are flowing strongly in this channel. My scientific
> interests are primarily biological, and I only work on molecular
> structure because I believe it to be the key to the really funda-
> mental biological problems.

Crick's cheeky solution was to ask the MRC to employ him as a researcher and immediately give him a year-long leave of absence while he worked in the USA. To his delight this was rapidly agreed.

Meanwhile, Perutz was pushing for the MRC to give Crick a permanent post 'with unlimited tenure', writing a glowing recommendation:

> F. H. C. Crick has just made his name through the structure of nucleic acid. It was he who suggested to Watson the geometric relationship between the two chains which led to the solution. His originality has been manifest on several other occasions and has been referred to in previous reports. Though a physicist by training, Crick has acquired a remarkably wide knowledge of biology and biochemistry. He does a vast amount of reading, has a retentive memory and a capacity for relating the facts he reads. His mathematical ability is also very considerable. I think Crick's presence would be an asset in any team working on biophysical problems, and his fertility of ideas is prodigious.[92]

However, the MRC was mulling over the future of its Cavendish unit, following Bragg's recent decision to join the Royal Institution in London. These strategic considerations, together with Crick's junior status, led them to give him only a seven-year contract.[93] Nevertheless, his future was secure, for a while.

Crick's life was now increasingly dominated by the problem of his thesis, which had to be examined before the transatlantic liner sailed in August. At the beginning of June, he told his son Michael of his progress: 'I am still writing – it is very tedious. I hope the examiners find it more interesting than I do.'[94] They did – Crick successfully passed his oral exam on the afternoon of 18 August, just four days before they all left for New York.[95]

Crick later described the thesis as a ragbag.[96] This is true, but in some respects, it looks quite modern. Rather than dealing with a single topic, each chapter focused on a different aspect of protein structure, using his published papers on haemoglobin, coiled coils and synthetic polypeptides – there was only one mention of nucleic acids, apart from the inclusion of the two *Nature* papers on DNA in the final bound version.[97] The opening paragraph set out Crick's worldview with a rare clarity and vision:

> A cell contains hundreds, probably thousands of different types of enzyme molecules. The central problem of molecular biology is the mechanism of synthesis of these highly specific proteins, and the manner in which the details of this process are passed on from generation to generation. Proteins and the nucleic acids are the key molecules of molecular biology.[98]

Those words – 'the central problem of molecular biology' – would stay in Crick's mind over the following years. Finding the solution would preoccupy hundreds of researchers around the world for over a decade. Crick had perceived the major scientific challenge of the age and was charting it out.

*

On 12 August, ten days before leaving for America, Francis put copies of the *Nature* articles into an envelope and sent them off to the man who, in some respects, had started it all – Erwin Schrödinger. An accompanying note explained:

> Watson and I were once discussing how we came to enter the field of molecular biology, and we discovered that we had both been influenced by your little book, 'What is Life?'. We thought you might be interested in the enclosed reprints – you will see that it looks as though your term 'aperiodic crystal' is going to be a very apt one.[99]

Schrödinger did not reply.[100]

THE CENTRAL PROBLEM

THE NEW WORLD

On 22 August 1953, Francis and a newly pregnant Odile sailed with Michael and Gabrielle from Southampton for New York on the Cunard ship *Mauretania*. Among the excitements on the week-long voyage were music by Geraldo's Orchestra and a screening of *The Beggar's Opera*, starring Laurence Olivier.[1] When they arrived in the docks at the lower end of Manhattan, they were greeted by Crick's new boss, David Harker, and driven to a flat that had been found by Harker's wife. Although it was spacious by New York standards, the Cricks were disappointed – on the top floor of a rather bleak 1920s apartment block in the furthest south-western corner of Brooklyn, their new home was a forty-five-minute subway ride from the centre of the city. With no money to pay for a car, even shopping was difficult. And as Odile recalled, the apartment had ghastly wallpaper, covered with huge leaves.[2] Portugal Place it was not.

To make matters worse, Odile suffered from terrible morning sickness and money was incredibly tight because Francis was inadvertently paying too much tax; some months they literally spent their last dollar.[3] As Crick told Watson in December, 'We live very quietly here, mainly because we are so broke.'[4] Even working in Harker's well-funded laboratory turned out to be much less attractive than expected. Rather than strolling into the Cavendish whenever it suited him, after a ten-minute walk past the glories of King's College, Crick was expected to be in the laboratory before 9:00 am, commuting on the noisy subway to Fort Hamilton. However, although they lived in boring suburban Brooklyn, the skyscrapers of Manhattan featured on the Christmas card painted by Odile and sent to Watson that winter, featuring herself, Francis, Michael and Gabrielle.[5]

Within three weeks of arriving in Harker's laboratory, Francis was off to California for the meeting on X-ray studies of protein structure that Pauling had organised in Pasadena. Scientists in this field were meeting for the first time since the publication of Crick's transformative theoretical work in 1952 with Cochran and Vand. As Kendrew put it in a review of the meeting in *Nature*:

The Pasadena conference revealed that the helix has now come into its own with a vengeance; finding helices is a game played by nearly everyone in the field, and there are now few biologically important structures which are not thought, by some workers at least, to be helical. This change – or it would be scarcely too much to say revolution – has of course been facilitated by the development of methods whereby the helical nature of a structure can be inferred, often at a glance, from its X-ray pattern.[6]

That last sentence referred to the Cochran, Crick and Vand paper. Understandably, Francis was very pleased with the article.[7]

At the meeting, Crick's influence was everywhere. He was given equal billing with Pauling in the discussion of coiled coils, while the double helix structure of DNA was considered of such importance that it had a whole session. Vittorio Luzzati, who had worked with Franklin in Paris and was now in Harker's group, joked to the audience: 'I thought I had some good ideas for this talk before I met Francis.'[8] In this small but significant sector of science, Crick had most definitely arrived.[9]

Unfortunately, he had also arrived in Harker's laboratory at the Polytechnic Institute of Brooklyn. On paper, everything looked great. It was a world-leading centre of X-ray crystallography that rivalled the Cavendish in terms of equipment and personnel. The group was focused on solving the structure of ribonuclease – an enzyme that cleaves RNA – within a decade.[10] The project turned out to be much more complicated than expected – in the end it took Harker seventeen years to resolve the molecule's structure.[11]

Crick worked with an expert crystallographer, Beatrice Magdoff, trying to identify ribonuclease crystals in which one kind of atom had been replaced by another – this isomorphic replacement method was Harker's preferred approach to revealing the structure of the molecule. Francis disagreed with Harker that this was the best way of proceeding – he remained wedded to the informed trial-and-error model building that had solved the α-helix and DNA. Furthermore, the practical work was extremely fiddly, and it was difficult to obtain consistent results. As Crick confided to Watson, 'It is terribly dull but I feel I owe it to my hosts.'[12] This work eventually led to the publication of four papers; the three uninspiring experimental articles each attracted less than a dozen citations in the following decade.[13]

Due to the lack of intellectual sparkle in the project, Francis spent much of his year in America not working on ribonuclease. After the conference in Pasadena, he went on a brief road trip with Magdoff and Luzzati – Max Delbrück lent them a car and they visited San Francisco, Berkeley (where Francis gave a talk) and Yosemite National Park.[14] When they returned to Brooklyn, Crick gave Kendrew long-distance advice about myoglobin – his letters teemed with technical suggestions.[15] He also went into Manhattan to see Chargaff in his office at Columbia University. To Crick's relief, Chargaff was surprisingly amiable ('He was really very friendly – we were asked to lunch, also to come again,' Crick told Kendrew.[16]) At the beginning of 1954, Francis went to a conference in Boston, then to Washington (accompanied by Odile), then he visited Philadelphia to talk with Arthur Lindo Patterson, who devised the analytical method for interpreting X-ray crystallographic data, before returning to Boston to give a talk at MIT on 'The Central Problem of Molecular Biology'.[17] In April he went to a genetics conference in Oak Ridge, Tennessee, then it was back to Washington for a meeting of the National Academy of Sciences on nucleic acids, at which he and Watson were invited to speak.[18]

Alongside all this activity, Crick was still thinking about other people's problems. Most notably, he made good on his March 1953 prediction that the structure of collagen would soon be solved by doing exactly that, in a brief article submitted to the *Journal of Chemical Physics* at the beginning of December, based on Pauline Cowan's data. Typically insouciant, Crick described his decision to work on collagen in a letter to Kendrew, revealing that he knew full well how it might look, but did not give a damn:

> The origin of the structure is quite amusing. One morning, over breakfast, I had a discussion with Hugh [Huxley], who was staying with us, on the question 'would it be ethical to try to solve collagen?' We decided it would be. I said I had an idea for the structure. After Hugh had gone I tried it out. It was quite hopeless. But the dilemma was so acute that within two hours I had arrived at the one I've written up![19]

Crick's collagen model was neither complete nor correct, but the arrival of the manuscript at King's College London – *after* it had been submitted to the journal – sent Randall into a rage and made Cowan so upset that she considered abandoning research on proteins altogether.[20] In January, Kendrew told Watson: 'I suppose you know that Francis has done it again. His collagen structure has reduced King's to a state of fury – Randall has written him a letter beginning "You will lose the respect of your scientific colleagues unless ..."'[21]

Crick confirmed this news, telling Watson that Randall had written him a very rude letter, accusing him of not giving sufficient credit to King's in his article.[22] (He said even Randall's secretary sent him 'a nasty little note'.[23]) In turn, Crick blamed the King's group for being unreasonable, explaining to Watson that he had 'tried hard to do them justice but their ingenuity at reading implications (or lack of them) into my words has defeated me'.

Six weeks later, after all his stifled anger over the double helix, Wilkins finally told Francis what he really thought:

> The collagen business appeared at this end as a very sharp piece of practise and I am sorry to say the impression you gave in it is of a decidedly mean person. (...) It has been said of you that you make friends with people so as to pinch their results but I think that is rather unfair on you. (...) Are you who have so much ability and good qualities, going to continue this rather dishonest 'theoretical' career, calculating the balance of offence against scientific ethics with economic expediency and in the process bringing out all the worst sides of your character and losing the goodwill of fellow scientists? Do you think you lack the ability to make a career in a nice way?[24]

Supremely confident, Crick took it all in his stride. He had already moved on.

Two new problems now preoccupied him: extensive collaboration with Luzzati in helping Kendrew interpret his myoglobin data, and the reading and writing of a weekly correspondence with Watson, who was struggling to solve the structure of RNA.[25] Frustrated by his intellectual isolation ('I have *no one* to talk to here,' he complained to Watson), Crick bombarded his friend with questions: 'Have you looked into the *quantitative* evidence on RNA and protein synthesis. How much RNA produces how much protein in 1 hour. Or, rephrased, how long does it take to produce 1 protein molecule from 1 molecule of RNA?'[26] He closed the letter with a heartfelt sigh, 'Am extremely interested in it all'.

In one letter Watson proposed a link between DNA and RNA, sketched out under the jokey phrase, 'In any case we now visualise the mysteries of life as follows'. Watson thought that one strand of the DNA double helix might be chemically transformed into RNA through the action of an enzyme. As he wrote: 'This is why we find 2 strands. One to keep code – the other to be transformed to RNA which sneaks to cytoplasm and makes protein.'[27] Underneath his little diagram Watson wrote, 'All of this is slightly mad'.

Despite Crick's appetite for distraction and their differences over the best strategy for studying ribonuclease, Harker urged Francis to stay beyond the end of his contract in September 1954. Pauling was also interested in bringing Crick to Caltech, although Watson's letters from California, describing Pasadena as 'a living hell, largely though not entirely, due to the smog', played their part in swinging the Cricks against the idea.[28] They clearly preferred Cambridge to Brooklyn and within four months of arriving, Francis informed Harker he would be returning to England in September, as planned. The Cricks also decided that Odile and Gabrielle should return in late January, so Odile would be near her parents when the baby was born.[29] The trip to America was turning out to be short-lived.

*

As well as becoming known to US scientists, Francis continued his conquest of the public; in the autumn, he wrote an article on the structure of DNA for *Discovery*, a British popular science magazine.[30] He name-checked those names that needed checking – Astbury, Bell, Chargaff, Wilkins and Franklin – and presented a more precise account of how he and Watson began their work: 'stimulated by the preliminary X-ray results of the King's College workers, we attempted to build models which would be consistent with their data for the paracrystalline form.'

The article brilliantly drew out the implications of the double helix for the ordinary reader; emphasising the two fundamental problems that now had to be understood – gene replication and function – Crick outlined the priorities that would be followed by the global scientific community over the subsequent decade:

> How do the two chains unwind? What holds a single chain in a helical configuration? (Watson and I suspect that the replication starts almost as soon as the unwinding, so that only a very short stretch is ever in a 'single' state at one time.) Most important of all, how does the DNA influence the rest of the cell? We believe that the sequence of the bases along the DNA is the code that carries the genetical information, but how does it produce its effect? We can see how the code may be copied, but as yet we cannot read it.

A few months later, he wrote a similar article, for the more academic readership of Scientific American, for which he received a fee. He invited Wilkins to co-author the piece, but his friend was still smarting over the collagen affair and turned down the offer.[31] Crick also forewarned Watson of his plan – after the row over the Third Programme broadcast, he was taking no chances. In his letter, he reminded Jim of their rather different circumstances: 'as a married man with two children (+1) I cannot afford to take your detached attitude about money.'[32] In this article, Crick explained how a double helix might unwind itself – replication of the genetic material was biology's greatest challenge, he claimed.[33] As to how they actually discovered the double helix, Francis explained they were 'convinced that we could get somewhere near the DNA structure by building scale models based on the X-ray patterns obtained by M. H. F. Wilkins, Rosalind Franklin and their co-workers'.[34] Perhaps the most striking thing about this article was its simple, bold title: 'The Structure of the Hereditary Material'. Liberated from the straitjacket of a scientific paper, for the first time Crick stated as fact something he was now convinced of, even if proof was lacking – genes were made of DNA.

One of the reasons behind this shift in perspective was Crick's encounter with the world-famous cosmologist George Gamow. Crick later recalled:

> Well, he was extremely convivial; used to drink a bit too much – by the time I knew him, anyway; and was fond of card tricks, which he showed to pretty girls – this sort of thing. (…) And he was what is called good company, was Gamow. I wouldn't quite say a buffoon, but – yes, a bit of that, in the nicest possible way. You always knew, if you were going to spend the evening with Gamow you would have a 'jolly time'. You know. And yet there was something behind it all.[35]

Gamow was also the author of some very successful popular science books, which explained physics through the eyes of an everyman character called Mr Tompkins. Now he was turning his attention to biology.

Gamow had read the second Watson and Crick *Nature* paper and had seized upon the idea of a genetic code that had been conjured by Crick, deciding he could crack the code just by thinking about it. At the beginning of July 1953, he wrote to Watson and Crick in Cambridge, asking if he could meet them there in September. His letter looked like the work of a crank, with its broken English expressed in childish handwriting, full of crossings-out, and his breezy suggestion that genes might not be separate units but instead be spread along the whole length of the chromosome – as Gamow cheerfully admitted, this would mean rejecting half a century of experimental results from classical genetics. Unsure how to respond and stymied by the fact that neither of them would be in Cambridge after August, Watson and Crick did not reply.*[36]

---

*Crick later claimed that after receiving Gamow's letter, 'Watson and I sat down over lunch one day at the pub and scribbled down a list [of amino acids] on the back of a piece of paper, and that's what we have today'. Gamow's July letter contained no mention of amino acids; it is possible that Crick's memory was mistaken, but it seems more likely that their Cambridge discussion of Gamow's first letter was more profound than this rather flip account suggested. Crick, The general nature of the genetic code, November 1964, PP/CRI/H/3/13.

In early November, Crick received another letter from Gamow, in which he put his finger on a fundamental question – the link between the four bases of DNA and the twenty-odd amino acids that make up the proteins which are encoded by genes.[37] As Gamow put it inelegantly:

> I was breaking my head for a while about the problem: how a long number written in a four digital system (i.e. DNA molecule) can define unickly a long word based on an alphabet of more than 20 letters.

Gamow's solution was that the four bases in the double helix produced twenty different diamond-shaped 'spaces' on the surface of the molecule, each corresponding to the shape of a particular amino acid. Twenty spaces, twenty amino acids; problem solved. Unfortunately, experimental evidence strongly suggested that DNA was not directly involved in protein synthesis, while RNA was.[38] However enticing the apparent coincidence of those twenty spaces on DNA and the number of amino acids found in proteins, the theory was a non-starter. Nevertheless, Francis invited Gamow to Brooklyn in early December – the suggestion that the genetic code could be solved by a theoretical approach had lit a fuse in his mind.

Crick's colleague Luzzati recalled these two minds meeting for the first time – the forty-nine-year-old Gamow, tall and bulky with an incongruously high-pitched voice, excitable and humorous (Watson later described him as a giant imp[39]) and Crick, twelve years younger, lanky and with a metallic laugh, the pair of them discussing animatedly for around two hours: 'It was amazing. These two spirited men debated, argued, and fought their way through the subject of the code, disposing of issues, one after another, in their exuberance their voices rising to shouts.'[40]

The thing they argued about was Gamow's diamond theory, which had recently been submitted to the *Proceedings of the National Academy of Sciences* (*PNAS*). Gamow loved making jokes, and had named Mr Tompkins as a co-author on his paper;* the Academy

---

*In 1948 Gamow had famously written a paper with his student, Ralph

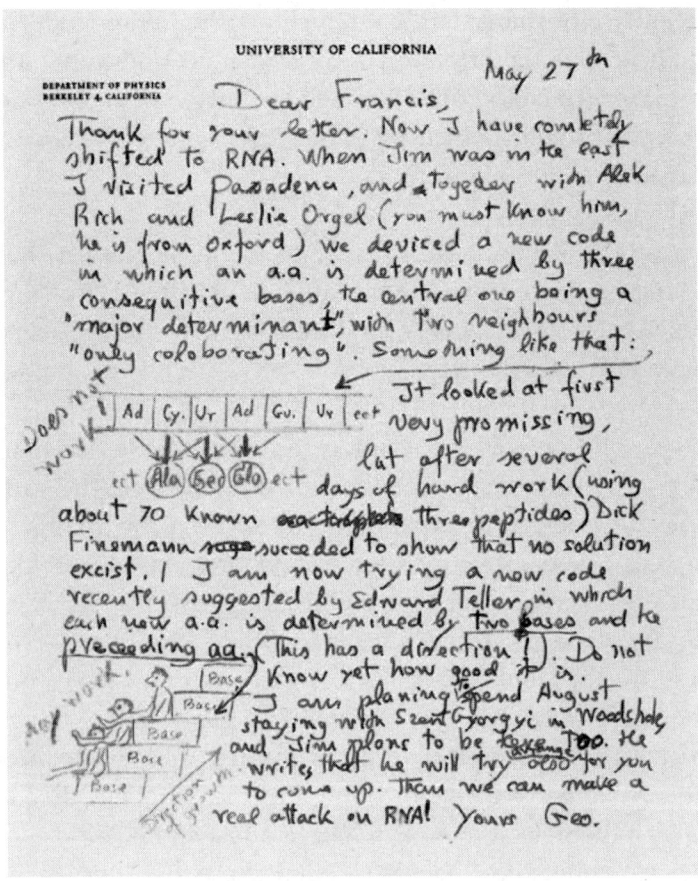

A typical letter from Gamow, 27 May 1954.

apparently took a dim view of such things and binned the article.[41] The Danish Academy of Sciences was less discerning and eventually published a different version, sans Mr Tompkins and including insights from Gamow's discussion with Crick.[42] In the meantime, a shorter account appeared in *Nature* in February 1954.[43]

    This theory – the first of many non-experimental approaches to

Alpher, on the origin of chemical elements. On a puckish whim, he contacted his physicist friend Hans Bethe to invite him to co-sign the article so the list of authors would read Alpher, Bethe, Gamow (α, β, γ). The editors of *Physical Review* either did not spot the joke or went along with the gag.

the genetic code that would be cooked up in the 1950s – had the great virtue of being testable. This could be done by comparing the schema with the first amino acid sequences that were being painstakingly produced by Fred Sanger in Cambridge (in 1958 he won his first Nobel Prize for this work; his second was in 1980 for sequencing nucleic acids). Crick was fairly certain that Gamow was wrong, but as he wrote to Watson: 'I explained all the doubts and difficulties but encouraged him to go ahead. After all, one never knows.'[44] (This was an approach Crick often used with ideas that seemed outlandish.) It turned out that some of the observed sequences in Sanger's insulin data were incompatible with Gamow's schema, and after a few weeks of struggling Gamow began to admit defeat: 'Thus the theory is still suffering from diabetes!', he told Francis.[45]

*

After Odile and Gabrielle returned to England, Francis and Michael left their unloved flat and moved into Luzzati's old apartment in Brooklyn Heights.[46] On 14 February, yearning for Odile and feeling lonely, Francis wrote: 'I am too settled for girl friends. It will be nice to be back at Portugal Place … Be my valentine!'[47] To keep himself busy, Francis saw four ballets, including *The Nutcracker* ('not much of a ballet'), went to an exhibition by the French painter André Marchand ('More interesting than I expected'), saw an off-Broadway musical called *The Bullfighter* ('very dramatic'), went uptown to see the medieval tapestries in the Cloisters ('wonderful') and became homesick when he watched the film *Genevieve* with Michael. And with Odile soon to give birth, he confessed he had 'little twinges of anxiety about you'.[48]

On 7 March, Crick gave Watson news of Odile who was in the last stage of her pregnancy, staying with her mother:

> Life is now pleasanter. I begin to feel as if I had a little leisure, but I am still not really in a state to do serious theoretical work. Odile writes to say that everybody says she looks very fit – she also writes a very cheerful letter. Gabrielle is becoming bilingual, and can switch from French to English depending on her audience. She cannot say whole sentences yet.[49]

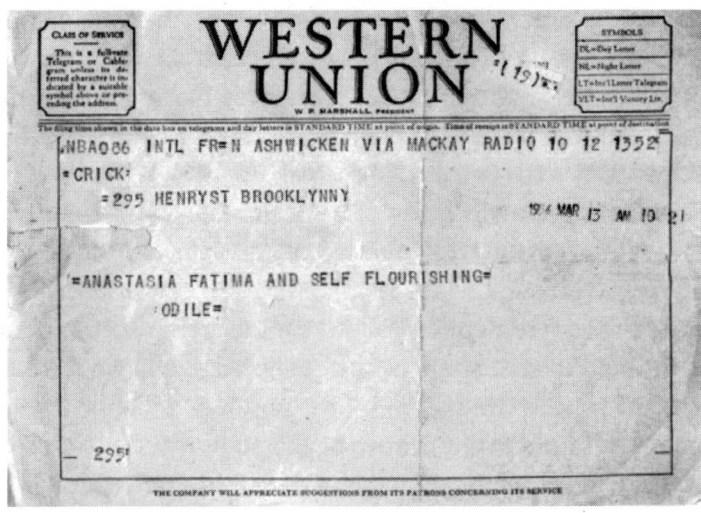

Then, on 13 March, a message arrived from England, in the shape of a brief, typically humorous telegram from Odile which read 'ANASTASIA FATIMA AND SELF FLOURISHING'.[50] (Michael opened the telegram and was unable to make head nor tail of it.[51]) This announced the arrival of Jacqueline ('Anastasia Fatima' was Odile's idea of a joke name for her new daughter) and Francis was inordinately proud. As he wrote to Odile the following day:

> My darling,
> You cannot imagine how delighted I am to have two daughters. All the fuss and bother about coming here, and your going back, and worrying about you while you are away, had quite disguised the fact that I was looking forward to it all. But when I got your telegram I was so pleased and happy that I was quite astonished![52]

It would be three months before Francis finally saw a photo of his second daughter.[53]

As his return to Cambridge crept closer, Crick began to feel more optimistic. In April, he wrote to Odile:

> My health, my temper and my general state of mind seem to have been improving steadily, so I hope you'll get back a really

renovated husband, after the ravages of Fort Hamilton on my morale. All my love and big kisses for The Girls!

Your adoring Francis[54]

Although Crick was profoundly disappointed by the Harker laboratory ('The atmosphere is rather second-rate after Cambridge,' he wrote) he began to lead a stimulating life outside of work. In spring that year he read French literature (Gide, Colette, Alain-Fournier), he saw Audrey Hepburn in a Giraudoux play, wandered the Botanical Gardens and visited exhibitions of pottery and glass. Nevertheless, all this had the air of marking time, of waiting to get back to his real life in Cambridge.[55]

In April, Kreisel wrote another of his letters, this time reminding 'Dear Prick' that payment was due for the £200 of IOUs from the previous year. A month later, still not having received the cash from his friend, Kreisel returned to the topic with the insistence of a loan shark: 'I never tell my debtors that I need the money, but prefer the dignity of "I want my money". WHEN DO YOU INTEND TO RETURN THE £200?'[56] The letter also included some cheerier news – Kreisel reported a conversation with Crick's wartime boss, Collingwood, who, on hearing of the birth of Francis's third child and thinking of the financial implications, made the following prediction: 'Crick will need the Nobel Prize which, rumour has it, he will one day get for his helices.'[57]

*

By the beginning of summer, Crick's American stay was approaching its end. Michael returned to the UK in the middle of June leaving Francis at a loose end. As he wrote to Watson, 'Am finding Brooklyn rather a bore.' To Odile, he was franker: with Michael gone, he wrote, 'Peace now reigns at no 295, and my temper is steadily improving, so that by the time I get back I hope I shall be my old cheerful self again. (…) I am quite tired of all this mediocrity and longing to be back with you at Cambridge.'[58] Still, there were distractions. A brief affair ended when the woman dumped him, saying she was not made 'for a gay interlude "en passant"'. Nonetheless, she did not feel bitter about it: 'My meeting you was one of the nicest things that has ever happened to me. I do not regret a single wonderful minute,' she wrote.[59] There were also pleasures that, for Francis, were more unusual. On a warm day at the end of the month, Sid Bernhard the young Caltech chemist who had conspired with Watson on the hoax letter from Pauling to Crick, took him to an atmospheric evening baseball game in upper Manhattan. Played under lights before a 50,000-strong crowd, Crick gave Watson his impression: 'Very dull until what should have been the last strike, when the game was suddenly transformed, became wildly exciting and lasted over an hour longer.'[60]

More significantly, Francis began to plan his return to Cambridge. Since the beginning of the year, he and Odile had been discussing the possibility of buying the house next door in Portugal Place – number 20 – but the owner was not keen to sell. Now there was a change of mind and the sale was agreed for £1,500, which the bank would lend.[61] Kreisel approved: 'It seems like a good idea to buy No 20, Portugal Place, because your family is steadily increasing and because, as your wife gets older, you may wish to hold orgies at a decent distance from the family seat, i.e. next door.'[62]

Francis had booked a ticket on a liner back to the UK on 8 September and had long planned to take August as his holiday, so he could devote himself to thinking about something other than the boring work on ribonuclease. As he wrote to Watson, his plans were 'to catch up a little on my arrears of reading, and to give some serious thought (for a change) to the whole coding problem etc'.[63] The best way of doing this was to be in the same place as Watson, who would be teaching a summer bacteriophage course at Woods Hole in Massachusetts, where Gamow would join him. That would be followed by the annual Phage Meeting at Cold Spring Harbor. To round it all off, there was also a conference in New Hampshire on Proteins and Nucleic Acids, at the end of August. Francis would then have just enough time to get everything in order before catching the boat back to England.

*

Woods Hole is a village on Cape Cod and is home to the Marine Biological Laboratory, founded in 1888, which puts on summer training courses for scientists. In 1954 Watson was there partly to run the phage teaching laboratory, partly to work on RNA with Matt Meselson, a pal from Pasadena, but, as things turned out, mainly to chat with Gamow and Crick. At the beginning of August, they both turned up, along with Sydney Brenner, who was taking the bacterial genetics course at Cold Spring Harbor and had been invited by Watson to come up to Woods Hole to be in on the discussions, which took place in the small seafront house where Gamow was staying. As Watson recalled, 'Francis, Sydney, and I joined Geo daily in the water-facing living room of the cottage for extended discussions of Geo's genetic codes.' These included ideas Gamow had developed with the hydrogen bomb pioneer Edward Teller, and which were becoming increasingly baroque; unimpressed, Crick repeatedly pointed out that the existing amino acid sequence data were incompatible with all the theoretical codes thus far developed.[64] A new approach was needed.

Although all these potential codes developed in the 1950s turned out to be profoundly mistaken, Crick was always positive about Gamow's influence. As he told journalist Horace Judson in the 1970s: 'The point, the contribution, of Gamow, was that he made one realise that there was – or that there might be – an abstract problem that was independent of the machinery. By thinking of it as an abstract problem of going from one thing to another, you might be able to deduce something about it.'[65]

During Crick's stay at Woods Hole, two interconnected issues began to push their way into his thinking, undermining his confidence in Gamow's approach. Firstly, the Russian-born French geneticist Boris Ephrussi asked Francis a question to which he had no answer: how did he know that the DNA sequence in a gene directly determined the amino acid sequence? Maybe the gene just encoded the individual amino acid components, and their order was determined by something in the cell. Crick thought this was unlikely, but he could not disprove it. Ephrussi's question challenged his assumption that the DNA sequence and the amino acid sequence were 'co-linear' and made him realise that an experimental approach would be necessary. As he later put it, 'It was because of Ephrussi's remark that I realised that we had to show that a change in a gene made a difference in the amino-acid sequence of a protein.'[66]

This question fizzed in Francis's brain as he listened to a second challenge, Brenner's description of some ingenious research on phage that involved creating mutants to map the structure of the gene. This was the work of Seymour Benzer – soon to become another of Crick's close friends and colleagues – who Brenner had met at Cold Spring Harbor that summer. Benzer had begun a complex research programme that would lead to the creation of phage mutants differing by a single base pair, thereby revealing the smallest possible difference between two genetic sequences. Brenner realised that this approach could be combined with studies of proteins to reveal the link between a given mutation and a change in an amino acid – an experimental route to cracking the genetic code, rather than the theoretical approach favoured by Gamow and his fellow physicists.

Brenner later recalled that Woods Hole was the moment where things gelled with Francis, 'where the interaction became strong, because it became clear that the ideas one was talking about were the same'.[67] Crick was so taken with Brenner that he immediately raised the possibility of bringing him to Cambridge to work in the MRC unit, a prospect that excited Sydney, who had to return to South Africa at the end of the year. For Crick, Brenner was 'just the kind of chap we wanted'.[68]

It was not all hard work – there were Gamow's card tricks and swimming in the ocean, and when Watson engineered a huge party at Gamow's place by sending out dozens of fake invitations imitating Gamow's handwriting, Crick ended up rather tipsy.[69] There was also the opportunity to rib Watson over his appearance alongside the actor Richard Burton in *Vogue* as one of a number of eligible young men, complete with a photo and the suggestion that he had 'the bemused look of an English poet'.[70] The teasing was made sharper by the contrast with Watson's hostility to Crick's proposed Third Programme broadcast the previous year, but it remained good-natured.

At the end of August it was all over and the caravan of molecular biologists moved on to the phage meeting at Cold Spring Harbor.

A photograph of the attendees gathered on the steps at the side of Blackford Hall shows Brenner in the front row, beaming like a schoolboy in what look like army surplus shorts; Francis stands just behind him. During a break, Crick, together with Joshua and Esther Lederberg and some others went down to the Sand Spit at the end of Bungtown Road; this long sandbar protects the inner part of the harbour, where the laboratory is, from the waves coming in from Long Island Sound; in the summer, scientific visitors play volleyball and hold beach parties there. Photos taken that day show Crick on the beach, slim and windblown, wearing a shirt with small red checks and a matching short-sleeved white top with a red and white striped collar, the whole thing tucked into high-waisted trousers. He looks relaxed and happy, completely at home.

*

Back in Brooklyn Heights, Francis found a letter from Odile waiting for him, written from Portugal Place.[71] The house had been let out during their absence and Odile had now returned from King's Lynn to get everything straight, leaving the children with her parents. Francis and Odile had not seen each other for over seven months:

> My Darling,
> Have just taken up residence again – lovely to wake up in our nice bedroom again but rather lonely by myself! Longing to have you home again – it seems almost incredible that you will be here in about ten days. (…) The house looks quite respectable now but will be absolutely full when the children arrive. (…)
>
> IloveyouIloveyouIloveyouIloveyou
>
> Odile

A few days later Francis embarked on the *Queen Mary*, crossing the Atlantic by sea for the second and last time.[72]

*

On 22 September Crick wrote laconically to Watson: 'Back safely. Family thriving (Gabrielle speaks beautiful French). House recovering, Cambridge wonderful.'[73] Ten days later, a slightly exasperated Kendrew told Watson: 'I wish you were here, if only to keep Francis in order. He is the same as ever – spends his whole day talking furiously about the secrets of life and about how he is going to become famous by writing best-sellers.'[74]

This book business had first emerged when Crick spoke to BBC producers in the summer of 1953; by spring 1954 he was in discussion with Kurt Jacoby of Academic Press, touting the title 'The Central Problem of Molecular Biology'.[75] Crick sent Jacoby a table of contents, a contract was drawn up, but nothing was written; over subsequent years an increasingly weary Jacoby repeatedly reminded Crick of promises made, by letter or phone. In 1955 Francis tried to let Jacoby down gently: 'I think you are overoptimistic to expect a first draft, but I might be able to show you *part* of a first draft.' He did write bits of a chapter, which he wafted under Jacoby's nose when their paths crossed in Brussels in the summer of that year, but a few months later admitted that he had been distracted: 'You must be only too familiar with authors who start and won't finish, but an author who never really starts is even worse,' he wrote. The two continued their dance for another few years before it became obvious that the book would never be written.

While Francis enjoyed writing short popular articles and making broadcasts, the mundane task of explaining in detail something that was already established could not hold his attention for any length of time. As he admitted many years later, 'I didn't get down to it. There were always too many distractions.'[76]

ET IN ARCADIA EGO

The Cricks' return to Cambridge began an exciting and happy phase of their lives. MRC salaries increased by a whopping 25 per cent at the beginning of 1955, freeing the family from their financial worries.[1] As Francis acquired a global scientific reputation, their house became the buzzing centre of a growing network of friends and visitors who enjoyed both the scientific discussions and the Cricks' taste for a party and good talk. Odile ran the household – cooking the meals, raising the children (with the help of au pairs) and making sure the bills were paid, while Francis carried on being Francis. That division of labour had been established in the early days of their marriage, but now Odile's culinary and party-organising skills moved to another level as she entertained a seemingly endless stream of guests in her new domain. In December, Odile drew a charming sketch of the building for the Cricks' Christmas card, featuring Francis, herself and the two girls, and Michael at the ground-floor window.*[2]

---

* That year, Francis decided that he was tired of Christmas trees, so Michael made a huge giraffe out of chicken wire and painted papier-mâché which replaced the tree; in subsequent years, other animals were made. Voll, D. (1994), Soul searching with Francis Crick. *Omni*, February 1994, 46–53. Michael Crick confirmed this story and gave me more details – e-mail to the author, July 2024.

Between 1954 and 1956, Francis was thinking about several scientific issues at once. Some of them were technical, relating to his
work in New York or to abstruse parts of crystallographic theory
– he described them to Brenner as 'rather dull', probably the most
damning phrase in his vocabulary.[3] But the most significant parts
of his work, the ones that have shaped how we understand biology,
related to the central problem – how genes do what they do. Francis
explored each of these questions with a different collaborator, each
of whom brought something different to his thinking.

There was Jim, again. Watson believed that the study of viruses
would provide the key to the structure of the RNA molecules most
of them contained.[4] He therefore wangled his return to Cambridge in
the middle of 1955, to work with Crick on this new topic. On hearing
the news, Kendrew wrote to Watson expressing his delight, although
he added, waspishly, 'Francis tells me he expects to collaborate with

you on RNA when you come. Delighted to learn that you feel able to cope with this.'[5]

There was Rosalind. While Francis was in the USA he had begun a friendly scientific correspondence with Franklin, soon signing off 'Yours ever', something he reserved for close male friends, like Kreisel or Watson. In response, Franklin sent Crick her latest results on Tobacco Mosaic Virus (TMV), as well as draft papers for his comments, something that continued when Francis was back in Cambridge. She became a regular guest at Portugal Place – Crick would close his letters to her with invitations, such as 'Come and see us some time' or 'Come again'.[6] Crick admired her sharp experimentalist's mind and skills and enjoyed testing his crystallographic knowledge with her latest results. When he went too far in his speculations, she scolded him – 'Facts are facts, Francis' – and they both relished the frank interaction.[7]

There was Alex. Alex Rich had met Francis at the Pasadena meeting in September 1953, and Crick agreed that he should come to the Cavendish in 1955 to study the structure of RNA. Fifty years later, Rich recalled their visit – apart from the scientific discussions, what stuck in his mind was Odile's cooking, and her singing and playing the accordion at the parties that took place in Portugal Place: 'Odile seemed to manage everything effortlessly. Things just flowed along, and people enjoyed themselves. Wine was freely offered, and good spirits abounded. Jokes were in the fabric of the parties. My memories of these gatherings are warm and glowing, even today.'[8]

And there was Sydney. For Francis, one of the most important things about his time at Woods Hole had been his intense discussions with Sydney Brenner. In November, Brenner returned to South Africa via Cambridge, staying in Portugal Place for a few days following an enthusiastic invitation from Francis ('Of course we'll put you up – we're really looking forward to it. Come when you like and stay as long as you can'), obligingly smuggling some of Crick's dollars through customs on his way.[9] During his brief visit, Brenner helped Francis explore ideas that were germinating in his mind – how DNA could lead to protein synthesis. In a letter to Franklin, Crick described Brenner's stay as 'A great treat. We managed to cover a lot of ground.'[10] Once Brenner was back in South Africa, Francis pursued these interactions through regular letters that were longer and more detailed than his correspondence with Watson. Crick wrote two or more letters a week to Brenner, sometimes cramming his ideas onto a fold-up airmail letter, the writing getting smaller as he ran out of space, sometimes sprawling across over a dozen pages or more. The impact of this correspondence on his ideas convinced Crick that he needed Brenner to come to Cambridge permanently; he spent much of the next two years trying to engineer the move, which eventually happened in December 1956.

*

After those few days of feverish discussions with Brenner in autumn 1954, Francis began work on a document that explored the theoretical ideas about the genetic code that had been cooked up by Gamow and his pals over the previous year, as well as developing his own notions about the molecular link between DNA, RNA and proteins. 'On Degenerate Templates and the Adaptor Hypothesis' (the term 'adaptor' was coined by Brenner) was duplicated and mailed out as a note to the members of the recently formed RNA Tie Club.[11] This was an informal group of researchers who were interested in the role of RNA in protein synthesis, set up by Watson, Leslie Orgel and Gamow.*[12] Known as the RNA Tie Club because each of its twenty members had a special RNA tie, bearing a woven sketch of an RNA molecule, the club never actually met, but it became an informal forum for the circulation of unpublished papers, or preprints.[13] While some of Gamow's physicist pals joined, Rosalind Franklin was never invited, even though she was eminently qualified through her new work on the structure of RNA viruses.

---

*The club later had headed notepaper that read in Gamow-esque style 'Rnatie Club' and carried the motto 'Do or die, or don't try' together with a list of Officers of the Club: Watson was 'Optimist' while Crick was 'Pessimist'. Gamow, appropriately enough, was 'Synthesiser'. Each member was allocated an amino acid at random and was able to purchase a tie-pin carrying its recognised abbreviation. Crick was Tyrosine, so his tie-pin – which it appears he never received – would have read TYR. Rnatie Club circular, 4 July 1955, SB/1/1/545.

Crick's note contained a prediction that embodied his understanding of the biological and chemical implications of the new outlook heralded by the double helix. Crick's starting point was that the structure of DNA was not a physical mould for the synthesis of proteins, as Gamow had initially suggested. Instead of spaces where amino acids would fit, both DNA and RNA carried a specific sequence of bases – genetic information. The challenge was to see how that information could get out of the nucleic acid and be turned into a sequence of amino acids – a protein. To solve this conundrum, Francis proposed that some kind of tiny molecular intermediary must bond with both a particular nucleic acid sequence and a specific amino acid. As he put it:

> Each amino acid would combine chemically, at a special enzyme, with a small molecule which, having a specific hydrogen-bonding surface, would combine specifically with the nucleic acid template. (…) In its simplest form there would be 20 different kinds of adaptor molecule, one for each amino acid, and 20 different enzymes to join the amino acid to their adaptors. Sydney Brenner, with whom I have discussed this idea, calls this the 'adaptor hypothesis', since each amino acid is fitted with an adaptor to go on the template.

Not everyone agreed – Watson responded tersely 'Dislike adaptors.'[14] Watson was concerned that there was no experimental support for Crick's hypothetical little molecules and felt that having a different type for each amino acid seemed wasteful and inelegant. However, a little more than a year later, Harvard biochemists Mahlon Hoagland and Paul Zamecnik found evidence for precisely such molecular intermediaries.* Crick's hypothesis had been circulated only to the RNA Tie Club, so had made no broader impact; when Hoagland excitedly announced his discovery to Watson, he learned to his amazement and annoyance that Crick had already predicted it.[15]

In his note, Crick also tried to use Gamow's theoretical approach to the genetic code, even though it had so far proved a dead end. But when he explored what kind of code might be implied by the

---

*They are now called transfer RNA or tRNA molecules.

existence of adaptors, none of the possibilities fitted the known protein sequence data. His final words were downbeat:

> Altogether the position is rather discouraging. Whereas on the one hand the adaptor hypothesis allows us to construct, in theory, codes of bewildering variety, which are very difficult to reject in bulk, the actual sequence data, on the other hand, gives us hardly any hint of regularity, or connectedness, and suggests that all, or almost all sequences may be allowed. In the comparative isolation of Cambridge I must confess that there are times when I have no stomach for decoding.

To emphasise his pessimism, Crick prefaced his note with a quotation from an eleventh-century Persian poet, Kai Kā'ūs ibn Iskandar: 'Is there anyone so utterly lost as he that seeks a way where there is no way?'[16] Coding might turn out to be a way of complementing future experimental evidence, he wrote to Brenner, 'but I don't think it is likely to go much further on its own'.[17] As Francis explained to Brenner, he was now convinced that the purely theoretical approach to the genetic code 'should be put on the shelf for a bit'.

He was as good as his word. From the beginning of 1955, Crick was busy in the laboratory, including on Saturdays, trying to isolate proteins from egg whites – centrifuging, analysing, scribbling down the results and then starting again the following Monday.[18] Together with Vernon Ingram, a protein chemist who worked in the room next door, Francis was trying to isolate lysozyme, a small enzyme found in mucosal secretions such as tears, which he had studied during his PhD.[19] They hoped to find variability in the structure of this molecule within a species, which they could then correlate with genetic differences, with the aim of showing how genes encode proteins.

This was a brilliant idea but, as Crick told Brenner, the results were discouraging.[20] It was easy to detect differences between lysozyme from human tears (Crick's own, obtained with the aid of an onion*) and the equivalent molecule from hens, guinea fowl or

---

*He had wanted to use the tears of his baby daughter Jacqueline, but Odile would have none of it. Crick to Brenner, 6 July 1955, SB/1/1/131.

ducks, but the enzymes appeared to have the same characteristics within each species.[21] And as Crick recognised, even if they did find a difference between individual animals, they would then have to link that to a genetic change – in a species like the chicken, with a slow generation time and poorly understood genetics, that would take forever. This project, which took up much of the first half of 1955 and lingered into 1956, seems to have been poorly conceived; it would surely have been better to start with an animal that had lots of mutations, such as *Drosophila*, and then find the associated protein changes.

While all this was going on, letters from Kreisel brought the usual scabrous descriptions of his activities and, in a novel twist, the first of a series of enclosures, which Kreisel called religious pictures. These were pornographic photographs that he arranged to have sent from Hungary via Vienna, sometimes featuring himself.[22] By the spring the Cricks' acquisition of 20 Portugal Place had been completed, a hole had been smashed through the wall connecting it to number 19 and a sliding door fitted. Odile was busy managing the transformation, but as Francis wrote to Watson, there was 'a lot of work still to be done'.[23]

The basement flat of number 20 had a separate entrance, used by the au pairs who came to help Odile with the children. First there was Fanny, from Austria, but she returned in early summer 1955. An unexpected replacement arrived in the shape of Linda Pauling, Linus's daughter, who was spending a year in Europe and suddenly needed somewhere to stay after a disastrous trip to Spain with her boyfriend (Odile painted a nude portrait of her).[24] In October 1955 she was succeeded by another Austrian, who came for a year.

At the end of June, Watson arrived. He had recently obtained a position at Harvard – despite Crick's letter of recommendation which described him as 'a rather strange young man' – and had somehow convinced his new employers to give him leave to work with Crick (this also brought him closer to his girlfriend, Christa Mayr, who was in Germany).[25] Watson recalled that when he walked into the laboratory he immediately encountered 'the buzz of Francis Crick holding court within his Cavendish domain'.[26] His arrival was followed a few days later by that of Alex Rich and his wife Jane; at the Cricks' insistence, the couple stayed in Portugal Place.[27] Their room was hardly luxurious – it had no carpet, just bare floorboards and, as Odile recalled, 'a scruffy table lamp on the floor as a bedside light'. Rich brought with him samples of synthetic RNA – a long chain composed solely of adenine bases, which had been created by Severo Ochoa and Marianne Grunberg-Manago at New York University School of Medicine.[28] The idea was that the powerful new X-ray source at the Cavendish would help reveal the structure of these monotonous RNA molecules.

At the end of July, the weather was unusually pleasant, and Alex Rich climbed over the railings on the other side of the path in front of the Cricks' house and photographed an unguarded moment when the whole gang apart from Watson were drinking punch on the steps at Portugal Place.* Francis is on the top step of number 20, with Michael just behind him, pointing a toy pistol at his father; Linda Pauling and Jane Rich are on the steps below. Sid Bernhard is standing on the left, Ann Cullis (Perutz's research assistant, and a member of the Cricks' circle) is standing on the right next to an unidentified man. Gabrielle is in the middle of the three girls sitting in front of the

---

*Why punch? There is a jug on the bottom step of number 19, the drink in peoples' glasses is darkish and cloudy, there appears to be fruit floating in Cullis's glass and whatever it is, only the adults are drinking it.

door to number 19. Odile is in the centre of the photo, and the focus of attention is Jacqueline, who is trying to drink from her mother's empty glass.

A week or so earlier, while Francis was on a brief holiday with Kreisel in the Swiss Alps, Odile had written him a rather dizzy letter:

> I am staying with some charming Americans at 19, Portugal Place. You should come here, it is quite delightful. Sid arrived tonight and is staying with Freddie. Hugh has fallen out with Eileen. Gabrielle's birthday party was a tremendous success in Aunt Ethel's garden. 13 children. Hope you had a wonderful time. I did. How are Kreisel's piles. Jim is sowing his wild oats. Jane is perfectly charming.
>
> I think I'm getting a little incoherent so good night darling.
>
> Lots of love from
>
> Your adoring and devoted
>
> Odile[29]

*

On the morning of Saturday 27 August 1955, the latest copy of *Nature* plopped through the letterbox at Portugal Place. Odile and the children were up but Francis was still in bed; breakfast was not yet ready, so Odile sent Gabrielle upstairs with the journal.[30] When Francis eventually came down with Alex Rich, who was still staying with them, Rich idly asked his friend if there was anything interesting in that week's issue. Francis replied 'No, not really', just a short X-ray diffraction study of a protein called polyglycine II, by researchers at the Courtauld company. As Crick and Rich lazily tucked into their breakfast, they read the article together, becoming increasingly animated, soon deciding to see if they could build a model that would solve the structure of the molecule, using the data in the paper.[31] They wandered over to the Cavendish, played around with molecular models for a couple of hours, and had the answer by noon. Francis hit upon the terrific wheeze of immediately writing up the structure, getting Bragg to submit it to *Nature* and trying to get it published the following week. Perhaps with the experience of DNA and collagen in the back of his mind, after a few moments of reflection he realised that this would sour relations with the Courtauld's researchers; he and Rich decided to invite them to see the model and then publish, with their agreement. Francis wrote cheerfully to Brenner a few days later: 'Things here are quite hectic in the extreme (Alex and I solved polyglycine II on Saturday – the same day the experimental data was published; it's quite uninteresting biologically).'[32] Within three weeks, the structure was submitted to *Nature*, and the article duly appeared less than two months after the original paper.[33]

Around this time, Rich, Watson and Crick were gathered in Portugal Place together with Leslie Orgel, who had recently joined the Cambridge Chemistry department. Someone – perhaps Odile or Jane Rich – took a couple of pictures of the four of them, or maybe Rich used the timer on his camera. Crick and Orgel were seated on the Cricks' stripey sofa, Rich and Watson were on the floor in front of them. They were all wearing their RNA Tie Club ties, except Orgel; Rich even wore his Tie Club tie-pin. Francis looked in need of a haircut, while bug-eyed, big-toothed, jug-eared Watson was every

bit the strange young man, down to the pens in the top pocket of his ill-fitting jacket.[34]

Solving polyglycine II gave Crick and Rich a clue to the structure of collagen, about one third of which is composed of glycine. The collagen structure Crick had published in 1953 was not correct and researchers around the world had begun to turn their attention to the problem, including G. N. Ramachandran of Madras, who had obtained his PhD at the Cavendish in 1949.[35] At the end of September 1955, he and his colleague Gopinath Kartha published an article in *Nature* in which they proposed a structure that Crick and Rich realised was basically correct but wrong in its details. In the space of two weeks they worked up two alternative models, taking into account some of Pauline Cowan's unpublished data.

Crick and Rich's article appeared in *Nature* within a month; Cowan was slightly less nimble – her response, with a similar solution, appeared three weeks later.[36] Despite talking to Cowan about the problems with Ramachandran's structure and citing her work, Francis admitted to Brenner that the affair had again led to 'difficulties with Randall's people'.[37] This was quite understandable – for the third time in two years, Crick had published a molecular structure using data from people in Randall's laboratory. Ramachandran seemed remarkably relaxed about the whole thing, as he wrote to Rich: 'We appear to have been thinking on very nearly the same lines as you and Dr Crick have done.'[38]

Crick later cheerfully remarked that this affair had all the elements that had made the discovery of the double helix so exciting: the difficulties in finding the right answer were just as great and 'the characters were just as colourful and diverse', but neither the structure nor the function of collagen were as significant as for DNA.[39] Pauline Cowan also drew parallels between the two discoveries, emphasising that in both cases it was the structure that attracted attention, not the underlying experimental work. In 1972 she told Randall that Crick and Rich behaved like 'two very adroit salesman', who were 'so carried away with their own enthusiasm, so "dizzy with success", that I do not think they themselves recognised their own indebtedness.'[40]

Crick was correct: both DNA and collagen involved an exciting race, there were friendships and the informal exchange of data, and deep upset was caused by what looked like breaches of scientific etiquette. He did not point out that both races also involved Francis Crick.

*

Two weeks after the collagen article was submitted, Francis was hit by a bombshell. His beloved Momma, Annie, fell ill and died on 27 October. Utterly distraught, Francis retreated to his room for three days.[41] A month later, he got a note from Kreisel: 'Sorry to hear about your mother's death. I sympathise with you, as much on account of the trouble ahead of you as on that which is past.'*[42] But despite his friend's gloomy prediction, Francis was soon able to put Annie's death behind him, partly by focusing on his work.

*

There was plenty to distract him.

In November, Francis recorded the first of four talks broadcast on the BBC European Service in which he highlighted the work of colleagues, using the opportunity to explore scientific problems that were at the forefront of his mind.[43] One talk focused on the work of Seymour Benzer in Indiana and of Guido Pontecorvo in Glasgow, who were each trying to demonstrate that the alteration of a single base pair could induce a genetic change. As Francis explained: 'the biological unit is getting down to the chemical unit, which only contains about forty atoms. We are on the threshold, in fact, of molecular genetics in its widest sense.' That sweeping sense of precision, the potential reduction of the complexities of genetics to the action of a handful of atoms, reveals the power of Crick's vision.

Another talk, given in April 1956, centred on a recent 'very important scientific paper' in which Berkeley researcher Heinz Fraenkel-Conrat separated the RNA and protein components of

---

*In typical Kreisel fashion, the same considerate letter included some earthier news: 'I have arranged to have more religious pictures sent to you.'

TMV and showed that the RNA component was required for the virus to be able to infect a plant.[44] He then swapped RNA from two different strains of TMV and showed – more or less – that it was RNA that determined the behaviour and structure of the virus. As Crick explained, disarmingly:

> This idea – that the RNA is a sort of code for the protein – has been a dogma to us for some years now, but the actual direct experimental evidence for it was negligible, and it was really held on faith – at least by the small minority, myself included, who held it rather strongly. You can imagine, then, how delighted we were to learn that here at last was an experiment which gave it strong support.

Benzer's study of the molecular structure of the *rII* phage gene was the subject of the fourth talk, and again Francis related the research to the fundamental problem he was grappling with:

> If we could find the protein controlled by Dr. Benzer's gene, we might be able to discover, with modern techniques, the change in the order of the amino acids produced by any particular mutant. If we *could* do this we could soon see if the two orders – the linear mapping of the gene and the linear arrangement of the amino acids – were related. Dr. Benzer is coming to work with us at Cambridge next year, and this is exactly what we shall try to do.

These radio talks reveal Crick's ability to communicate with the public – he had a real knack for explaining complex issues to non-specialists. This could involve quite dramatic gestures. In 1955 he gave a talk about DNA; to demonstrate that it was a very, very long molecule, in the middle of the lecture he suddenly hurled a toilet roll across the room. As it unravelled in the air, it became clear that the whole length was covered with a double helix.[45]

Francis was also busy trying to arrange a place in the MRC unit for Sydney Brenner, although this was proving difficult. The new head of the Cavendish, Nevill Mott, wanted the unit to leave, and government spending cuts threatened its future. Furthermore, Crick's own position within the unit was, as he put it to Brenner, anomalous – 'I still do theoretical crystallography,' he wrote – and he was wary of drawing the attention of the MRC high-ups if he pleaded Brenner's case too strongly.[46]

But in October 1955 the situation suddenly changed. Hugh Huxley left the unit, freeing up one salary, and the Rockefeller Foundation awarded the unit a four-year grant totalling $40,000. 'This changes a position of acute financial stringency into one of comparative plenty,' Francis explained to Brenner, as he seized the opportunity and asked Perutz to recruit the young South African.[47] Perutz agreed in principle, but there was no space for the new arrival; this was partly resolved by Brenner insisting that he was prepared to work in a cupboard if necessary.[48] By December 1955 it seemed certain that 1956 would be the year that Brenner came to Cambridge, which it was, if only just.[49]

There was more excitement over RNA, as Watson and Rich tried to find a structure using Ochoa's synthetic RNA molecule having adenine as its sole base, polyadenylic acid. After the pair had dashed off a manuscript for Francis to read, it was time for Alex and Jane Rich to return to the USA, which inevitably required a farewell party at Portugal Place.[50] A period of calm followed around Christmas, as Watson left for Scotland where he hoped to stoke the flames with Christa Mayr, but instead was unceremoniously dumped. Jim's cause cannot have been helped when, after walking wordlessly beside Christa on a Scottish hillside for some time, he blurted out that Francis was the only person he could really talk to.[51]

Odile, who was recovering from bronchitis, decided to take the girls to King's Lynn for Christmas; Francis remained in Portugal Place, overseeing the work on number 20.[52] Odile wrote giving clear instructions to pass on to the decorators: 'Front room should have inside front door yellow like the curtains but should prefer the topcoat to be done when return. Other doors & skirting grey.'[53] She went on to tell Francis which tiles should be used for the basement and which wallpaper for the kitchen, before signing off 'Look after yourself and don't work too hard.' She also included a thoughtful remark about the Austrian au pair, who she feared might be homesick at Christmas, suggesting that Francis should take her to Marks &

Spencer to buy a present. Odile might not have been so kind had she known that at some point the au pair and Francis had a brief affair.[54] Or maybe she did know and was kind anyway.

*

In the New Year, there were lots of distractions from science. Watson returned heart-broken from Scotland, Odile had bronchitis again, new tenants had moved into the basement at Portugal Place, a lodger – 'a young man (who acts)' – was living in Michael's room during term-time and Francis was now being invited onto the BBC to speak on non-scientific programmes. At the beginning of the year, as Francis excitedly reported to Rich, he did 'an (unscripted) broadcast with a bishop' and a few weeks later he recorded an episode of a long-running general discussion programme called *Questions in the Air*, alongside the Tory politician Lord Hailsham and the composer Antony Hopkins.[55]

Meanwhile, Crick and Watson had to get on with an article on plant viruses for *Nature*. Francis had written an initial draft back in November 1954, but it had lain dormant since then. Now they had a dual objective – getting the damned thing finished and having something to say at an upcoming ultra-select Ciba Symposium on 'The Biophysics and Biochemistry of Viruses', to be held in London at the end of March, to which they, and Franklin, had been invited.[56]

The article eventually appeared a couple of weeks before the symposium and set out Crick and Watson's hypothesis that the outside of small viruses is made up of identical or near-identical protein sub-units.[57] Their presentation to the meeting, given by Crick, was highly pedagogical, partly because of the composition of the audience. There were the well-established virologists who used biochemistry to study their favourite microbes,* and there were the irritating upstarts like Crick, people with no experience of viruses, who wielded X-rays to describe viral structure.

---

*Franklin had already had a run-in with one of these types, N. W. Pirie of the Rothamsted Experimental Station, who had made tetchy comments about her articles and then refused to share samples with her (FRKN/2/33).

Crick lectured the virologists about the 'general principles' of the structure of the things they had been studying for decades, explaining that RNA encoded protein, but the amount of RNA in a virus was very small compared to the large protein coat.[58] There was not enough RNA to code for the amount of protein unless the viral shell was composed of repetitive sub-units – the same bit of RNA would produce the same bit of protein, over and over again, which would then self-assemble to form the viral coat. As he put it: 'The essential point is that you cannot carry an unlimited amount of information in a limited amount of RNA.'

As with DNA three years earlier, Franklin provided the experimental evidence to back up Crick's insight, showing that Tobacco Mosaic Virus was indeed composed of many protein sub-units, arranged in a helix, with RNA threaded through them. The old guard were not convinced, dismissing Franklin's results as an artefact – Crick defended her, insisting that the virus had the same shape with or without RNA.[59] The critics even argued that viruses could be infectious without any functioning nucleic acid. Francis carefully picked apart their claims, obliging them to accept that the key question was whether pure RNA would be infective; within two weeks this was shown to be the case.[60] Throughout the meeting Crick kept on bobbing up in the discussions, calmly responding to the criticisms from the more traditional attendees, showing the power of the new approach. He must have been infuriating.

No sooner was the Ciba meeting over than Franklin and Crick – and Odile – were off to Madrid for a large symposium organised by the International Union of Crystallography.[61] Also attending the meeting were people from the Cavendish, King's and Birkbeck, including Kendrew, Ann Cullis, Wilkins, Bernal, Klug and Don Caspar, a US scientist who had been working at the Cavendish and with Franklin. Caspar gave a joint paper with Crick and Watson on virus structure, while Franklin repeated her Ciba symposium talk for a new audience. A photo taken at the symposium shows Klug, Kendrew, Cullis and Caspar, with Odile and Franklin standing next to each other, while Crick grins and points. Afterwards, Francis and Odile went on a brief holiday with Franklin, visiting Toledo, Seville, Cordoba and Granada, travelling by train and bus. Klug, with a penchant for Hemingway, decided to stay in Madrid and watch a bullfight.[62] A few weeks later, Crick told Rich that the three of them had a splendid time.[63]

L-R: Ann Cullis, Francis, Don Caspar, Aaron Klug, Rosalind Franklin, Odile, John Kendrew.

*

On his return, Crick broke his promise to lay off theoretical approaches to coding and dashed off a brief note for the RNA Tie Club, written with Leslie Orgel and John Griffith. Entitled 'Comma-less Codes', this was Crick's last adventure in theoretical coding, and it was a cracker.[64]

The implication of the double helix was that a particular sequence of bases somehow corresponds to a particular amino acid. Each base in a DNA sequence clearly does not code for a single amino acid, as there are only four bases, but twenty amino acids. Similarly, a sequence of two bases produces only sixteen possible combinations, but there are sixty-four possible combinations of three-base 'triplets'. The challenge was to reduce those sixty-four combinations to what Crick called 'the magic number 20'. In their ingenious paper, Crick, Griffith and Orgel explored the implications of the assumption that the genetic code was 'comma-less' – there were no instructions telling the cell where one triplet began and another ended, not even a signal that said 'start here' – and non-overlapping (each triplet was read separately). In the absence of a 'start here' signal, each triplet would have to be distinguishable from the preceding and succeeding sequences. Using logical arguments, the trio excluded all triplets that would be ambiguous under such conditions (for example, all four triplets composed of a single base – AAA, CCC etc.) and found that twenty combinations remained. They must have been very pleased with themselves.

Finished in May 1956, the note made a great impression on its RNA Tie Club readers and despite its caveats (the title page carried an epigraph from the seventeenth-century thinker Francis Bacon warning about the danger of relying on theories) it was soon published in the *PNAS*. This elegant and stylish hypothesis dominated thinking about codes, reinforcing Crick's reputation as the intellectual powerhouse of the growing molecular genetics community.[65] It also turned out to be completely wrong.

After completing this tour de force, Francis was on his travels again; he spent May to July 1956 in the USA, working with Rich in Maryland, giving some lectures in Ann Arbor and going to three conferences. One of the meetings was in Baltimore, where Crick and Watson found themselves sharing a huge suite in the conference hotel. As Watson recalled, 'Francis beamed, pointing out that we were getting the recognition the double helix deserved.'[66] That recognition was also seen in some of the lectures he gave – at the University of Wisconsin Madison his talk on small viruses was expected to attract an audience of fifteen; over two hundred people turned up.[67]

While he was in the USA, Crick continued writing his intense letters to Brenner, keeping him up to date with all the latest scientific gossip. For example, in the middle of July he wrote a sixteen-page letter summarising the conference talks he had heard, going into great detail about the experiments and the conclusions from various presenters, including little sketches of the results and adding his own views: François Jacob gave 'a beautiful talk', while of one of Gunther Stents ideas, he wrote 'Personally, I don't like it for a number of reasons.'[68] The most exciting thing he heard was Arthur Kornberg's claim to have replicated DNA in the test tube. Crick summarised the steps involved in the experiment and concluded, 'Everybody was greatly impressed by the great competence of Kornberg. It's my belief that he really has DNA replication', thereby opening the way to studies of nucleic acid replication and of gene function. Crick concluded with a heartfelt plea: 'There are so many things I should like to do that I can hardly wait for you to arrive. Is there no chance of you arriving a month or so earlier?'

Francis also received letters from Odile while he was on his trip, describing her outings (she had seen Laurence Olivier's *Richard III* and Orson Welles' *Othello* at the local cinema) and listing the bills that made her head buzz – the decoration of Portugal Place and the refurbishment of Croft Lodge on Barton Road that the Cricks had bought with an inheritance and now rented out, the running of the household (£28/9/- on wine for April), the book-buying habit (a Heffers bill of £40/4/4) and the cost of getting a second child's seat put on her bicycle so she could transport both girls around town.

Most of Odile's letters, however, were amusing and full of gossip – exactly as Francis liked. To mark the departure of Caspar and Watson at the end of May, Odile held a 'terrific party' of around eighty people. Watson was 'horribly temperamental' and arrived late, having been to another party nearby. And when he did turn up, accompanied by biochemistry student and Crick family friend Belinda Bullard*, he complained about the dullness of Cambridge conversation.[69] At one point in the evening Odile popped into the other party and performed a toreador dance with Caspar. When she returned to Portugal Place, Gabrielle was still not in bed, so Odile sat her daughter on her lap until the last revellers left, at around four in the morning. Odile remarked: 'Rosalind F. came to the party and stayed the night. Invited me again to go to London and stay with her so maybe I will next week. Gabrielle liked her "very very much."'

---

* Belinda's father was the geophysicist Edward Bullard, who had recently returned to Cambridge as a Fellow at Gonville and Caius.

A week later, Odile told Francis of her London theatre trip with Franklin, which unexpectedly involved her dress-making skills:

> I went to collect her at her lab and we went to see a fine bit of nonsense called Romanoff and Juliet. Peter Ustinov having a wonderful time. When we got back to the flat, Rosalind asked me if I would fit a dress for her as the friend who usually does this for her was on holiday, so I took a bit in here and a bit in there, nipped in the waist and gave her a lesson in deportment (she said it's a little difficult to alter the habits of a lifetime!) If you breathe a word of this to her I'll never forgive you.

A few weeks earlier, Francis had written unusually affectionate letters (now lost); in the same letter, Odile remarked on the change: 'I don't think I've ever had such nice letters from you before – who would have thought the US would inspire you in this way!'[70] One inspiration may have been another adventure that Crick had at the time, with a divorced researcher. Their affair continued intermittently for a couple of years, mainly through cheerful correspondence about scientific, social and sexual matters and occasional hotel trysts when their travels coincided.[71]

Whether Odile knew, suspected, or was in ignorance of this, on 8 June, Crick's fortieth birthday, she sent him a greetings telegram that was either a joke or a misprint – 'MANY HAPPY HAPPY RETURNS', with the whimsical family signature 'FIFI, FINELLA AND FIFINETTE'. A few weeks later she gave some insight into Crick's views about the power of sex: 'So you think the ability to enjoy sexual intercourse is a panacea for all kinds of troubles – well, perhaps you are right,' she wrote.[72] This led into a discussion of the work of Simone de Beauvoir, who Francis had suggested she read. She replied sharply that not only had she read de Beauvoir's *Les Mandarins*, she talked to him about it at the time. She was currently reading de Beauvoir's *The Second Sex* ('very fascinating – much much more readable than Kinsey') and Norbert Wiener's *The Human Use of Human Beings*. Francis was not always quite on the same level – in July he sent her a postcard of the Washington Monument (an immense obelisk), with the saucy message 'American symbolism at its best. Hope it reminds you of me!'[73]

In return, Odile continued to write letters full of domestic trivia – the details of Gabrielle's birthday party, 'beastly bills' for light bulbs and name tapes, as well as another hefty bill from Matthews the wine sellers. There were also hints of the usual conflicts in any couple:

> If only you would try to be a little more considerate at home and loving too, I would be quite happy to get on with my work and not expect too much of your company. But when the little time we spend together is full of nervous tension I just have to get away and fritter away my time in a lot of useless ways.[74]

But as his return became imminent, Odile became increasingly excited: 'I see I am going to get a new, healthy and reformed husband! I'm absolutely terrified! What has the USA done to you. (…) Lots of exuberant love'.[75]

There were also the usual unusual letters from Kreisel, including one describing his encounter with Rosalind Franklin in Stanford: 'I have just seen Miss Franklin. When I heard about her sleeping troubles, my heart went out to her (though not my cock). But as time went on, it began to sag (my heart): I believe she is a socialist or something.' When Kreisel tried to shock her by asking if she had visited any brothels for women in Spain, she refused to rise to the bait and he concluded that she was 'impregnable'.[76] Her impression of him was not recorded.

*

When Francis returned from his US trip, he soon found that his scientific and personal lives were piling up.

There were the domestic worries associated with parenthood – Gabrielle broke her arm, but soon recovered. There were still more letters, some intimate and discreetly sent to the Cavendish. The Austrian au pair, who had returned to Vienna, explained how much she missed the girls and naively wondered why Odile had not replied to her last three letters.[77] In a later letter she provided eye-popping descriptions of her recent sexual adventures; she then pretended to be shocked at Crick's reply, before admitting the truth: 'You are a devil, a monster to write such a letter to me – though it was quite exciting.' His scientist lover wrote from the USA, mainly about science, but including a rude limerick:

> Dr Crick was once quoted to say
> To a lady he had in the hay
> 'It's not caloric counting,
> But old-fashioned mounting
> That keeps excess poundage away!'[78]

The letters that Sir Lawrence Bragg sent were also exciting, but not in the same way. In April 1958 the World's Fair – Expo 58 – was to open in Brussels. Bragg had been put in charge of British contributions to a display entitled 'The Living Cell', as part of the International Hall of Science. He wanted to make a big feature of DNA and hoped that Crick could help. Crick responded by suggesting that Wilkins could provide material on DNA and Franklin on RNA virus structure, while he would cover collagen.[79] Although Wilkins and Franklin were both involved in the development of huge models for the exhibition, the collagen idea got dropped along the way.

Francis was also busy putting the finishing touches to a long review article he had been writing for around a year with Kendrew, 'X-ray Analysis and Protein Structure'. This paper, aimed at biochemists, explained X-ray crystallography in relatively simple terms, highlighting the Cavendish work on haemoglobin and myoglobin and Franklin's studies of virus structure.[80] At eighty pages long – around thirty thousand words of text – it was hard going for the uninitiated, despite Crick's attempts to make the technique sound simple, reassuring the reader that it was 'easy to the point of tediousness' and that no 'three-dimensional imagination' was required.

There was breezy talk about the 'hokey-pokey' required to get a good image, descriptions of high-speed computers as being like mathematical sausage machines, and a joke about what an image would look like if a crystallographer stood on their head, but after all the underlying physics and mathematics had been explained,

Crick emphasised that in only rare, simple cases was it possible to directly deduce a structure from X-ray data. His disarming conclusion must have disoriented more than one reader: 'guesswork is always involved, and it is this which makes crystallography something of an art.'

To explain two of the basic terms of crystallography – unit cell and asymmetric unit – Francis asked Odile to provide an illustration. She obliged using a motif that appeared in her drawings at this time – a pair of mermaids, which she repeated four times for the purposes of the paper. Each symmetrical pair represented the unit cell, while each mermaid was an asymmetric unit; this was light-heartedly captioned as 'an example from everyday life'. Everyday life in Portugal Place, perhaps.

Fig. 2. An example from everyday life to illustrate the difference between unit cell and asymmetric unit. There are two mermaids in the unit cell, but only one in the asymmetric unit. Notice that this pattern is the same upside down.

Although Francis clearly enjoyed exercising his explanatory powers in the more technical descriptions, the final section on viral structure showed where his interests now lay. Reflecting his many discussions with Franklin over the previous months, the review cited seven of her recent papers on virus structure, emphasising the high technical quality of her data, particularly the successful use of iso-morphous replacement – twice – in her work with Don Caspar, and the 'ingenious interpretation' of her unpublished results with Klug. Even though many of the studies discussed in the review focused on the structure of the protein shell, what increasingly interested Francis was its link with the viral nucleic acid. His focus was moving away from X-ray crystallography and towards resolving the 'central problem' of molecular biology that he had identified in his PhD thesis and had begun to explore with Sydney Brenner.

As Brenner's arrival approached, their correspondence grew increasingly detailed and somewhat frenetic as they argued over what equipment Brenner would need, how much it would cost and where it could all be housed. They also discussed where the Bren-ners would live when they arrived (with two small children, Stefan and Belinda, and May's ten year-old son, Jonathan, Portugal Place would not be big enough, even for a short time) and what school Jonathan might go to. And, as always with Francis, there was scien-tific gossip, this time relating to the research that Vernon Ingram was doing. Unable to find variation in lysozyme within a species, Ingram had turned to a protein for which there was known variability with a clear genetic basis, and which was well studied at the Cavendish – haemoglobin. Ingram and Crick were interested in the altered form of the protein found in sickle cell disease, which was known to have a slightly different structure and a genetic cause.[81] Francis excitedly spread news of this work, writing for example to Sol Spiegelman in October 1956:

> Nothing much going on here, except that Vernon Ingram has got very good evidence that sickle cell anaemia haemoglobin has a (slightly) different amino acid sequence from normal human haemoglobin. This will be the first case where an authentic genetic difference has been shown to produce an authentic change in an amino acid sequence, as opposed, say, to a difference in the folding without a sequence change. He hopes to pin down the difference within the next month.[82]

The real world impinged on all this excitement, as at the end of October

Israel invaded Egypt and the French and the British launched a disastrous attempt to seize the Suez Canal following its nationalisation in
the summer. This move was opposed by the USA, which put immense
financial pressure on the UK to withdraw; the failure of the campaign
highlighted Britain's decline as a world power. The prime minister,
Anthony Eden, had to resign, and petrol rationing was imposed as
supplies dried up with the canal out of action for months. Normally so
disconnected from politics, for once Francis noticed what was going
on. At a party in Portugal Place in early 1957, he got into an argument
about the Middle East; Belinda Bullard, who was present with two
friends, Janet and Lorna, described the scene to Watson: 'Janet told
Francis she was going to Israel because it was the promised land and
there were good opportunities for women, especially in embroider-
ing duffle coats. (…) In spite of not reading the newspapers, Francis
certainly got the better of Janet over Israel.' The festive atmosphere
was not spoilt for long – Bullard's letter continued: 'Lorna played the
accordion in Odile's kitchen. Lorna is terribly good.'[83]

Meanwhile, Kreisel's life was in turmoil. He had been having
an affair with Verena, the mathematician wife of his friend, the
physicist Freeman Dyson; she had confessed to her husband, who
was now divorcing her. At least once a week, Crick got an agitated
letter from Kreisel, asking for advice and so on. And then, when his
desires led him astray again, Kreisel described the various STDs he
had acquired. The bizarre background hum of Kreisel's letters contrasted with Crick's world, providing amusement and the occasional
cautionary tale.[84]

*

In September, the Cricks had a visitor who was very welcome, but
who came for very unwelcome reasons. During her trip to the USA,
Franklin had begun to feel abdominal discomfort; on her return to
London, she went to see her doctor and soon underwent investiga-
tive surgery. In the words of her surgeon, the outcome was most
unfortunate – he found a cancer on one ovary, and a large cyst on
the other. The cancerous ovary was removed, along with part of the
other, less damaged organ. To recover, Rosalind went to Cambridge

to stay in Portugal Place with Francis and Odile. But within a month she was back in hospital for a hysterectomy and the removal of the rest of her remaining ovary. After two weeks convalescing with her parents in north London, at the end of October she again went to stay with the Cricks, telling her friend Anne Sayre, 'I've promised them I won't do it a third time'.[85] Like Franklin's colleagues, Francis seems to have been completely in the dark about the nature of her illness; as he told Watson, 'Rosalind has had two mysterious operations, but is now much better'.[86] Odile may have known some of the details; if so, either Franklin swore her to secrecy, or Crick was playing dumb.

During her second stay with the Cricks, Franklin met Dorothea Raacke, a chemist who worked on protein synthesis and had recently arrived in Todd's Chemistry department. Raacke's recollection of her first meeting with Francis was that they went to a restaurant and Crick, rather drunk, mistakenly gave the waiter a £5 tip for a meal that cost less than that.[87] Raacke and Franklin met at the Eagle, drinking with Crick; they became friends, and Raacke stayed in Franklin's flat several times.[88] After a few weeks in Cambridge, Franklin felt sufficiently recovered to return home, intending to 'drift back to the lab' towards the end of November (half-days only, at first).[89] She even planned walking expeditions – early in 1957, Raacke told the Cricks that she was going hiking with Franklin 'in order to keep young'.[90] Raacke, apparently like Crick, never knew the nature of her friend's illness; it was a year before she learned of Franklin's hysterectomy.[91]

Francis and Rosalind's friendship continued: in January 1957 he returned from New York with a present for her – a precious gift of frozen rat liver nucleoprotein from some cancer researchers, carefully stored in a thermos flask.[92] She was still working hard, sending draft papers to Crick for comments and advice. According to Klug, 'She would do nothing without clearing it with Francis',* although that did not stop her ignoring him when she disagreed.[93] Sometimes,

---

*I feel this gives a stronger impression of Franklin's attitude to Crick than the facts imply. Franklin's biographer Brenda Maddox drew on Klug's view to suggest that Crick's intellect 'stirred her hero-worshipping tendency', but I don't find this convincing, either. Much later, Crick said that he acted as 'Rosalind's (unofficial) scientific advisor'. That seems a bit more accurate. Crick to McClain, 10 February 1998, PP/CRI/J/2/18/1.

his views were brusque – in May 1957 he told her that publishing a particular article would be 'rash in the extreme' because if 'it turns out wrong your whole research programme will be discredited'.[94] She appears to have abandoned the article. In 2001, Crick told Brenda Maddox, 'I now believe Rosalind was pressing to publish this because she thought she had only a little time left to live, and that I was too stupid to perceive this.'[95]

Franklin was soon hospitalised again and a new abdominal mass was found. Her surgeon gave her little hope, but she had cobalt radiotherapy and became strong enough to visit Europe for two conferences and a driving holiday in Italy. In the autumn, she became unwell again and was admitted to the Royal Marsden Hospital, where she received a new treatment – chemotherapy.[96] Through all this she continued work on her new project, the structure of polio, overcoming technical problems and the understandable concerns

Rosalind Franklin's laboratory at Birkbeck College,
shortly after her death in April 1958.

of Birkbeck staff about potential leaks of the terrible virus. Friends wondered about her illness, but no one outside her closest friends and family knew exactly what the problem was.[97] Oblivious to the gravity of her condition, Crick invited Franklin and her group to join the Cambridge MRC unit when it moved into a smart new building.[98]

Tragically, the cancer won. On the last day of March she was re-admitted to the Marsden; she died there on 16 April 1958, aged only thirty-seven. According to her friend the physician Mair Livingstone, who visited her in those last days, her end was not peaceful: 'I have known people in greater physical distress, but never in greater anger about the unwanted, inconvenient, unjust and cruel sentence of dying young,' Livingstone recalled.[99]

Slowly, her friends, colleagues and enemies heard the terrible news. At the National Institutes of Health (NIH) in Bethesda, Alex Rich wrote to Francis that he was 'profoundly saddened' when he learned of her death from an obituary in *The New York Times* on 20 April (the previous day, *The Times* had carried a heartfelt obituary by Bernal, who also wrote a long obituary for *Nature*).[100] Rich's colleague David Blow was equally upset, telling Crick that, 'Not being given to asking questions about people's illnesses, I hadn't even known she had cancer.'[101] Nearly two weeks after her death, Wilkins wrote a letter to his friend Leonard Hamilton and added at the end 'You may have heard that Franklin died at Easter. Poor girl she had a hard life and it made me very sad.'*[102]

It is not known how Francis and Odile were informed or if they went to the funeral, which in line with Jewish tradition was held the next day, but Crick's laboratory notebook bears no entry for 17 April.[103] The death notice in the *Manchester Guardian* was terse:

> FRANKLIN – On April 16, at the Royal Marsden Hospital, Dr. ROSALIND FRANKLIN, aged 37 years, dearly loved elder daughter of Mr and Mrs Ellis A. Franklin, 13 Hocroft Road, London N.W.2. Funeral private. No flowers.[104]

---

*These are the only references to Franklin's death I have found in any correspondence from the time. Either people did not mention it in their letters, or those letters have been lost.

MAD SESSIONS
WITH SYDNEY

One of the things that made Crick so influential was his ability to see into the heart of a matter and extract general principles and underlying tendencies. That talent was first glimpsed publicly in his work with Watson on DNA, but it really developed with the arrival of Sydney Brenner in Cambridge. Brenner and Crick rarely worked on joint laboratory projects, or even joint publications ('Every now and again we wrote a paper together,' Sydney told me nonchalantly in 2017).[1] Instead, every day, except for when one of them was travelling, the pair would talk intensely about anything that interested them. And when they were apart they would write letters, gossiping about science, outlining novel hypotheses and devising potential experiments. There were few hints of personal matters in their correspondence: Crick's close relationship with Brenner, while deep and productive, was more formal than his friendship with Kreisel. Their collaboration was essentially about exploring and clarifying their ideas, and along the way they produced answers to some of the most crucial issues that faced biology.

Their discussions involved a freestyle way of examining different aspects of a topic, sometimes raising apparently absurd possibilities. Brenner explained: 'The thing we did have was a rule that you could say anything that would come into your head. Now most of these conversations were complete nonsense but every now and then … a half-formed idea could be taken up by the other one and really refined.'[2] Swapping ideas is one thing, having your ideas subjected to forensic or brutal criticism is another. And yet, for over two decades, that is how Brenner and Crick worked. As Crick put it: 'Of course you have to be candid. This is perhaps the most important thing. You have to be candid without being rude. (…) And you must of course try and attack the other person's ideas because it's getting rid of the false ideas which is the most important thing in developing the good ones.'[3]

This was what Crick had done with Watson earlier in the decade and, to a lesser extent, with Rich in 1955. He would later use a similar approach with Leslie Orgel, Graeme Mitchison, Pat Churchland, Christof Koch and others, but it was in his two-decade-long relationship with Sydney that this method reached its peak. For Brenner, this represented 'the most important thrill of research, the social interaction, the companionship that comes from two people's minds playing on each other'.[4] For Crick, 'collaborating with Sydney not only made all the difference to my ideas and my few experiments, but it was all such fun. It says much for his tolerance and good temper that there was never an angry word between us. Happy days!'[5]

This frenetic exchange of ideas was not merely some kind of superior scientific banter – it had real consequences for discovery and even for the future of biology. Brenner's quiet, almost wistful summary of how they worked captures its significance: 'I think a lot of the good ideas that we produced were produced in these completely mad sessions.'[6]

*

Some of the insights that emerged in their early discussions were contained in a lecture given by Crick in September 1957, a lecture that, according to the journalist and historian Horace Judson, altered the logic of biology.[7] In his talk Crick presented a new way of thinking about how life works, shaping future research in some of the most thrilling parts of science and making a bold prediction about the appearance of an exciting new discipline that now informs everything we know about evolution. Not bad for a single lecture. The understated title of the talk – 'Protein Synthesis' – might suggest something dull, but that would be reckoning without Crick's uncanny ability to detect connections and reveal deep truths.[8]

The hour-long lecture was given at University College London, as part of a symposium on the 'Biological Replication of Macromolecules'. What Francis actually said that day is unknown – all that survives is the published version of the talk, which was written following long hours of excited discussion with Brenner.[9] At nearly seven thousand words, the printed article could not have been read in sixty minutes, even with Crick's rapid diction and the fact that he ran overtime.[10] François Jacob sat in the audience, stunned:

> Tall, florid, with long sideburns, Crick looked like the Englishman seen in illustrations to nineteenth-century books about Phileas Fogg or the English opium eater. He talked incessantly. With evident pleasure and volubly, as if he was afraid he would not have enough time to get everything out. Going over his demonstration again to be sure it was understood. Breaking up his sentences with loud laughter. Setting off again with renewed vigour at a speed I often had trouble keeping up with. (…) Crick was dazzling.[11]

The opening of the lecture summarised recent work on the biochemical mechanisms of protein synthesis, but Francis soon moved on to the really interesting stuff, some of which had first been outlined in a two-page document he typed up in October 1956.[12] This piece – never circulated – was partly inspired by Sol Spiegelman of the University of Illinois, who in a talk in Baltimore that year had referred to the widespread assumption of the existence of a link between DNA, RNA and protein as a 'dogma', because there was little concrete evidence for it. Crick had already referred to this in his April 1956 BBC radio talk.[13]

Riffing on Spiegelman's ideas in that brief document, Crick had sketched a little diagram showing how genes do what they do. This figure was not included in the printed version of his lecture and he may not have used it when he spoke. The most important point was

what Crick called the Central Dogma: the claim that 'once information has got into a protein it can't get out again.'* To explain his point,
Francis focused on what he called the flow of information between
the macromolecules found in cells – DNA, RNA and proteins. This
information, he said, was simply the sequence of nucleic acids and
the sequence of amino acids that were related to it.

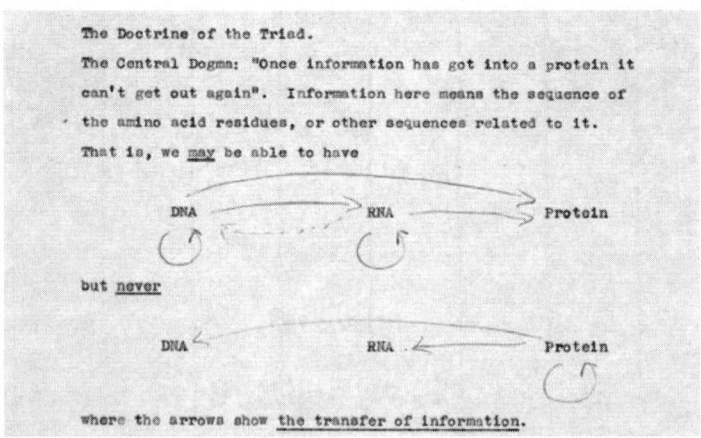

The Doctrine of the Triad.
The Central Dogma: "Once information has got into a protein it
can't get out again". Information here means the sequence of
the amino acid residues, or other sequences related to it.
That is, we may be able to have

but never

where the arrows show the transfer of information.

This was very different to Watson's suggestion two years earlier
that DNA might be chemically transformed into RNA. Crick's vision
was focused on the movement of that utterly modern, intangible
quantity – information – through the synthesis of new macromolecules. According to Crick, there were four kinds of information
transfer: DNA → DNA (DNA replication), DNA → RNA (the first
step of protein synthesis), RNA → protein (the second step of protein
synthesis) and RNA → RNA (RNA viruses copying themselves).
Crick also argued there were two steps for which there was no evidence, but which were possible: DNA → protein (this would mean
RNA was not necessarily involved in protein synthesis) and RNA →
DNA (structurally possible, but at the time without any conceivable

---

*Crick's friend the French geneticist Jacques Monod later told Francis that this
was not in fact a dogma – something that cannot be challenged. Crick admitted
that he had got it wrong, explaining: 'I used the word in the way I myself
thought about it, not as most of the rest of the world does, and simply applied
it to a grand hypothesis that, however plausible, had little direct experimental
support.' Crick, F. (1988), *What Mad Pursuit: A Personal View of Scientific
Discovery* (New York: Basic), p. 109.

function). Just as striking were the three flows of information that Crick considered to be impossible, due to lack of evidence and lack of a biochemical mechanism. These were protein → protein, protein → RNA and, most significantly, protein → DNA.*

This last point was what Crick meant when he said that once information had gone from DNA into the protein, it could not get out and go back into the genome. There was no known biochemical mechanism by which the sequence of a protein could be translated into a nucleic acid; this was the key point of the central dogma. Information flowed only in one direction, from nucleic acids to proteins, a fundamental concept that remains true. An evolutionary implication helps to explain the significance of Crick's idea: whatever might happen to an organism's proteins, those changes will not alter its DNA sequence. Organisms cannot use DNA to transmit characteristics they have acquired during their lifetime to their offspring. Although Crick did not state this, it became a fundamental part of the modern conception of Darwinian evolution.†

Crick admitted that the evidence for his central dogma hypothesis was negligible, but he defended his approach by pointing out that cosmologists had no qualms about constructing theories without adequate experimental data. That implicit comparison with grand theories of the universe is justified, for Francis was laying out the foundations of a new way of understanding life. Hundreds of scientists around the world were aware of the experimental data that Crick summarised in his lecture, but he was the only one to think in such a profound way about the implications. That was the power of Crick's mind, especially when it had been catalysed by that of Brenner during their 'mad sessions'.

Crick also outlined some adjacent issues that are still immensely significant. First, he described the adaptor hypothesis he had

---

*As Crick later recognised, infectious proteins – prions – can spread by altering the conformation of otherwise identical protein molecules, but they do not change the amino acid sequence, which was Crick's definition of information.
†Recent popular interest in epigenetics – the potential transmission of gene regulation mechanisms over a few generations in a handful of animal species (not humans), which never alters the DNA sequence – has done nothing to change this.

developed with Brenner, but which he could now reinforce by referencing the dramatic confirmatory experiments of Mahlon Hoagland
and Paul Zamecnik.[14] Then he explored a fundamental aspect of
the link between nucleic acids and proteins: proteins are three-
dimensional structures – the string of amino acids folds upon itself
– whereas a DNA sequence is one-dimensional. Francis homed in on
the problem of how a one-dimensional nucleic acid sequence could
produce a three-dimensional structure of amino acids. He accepted
there might be some unknown source of folding information, but
emphasised that the 'more likely hypothesis' was that *folding is simply
a function of the order of the amino acids.'*[15] In other words, 3-D protein
structure is an emergent property of the 1-D amino acid sequence,
which in turn is a direct product of the nucleic acid sequence. This
sequence hypothesis, as he termed it, remains essentially true today.

Finally, he foresaw the development of what is now called
phylogenetics – the study of the evolutionary relations of organisms
using nucleic acids – which has transformed our understanding of
every branch of life, from crustaceans to coronaviruses. Nucleic acid
sequencing was still a dream when Crick spoke, but he could see the
way things would go:

> Biologists should realise that before long we shall have a
> subject which might be called 'protein taxonomy' – the study
> of the amino acid sequences of the proteins of an organism and
> the comparison of them between species. It can be argued that
> these sequences are the most delicate expression possible of
> the phenotype of an organism and that vast amounts of evolu-
> tionary information may be hidden away within them.[16]

This prediction had an immediate impact: zoologist Charles Sibley of
Cornell University wrote enthusiastically to Crick, explaining that he
had data from egg white proteins for 370 species of bird. This led to a
rapid exchange of letters and what Sibley called a flurry of activity in
his laboratory, culminating in the appearance of two papers – a study
of proteins from twenty-three breeds of chicken and a far-reaching
paper that encouraged zoologists to use proteins in their studies of
systematics.[17] Every part of biology, from the intricate molecular

activity of a cell to the broad sweep of billions of years of evolution, was caught up in Crick's vision.

*

Crick spent much of 1957 and 1958 in the laboratory, helping visitor Mahlon Hoagland work on transfer RNA in the nearby Molteno Institute. This was not very successful, and Crick did not enjoy the work – it involved killing rats to obtain samples, which he did not like at all. Much more to his taste was the talking he did with Vernon Ingram and with Seymour Benzer, who was on a year's sabbatical at the Cavendish.[18] They were both trying to prove the colinearity of the gene and its protein by showing that a change in a DNA sequence led to a change in an amino acid sequence.

Benzer's experiments on mapping the *rII* gene in phage, down to a single base pair, was done with Sydney Brenner and involved a new technician, Leslie Barnett, who would play a vital role in Brenner and Crick's work. However, Benzer's mapping project only solved half the problem. As Crick had excitedly explained on the BBC, to complete the story, they needed to find the protein encoded by *rII* and then identify amino acid changes that corresponded to the precisely identified mutations that Benzer was creating. That goal continued to elude them, and Benzer's sabbatical ended with that part of the problem unresolved.

Greater success came from Ingram's work on haemoglobin; in October 1956 he published an article in *Nature* showing that there was a difference in the amino acid sequences of normal and sickle cell haemoglobin.[19] The following August, he showed that this differ- ence – carried by people with two copies of the sickle cell gene (this is called being homozygous) – was due to a change in a single amino acid, as glutamine was changed to valine.[20] *The Times* was ecstatic: 'Dr Ingram's demonstration of a single, identified difference between genetically determined haemoglobins is thus the nearest that has been got to a direct view of one of Mendel's genes in action. This is indeed a landmark.'[21] Crick did not sign Ingram's paper – like many scientists at the time, he never signed articles that he had not directly contributed to, even if he had played a decisive role in the gestation of the work.

This breakthrough study did not completely resolve the colinearity problem – Ingram could not identify the nature of the sickling mutation in the haemoglobin gene – but it did tighten the link between changes in a gene and changes in a protein. As Crick explained in his central dogma paper: 'It may surprise the reader that the alteration of one amino acid out of a total of about 300 can produce a molecule which (when homozygous) is usually lethal before adult life but, for my part, Ingram's result is just what I expected.'[22]

In the middle of November 1957, Crick wrote to Watson describing this activity:

> Everybody here is very busy. Seymour is studying a model of DNA. Sydney and George [Streisinger] are hard at work on phage tails. Leslie Barnett and Alice Orgel are learning phage techniques. Mahlon is working full steam with Muriel in the Molteno. Tomorrow John talks about his three-dimensional Fourier of myoglobin. Vernon has just left for the States. The bacterial flagella look very promising. How are things at Harvard?[23]

Watson responded with an excited letter that contained news of a major breakthrough – in an extremely elegant experiment, Matt Meselson and Frank Stahl of Caltech had shown how DNA replicated, tying up one of the major loose ends left by the discovery of the double helix. Francis also heard about the discovery from Meselson himself, and in a letter from his scientist lover in the USA, who described it as 'the most exciting thing being done just now' and sketched a diagram of the key result.[24]

Crick remained intensely busy, juggling research, domestic life and growing attention from a broader audience. As he wrote to Watson in March 1958: 'You will be amused to hear that in February I gave three public lectures in U. C. London on "The Nucleic Acids" which were crowded out. (...) Gabrielle and I have had German Measles, Jacqueline has mumps, Odile is covered with spots of unknown origin but otherwise we are all well.'[25] Together with Brenner, he was also giving Fred Sanger and his group 'a short sharp course on simple modern genetics'. Sanger soon had other things on his mind – he was awarded the Nobel Prize in Chemistry for his work on the structure of proteins, in particular his sequencing of insulin. To celebrate, the Cricks held a party and there was much gaiety. Too much. As Hoagland recalled: 'At the height of the festivities, someone set a rocket off from the roof of the house. Its ill-planned trajectory caused it to lodge, still smouldering, in the tower of the nearby church, and this necessitated calling the fire brigade.'[26]

*

Most of this work by Crick and his collaborators was done in a new MRC facility: an unprepossessing one-storey structure in the Cavendish courtyard, previously occupied by the metallurgists and known simply as 'the Hut', with brick foundations, white windows and corrugated asbestos roof and gables. A name plate was eventually screwed onto the front door, reading 'Medical Research Council Unit for Molecular Biology'.[27] Conditions remained cramped – there were seven researchers working in an area the size of two parking spaces. While this made life difficult, it meant that everyone knew what was going on and could lend a hand if necessary. Benzer's memories of his sabbatical were almost blissful: 'It was great, because Crick and Brenner were arguing all the time. We would all read Crick's mail that would be sitting on his desk. It was a tremendously stimulating environment.'[28] And at the centre of the hubbub was Francis. As Benzer recalled:

> We could always tell when he was in the building; you could hear his 'Ha, ha, ha, ha' down the hall. He was tremendously brilliant and stimulating – his mind was working all the time. (…) He was into all kinds of adventures on the personal level. He was very urbane, well educated. He reminded me most of Henry Higgins in My Fair Lady. There was quite a resemblance. That kind of style. No shrinking violet, that's for sure.

For a US night owl like Benzer, the very English set-up at the MRC unit seemed positively quaint: 'You'd come in in the morning, about 10:30 or so, and there would be coffee time. Then there was a little

Vernon Ingram (left), Sydney Brenner and his children,
Stefan and Belinda, in front of the Hut, in 1957.

time to work; then it was lunchtime. Then you'd come back after lunch and before you knew it, it was tea time. And then you were home.'

No sooner was the unit housed in the Hut than Perutz began to push the MRC to build a new, permanent laboratory, drawing on advice from Fred Sanger and Crick – an indication of the status now accorded to Francis by both Perutz and the MRC.[29] At the end of 1957, Crick and Perutz wrote a document explaining that a large new facility would enable researchers from different disciplines to develop a common approach to 'the molecular basis of *simple* living systems'. It would be independent of any university department or college and would also train postgraduate students. Such an institution would allow the UK to maintain its lead in the field; if it were not created, Crick and Perutz warned, researchers would leave not only Cambridge but probably the country, attracted by more spacious and modern facilities.

Crick was writing from experience. Earlier in the year he had applied to be Chair of Genetics at Cambridge, but he was deemed not to be a geneticist* and his candidacy was rejected. He probably had a lucky escape – Guido Pontecorvo told Crick he had turned down the Chair because the facilities were awful and university intrigue was rampant.[30] Aware of the university's rejection of Crick and of the cramped conditions in the MRC unit, American suitors began to circle.[31] Francis soon received generous job offers from NIH, Chicago and Harvard, as well as a joint offer to Crick and Brenner from Wisconsin.[32] Initially, Francis politely turned down these invitations, but as time went on, the offers became increasingly alluring, despite the MRC giving him a permanent contract in April 1958 and increasing his salary.[33] The MRC became alarmed that he might leave; his closest colleagues were dismayed – Brenner told him 'I hope you don't succumb to the temptation', while Aaron Klug, who was due to join the MRC unit, explained 'I suppose it is really unnecessary for me to add that I would very much like to "find" you there when I come to Cambridge.'[34]

Crick remained ambiguous about Cambridge. He liked working for the MRC but he cared little for the flummery that abounded in the colleges. He did not butter up the dons – as he told Georgina Ferry shortly before his death, most people in his position would have cultivated the university by inviting heads of colleges to stuffy dinner-table talk, but he never did.[35] When asked to write an article on relations between arts and science dons, Crick explained he knew little of such matters, being neither a Fellow nor a lecturer: 'I do dine occasionally but it is well known that at High Table they only talk about college drains or such topics as "can an elephant jump?" and any serious conversation is regarded as bad form.'[36]

---

* There was some truth to this. One of the first things Crick did on returning to Cambridge in 1954 was to enrol on R. A. Fisher's genetics course, taking copious notes about relatively simple matters such as Mendel's experiments and various forms of sex determination. None of the lectures dealt with Fisher's interest in eugenics. Crick's attention was not fully engaged – there are notes reading 'several lectures missed' (Crick, notebook, 1951–54, PP/ CRI/G/1/6). To continue his education, Crick attended a course on microbial genetics at the beginning of 1955 (Crick, notebook, 1955, PP/CRI/G/1/10).

*

American interest in Crick was reinforced in the first half of 1959, when Crick was a guest lecturer at the Department of Chemistry in Harvard.[37] This time the whole family – including Michael and the new French au pair, Renée – crossed the Atlantic. That meant sorting out a house to live in, renting out Portugal Place, organising a temporary place for Michael at Harvard, finding a school for the girls and finally arranging transport – the world had changed since the Cricks' transatlantic sea voyage of 1953, and this time first Francis, then Odile and the girls, took a plane (Michael and Renée went by sea).[38]

Once settled in the other Cambridge, Crick began grappling with an utterly novel task – teaching an undergraduate lecture course. He had given plenty of research talks in his life, but never taught. His solution was to give twenty-four lectures on the questions that had been consuming him for the previous decade – proteins, nucleic acids and their functional links. He began with Avery's work on the transforming principle from the 1940s, explained X-ray crystallography and its role in the study of proteins and nucleic acids, and brought the story up to date with whole lectures on Benzer's work on *rII* and on Ingram's work on haemoglobin. It must have been marvellous for the students.

With three lectures a week, and the first exam in mid-March,* Francis still found time to visit scientists in other universities and go to various conferences.[39] There were around twenty such trips, on which he generally talked either about virus structure or about the structure and replication of DNA. Some invitations had to be turned down – Francis explained to a colleague from St Louis: 'I have agreed to take Odile to New Orleans, and she would shoot me if I backed out now!'[40]

Throughout his stay, Francis wrote letters to Brenner, full of scientific gossip. For example, on 8 February he wrote an eight-page letter, detailing various things he had heard, each briefly summarised with

---

*Crick set the exam but will not have marked it. When I asked Brenner in 2017 if he had ever marked an exam, he cheerily replied 'Nope!'

the promise of more in the future: 'I will write more fully ... More when I hear the full story ... More details when I have read the pre-print ... I have picked up lots of trivial scientific news ... but nothing very striking.'[41] However, the pressure of all that travel soon began to tell, and within a few weeks Crick had to apologise to his friend: 'I'm sorry not to have written but life here is far too busy. I hardly even have time to prepare my lectures, let alone do any serious reading or thinking.'[42] A month later, things were no better: 'I'm afraid your man in Havana is letting you down, but the fact is that I am living a dog's life, with no time to myself, and this is likely to persist till about the end of the month.'[43]

Correspondence also flew in the other direction, sometimes carrying good news. First, in early March, Crick got a telegram from Perutz and Royal Society committee member Alan Hodgkin telling him in confidence that he would be proposed as a Fellow of the Royal Society, with the inevitable confirmation to be announced in a couple of weeks – PLEASE KEEP QUIET UNTIL THEN DELIGHTED WARMEST CONGRATULATIONS = ALAN AND MAX. Then on 19 March the official telegram arrived. Less than six years after getting his PhD, Francis had received the highest award of British science: fellowship of the Royal Society.*

Crick's nomination, proposed by Perutz and seconded by Todd, included the support of both friends and foes – Bragg, Mott, Sanger, Pauling, Pontecorvo, Bernal and Randall.[44] The qualifications described on the nomination, written with typical generosity by Perutz, began with the elucidation of the structure of DNA before concluding with a perceptive description of his current role: 'By his searching criticism and wealth of ideas he is exercising a wide and stimulating influence on the development of molecular biology in general.'

As the news of Crick's award became known, dozens of letters from all sorts of people came winging in, including from those who had played significant roles in his career – Bragg, A. V. Hill, the

---

*Wilkins was also made an FRS at the same time. As Perutz astutely observed, this ensured there would be no bitterness. Perutz to Crick, 11 March 1959. CRI/D/1/1/16.

editor of *Nature*, friends from the war and many others. Crick was clearly grateful for all the congratulations – although many of his correspondents insisted that he should not bother responding, every letter is marked 'replied'.[45] He explained his feelings in a letter to Brenner: '*You* may have expected it but *I* certainly didn't expect it so soon. It's nice that Maurice got in as well. I have celebrated by buying a bowler hat.* (…) We had been secretly accumulating champagne, and plan to have people in on Sunday …'[46]

In March, the MRC approved the construction of the new laboratory, near Addenbrooke's Hospital, leading Crick to promise Brenner that he would stay at Cambridge if Sydney did.[47] He then began to think furiously about how the new building should be organised – as ever, he turned even a mundane problem into something with more fundamental implications. As he explained to Brenner:

> I favour your plan of big labs and small offices. (…) The general principle should be: *not* that things needed together should be very close together, as this makes everything hopelessly complicated, as one soon finds that everything has to be next to almost everything else, but that rooms very far apart should be the ones that need *not* be close together.[48]

After his students had sat their final exam, all that remained for Francis was to turn down an extremely generous job offer from Harvard: 'As you know, I have been greatly tempted to accept this offer, but I have now reluctantly decided that I must decline. I am so sorry that you have been put to all this trouble for nothing.'[49]

There was one more conference to attend – the Brookhaven Symposium on Biology, held on Long Island – where Francis gave a talk with a typically Crickian title: 'The Present Position of the Coding Problem', in which he focused on a recent report that although the

---

* This did not prove a success. Although shortly afterwards he wore it to Freddie Gutfreund's wedding, it did not suit him, perching on his head – Olby, R. (2009), *Francis Crick: Hunter of Life's Secrets* (Cold Spring Harbor, NY: Cold Spring Harbor Laboratory Press), plate 51. The next time he wore it was fifteen years later, at an Orthodox Jewish wedding. Crick to Orgel, 21 March 1974, MSS 176, Box 40, Folder 16.

base ratio (A+T):(G+C) was constant in the RNA of different micro-organisms, the same ratio in their DNA differed wildly. He put forward six possible explanations for this unexpected result, two of which turned out to be on target – 'only part of the DNA codes proteins', either coding 'nonsense' or having some other function, and 'the code is degenerate', in other words most amino acids have several representations in DNA. He was not convinced by any of his explanations ('they all, at the moment, appear rather unattractive') and to reassure his audience that it would eventually be possible to make sense of the whole business, he repeated three well-established facts: RNA from TMV controlled the viral protein capsule, Avery's transforming factor was made of DNA, and the sickle cell gene controlled the amino acid sequence of human haemoglobin.[50] Nucleic acids were at the heart of protein synthesis, but the exact details remained a mystery.

*

Once the Harvard adventure was over, Francis and his family crossed the continent to California for a couple of months. But not all of them went – eighteen-year old Michael decided to work his passage on a Danish freighter that was travelling from Boston to Hong Kong via Panama, briefly meeting up with his family when his ship docked at San Francisco.

Although Francis was supposed to be working with Gunther Stent in the Berkeley virus laboratory, he spent most of his time relaxing. In July he told Brenner, 'The family are all in excellent spirits. The weather is wonderful – I do very little work, as I need a holiday.'[51] Three weeks later, he told his friend: 'I seem to do less and less, so forgive me if my letters are not very informative', before signing off with a reference to the radical literary world of San Francisco – 'We spend our time reading about Beats.'[52] The house, which had sensational views, suited them down to the ground. And on the weekends they visited the city, where one day Francis went to City Lights bookstore and bought 'Peyote Poem' by Michael McClure, with that phrase that struck such a chord within him:

THIS IS THE POWERFUL KNOWLEDGE

---

*

In September, back in Cambridge, Odile regained possession of Portugal Place and Francis pinned McClure's poem to the wall, while the girls went back to school with the allure of exotic creatures who had been to America. In the laboratory, Francis returned to the daily sessions with Sydney, which would soon lead to two decisive breakthroughs in our understanding of how genes work.

AN APOTHEOSIS
OF GENETICS

For years, Crick's mind had been circling around the relationship between genes and proteins and how information flowed through the cell. He had explained the general framework in his 1957 central dogma lecture, but it still lacked detail and experimental evidence. How the cell turned genetic information into proteins, and the exact nature of the genetic code, remained unclear.

The first two years of the 1960s saw both these questions answered, with some of the main insights coming though intense discussions between Crick and Brenner. These discoveries propelled Crick into the media spotlight, transforming him from a mere leading figure in molecular biology to an important scientist with a global public renown. By dramatically confirming the significance of the double helix, this was another turning point in Crick's life and in the history of biology. Everything afterwards revolved around the insights he made in those months.

The first breakthrough emerged from a contradiction between Crick's ideas and a complex set of experimental results. The double helix had shown in principle how genetic information might be encoded in DNA, and many strands of experimental evidence, combined with Crick's theoretical ideas, suggested that RNA played a role in protein synthesis, perhaps through tiny particles made of

RNA and protein called ribosomes. Crick and Brenner – like many others – thought each gene produced a particular kind of ribosome, which enabled the cell to produce a particular protein.

Experimental evidence was beginning to contradict this view. For a start, all ribosomes seemed to be composed of two kinds of RNA, each of which was always of the same size. This was not what Crick and Brenner predicted – because proteins are different sizes, they expected that genes and their related ribosomal RNA would vary in size, too. Then, towards the end of 1959, Jacques Monod visited Cambridge and explained his latest results to Crick and Brenner over a meal at Portugal Place. Together with Arthur Pardee, an American visitor at the Institut Pasteur, Monod and François Jacob were studying how genes are activated under different environmental conditions, focusing on β-galactosidase, a lactose-metabolising enzyme that was produced only in the presence of lactose.

The group had shown that bacteria with a mutation in the *lac* gene that encoded the response to lactose could still synthesise β-galactosidase if they were given a gene called z+. Crick and Brenner's ribosome model suggested that following the introduction of z+ into the bacterium, there should be a slow build-up of the enzyme as growing numbers of ribosomes were synthesised. Instead, the Pasteur researchers found that enzyme synthesis began within a minute, at a high, constant level, suggesting that some chemical signal passed rapidly from the introduced gene to the host cell's protein synthesis system. They had not been able to identify the signal's composition as it was extremely short-lived, so they called this mysterious molecule X (even British and American scientists used the French pronunciation 'eex').

This was not new – Jacob had presented these results a few weeks earlier at a meeting in Copenhagen in front of Crick, Brenner and others, without a murmur of dissent.[*1] But when Crick and Brenner now heard Monod talk around the dining table they were perplexed and even suspicious of the findings. A few weeks later, Crick and

---

*Crick may have been distracted; one of his lovers flew from Tehran to spend the conference with him. Letters to Crick, undated [September 1959], MSS 660, Box 11.

Brenner produced a brief note for the RNA Tie Club, summarising the problems with their ribosomal view of the role of RNA in protein synthesis and trying to find explanations for the constant size of ribosomes.[2] All of their ingenious ideas turned out to be wrong.

They finally realised the truth a few months later, in April 1960. After attending a meeting in London, Jacob took the train to Cambridge and a small group of researchers, including Crick, met in King's College on Good Friday to discuss each other's work. Jacob again explained that the z+ gene did not encode a ribosome; it produced only X, which was extremely short-lived. This was the third time that Crick and Brenner had heard more or less the same story. Finally, the penny dropped. 'At this point,' said Crick, 'Brenner let out a loud yelp – he had seen the answer.' Jacob vividly described the excitement and his own confusion:

> Francis and Sydney leaped to their feet. Began to gesticulate. To argue at top speed in great agitation. A red-faced Francis. A Sydney with bristling eyebrows. The two talked at once, all but shouting. Each trying to anticipate the other. To explain to the other what had suddenly come to mind. All this at a clip that left my English far behind.[3]

Brenner's insight – which Crick instantly shared – was that the X intermediate might be identical to a short-lived and mysterious form of RNA that appeared when phage infected a bacterium, as reported a few years earlier by Ken Volkin and Lazarus Astrachan. What Brenner and Crick gabbled to each other was that each gene might not produce its own ribosome but instead an RNA molecule – X, soon referred to as 'messenger RNA' or mRNA – which would then be 'read' by the ribosome, like a tape recorder head 'reads' a piece of magnetic tape. Rather than being the specific products of each gene, ribosomes were simply a constant part of the cell's machinery.

This radical new vision represented a decisive development of the informational view of life that Crick had pioneered. Nucleic acids were information, Crick had announced in 1953; now he and Brenner saw how that information might be read and turned into action. Reading heads and tapes might seem old-fashioned today, but at the time they represented a key part of information technology. Cells were seen as tiny, sophisticated machines, full of molecules containing information.

This was not some minor piece of a biochemical jigsaw but a profoundly novel way of thinking about a process that is fundamental to life. It represented another step in the shift away from conceptions of life as some kind of magical, vital process, to the informational view that Crick had outlined almost exactly seven years earlier.

As Francis put it, once the role of the ribosome was realised, the world never looked the same again.[4] Everything made sense, in a new way.

*

After this explosion of realisation, Crick, Brenner and Jacob immediately began planning how to test the idea. This would involve radioactively labelling RNA molecules and using powerful centrifuges to separate the different kinds of RNA – ribosomal RNA and the predicted smaller form, which was an intermediate between the gene and the protein. That evening, Francis and Odile held one of their parties. Jacob recalled:

> A very British evening with the cream of Cambridge, an abundance of pretty girls, various kinds of drink, and pop music … It was difficult to isolate ourselves at such a brilliant, lively gathering, with all the people crowding around us, talking, shouting, laughing, singing, dancing … A euphoric Sydney covered entire pages with calculations and diagrams. Sometimes Francis would stick his head in for a moment to explain what we had to do.[5]

In the weeks that followed, as Brenner made plans for the trip to Pasadena where they would use the ultracentrifuges that their friend Matt Meselson had access to, Crick wrote up their ideas in a brief note entitled 'What Are the Properties of Genetic RNA?' (this referred to RNA produced by a gene rather than the RNA in a ribosome).[6] The note outlined the fragmented evidence that they had suddenly seized upon, such as the existence of X and the fact that the transitory RNA molecules that researchers had observed when phage infected bacteria had the same base composition as phage DNA. All this led to a three-point hypothesis that generalised these findings: '1. Genetic RNA has the same overall base ratios as genetic DNA; 2. It passes into the ribosomes, but it is only a minor component (…); 3. Genetic RNA is (at least in some circumstances), 'unstable', that is, it may have only a limited life.'

The implication was that ribosomes could rapidly switch from producing one protein to another – they were 'the main part of the machinery for protein synthesis into which genetic instructions can flow'. All this was basically correct. The note was intended for the RNA Tie Club, but in the end Francis did not circulate it, or even type it up. Perhaps he – or Brenner – felt that it could wait until the results from the Pasadena trip were known, or perhaps they were wary of treading on the Parisians' toes. Whatever the case, this readout of that Good Friday mad session remained unseen.

*

In early summer, Brenner and Jacob were in California with Meselson, successfully proving the existence of mRNA. There would be no rapid publication of their result, however. Watson and French researcher François Gros were using a different method with the same objective but were making slow progress; Watson convinced his friends to delay submitting their article to *Nature* until his experiment was complete; this took several months and the two papers eventually appeared in the same issue of the journal in May 1961.[7] Meanwhile, Crick also travelled to the USA, presenting the big picture view of his work at a conference at Purdue University in Indiana (the home of Seymour Benzer) where he talked about DNA, proteins and natural selection. He also went to the Gordon Conference on Proteins and Nucleic Acids, held in New Hampshire, as well as to multiple institutions in New York and Massachusetts. When he returned to England, he felt exhausted. 'I seem to travel far too much,' he wrote.[8]

He now had two radio broadcasts to record for the BBC, one on 'Genes and Atoms' for the Third Programme, the other for the

European Service on 'Living Matter' – one of six talks by Fellows of the Royal Society, to mark the tricentenary of its foundation. Both these radio talks were really on the same topic – the nature of molecular biology and how Francis felt it could explain fundamental biological processes, indeed the nature of life itself.

In his first talk, Francis explained the relationship between the one-dimensional information in DNA and the three-dimensional structure of proteins and accurately speculated about the possibility of synthesising DNA ('horribly difficult'), the timescale within which the DNA of a bacterium might be precisely altered ('ten or twenty years') and even the chance of synthesising a human genome ('remote').[9] One phrase was particularly dramatic and is still surprising, over half a century later:

> Suppose we took all the genetic material in the world – that is, if we extracted all the DNA from one cell of every human being alive today, and packed all this DNA together, to give a file-copy of the blue-prints for the human race – it would fill a space about the size of a rather small drop of water.

After the broadcast, Mr G. Taylor, of Ross-on-Wye, wrote to Francis with some questions.[10] Was it true that French scientists had turned a chicken into a duck by injecting duck chromosomes? Given that crabs can regenerate their legs, 'is there any chance of modifying crab chromosomes so that people with limbs missing can grow more? (…) How far away is the genetically modified superman?' Crick's response was reassuring, explaining that although French researchers said they had turned one breed of duck into another using DNA injections, he doubted that the claim was correct.* He went on to point out that 'it will be a very long time before we could make use of crab chromosomes, modified or otherwise. The chromosomally modified superman is unlikely to appear this century.'

During the recording of the second talk, Crick was evidently

---

* This 1956 report was at the origin of Brenner's later joke that French researchers had tried to fuse the DNA of a duck and of an orange, for culinary purposes.

extremely relaxed, for he allowed a photographer to take two portraits of him posing in front of the microphone. In both photos he
looks happy and confident, with no trace of his usual reluctance to
perform for the camera. The talk began with the biochemical similarities between organisms and the roles of nucleic acids and proteins.
Francis then explored the problem of how genes synthesised proteins and the nature of the genetic code, which he predicted would
be known within ten years.[11] The conclusion was again dramatic,
this time providing the first public hint of his deeply critical view of
religion:

> It now seems very probable that the understanding of living
> things in terms of atoms and molecules will be essentially com-
> plete before the Royal Society celebrates its next centenary,
> and with that understanding man's whole view of himself – of
> his nature and of his place in the universe – will be radically
> changed. And a good thing too, I would say, considering all the
> superstition which still permeates our whole society.

*

In October, there was yet more travel, first to North Carolina to lecture
at Duke University and then on to New Orleans. In the Duke lecture,
'The Genetic Control of Protein Synthesis', Crick asked the question
'What are genes made of?' and, according to his notes, gave the striking answer 'don't fully know / nucleic acid esp DNA'.[12] Despite all
the progress since 1944, when Avery suggested that bacterial genes
were made of DNA, there was little proof that genes were composed
of DNA alone. Part of the problem was that none of the steps in
protein synthesis were clear. The discovery of mRNA and the realisation of the role of the ribosome had confirmed Crick's informational
interpretation of nucleic acids but the fundamental question of the
nature of the genetic code remained. This led Crick to think about a
project that produced a second decisive breakthrough.

The starting point was a complicated and now-forgotten theory
of the genetic code developed by Crick and Leslie Orgel which they
called loopy codes.[13] The central prediction of the theory was that

the effect of a mutation at one end of a gene might be compensated (or suppressed, in the jargon) by the effect of a mutation at the other end, because the two regions of DNA would each unravel and would then pair up in a loop. To test this prediction, in February 1961 Crick began work in the phage laboratory, instructed by Leslie Barnett. This was the first time that Francis had worked with phage, and the procedure appealed to him because it was quick and relatively straightforward.[14] It only took twenty minutes for the phage to infect the bacterium, multiply inside it and then burst out of the cell in vast numbers. If phage infected a sample of bacteria, a patch or plaque of dead bacterial cells rapidly appeared on the petri dish where they were growing, whereas if a phage mutation affected that ability, the bacteria would survive. Crick soon discovered that the loopy code theory was wrong – suppressors were predicted to be far from the mutation they affected, but the first three suppressors they found were close to their mutations. A not-so-beautiful idea had been killed by an ugly fact.

To overcome his disappointment, Francis could amuse himself by reading the latest batch of letters from Kreisel, who was working at the Sorbonne in Paris. Kreisel's girlfriend – an ex-model – invited him to dinner with Ingrid Bergman and Yves Montand ('adorable'); he also dined with the Aga Khan ('a pompous fellow'), crashed the Dior and Givenchy fashion shows posing as the fashion correspondent of *Mathematical Reviews* and had sex with a mutual French friend.*[15] Other distractions for Francis included reading *Brecht: A Choice of Evils* by Martin Esslin, sent by Max Delbrück, and Laurie Lee's recent novel *Cider With Rosie*, the story of a boy's rural childhood in the 1920s that no doubt produced a rush of Northamptonshire nostalgia. He also read *Pornography and the Law*, a book by two US psychiatrists that explored the distinction between erotica – which they claimed had a positive social function – and what they termed hard core pornography.[16]

Among Crick's scientific correspondence there was a letter from

---

* From this point, Crick's archive of his friend's correspondence is virtually empty until the beginning of the 1980s, by which time Kreisel's style, and perhaps his interests, had mellowed.

Edward Albritton, an administrator at NIH who invited Crick to join something called an Information Exchange Group (IEG).[17] The idea was that preprints in the field of DNA coding would be sent to NIH, where they would be distributed to anyone who was on the IEG mailing list, thereby allowing scientific ideas to flow more freely and rapidly. Crick was appalled and, replying on behalf of himself and Brenner, bluntly stated that they were strongly opposed to such a scheme. As he explained: 'There is far too much careless and rapid communication in every area of this field of study. The idea of increasing it even in this semi-public manner fills me with horror.' Although Crick had been enjoying precisely this kind of exploration of his ideas, through the RNA Tie Club, the Tie Club was basically correspondence between friends; the IEGs were intended for everybody.[18]

One of the reasons why Crick was so opposed to Albritton's idea was that he feared there would be even more baseless speculation about the nature of the code – this had been going on for years and had led to no insights whatsoever. Instead, the idea of using an experimental approach continued to tug at Crick's mind, and in yet another mad session in the Eagle, Crick and Brenner began thinking about studying suppressors using dyes known as acridines, which Brenner suggested could induce a mutation by adding or subtracting a single base.*[19] What Crick and Brenner now realised was that adding or subtracting a base could render the genetic message after the mutation nonsensical, altering the characteristics of the mutation.

Crick began furiously experimenting, working late into the night in part of the laboratory known as the Gallery. He soon found an acridine mutant he named FC0 that destroyed the ability of phage to infect one strain of bacteria.[20] He then began to look for suppressor mutants that would revert the FC0 strain back to wild-type and enable it to infect once again. The satisfaction and enjoyment he gained from doing this work was clear to everyone. As US visitor Wendell Stanley recalled: 'You would have to be in that hut over there in Cambridge, though, late at night when Francis comes in with

---

*They could not actually tell if a base was added or subtracted in any given mutation, but by comparing the effects of combinations of mutations they could class them arbitrarily as either + or –.

a new mutant, you know, and you wouldn't recognise him as the same fellow. He is just like – you know the way many of us get with a newborn baby?'[21] However, although Francis began to sense that the experiment might reveal something fundamental about the genetic code, he could not pursue the work for long as he had various foreign jaunts coming up. Brenner would have to pick up the experiments.

On the first of his trips, Crick went to a DNA conference in the shadow of Mont Blanc, which involved a specially chartered train from Paris; he was accompanied by Odile, who had a great time (Watson, Wilkins, Monod, Benzer and Jacob were all there, so there were plenty of people she knew).[22] During the discussion of one presentation, Francis briefly described the suppressor experiments, an account that appeared in the conference proceedings:

> The code is read in short groups, starting from one end of the gene. The exact starting point is supposed to determine which group is read. The deletion of a base would then alter the active reading from this point onward. The double mutants produced by the reversion of acridine mutants would then, on this hypothesis, be altered not just in two, separated amino acids, but in a short stretch of amino acids in sequence.[23]

Once the conference was over, Francis and Odile, now accompanied by Gabrielle and Jacqueline (there had not been room for the girls at the conference) and by the German au pair, went on their first real holiday, to a mountainside villa near Tangier in north-western Morocco.[24] For Francis the setting was perfect – the girls went swimming every day, while he lay in the shade of the palm trees, reading Brecht plays that Delbrück had sent him and studying letters from Brenner that described his progress – or rather the lack of it – on the suppressor experiment.[25] After a holiday that lasted over a month, on 7 August he left for Moscow, where he was due to chair a major session of the five-thousand-strong International Congress of Biochemistry.

The Moscow meeting, which was marked by a commemorative Soviet postal stamp, was also attended by Watson, ostentatiously wearing his RNA Tie Club tie, as well as Meselson, Perutz, Jacob,

Benzer and many other leading figures in molecular biology. Snap-shots taken around the meeting show Crick, cigarette in hand, deep in conversation with other delegates.*[26] Activities outside the confer-ence hall included parties with Russian scientists, as well as official events, such as a huge parade on Red Square to mark the return to Earth of the world's second cosmonaut, Gherman Titov, who had spent over a day in space. Robert Maxwell, the businessman and boss of Pergamon Press, which was publishing the conference pro-ceedings, invited Watson to watch the parade from his hotel suite overlooking Red Square. Francis was unsure if he would be welcome, but Maxwell boomed that any friend of Jim Watson's was a friend of his and ushered Crick in to join the party.[27]

In the middle of the marathon week-long meeting, the delegates were rocked by a scientific paper that was as astonishing, unexpected and game-changing as Yuri Gagarin's spaceflight four months earlier. Marshall Nirenberg, a thirty-four-year-old researcher from the NIH, announced that he had read the first word of the genetic code.

Adapting a recently developed technique that allowed pro-teins to be synthesised in a test tube, Nirenberg and his colleague, German post-doctoral researcher Heinrich Matthaei, had added a stretch of synthetic RNA composed of only one base, uracil, to a mixture of enzymes, ribosomes and amino acids. To their delight and excitement, they found that the stuff in the test tube had produced a polymer composed solely of the amino acid phenylalanine. The code had been broken: some combination of U bases was the code for phenylalanine.

Nirenberg's result was an astonishing breakthrough, but virtu-ally no one heard him talk about it. Neither the title nor the abstract gave any indication of what he had done (both had been written long before the key experiments were performed), so as an unknown speaking about something apparently not very interesting, Nirenberg

---

*After taking heed of the first demonstrations of a link between smoking and cancer in the 1950s, Crick repeatedly tried to stop smoking, eventually succeeding in the 1960s. In 1979 he advised Brenner – an inveterate smoker – that giving up smoking was only half the battle: 'The other half is to learn how not to start again! After one or two failures one learns how to outwit oneself.' Crick to Brenner, 6 November 1979, SB/1/1/133.

was put in a small lecture theatre.[28] Barely two dozen people, mainly Russians, heard him. By chance, Matt Meselson was passing as Nirenberg began speaking and, his curiosity piqued, he sat down and listened. Meselson recalled: 'I heard the talk. I think that no one whom I knew well heard it (...) I was bowled over by the results, and I went and chased down Francis, and told him that he must have a private talk with this man.'[29]

Crick later described Nirenberg's discovery as 'spectacular'. The following day he was due to chair a major session of the Congress, so he used his position to change the programme, putting Nirenberg onto the main stage. Despite the plea from Congress organiser Perutz to leave plenty of time for discussion in the sessions, Crick had no compunction in giving Nirenberg the entire discussion slot.[30] Perutz was quite happy with this – he described Nirenberg's plenary presentation as a tremendous climax; according to Crick, the audience was electrified, while Meselson ran up to Nirenberg when he had finished speaking and hugged and congratulated him. 'It was all very dramatic,' recalled Meselson.[31]

Nirenberg and Matthaei's discovery was indeed dramatic, and amazing. It proved the role of mRNA in protein synthesis in the clearest way possible. It broke with eight years of theorising about the genetic code and showed that the problem could be tackled experimentally. It also triggered a race among US laboratories to discover more links between RNA sequences and amino acids.

What it did not do was show exactly how the code was read. The synthetic RNA molecule used by Nirenberg and Matthaei was of an unknown length; the question about the genetic code that had been troubling scientists since first being posited by Crick – how a sequence of bases in a nucleic acid could represent one of twenty amino acids – remained unanswered.

*

When Francis got back to Cambridge in the middle of August, his head was buzzing. Nirenberg and Matthaei had not only confirmed the insight that he and Brenner had had fifteen months earlier, their discovery clarified the meaning of the experiments he had been doing. Francis now realised that with a slight twist the deletion/ addition technique could reveal the number of letters in each 'word' in the genetic code.

For example, if there were a triplet code, with a sequence that began ATG CAT CCC TGA and the first C were deleted, then the sequence would become ATG ATC CCT GA and so on. The first word would be the same but the message after that point would be garbled. As Crick put it in the article that eventually described the work: 'The simplest postulate to make is that the shift of the reading frame produces some triplets the reading of which is "unacceptable"; for example, they may be "nonsense", or stand for "end the chain", or be unacceptable in some other way to the complications of protein structure.'[32] But, he reasoned, in principle it should be possible to make the message acceptable again by adding or subtracting enough bases so that only one amino acid would be added or removed from the protein encoded by the gene, leaving the remainder of the molecule intact. Nirenberg and Matthaei had read the first word of the genetic code, but they did not know how many letters it contained. Crick's experiment would provide the answer.

The task was substantial – Crick and Barnett had to map the effects of eighty suppressor mutants and combine them in increasingly complex crosses. As they described it, these mutations 'were all suppressors of FC0, or suppressors of suppressors, or suppressors of suppressors of suppressors.'[33] After a great deal of effort, Crick and Barnett constructed six triple mutants in a suppressor gene – five of the +++ type, and one triple negative.[34] If the genetic code was read in blocks of three letters, they reasoned, both kinds of triple mutation should restore the reading frame and make the phage behave like FC0. Which is what they found.

Crick recalled how, in late September, he and Barnett observed the first mutant virus carrying triple mutations:

And all we had to do was look at one plate. And see if it had any plaques on it. So we came in late at night, ten o'clock at night, or something, and there were plaques on the plate! So I said to Leslie, 'Let me check; we may have got the plates mixed up,' and she checked it, and then I told her, 'We're the only two to know it's a triplet code!'[35]

Even before the experiments were finished, Crick was excitedly spreading the news to colleagues around the world. On 9 October he wrote to Bob Sinsheimer at Caltech: 'We now have convincing genetic evidence that the coding ratio is 3 or a multiple of 3.'[36] He was vague about the actual number of bases per word because although their results strongly suggested that the code was based on units of three, the experiments did not prove this – a code using groups of six bases was also technically possible. However, the code only needed twenty combinations, one for each amino acid, so a six-base code would massively increase the number of either meaningless or redundant sequences. In Crick's words, this was hardly likely to be taken seriously.[37] The final, conclusive experiment was apparently carried out on 13 October when Francis recorded the results and wrote at the bottom of the page '∴ coding ratio is 3'.[38]

Francis enjoyed working in the laboratory, revelling in the experiments and often working until midnight – Odile later said she had never seen him so cheerful.[39] He put this down to the fact that the experiments seemed to work so well, but other distractions may have helped, as he recalled:

> One evening, after dinner, I was working away in the lab when a glamorous friend of mine turned up and stood behind me while I continued to manipulate the tubes and plates. 'Come to a party,' she said, running her fingers through my hair. 'I'm far too busy,' I said, 'but where is it?' 'Well,' she said, 'we thought we'd hold it in *your* house.' Eventually a compromise was reached. She and Odile would organise a small party and I would join them when I'd finished.[40]

At the beginning of November 1961, when all the experiments were completed, Crick wrote up the article, with editing input from Brenner.[41] Benzer responded enthusiastically when he read the draft: 'The result with triple mutants is a real knockout punch,' he wrote.[42] But Benzer was less impressed by Crick's decision to exclude findings that did not fit with the triplet explanation (Crick and Brenner called these results 'barriers'). Crick replied in a long, dense letter, explaining that because they had submitted the article to *Nature*, rather than a specialist journal, the paper had to be succinct and intelligible to the general scientific reader. As he explained spikily to his friend: 'I disagree with almost all your points on presentation for the audience I have in mind, so don't be offended if we ignore them.'[43]

Apart from lack of space in *Nature*, there was another reason for not including those annoying results. While they did not fit the theoretical explanation, they did not represent a coherent alternative. Presenting them unexplained would distract from the fundamental argument, so they were simply excluded. The α-helix affair had taught Francis not to obsess about accounting for every data point, but scientists are not supposed to hide results that 'do not fit'. Brenner later spoke frankly about they how they viewed these irritating exceptions:

> Well, you have the 'don't worry hypothesis' – there'll be an explanation for them. As it turned out it took about five more years to work through all the exceptions, and the remarkable thing is that each one of them had a different and special explanation (…) it was wise of us to take all those exceptions, which showed no relationship amongst each other, and put them to one side.[44]

As Crick promised Benzer, these exceptions were eventually published – six years later – in a mammoth seventy-three-page paper, where the weird exceptions and barriers were successfully explained in mind-numbing detail.[45] Convinced that no one would actually bother reading their turgid article, Crick and Brenner attempted to smuggle a personal communication from Leonardo da Vinci into the paper, but the eagle-eyed editor spotted the jape and it was removed.[46]

*

Crick's behaviour as he wrote up the article shows how he had changed over the previous decade. His sense of joyous culmination as he grasped the new view of life was mingled with a recognition of his responsibility as the emerging intellectual leader of the field – it was time to do the right thing, and to be seen to be doing it. He therefore gave clear credit to other researchers for the underpinning argument and he prominently emphasised the significance of Nirenberg's breakthrough, ignoring Benzer's urging that they cut passages relating to this because everyone knew about it.[47] Instead, Francis added a whole paragraph, describing how he had been startled by Nirenberg and Matthaei's presentation of their discovery in Moscow, summarising their experiment and concluding that their results implied 'that a sequence of uracils codes for phenylalanine, and our work suggests that it is probably a triplet of uracils'.[48]

As soon as the manuscript was submitted, Crick sent a copy to Nirenberg, accompanied by a letter describing the American's paper as an epoch-making discovery and emphasising that he had the essential idea of using the deletion mutants before the announcement of Nirenberg's astonishing result, as shown by his contribution to the French conference in June.*[49] Francis was clearly keen that Nirenberg should not feel that he had been robbed, scooped or snubbed in any way. However, he was equally keen that the article should appear in the same year as Nirenberg and Matthaei's paper, so he pressed the *Nature* editor to squeeze the article into the last issue of 1961.[50]

The paper duly appeared in *Nature* at the end of December, and was signed by Crick, Brenner, Barnett, and by a theoretical physicist, Richard Watts-Tobin, who had helped out. It was entitled 'The General Nature of the Genetic Code for Proteins' and unlike the work by Nirenberg and those who were following his lead, the results from the Cambridge group said nothing about the specific nature of the code – there was no link between a particular DNA sequence and a given amino acid. Crick and Brenner were thinking on a higher level.

---

*Mark Bretscher recalls Crick saying in autumn 1961 that his summer holiday in Tangier had been wrecked when he realised that a combination of mutations might reveal the number of bases read at a time. This would put Crick's insight as occurring before he heard Nirenberg's bombshell presentation in Moscow.

The article began with four fundamental conclusions, which were then explored and justified by a series of experimental results, each of which contributed to the overall argument:

(a) A group of three bases ... codes one amino acid; (b) The code is not of the overlapping type; (c) The sequence of the bases is read from a fixed starting point; (d) The code is probably 'degenerate'; that is, in general, one particular amino-acid can be coded by one of several triplets of bases.[51]

One of the reasons why the paper has been loved by scientists down the decades is the clarity of its argument and the logical steps that the reader follows as hypothesis and experimental evidence are melded, all leading to a logical climax and an inescapable conclusion. The reader is seduced into believing that the experiments were designed this way from the start, with each test of the theory carried out in a logical order.

Reality is more complicated. All scientific articles are constructions that select evidence to prove a point, this one perhaps more so than most; indeed, in many respects this is a virtuosic display of the art of writing a scientific paper. The idea of testing the hypothesis that the genetic code is based on groups of three bases, which seems to be the point of the experiment, emerged only towards the end of the process. As Crick breezily admitted: 'It's the usual business – it seems very straightforward, and when you actually look what happened, you did it for a lot of *silly* reasons that led you to the right thing.'[52]

Some people found the logic hard to accept. Brenner said: 'it was a real "house of cards" theory. You had to buy everything. You couldn't take one fact and let it stand by itself and say the rest could go. Everything was so interlocked.'[53] For most readers, however, the argument contained in the paper was immensely attractive, as Brenner explained:

This I think is the kind of apotheosis of a genetic analysis, because you have to consider what you're doing here: you're taking these viruses and you are just mixing them together and you are simply recording plus and minus. And from this pattern it seems mad that you could deduce the actual triple nature of the genetic code. But this is simply the logic of how the genetic information is transferred – it's a non-overlapping triplet code.[54]

A fundamental molecular aspect of life had been understood by a relatively simple genetic experiment.

The article's conclusion was audacious, conveying the optimism felt by many scientists after Nirenberg and Matthaei's breakthrough: 'If the coding ratio is indeed 3, as our results suggest, and if the code is the same throughout Nature, then the genetic code may well be solved within a year.'[55] That view was shared by Nirenberg, who shortly afterwards predicted to Crick that 'within another six months or so most of the genetic code will be cracked.'[56] Both men severely underestimated the difficulties ahead.

*

Even before the article appeared, Crick sent copies of the manuscript to his correspondents around the world and gave talks describing the findings. Jacob wrote enthusiastically to Brenner: 'We had the visit of Francis who gave a remarkable seminar. This story really is astonishing.'[57] In California, Gunther Stent found the paper 'historic' and was tempted to immediately send Crick a congratulatory telegram to express his 'limitless admiration' for the clever way the experiment was designed; instead, he sent Francis a letter saying 'Man, it's cool.'[58]

One of the reasons for the excitement was that, following Nirenberg's initial breakthrough, more links between RNA sequences and amino acids were being discovered, both by his laboratory and by that of Severo Ochoa in New York. In December, Crick and Brenner received a postcard of a chipmunk from Kendrew, who was visiting Harvard, excitedly summarising the latest findings (most turned out to be incorrect).[59]

This flurry of results, combined with Crick and Brenner's experiment, set off a media avalanche. Although Nirenberg's Moscow

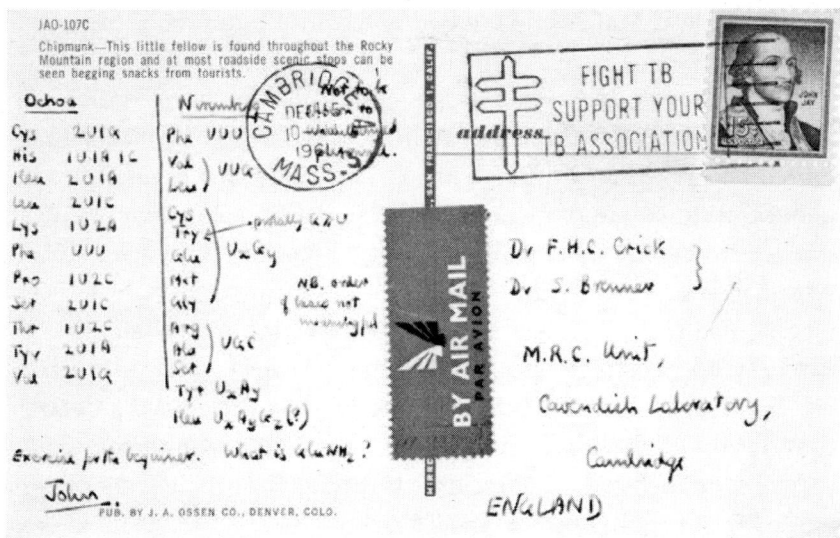

announcement sent a wave of excitement through the scientific community, the media had remained silent. That now changed dramatically as journalists from around the world swarmed all over the story.[60]

First out of the blocks was the *New York Herald Tribune*, which on 18 December described the latest results from Nirenberg and Ochoa and proclaimed 'Code of Life Deciphered by Biochemists'. Two weeks later the UK *Sunday Times* took a similar line – 'Scientists Have Cracked the Code of Life' – while the *Observer* gave a whole page to the discovery, highlighting the distant possibility of controlling heredity, which would put 'new and alarming powers into our hands'. Both newspapers emphasised Crick's role – the *Sunday Times* even included a rare photograph – and highlighted the importance of Crick and Brenner's *Nature* paper, published the day before.[61] The next day, *The Times* heralded a 'new stage in research on heredity', singing the praises of the Cambridge group.[62] On 2 January, the BBC broadcast a television programme, *Challenges*, which explored the main scientific discoveries of the previous year and featured Crick and Brenner's work.[63] Three weeks later, Crick gave a talk on the BBC European Service in which he described Nirenberg and Matthaei's 'spectacular' result and his own work with Brenner.[64] Crick and Brenner's coding paper and the cracking of the genetic code by

Nirenberg and Matthaei were combined in the minds of the global public.

The clearest expression of the significance of the recent discoveries, and of Crick's fundamental role, came in *The New York Times*, which published a front-page article describing the breaking of the genetic code as 'among the greatest scientific achievements of all time'.[65] It began dramatically: 'Biology is undergoing a revolution whose meaning and magnitude have become apparent only in recent weeks. The pace has been so swift, in fact, that many scientists do not fully appreciate the potential of the powder keg they are sitting on.' Spilling over onto a full inside page, the article gave a detailed description of the research that had been done around the world, focusing on the work of US scientists. But as the article went on, one name kept cropping up – Francis Crick.

To introduce Crick to American readers, the newspaper included the first profile of him, in which he was described as 'Hunter of Life's Secrets'. The journalist claimed that Crick's home in Portugal Place was 'the constant focus of newsmen and broadcasting men, clamouring for details of the news that Dr. Crick has wrested portentous secrets from the ultimate particle of life, the gene.' This was somewhat exaggerated, but Crick's dislike of publicity and Perutz's role in creating an intellectual powerhouse in the dingy Hut ('an outdoor washhouse in a dour Cambridge courtyard') were both well captured. Equally accurate was the description of 'Crick's corner' of the Hut – it looked like 'an owl's aviary' in which 'model helixes hang from the roof on strings, and scholarship is apparent only from books and untidiness.' The final paragraph of the profile succinctly sketched Crick's appearance, character and outlook: 'To intimates, this unraveller of the coil of life is elegant in explanation and, with his fondness for sideburns and Italian suits, somewhat Edwardian in manner. In his forty-fifth year, he lists as his sole recreation "conversation, especially with pretty women."' Although Francis insisted that he hated any personal publicity, he told a colleague that it was 'Not a bad article, I thought.'[66]

It is striking that the media focused on Crick, the slightly eccentric Briton, and on the code, that sexy-sounding but cryptographically inaccurate term for how cells turn genetic information into proteins.* The discovery that each genetic word was composed of three letters was indeed incredibly significant and Crick's intelligence and manners made for good copy (in the case of the British papers, his nationality helped, too). But, as he emphasised in the *Nature* article and to reporters, it was Nirenberg and Matthaei who provided the breakthrough in understanding what those genetic words actually meant.

All this was in contrast to how another fundamental discovery in molecular genetics, also made in the summer of 1961, had been completely ignored by all but the scientific community. François Jacob and Jacques Monod published a theoretical and experimental description of what genes actually do, showing that while some produced structural proteins, others appeared to regulate the activity of those structural genes, determining where and when they were activated, and for how long. This way of thinking about gene function gave the key to how multicellular organisms could develop, with different cell types being determined by the same genome that was present in every cell, and how uncontrolled growth could occur, as in cancer. And yet this breakthrough was not covered by any newspaper or radio or television station. The public, journalists and scientists were all swept away by fascination with the code, with Crick at the centre of it all.

*

Crick's fame was becoming global – within a few weeks he ordered an astonishing one thousand extra reprints of the *Nature* article to meet the demand for copies – and when he arrived in San Francisco in March 1962 he had to give a televised press conference.[67] As well as academic lectures, he was increasingly asked to talk to general audiences, where, as he put it, 'everybody and his girl-friend has turned up and I am forced to give a popular lecture'.[68] There was

---

*Strictly speaking, the genetic code is a cipher, not a code. In coining the term 'genetic code', Francis had in mind something like the Morse Code, although this is also a cipher, not a code. He later admitted that 'genetic code' sounded a lot more intriguing than 'genetic cipher'. Crick, F. (1988), *What Mad Pursuit: A Personal View of Scientific Discovery* (New York: Basic), pp. 89–90.

also recognition from leading academic bodies around the world. Already, in autumn 1960, he had received the prestigious Albert Lasker Award from the American Public Health Association, along with Watson and Wilkins. A year later, there was a ceremony in Paris where the French Académie des sciences awarded Crick – and Crick alone – the Prix Charles-Léopold Mayer. (Crick told Benzer 'there were soldiers, and drums and Academicians in uniform! Almost as antiquated as Cambridge.')[69] At around the same time he was given an Honorary Fellowship by UCL, and in May 1962 he was made a Foreign Honorary Member of the American Association for the Advancement of Science.

The official celebrations began to pall – although Crick was given the US Research Corporation Award along with Watson in April 1962, he chose not to attend the ceremony. He had a prior arrangement to give lectures at the University of Oregon, where Sid Bernhard had promised him 'quite spectacular' weather, together with 'the advantages of a co-educational institution abounding in parties without formalities'.[70] Odile told Francis clearly that this behaviour did not impress her or Watson ('JDW'):

> I am sorry to hear you have decided not to attend the presentation on April 18th. I suspect you just don't want to be bothered but it does seem not only impolite (bad manners on a really JDW scale) but distinctly insulting in view of the fact that you will actually be in the States at the time. These are my personal views not those of Jim who evidently thinks it is also personally unfriendly towards him. I think if you accept the prize at all you should accept it with grace.[71]

Odile's sharp words had no effect, and when Francis eventually received the commemorative plaque that came with the award, he gave it to his Aunt Ethel who was setting up a shrine to her nephew in her sitting room.[72]

Crick's absence from the ceremony had an unexpected consequence. Alone on the platform, Watson abandoned his usual lecture on nucleic acids and viruses and improvised a talk about the personalities involved in the discovery of the double helix and their role in 'determining the winners and losers', a typically Watsonian framing of events.[73] That moment, he claimed, was when he realised he wanted to write 'a real and gripping *story* as opposed to a contribution to the history of science' – the book that would become *The Double Helix*.

All these awards suggested that the ultimate prize was coming closer. In December 1961, Francis learned how soon that might be. Monod wrote explaining that he was nominating Crick, Watson and Wilkins for the Nobel Prize for the discovery of the double helix, asking Francis to provide an outline of what exactly each of them had done, to simplify his task as a nominator.[74] Crick's response was a nine-page 'brief screed', in which he emphasised the fundamental role of Rosalind Franklin in their 1953 discovery: 'the data which really helped us obtain the structure was mainly obtained by Rosalind Franklin'.[75] Franklin herself was tragically excluded from Monod's nomination because of her death nearly four years earlier.

Franklin's role was probably clear in Crick's mind because earlier in the year he had twice given that lecture on the events surrounding the discovery, first in Cambridge, then in Oxford.[76] In his talk he emphasised the role of collaboration and good relations with other researchers, something that Franklin had not enjoyed while working on DNA. Crick had matured over the intervening years; he retained his excitement and sometimes bullish enthusiasm, but increasingly recognised that he now had a position of influence and of leadership among scientists, and that responsibilities flowed from his growing reputation.

Even before DNA's Nobel moment, there was already the sense of an ending, the feeling that something profound had shifted in the world of science. Many of the old problems and questions had now been resolved and a new approach to biology was taking shape. For the science correspondent of the *Guardian* – the one-time University of Manchester lecturer and the future editor of *Nature*, John Maddox – Crick and Brenner's paper marked the culmination of a major phase in scientific research, the consequences of which were uncertain, but which were sure to be exciting and incredibly far-reaching: 'If the research puts an end to an era, it also marks the simultaneous beginning of a dozen others.'[77]

THE SWINGING
SIXTIES

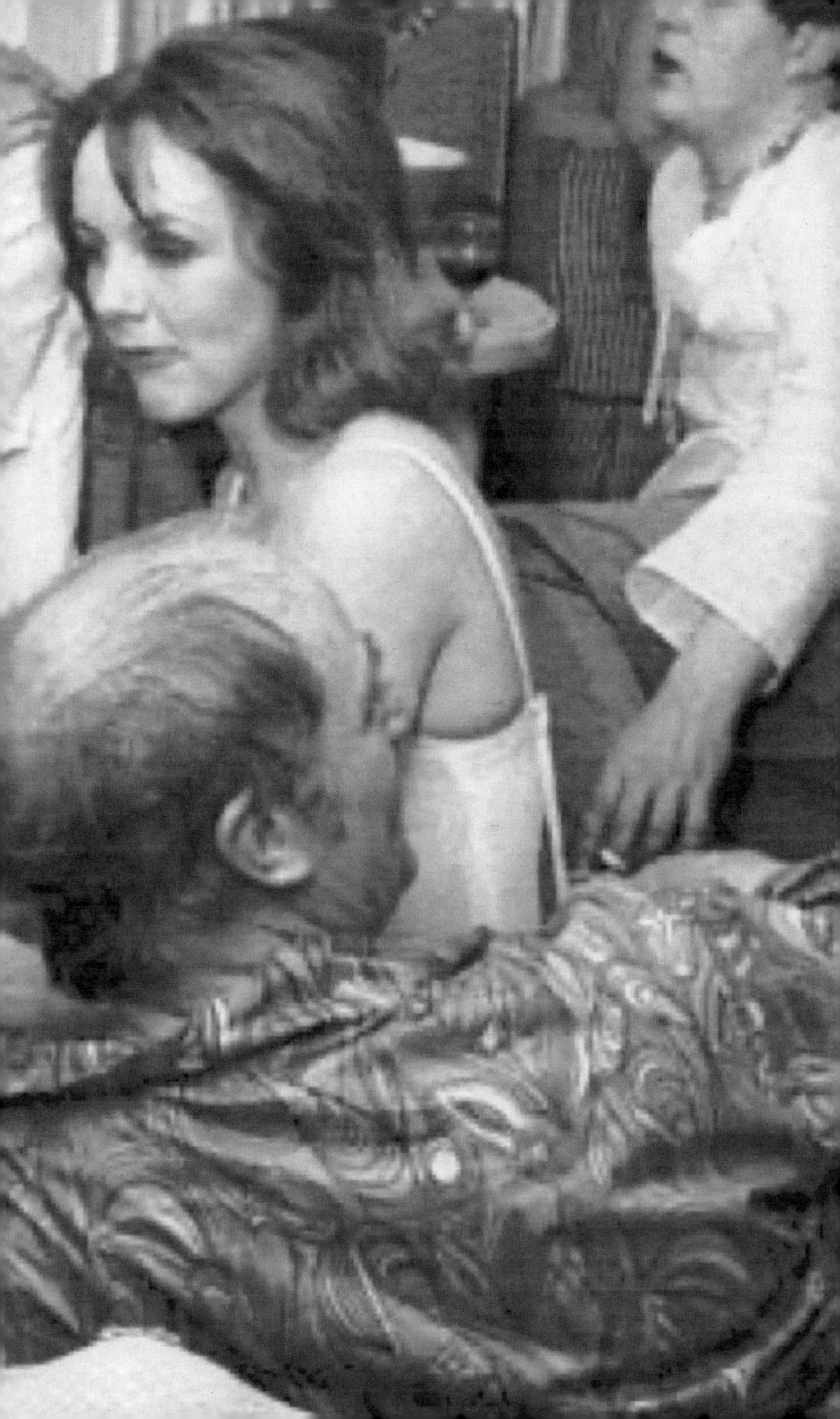

FAME

In January 1962, Francis announced to a friend: 'Odile now has a car' – an Austin Mini, soon to become a popular symbol of British cool.[1] In the summer they entered the world of stereo hi-fi, exploring various state-of-the-art systems.[2] The times were changing, and the Cricks' lives were changing, too.

When Francis returned from his US trip in spring 1962, it was to the shiny new Laboratory of Molecular Biology (LMB) on Hills Road.[3] His secretary, Alison Auld, had told him what to expect:

> Your room is in an awful mess with some drawers and the wall cupboard and that's all. Everything is full up and there are still heaps of papers, books, pamphlets, etc. with nowhere to go. Sydney won't unpack his things which are just sitting in huge packing cases on the floor. With any luck we will have things sorted out a bit before you get back.[4]

Built on a vast open plot in the south-east of the city, the LMB was four storeys of brick and glass. Its spacious modernist structure – early sixties UK office style – lacked architectural panache but was functional; there was ample room for the new groups led by Fred Sanger and Aaron Klug. Everyone was pleased to be moving in, despite being far from the centre of town – there would be no more sloping off to the Eagle for lunch. Instead, one of the successes of the new building was a top-floor canteen for all members of staff, where informal conversations could flourish.*

The LMB was officially opened by the Queen on the morning of 28 May 1962. Crick and Brenner, who disapproved of the monarchy, ostentatiously absented themselves, but they attended the guest lecture given by Watson (he was on a brief visit) and, of course, the lab party, unlike the Queen.[5] Crick's hostility to the British establishment surfaced again the following year, when he turned down an offer from 10 Downing Street to make him a Commander of the British Empire in the forthcoming Queen's Birthday Honours List.[6] (Perutz, Kendrew, Wilkins and Sanger all accepted their awards.)

With the new building came a new way of working: Perutz gave the laboratory a more open and democratic organisation, with a four-man governing board composed of three heads of Division and himself as Chairman.[7] Although administration and organisation were never Crick's strong points, he was now one of those three Division heads, in charge of Molecular Genetics (the other two heads were Sanger and Kendrew; Kendrew was also Deputy Chairman). The new building and the organisation of the laboratory were designed to remove obstacles and to foster what Crick thrived on – intense intellectual interactions. This was the kind of thing that Harold Wilson, the opposition Labour Party leader, had in mind the following year when he foresaw a new Britain forged in the 'white heat' of a new scientific revolution, which would require modernised facilities and working practices. This flatter, more collective structure, where everyone used each other's first names, was not only a sign of the LMB's independence from the traditional hierarchies of the university; it also hinted at the profound social changes that were taking place in British society.

Sharing an office with Brenner meant that the pair could enjoy

---

*A few years later, Crick told Benzer, 'There is nowhere to eat or drink within a reasonable distance, so most people have their meals at the canteen, which at least mixes them together a bit. Fish and chips are provided on Fridays.' Crick to Benzer, 2 April 1970, PP/CRI/D/1/1/2.

their daily discussions without disturbing their colleagues quite so much. In the summer of 1962, US biophysicist John Platt visited Cambridge and watched how Brenner and Crick interacted, as part of a study of scientific thinking:

> On any given morning at the Laboratory of Molecular Biology in Cambridge, England, the blackboards of Francis Crick or Sidney Brenner will commonly be found covered with logical trees. On the top line will be the hot new result just up from the laboratory or just in by letter or rumour. On the next line there will be two or three alternative explanations, or a little list of 'What he did wrong'. Underneath will be a series of suggested experiments or controls that can reduce the number of possibilities. And so on. The tree grows during the day as one man or another comes in and argues about why one of the experiments wouldn't work, or how it should be changed.

Shortly after the Cavendish site was abandoned by the molecular biologists, Crick's PhD student Hans Boye went back and took some photos, including one of Crick's blackboards, propped up against the outside of the Hut and destined for the bonfire.[8] Covered in chalk of

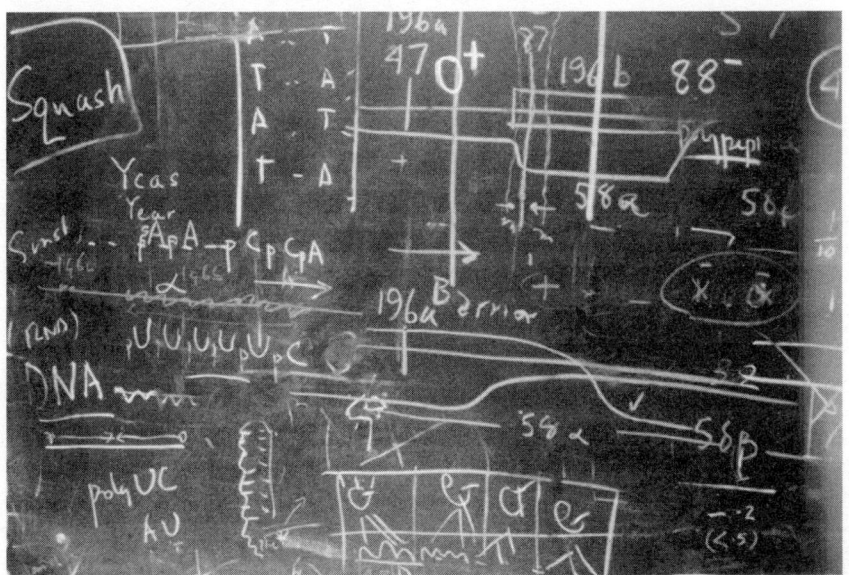

many colours, it showed bits of experiments on the genetic code, bibliographic references, and a sporting reminder in the top left corner: 'Squash'. You can sense the squeak of the chalk as the lines were drawn, hear the high barking of Crick's voice and the drawly mumbling of Brenner's as they argue over a particular point. Here was a mad session made solid, the excited interactions frozen in time.

*

On Thursday 18 October, Francis received a half-expected telegram announcing that, together with Watson and Wilkins, he had won the 1962 Nobel Prize in Physiology or Medicine, 'for your discoveries concerning the molecular structure of nuclear acids and its significance for information transfer in living material'.[9] Francis was overjoyed and that evening there was a wild party at Portugal Place, with fireworks let off from the roof garden, thrown down into the street, and even aimed at the nearby St John's College, all accompanied by lots of alcohol and even more noise.[10] A police officer turned up to see what all the fuss was about and was invited in to join the celebrations. At some point, Watson phoned up excitedly; Crick responded but could not make himself heard over the racket from the party.[11]

Four days later, joy at the award was overshadowed by President Kennedy's alarming announcement that Russian nuclear missiles were being installed in Cuba, within striking distance of the USA, and that a naval blockade of the island would be imposed. For a week, a terrified world teetered on the brink of nuclear confrontation. Even news-averse Francis was affected – he sent no letters during the crisis. Then it was all over, although everyone was shaken by this brush with catastrophe.

Crick could now turn his attention to the blizzard of congratulatory letters he had received from around the world, some from old colleagues, others from randoms such as teachers in Italy or the Valparaíso Rotary Club. Soviet scientists also sent letters and telegrams; Francis responded warmly, urging that scientific friendships should not be affected by 'the ups and downs of international affairs'.[12] For once, he even sent his signature to lucky autograph hunters, but he still refused to send photographs.

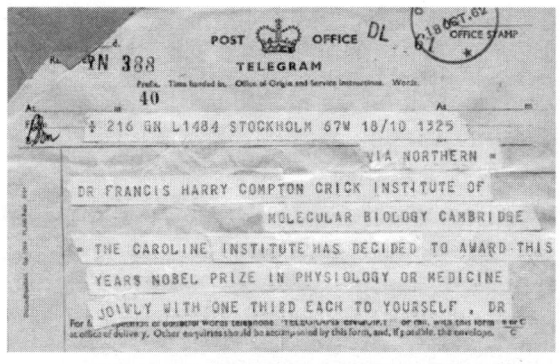

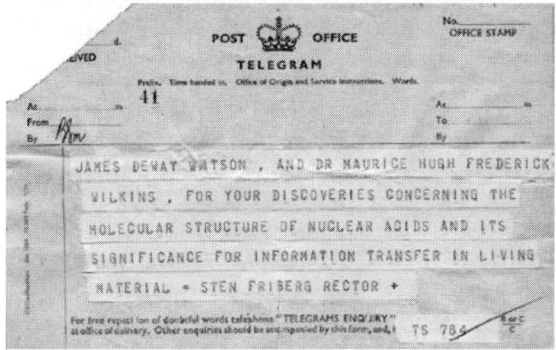

The excitement in Cambridge was not over yet: on 1 November, Perutz and Kendrew learned that they had won that year's Nobel Prize in Chemistry for their work on haemoglobin and myoglobin; at the LMB party to celebrate their award, a grinning Perutz, a carnation in his lapel, triumphantly held up the telegram and a glass of champagne.[13] Together with the award for DNA, this was an extraordinary recognition of the vision of Sir Lawrence Bragg, of Perutz's patient management style and of the consistent support of the MRC.

The Nobel ceremony took place in the second week of December (Crick laconically noted in his diary for 8–14 December, 'Stockholm'), and the whole Crick family went along. The celebrations began with two days of parties and receptions, including a meal at the British Embassy – when the Ambassador invited them all to lunch, Crick enquired, 'Do you really want my two small daughters (aged 11 and 8)? They are quite house-trained but have no conversation.'[14]

The Prize-giving took place on Monday 10 December, in the presence of the King and Queen of Sweden, with lots of pomp, trumpets and playing of the Swedish national anthem. Francis shook the hand of King Gustaf VI Adolf and bobbed his head up and down as protocol demanded, looking dapper and pleased with himself in his white tie and tails.[15] At the grand banquet that followed, Odile was seated beside the King, while Francis was placed next to twenty-four-year-old Princess Desirée. Watson gave a brief speech of thanks on behalf of the three DNA winners; as he sat down, Francis scribbled a note on the back of his place card and passed it to his friend: 'Much better than I could have done. – F.'[16] After the speeches it was time for the celebration ball, which went on into the early hours; Francis danced with Gabrielle, who looked smart in her white ruffed dress and ankle socks.

In their official Nobel Lectures the following day, neither Watson nor Crick referred to Rosalind Franklin. This might seem ungracious, but tradition demanded their lectures focus on more recent work: Watson spoke about RNA, Crick described developments in coding, while Wilkins explained the precise structure of DNA.[17] Wilkins' lecture, however, began with the historical context, in which he merely stated that Franklin 'made very valuable contributions to the X-ray analysis'.[18]

After that, it was time for the Cricks to return home from freezing Stockholm, elated and slightly stunned by the whole affair. They obviously had a taste for the cold, for at the end of the year they went on a two-week family holiday to Cortina in the Dolomites, where the Nobel aura attracted the attention of the press photographers – Francis, Odile and Gabrielle were photographed looking stylish at an ice rink.[19] They returned to a country that was in the grip of the worst winter for decades. In February the Cricks could even go skating on the frozen Cam.* Snug in Portugal Place, Crick wrote to Kreisel ('My Dear Boy'), summing up the Nobel experience in terms his friend would understand: 'Stockholm was not quite as bad as I feared, but no adventures. Cambridge is *far* better for that!'[20]

---

*Crick told a friend: 'The Professor of Theoretical Chemistry has broken his leg skating but fortunately all our bones are intact.' Crick to di Mayorca, 5 February 1963, PP/CRI/D/1/1/13.

*

On the same day that Crick gave his Nobel lecture, BBC TV broadcast *The Prizewinners*, an hour-long celebration of the awards. Presented by Raymond Baxter, and with expert commentary from Crick's friend Michael Swann, the programme was produced in a rush by Philip Daly, who had begun recording interviews with all five men virtually as soon as the announcements were made.[21] Daly was jubilant at getting an interview with Crick, as he explained to his bosses: 'This is the first time that Francis Crick has agreed to appear on television, and it may well be his last. He will go down in history as one of the great scientists of our time – possibly as great as Darwin – and the material is therefore of inestimable archive value.'[22]

The programme opened with Baxter dramatically promising an intimate portrait that was unheard of at the time:

> This is to be a personal programme about these men. Their faces may be unfamiliar to you. To our children and our grand-children their names may well be as familiar as Darwin and Mendel and Pasteur are to us today. (…) In a few moments you will be able to meet them, to judge for yourselves what manner of men they are.[23]

Watson's interview, recorded in New York, had been beset by technical problems and was less than two minutes long, most of which consisted of the young American rolling his eyes, pausing, and talking about Crick ('I always liked working with Francis. He was … well, Francis likes to talk. It's his dominant quality; he doesn't stop unless he gets tired or thinks the idea is no good.'). Wilkins was seen in his garden on a freezing cold autumn day, sounding as tight-lipped as his overcoat was closely buttoned. Kendrew seemed the archetypal academic, sitting in an armchair, puffing on his pipe and listening to seventeenth-century music on his gramophone. Perutz – introduced by Baxter as 'the most romantic of the five' – came over as a warm and likeable man, explaining how in the 1930s he fled Austria out of fear of Hitler and became a refugee in Britain, unable to take up a post if a UK citizen could fill it. Putting his Nobel award into context, Perutz explained that his greatest prize 'was being able to live and work in this country'.

Crick's interview was the longest – over twelve minutes with psychologist Stephen Black – and was shown at the beginning of the programme. Seated at his desk in the LMB, Crick was deftly sketched in the *Observer* by journalist Anthony Sampson: 'Tall, sloping shoulders, a nervous, oddly Edwardian charm, twinges of eccentricity'.[24]

Black began by asking Crick about whether he believed in God ('No, certainly not,' Francis replied, with an embarrassed smile and a shake of the head). Whenever more personal matters were broached, such as whether the MRC took a gamble employing him in 1947, Francis displayed a shyness that contrasted with his confidence on scientific issues:

> Black: Do you think they were putting money on an outsider who came home?
> [Crick laughs, looks away, shifts in seat, smiles]
> Crick: Certainly I wasn't an insider in those days.
> [Crick laughs embarrassedly]

These mannerisms were picked up by journalist Cyril Connolly, who wrote a witty column in the *Sunday Times* spoofing Crick's odd mixture of boyish enthusiasm and sudden flashes of self-effacement.[25] A more negative view of Crick's performance came from the novelist Angus Wilson, who described the 'quick-thinking, fast-talking' Crick as 'almost a caricature of the obsessively talking, idea-throwing-out don with a lot of disarming boyishness and bounce' (he also said Watson was a 'real weirdie').[26] Two female reviewers were more positive: in the *Newcastle Journal*, Anthea Hall said that Crick was 'the star of the evening' – 'charmer and extrovert, and a "natural" for television' – while the *Guardian*'s Mary Crozier considered him to be a 'tremendously intelligent and vigorous-looking man'.[27]

One of the issues that most shocked Crick's critics was his dismissive attitude to religion – the reviewer in the *Belfast Telegraph* was alarmed by his 'god-less, scientific approach'.[28] In contrast, younger reviewers found Crick's attitude invigorating: in the *Daily Herald*, the future playwright Dennis Potter detected 'fascinating hints of the intellectual passion and arrogance which makes ideas so explosive', while Anthea Hall considered it 'about the most 20th Century thing to have happened on television while I've been watching'.[29]

For a few minutes, Crick, with his confidence in the power of science and his insouciant disregard for centuries of Christian tradition, became an unlikely symbol of the changing cultural and class divisions in British society, which appeared as the country emerged, wide-eyed, into the swinging sixties. A couple of weeks earlier, the ground-breaking satirical TV show *That Was the Week That Was* had exploded onto British TV screens – according to Tory MP Edward Heath, its biting attacks on the Establishment led to the death of deference.* As 1963 dawned, there was soon the outbreak of Beatle-mania and, according to the poet Philip Larkin, the invention of sex. None of this was very important for Francis – although he did buy Beatles LPs for his daughters and later loved The Beatles' music, he was not interested in satire, he had no television, and he needed no lessons about sex.

*

Crick's hostility to religion became well known following the founding of a new Cambridge college – Churchill College. Science-focused, modelled on MIT, and men-only, its aim was to help make the country scientifically and technologically competitive. Crick was one of the first Fellows, but his affiliation came into doubt over the question of whether the college buildings should include an Anglican chapel – in 1960 there was an outcry because there would be nowhere for Christians to pray.[30] A campaign was launched by fuddy-duddies to gather funds to build a chapel; this dismayed Crick, but to his relief the appeal was largely unsuccessful. However, following a large donation from a wealthy Anglican vicar, the college trustees approved the project. Dismayed but bull-headed, in August 1961 Crick wrote to Sir Winston Churchill (after whom the college was named), resigning his fellowship.[31]

---

*TW3, as it was known, even used the bunch of Nobel Prizes to British scientists as the premise for a (not very funny) sketch.

The eighty-six-year-old Churchill was puzzled by Crick's resignation and pointed out that a chapel would simply be an amenity for those that wished to use it. Crick's response was to send Sir Winston a cheque for ten guineas as a contribution to 'the Churchill College Hetairae fund' (in Ancient Greece a hetaira was a highly educated female courtesan).*[32] Francis explained his gesture: 'My hope is that eventually it will be possible to build permanent accommodation within the College, to house a carefully chosen selection of young ladies in the charge of a suitable Madam' – an amenity for those who wished to use it. He insisted that although the trustees might find his joke in bad taste, 'that is exactly my view of the proposal of the trustees to build a chapel, after the middle of the twentieth century, in a new College and in particular in one with a special emphasis on science.' Churchill did not respond, but merely returned Crick's cheque, 'with comps'. Francis later admitted that perhaps he should have remained a Fellow and argued his case (a non-denominational chapel was eventually erected just outside the college grounds).†[33]

While all this was initially a minor storm in the Cambridge teacup, it became known nationally at the time of the Nobels, when Anthony Sampson in the *Observer* quoted Francis's confidently Crickian comment about the chapel, 'Why should I support the propagation of error?'[34] This all added to Crick's growing reputation as a freethinker.

No sooner had Francis abandoned one prestigious fellowship

---

* At first, Churchill College did not even allow women to dine in college; partly as a result of Crick's arguments, this policy changed and he was able to invite Dorothy Hodgkin to dine as his guest. Crick to Kelly, 14 June 2000, PP/CRI/J/2/20/1.

† In 1965, Crick accepted an Honorary Fellowship at Churchill (he was not a member of the university, so the title was honorary) – *Daily Telegraph*, 19 May 1965. Much later, he said this was 'to let bygones be bygones' (Crick to Kelly, 1 August 2002, PP/CRI/J/1/8/3). In 1963, Crick had refused the offer of an Honorary Fellowship at Gonville and Caius. As he explained to Nevill Mott, the Master of the College, he 'would accept with great pleasure but for the unfortunate matter of the Chapel. (…) It's a bore, but what else can I do?' Crick to Mott, 13 February 1963, MSS 660, Box 3, Folder 47. Crick eventually relented in 1976, when he was about to leave Cambridge, becoming an Honorary Fellow of Gonville and Caius despite the continued presence of the chapel and its attendant Anglican rituals.

than he took up another, this time at an institution that would eventually change the course of his life. On the same day in April 1960 that Crick and Brenner were jumping up and down about messenger RNA, Jonas Salk, the pioneer of the polio vaccine, announced that he was setting up a biological research institute. It would have a small number of resident members and a larger number of visiting Fellows, all devoted to 'research in fundamental biology, and in the cause, prevention, and cure of disease, and in the factors and circumstances conducive to the fulfilment of man's biological potential'.[35] The institute would be housed in a new building on a coastal cliff site near La Jolla, a small town north of San Diego.[36] In October 1961 Crick was invited to become a non-resident Fellow 'of special quality' who would advise Salk on the choice of future institute members.[37]

By 1963, a striking low-rise building made of concrete, hardwood, glass and steel, designed by Louis Kahn, began to emerge from the idyllic site overlooking the Pacific.[38] Some felt that the building looked like a prison, but it is now seen as a classic of Californian modernism. It also became the workplace where Crick stayed the longest.[39] One wag at the MRC noted on a memo about Crick joining the Salk, 'I only hope it has no ecclesiastical intentions!'[40]

The terms of Crick's Salk fellowship were extremely generous: in return for spending an unspecified period each year at La Jolla, where he was provided with a study, laboratory space and accommodation for himself and Odile, Francis would receive $3,000* a year in compensation and a similar amount to cover expenses. The bean-counters at the MRC agreed that Crick could swan off to California each year, on condition that his salary was reduced by one-sixth.[41] The money from the Salk easily made up for this reduction.[42]

Together with a recent MRC pay rise and Francis's share of the £17,000 Nobel award (worth over twice his annual salary), the Cricks' financial worries were so far behind them that they began to splash out. In early 1963, while Odile was teaching Francis to drive in the Suffolk countryside, they came across a pair of dilapidated eighteenth-century cottages in Kedington, south-east of Cambridge, which they eventually bought, restored, and turned into a single

---

*The current equivalent would be around $31,000.

house, Well Cottage.[43] This project involved a lot of the Cricks' time in 1963–4; Francis not only supervised the building work, including trying his hand at bricklaying, but also designed the garden, a first sign of what became a lifelong interest in horticulture. They even built a swimming pool in the cottage grounds – quite daring for the time.

The Cricks' new financial ease, together with Francis's friendship with Jacques Monod, led to another new passion – sailing. Monod was an experienced sailor who regularly invited his friends to join him on Mediterranean trips. Crick's interest led Monod to rashly suggest that they might go halves on his new 11-metre cutter, designed for crossing the Atlantic at high speed. Crick sheepishly admitted that he and Odile lacked any experience of sailing – 'the biggest thing we've sailed so far is a sailing dinghy, and that was some years ago.'[44] Monod wisely said they should not make any decision about buying a boat without *'serious experience'*.[45]

Francis appreciated this advice a few years later on a trip with Monod along the Côte d'Azur. The outward leg of the voyage was idyllic – they were accompanied by whales – but as they returned to Saint-Tropez overnight a huge storm broke. Monod had boasted that they would be back in port before the nightclubs closed, but Crick began to think that they might not make it back at all. In contrast, Monod was full of derring-do, dashing around the deck, clipping himself onto the boat as it rocked, his movements lit from above by the boat's lights and the sharp flashes of the electrical storm. Crick recalled:

> Finally I said to him, 'Jacques, exactly what do I do if you fall overboard?' (I didn't think that he would, but I felt I'd better know.) He explained to me what manoeuvres to make and I felt a little more relaxed. … Eventually we located the channel and slipped into St. Tropez a little after dawn. The nightclubs were closed, but even if they'd been open we would probably have been too tired to go to one.[46]

Odile and Francis eventually bought a half-share in a six-berth powerboat called *Kiwi II*, which was moored in Naples and crewed by an ageing Italian who spoke little English.[47] Francis, Odile and the girls used the yacht for their summer holidays until they replaced it in 1967. Although Francis was never a very confident sailor (he described himself as 'a rather bumbling amateur'[*48]), their cruises round the Mediterranean show they were far from the typical Cambridge academic couple.

*

Crick's life in the mid-1960s was not just devoted to science and travel – the parties at Portugal Place and Well Cottage gradually became even more renowned or infamous, depending on your point of view.[†] Not only was there lots of music, dancing and alcohol (and, later, maybe other drugs), they often had a theme, sometimes involving fancy dress, such as the South Seas Party, at which guests had to dress as either Missionaries or Native Girls.[49] Sometimes the printed invitations, illustrated by Odile, hinted at risqué entertainment – at the 1962 Studio Party one of Odile's life models was in attendance, naked, and guests, who were invited to come disguised as artists, models or dancing girls, had to draw her.

Francis and Odile Crick
invite you to

A STUDIO PARTY

at

The Golden Helix
19 Portugal Place

on Friday, 1st June 1962 at 9. p.m.

Dress : Artists, Models
or Dancing Girls   R.S.V.P.

---

*Many years later, a friend recalled 'it is clear that when Watson made his famous remark about Francis's modest mood he had never seen him on a boat.' Jeffries to Crick, MSS 660, Box 11, Folder 12.
†In 1965, the *Sunday Times Magazine* published a two-page photo of Crick describing him as 'a famous partygoer' and 'Cambridge's most flamboyant scientist'. The title of the article, which was about arguments over the future of Churchill College, was 'Girls: Yes! Gowns: No!'

There could be a fair amount of sex at these parties – not only the usual canoodling in corners, but also the occasional projection of pornographic films, which were jointly owned with the Cricks' friend, the potter John Gayer-Anderson.[50] In 2005, the geneticist Michael Ashburner, who knew the Cricks as a student, implied that sometimes sex was not only watched on celluloid. Crick and Gayer-Anderson, he recalled, 'both liked to engineer situations between couples, triples, and quadruples. I mean I probably shouldn't go much further than this.'[51] In 2011, the historian Lisa Jardine, who was the daughter of Jacob Bronowski and a student at Newnham College at the time, described the parties for BBC TV – they were 'insanely wild', she said, concluding with a grin and a twinkle in her eye: 'I'm telling you, I shouldn't have been at those parties aged eighteen.'[52]

In other respects, the Cricks' cultural world was quite mainstream. At the Flower Party in April 1968, Francis was photographed lounging near a gas fire; on the turntable was some decidedly middle-of-the-road music from Herb Alpert and from Herman's Hermits.[53] Although he did buy a copy of the trendier 1968 double LP *Electric Ladyland*, by Jimi Hendrix, it was apparently because of the gatefold cover, which in the UK scandalously featured nineteen naked women.[54]

Much more in keeping with their age and tastes, Francis and Odile enjoyed the film of *My Fair Lady* (they had seen the original London production in November 1959) and *The Many Voices of Miriam Makeba*, a popular LP by the South African singer.[55] Similarly, the books they read were very much of their time; they noted the titles they lent to friends in a Lending Book, including novels by Turgenev, Colette, Thomas Mann, George Orwell, Proust and Henry Miller.[56]

*

Following the Nobel Prize, Crick's fame grew, and he soon found himself locked into a punishing schedule of travel and invited lectures. Between 1963 and 1966, he gave nearly seventy lectures in scores of different cities.[57] Each trip involved detailed negotiations with the organisers, such as ensuring that the sometimes substantial honorarium would incur the lowest tax burden, checking whether he needed to bring evening dress or discussing what kind of reception he would like – 'a quiet evening at home or a brass band' was one offer (Crick replied 'Please, no brass band. A quiet evening at home would be just the thing, although an occasional dancing girl would do no harm').[58] Francis even had tussles with the British government, which wanted him to give extra lectures and write articles, and insisted on knowing exactly where he would be when.[59] Crick would have none of this, as he told R. W. Ford of the Foreign Office: 'As for the programme of my tour, this is a closely guarded secret, and you are the last person I would give it to! So sorry.'[60]

Invitations from friends were turned down – Sir Lawrence Bragg, Marshall Nirenberg and Robert Oppenheimer all got the brush-off; even the promise of 'sailing and especial gastronomy (grilled lobster with cognac)' at a Brittany research station met with a refusal.[61] Many of the rejected invitations were from tiny student groups such as the Socratic Society or the Lemuel Gulliver Society, or from intriguing commercial organisations like the International Union of Leather Chemists Societies or the Natural Rubber Producers' Research Association.[62] There were also hopelessly misguided people who clearly had no idea about Crick's views – the Impington Village College Further Education Programme on Religion and Politics, the Committee of Sponsors for the Centenary of the Jewish Theological Seminary of America or the Society for the Study of Theology in Strasbourg.

Some of the letters smell of another age, such as the invitation from NASA to visit the Manned Spacecraft Center in Houston, with a view to devising an experiment for the Apollo missions, or the request from *Playboy* to write an article on President Johnson's 'Great Society' project (Crick replied that he was a regular and enthusiastic reader of *Playboy** but turned them down).[63] Cheekier letters came from Petfoods Limited, inviting him to join their management awayday at Ragdale Hall Country Club, or from the University of Minnesota professor who wanted Francis to give fifteen lectures in five weeks and pompously signed off: 'Think deeply on it, consider the time, the place and your duty to society, and let us know your decision. I fail to believe that you can find it in your heart to deny us this request.'[64]

There were also the inevitable letters from cranks, kept in a file labelled 'Eccentrics' (in one case Francis scrawled on the letter 'File under madmen').[65] These were sometimes met with a brusque reply signed by his secretary ('his point of view is so different from yours that any correspondence would be a waste of time'), but more often the aim was to gently prevent any further communication, such as the reply to a letter urging everyone to eat 'pre-digested beef' which

---

*Crick was a long-standing subscriber to *Playboy*, which he felt was 'a serious magazine, with an excellent record for considered articles and interviews'. Crick to Pohl, 31 December 1968 and 2 December 1969, PP/CRI/E/2/8.

From:
M.R.C., *Laboratory of Molecular Biology, Hills Road, Cambridge.*

Dr. F. H. C. Crick thanks you for your letter but regrets that he is unable to accept your kind invitation to:

send an autograph	read your manuscript
provide a photograph	deliver a lecture
cure your disease	attend a conference
be interviewed	act as chairman
talk on the radio	become an editor
appear on TV	contribute an article
speak after dinner	write a book
give a testimonial	accept an honorary degree
help you in your project	**Go to stud**

told the correspondent that Crick had 'temporarily retired from public life and is in retreat in Fulbourn [a psychiatric hospital near Cambridge] for an indefinite period'.

Letters asking for photographs became frequent – in a pre-digital world it was hard to obtain good-quality photos without access to the negatives.[66] Crick's response was virtually always a refusal, although he never explained his aversion to having his portrait reproduced, beyond a claim of being shy. Because he was not consistent – he would pose for press photographers while travelling, including with his family – the motivation for his refusals remains unclear.

To ease the burden of rejecting requests that would never be considered, a response card was devised which listed the various things Francis would not do (this was not Crick's idea – he copied it from the American writer Edmund Wilson).[67] 'Provide a photograph' was second on the list, after 'send an autograph' with the remaining sixteen no-no's including 'accept an honorary degree' (he consistently refused these), 'appear on TV' or 'speak after dinner'.[68] As Crick later explained, he soon decided it seemed rude if he just put a tick next to a reason, so he would write something like 'Sorry, I can't manage it this time' on the back.[69] These cards were used quite regularly, sometimes prompting a good-humoured reply: one television producer responded 'Thank you for your card, which gave this office a very happy five minutes!'[70] Someone amended one of these cards to include 'Go to stud', which amused Francis so much he kept it.

TRIUMPH AND BETRAYAL

Following Nirenberg and Matthaei's breakthrough in 1961, there was huge excitement in the scientific community as researchers flocked to study the genetic code. This enthusiasm was not always matched by clarity, and Francis realised that there was a lack of rigorous thinking about how to proceed. To set his ideas out clearly, in 1963 he wrote an article entitled 'The Recent Excitement in the Coding Problem'.[1] Despite his admiration for Nirenberg's discovery, when he studied the experimental claims from the various laboratories regarding which codon (the new term for a sequence of three bases, coined by Crick*) coded for which amino acid, Francis was dubious: 'There are so many criticisms which can be brought against this type of experiment that one hardly knows where to begin,' he wrote. The sequence of the artificial RNA – the input of the experiment – was known only where a single base was involved (for example, UUU), while the amount of amino acid produced in each experiment – the output – was often barely measurable. Crick therefore accepted only two of the

---

*The first use of 'codon' in print was in a July 1962 article by Mark Bretscher and Marianne Grunberg-Manago (*Nature* 195:283–4). Bretscher told me that Francis inserted the word into the manuscript, saying that was what a triplet would be called in future.

links between codons and amino acid that were being claimed at the time; as it turned out, only one of these was correct – Nirenberg and Matthaei's original suggestion that UUU codes for phenylalanine.

Surveying the resurgence of theoretical approaches to the code that had appeared in the wake of Nirenberg's breakthrough, Crick was even more critical:

> In the long run we do not want to guess the genetic code, we want to know what it is. (…) Whether theory can help by suggesting the general structure of the code remains to be seen. If the code does have a logical structure there is little doubt that its discovery would greatly help the experimental work. Failing that, the main use of theory may be to suggest novel forms of evidence and to sharpen critical judgement. In the final analysis it is the quality of the experimental work which will be decisive.

Francis could not himself find solutions to the problem of the genetic code – he did not possess the necessary biochemical skills and was spending too much time travelling. But he played to his strengths – talking with colleagues, especially in the USA, about their latest results, keeping Brenner informed about all the scientific gossip he heard. Without planning it, he became the central point around which all the researchers in the field revolved. Because everyone sent him their results, either in letters or in preprints, he was better informed about progress than anyone else and became an informal arbiter of priority – who got the credit for each advance.[2]

For example, in 1964 he went on a long tour that began with a Symposium on Nucleic Acids in Hyderabad, which he attended with Seymour Benzer, Alex Rich and others.[3] Although he enjoyed the visit, the meeting was not interesting: 'Nothing you would find wildly exciting,' he wrote to Brenner.[4] After leaving India, he then went on to Harvard, where he found ample sources of the scientific gossip he craved so much, as he told Brenner: 'News at last. (All these trips to India, Princeton etc are a waste of time. This is where we should be.)'[5] One of the bits of news he heard was that Nirenberg and his colleague Philip Leder had been able to discover which amino acid bonded with the relevant RNA adaptor molecule (now called transfer RNA or tRNA), using synthetic RNA molecules composed of just three bases in a known sequence. Although this apparently enabled Nirenberg to identify the function of some codons, doubts remained about whether the experiments really represented what happened in a cell. A contrasting, complementary and more complicated technique was developed by Gobind Khorana at the University of Wisconsin; put very simply, his group made synthetic mRNAs having short repeating sequences, which were then added to a test tube full of ribosomes, enzymes and amino acids to see what polypeptide was produced.[6]

Crick's trips primarily consisted of talking and the sifting of scientific gossip, but they were also punctuated by letters to and from Odile, full of tedious detail about sofas, bathroom fittings and bills: 'Dull letter full of business – Damn Damn Damn' she wrote in one letter, but added a PS: 'Just got your letter – I see you are quite living it up but you don't tell me all the interesting bits. I have to read between the lines.'[7]

In February 1965, when he was in La Jolla with Odile, Francis began writing a letter to Sydney, explaining how one set of results he had heard of supported their theories and encouraging Brenner to pursue a rather difficult experiment, when he suddenly broke off. He returned to the letter the next day: 'At this point Odile walked through a glass door!! Fortunately nothing serious and no injuries to her face or neck, but she had to go to hospital and have about a hundred stitches. She hopes to be back in Cambridge on Wednesday as planned.'[8] He then returned to the theme of the letter, making suggestions for Brenner's next experiment. Odile was indeed not badly injured, although she did have painful cuts to her left arm and leg; within a few weeks she had made a full recovery.[9]

Throughout his travels, Crick had collected results, information and gossip from colleagues around the world, drawing up his own versions of the emerging genetic code. To keep track of the rapidly changing evidence, he duplicated a set of grids with space for all sixty-four codons, into which he could insert the relevant amino acid when the latest data came in. The design of this table has since become canonical and it is known all over the world.[10]

Because Crick had no skin in the game, competing groups were prepared to trust him with their unpublished data, while his well-established focus on the topic led him to be the Godfather of the code – cajoling colleagues, encouraging certain lines of research and criticising others. As he later put it – 'It was a most exciting occasion for me, travelling about the country and seeing how the various lines of evidence fitted together.'[11]

When writing to Nirenberg and Khorana, the two main drivers of the new wave of experimental studies, Crick was careful to praise their work even when he had doubts. For example, he described Nirenberg's initial draft of the whole genetic code as 'a wonderful piece of work' while pointing out minor errors and urging Nirenberg to be '*most* careful to distinguish between the triplets you have tested and those you guess'.[12] When Khorana sent Francis some of his latest results, around the same time, Crick said they left him puzzled. To both men, he emphasised the problem of using methods that often produced unreliable results.[13]

The pace of discovery and the intellectual excitement of working on a problem with constantly changing parameters but one central, knowable solution – the meaning of each of the sixty-four possible codons – led Francis to change his mind about the parallel world of scientific communication represented by the Information Exchange Groups (IEGs). In 1961, when invited by NIH administrator Edward Albritton to set up an IEG in which scientists could informally exchange results and ideas around the genetic code, Crick had brusquely rejected the idea. But now contradictory experimental results were tumbling out of laboratories, leading to inconsistent interpretations, with wildly different draft codes circulating in private correspondence. Often, these findings were too preliminary or uncertain to justify submitting to a journal, and anyway, going down the official route would inevitably lead to delays and the eventual appearance of conclusions that were known to be incorrect even before they were published.

Faced with this situation, at the beginning of 1965 Watson and Nirenberg set up a seventh IEG devoted to Nucleic Acids and the Genetic Code, and hundreds of scientists soon signed up. Within fifteen months, IEG7 had circulated over four hundred memos, as

IEG documents were called.*[14] Crick not only joined IEG7, he began writing a memo about the molecular basis of the most puzzling feature of the genetic code: how a codon could code for more than one amino acid.

Crick's solution related to the structure of the transfer RNA molecule – the adaptor that brought the amino acid to the ribosome and recognised a particular codon on the mRNA molecule. Each tRNA molecule carried an 'anti-codon' which paired up with an mRNA codon, so if the mRNA codon was UAG, the tRNA anticodon would read AUC. One of the great surprises of the work on the genetic code was that the code was redundant, or degenerate as they called it at the time. In many cases the final base in a codon did not matter – for example, UUU and UUC both coded for phenylalanine, AGU and AGC both coded for serine, while CUU, CUC, CUA and CUG all coded for leucine. By closely studying the atomic forces involved in a brief stretch of base pairing between tRNA and mRNA molecules, Crick realised that there could be a degree of play in the pairing of the bases in the third position, permitting the same tRNA molecule to pair with more than one mRNA codon. In spring 1965 Francis wrote this idea up as a chatty memo for IEG7 and called his idea 'The Wobble Hypothesis'.[15] To aid those who might not understand his terminology, he included a tongue-in-cheek footnote: 'Those non-English speaking readers who are not too familiar with the word "wobble" may prefer to use the term "anticodon ambisterique" instead.'

Eight months later, Crick submitted a version of the IEG memo to the *Journal of Molecular Biology*, written in a staider style.[16] Nevertheless, in the published version, Francis could not resist adding a closing Crickian flourish: 'In conclusion it seems to me that the preliminary evidence seems rather favourable to the theory. I shall not be surprised if it proves correct.'

---

*The circulation of preprints by the IEGs ended in September 1966, when a cartel of journal publishers agreed not to publish articles that had previously been circulated by the IEGs. Faced with this ultimatum, the scientific community rolled over and NIH closed the system down. It would be nearly half a century before biologists began to circulate preprints again. Cobb, M. (2017), The prehistory of biology preprints: A forgotten experiment from the 1960s. *PLoS Biology* 15:e2003995.

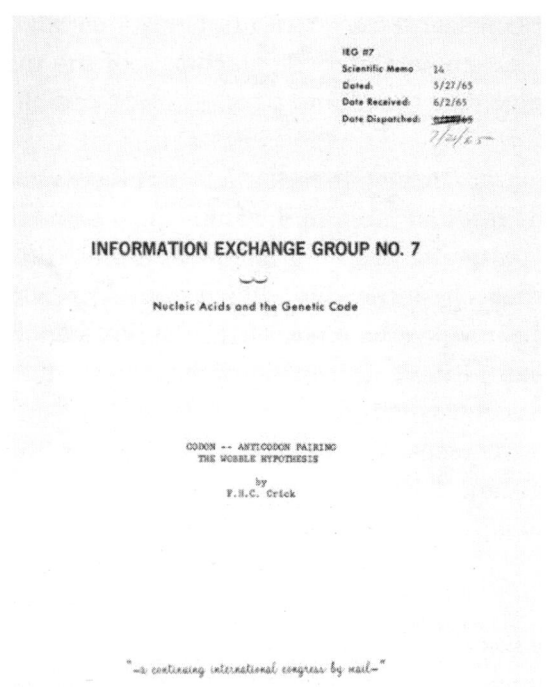

While quietly satisfied with many of his own ideas, Crick could be impatient with colleagues who published mistaken claims. At the beginning of May 1965, Edwin Osgood of the University of Oregon Medical School argued in *Nature* that the genetic code was not redundant at all.[17] Unimpressed, Crick wrote to Osgood scolding him for his feeble paper, pointing out that a quarter of his proposed triplets were wrong, that his idea that up to half the codons might be nonsense was simple-minded, and that it was rash to speculate about the evolutionary advantages of his version of the code when there was so little evidence it was correct. Crick concluded: 'It is a great pity that you did not submit your version before publication to somebody more intimate in the subject, as this would have saved you much subsequent embarrassment. Never mind, it will soon be forgotten!'*[18]

The widespread uncertainty about the experimental results from studies of the code that had so misled Osgood encouraged Crick to try and put some order into a chaotic situation. Shortly before the

---

*Harsh but true. Poor Osgood's article has been cited only once.

June 1965 Gordon Conference on Nucleic Acids, held in New Hampshire, he proposed that at the end of the meeting a short statement on the current state of research on the genetic code should be adopted. This suggestion was sent to Watson and Nirenberg, as Chairmen of IEG7; Khorana, the organiser of the conference, was copied onto the correspondence.[19] Francis explained:

> As you know I have found myself involved in this, but as a collator of information rather than as a producer. I am constantly having to provide copies of my private version of the code to interested people. (...) This year's Gordon Conference should provide an ideal opportunity, not to present a final version of the code, but the best version of most of it.

Watson replied positively, but Nirenberg pointed out that discussions at Gordon Conferences are not summarised or published and instead suggested to Francis, 'Why don't you write it'.[20] Crick was wary of appearing to claim credit for the work of others so nothing came of the suggestion, for a few months, anyway.[21]

*

Crick was repeatedly invited to give lectures around the world as his lecturing style became renowned. Hardly any of these talks survive in written form – he did not read them out but extemporised from detailed notes. In only one case, a talk for the National Research Council in Ottawa in September 1966, did he permit an archived audio recording.[22] In this apparently unique record of Francis at the height of his powers, he explained the links between the 'two great families of molecules' – proteins and nucleic acids – in terms that anyone could understand. Speaking in his slightly high-pitched, metallic voice, he used simple analogies to make his point – 'sausages' to describe the structure of haemoglobin, 'spaghetti' to describe DNA spooling out of a bacterium following a phage attack, and so on. When he made a joke, it was accompanied by his typical breathy snorting as he laughed along with the audience.

Avoiding experimental detail, Crick brilliantly explained the central dogma and the sequence hypothesis, the proof that the code is non-overlapping, the redundancy of the code and the co-linearity of the nucleic acid and amino acid sequences. The final section was a tour de force showing how the outline of the genetic code could explain amino acid data from human haemoglobin variants and from mutations in Tobacco Mosaic Virus. In both cases, Crick's careful analysis of the code showed that those variants were caused by single base-pair changes – all this long before DNA sequencing.

Another impression of how Crick spoke can be gained from a more academic lecture he gave in November 1964 in front of 1,600 biochemists in Houston. For once, he wrote up his talk, using a verbatim record provided by a transcription service.[23] A comparison of the two versions reveals the contrasting voices he used in speaking and writing – the taut precision of the written version and the genial informality of the actual lecture:

Published:
I have taken as my title 'The *General* Nature of the Genetic Code' because we do not yet know the genetic code in detail, although we certainly hope to do so before very long.

Verbatim:
The topic I have is The General Nature of the Genetic Code and the catch in that is, of course, if you know how to read titles, it is simply our way of saying we don't know what the genetic code is. If we knew what the genetic code is I'd just have to say, 'First Slide', and there would be the genetic code on the screen. But as you will see, we aren't quite yet in that happy state.

It was this warm, confident, but intense voice that filled the scores of lectures he gave, entrancing and informing audiences, whether they were his peers or the public.

Sometimes his usual vim deserted him. For example, in 1963 he gave the keynote lecture at Cold Spring Harbor, where the annual symposium discussed the Synthesis and Structure of Macromolecules. Although this should have been right up Crick's street, he could not rise to the occasion. There is no trace of that lecture, not even a title.[24] All that remains is a photograph of Francis standing in front of a blackboard on which he had chalked a diagram of the central dogma.[25]

*

At the beginning of 1966 Francis was back on the road again, flying to La Jolla for his annual visit to the Salk Institute. While he was away, Odile wrote to him reflecting on their relationship: 'I really am very proud of you. I suppose that prolonged co-habitation tends to obscure the important things and one gets enmeshed in lots of little details which are relatively trivial. I only get a chance to take a good look at you when you're away.'[26] But soon there was terrible news: his brother Tony was gravely ill. Odile wrote: 'Your brother phoned in the middle of the night hoping to catch you before your journey. (…) His time may be very short and he would urge you to take a trip to New Zealand,' explaining that Tony wanted Francis to have tests as soon as possible.[27]

Odile was understandably concerned – 'please, don't leave anything to chance Darling. I shall be very anxious about you.' A few days later Francis felt unwell and was admitted to the Scripps Clinic in San Diego for tests.[28] Distressed that he could not travel to his brother's bedside – they had not seen each other for years – he was now deeply worried about both Tony's health and his own. Although Francis's tests turned out fine, his brother died of cancer on 8 March 1966, aged only forty-seven.[29]

*

A few weeks later there were two pieces of good news from the Royal Society – Kreisel was elected a Fellow (the citation described him as 'the most distinguished of the British mathematicians currently working in mathematical logic') while Crick was awarded the Croonian Lecture, one of the Society's highest honours, which he gave in May 1966.[30] Francis could not immediately begin preparing the lecture, as he became deeply preoccupied by Odile's health. While he was away, she underwent what should have been a routine minor operation, but severe complications required a prolonged hospital stay and appointments extending into May.[31] Together with the death of his brother and his own health scare, all this made Crick's life feel a bit less stable.

With Odile still not wholly recovered, Francis gave his Croonian lecture in May, on the genetic code.[32] The published version lacks his usual flourishes, perhaps reflecting his worries over Odile. He explained the basic mechanisms of protein synthesis, before focusing on the nature of the genetic code and the experimental results upon which it was based. The table of the genetic code he presented, with abbreviations for each amino acid corresponding to all but three of the sixty-four possible codons, revealed a bizarre degree of redundancy (for example, arginine was encoded by six codons, whereas tryptophan had only one). He then showed how the 'phase shift' mutants he had studied with Brenner and Leslie Barnett in 1961 could be used to explain changes in amino acid sequence, before culminating in the most enigmatic part of the code – what he called the punctuation marks, codons that seemed to initiate or terminate the assembly of the amino acid. The START codon appeared to be AUG, which oddly also coded for the amino acid methionine. The STOP codons were UAG and UAA, which were whimsically called amber and ochre, respectively, while a third class of STOP mutations was called opal – it was suspected but not certain that opal was UGA – hence the question mark in the table.*[33]

Crick's closing argument emphasised how the central dogma and the molecular understanding of protein synthesis and the genetic code fitted neatly with how natural selection operated and also explained why there was no inheritance of acquired characteristics.

---

*Amber mutants were named after a student, Harris Bernstein, who had helped in a tedious mutagenesis experiment in a US phage laboratory that led to the discovery of the mutation – 'Bernstein' is the German word for amber. Two other mutants that also stopped protein synthesis were named ochre and opal as jokes. The article announcing the amber mutants was variously described as 'in press', 'in preparation' or 'in contemplation' for over half a century; it eventually appeared in 2012. Epstein, R. H., Bolle, A. and Steinberg, C. M. (2012), Amber mutants of bacteriophage T4D: their isolation and genetic characterization. *Genetics* 190:831–40.

2nd → 1st ↓	U	C	A	G	3rd ↓
U	Phe	Ser	Tyr	Cys	U
	Phe	Ser	Tyr	Cys	C
	Leu	Ser	ochre	?	A
	Leu	Ser	amber	Tryp	G
C	Leu	Pro	His	Arg	U
	Leu	Pro	His	Arg	C
	Leu	Pro	GluN	Arg	A
	Leu	Pro	GluN	Arg	G
A	Ileu	Thr	AspN	Ser	U
	Ileu	Thr	AspN	Ser	C
	Ileu	Thr	Lys	Arg	A
	Met	Thr	Lys	Arg	G
G	Val	Ala	Asp	Gly	U
	Val	Ala	Asp	Gly	C
	Val	Ala	Glu	Gly	A
	Val	Ala	Glu	Gly	G

FIGURE 1. The four standard bases, uracil, cytosine, adenine and guanine are represented by the letters U, C, A and G respectively. The first base of any triplet is indicated on the left, the second base at the top and the third at the right of the figure. The twenty amino acids are represented by their standard abbreviations. Thus 'Phe' stands for phenylalanine, etc. The triplets marked 'ochre' and 'amber' are believed to signal the termination of the polypeptide chain. Those associated with chain initiation are not marked in this figure.

Although the exact role of the punctuation mark codons had to be verified, and the code needed to be studied in other organisms, the circumstantial evidence from tobacco plants and human haemoglobins left little doubt that the genetic code was universal. 'We can now confidently look forward to placing increasing areas of biology on a molecular basis,' he concluded.

A little over six weeks later, Francis gave a similar talk at the opening of the Cold Spring Harbor symposium, which was on the genetic code, but with a bit more swing – this time he was speaking in the relaxed and excited company of well-informed friends. He promised to put on a better performance than in 1963 – even the title of his lecture suggested a degree of confidence that had apparently been lacking three years earlier: 'The Genetic Code. Yesterday, Today and Tomorrow'.[34]

Crick's bold opening words summed up the excitement at the meeting: 'This is an historic occasion.' It was. The accumulation of data over the previous two years meant that, to all extents and purposes, the genetic code was now known. That work had not been organised by any official body, nor had it been the subject of any focused funding. Instead, for more than a decade, hundreds of researchers around the world had devoted their time and ingenuity to trying to solve the problem. One man had been involved throughout, and his ideas had shaped the whole field: Francis Crick.

Although some self-congratulation would have been understandable, Crick's title showed what he intended to do in his lecture – give credit to everyone who had contributed, from the earliest conceptual approaches through to the most recent identification of precise codon–amino acid relations. He singled out Nirenberg and Khorana and highlighted the work of Robert Holley, who had recently sequenced the first tRNA molecule. Their results, which had come in a rush over the previous two years, were decisive in enabling the full code to be drawn up. In 1968 all three men shared the Nobel Prize in Physiology or Medicine 'for their interpretation of the genetic code and its function in protein synthesis'.

As the person who had been thinking the most intensely and the longest about the code, Crick allowed himself to give some advice to those who were venturing into more controversial areas such as the origin of the code, warning them that without experimental evidence, excited theoretical speculation would be unhealthy – 'One of the reasons why I enumerated, in this introduction, something of the early history of the code was to show how little theory was able to contribute,' he said.

Understandably, his conclusion had an elegiac air. He had been working on this topic for thirteen years, beginning when some in the audience were still students. Now it had all been resolved, in part (although he did not even hint at this) through his inspiration and intellectual leadership. This was a great achievement, he said, allowing a glimmer of pride to appear in the final sentence, as, without saying so, he described how the 'central problem' he had identified in his PhD thesis had now been resolved through the cracking of the genetic code:

It is, in a sense, the key to molecular biology because it shows how the two great polymer languages, the nucleic acid language and the protein language, are linked together. It is not only important to know the details for their own sake, but by knowing these details we become quite confident that our general ideas, such as the sequence hypothesis, are indeed correct. It will be difficult, after this, for doubters not to accept the fundamental assumptions of molecular biology which we have been trying to prove for so many years.

The penultimate day of the meeting was 8 June 1966 – Crick's fiftieth birthday. To mark this event and his role in cracking the code, a party was organised on the lawn outside the lecture hall. A telegram arrived, supposedly from London and signed 'Elizabeth', congratulating Crick on reaching the age of *sixty*. Then a scantily clad dancer burst out of a large pretend cake, celebrating the birthday boy in front of the nearly all-male crowd.[35] This was followed by DNA pioneer Rollin Hotchkiss reciting a piece of doggerel he had composed for the occasion, 'Merry Crickmas'.[36] The poem described the winding road from the double helix to the cracking of the code; it was long and not very good, but it revealed the warmth of feeling towards Francis in the scientific community.

All these japes were Watson's doing. A little over a week later, Crick wrote to the Director of Cold Spring Harbor, John Cairns: 'I look forward with some trepidation to the photographic illustrations! It was nice of you to go to so much trouble to produce a really memorable birthday celebration. I hope when the time comes I can rely on your help to spring something on Jim on one of his birthdays.'[37] Crick need not have worried; although there were photographs of himself and 'Fifi' the dancer, they did not become public until now (the copies in the Cold Spring Harbor Laboratory Archive are restricted until 2054).[38]

*

At the same time as Francis basked in the triumph of cracking the code, he began to realise that the public was about to get a view of him that he felt to be unfair and deeply intrusive, in the shape of Jim Watson's planned book about the discovery of the double helix.

Watson had first told him of this in summer 1965; the pair were dining in a restaurant near Harvard Square when Watson read out a brief chapter from his gossipy account, which was then called *Honest Jim*.*[39] Crick was bemused; 'Who could possibly want to read stuff like this?' he wondered.

The draft contained striking pen-portraits of Crick, beginning with the intimate opening phrase, 'I have never seen Francis in a modest mood', continuing with the claim that 'he was given to stealing other people's ideas' and that 'for 35 years he had not stopped talking and nothing of value had emerged', culminating in the statement that 'there was no restraint in Francis's enthusiasm about young women' (Odile, Watson said, did not mind Crick's predilection).[40] This was clearly not your normal piece of writing about scientific discovery, nor even a straightforward memoir; it was something utterly novel.

Unlike Francis, many people who read Watson's manuscript, especially the younger generation, adored his way of telling the story.[41] A young Cambridge friend of Watson's said the first chapter was tremendous; absorbing the book's intimate use of first names, she told him: 'I don't know Francis, but had this been written about me I would be highly delighted.'[42] Watson's studiedly familiar descriptions of the participants, all Francis and Maurice and Rosy and Max, was daring at the time – scientists were still respectfully referred to by their surnames and titles. And the book was not solemn, but really rather funny – Watson's friend told him that although she had followed his instruction to keep the draft confidential, 'it was hard because I couldn't conceal my laughter and I was longing to share the joke by reading out little bits'. As she read on, she began to wonder about Crick's potential reaction: 'I wonder if Francis has seen any of this yet – his reactions to it might almost provide you with a sequel!'

---

*Watson was partly referencing the Kingsley Amis comic novel *Lucky Jim*, about a hapless young British academic, which came out in 1954. There are structural parallels between *The Double Helix* (which in some respects is a campus novel) and *Lucky Jim*, including Amis's misogynistic description of a central female character, Margaret Peel, and Watson's distorted portrayal of Franklin. Maddox, B. (2002), *Rosalind Franklin: The Dark Lady of DNA* (London: Harper Collins), p. 315.

Eventually she warned Watson that she was sure that the book was libellous, although she felt this was 'tragic', because 'the libellous bits are so hilarious. I hope the lawyer doesn't mutilate it too much.'[43]

Watson first considered writing about the discovery of the double helix in 1962, after going off-piste in his lecture accepting the Research Corporation award; within two years he was sending draft chapters of his 'novel about the discovery of DNA' to an enthusiastic editor.[44] By the end of 1965, a first draft was circulated to dozens of colleagues, including Francis, Pauling, Perutz, Kendrew and Bragg. Busy with his hectic travelling and disturbed by the death of his brother, Crick had neither the time nor the inclination to read it closely. Nevertheless, after he returned to Cambridge at the end of March 1966, Crick sent Watson a fifteen-page list of errors and differences in interpretation, together with some fundamental objections to the kind of book his friend had written. Francis contrasted *Honest Jim* with his own account of the discovery, given in those lectures at Oxford and Cambridge five years earlier:

> The difference between my lecture and your book is that my lecture had a lot more intellectual content and nothing like so much gossip. (...) Your book on the other hand, is mainly gossip and I think it a pity in this way that there is so much of it that it obscures some of the important conclusions which can be drawn of what we did at the time.[45]

Surprisingly, Crick said nothing about Watson's portrayal of 'Francis' – neither the mixture of arrogance and incompetence, nor the accusation of intellectual theft, nor even the descriptions of his womanising and of Odile's flirtatious nature.

Watson replied amicably, accepting some of Crick's suggestions, disputing others and promising to rewrite the opening chapters.[46] All seemed to be going smoothly. In the summer, both Watson and Crick attended a NATO-sponsored molecular biology summer school on the Greek island of Spetsai* – Francis sailed there in his new blue and white motorboat, the *Eye of Heaven*, as part of a trip around the Greek islands.[47]

---

*Now transliterated as Spetses.

During the breaks between lectures, Watson's book was a topic of conversation; but Francis seemed 'detached, patient and bemused' when he discussed the book with Watson, according to a friend.[48]

Relations between Watson and Crick remained good – at the end of September 1966, Francis sent Watson a friendly letter saying he did not approve of the new working title (*Base Pairs*).[49] He also felt that *Honest Jim* was an 'excellent' title, although he does not seem to have realised the ironic implication that Watson sought to put into the reader's mind. Equally significantly, Crick was merely 'not at all keen' about letting Watson use his photograph. Given his usual hostility to such requests, the fact that he said he would reflect further on the matter was surely positive, as was his signing off – his usual 'Yours ever, Francis'.

It would be three years before Crick was again so friendly with Watson.

*

Less than two weeks later, Crick wrote angry letters to both Watson and the publishers, Harvard University Press.[50] He told Watson he was opposed to publication because of the style of the book – there was 'far too much gossip' and 'the intellectual content is too low' – and because it would expose him to personal publicity. To the publisher, he was clearer: 'I am sure you will agree that any law court will find it defamatory. In addition I regard it as a gross invasion of my privacy.' Watson could be forgiven for feeling bewildered.

Crick's dramatic turnabout came after he spoke to Maurice Wilkins, who had just read Watson's latest draft. When Watson first sent Wilkins the manuscript, he predicted that Wilkins would want to shoot him.[51] That was pretty much what happened now. In the space of a few days, Wilkins and Crick worked themselves up into a righteous fury, prompted by the request from the publishers that they sign release forms approving the book. Wilkins particularly objected to Watson's descriptions of 'Francis as a feather-brained hyperthyroid, me an overgentlemanly mug,' but irrespective of the accuracy of Watson's pen-portraits, Wilkins and Crick were really concerned that by putting gossip before science, Watson's account would affect

1. On the beach at Cold Spring Harbor, summer 1954.

A structure for D.N.A.

Pauling and Corey[1] have recently proposed a structure
for nucleic acid. ~~Their manuscript~~ They were kind enough to make ~~was very kindly made~~

Their manuscript
available to us in advance of publication. ~~We feel that~~ In our opinion their

structure is unsatisfactory for two reasons:

① the ~~structure~~ material which gives the x-ray diagrams is the
~~sex~~ salt, nor the acid. The absence of the hydrogen
atom means that there is nothing to hold the structure

some of together.
② the Van der Waal ~~contacts~~ distance ~~in this structure~~
appear to be too ~~close~~ small.

~~So~~ We wish to put forward a radically different structure
for the salt of deoxyribose nucleic acid (D.N.A.). This
each coiled round the fibre axis.
structure has two helical chains ~~a around a common axis~~
~~which is also the fibre axis~~.

2. The first draft of the Watson and Crick paper on the
structure of DNA, March 1953, written by Crick.

3. Model of the double helix, made by Crick in April–May 1953 for a talk in Edinburgh.

4. Fiftieth birthday celebrations for Francis at Cold Spring Harbor Laboratory, June 1966. 'Fifi' the dancer is standing next to Crick (*centre*); the white 'cake' from which she emerged is on the floor. Crouching on the right in a white shirt is Watson.

5. LMB Governing Board, 1967. *L-R*: Hugh Huxley, John Kendrew, Max Perutz, Crick, Fred Sanger, Sydney Brenner. Note Brenner's very different attire and footwear, and the cigarette he is attempting to hide in his left hand.

6. Crick and Christof Koch, early 1990s.

7. Crick and Watson on the fortieth anniversary of
the discovery of the double helix, 1993.

8. Sketch of Kreisel by Odile, late 1940s.

9. Captain Crick, mid-1960s.

10. Sketch of Crick in the Green Door by Odile, late 1940s.

11. Odile, Francis and Jacqueline punting down the Cam from Mill Pond, mid-1950s. They have just passed under the old Silver Street bridge.

public perception of their profession. Raised in a pre-war English world of respect for authority and science, they were shocked that their young American friend did not share their outlook. In a way, their dignity was under attack.

In reply to Crick's letter, Watson calmly emphasised that he wanted to portray the people and events as he saw them at the time and to 'tell people how our brand of science was done'.[52] This was one of the points that was highlighted in a letter to Crick from a graduate student at Harvard who had read the manuscript: 'Like so many others who consider you and Jim our heroes, I was terribly interested to read about the human side of the DNA story and the complex interactions occurring between people involved in a great discovery. This is something we never learn through scientific publications. I do not know how you could consider the book defamatory.'[53] Watson, younger than Crick and Wilkins and from a less deferential culture, was immersed in undergraduate teaching and sensed the deep changes that were taking place among young people. He was far more in touch with what the coming generation thought about the world than the two stuffy quinquagenarians in England.

Watson pointed out that the book teemed with positive comments about Francis, beginning with the third sentence, which claimed that Crick 'is much talked about, usually with reverence, and soon he may be considered in the category of Rutherford or Bohr', and he promised to add an Epilogue 'that would put Rosalind's first-class mind into better perspective'.[54] Finally, Watson pleaded that his friend should act like a gentleman and prevent 'the ugly spectacle of a Crick-Watson duel'.

But a duel is exactly what ensued. Crick warned that he might sue Watson for libel and his letters became sharper as the wound smarted: 'I can assure you that if I had known you were going to write the sort of book you have written I would never have collaborated with you.'[55] Watson sorrowfully replied that the prospect of 'our long, most productive, and thoroughly enjoyable friendship coming to an unnecessary end thoroughly depresses me,' but there was no room for compromise, it seemed.[56]

Other people began to get involved, stoking the fire by sending Francis copies of their letters to Watson. Linus Pauling took issue with many parts of the manuscript, listing Watson's scornful language around his incorrect structure for DNA: 'blooper ... stupid ... blunder ... unbelievable mistake ... nonsense ... screwy ... infantile ... looking like an ass'.[57] Pauling insisted to Watson that, contrary to the suggestions in the book, he had not made a schoolboy chemical error with his proposed structure, and that Watson's abusive terms were quite unjustified.

Meanwhile, Watson had overcome Sir Lawrence Bragg's initial hostility to the project and persuaded him to write a Foreword, providing the scientific establishment's seal of approval.[58] Feeling abandoned, Crick wrote to the President of Harvard, Nathan Pusey, pointing out that the publication of an account of joint work where the collaborators objected would damage the university's reputation.[59] With no sign of a change of position from Harvard, the publisher, or Watson, Crick became incandescent with rage, lashing out at his friend in ways that were intentionally hurtful:

> Before long the New York Review of Books may be wondering whether the tone of your book (which certainly needs some explanation) can be accounted for by, say, the hypothesis that you are a latent homosexual. Your strange behaviour with young women and the fact that at 38 you are still unmarried could easily suggest such an idea.

Crick next descended into playground abuse, satirically saying he was planning to write a book called *The Loose Screw*: 'The first chapter will deal with your lack of manual dexterity, your juvenile handwriting, your speech impediment, your early failures in public speaking,' and so on.[60] By this stage, letters between the two men were signed with cold civility 'Yours sincerely'.

By the beginning of 1967, Crick's fury was burning out – he told Wilkins that it would be difficult to prevent publication and suggested they concentrate on 'eliminating the more offensive and misleading parts'.[61] That goal seemed to have been achieved in March, when Watson said that he had extensively revised the manuscript 'to meet virtually every *specific* objection' made a year earlier.[62] But when Francis read the new version he went ballistic, sending Watson a furious six-page letter, pompously describing the book as 'vulgar popularisation … indefensible'.[63] As the letter went on, Francis became increasingly angry, claiming that a psychiatrist who had studied Watson's collection of modern art thought 'it could only have been made by a man who hated women,' and making a vicious insinuation that suggested that Crick had become slightly unhinged: 'In a similar way another psychiatrist, who read *Honest Jim*, said that what emerged most strongly was your love for your sister. This was much discussed by your friends while you were working in Cambridge, but so far they have refrained from writing about it. I doubt if others will show this restraint.' Evidently feeling pleased with himself, Francis sent copies of his incendiary letter to ten people involved in the dispute.[64] Watson, unfazed, supposedly pinned it up on a Harvard noticeboard.[65]

In April, with Bragg, Perutz and Kendrew all backing publication, Crick accepted defeat, admitting to Bragg that he should have taken a firmer line from the outset.[66] With the exception of Wilkins, Francis had few supporters among his friends – even Brenner, who had enjoyed a bit of banter about possible titles for Crick's imaginary riposte, said nothing to Watson. Crick was isolated and his raging letter of April 1967 had gone much too far.*

Then matters took a surprising turn. For months, Wilkins had been writing about the affair to his friend and confidant, the US-based chemist Leonard Hamilton. Hamilton now decided to get involved and – presumably with the agreement of Wilkins and Crick – engaged Robert Montgomery of the US law firm that a few months earlier had represented Jackie Kennedy in a public spat over a book about her husband's assassination. It seemed the row between Watson and Crick might similarly be heading for the courtroom, and the newspapers.

In mid-May, Montgomery sent a letter to Harvard University Press threatening legal action if the book were to appear. Surprisingly, this seemed to have the desired effect – the Press decided not to

---

*Crick completely forgot about this letter. When shown it later by Robert Olby, he said 'I see it contains some good points.' Crick to Olby, 8 July 1985, PP/CRI/J/2/5/2.

publish, although they insisted that this decision was simply because the university did not wish to take sides in a dispute between eminent scientists.[67]

Crick was pleased at the outcome, but his relief was short-lived.[68] Watson's publisher at the Press had left for a new company, taking Watson's book with him, arranging for it to appear under the blander title *The Double Helix*.[69] Urged on by Hamilton and Wilkins, Montgomery wrote to the new publishers, again threatening legal action.[70] This was a bluff – Montgomery told Wilkins and Crick that their case for an injunction was hopeless and urged them to drop the matter. The blistering letter Francis had written Watson in April was probably actionable and could easily lead to a countersuit if things got ugly, the lawyer advised.[71] Defeated, Wilkins and Crick withdrew their opposition.[72]

The Double Helix was now substantially improved by Bragg's Foreword, the removal of the more offensive passages, two additions from Watson – a scene-setting Preface explaining the kind of book he had written and a considered Epilogue highlighting Franklin's contribution, no longer misnaming her as 'Rosy'. Hamilton tried to stir things up one more time, sending Crick a cutting from *The New York Times* about the row and deploring what he saw as 'a transparent example of the crass commercial interest of your friend Jim Watson'.[73] Crick's reply was downbeat: 'The book seems to be arousing a lot of interest. I expect it will all die down soon.'[74]

There was one final twist. The UK edition would be subject to the far stricter English libel laws so the British publishers, Weidenfeld and Nicolson, had instructed a rising star in English libel law, Peter Carter-Ruck, to study the affair. After showing the book to someone who knew Crick well and considered that Watson's portrayal was 'as large and true as life', Carter-Ruck concluded that publication could go ahead.[75] The book appeared in two parts in *The Atlantic* magazine in January and February 1968 and was published in the USA immediately afterwards. British publication was scheduled for the end of April, and the publishers proudly sent Watson copies of the cover – the front carried a glowing quote from Crick's friend C. P. Snow and, on the back, there were three teasing questions relating to the behaviour of an unnamed scientist: his loud voice, his love of gossip about women and his taste for kissing them at parties.[76] Watson was livid, immediately firing off a telegram to Weidenfeld and Nicolson, threatening legal action against them if the cover appeared.[77] He was not only upset about hurting a man who he cared for greatly, he still feared that Francis might sue, and told the publisher that 'if it is your outrageous jackets which set him off, I shall insist that *you* pay all the costs of any libel battle'.

The publishers instantly promised, on the personal responsibility of Mr Weidenfeld himself, to destroy all copies of the cover and to ensure that publicity for the book avoided any hint of scandal or mischievous gossip.[78] In fact, the London *Evening Standard* had already quoted the jackets and their supposedly scandalous content in an article about the book back in January.[79] Crick knew nothing of all this, and there was no lawsuit. The offending covers, which Watson kept in his archives at Cold Spring Harbor, are still redacted from online viewing.

The public response to *The Double Helix* was overwhelmingly positive. As Watson hoped, younger readers were particularly enthusiastic; the frankness with which he described the people involved made the book seem somehow part of the burgeoning counterculture. In California, poet Michael McClure wrote to a friend that he was sitting drinking wine, listening to an LP by Nico and 'reading DOUBLE HELIX by Watson & putting up Sir Francis Crick's picture on my wall.'*[80] The book spent seventeen weeks on *The New York Times* best-seller list, with over seventy thousand hardback copies sold in the first year; over thirty thousand copies of the British edition were sold in the same period.[81] It went on to be translated into nearly twenty languages and to sell more than a million copies; over half a century later, it is still in print.

---

*It was often assumed, particularly by Americans, that Crick had been knighted – in fact he turned down the honour. He would often correct this mistake, for example 'P.S. Not knighted yet.' Crick to Greenblatt, 13 March 1970, PP/CRI/D/1/1/7. The pinnacle of this confusion came in 1979 when 'Sir Francis Crick' was the answer to a clue in *The New York Times* crossword. Crick pointed out the error, to the embarrassment of the setter (PP/CRI/D/1/4/18).

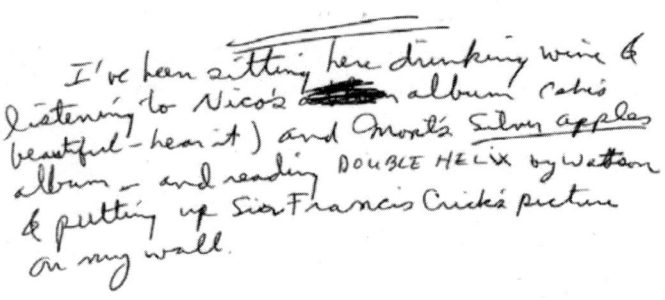

I've been sitting here drinking wine & listening to Nico's ~~new~~ album (this beautiful — hear it) and Monti's Silver apples album — and reading DOUBLE HELIX by Watson & putting up Sir Francis Crick's picture on my wall.

*

Crick's conflict with Watson was sharp and long, partly because they had been friends for fifteen years, but also because there was no movement on Watson's side. Like a child having a tantrum faced with a reasonable but implacable parent, Crick could only escalate the argument, throwing verbal furniture around until, exhausted, he accepted the inevitable.

The reasons underlying this extreme behaviour were complex. On the surface, the row was about the book's content. Apart from the issue of his privacy, Crick was concerned about its gossipy tone and its portrayal of scientists. This was not because he disliked gossip, but because of how he thought science should be presented to the public.[82] But this was not just a difference of style, it was also a difference of generation. Crick's pre-war English reserve put personality in the background; Watson's brash young American approach chimed much more with the growing mood of the 1960s, and it chafed Crick profoundly.

This difference in attitude also revealed an uncomfortable truth. Francis was a man used to being at the cutting edge of things, but he was now in his fifties and beginning to look out of touch. A year earlier, the artist Françoise Gilot* had written an intimate account of her years with Pablo Picasso; when the book was translated into French, Picasso became furious, attempting to get it banned by the French courts, dragooning his intellectual and artistic pals to write articles and to sign the inevitable petition. Crick's response was less extreme, but it had the same roots in a clash of generations and the betrayal of intimacy, even love.

---

*Gilot became a friend of the Cricks after her marriage to Jonas Salk in 1970.

Crick's view of the book gradually mellowed and in his own memoir, published twenty years later, he accepted that he had been wrong to think that the personal side of science should remain hidden: 'I now appreciate how skilful Jim was, not only in making the book read like a detective story (several people told me they were unable to put it down) but also by managing to include a surprisingly large amount of the science, although naturally the more mathematical parts had to be left out.'[83]

Friendly relations with Jim were eventually restored, and at the end of 1969 Watson and his new wife, Elizabeth, stayed at Portugal Place.[84]

*

During the row over *The Double Helix*, Crick's increasingly irascible mood seeped into his relations with other researchers, leading him to completely lose his cool on two other occasions. At the beginning of 1966, Khorana got into a spat with Nirenberg over a set of articles on the genetic code which they had all agreed to send to the *Journal of Molecular Biology*.[85] Khorana claimed that Nirenberg had pulled a fast one on his competitors by rushing his article into print in a more prestigious journal.[86] Crick immediately took Khorana's side and scolded Nirenberg: 'I feel you owe both Gobind and me an explanation, if not an apology. Would you please write to me to explain your position.'[87] Nirenberg was outraged, insisting that Crick's interpretation of his behaviour was 'wrong in every respect – and thoroughly unjustified'.[88] Crick's reply reads ironically in the light of what had been happening with Watson: 'Relax! Relax! I didn't really believe you had acted in an elaborate underhand way, but I had to point out to you how it might appear to someone looking from the outside.'[89]

The argument with Watson had primed Crick for a fight, even over minor issues, and a few months later it happened again. When Stephen Pelc, of the King's College London biophysics unit, published two articles in *Nature* on the structure and function of tRNA molecules, Crick immediately realised they were completely wrong and sent a condescending letter to the King's researcher:

I hope you will forgive me if I say as you have no previous experience of model building and no special knowledge of stereochemistry one is not inclined to accept your claims without checking them. I can see that this might take your small group a certain time, but this is no excuse for publishing sloppy papers. If the problem is too difficult for you, you should not undertake it, let alone publish on it.[90]

Pelc calmly replied that Francis should take the time to write a 'reasonably worded letter'. Admonished, Crick apologised and subsequent letters were more friendly ('Dear Stephen'), but with Pelc refusing to retract his article, Crick submitted a crushing letter to *Nature*, pointing out that Pelc's model was impossible and that the nucleotide sequences had been built backwards – 'their AAG was in fact GAA'.[91] Crick even wrote private letters to Wilkins, suggesting he should investigate Pelc's previous work and implying that the MRC should sack him.[92]

These incidents with Watson, Nirenberg and Pelc show Crick at his most aggressive and over-confident. They demand explanation, for although one furious row may be regarded as a misfortune, three implies an appetite. Crick could certainly lose his temper in academic disputes, but something deeper was going on in 1966–67.

As Francis had sensed for several years, the glory days of molecular biology were drawing to a close, and the completion of the genetic code in 1966 clearly marked a watershed. Crick's leading role was celebrated at the Cold Spring Harbor meeting in June of that year, but seen in another light his birthday party was also a wake. These intellectual problems, combined with the health worries brought on by his brother's death and Odile's illness, suggest that underneath Crick's aggressive, hyper-confident responses there lurked a profound doubt about his future. After twenty years of extraordinary success, he was now faced with the challenge of, if not repeating that success, at least having a coherent strategy that might perhaps enable him to do so. That nagging anxiety, that night-time doubt, seems to have impelled his enraged over-reactions.

FINDING A
NEW FOCUS

In October 1963, following a series of discussions with Francis, Sydney Brenner submitted a document to the MRC outlining their future research plans. After accurately predicting that 'no major discovery comparable in importance to that of, say, messenger RNA, now lies ahead,' Brenner concluded that the *'new major problem* in molecular biology is the genetics and biochemistry of control mechanisms in cellular development.'[1] Brenner proposed to study a small nematode worm which contained around one thousand cells, beginning by identifying all the cells in the worm, and their lineages, and to start looking for mutants. This eventually became a massive research area involving thousands of scientists around the world, and led to Brenner's Nobel Prize in 2002.

Although Crick was heavily involved in developing Brenner's idea, he did not join his friend in this endeavour.[2] This might look odd given the subsequent success of nematode research, but Crick and Brenner rarely studied the same problem, despite their close working relationship. Furthermore, Brenner's new project involved a vast amount of fiddly experimental work as he toyed with the rearing conditions and then began creating mutants. The work was painstaking, and progress was so slow that at the end of 1968 Brenner reported to a colleague that after four years' work, the anatomical side was only 'reasonably well advanced', and while over two hundred mutants had been found, most involved movement defects, probably to do with muscle function.[3] There was little sign of fundamental insights into development or nervous system function; the first paper about Brenner's work did not appear until 1974. Such ponderous progress was not to Crick's taste.[4]

Instead, Crick initially thought about working on 'the complete solution' of the bacterium *E. coli*.[5] Brenner, ever the wit, called this 'Project K' (for 'koli'), because he and Crick had already discussed projects on phage lambda ('L'), the mouse ('M') and the nematode ('N').[6] The aim was to understand everything about how the single-celled organism functioned, from the activity of its membranes, through its genetic and physiological control mechanisms to the behaviour of populations of cells. Although the approach flowed from the reductionist methods that had dominated Crick's thinking, and molecular biology, Francis admitted that it was unlikely that literally everything about *E. coli* would ever be known (for example it was improbable that every protein it contained would be characterised, never mind all their interactions). This idea was extremely ambitious – so much so that Crick later suggested that the future European Molecular Biology Laboratory (EMBL) might be entirely devoted to the idea – and Francis never worked on it.*

Instead, he became interested in how patterned, organised sheets of cells appear during embryonic development. In the summer of 1968, he became temporarily fixated by fingerprints, with their unique patterns that are determined by a mixture of genetic and environmental factors. Trying to find a short-cut to expertise, Crick contacted the medical geneticist Lionel Penrose and asked for some references that would get him up to speed on the topic – 'A few titles on a postcard would be all I want,' he explained.[7] He also borrowed *Finger Prints, Palms and Soles: An Introduction to Dermatoglyphics* from the Police College Library, but it soon became evident that while

---

* Various scientific consortia have explored this project over the years; it still has not been realised. Much later, Crick recognised that his suggestion was 'hopelessly premature' given the lack of genetic and computing tools at the time. Crick to Wanner, 1 October 2002, PP/CRI/J/2/22/2.

there was a vast amount of data available, it would be extremely difficult to develop an experimental approach to the topic.[8]

A solution appeared in the work of Peter Lawrence, a young insect biologist in the Genetics Department at Cambridge. Lawrence did not study fingerprints, but another two-dimensional problem – the patterning of insect cuticle – using delicate experimental techniques.[9] Shortly after Crick's brief fascination with fingerprints had faded, Lawrence gave a talk at the Genetics Department; having heard about his deep understanding of insect biology, Crick and Brenner went along (their unusual presence combined with their late arrival caused a minor disturbance). Enthused by Lawrence's lecture, in particular his suggestion that a chemical gradient within the insect cuticle determined the orientation of the hairs on the outside of the insect, Crick and Brenner decided on the spot to recruit the young man as an MRC researcher.[10]

Since the beginning of the century, the role of chemicals in development had been suggested as a way of explaining one of the fundamental problems of embryology – how a cell knows what it needs to turn into. In 1924, Hans Spemann and Hilde Mangold showed that in amphibians, a group of skin cells known as the organizer influenced the development of surrounding cells. Although this discovery led to Spemann's 1935 Nobel Prize, it proved extremely difficult to identify how the organizer exerted its influence and scientists eventually drifted away from the subject. In 1952, Alan Turing published a paper on the role of chemicals in producing patterns during development; Francis heard Turing talk on the topic, and was greatly impressed (this was the only time the two men met) but Turing's ideas had little immediate impact.[11] By the middle of the 1960s, most leading developmental biologists viewed the idea that chemical gradients shaped development as very old-fashioned.

However, Lawrence and a number of younger researchers, including Hildegard Stumpf at Göttingen, Michael Locke in Cleveland and Lewis Wolpert at King's College London, were becoming interested in the topic.[12] In 1968 and 1969, Wolpert published papers suggesting that a chemical gradient, combined with different response thresholds to that gradient in each type of cell, could produce what he described as positional information – telling the cell where it is

– and lead to the appearance of patterns.[13] This idea got a very rocky reception – when Wolpert gave a talk to developmental biologists at Woods Hole, it was 'a total and utter disaster,' he recalled.[14] Everyone ignored him after he spoke. The next day a friend explained that the assembled experts '*hated* the idea of gradients'; this made Wolpert utterly miserable, but his morale was boosted when Brenner told him that Crick was impressed by his hypothesis, although that was not enough to prevent Wolpert from putting the idea to one side for some time.

Francis was attracted by the apparent simplicity of the theoretical explanation and the implication that complex effects could be explained by molecular activity. The sexy-sounding term positional information was also right up Crick's street – a developmental application of the informational approach to biology that he had pioneered. While Lawrence pursued his experimental work, Crick thought about the practical and theoretical problems raised by the diffusion of chemicals in biological tissues, relying on Lawrence to put him right on the technical detail – 'An amateur like myself could easily go astray but for his guidance,' he wrote.[15] Lawrence did not have an intense collaboration with Francis but they shared common interests in theatre and gardening, especially the cultivation of roses, and became good friends. Above all, as with Brenner, the experimentalist and the theoretician were able to enrich each other's thinking.

*

As Lawrence's rapid recruitment suggests, life at the LMB was very informal. Following a reorganisation in 1964, Crick and Brenner were now joint leaders of the new Division of Cell Biology.[16] Mark Bretscher, who had worked with Francis since the days of the Hut, recalled Crick's relaxed routine:

> He would come to his office around 9.30 – 10am and the day would seem to be filled with writing letters and maybe looking at journals, interspersed with coffee at 11am, lunch at 1.00 pm and tea at 4 pm. (...) He would sometimes wander round to ask people what they thought about this or that problem. In

so doing, he was always circumspect and most courteous: he would peep into your lab to see if you were busy and, if you were, wait until you saw him and then he would ask if you could pop by his office when you were free.[17]

Crick and Brenner's style helped produce a thriving laboratory culture, as one visitor told Francis: 'I envy the sense of excellence and excitement which you and Sidney create around you.'[18] As well as informal discussions in the canteen, Crick introduced a more formal informality – an annual week-long set of internal LMB seminars at which everyone presented their recent findings, soon known as Crick Week. Together with Brenner he also encouraged the development of new research areas, each of which would require the 'right' organism – the system that could provide the best way of approaching the problem, combining manipulability and simplicity.[19] Inevitably, a different organism would be best for each sub-area – 'the actual choice involves a deep intellectual analysis of the nature of the problem and the sort of methods likely to be required to solve it,' he told a colleague.

New recruits were not necessarily focused on a particular project, as Crick explained to a colleague:

It is better to start a new line of work with some hope of interacting with work already going on in the same place. (...) However, the most important rule of all is not to worry overmuch about exactly which subjects should be followed, provided the subjects chosen are acceptable, but to find good people who already want to do them, and preferably good *young* people, in their late twenties or thirties.

There were problems, however, as LMB colleagues became frustrated at the length of Crick's annual trips to the Salk; heeding their complaints, Francis eventually reduced the time he spent in La Jolla.[20] Furthermore, Crick and Brenner's habit of inviting suitable researchers to work with them, and only then finding space and funding, became increasingly difficult to maintain – by 1972 they had to find room for thirty-eight researchers and visitors in their Division.[21]

As well as his administrative responsibilities and keeping up with the different research areas being pursued by members of the Division, Francis also had to deal with countless letters from fellow-scientists and members of the public. The requests for information ranged from the trivial, such as his opinion on psychokinesis ('there is nothing in it,' he replied), to the moving – an old lady from Connecticut asked Francis about Huntington's Chorea, a lethal degenerative genetic disease that she feared her grandchildren might have inherited.[22] Crick replied kindly, explaining that work on the disease was very difficult; he also described how it was transmitted, and showed that with luck none of her loved ones would be affected. Her response was fulsome:

> I found your wonderful letter awaiting me. How kind of you in the middle of your busy days to take time out to write it … You explained so much to me that I have never known and really gave me a tiny bit of hope … Maybe some day we may meet and I can tell you how grateful I am.

One of Crick's occasional correspondents, an octogenarian Major from Southport, had heard a radio programme which claimed that a man aged one hundred had been able to memorise a twenty-minute speech following an injection of RNA. Keen to continue with his studies of mathematics, the Major offered himself as a guinea pig and asked Crick to put him in contact with someone working on the topic. Amused, Crick did as he was asked but emphasised that he did not think it very likely that the injection would work. Furthermore, he continued, 'I suspect from the liveliness of your letter that you might not find it much help. However, you might find it fun to try, and I certainly think it would be unlikely to do you any harm.'[23]

Crick also showed his respect, admiration and affection for Bernal, whose retirement was feted at a dinner in London in January 1969. Francis was in the USA and unable to attend, but he wrote a warm letter highlighting Bernal's significance for all those working in Cambridge:

> In this lab we have always regarded you as the scientific father

of our subject. If it was not for your imagination in thinking about what seemed to be impossibly difficult problems, and the encouragement that you gave to Max and Dorothy and the others, people like myself would never have had the opportunity to work in molecular biology, and would have been too timid to tackle the really interesting questions.[24]

*

An impression of Crick's thinking about development can be seen in notes he wrote in the summer of 1968, in which he suggested that while neurons were guided to roughly the right position by diffusing chemicals, their final location was determined through random effects.[25] Francis concluded that neuronal growth responses to a chemical gradient must be simple, whereas contacts between cells might rely upon more complex responses to mixtures of gradients. The point about these notes is not the value of the ideas – they turned out to be either wrong or not entirely correct – but the approach he was using as he entered this new field. The search for fundamental postulates was what underpinned his scientific approach, revealing his ambition and his confidence that, as a newcomer, he could understand things that the established experts in the field could not.

In 1969, Crick decided to publish an article about his work with Lawrence. This would not be a traditional scientific paper, full of experimental detail. Instead, he decided to send an article to *Nature* highlighting the growing interest in gradients as a mechanism for organising cells and as a potential source of positional information. He would also provide a theoretical framework to estimate over what distances diffusion might function and how quickly it might exert its effects.

Written in autumn 1969, with advice from Lawrence and contributions from mathematician Mary Munro, the paper opened with a quote from Wolpert's 1969 paper on positional information, which suggested that the gradients might exert their influence over a distance of at most one hundred cells.[26] Crick had arrived at a similar conclusion on purely theoretical grounds, which he set out in the paper. With typical clarity he explained what interested him: 'The problem can be stated in this way: what is the maximum distance over which a steady concentration gradient could plausibly be set up in the times available during the development of the embryo?'

To come up with a rough answer, Crick simplified his model even further, focusing on the effects of a chemical ('which I shall call a morphogen'*) down a line of cells, thereby reducing development to a one-dimensional phenomenon. Using his knowledge of the viscosity of cell contents, and with help from Munro, Crick calculated that in many cases of development, the times and distances involved were small and compatible with a diffusion model. In a rare printed joke, Crick admitted that other mechanisms might exist in 'cases of "mushroom growth" (as, for example, the growth of mushroom)'. Unfortunately, the model, implemented on a primitive computer along with slide rules and graph paper, did not entirely fit Lawrence's data. Nevertheless, it was a start, and it helped Crick recognise that for the idea of gradients to gain traction, the molecules involved would have to be identified. He concluded: 'If this approach serves to make the idea of diffusion gradients respectable to embryologists it will have served its purpose.'

Francis submitted the article to *Nature* on 1 January 1970.[27] The journal received the manuscript the following day and accepted it immediately, with no changes.[28] Whatever consideration *Nature* gave to the paper, it cannot have lasted more than a couple of hours.[29] Crick's article was sent straight to production and appeared at the end of January as the first major item in that week's issue, following a three-page paper on the doomed British Rail Advanced Passenger Train. It is hard to imagine any other scientist getting such treatment by *Nature* or any other journal, then, before or since.

The responses to the article were varied. Developmental biologists who worked on gradients were happy that someone famous was taking their research seriously, and in such a prestigious location.[30] Wolpert was pleased with how his work was presented and that Crick had picked up an idea that he had abandoned too lightly:

---

* 'Morphogen' had been coined by Turing in 1952. Francis later recalled Turing's paper and his talk on the subject but appears to have forgotten the origin of the term. Crick to Laing, 3 March 1976, PP/CRI/D/1/3/11.

'It is now clear that I was wrong and I find your arguments very persuasive,' he wrote.[31] However, the more conservative developmental biologists – the same crowd who had snubbed Wolpert at Woods Hole – were not impressed. One of them, Elizabeth Deuchar of the University of Bristol, wrote a letter to *Nature* in which she suggested that Crick had canonised a long-discredited idea 'with the double halo of his own reputation and some elegant mathematics'.[32] Diffusion processes were extremely rare, she insisted.

The pair began a brief correspondence, but there was little movement on either side. Deuchar emphasised that Crick's model was at best valid only for a two-dimensional system whereas development was a three-dimensional process. Crick's response highlighted the fundamental difference between them: 'one of the mistakes embryologists have made in the past is to concentrate on the system that they happen to be interested in instead of trying to discover the simplest system which displays the properties they are interested in.'[33] That was one of Crick's key credos, summed up in a snappy riposte.

Crick's paper was undoubtedly important, contributing to the emerging interest in gradients and, as he hoped, drawing the attention of established embryologists to the importance of this approach, even if some of them did not appreciate it. But the article did not have a transformational impact, because there was no overwhelming experimental evidence to back it up. A year later, Lawrence, Crick and Munro published an experimental paper in which the development of insect cuticle seemed to fit fairly well with their gradient model, but the role of morphogens and their mode of function turned out to be more complex than Crick had hoped.[34]

To simplify the problem of development down to one dimension, Francis next explored the way that a blue-green alga, *Anabaena*, produced short chains of cells. This work was done by two new LMB recruits, Michael Wilcox and the mathematician Graeme Mitchison, who would become a close collaborator of Crick's. But even *Anabaena* turned out to be very complicated and Francis began to realise that there would not be a simple set of fundamental postulates that would explain development, even in one dimension. It seemed as though the detail of development *was* the bigger picture – there was little room here for Francis to set aside troublesome results.

A final opportunity to exert a significant influence on the thinking of developmental biologists came two years later, when Peter
Lawrence visited the Madrid laboratory of Antonio García-Bellido,
who studied *Drosophila*. By using mutants, the Spanish group had
shown that the fly wing developed in two parts, each formed by the
descendants of a different set of progenitor cells. While this was no
surprise – Lawrence had described similar effects in the milkweed
bug using a different technique – having two approaches to the topic
helped bring out the underlying issue.[35] During the long debates
in a smoke-filled laboratory room, the Spanish researchers asked
Lawrence what word they should use to describe these regions –
'compartments' or 'boxes'? Lawrence preferred 'compartments', and
the term stuck.[36]

On his return to Cambridge, Lawrence explained the new
insights to Crick, who was excited at the implication that there was
a common process in insect development; he also realised that the
ideas of the García-Bellido group were not widely appreciated,
despite having been published in *Nature*. This was partly because,
despite his brilliance, García-Bellido was not always clear, as Crick
later explained:

> Garcia Bellido is really very good. A man of great originality,
> energy and enthusiasm; he is undoubtedly outstanding. His
> main fault (apart from speaking too fast) is that he is rather
> difficult to understand. I am willing to believe that it is all clear
> in his mind but his thinking appears so convoluted that others
> often have difficulty in grasping his ideas. It was because of
> this that I persuaded Peter Lawrence that he and I should
> write an intelligible exposition of (part of) Antonio's work for
> *Science*.[37]

Crick and Lawrence's article focused on compartments and their
creation by cell lineages consisting of several clones – copies – of
a small group of progenitor cells.[38] The central point was that cell
identity was determined by the position of the cell within the organism – not by a precise anatomical location, but by the membership of
a particular compartment. That membership was transmitted to the

progeny of each cell, so cell lineages produced compartments. The underlying mechanisms were unknown, but Crick and Lawrence speculated that compartments might be a readout of gradients, produced through specific patterns of gene activation.

The article was planned by Crick and key parts bear his hallmark clarity, but the ideas it contained were the product of many hours of discussion with Lawrence, who recalled that the article was truly a joint effort: 'Neither of us could have written it without the other.'[39] This was particularly true of the technical detail, which was Lawrence's area – Crick was not at all familiar with this material. As with many of Crick's articles, it included a hefty dose of speculation that was presented with disarming honesty:

> For the first time there is the real prospect of understanding the logic behind gene deployment in pattern formation. As we have seen, the speculative ideas about compartments in this section are not supported by hard evidence. But it is exactly this possibility, that compartments may have a wider significance, which makes the study of them at the present so important and so interesting.[40]

Despite his enthusiasm, this was Crick's swansong in developmental biology. He never wrote another research paper in the field.

*

Although Crick was in his early fifties and not generally interested in the latest cultural developments, in the second half of the 1960s he did become entangled with two of the main features of the time – recreational drug use and protest politics. From the mid-1960s, he had occasionally smoked marijuana for fun and relaxation, and in 1967 he took his first LSD trip.*[41] Safe and secure in Well Cottage, Francis had an amazing experience and was profoundly marked by the effects on his perception, and used the drug several more times; in California a

---

*The acid was supplied by Henry Barclay Todd, who a decade later would be jailed following a massive drugs bust, Operation Julie.

year later, Odile tried it too.[42] Francis was well aware that his drug use
was illegal, but considered that cannabis in particular was no more
dangerous than alcohol, and that the laws prohibiting its use were
outdated. He was so convinced of his view that, unusually, he took
a public stand and in July 1967 signed a petition from a small, short-
lived organisation called the Society for Mental Awareness (SOMA),
which was published as an advertisement in *The Times* (paid for
by Paul McCartney) under the title 'The Law Against Marijuana Is
Immoral in Principle and Unworkable in Practice'.[43]

Crick was the only FRS to sign the SOMA petition, alongside the
novelist Graham Greene, two MPs and a sprinkling of 1960s London
bohemian glitterati (virtually all men). There were all four Beatles
and their manager Brian Epstein, the revolutionary Tariq Ali, photographer David Bailey, artists David Hockney and Richard Hamilton,
the jazz singer and satirist George Melly, theatre director Peter Brook,
physician and comedian Jonathan Miller, the psychiatrist Anthony
Storr and the anti-psychiatrist R. D. Laing. The petition appeared at
what seemed like a turning point in British debates over drug use.
The government had recently set up a committee to investigate the
use of cannabis and LSD, while a notorious drug trial saw Keith
Richards of the Rolling Stones sentenced to a year's imprisonment
for allowing marijuana to be smoked on his premises. In the same
case, Mick Jagger was given three months for possession of ampheta-
mines, prompting an editorial in *The Times* criticising the severity of
the sentences.*

The petition did not change the debate over the legalisation of
cannabis in the UK, but it did draw media attention to the question,
although the preference of politicians for a repressive response led
the police to focus on harassing the Black community and carrying
out attention-grabbing raids on pop stars. Crick would undoubtedly have been a high-profile trophy for the police, but his discretion
ensured he never had a brush with the law.† Nevertheless, his

---

*On appeal, Richards' conviction was quashed, while Jagger was given a
conditional discharge.
†Crick committed two minor traffic offences (a parking violation and 'driving
without due care and attention'), both in 1972, the latter leading to a conviction
in the Magistrate's Court in April 1973. According to his diary, in June 1975 he

involvement with the petition, and the implication that he indulged, added to his reputation as a freethinker and an unlikely symbol of changing values.

Crick's involvement in the SOMA petition was unusual. As he explained a few years later, 'I feel that signing things, at least in most cases, does very little good except quieten the conscience of the person signing. I therefore usually make it a rule not to sign declarations unless it can be shown that it will make a significant contribution to the end in view.'[44] For example, at the end of 1967, his friend the Mexican anthropologist Santiago Genovés invited Francis to endorse an appeal for world peace; Crick politely declined, saying 'I do not feel that my opinions on this subject are worth very much.'[45] In 1969, however, he signed an appeal calling for the release of Professor Shlomo Samueloff, an Israeli physiologist who was imprisoned in Syria.*[46] On the more prosaic end of politics, Francis also signed a petition against Cambridge council's proposal to allow parking on the city's medieval Market Square.[47] That was something he actually knew about and on which he felt that his opinion might carry weight.

Despite Crick's reluctance to become involved in politics, the hurly-burly of late 1960s political protest gently impinged upon his world. After the success of the 1966 NATO summer school on molecular biology in Greece, Francis agreed to organise another meeting in the same location the following year. But in April 1967 a group of Greek army colonels launched a coup and installed a dictatorship that imprisoned and tortured political opponents, while hundreds of academics and teachers were summarily dismissed. Faced with the upheaval, Crick and the other organisers decided to postpone the school for a year.[48]

It soon became apparent that a meeting in 1968 would be equally

---

was on jury service. In England jurors are forbidden from revealing any details of the cases they are involved with; it is therefore not known if Crick actually served in a case, and if so, what impact he may have had on the deliberations. MSS 660, Box 17, Folder 10; MSS 660, Box 12, Folder 18; MSS 660, Box 14, Folder 21.
*After Samueloff was released he wrote Crick a thankful letter, although the appeal had not in fact been sent and had therefore played no part in his liberation.

impossible, as scientists and students refused to travel to Greece because of their hostility to the regime. Jim Watson pulled out of the organising committee, while Crick's co-organiser, Marianne Grunberg-Manago, told him she could not visit a country 'where even musicians are being arrested'.[49] Spock-like, Crick said he considered such views illogical and went on a Greek sailing holiday with Odile, giving a lecture in Athens.[50]

In autumn 1968, as the situation in Greece began to stabilise, the school was rescheduled for July the following year, with Crick as Chairman and LMB researchers Mark Bretscher and Brian Clark doing the organisational work. Around this time, Francis published a light-hearted article in *Nature* on how to run a summer school – mainly obvious stuff like having students discuss in small groups, leaving plenty of time for informal discussion and making sure that there were no morning sessions after late-night parties: 'Personally, I love dancing in rather dimly lit cellars,' he wrote, 'but I find that I cannot stay up all hours of the morning and still be fresh and receptive the next day.'[51]

Shortly after Crick sent his chirpy article to *Nature*, a group calling itself the European Committee of Scientists for Democracy in Greece called for a boycott of all scientific conferences in the country and explicitly targeted the Spetsai summer school. Led by François Gros, the call was supported by hundreds of scientists, including many of Crick's French friends.[52] Alarmed, Crick obtained reassurances from the Greek government, via their Ambassador in London, that the meeting would not be addressed by any official, that there would be no government propaganda about the school and that students from Eastern Europe could attend. In return, he promised there would be no anti-governmental protest during the event.[53] Explaining this agreement to Gros, Francis puckishly pointed out the contradictions in such campaigns – 'I do not relish the spectacle of people who take a stand on moral principles about not visiting Greece, but who are prepared to go to meetings in Madrid or Warsaw, or organised by the Vatican,' he snarked.[54]

The row subsided as Gros and the other signatories agreed that meetings in Greece were permissible if there was no official involvement; despite opposition from some expatriate Greek scientists, two dozen Greek students signed up for the school, along with many others from Europe, the USA and even from behind the Iron Curtain.[55] The meeting went ahead smoothly, but the political issues around boycotts would not go away, so an evening slot for a students' political meeting was found ('lecturers welcome,' Crick noted).[56] The students were concerned by two things. First, as Crick had explained in his welcoming remarks, the Greek regime had provided financial support for a reception, and for two excursions.[57] Crick therefore announced he would pay for the reception himself and that if people did not wish to go on the excursions, they did not have to.

All that was well received, although, as Francis later pointed out, 'the main financial effect of this action was to transfer $500 from our pockets into that of the Colonels.'[58] The second difficulty was that some students wanted to organise a protest against the regime; Crick said that if this happened, he would stop the school immediately, but they were welcome to protest once the programme had ended. The students accepted this situation and the whole thing blew over.

A few weeks later, one of the lecturers, US biochemist Maxine Singer, wrote Francis an appreciative note, enclosing a cheque to help cover the costs of the reception: 'I wanted to tell you how well I thought you handled the "political" matters with the students. (…) Watching and listening to all of it, your patience and understanding came clearly through. But most of all it seemed that your extraordinarily straightforward approach to the situation was the main component in keeping heads and hearts cool.'[59]

Diplomacy and tact are not qualities that are immediately associated with Crick, but faced with the strength of feeling among the younger students he was able to find a way of resolving the issues to everyone's satisfaction.[60]

Nature published a series of letters and an editorial about the issue of boycotts (that year there had been opposition to scientific meetings in Franco's Spain and in Chicago, following police violence against demonstrators at the 1968 Democratic Convention).* Having

---

*The call to boycott Chicago as a meeting site for ten years emerged from the Cold Spring Harbor phage meeting in September 1968, and was co-signed by Jim Watson. Eigner, J. et al. (1968), Boycott Chicago! *Science* 162:511.

had practical experience of the arguments, and sure that logic and facts could overcome political differences, Crick corralled some Nobel pals – including Kendrew, Perutz, Sanger, Jacob and Monod – to set out criteria for attending conferences in problematic places, which were duly published in *Nature*.[61] But despite Crick's confidence, their proposals were vague and unoriginal, hedged about with conditional clauses to enable everyone to agree, and came to no clear conclusion. The Nobelists' letter caused barely a ripple – a handful of letters dribbled into the *Nature* offices and there was a brief article in *The Times*.[62] In fact, there were no great lessons to be learned from the Spetsai affair. Crick could not even persuade his colleagues of his case – there was no further summer school on the island until 1972, and the meeting returned permanently to the island only after the restoration of democracy in 1974.

EDWARDIAN IDEAS

As the Spetsai incident showed, Crick paid little attention to politics. However, for about a decade from the early 1960s he became publicly involved in discussions of the social implications of science, exploring two issues in some depth: how growing scientific knowledge might affect morality and the implications of genetic differences between individuals. In both cases his ideas were somewhat naïve; he eventually decided that he could make no useful contribution to debates around these matters, and in the early 1970s he ceased all public comment. These episodes are significant, because they reveal the limits of Crick's intellect in a way that was rarely the case in his scientific thinking.

Francis had long been interested in the link between scientific discovery and morality and beliefs; when he outlined his intention to study the nature of life and of consciousness in 1947, it was partly because both these fields were shrouded in religious, non-materialist explanations. Even scientists were not immune to the semi-mystical suggestion that these phenomena could not be properly explained by existing scientific laws and that some new approach would be needed – for example, in the 1930s and 40s, Delbrück and Schrödinger both expected this would be one consequence of understanding the nature of the gene. Similar speculative ideas emerged repeatedly over subsequent decades. In 1958 the theoretical physicist Walter Elsasser claimed that information could not be reliably stored in DNA, nor transferred from genes to proteins, because of the irreducibly complex and unstable nature of the cell. New non-physical explanations, or biotonic laws, were needed, he said.[1] Crick told him that existing approaches, coupled with mutation and the principle of natural selection, could account for what he thought was inexplicable. For Francis, Elsasser's ideas were a revival of the vitalist, non-materialist explanations that affected science at the beginning of the twentieth century and which molecular biology had helped replace.

In a similar vein, a few years later NIH researcher Peter Mora published a six-page article in *Nature* exploring the 'urge or drive towards self-fulfilment (…) the relentless striving to survive, to absorb, to expand, to dominate', that he claimed characterised living organisms.[2] For Mora 'the present scientific method used in physics may not be sufficient' to understand the nature of life. He sent a reprint of the article to Crick with the evangelical dedication: 'Francis Crick – That you may *see.*' Francis was not impressed by Mora's claims, but he became concerned that there was a revival of vitalism – when Warren Weaver, the chairman of the Board at the Salk, proposed the institute should appoint what he called a 'biologists' biologist', Crick's reply was sharp: 'I would not be keen to have a "neo-vitalist"; that is, a man who thinks that the whole is greater that the parts in some manner which it is impossible to comprehend. (That the "whole is greater than the sum of its parts" is true, in the sense normally used, of the benzene molecule.)'[3]

In 1965, Francis decided to present his views on the subject in three lectures at the University of Washington in Seattle under the title 'Is Vitalism Dead?', later published in his first, slim book, *Of Molecules and Men*.[4] The opening lecture emphasised the power of the 'beautiful mechanism' of natural selection, the discovery of which was 'one of the great intellectual triumphs of our civilization'. Crick told his audience that the aim of the modern movement in biology was to explain '*all* biology in terms of physics and chemistry'. This did not mean a relentlessly reductionist programme – 'one should study both the whole and its parts, the relative emphasis in any particular case being a matter of tactics,' he said.

In the second lecture – which even his critics regarded as a tour de force – Crick described cell function and the role of genes, emphasising that there was 'very little that we have been unable to explain'. Processes such as the growth of membranes or cell division were still poorly understood, but all previous experience suggested that there would be nothing mysterious underlying them.[5] In its published form, this lecture had as its epigraph that stanza from McClure that had caught Crick's eye in 1959:

THIS IS THE POWERFUL KNOWLEDGE
We smile with it.

The final lecture dealt with the challenges to the collective world-view that would be produced by future scientific discoveries, such as explaining consciousness, or finding the origin of life. One way to ensure that people were able to understand these developments, he argued, would be for everyone at university to study a broad scientific curriculum, including the study of animal behaviour.* On the other hand, he did not suggest that science students needed to study history, philosophy or literature, all of which are essential for putting science into context, nor did he extend his proposal to high school students or the general public.

The conclusion of the lecture foresaw the endless progress of scientific understanding, especially with regards to the molecular biology of the cell, the origin of life and the nature of consciousness. Crick confidently predicted that while vitalism would undoubtedly persist, it would eventually be restricted to a lunatic fringe: 'There are still people today who believe the Earth is flat, in spite of all the

---

*Crick's underwhelming prescription prompted one reviewer to remark:
'The social programme that is supposed to carry out the cultural revolution is pure milk and water. It consists of a course of study in general science and animal behaviour for all university students. The message of the apocalyptic angel turns out to be a report from the Committee on the Revision of the Undergraduate Curriculum.' Murray, J. (1967), War between the two cultures. *The Virginia Quarterly Review* 43:514–17.

enormous accumulation of scientific evidence to the contrary. And so to those of you who may be vitalists I would make this prophecy: what everyone believed yesterday, and you believe today, only cranks will believe tomorrow.'

When the book appeared later in the year, reviews were generally polite, although believers could be tetchy – the Catholic neurophysiologist Sir John Eccles was scornful of Crick's views, including his predictions about the future abilities of computers, which turned out to be quite accurate.[6] There were friendly but critical reviews in *Science* and *Nature*, but there was no real buzz about the book and sales eventually plateaued in the thousands.[7]

Francis lectured on vitalism on only two more occasions, both the following year, first in Illinois, then to the Cambridge Jewish Society (the future British Chief Rabbi, Jonathan Sacks, described it as 'a superb talk ... exceptionally stimulating').[8] However, Crick did return to the link between science and morality. In 1968, at the invitation of his friend Lord Annan, Provost of University College London, he gave a public lecture on 'The Social Impact of Biology'.[9] There was huge interest in the event, with people turned away at the door.[10] Those lucky enough to get in were perhaps disappointed; intended as a showpiece for Crick and for UCL, the talk instead revealed that he had not thought sufficiently about the ethical or sociological issues and marked the beginning of a turning point in his willingness to express his views in public.

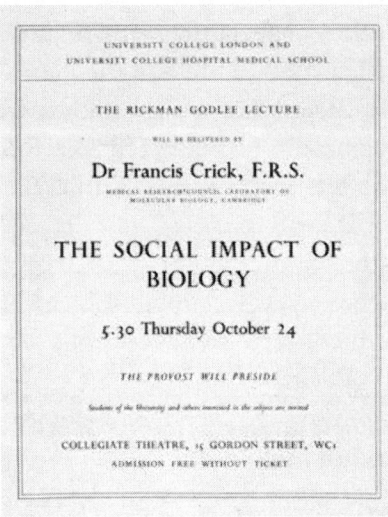

UNIVERSITY COLLEGE LONDON AND
UNIVERSITY COLLEGE HOSPITAL MEDICAL SCHOOL

THE RICKMAN GODLEE LECTURE

WILL BE DELIVERED BY

Dr Francis Crick, F.R.S.
MEDICAL RESEARCH COUNCIL LABORATORY OF
MOLECULAR BIOLOGY, CAMBRIDGE

THE SOCIAL IMPACT OF
BIOLOGY

5.30 Thursday October 24

THE PROVOST WILL PRESIDE

Students of the University and others interested in the subject are invited

COLLEGIATE THEATRE, 15 GORDON STREET, WC1
ADMISSION FREE WITHOUT TICKET

The lecture opened with a conventional outline of the current state of biology and its increasing rate of progress. Francis had a spring in his step when he discussed recreational drugs and joked about how, at Well Cottage, he had called out to Odile, 'have you put the acid in the pool?' to the alarm of their younger guests (this got a laugh). He attacked the laws against the possession of cannabis, asked the audience to think about why new psychedelic drugs were not being developed, and complained that there was no money being spent on the creation of aphrodisiacs (that got an even bigger laugh). However, his central argument, as in *Of Molecules and Men*, was that existing morality, with its origins in religion, would be unable to respond to future scientific developments. He was scornful of the place of religious education in school and its widespread presence on the BBC, although he did accept that 'Christianity may be OK between consenting adults in private' (this got the biggest laugh of the night).[11] Instead of teaching religion, Francis suggested that by educating children about science, together with the presentation of unadorned facts, 'a *new ethical system* based on modern science' would emerge, able to resolve the difficulties that were to come. The most significant parts of the lecture consisted of his attempts to show the kind of ethical approaches that would be needed.

To limit population growth, Francis advocated the use of the contraceptive pill – still illegal in many countries – and took a side-swipe at the Pope's opposition to contraception. He insisted that there was no right to have as many children as you pleased, but he did not explain how this could be enforced. He then explored the need for 'quality control' of human life, focusing on the terrible dilemmas raised by babies born with awful deformities, or people living with dementia. At both ends of life, Crick considered that some lives might not be worth living; the difficulty was who should decide what to do – the family, society, or doctors?

In a deliberately provocative suggestion, he proposed that babies might be 'legally born' only after appropriate health checks had been made in the first two days of life. He accepted that every-one felt uncomfortable with this idea, but he wanted the audience to wonder why, when the idea seemed so logical – 'we do this with motor cars, why not for people?' he trilled. On the other hand, 'legal death' might come into operation at say eighty or eighty-five, after which euthanasia or assisted dying would be permitted, if circumstances were appropriate. While all this was dealt with in a very flippant, Cambridge common room kind of way, he raised issues that we are still grappling with.

The lecture made few waves; *Nature* summarised the talk but passed no judgement beyond the implicit approval of appearing in its pages, while when the lecture was broadcast on Radio 3 four months later, the sole comment in the media was about the sound quality.[12] His views were not seen as particularly unusual, at the time. However, Lord Annan sent Francis a letter criticising his naivety about the power of facts and rational argument to change opinions. Subjecting his friend to a gentle history lesson by outlining the ideas of J. S. Mill, Marx, Weber and Durkheim (Annan pointed out that Crick's view was basically that of the positivist philosopher Auguste Comte), he explained that no matter how sensible the ideas in a debate might be, 'they will not be accepted as conclusions unless considerable changes have also taken place in our social structure and relationships.'[13] In reply, Crick began by disarmingly downplaying the whole business – 'The things one says in lectures!' – before admitting that he was in 'almost a total state of confusion' about how changes occur in society.*[14]

*

Crick's positivist conviction that increasing scientific knowledge would lead to the emergence of a new morality was the kind of assumption that would have fitted with the ideas of H. G. Wells. Despite Annan's philosophy lesson, in 1971 Francis became more convinced of his view following the appearance of *Chance and Necessity* by Jacques Monod, who shared Crick's outlook.[15] Francis was so impressed by Monod's ideas that he toyed with the possibility of

---

*Towards the end of his life, Francis recognised that 'legal birth' was a non-starter and that the feelings of the parents and of society had to be taken into account; as to 'legal death', he emphasised the right of the terminally ill to take their own lives. Crick to Hargittai, 28 June 2001, PP/CRI/J/2/21/1.

writing a book about them, encouraged by the literary critic Frank Kermode, editor of the Fontana Modern Masters book series.[16]

Nothing came of the proposal, but an outline of the book that never was can be seen from the notes for a lecture Francis gave to the Cambridge Humanists in 1972.[17] Crick's central theme, taken from Monod, was the conflict between scientific knowledge and the views of established religious and political ideologies. In his notes, Francis dialled up the rhetoric as he railed against those who rejected the Darwinian view of life: 'We live in a barbarian culture. We are surrounded by barbarians. Sophisticated, erudite and passionate but basically barbarians because they cling to the old knowledge which (as Monod has shown) imposes a particular purpose to man or to the Universe. They cannot stomach the idea of Nature evolving in any open-ended way *without* any foreseeable target.'

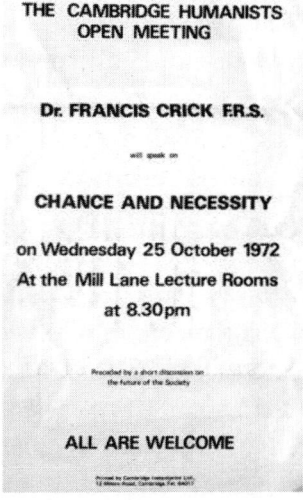

THE CAMBRIDGE HUMANISTS
OPEN MEETING

Dr. FRANCIS CRICK F.R.S.

will speak on

CHANCE AND NECESSITY

on Wednesday 25 October 1972
At the Mill Lane Lecture Rooms
at 8.30pm

Preceded by a short discussion on
the future of the Society

ALL ARE WELCOME

Because of these clashes, Crick claimed, 'society accepts the prodigious power of science but rejects the profounder message.' That profounder message was composed of the materialist basis of scientific discovery and the implication that new discoveries would lead to a new ethical system. Crick considered that the key to this development would be understanding the human brain. For Francis, neuroscience had immense practical, political implications – it would eventually undermine existing morals and ethics, opening the road to a scientific new Jerusalem. Research into the brain, he argued, was far more important than dealing with any of the immediate problems that were pressing on the world in 1972: 'This then emerges as the major scientific knowledge we require (not urban renewal, or pollution or even population control). Moreover <u>when</u> this knowledge is obtained it is virtually certain that man's whole view of himself will be radically changed.'

While such predictions may be thought-provoking, they do not lead to any particular ethical position and until scientific developments drive the promised ethical changes, you could say this kind of thing only so often before its impact faded; this may have contributed to Crick's decision to abandon his planned book following Monod's death in 1976.[18] He never returned to the subject.

*

Crick's most controversial views about science and society related to the significance of genetic differences between people. The first public expression of these interests came in 1962, when the Ciba Foundation invited him to a small meeting in London on 'The Biological Future of Man'. Francis cheerfully accepted, despite having no particular knowledge about the question: 'This sounds as if it might be rather fun (…) I would certainly like to join in. Whether I have anything useful to say I am not sure, but could think about it during the summer.'[19] The meeting involved some of the leading British scientific intellectuals of the period – Peter Medawar, Jacob Bronowski, Sir Julian Huxley and J. B. S. Haldane, together with the US Nobel Prize-winning geneticists Hermann Muller* and Joshua Lederberg. Also in attendance were Alex Comfort, the anarchist physician and future author of *The Joy of Sex*, and the nominated representative of the Archbishop of Canterbury – the Reverend H. C. Howell, the Perpetual Curate of Stratford-sub-Castle.[20]

In his opening address, Huxley, a keen eugenicist, highlighted environmental destruction and the need to reduce population growth by making oral contraception widely available, but all this was background to his support for 'the improvement of human

---

*Muller was unable to attend, so his contribution to the meeting was read out.

genetic quality'. His central objective was to produce 'a marked increase in the number of the outstandingly intelligent and capable people needed to run our increasingly complex societies' by adopting Muller's proposal for 'multiple artificial insemination by preferred donors of high genetic quality' – a sperm bank.[21]

Muller justified his initiative by claiming that modern medicine was keeping people alive despite their genetic defects and that 'genetically based ability' was therefore declining across the globe. To meet this supposed challenge, Muller – who was a socialist – advocated a system of voluntary artificial insemination from donor sperm (he had drawn up lists of the supposedly high-quality men who would be called upon to donate – these changed over time as Muller's views as to what was desirable also altered). This would enable couples 'to give their child as favourable a genetic prospect as can be obtained for it,' he claimed. Although Muller also raised the possibility of storing and fertilising eggs, and even of human clones, in the absence of such technology his proposal amounted to supposedly high-quality men finding vessels for their semen.

Francis had promised the organisers that he would think about the issues over the summer, but he showed little sign of having seriously considered matters when he began, 'I agreed with practically everything Muller said'. In fact, he wanted to go further, proposing to 'encourage by financial means those people who are more socially desirable to have more children … The obvious way to do this is to tax children.'[22] Crick claimed later in the discussion that this was said 'playfully', while Bronowski generously interpreted this idea as akin to Jonathan Swift's 'modest proposal' that the Irish could solve their financial woes by selling their children to the rich as food.[23] However, there is no sign that Francis was being satirical, even when he suggested it would be possible to make everyone sterile by putting a drug in food, and then give the antidote only to people who were licensed to have children.[24] A more accurate description of his ideas was given two decades later by Germaine Greer: 'schoolboy silliness'.[25]

Although Francis obviously found the discussion fascinating, he did not take it seriously enough. It was Bronowski – not Crick – who challenged Muller and Huxley to provide a jot of evidence that the human population was deteriorating. In fact, their ideas flowed from the declinist fears that had driven Huxley's intellectual forebears, the Edwardian eugenicists like Galton. Although these obsessions were now dressed up in the language of recessive alleles and radiation-induced mutations, there was no proof that any such decline existed.

The eugenics advocated by Huxley and the others was not racial, but the policies they outlined would inevitably reinforce inequalities in society that were supposedly based on genes.[26] This was pointed out by the French endocrinologist Marc Klein, who had been deported to Auschwitz and had witnessed the horrific sterilisation 'experiments' that were carried out there: 'Once you have seen with your own eyes where those problems can lead, you are always very cautious, even when you hear about the very beginnings of this type of experiment,' he told the meeting.[27] Unlike Crick and the others, Bronowski and Klein – both European Jews – were alive to the dangers of these ideas and to the poor science that lay behind them.

The ideas that were discussed at the Ciba meeting were tragically typical of thinking at the time about how to deal with genetic diseases ('negative eugenics'), although many, like Muller, Huxley and Crick, also advocated encouraging certain groups to reproduce ('positive eugenics').[28] By the 1980s, all these ideas had been debunked and had become unacceptable in most countries, but at the time they were widespread, particularly among scientists.[29] This is shown by the reception given to the published proceedings of the meeting – the *Journal of the American Medical Association* claimed the book 'brims with sage comments and judgments', the reviewer in *Perspectives in Biology and Medicine* praised the 'lively discussion' by Crick and others, which contributed to the 'stimulating and provocative' ideas on offer, while *Science* found the discussions to be 'often profound and original'.[30]

There were dissenting voices. The physician Louis Lasagna skewered 'the perfect nonsense' uttered by 'the Nobelists and near-Nobelists' at the meeting – he considered their comments were 'sufficiently appalling' to make him glad the world was not run by scientists. He also usefully recommended that in future no Nobel Prize winner be allowed to pontificate about humanity's problems for five years after the award.[31] More explicitly, the German physicist Friedrich Wagner pointed out that 'such genetic visions of the "second cycle" of eugenic theory remind us, however, of the "first cycle" which led, a generation later, to Hitler's mass exterminations.'[32]

Crick repeated some of his Ciba ideas in his 1968 UCL lecture, in which he called for more research on the origins of individual differences between people – nature or nurture, genes or environment. The best way of investigating this question, he argued, was to study identical twins separated at birth; to do this on a sufficiently large scale would require society to encourage parents of twins to give up one of their children for adoption. 'I don't say they should be compelled,' he said, before adding to laughter, 'they might be bribed.'[33] (He later expanded on his plan in a letter to a colleague: 'I can imagine an advertising campaign to this end along the lines of "donate a twin".'[34])

After stating that people are born very unequal in their abilities and that it would not only be difficult but also highly undesirable to make them equal ('diversity is necessary as an insurance against the future,' he explained in his notes), Francis slipped in a claim that at the time was unremarkable: 'it is by no means clear, let me say, that all races are equally gifted.' He did not say which races he considered to be particularly gifted and which less so, but a few months later he explained to his friend C. P. Snow, using language that was typical of the time: 'Had I enlarged on the subject I would have dwelt on the probable positive differences, such as, for example, the Jews and the Japs, rather than speak only about Negroes.'*[35]

A brief account of Crick's talk appeared in the Californian newspaper *The Riverside Daily*, under the title 'Scientist Says Not All Men Equal'. This caught the eagle eye of the avid racist William Shockley, who in 1956 had won the Nobel Prize in Physics for his work on the transistor.[36] Shockley was convinced that Black people were genetically inferior to White people and although there was no mention of race in the article, seized upon Crick's comment as a sign of agreement. He soon sent an unctuous letter to Francis: 'I believe that you

---

* There was no mention of race in Crick's notes or in the (slightly shortened) broadcast version. This may have referred to his passing comment about the experimental evidence for genetic differences in IQ, which was based on studies of Black and White populations in the USA.

and I are the only Nobel Laureates who are in print with views that racial differences in intelligence are significant.'[37]

Shockley began bombarding Crick with packs of photocopied documents – often the same ones in different dispatches – with the important bits underlined in red. This material, which smelt of the crank, was accompanied by self-important and equally cranky letters – '20,000 illegitimate slum babies per year with IQ ≤ 70 and only one Laureate who will speak out?' wailed Shockley. Crick initially declined to engage, explaining that he had decided not to speak or write on social problems for a year or two.[38] However, a little later he asked Shockley for information about Arthur Jensen, a US educational psychologist who used serious-sounding statistical evidence to justify his view that attempts to increase educational achievement by Black children were doomed to failure, because of genetically based IQ differences between races.[39]

In February 1971, Francis telephoned Shockley because he had discovered that Jensen had *over*-estimated the supposed genetic component in IQ scores and wanted to alert Shockley to the error. Shockley recorded their long conversation and stored it in his archive.[40] Much of the call involved an obscure discussion about statistics in which neither man understood the other, although Shockley ended up saying he agreed with Crick's point. As the conversation went on, Shockley became increasingly unbuttoned in his discussion of Black Americans and Crick's responses became politely neutral – 'unh-huh', 'mmm' and so on. When Shockley claimed he could do more than anyone else to 'reduce Negro agony in this country for the next generation', by showing the Black population that their social condition was inevitable, Francis clearly felt uncomfortable at the turn the conversation was taking.

Jensen's apparently scientific approach to genes and IQ was more to Crick's taste than Shockley's cruder racism and the pair corresponded until the middle of 1975. Francis gradually warmed to Jensen – his letters shifted from 'Dear Dr Jensen' to 'Dear Arthur' before becoming 'Dear Art' in 1974, although he never used his most intimate sign-off of 'Yours ever'.[41] Jensen's views provoked student protests whenever he tried to speak, including at the Salk while Crick was visiting, which Francis was sympathetic about in his letters – 'You do have a rough time! It's lucky you can take it all so philosophically.' But what eventually provoked Francis to publicly associate himself with Jensen's ideas was the refusal of the National Academy of Sciences (NAS) to support research into genes and IQ.

At the beginning of 1972, educational psychologist Ellis Page circulated a 'Resolution on Scientific Freedom Regarding Human Behaviour and Heredity'.[42] This document – effectively a petition – argued that hereditary influences on human abilities and behaviour were very strong and urged the financing of research into the topic. Although neither Shockley nor Jensen were named, the resolution clearly suggested they had a right to receive research funding and to speak. At Jensen's invitation, Crick signed the appeal and promised to try and get some of his close colleagues to sign, but he was not optimistic about their response.[43]

This proved accurate. Perutz refused, telling Francis that he did not think that tests on racial groups were useful, and that loyalty, good nature, and trust were more important to society than intelligence.[44] Although Kendrew and Monod did sign, Sydney Brenner, with his far-left South African background, did not, and neither did Jim Watson, perhaps surprisingly given his later views. The resolution and its list of signatories was published in July 1972, leading Jensen's opponents to send Crick shoals of documents, many of which he filed away, apparently unread.[45] It also prompted students opposed to Jensen's ideas to target Crick when he visited campuses to speak on entirely unrelated matters; for example a 1973 protest leaflet was titled 'Nobel Prize Winner Crick Backs Jensen's Racist Theories'.[46]

The Page petition marked the end of Crick's brief public involvement in the race and IQ debate. As he explained in September 1972, he was becoming 'less and less inclined to get involved in controversies of any sort'.[47] When John Maddox of *Nature* tried to involve him in a public debate over eugenics, Francis declined, revealing an unusual degree of self-perception: 'As you know, I've tried to take an interest in problems concerning science and society but I've reluctantly come to the conclusion that I have little talent for them and no taste at all. I have a horror of political matters, mainly because my nature leads me spontaneously towards actions which would be

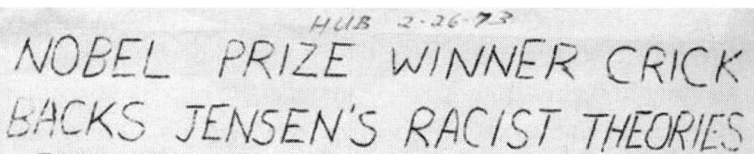

HUB 2-26-73

NOBEL PRIZE WINNER CRICK BACKS JENSEN'S RACIST THEORIES

The new wave of racial inferiority theories, which are being used now by the Nixon administration to justify policy such as HEW cuts and lobotomy studies on prisoners, are backed by Nobel laureate Francis Crick, who will speak today at 3:30 in the Health Sciences Auditorium.

Crick lent his signature and his prestige to an ad which was pub-

3:30, today, Monday, in the Health Sciences Auditorium

CONFRONT CRICK   sds

politically inept.'[48]

As Matt Ridley has pointed out, Crick's reputation survived intact partly because he made no public declarations about racial differences and eugenics after 1972.[49] Furthermore, in the 1970s his views were part of mainstream thinking – the idea of 'positive eugenics', of reversing the supposed genetic degeneration of the human race, was widely accepted by scientists at the time, including by those like his friend John Edsall or the evolutionary biologist Ernst Mayr, who were openly hostile to Jensen and Shockley's views.[50] For example, in a letter to Crick, Edsall bemoaned the 'bad name' acquired by eugenics through 'the misfortune that the Nazis promoted something to which they gave the name of eugenics'.[51] Francis agreed: 'The main difficulty is that people have to start thinking about eugenics in a different way. The Nazis gave it a bad name and I think it is time something was done to make it respectable again.'[52] In this respect, Crick's ideas were simply not unusual enough to draw attention. They were certainly no more surprising than the suggestion of Linus Pauling, like Muller a left-winger, who sought to reduce the transmission of genetic disease by obliging any carrier of a genetic disorder to have a tattoo on their forehead indicating their condition.[53]

Although Francis did not discuss such matters in public again, there were those who remembered what he had said. In 1976, the National Front, a British fascist organisation that was growing at the time, used a supposed quote from Crick about the genetic basis of racial differences in one of its leaflets.[54] For Francis the link between

race and IQ was a purely intellectual matter, but those intent on pro-
moting race hatred could make those ideas have consequences.

As with his exchange with Lord Annan over changes in society,
Crick backed down whenever his ideas on genes and IQ were challenged in private. Crick told his friend John Edsall that he believed
that half the average difference in IQ between Blacks and Whites
was due to genetic factors and needed investigating; when Edsall
pointed out the weaknesses of Jensen's methods and the unreliability
of IQ tests, Francis claimed he accepted most of this, but illogically
felt it did not undermine his confidence in Jensen's conclusions.[55]
He did not rebut any of Edsall's arguments. A few years later, in a
personal letter, Crick's friend Peter Medawar gave him a hard time
over his views. In 1977, Medawar reviewed two books on race and
IQ, prompting Francis to suggest to him that a policy was needed
that would encourage 'the bulk of people generally regarded as
valuable to society' to have more children, while 'those who are a
handicap' should be encouraged to have fewer.[56] His emphasis was
not on race, he explained, although he felt that 'the supposed differences between Chinese and Jews, Caucasians, American Indians and
Blacks, to name a few poorly defined categories, are probably real.'
Instead, he told Medawar that what really counted were class differences – 'very broadly, between the rich and the poor'. As he had
explained to Ernst Mayr six years earlier: 'I myself do not feel very
strongly either way about the Black-White distinction. If I have a
prejudice it is against the poor, and in favour of the rich, but such an
attitude is almost equally unacceptable to most people.'[57]

It may seem surprising, but Francis was somehow convinced
that the wealthy somehow had a better genetic endowment than
the poor. His eugenics, like that of the Edwardians, was rooted in
unscientific declinist fears and focused primarily on class, not race
(however, whether he realised it or not, the two are connected).
Medawar had the measure of his friend and replied caustically: 'Very
many thanks for your letter about IQs and the like. I hadn't realised
you were christened "Francis" after Francis Galton.'[58] Crick ignored
Medawar's barb, responding that he found it difficult to believe that
the present human gene pool was at any kind of optimum composition and that it was surprising that 'no one dares' to consider if

a different gene pool might be preferable. Somewhat wearily, he concluded: 'However, we shall never agree on all that by correspondence. I appreciate your good sense in not wishing to get involved publicly with the issue. I feel exactly the same way but I don't feel comfortable about it.'

Although Francis did not appear to think much more about such issues, what evidence there is suggests that his views slowly changed. In 1981, he told an Australian politician that the best way of improving life expectancy was to focus on public health measures – clean water and discouraging smoking – not genes. Even his continued advocacy in this interview of a kind of eugenics merely suggested that society should 'try to decide the sort of citizens we want and encourage people to have them in some way'.[59] In the late 1980s he was invited to air his views once more, for a German television programme, *Die stillen Stars* (*The Silent Stars*), but his responses were circumspect.[60] In 1994, a young correspondent wanted his opinion about de-extinction à la *Jurassic Park* and the possibility of controlling genetically determined traits in humans.[61] Francis considered de-extinction to be 'extremely remote and not worth considering' and produced a nuanced response on the question of human genetic engineering:

> We can already alter the DNA of a very few people (with their consent) who have life-threatening diseases, and more of this is likely in the future. We have, at the moment, no good techniques for altering the DNA of the next generation (before they are born) and, even if we had, no one is keen to do this, if only because of the ethical and social problems involved.

Although these late positions showed some insight and reflection, for most of his life Crick's views about these matters revealed the limits of his understanding. When his arguments were criticised by his friends, he would claim to accept the points being made, but there is no sign that he made the intellectual effort to re-examine his positions. His reluctance to engage in debate hints at either a lack of confidence in his ability to argue his case, a reluctance to expose himself to the public gaze, or both – in striking contrast with his confident and clear exposition of more neutral scientific matters. Crick's attitude to political and social issues was often naïve, relying on attitudes he had absorbed as a youth and had never seriously questioned. When confronted with the complexities of such matters, he found himself unable or unwilling to explore them and learned not to get involved. The ultimate explanation is that he did not find these issues sufficiently interesting to think about them in any depth; tractable scientific questions were what really excited him.

NONSENSE IN *NATURE*

Throughout Crick's career, *Nature* gave him a global platform, publishing thirty of his research or opinion articles. It also gave space to some of his severest critics – in the late 1960s the structure of the DNA molecule, its role as the genetic material, and the central dogma, were all attacked in leading journals, starting with *Nature*.

Crick's most consistent opponent was the virologist Barry Commoner, who in the 1950s claimed that both RNA *and* protein were involved in Tobacco Mosaic Virus replication (this was not true).[1] In 1964 Commoner published two long articles – again in *Nature* – arguing that DNA could not be the source of genetic information because its replication required an enzyme, DNA polymerase, which affected the pattern of inheritance (this was not true, either).[2] When Commoner repeated these claims in 1968, *Nature* stated that his arguments had been experimentally refuted and that giving publicity to his views would confuse and delay research. 'That should not be allowed to happen,' thundered the journal.[3]

Commoner must have insisted on a right to reply, for six months later he published a seven-page article in *Nature*, 'Failure of the Watson-Crick Theory as a Chemical Explanation of Inheritance,' complete with a Zen-like conclusion: 'The inherited specificity of life is derived from nothing less than life itself.'[4] Although annoyed responses soon appeared, Crick limited himself to private sideswipes, saying Commoner was 'misguided', 'ridiculous' and 'beyond hope'.[5]

More serious attacks followed. In early September 1969, Francis was having breakfast in Portugal Place, browsing through a recent issue of *Proceedings of the National Academy of Sciences* (*PNAS*), when his Friday morning calm was disrupted by an article by one Tai Te Wu, which argued that, at 92 per cent humidity, DNA was in fact a *quadruple* helix.[6] Crick was no longer a practising crystallographer and did not follow the literature on DNA structure so he fired off a letter to Maurice Wilkins, asking his old friend to respond.[7] Wilkins and his colleagues soon published a brief rebuttal that opened with a terse, one-sentence abstract: 'The X-ray diffraction patterns of DNA do not support a four-stranded helical structure.'[8] Again, Francis said nothing in public, but in private he suggested that Wu should try and build a four-stranded model and then calculate what diffraction pattern it would produce, thereby revealing if his proposal was correct.[9]

Crick could not remain aloof from the next attack on the double helix, which appeared in *Science* and came from Jerry Donohue, the chemist who had put Watson right about the structure of the bases back in February 1953.[10] Donohue argued that the mathematical tool known as Fourier analysis was not appropriate for X-ray diffraction studies, thereby undermining the work of Wilkins and his colleagues that had put the double helix on a solid footing. He also claimed that novel atomic forms of A–T and G–C base pairing, different to those described by Watson and Crick, could equally account for the X-ray diffraction data, giving the molecule an hourglass shape.

Within a few months, Crick and Wilkins both published responses robustly defending their work.[11] Crick's brief riposte had a wry, even sorrowful, tone: it would be fruitless to have a 'long, involved, and possibly acrimonious theoretical argument,' he said, but, as with Wu, if Donohue considered that his idea could produce an effective structure, 'let him build such a model and publish the coordinates'.[12] Two weeks later, the affair was amplified when *Nature* published a rather snotty summary of the exchanges.[13] The anonymous article described the dispute as a brawl involving the hurling of custard pies, and disdainfully referred to the 'crystallographic dialectic' on display. Donohue was described as a fundamentalist and his idea as heresy ('*odium theologicum*'), while Crick was said to have put 'an Olympian boot into Donohue's ribs' with his request for a model.

Despite this attempt by *Nature* to stir up trouble, Crick and Donohue began an exchange of letters that on Crick's part was initially coolly condescending – Olympian, in fact. However, both men soon became increasingly irate; Crick's final letter was a five-pager which concluded:

> I have established to my own satisfaction that you do not yet have an adequate grasp of helical diffraction theory, that your arguments from hypothetical models of base-pairs are theoretically not to be trusted without further justification, that the theoretical position is complicated and indeed likely to lead to 'long acrimonious arguments,' whereas the production of an acceptable alternative model by you would settle the argument in your favour.[14]

Donohue shot back: '*You* are not aware that there is no such thing as helical diffraction theory.' Donohue's only response to Crick's legitimate request that he build a structure came in a letter to *Nature*, where he said that being asked to produce a model was like demanding that a critic of a Wagner opera put on their own production.[15] Neither Donohue nor Wu ever accepted Crick's challenge.[16]

*

While all this was going on, in June 1970 *Nature* published yet another snotty anonymous article, this time aimed at Francis.[17] Recently, David Baltimore on the one hand, and Howard Temin and Satoshi Mizutani on the other, had simultaneously discovered a viral enzyme, later called reverse transcriptase, that had the surprising ability to copy information from RNA into DNA. With an inflammatory title ('Central Dogma Reversed' – clickbait before clickbait), the *Nature* article claimed that this discovery was a major blow to the central dogma, which it erroneously described as the idea that genetic information flowed from DNA to messenger RNA and then to protein.

Within two weeks Francis had submitted a response, accompanied by a letter to *Nature* editor John Maddox accusing the journal of misrepresenting his views.[18] Although Crick light-heartedly reassured Maddox he did not require a public apology, he did want his riposte to be published quickly 'while the matter is still topical'. It duly appeared four weeks later, virtually unchanged.[19] Crick began by insisting that he never claimed that the flow of information went solely from DNA to RNA to protein, and that neither he nor any of his colleagues had ever suggested that the transfer from RNA to DNA could not occur.* The discovery of reverse transcriptase was important, but did not affect the central dogma, which flowed from the recognition that some kinds of information transfers had never been observed and seemed structurally improbable (especially, protein → DNA). In other words, the central dogma was 'a negative statement, saying that transfers from proteins did not exist,' he wrote. He had explained this at a meeting in 1964, when Temin's original suggestion that RNA viruses might copy themselves into DNA was put to him: 'I was just going to say for the record the central dogma doesn't say you can't go back from RNA to DNA. It merely says you can't go back from protein to nucleic acid.'[20]

To underline this point, in his *Nature* article Francis presented a new version of the unpublished diagram he had created in 1956. To truly reverse the central dogma, Crick argued, a cell would have to be found that used one of the three unknown transfers of sequence information from protein (protein → protein, protein → RNA, protein

---

*Microbiologist Horst Malke pointed out to Crick that Jim Watson, in his best-selling textbook *Molecular Biology of the Gene*, stated 'RNA never acts as a template for DNA' and described the central dogma as DNA → RNA → protein. Abashed, Crick admitted that Malke was correct and said that Watson 'must take a large degree of responsibility for the term "the central dogma" being incorrectly used.' Malke to Crick, 29 September 1970; Crick to Malke, 20 October 1970, PP/CRI/D/1/1/13. Crick read Watson's book when it came out in 1965 but does not appear to have noticed Watson's error. Crick to Watson, 25 October 1965, JDW/2/2/404.

→ DNA). Over half a century later, we still not have found such a cell, and Crick's concept looks increasingly well-founded.

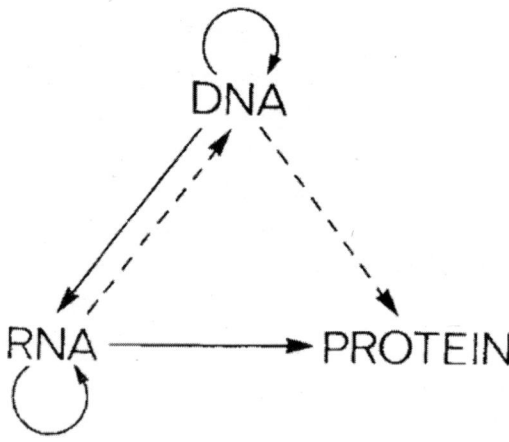

Fig. 2. The arrows show the situation as it seemed in 1958. Solid arrows represent probable transfers, dotted arrows possible transfers. The absent arrows (compare Fig. 1) represent the impossible transfers postulated by the central dogma. They are the three possible arrows starting from protein.

In a personal letter to Temin, Francis developed his thinking with such clarity that, had these passages been published, they might have prevented many subsequent misunderstandings:

> I do not subscribe to the view that all 'information' is necessarily located in nucleic acid. The central dogma applies only to the residue-by-residue sequence. In fact, I suspect that the cell cortex holds 'information' in the broad sense. (…) For example, the activating enzymes, the transfer RNA and the ribosomes are necessary for protein synthesis, and also define the genetic code, but they are not the sequence information itself, which resides in the mRNA.[21]

And as he emphasised, because enzymes can modify protein sequences after the molecules have been synthesised, not every amino acid in a protein has been specified in the corresponding DNA sequence.

Francis also engaged Temin in what he described as a 'rather highbrow' discussion, flowing from his conviction that DNA did not contain '*all* the information'. As for where the additional information came from, his mind reeled:

> Was it coded by the DNA (though indirectly) at some previous time, or was there an infinite regress back in time *not* depending entirely on the DNA? For example, the cortex of an egg probably contains (in many cases) essential information for the development of the egg. Was this controlled by the DNA in the oocyte? Or was it due to the cortex in some previous cell, which depended again on the cortex of some previous cell, etc. (…) It is extremely difficult even to state the problem in a really rigorous way, and the above remarks should only be regarded as a sketch.

Sketch or not, this shows that Crick was not the double helix obsessive portrayed by Commoner and others. He fully understood the essential role of cells and the proteins they contain, and the difficulty of conceptualising how the whole complex system might have evolved.

Crick had been tussling with this problem for some time – in 1966 he had given a lecture on the origin of the genetic code, which formed the basis of a 1968 article that appeared in the *Journal of Molecular Biology*, together with an accompanying paper by Leslie Orgel.[22] Francis explained why the code is the way it is, with no apparent logical structure, and why it is (nearly) universal – either there is some hidden structural, molecular explanation, or, as he considered, it is a frozen accident. By this, he meant that once the code was established, for a series of specific or even random reasons for each codon/amino acid pair, any change would so disrupt gene function that it would be lethal. As a result, life is stuck with a highly redundant code that looks illogical. He also emphasised the importance of nucleic acids in protein synthesis, including the role of tRNA and the preponderance of RNA in the composition of the ribosome. This led him to wonder whether the primitive machinery of life involved only RNA, and that the first enzyme was an RNA molecule that could catalyse nucleic acid replication. Crick, like his friend Orgel and the microbiologist

Carl Woese, was thinking that before life-forms based on DNA, RNA and protein, there had been an RNA world, now lost.

The article was also notable for its emphasis on the power of natural selection. Crick had learned a profound lesson from rubbing shoulders with biologists over the decades and realised not only that random events could have significant consequences for the pattern of evolution, but also that even with natural selection, the outcome would often be messy.

*

In October 1969, *Nature* celebrated its centenary, and John Maddox invited Crick to a two-day bash that included a cocktail party at the British Museum, a banquet at the Royal Society in the presence of Sir Harold Macmillan (one-time British Prime Minister and Chairman of the magazine's publishers), and a set of talks at the Royal Institution, where Francis gave a lecture entitled 'How Molecular Is Biology?' which, as Maddox requested, included a 'peep into the future'.[23] Afterwards, Maddox told Crick that his talk was the best thing he had heard for years.[24]

The Editor of NATURE
requests the pleasure of the company of

Dr. F. Crick

at a cocktail party to
celebrate the centenary of

on Friday 31st October 1969   6.30 - 8.30
at the British Museum (Natural History), Cromwell Road London SW7

RSVP

In the following months, many people asked Francis what he had said that made such an impression. Becoming tired of repeating himself and having recently acquired a Dictaphone, he used his notes to re-improvise the talk, which was then typed up.[25] After a few weeks of polishing and redrafting, he sent the article to *Nature* where it eventually appeared with a bold prophetic title, 'Molecular Biology in the Year 2000'.[26]

Some of Crick's broad predictions were quite accurate – China would become a major scientific power, the role of DNA control sequences and of repetitive DNA would be understood, as would the mechanisms of muscle contraction and of synapse modification during learning.*[27] Crick was equally correct in identifying areas where he expected that little progress would be made – understanding the complex interactions between evolution and ecology, the origin of life on Earth and the nature of consciousness.

Progress on our knowledge of genomes – not dealt with in the article but mentioned in the lecture – has far surpassed his expectations.[28] Francis predicted that by 2000 we might have the sequence of a few viruses and of some genes, but certainly not of whole chromosomes, never mind of a multicellular organism. Given his talk was given eight years before DNA sequencing became a reality, his pessimism is not surprising. Furthermore, the breakthroughs that allowed the sequencing of whole chromosomes and then whole genomes, culminating in the first draft of the human genome in 2003, involved the development of new computers and automated sequencing, both of which would have been hard to predict, even for Crick's galaxy brain.

*

One of the issues that Crick expected would be solved by the year 2000 was the organisation of chromosomes. In 1965, Jacob and Monod had won the Nobel Prize for their work on the mechanisms that controlled the activity of bacterial genes. In their model there were structural genes, which encoded proteins, and regulatory genes

---

*On Crick's death in 2004, *Nature* described his predictions as 'a remarkably accurate summary of the issues that have occupied biologists over the past three-and-a-half decades'. Anonymous (2004), Passing the torch, *Nature* 430:815.

that controlled their activity. How these different kinds of genes might be organised, in terms of both their interaction and their chromosomal distribution, was the subject of speculation. The problem was particularly intriguing because it was becoming apparent that in many organisms much of the genome was not involved in coding proteins – huge chunks of DNA seemed to be composed of repeated, apparently non-sensical sequences.[29] Many people began to wonder if the distribution of the different kind of genetic sequences – structural, regulatory and non-coding – on the chromosome might reveal something about gene function. In 1971 Francis became interested in this idea and, using his influence at *Nature*, quickly published an article on the topic that he expected to be of immense significance. But it all turned out to be hopelessly, uselessly mistaken, prompting a major mental crisis.

It all began in May, at a small meeting on DNA in eukaryotes (organisms with a cell nucleus, including all multicellular organisms) held on Port-Cros, a tiny island on the French Riviera.[30] Most of the people who had been speculating about chromosome organisation were there, and Crick's job was to act as ringmaster in the final session, synthesising the sometimes contradictory ideas that had been presented. According to a report in *Nature*, he did this with aplomb – 'Dr Francis Crick accomplished the near miracle of presiding over a final discussion which genuinely stimulated the participants to reconsider and probe the earlier contributions.'[31] He also uttered a few words of warning, pointing out that the field resembled the ultra-speculative period before the discovery of mRNA, when 'all kinds of controversial new ideas were being canvassed', virtually all of which turned out to be wrong. His audience may have heeded his words, but he did not.

After a month-long holiday in Greece with Odile, he was off again on the merry-go-round of meetings. After first attending an MRC panel in Edinburgh to discuss progress on mapping the mammalian genome, which focused in part on the function of non-coding DNA (estimated at up to 99 per cent of the genome), Francis then went to the NATO summer school, which had been moved from Spetsai to Erice on Sicily.[32] That was where his brain began to fizz.

During the school, 'Gordy' Tomkins described a potential link between RNA gene regulation mechanisms in E. *coli* and those in mammalian cells.[33] As Crick listened, he put together the ideas he had heard at Port-Cros, Tomkins' data-rich speculation, and recent work on histones, the proteins involved in chromosomes.[34] Cogs clicked and wheels whirred in his head and he immediately scribbled a hasty letter to the one man who would understand him, Sydney Brenner.[35] The opening was quite something: 'My Dear Sydney, I think I have solved, in outline, the structure of the eukaryotic genome.'

As Francis explained feverishly, his idea was that gene regulation by proteins and RNA occurred only when the two DNA strands were separated. Chromosomes therefore had a three-dimensional structure that consisted of normal paired DNA strands, separated strands and paired DNA strands established between different regions of repetitive DNA. All this changed dynamically during gene regulation, he claimed.

No sooner was Crick back in Cambridge than he and Brenner launched into days of intense work, attempting to turn the insight Crick had sensed developing in his imagination into a theory of gene regulation and chromosomal organisation in higher organisms. Shut away in their office, the pair argued back and forth, scribbling furiously on the blackboard, filling the air with chalk dust and crazy ideas. As in the Cavendish in March 1953 with Watson, steam seemed to be rising. Exactly what they were discussing was kept from everyone in the LMB.[36]

After a little over a week, Francis broke cover and presented his idea to a small group of colleagues. He and Brenner had come up with a model of chromosome structure based on a series of numbered postulates or assumptions about gene function.[37] Apparently hoping to repeat his success with the central dogma, he coined a couple of fancy-sounding phrases that formed part of the scaffolding of his idea – the 'Principle of Abundant Variability' (highly successful molecular systems must have great variability to adapt to different situations) and the 'Unpairing Postulate' (coding DNA strands must be totally unravelled to be regulated). Both are now completely forgotten.

After explaining their model, Crick and Brenner retreated to their office to write up a long article, rattling off several versions,

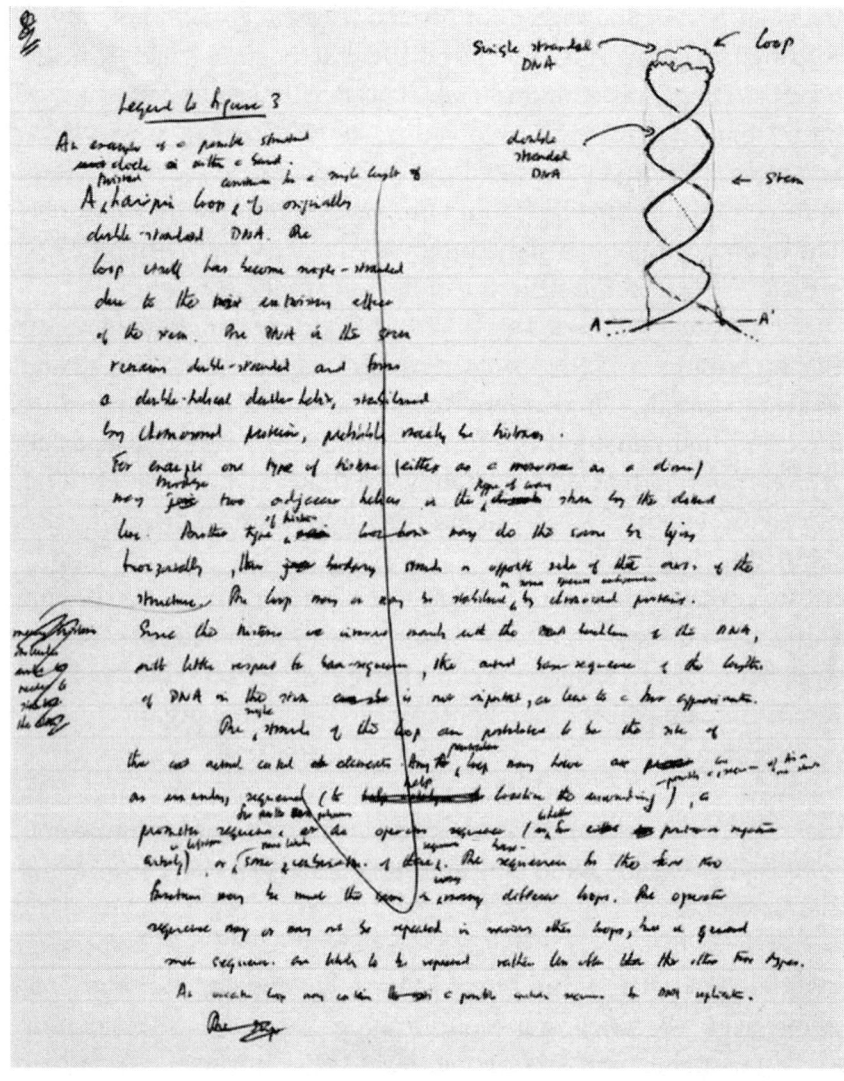

parts of which were written by Sydney.[38] Crick's handwriting on the drafts was hasty, even frenzied, full of crossings-out and additions. At the same time, Brenner drew up a supporting article in which he used his experiments on mutation frequencies in *C. elegans* worms to support the growing conviction in laboratories around the world that much of the genome did not code for anything important. This data, he claimed, fitted with Crick's model.[39]

By the end of the month, Crick and Brenner had accepted defeat

– the baggy monster they were producing was far too long to be published by *Nature*. Instead, they decided to write a 'summary' that included the promise of a longer account to come. In four days of frantic activity, Crick, with help from Brenner, Perutz and two courageous typists, successively hammered out what Francis described as 'three and a half' versions of the article.* The manuscript was finally ready the day before he left for a two-week trip – first to Yerevan in Soviet Armenia for a strange meeting on communication with extraterrestrial intelligence (CETI), then on to a conference on cell differentiation in Nice.[40]

That same day, Francis summoned the members of the LMB – along with journalist Horace Judson, who was beginning work on his oral history of molecular biology, *The Eighth Day of Creation* – to hear an outline of the new version of his paper, which no longer featured all those pretentious postulates.[41] The idea was still surrounded by secrecy: although two copies of the manuscript were left in the LMB coffee room and Crick emphasised that the article was 'NOT SECRET', he insisted that it should not be photocopied until after his return.

The paper – 'General Model for the Chromosomes of Higher Organisms' – began by explaining that this was merely the conclusion of a longer article that would appear later. Crick claimed that the DNA in chromosomes came in two states, 'fibrous' – sections of classic double helix – and 'globular', where the DNA was all wrapped up, forming the dark chromosomal bands that can sometimes be observed. While fibrous DNA was the protein-encoding nucleic acid that Crick had been thinking about over the previous two decades, the more extensive globular DNA corresponded to the control sequences, which included vast stretches of repetitive DNA. Fibrous DNA, he suggested, was composed of sections where the two strands were separated by the action of histones, enabling RNA

---

*This was one of the last official services that Crick's secretary, Pauline Finbow, performed for him. A couple of days later, she left the LMB to have a baby. She remained close to the Cricks, later managing their affairs in Cambridge. On leaving the LMB, she told Francis: 'the last four years working for you and Sydney have been the most happy and memorable of my working career.' Finbow to Crick, 10 September 1971, MSS 660, Box 3, Folder 33.

molecules to bind with a particular gene and thereby control its activity. Virtually all of this was wrong.

The submission letter to *Nature* that accompanied the manuscript was remarkable for the intensity with which Crick wrote (he signed off 'Excuse the excitement').[42] For example, he explained that despite his best efforts to keep the work confidential, word had got out and now people were inviting him to speak on the topic and sending him their articles to be included. 'I am therefore anxious to get something into print rapidly,' he wrote. Then, apologising for the fact that the legends to the three schematic figures were as long as the rest of the paper, he asked for them to be printed in larger type than usual, 'since so many important points are contained in them'. In a similar vein, he pleaded that sub-editors should not tinker with the text – 'Sydney and I have spent a lot of time on the exact wording in order to convey precisely what I mean and no more.'

Two additional points in the letter revealed Crick's great state of excitement. First, he gave instructions for dealing with the proofs during his two-week absence, as though the journal would be rushing the article into print (they did not – it appeared two months later). Second, he insisted that a footnote be included pleading that readers with access to photocopiers should not request reprints. Francis expected ten thousand reprint requests; 'This would impose a heavy burden on our secretaries,' he explained. *Nature* did not comply.

*

Crick's mind was in overdrive. At the Yerevan meeting on CETI in early September he repeatedly bobbed up in the biology-focused sections, at one point bubbling over with excitement about his work on chromosome organisation even though it had nothing to do with the discussion.[43] One night it was so hot that Francis could not sleep; his brain buzzed some more and he came up with an explanation of the origin of life on Earth.[44] This was an apparently brilliant idea with little evidence, the kind of thing we all dream up in the middle of the night but then think better of the next morning. Not Francis.

Over lunch a few days earlier, Francis, Leslie Orgel and Carl

The meeting on Communication with Extraterrestrial
Intelligence in the USSR, September 1971. Crick said of the
photo, 'it is obvious we were all enjoying ourselves'.

Sagan had discussed the theory of panspermia ('sperm' means
'seed') – the idea that life came to Earth accidentally from outer
space – and the main problem with this suggestion, which was that
cosmic radiation would damage any alien microbes, even if they
were embedded in a comet.[45] Crick's fevered night-time solution
was that the microbes had been deliberately sent to Earth on a pro-
tective spaceship, by an alien civilisation motivated by missionary
zeal. Orgel was somehow impressed by this nonsense and the pair
decided to turn Crick's flimsy idea into an article as soon as they
returned to England.[46]

Francis was now thinking hard about three major articles on
wildly different subjects. There was the *Nature* chromosome mas-
terpiece, the panspermia idea produced by Crick's boiling brain and

Lawrence's draft of their article on development, which Francis had just completely rewritten.[47] And there was a whole new area that was beginning to enthral him. The Japanese population geneticist Motoo Kimura had recently published an article on the role of mutations and gene duplication in evolution; Francis immediately wrote an enthusiastic letter to Kimura – he felt that Kimura's results supported his chromosome model.[48] Crick also expressed his excitement at the possibility of using genetic variation to study the pattern of evolution, something that he pointed out he had first suggested in 1957.* Francis immediately resolved to get to grips with population genetics, in order to pursue this work.

The first indications that all might not be well with either Francis or his beloved chromosome model came at the Nice meeting in mid-September, where he gave a brief presentation on the still-unpublished paper. In its report on the meeting, *Nature* mocked his responses to questions from the audience: 'On being questioned after his presentation, Dr Crick successfully destroyed all attempts to introduce facts as counter-evidence by demonstrating, or just by stating, that the facts were predicted, indeed demanded, by his model.'[49] Francis might have seemed ultra-confident, but he was beginning to have doubts. On his notes for the talk, next to the description of the final slide in which he claimed histones might distort the structure of DNA to reveal a single strand, he later scrawled 'UTTER NONSENSE'.[50]

---

*This was news to Kimura who told Crick he was 'deeply impressed with your remarkable foresight'. Kimura to Crick, 2 November 1971, PP/CRI/D/1/2/6.

Once back in Cambridge, Crick sent *Nature* a slightly revised version of the chromosome article and was soon pestering the journal for news of the article's progress. 'We will publish your piece as soon as possible,' Maddox replied patiently.[51]

Francis also began work with Orgel on the aliens article, now entitled 'Directed Panspermia'. They initially thought about sending it to *Playboy*, before deciding on a more academic forum.[52] A key piece of their argument was that many enzymes require the trace element molybdenum to function, but this metal is extremely rare in the Earth's crust, implying that it was unlikely that life could have evolved on Earth to rely upon it. This impressed Kreisel but it turned out to be a dead end – the levels of molybdenum in the oceans, where life began, are much higher, so there was no mystery. Crick's friend Tom Jukes scolded him that this was 'an ancient and well-known fact'.[53]

The largely impenetrable chromosome article appeared in *Nature* on 5 November 1971, accompanied by a page-long editorial.[54] But the trumpeting was somewhat muted; the journal hoped the paper would focus researchers' attention on critical issues in chromosome organisation, but added a sting: 'Unhappily, it is not obvious how this will be done.' It was even hard to see how the model could be tested.

This problem was brought home to Francis a couple of weeks later, when *Nature* sent him an article on chromosome organisation to review. Written by John Paul of the Institute of Cancer Research, this paper used pretty much the same evidence as Crick's but came to the opposite conclusion – the dark bands of chromosomes contained structural genes and the light bands contained regulatory sequences.[55] There was no way of choosing between these two equally clever, and, as it turned out, equally wrong models.[56]

Crick was late returning his review of Paul's article to *Nature* because something had happened. On 15 November, he attended the opening session of an ambitious symposium in London on cell interactions, which featured friends like Seymour Benzer and Lewis Wolpert, as well as some leading figures of early neuroscience, such as Eric Kandel and Adrian Horridge. Crick had agreed to sum up the disparate threads of the three-day discussion, but on the first afternoon, he abruptly walked out and went home. Ten days later he wrote to the conference organiser, apologising for abandoning the meeting and explaining: 'I am afraid I have been overworking too much – my doctor has now told me to have a complete rest for several weeks.'[57] The unusual stylistic slip – 'overworking too much' – is telling.

There had been warning signs. Earlier in the year Francis repeatedly complained in letters to colleagues of being 'hopelessly over-worked', while photographs taken at the CETI conference in Yerevan show him looking gaunt.[58] At the Nice meeting he missed a reception at which he was to receive an award, and just before his crisis, at the beginning of November, Francis spent the weekend in bed, unable to get up, despite having an imminent trip to Tübingen.[59] As he admitted to John Maddox, 'in spite of all my efforts to be lazy I am hopelessly over-worked, mainly because of these recent ideas about chromosomes.'[60]

Crick explained his breakdown in varying ways: 'I've worked myself to a standstill,' he said to one colleague, while to another he wrote, 'Last year I had so many ideas that I seriously overworked myself and for the last two or three months I have had to take a rest.'[61] His busy mind had ground to a halt, as he confirmed to a friend in March:

> As you may have gathered the meeting at Port-Cros had unexpected results for me. A few months later, while at a summer school in Sicily, I began to think about chromosome structure and eventually, in a great rush, published the enclosed paper. The whole proved so difficult that I overworked myself and was told by my Doctor, before Christmas, to take six weeks holiday.[62]

An additional factor, which may have provided more stress, was an unusually intense affair that he began around this time with a married woman.[63]

*

It took Francis many months to recover from his crisis. This was partly because he did not obey his doctor's instructions to stay away from the laboratory – within two weeks of walking out of the London conference, he was writing long letters to colleagues about his chromosome model.[64] He also wrote a detailed two-page letter about free will – despite his collapse, he was able to muster some fairly cogent views, essentially arguing that without knowing more about brain structure and function, 'any judgement made at the present time is likely to be valueless'.[65] None of this helped his recovery.

Francis said that he had felt 'a bit dim' over Christmas, and even in February he had little enthusiasm for work.[66] If all this sounds like Francis was depressed, perhaps he was. That was certainly the impression of Mark Bretscher: 'During this period I only remember seeing him once; he came to ask me my opinion about something of no consequence at all. He was very pale; I was astonished by this consultation and lack of self-assurance.'[67] Members of the Division of Cell Biology at the LMB were so concerned about Crick's state that they sent him some get-well flowers, for which he was very grateful.[68]

Although his new secretary, Sue Barnes, noted in her diary that Francis was occasionally in a very good mood, he was rarely in the LMB, instead summoning her to Portugal Place where she would type for hours on end.[69] When he was in the office, the atmosphere was often chaotic – 'Extremely busy could hardly find time to breathe' and 'So busy could've screamed' were among Barnes' diary entries. Crick's mood was further affected by the death of his Aunt Ethel, who had been frail for some time, and by Odile experiencing problems with her vision – she had a torn retina that needed an operation. As Crick told Leslie Orgel, it was only a small operation, but it was worrying.[70] When it all went well, Barnes recorded that Crick was singing; however, Odile ended up with weeks of complications due to an infection.

The emotional, intellectual and physical crisis of late 1971 left lasting scars. In May 1972 Francis decided that he would not accept any invitations to speak or attend conferences from May 1973 onwards.[71] The remaining months were very tiring, with twelve unavoidable engagements, several lasting more than a week and all but one of them abroad.[72]

Francis seemed to have lost his mojo, and even the award of the Royal Medal by the Royal Society for his work on DNA and molecular biology did not seem to give him a boost.[73] Although colleagues were polite about his chromosome paper, the opinion at the LMB was that it was not his finest work. He never tried to write up the promised longer version and when people asked when it would be published, he first made excuses, then promised to work on the paper in the summer before eventually ignoring the question.[74] His subsequent lectures on the topic became less assertive, emphasising the need for caution, noting the lack of experimental support and the absence of any *'compelling* theoretical arguments' for his beloved model.[75] A year after it appeared, Francis admitted in private that he had reservations about the article and that the evidence for the unwinding idea at its heart was weak.[76]

There was no brilliant experiment that disproved Crick's grand chromosome theory, only the slow realisation that everything about it was profoundly mistaken. In spring 1972, Bretscher gave Crick's paper to Roger Kornberg, an American post-doctoral researcher who had recently joined the LMB; Kornberg recalled that he could not make head nor tail of it, but he became intrigued by the question of the structure of the proteins that were bound up with DNA.[77] Within two years, Kornberg helped show that rather than histones protecting DNA as Francis and everyone else assumed, they in fact formed tiny bead-like structures called nucleosomes, which DNA was wrapped around.[78] All of Crick's clever imaginings about the coding parts of DNA having to be unwound by histones turned out to be wide of the mark.* Although Crick's *Nature* chromosome article has been cited in over four hundred publications,† most of those citations occurred in the two years following publication, when it was still possible it might be correct. It was never cited by F. H. C. Crick.

The draft of the directed panspermia squib was also affected by Crick's damaged confidence. The style was flattened: a jokey

---

*When DNA is transcribed, chromatin (DNA + histones) becomes less tightly packed, allowing transcription factors and RNA access to the DNA strands to regulate transcription.

†All citation data are taken from the Science Citation Index. Figures from Google Scholar are generally higher but less accurate.

Crickian phrase – 'Perhaps – after all – God is not dead but is alive and well and living in Andromeda' – was deleted in the editing, while the aliens who might have sent the microbes were no longer referred to as 'the Senders'.[79] Shorn of the brash certainty of the stifling Yerevan night when the idea wriggled into his head, Crick now sought merely to show that the suggestion was not totally implausible. This relied upon what he called the 'Theorem of Detailed Cosmic Reversibility', which simply stated that because we might engage in such a project, aliens might do so, too. Despite the criticisms of a reviewer who suspected the whole thing was a joke, the article was eventually accepted by *Icarus*, the International Journal of Solar System Studies, and appeared in 1973.[80] This rather obscure choice of journal was deliberate and probably reflected Crick's declining confidence in the article – a year later he explained that they tried 'not to give it a very wide circulation', while in 1977 he admitted to Kreisel that the whole thing was 'an exercise in imagination' that 'lacks any serious scientific support'.[81]

ADVANCE NOTICE

SIO Marine Biology Seminar

Direct Panspermia

Professor Francis Crick

Nobel Laureate, 1962

Non-resident Fellow, The Salk Institute

Medical Research Council
Laboratory of Molecular Biology
Cambridge, England

Friday, November 5, 1976
12:05
Sumner Auditorium
Scripps Institution of Oceanography

Francis's two brilliant ideas from the summer of 1971 had blown up in his face, leaving him exhausted and subdued. Crick had reached a crux in his life.

*

Crick's chromosome theory was not the first time that he had been hopelessly wrong. In November 1951 his triple helix model of DNA had made him look ridiculous; in 1957 he had proposed the beautiful comma-less theory of the genetic code which was soon destroyed by experimental facts, while in 1961, together with Leslie Orgel, he had proposed the utterly mistaken coding theory called loopy codes.[82] But these were mainly private fiascos. Even the elegant comma-less code, which was published in the *PNAS* in 1957, was hedged with warnings that it was almost certainly wrong.[83] Furthermore, the Crick who made these mistakes was not the Crick of 1971, the man who could telephone the editor of *Nature* and get an article accepted instantly, the scientist who was feted by his peers and viewed with awe by many. Paradoxically, because Francis was now so well established, with such a planetary reputation, there was more at stake than when he was an obscure rank-and-file scientist.

The events of 1971 can be explained by Francis not heeding his own warnings. In his *Nature* article defending the central dogma, he correctly explained that 'well-constructed theories can play a really useful part in stating problems clearly and thus guiding experiment'. But as the *Nature* editorial highlighted, the all-encompassing theory in the chromosome paper pointed to no particular experimental test. At Port-Cros, Francis warned his colleagues that the field of gene regulation and chromosomal structure was afflicted by 'all kinds of controversial new ideas', but then went on to produce just such a new idea, with no experimental backing.

Once, Francis had known the dangers; the cover of the 1956 preprint of his doomed comma-less code paper carried a warning from the seventeenth-century thinker Francis Bacon, advice that fifteen years later Francis appears to have forgotten: 'It cannot be that axioms established by argumentation can suffice for the discovery of new works, since the subtlety of nature is greater many times than the subtlety of argument.'[84] Bacon emphasised that thinkers should avoid a purely logical approach to discovery, but that was exactly the trap that Francis had fallen into. This time his mad sessions had produced only madness. Trying to think about too many things at once while rushing around the planet, Francis had lost his bearings and his scientific judgement, had become supremely over-confident and had finally crashed and burned. Emotionally and physically diminished by the crisis and abashed by the gap between his expectations and reality, Crick took months to recover. It would be four years before he submitted another scientific article to *Nature*.

INTERLUDE

In   or   in   in
   b   p   e   g O   m
     e   u   k   a   f
       n   r   a   s r
         d   s   n   d   d
           i   u s   n   e
             n   e   a   n
               g   a d   h   s
                 as   by   a

                   so   in
                 E   b   s
                   n   r   e
                     t   a   t
                       w   i   a
                         i   d F
                           n   e   e
                             e   O d   b
                               us   is

```
    on      am
d   f I     c           b
      o         h       m
      h r       a    i       e
     c w     i    l          m
   i      a       n c        y
   h       r      e        h
  w         d    I d     r
          as      in



            d
  t        a
  u      e
   r     r
    n h     d
     i t    a
      n    e
 s  a g  d
   of    is
```

CREATIVE WRITING

Francis was not just a scientist; poetry always interested him, often in ways that might seem to belie his rigorously materialist outlook. For example, while on honeymoon in 1949, he fell into discussion about poetry with an Italian man and ended up recommending the verse of the English Jesuit mystic Gerard Manley Hopkins.[1] By the mid-1960s, however, Crick's views seemed to have changed. In a letter to the British intellectual C. P. Snow, he described how he had fallen out of love with some of the greats of world literature:

> Personally, I am quite unable to read, say, Sophocles or Dante. They are not merely irrelevant, they are distinctly unpleasant. I can still enjoy Dostoevsky, Tolstoy or Proust (though I notice I haven't read them for some years) but I doubt if my descendants will. (…) It would almost appear that you can't be a major poet without a solid foundation of silly ideas (almost everybody thinks Yeats's ideas silly but to me Eliot's are just as bad).[2]

Crick went on to explain that his alienation from literature flowed from his conviction that future studies of the brain would make the 'old culture completely bankrupt', using an Ibsen quotation to high-light his feeling of isolation: 'I feel that before long most educated intelligent men will feel as I do; that I am "in league with the future". I know this is a common delusion, but I don't feel this because I consider myself a prophet, but because the point of view I hold seems to me to be obvious.'

That 'obvious' represents an important blind spot in Crick's thinking. When something appears straightforward but is not evident to others, the challenge is to understand the factors that cause others to disagree. Only then can one properly comprehend their point of view and work out arguments that might change their mind. Crick did this highly effectively in scientific matters, but as seen in his private discussions of science and society, on social, political and cultural questions he was often nonplussed by the apparent incommensurability of his self-evident views and the attitudes of others, but made no further effort to understand.

Crick's letter to Snow was sent during the British intellectual debate known as 'the two cultures', after the title of Snow's 1959 lecture which highlighted that while a knowledge of history and the arts was assumed essential for a well-rounded education, many intellectuals, civil servants and politicians were profoundly ignorant of basic scientific principles, such as the Second Law of Thermodynamics. In 1962, a Cambridge lecturer in English Literature, F. R. Leavis, wrote a bad-tempered response, attracting a great deal of media and intellectual attention, and propelling the issue onto the public stage.[3]

Crick was even used as a symbol in the debate: Snow published an updated version of his essay, now arguing that everyone should understand the structure of DNA and its implications, while Jacob Bronowski – another British intellectual who was close to Crick – dramatised the arguments in a BBC radio play, *The Abacus and the Rose*.[4] This occasionally stilted three-hander featured a high-ranking civil servant who represented Snow, a spikey Leavis character, and a scientist who, although he spoke in Bernal's Irish brogue, was modelled on Crick.

In the late 1960s, Francis became increasingly fascinated by modern poetry, partly because some poets were using their writing to explore their interest in science. For Francis, the most significant of these writers was Michael McClure. Crick never explained how he could find the mystical ideas of Yeats and Eliot silly and yet revel in McClure's mystical psychedelic Beat poetry, but it seems that McClure's materialism was what counted – whatever the fluid heat of the poetry, marked by the hallucinogenic experience, it contained no Celtic spirits or Anglican mumbo-jumbo, only what Francis later called 'the howling mammal, contrived out of "meat" by chance and necessity'.[5] Already intrigued by McClure's work, by the end of the 1960s Crick's mind was now sufficiently tuned – blown – to meet McClure in person.

It was McClure who made the first move. In 1966 Francis had written to McClure's publisher asking for permission to use the *THIS IS THE POWERFUL KNOWLEDGE* stanza from 'Peyote Poem' as an epigraph in *Of Molecules and Men*. McClure responded enthusiastically, saying he was fascinated by molecular biology and was sending Francis a 'poem in the form of a molecular chance deck'.[*6] Crick responded to the publisher with slight bemusement – 'I cannot say I fully grasp this but I have sent a postcard to Michael McClure thanking him for it.' McClure seems to have forgotten all this, for in September 1970 he came across *Of Molecules and Men* with the epigraph from 'Peyote Poem' and was overjoyed, immediately sending Francis a copy of 'The Surge', a poem he had sent to *Scientific American* in 1961 (they had ignored it). McClure had recently published it as a slim brochure and he sent a copy to Cambridge, dedicated to Sir Francis Crick.[7] Among the lines that will have caught Crick's eye was this stanza:

> Genetics and memory
> are the same
> they are degrees of one
> molecular unity

---

*This was DREAM TABLE, a deck of thirty cards in an envelope, created by McClure in 1965 with Dave Haselwood. Each card bore two words (WINE DARK, BREATH ROAR, FLASH SMILE, etc.) on one side, a small engraving of a lion's head and of a tree and four small squares (one on each corner) and two dots on the other. Crick kept it for the rest of his life. MSS 660, Box 7, Folder 12.

Francis replied enthusiastically, thanking the poet for the gift and explaining that he owned several of McClure's books including *The Beard*, his notorious play involving a sexual encounter between Jean Harlow and Billy the Kid (Francis regretted that he had missed the play when it was performed in London in 1968).[8] He also said that he and Odile would be in La Jolla in January 1971 and that it would be fun to meet.

McClure's reply was equally positive, saying it was terrific to hear from him: 'Your work has made so much possible for me in poetry – and personally-spiritually,' McClure wrote, before concluding: 'Your discoveries have made it possible for thinking persons to re-evaluate their stance towards nature – it's as if a core were put into the possibilities of perception.'[9] McClure also enclosed a poem, 'Moiré', dedicated to Crick, and promised to send an essay, 'WOLF NET', which he said was 'a poet's view of biology', hoping that Francis might comment on it.

Even by McClure's standards, 'Moiré' is a rather odd beast – it consists of eighty-two numbered phrases, each composed of five to ten words, all in capitals. It is full of references to animals (sea otters, dragons, wolves, planarian flatworms) and perceptions, and although the 'point' is not immediately obvious, there was enough style and nods in the direction of Crick's interests for him to embrace it by immersing himself in the words.[10] As Professor Geoff Ward, an expert on American poetry, explained to me, McClure's poetry 'is very straightforwardly, ecstatically assertive, and calls for recognition rather than analysis'.[11] These lines from the middle of 'Moiré' give an impression:

35. THE DESERT IS ALIVE.
36. THE FIR FEELS THE SOLSTICE.
37. SENSE HORIZONTALLY, ASPIRE VERTICALLY
    – *AGNOSIA*.
38. KEATS, DIRAC, DIONYSIUS THE AEROPAGITE.
39. TRUMPETS, CYMBALS, WARM GRASS, ROAR OF A
    MOTORCYLE.
40. LEATHER, QUARTZ AND CINNAMON.
41. DISSOLUTION IS A PRIVILEGE.

42. HAIL PLANARIAN!

You can imagine Francis reading this out to Odile while they smoked a joint in the solitude of Well Cottage, with Hendrix blasting out of the speakers. Francis was very happy with the poem, as he told McClure:

> Both Odile and I enjoyed Moiré very much, and I was very flattered that you should dedicate it to me. It expands on repeated readings, and the succession of images has a tremendous impact. (...) Yes, do send me a copy of WOLF NET, though I'm not very good at commenting – but I'd love to see what it's like.[12]

'WOLF NET', which arrived a few weeks later, opened with a bold statement of McClure's outlook – 'When a man does not admit that he is an animal, he is less than an animal' – then developed its emphasis on humans as the product of evolution – 'We are born out of physical matter from a spectrum of inorganic matter that shapes itself into amino acids, bacteria, viruses, sponges, and ultimately projects the vertebrate' – before focusing on sensory perception (in this case, perceiving an apple). Crick told McClure: 'I enjoyed WOLF NET, mainly by letting it flow along as I read it. Occasionally my sense of "logic" got the upper hand, but most of the time I was delighted to see that we have the same viewpoint of many things.'[13]

This was not mere flattery. McClure's stance echoed Crick's own views, explained to Snow in 1963:

> Can it really be said that any modern imaginative writing has been influenced by Darwin? Is any thought given in literary articles to the fact that while being men we are also mammals? (...) I think the most powerful criticism one can make of literary intellectuals is that they are like children, merely playing with problems and fundamentally not serious. (...) The reason most poets are nowadays mainly ignored is that they either deal with trivialities or, if they do go deeper they merely appear ridiculous to any educated man.[14]

Michael McClure in 1970.

McClure's approach to the link between science and literature, his interest in and understanding of biology, was exactly what Crick had been looking for.

By this stage in his career, McClure was, in the words of the editor of the London underground paper *International Times*, 'the Prince of the San Francisco poetry scene'.[15] Strikingly good-looking, charismatic, a friend of Janis Joplin and Jim Morrison, the ghost-writer of Hell's Angel Freewheelin' Frank, McClure was extremely well-connected with both the older generation of Beat Poets and the younger countercultural community.

Some of those connections surprisingly spiralled their way back to Crick. For example, one of McClure's good friends was the poet Charles Olson, who in turn was close to J. H. Prynne, a Fellow of Gonville and Caius, who wrote what the *New York Review of Books* called 'famously opaque' poetry which broached scientific themes; the work of both Olson and Prynne focused on what has been described as 'the leap from empirical to mystical revelation' – exactly what Crick took from McClure.*[16] Crick knew Prynne well and considered him to be one of the cleverest men in Cambridge. The respect was mutual; when the pair first met in 1963, Prynne reported that the 'range & penetration' of Crick's mind was 'something close to genius'.[17] Prynne was equally impressed by Crick's knowledge of contemporary American poetry – not only the Beat movement but also the experimental Black Mountain College in North Carolina, where Olson had been the Rector.[18] Prynne also shared Crick's interest in McClure (Prynne showed Francis a copy of McClure's *The Surge* in early 1970).[19]

Or again, one of the people McClure most wanted Crick to meet when in San Francisco was his one-time teacher, the poet Robert Duncan, who had mentioned the imagery of the double helix in his 1962 poem 'A Set of Romantic Hymns'. But Crick had already met Duncan several years earlier – the Zelig-like Kreisel, who was at Stanford at the time, had taken Crick to see Duncan and the pair spent a day together.[20]

Francis was developing a kind of awestruck poetic crush on McClure and thoroughly got into the early seventies Californian groove; shortly before the pair met for the first time in early 1971, he wrote to the poet: 'Your new poem is terrific – a real lyrical outburst. I find I am beginning to live in your image world. Almost to dream your dreams.'[21] That could have been a line from a Grateful Dead song.

The meeting with McClure was a great success, cementing the two men's mutual admiration. Over the years, McClure introduced

---

*In 1992, Prynne gave a lecture in which he drew clever parallels between the 'asymmetrical direction of intracellular data flow' in Crick's central dogma and Ferdinand de Saussure's linguistic theory of the sign and the signifier. However, in a note he suggested that the discovery of reverse transcriptase had compromised the central dogma 'in its strong form', showing he had not fully understood Crick's idea. Prynne, J. H. (1993), *Stars, Tigers and the Shape of Words* (London: Birkbeck College). Prynne, J. H. (2016), The Art of Poetry No. 101, *The Paris Review* 218:174–207.

HOTEL **Del Charro**

2380 TORREY PINES ROAD, LA JOLLA, CALIFORNIA 92037 · TELEPHONE 454-6134

ARTHUR L. FORBES
Manager

Wednesday 3rd Feb 1971

Dear Michael,

Your new poem is terrific — a real lyrical outburst. I find I am beginning to live in your image world. Almost to dream your dreams.

About the weekend. We plan to have dinner with friends in Berkeley on the Friday ~~night~~ evening, so possibly the best thing would be to spend Friday night there. We could arrive at Downey at about midday on Saturday 13th, if that would suit you. I think we ought to fly back to San

Francis to his artistic and scientific friends and collaborators in California; the impression Crick made was often indelible. After seeing a show by McClure and the renowned photographer of the San Francisco scene Larry Keenan, Francis asked McClure to be introduced. Keenan recalled the meeting: 'We spent his visit talking about shadow worlds and dual realities. After they left, I walked around in my house for hours because I was so up, I could not sit down.'[22]

After Francis returned to Cambridge in February, he regretted that he had been too shy to ask McClure to read any of his poetry; McClure promptly sent a tape recording, much to Crick's delight.[23]

Like his poems, McClure's correspondence gave Francis a glimpse into a world in which emotion and sensation surged and shimmered, sometimes in a bizarre fashion. In one letter, McClure enclosed a twenty-two-page stream of consciousness splurge, 'Xes', an 'act of nature' proclaiming we are all 'Pseudopods of Messiah' that was inscribed to Crick.[24] In another, McClure described his latest play in terms that must surely have amused Francis: 'GORF has naked tap-dancers, Giant Penguins, the hero is a flying purple phallus, and the heroine is a blind, sapphic motorcyclist.'[25]

There were moments of incomprehension in their relationship – McClure enthused to Francis about his discussions with the German Marxist philosopher Herbert Marcuse ('the greatest treat in La Jolla'), urging Crick to talk to him and getting Marcuse's agreement to a meeting.[26] Francis was polite – after all, 'there might be something in it,' as he often said – although it is not clear if the two men did ever meet and, if they did, what on earth they might have said to each other. Nevertheless, Francis acquired a copy of Marcuse's book *One-Dimensional Man*, although he may not have read it.[27]

In 1974 Crick was asked to write an article for a special issue of the US magazine *Margins* which would be entirely devoted to McClure; unusually, he accepted the invitation, and a brief article about his responses to McClure's poetry appeared the following year.[28] The cover of the magazine showed McClure, clad in a leather jacket, staring out at the viewer.

In his article, Crick explained how he first encountered McClure's work in City Lights and was subsequently delighted to discover the poet's fascination with science. According to Francis:

> McClure is so at home in the fantastic world that science has conjured out of ourselves and our surroundings – a world which makes that of other cultures seem contrived and pedestrian – that he takes it all in his stride. When he writes lines like LIFE BEGINS WITH COILING – MOLECULES BE NEBULAE or ACTION IS PROTEIN someone like myself can accept them as naturally as a non-scientist can accept CITIES ARE SWIRLS OF POPULATIONS ...

Crick also paid his friend the ultimate compliment: 'If I were a poet I would write like Michael McClure – if only I had the talent.'

That did not mean that Francis was uncritical. Around the same time he responded to a new collection by McClure:

I am not yet quite at home with Organism. I find I resent the pattern of repetition within each poem. In fact when I have got half way I want to stop and not encounter the same lines again. Also I think the images are more disjointed than in some of your poems. But I like the repetition of the pattern from poem to poem and there are many wonderful lines.[29]

McClure took it on the chin, replying that 'Organism' was written 'strictly as an experiment. I was hoping to touch some vein of bio-alchemy in words. I missed, so it stands as it is.'[30] Perhaps he was mollified by Crick's mid-seventies mellow – the letter was uniquely signed, 'Blessings, Francis'.[31]

A few months later, at the end of October 1975, McClure visited the UK to read at the Poetry of the Americas conference in London. At the invitation of Crick and Prynne, he then travelled on to Cambridge where he gave a private reading in Gonville and Caius College – he was looking forward to this, writing in his travel notebook just before he left London, 'will see Francis Crick in less than half a day'.[32] Geoff Ward – then a student – was profoundly struck by the inter-actions between the two men:

I could see a certain affinity between Crick and McClure; with neither was it the easiest of tasks to get a word in, both were supremely self-confident, and both possessed a strong sense of the underlying interconnectedness of things.[33]

After the reading there was the inevitable party in Prynne's college rooms; on leaving the festivities, Ward reflected: 'we had an extraor-dinary evening, not simply in terms of listening to some powerful personalities but people who restored the possibility, generally con-sidered lost, of conversation and shared understanding between and across the Arts and Sciences.' He later recalled: 'Crick was great. Voluble, but fast, crisp, letting the conversation go wherever it felt like going. Great for me as basically a kid of 21 or whatever to be able to be at a conjunction like that.'[34] McClure was equally happy with how the visit went, telling Crick, 'Being able to read those poems to you at Caius College is a gleaming highlight of it all.'[35]

*

Other poets Francis encountered also wanted to explore how poetry and scientific understanding might interact. In September 1968, the poet John Hollander dedicated one of his typed graphematic emblems (a poem in a shape), 'A Shape of Life', to Francis.[36] It consisted of two stanzas, each made up of a double helix; the intricate and elaborately executed form had two strands, which were typed using the black or the red part of the ribbon, each strand alternately appearing at the front.

Around the same time, Francis received a canto of a long poem by the British playwright and poet Ronald Duncan, which was dedicated to Crick – 'your own work has stimulated, even if it has not inspired, me,' Duncan told Crick with odd precision.[37] Duncan explained to Crick that he wanted the work, entitled 'Man', to bring science and poetry together by encompassing no less than the whole history of the Universe and humanity's place within it.[38] Francis replied he had read the canto with considerable interest, and enjoyed reading it, despite finding the scientific passages too didactic.[39] Duncan promised to revise the overly factual sections, although he pleaded for understanding: 'it is damned difficult to digest the scientific matters and make poetry out of them … but I think it's a job that must be attempted unless poetry is to become a mere mush of subjective hosannahs, decorative irrelevancies.'[40] He told his diary that Francis was 'a better poet than I am'.[41] When it was eventually published in 1971, this part of Duncan's poem covered the history of the Earth and the appearance of life, as well as his literary spat with T. S. Eliot over the nature of poetry.[42] Crick felt that, unlike McClure's work, it was only a partial success, but he still bought an expensive copy of a limited edition of Duncan's poems.[43]

A few months later, Francis received another flattering and intriguing letter, this time from Dr Martin Bax, a paediatrician who was also the editor of the poetry magazine *Ambit*. Bax explained that he was organising a happening at the Institute of Contemporary Arts on the Mall in London, at which scientific papers would be read out to a jazz accompaniment.[44] Bax wanted Crick's permission to read out the 1953 *Nature* paper on the structure of DNA; Francis replied enthusiastically and said that although he was otherwise engaged, he would like the details, in case his plans changed.

There is no evidence that Francis was there, but it sounds like it was a blast – as well as the DNA paper, Bax read out articles on viper venom and on the sensory processes of young children, accompanied by a five-piece group that included the bass player from Manfred Mann and the legendary jazz musician Henry Lowther on trumpet, flugelhorn and violin. There are no traces of how the event was received, nor whether Bax's desire to 'wake up' the presentation of science 'so that non-scientists can appreciate it' was achieved.

Duncan's poem and Bax's happening suffered from the same problem – both men seemed to want their work to involve more science than poetry. Duncan sought to encompass the history of the universe, including lots of equations from physics and chemistry, while Bax hoped that phrases such as 'The distance of a phosphorus atom from the fibre axis is 10 Å' would impart their meaning to the uninitiated when proclaimed over the noodling and tooting of improvised jazz. What neither man focused on sufficiently was the poetry of poetry. And no matter how difficult McClure's work might sometimes have been, it was full of poetry.

There were also women artists in the Cricks' circle. At the beginning of 1970, their friend Shusha Guppy, an Iranian writer and singer, invited Francis to attend the Westminster Poetry Festival, where she was performing on the same bill as Ted Hughes.[45] A few months earlier, Guppy wrote to Francis about her meeting with Jonas Salk in La Jolla, using language that was very much of the time: 'Yesterday I had breakfast with Jonas (…) everybody talks about you as the supreme genius, the big-shot who started it all! Not that I didn't know you were great, but I thought because you are so good and generous and life-giving like all good things – trees and flowers and birds and babies …'[46]

With all this poetry floating around in Crick's non-scientific world, it was probably inevitable that he would try writing some himself. Indeed, he was encouraged by McClure, who told him: 'It would be fascinating if you wrote an essay – or drama – of the life system at the chemical-molecular level "speaking" outward toward us.'[47] Francis produced several pages of outline notes for 'The Story of A'*, which appears to have been a novella, or perhaps a play, projected to be around thirty thousand words long.[48] On the first sheet, after indicating a La Jolla influence (he wrote 'By the pool' and 'Hang-gliding' at the top of the page), Crick listed a dozen characters, all of whom had titles – The Horse, The Bishop, The Camel, The Female Masturbator and so on – then provided further details for some of them in a series of bizarre sketches such as:

The Horse
The Horse's name – Horse, Hoarse, Horace
Erasmus
Its last name – known only to the Horse
Hirohito

The Bishop
Almost naked, his mitre, collar, bathing slip (colour?)
(…)
DNA – controls the body
ESP – controls the soul

Sadly (or thankfully) Francis did not pursue matters any further – writing was obviously harder than it looked. A possible explanation of the project can be found under his notes for a character called The Fat Man: 'Are you stoned?'

One piece of writing that Crick did not even begin might have raised some eyebrows, had it appeared. In early 1978, McClure invited Francis – and Odile – to contribute to a revival of a magazine that he had co-edited back in 1961, *Journal for the Protection of All Beings*. This new version of the journal, which would be published as a special issue of Stewart Brand's *Coevolution Quarterly* magazine, was centred on 'how to liberate mind and body and protect endangered species (including ourselves) from pathogenic industrial civilisation'. The way this would be done, said McClure, would be

---

*The title may have been a reference to the pornographic French novel, *The Story of O*.

to put the art of poetry and the art of science side by side in the same journal.[49]

Crick and McClure agreed that he would write an article for the magazine, but within a few weeks Crick's plans changed, leaving him unable to meet the deadline.[50] Whatever he was supposed to be writing about, it would have rubbed shoulders with an article co-written by Allen Ginsberg and a pseudonymous Hunter S. Thompson, articles about anarchy in the UK and the USA, about natural history and ecology. That might seem strange company for Crick, but it was clearly something he was happy to countenance until events conspired against him.

*

Francis also tried his hand at writing for children. It began in 1975, when the publishers Dorling Kindersley invited him to write a brief introduction to an ambitious children's book, *The Origin of Johnny*, which would use graphics and simple writing to explain the history of the Universe and of life.[51] The book was not yet finished, and Francis grew embarrassed as he realised the draft was error-strewn and that he did not share the author's approach. He repeatedly tried to back out of his commitment but was eventually persuaded to go ahead after an hour-long telephone conversation with the publishers. The introduction he finally produced was brief and banal; the book itself was eventually published by another company.[52]

However, Dorling Kindersley felt they were on to a good thing with Crick; in October 1975 they invited him to work on another children's book, provisionally titled *Where Am I?* which would use drawings and text, zooming into the microscopical and out to the astronomical, showing the different scales of matter in the Universe, with a child at the heart of the book. Francis initially thought he was being invited to write another preface and was somewhat downbeat, but when his agent explained that they wanted him to write the book, he reacted enthusiastically. Detailed storyboards were produced and in between various holidays and overseas trips, Francis churned out several drafts in the first half of 1976.

This was his opportunity to emulate the style and clarity of *The*

Children's Encyclopædia, to produce something that could be as inspirational for the next generation. But there were arguments about how the book was to be organised and how Francis should write. He was acutely aware that his style was often dry, and the publishers repeatedly nudged him to put more of himself into the writing. Keen to show that he could fix the problem by writing in any style required, Francis produced a draft section on the Moon which included a free verse poem, 'Lines from an Old Lunar Hand'. This was written from the point of view of a settler on the far side of the Moon, who had never seen the Earth, contemplating what life must be like on the home planet. Composed in the bath, the poem drew appreciative comments from the publishers.[53] It concluded:

> Life must be dangerous there, upon all sides
> Surrounded by a million living things
> So various, so hostile, so green;
> Not a nice colour. Here the violet light
> Shows the true spectrum of our stony world
> And throws sharp shadows on the glassy dust.
> This lunar beauty can't be matched on Earth.
>
> Yet these young lunatics still want to roam.
> I'll stay just where I am. The moon's my home.

Despite the success of this poem, Francis continued to write in his didactic style and still could not make it work. The publisher complained that he needed to make the writing more like his draft conclusion to the whole book, a section called 'The Void', which they liked because it contained this kind of thing: 'All these facts have to be put together like an intricate, unending detective story. If the Universe is a crime we have yet to discover who committed it.' Francis tried out the more austere passages on Odile and a friend and was pleasantly surprised by their enthusiastic response. The publishers, unconvinced, proposed so many changes to the manuscript that they eventually asked Francis to start again.[54]

Part of the problem was that nobody could agree who the book was aimed at. A consultant brought in to help salvage the project suggested Crick write for a nine-year-old, the publishers wanted to target twelve-year-olds, while Francis felt the book should be aimed at the intelligent adult. They were not even agreed on what kind of title the book should have – the publisher's working title was *The Scale Book*, while the consultant proposed the jaunty *A Journey through Space and Time with Francis Crick*, to attract young readers and to encourage Francis to write in a more personal style.[55] Crick's suggestions, scribbled on the back of an envelope, revealed a very different conception: *Dr Crick's Sunday Morning Sermon, Crazy Like the Cosmos* and *How to Blow Your Mind Without Really Trying*.[56]

As the year wore on, it became increasingly clear that the project was going nowhere, even though an artist made beautiful pencil drawings of a child lying in a woodland glade, full of botanical detail, which then zoomed out to show the countryside at varying scales, and ultimately the whole planet.[57] But the writing was the problem. It could have been a very fine book, if only Francis and the publisher had agreed on what exactly it was to contain. As he put it: 'We all feel that if we get everything just right we might perhaps have a winner.'[58]

At the beginning of 1977, Peter Kindersley told Francis that they were still keen on publishing and that he should relax until there was further news.[59] This just irritated Francis who, after first threatening to 'withdraw from the enterprise', then insisted that there be a clear timetable of progress and that if the publisher's revised version did not arrive by September, their rights would lapse and he would be free to approach another press.[60] His agent gently pointed out to him that this was not possible, as it was their book, not his.[61] Apparently coincidentally, a brief film called *Powers of Ten* was released that year, using a near-identical conception, reducing the originality of the proposal. Whatever the case, the book never appeared.

Shortly after the project was abandoned, Francis did write an unusually personal piece for a particular child, in response to a letter from one James Wassmuth of Staten Island.[62] Wassmuth explained that, after many years of hoping for a baby, his wife had recently given birth to a son; in recognition of Crick's contribution to furthering the bounds of man's knowledge, the infant had been named Francis Crick Wassmuth. Francis the elder was invited to write a letter of advice to the child, which would be included in the boy's family photo album. Deeply touched by the request, Francis pondered how to respond for some weeks, then did his best, trying to relieve any pressure the child might later feel from having such a famous namesake:

Dear Francis

Some day you will be old enough to read this letter. I am a scientist but you may grow to be a musician, a businessman, an athlete – who knows. So what can I say which might help you in some way?

I can only pass on to you my own experiences. Try to find what you really want to do in life and then do your best at that. It doesn't matter if you don't win prizes. The important thing is that you're attempting something that really matters and you enjoy doing it.

Beyond that all one can hope for is a little luck and the blessing of good health.

So don't feel in any way that you ought to continue the work I have been trying to do – to understand the basic problems of biology – it's what you feel that is important. And good luck to you in the attempt.

Affectionately,

Francis Crick

While this letter was heartfelt, thoughtful and kind, it seems that Francis had been duped. A US autograph hunter had hit on the wheeze of sending letters to famous people (Picasso, Kissinger and so on), claiming to have named their child after them and asking for a reply.[63] This appears to have been such an instance.

CALIFORNIA
DREAMING

THE LAST OF ENGLAND

Long after his 1971 crisis was over, Crick still travelled as little as possible, so when his term as a non-resident Fellow at the Salk came to an end in 1973, he decided he would not renew his affiliation. The president of the Salk, Frederic de Hoffmann, attempted to convince him to maintain some kind of connection, but Francis refused and for some time he seemed satisfied with life in Cambridge.[1]

However, Crick retained his appetite for novelty, and despite his hostility to personal publicity and his general lack of interest in looking to the past, he agreed to appear in a documentary about the discovery of the double helix. This was the brainchild of film producer Ronnie Fouracre, who had made his name working on *The Benny Hill Show*.[2] In summer 1972, Watson was flown over to Cambridge, and the pair were filmed chatting over a beer in the Eagle and strolling along the Backs as punts drifted by.[3] The *Guardian* printed a photograph of the pair in a lecture theatre, Francis looking dapper in his Paisley kipper tie.[4] As the newspaper pointed out, this was the first time that the two friends had been filmed together. Two versions were made, one for the public, the other for students. The university edition opened with Francis standing next to a churn containing straws of frozen bull semen, grinning as he described the tiny genetic language in the head of each sperm.[5] Forty-five minutes long, *The DNA Story* was released in early 1973.[6]

The BBC decided it should be broadcast, adding an interview with Aaron Klug on Franklin's contribution and a commentary by Crick's friend Sir Michael Swann, who was now Chairman of the BBC. Retitled, to Crick's irritation, *The Race for the Double Helix*, the programme went out in July 1974 and was well received by the critics – in the *Observer*, Clive James said it was 'consuming viewing' while for Nancy Banks-Smith of the *Guardian*, Crick was 'a laughing talking-machine' and Watson had 'the vague look of a large flight-less bird, which is just going to become extinct by absentmindedly stepping on its own egg'.[7] *Nature* was more sober, praising the pro-gramme as 'an excellent exercise in demonstrating the foibles and failings of scientists', including its exploration of the personalities involved.[8] Fouracre was less happy, complaining to Francis that there was too much science in the programme and not enough gossip.[9]

Philip Daly, the producer of *The Prizewinners* and now Head of Science and Features Television at the BBC, was deeply impressed by Crick's performance and invited him to host a TV series 'similar in scope to Bronowski's *The Ascent of Man*', perhaps on the search for extraterrestrial life.[10] *The Ascent of Man* had been a landmark thir-teen-part BBC series on human history and science, made in 1973 by Crick's friend Jacob 'Bruno' Bronowski, to whom Francis now turned for advice. Bronowski encouraged Crick to consider Daly's proposal but warned Francis that his series had taken three gruelling years to make.[11] Nothing came of Daly's offer, but Francis did make another film, on the triplet code experiment. Broadcast late at night, highly technical and produced by the UK's distance learning institute, the Open University, this was not what Daly had in mind.[12]

There was more retrospection when *Nature* published a set of essays to mark the 'coming of age' of the double helix (it was the twenty-first anniversary of the discovery).[13] Crick's article, which opened the collection, filled in some of the background to the four articles he and Watson wrote in 1953, declaring that he had enjoyed every moment of the discovery and quoting an artist, John Minton, who said that 'the important thing is to be there when the picture is painted'.[14] And that, argued Francis, was a matter of luck, judge-ment, inspiration and hard work.

Although Aaron Klug's contribution to the collection was a

useful piece on Franklin's work, many of the other articles were a bit wacky. Gunther Stent attacked Crick's critique of vitalism (Francis told Stent, 'you have no talent for this sort of intellectual activity and are not only making an ass of yourself but are embarrassing us all as well'), while in a very seventies touch, the final article claimed that molecular biologists tend to be born under Aries and called for more research on astrology.[15]

*

In the middle of the anniversary celebrations, Crick found himself embroiled in an unpleasant squabble between Klug's group and Alex Rich's team at MIT over the structure of tRNA. Although Francis was not directly involved, his position and reputation, as well as his long friendship with Rich, made the whole thing particularly delicate.

In March 1974, Rich's group published a structure of tRNA in *Nature* which Klug's team knew was wrong; in June, Klug submitted the correct structure to *Nature*, where it languished in the press.[16] Confident they had won the race to publish the right structure, Klug's group presented their data at a conference where, to their relief, Rich and his colleagues again described their mistaken model. However, a little over two weeks later, the Rich group submitted a paper to *Science* containing a structure identical to that proposed by Klug. This appeared, with no reference to the work of the LMB group, a mere ten days later – before Klug's *Nature* article finally crawled into print.[17]

Klug and the other LMB researchers were convinced that the American group had used the Cambridge structure; David Blow, who had worked with Rich, was so outraged that he sent a letter to *Science* accusing Rich's lab of plagiarism.[18] Rising tempers were further stoked when Francis wrote a sharp letter to Rich, echoing Klug's fury:

Dear Alex,
Does your name stink. Aaron was convinced that once you had wheedled out the details of his structure you would attempt to publish it as your own. This is exactly what has happened. (…) There is absolutely nothing to suggest that you would

have actually published a revised structure at this time except for the knowledge you obtained of the Cambridge structure. Moreover you did not even have the elementary courtesy to acknowledge the Cambridge work. (...) Unless you are prepared to make a suitable apology in public I must tell you that your visits to Cambridge in future will not be welcomed.[19]

Surprised and distressed by his friend's accusations, Rich sent Francis an eleven-page letter, defending his group but accepting that they should not have presented a model they knew to be incorrect.[20] Meanwhile, *New Scientist* published an article about the row, including quotes from the angry letters sent by each side.[21] With the situation getting out of hand, Francis now decided to play peacemaker, suggesting there should be no further comment.[22] Rich disagreed, pointing out that the accusations of plagiarism in Crick's letter were being circulated among British scientists ('a very dirty business').[23] In the end, Crick's view prevailed.

Apart from being a textbook example of scientists behaving badly, becoming absurdly obsessed with priority even down to a matter of days, the affair showed Crick not only at his crossest, but also – eventually – at his most thoughtful, calming emotions and drawing out lessons. As he explained to Rich:

I think you should try to bend over backwards to acknowledge the ideas and influence of others, not only about work in other laboratories but also by junior people in your own. I know from personal experience how very important this is, since one can by carelessness and forgetfulness easily upset one's co-workers, who can come to feel, rightly or wrongly, that one is stealing their ideas.[24]

The shade of Rosalind Franklin must have given a faint smile.

*

Following the realisation that development was unlikely to provide the kind of insight into fundamental processes that he thrived on,

Crick continued his quest for a new scientific project. He published three scientific papers during the mid-1970s, all on the coiling of DNA or chromatin (DNA in combination with proteins), but despite his enthusiasm they were either mistaken or obscure.

The obscure paper was based on the work of mathematician F. Brock Fuller, who had described how a double helix might twist round itself to become a supercoil. To ensure that he fully understood Fuller's complex topological arguments, Crick wrote a simplified summary, focusing on something he called the Linking Number which described the topological property of ribbon (an approximation to a double helix); Francis decided to publish the article in the *Proceedings of the National Academy of Sciences* (*PNAS*) without going through peer review (a privilege of Academy membership).[25] There were occasional flashes of Crick's hallmark clarity, but the argument was dense and his tales from topographic oceans seemed devoid of biological implications. To help the mathematically challenged, Crick included a physical explanation, which had clearly been developed with Odile in Portugal Place before being rolled out in the LMB:

> It is fortunately easy to obtain an approximate value for a structure by constructing it from a piece of flexible ribbon of, say, some dressmaking material. One then simply pulls the ribbon 'straight' and counts the number of twists. This will show if a gross error has been made and can also be used to astonish one's colleagues.

Despite this clever suggestion, the article surely bewildered rather than astonished most readers.

Shortly before this paper appeared, Crick returned to the pages of *Nature* for the first time since 1971, in an article with Aaron Klug that presented a theoretical explanation of the suggestion by their LMB colleagues Roger Kornberg and Markus Noll that chromatin formed a jointed or kinked chain.[26] Bearing a striking, ultra-brief title – 'Kinky Helix' – the paper's fame was short-lived, as within months new LMB data undermined Crick's confidence in the reality of kinked chromatin. Much later, Crick said it 'was a nice idea but as far as I know doesn't actually exist'.[27] Part of the problem was that

Francis was too hasty, excited by the idea of rapidly publishing an explanation of something that, it turned out, was not actually there – or least not in the form that Crick imagined. He was abetted in this by the new editor of *Nature*, David Davies, keen to publish his first article by Crick. When Francis insisted that the paper be published rapidly, Davies responded that he expected it would get through review in two weeks and be published in five, which was exactly what happened.*[28]

The worst paper of the bunch, the one that for some people threatened Crick's reputation as a serious scientist, appeared early in 1977. The year before, Danish microscopist Arne Leth Bak reported that human chromatin spiralled round itself and then folded back to form a loop.[29] This caught Crick's eye, as he explained enthusiastically to Klug: 'Guess what! Another breakthrough.' Crick thought Leth Bak's microscopic images of chromosomes were amazing: 'They are so striking (…) I can't believe it's an artefact.'[30] The data were too good *not* to be true. Bubbling with excitement, Francis told chromosome expert Mick Callan that great things were just around the corner: 'This is just to alert you to the possibility that there may be a breakthrough on chromosome structure (…) if I am correct, by Christmas everyone will be working on the idea.'[31]

Crick contacted Leth Bak and decided to write a joint article explaining the significance of the discovery, to be published without peer review in *PNAS*. However, Crick's colleagues were shocked at his enthusiasm for Leth Bak's claim. One told him: 'If I believed that you could really take seriously the kind of bullshit that is presented in the Bak and Zeuthen paper, I would tend to discount your future publications as probably not worth the paper they get Xeroxed on.'[32] Callan was equally clear: 'the story is a load of rubbish … All the evidence which I know goes against this.'[33] One major problem with Leth Bak's idea was that it contradicted a great deal of well-established genetic data; Crick took this problem seriously and urged

---

*This episode again showed Crick's immense prestige at *Nature*. A couple of years earlier, the Publishing Director of Macmillan had put astonishing weight on Crick's view as to who should replace John Maddox as Editor: 'I would not want to go too far in this consultative process without talking to you,' she wrote. Hughes to Crick, 16 February 1973, PP/CRI/D/2/27.

Leth Bak to perform all the necessary control experiments: 'You must realise that what you are proposing is not a small modification of existing ideas. It is quite revolutionary. It will be ignored unless you can produce strong evidence that you are right.'[34]

Eventually, having inspected over a thousand photographs from his Danish collaborators, Francis bluntly informed them that their observations were probably an artefact caused by using the optical microscope at the limits of its resolution. Nevertheless, he submitted the paper, telling Watson he hoped that at least some of the observations might turn out to be correct.[35] As he told a colleague, 'The problem, as I see it, is to decide what is artefactual and what is real.'[36] Scientists normally do this before publication.

That summer, after the article had appeared, Francis took a long-planned trip to Denmark where he met Leth Bak and his colleague Jesper Zeuthen and inspected their data. The situation was even worse than he had feared. Their procedure yielded poor-quality samples that were highly variable, whereas what was required was large quantities of consistent, pure material. Crick suggested ways of improving this, but Leth Bak did not understand what all the fuss was about. Faced with such poor data and the incompatibility of the model with so many well-established findings, Crick admitted to Klug that the whole thing had been a wild-goose chase: 'Talking with them and looking at their slides soon revealed a number of things which my previous extensive correspondence had not uncovered. ... Anyway, it was a lesson to me not to write papers with people you've never met! It never occurred to me to ask what their yields were. The point is so elementary.'[37]

Crick's judgement seemed to be failing. He no longer had anyone to work with who could shoot down his crazier enthusiasms and cast a sceptical eye on his ideas – his preferred partner, Sydney Brenner, was heavily involved in the politicking around the development of genetic engineering, which consumed him for several years. The Cambridge magic was no longer working for Crick.

*

As the decade wore on, Francis had to face up to the inevitable – he was getting old, and even his red Lotus Elan sports car could not hold back time.[38] Decisions were going to have to be made about what he would do and where he and Odile would live. For a while, they flirted with the idea of buying a house in Morocco, so as not to spend their winters in Cambridge.[39] Francis even drew up detailed plans of their future home, grandly titled 'The Design of a Small Arab House'.[40] But although they enjoyed a visit to Marrakech, scouting out potential locations, they decided against making it their home.

There were more significant issues. Francis's persistent gastric reflux, due to a hiatus hernia, was not only painful but had also led to a build-up of scar tissue, making it difficult to swallow. Sometimes he vomited blood. He avoided strong alcohol and spicy food, but he still required annual operations on his oesophageal sphincter. The last of these took place in June 1975, when he was taken ill in the night in London following a meeting at the Royal Society; he had severe bleeding from a ruptured polyp and was rushed to hospital in an ambulance.[41] After two weeks he was well enough to go home but still needed weeks of convalescence.[42]

Life in Portugal Place was also changing as the girls grew older and became independent; Gabrielle was now at Cambridge School of Art, while Jacqueline was thinking of studying biology.[43] There were also new lodgers, including Kirsti Simonsuuri, a Finnish poet who was finishing her PhD on Homer's lyric poetry at Newnham College. She became a close friend of the Cricks, renting an upstairs room at Portugal Place and then moving into Well Cottage.[44] A few years later, after she had left Cambridge, she wrote Francis and Odile a nostalgic letter about her time with them: 'Sometimes when I close my eyes I can see an afternoon in the roof terrace at Portugal Place, and it is very warm, the passion flowers are tumbling along the bamboo roof, and the sun melts into a thin mist, getting redder …'[45]

The question of what Francis and Odile would do next became acute as Crick's sixtieth birthday loomed in 1976. For the MRC at the time, hitting sixty meant retirement, with the possibility of a five-year extension by mutual agreement – the MRC administration had begun making discreet enquiries about Crick's wishes shortly after his fifty-seventh birthday in 1973.[46] Francis considered retiring, but soon changed his mind as he found he still had an appetite for work and, more prosaically, he realised that because he joined the MRC in his late thirties, his pension would be cripplingly small.[47] Despite the various bits of property he owned, he could not afford to retire. By the time the MRC increased its staff retirement age to sixty-five, Francis had already decided to make his future elsewhere.

At first, that future seemed to be in Cambridge. In the summer of 1975, two of Crick's friends, Jeremy Prynne and Richard Le Page, approached him about the post of Master of Gonville and Caius, which would soon be vacant.[48] Over a series of discussions in Portugal Place, Crick gradually grasped what the job entailed and realised it was not for him. He was apparently prepared to utter the traditional Latin grace at Feasts but chairing dull committee meetings, glad-handing donors and applying the tedious college rules would have been very much not Francis Crick.

Another possible future glimmered when Francis was contacted by the director of the Salk Institute, Frederic de Hoffmann, who wanted to get Crick back to California without the annual brief visits that Francis now found so exhausting. 'It is very important that you spend time here and I will make this possible,' de Hoffmann wrote, somewhat peremptorily. Leslie Orgel, who was a Salk Fellow, suggested an extended sabbatical visit and Francis soon agreed to an eight-month stay.[49] Max Perutz reluctantly accepted the proposal but insisted that if Francis was needed at the LMB, the California trip would have to be postponed.[50]

In early April 1976, Crick and de Hoffmann dined at Claridge's to seal the deal; Francis would be a Visiting Professor (the post would be created especially for him; this would be the first time he was given the title Professor) at $50,000 per annum, about three times his MRC salary of £9,000.[51] But over the course of the meal, de Hoffmann revealed that he had a longer-term arrangement in mind. Confident that Crick could help change the direction of the Salk, he wanted Francis to move there permanently – the sabbatical was merely a way of getting the Cricks to test the water.*[52] Francis was immediately

---

*For Suzanne Bourgeois, a long-time Salk researcher, Crick's return was part of de Hoffmann's Machiavellian plan to undermine Jonas Salk. However,

attracted to the idea, but the whole thing was extremely delicate – first, he had to get Odile's agreement and, in the meantime, his LMB colleagues must not get the slightest hint of what was afoot. De Hoffmann was therefore instructed to send letters regarding 'possible longer-term arrangements' to Portugal Place rather than the LMB.

Odile was not keen. A couple of weeks after the meeting at Claridge's, Francis reported to de Hoffmann: 'She is quite prepared to spend four months every winter in La Jolla but is reluctant *at this stage* to commit herself to longer stays. She is anxious to keep some contact with Europe, as am I.'[53] As a compromise, Francis suggested that in the five years following his sixtieth birthday he would spend at least twenty-five months at the Salk, with up to three months' unpaid leave each year. De Hoffmann turned this down – he wanted Crick there for longer periods.[54] Taking one step at a time, Francis suggested extending his sabbatical slightly, to meet Odile's concerns: 'Odile tells me that she is not yet prepared to say whether she feels she could settle down living mainly at La Jolla (as opposed to visits of four to five months each summer) until she has lived there for some six months.'[55]

All this was kept secret from Perutz, Brenner and the rest of Crick's LMB colleagues.[56] They knew only that Francis and Odile were going to La Jolla for an eight-month sabbatical in September 1976, and that they would be back the following year. Nobody imagined Cambridge without the Cricks, or vice versa.

*

Leslie and Alice Orgel found a rented house for Francis and Odile on Roseland Drive, just north of La Jolla village, a little over three miles from the Salk Institute (they soon bought a car and passed their California driving tests).[57] The house seemed rather dark at first (they fixed this by buying brighter light bulbs), but compared to Portugal Place it was huge – it had four large bedrooms and three bathrooms.[58]

---

she admitted that Crick's subsequent influence at the Institute was very positive. Bourgeois, S. (2013), *Genesis of the Salk Institute: The Epic of Its Founders* (London: University of California Press), pp. 179–80.

The facilities at the Salk were equally sumptuous, as Francis boasted to Aaron Klug: 'I have an immense office (by Cambridge standards) – almost twice as big as Max's – with a lovely view over the ocean.'[59] And Californian geography meant that virtually any trip included extraordinary opportunities for sight-seeing. For example, when Francis gave a talk in San Francisco, the journey back was delightful: 'After we visited Berkeley and San Francisco we had a very pleasant day in the Napa Valley and a perfectly splendid time in Yosemite. The sun shone all the time.'[60]

Despite her reservations, Odile seems to have relaxed into the new way of life, enjoying the bright sun and the possibilities that provided for her art.[61] Although the Cricks' social circle was more restrained than it had been in Cambridge, their friend Kirsti Simonsuuri perceived a potential advantage for Odile: 'I was delighted to hear that you had found some artist friends with whom to collaborate. Perhaps your social life is not too overwhelming so that you can work on your own projects.'[62]

Within a few months of arriving in La Jolla, Odile accepted that they would be living in California for some time, punctuated by three-month annual vacations in Europe to keep in contact with family and friends, and in November 1976 the Cricks bought a small apartment in a condominium, although Crick assured Brenner that they had not made any decision about staying permanently in California.[63] In December 1976, Francis wrote discretely to Perutz, explaining their decision and exploring what he had to do to resign from the MRC.[64] Although Sydney came over to talk the matter through, keen to persuade his friend to accept Perutz's compromise proposal of a two-year leave of absence, Francis was adamant.[65] However, Brenner did get Perutz to agree to a secret, unofficial agreement to keep a post open for Crick at the LMB until his sixty-fourth birthday, 'in case there might be some change in his plans'.[66]

In February 1977, Francis wrote an official letter to Perutz announcing his resignation from the MRC:

> I have now been offered a full-time appointment here on such favourable terms that I feel I must accept. (...) I am therefore writing to give notice of my intention to resign my job with

the MRC. (…) When I reach the stage of sending my formal resignation direct to the MRC I will express to them my great appreciation for the constant and massive support they have given me for so many years.[67]

Perutz transmitted the news with a heavy heart: 'This is a great shame as we shall miss the stimulus and forceful criticism which he provided, not to speak of his bounding vitality.'[68]

The deal that de Hoffmann finally proposed was that Francis would be named Kieckhefer Distinguished Research Professor until he reached the age sixty-five, in 1981, with a three-year rolling contract after that date. The Kieckhefer Foundation also created the Kieckhefer Center of Molecular Biology to 'carry out theoretical studies in biology with primary emphasis in the field of molecular and cell biology, with Dr. Crick as the focus' and agreed his salary would increase to $55,000.[69]

Although Crick's desire to carry on working and earning was clearly the main motivation for the move, living in California brought Francis and Odile a little closer to their grandchildren – Michael, his wife Barbara and their family lived in Seattle, and soon had four children, Alex, Camberley, Francis and Kindra. But California also separated Francis and Odile from their daughters. The girls were no longer living in Cambridge (Jacqueline had given up her studies and was travelling, while Gabrielle was at Dartington College of Arts), but they joked that they were not ready to leave home, so their parents left instead.[70] Behind the joke was an understandable feeling of abandonment, of physical distance from their parents.

For Francis and Odile, a fresh opportunity had arrived. Their new home had a shared swimming pool, jacuzzi and gardens; it was not Portugal Place, but perhaps that was the point. The weather was nicer, and Francis was happier. They were still in love, and life was still good.

CRICK RE-IGNITED

The Cricks hoped that the balmy climate of southern California and the security of long-term support from the Salk would
reinvigorate Francis. They did. The doubts, soul-searching and
exhaustion of the previous decade were chased away by the Californian sunshine, replaced by the stimulation of new colleagues and
new ideas.

Crick's scientific output in the four years following the move
was marked by an extraordinary surge in energy and appetite. In
terms of the quantity, quality and range of his publications, this
was by far the most productive period of his life. He published
research articles defending the reality of the double helix and, in collaboration with one of the brightest young thinkers in neuroscience,
explored how visual signals are processed by the brain. He wrote
two extremely influential papers describing the evolutionary implications of the latest astonishing discoveries in molecular genetics
– a mini-revolution, he called it. He produced pieces for the general
reader on the discovery of the double helix and a long summary of
classical and recent molecular biology. He even published a book –
Life Itself, a successful popular account of his outlandish Directed
Panspermia hypothesis. He also wrote a piece for *Scientific American* that outlined the problems faced by brain science and brilliantly

charted its future – an article that is as striking today as it was nearly half a century ago.

In other words, the move worked. Crick's mind was re-ignited.

*

Crick's departure for the USA was front-page news even before it was officially announced. The *Sunday Times*, which broke the story, accurately proclaimed 'Nobel prize-winner quits Britain' in its head-line, but managed to mangle the truth from the very first sentence:

> Dr Francis Crick, the man who shared a Nobel Prize for what
> has been called the most important scientific advance of the
> century, has left Britain because of our tax laws.

This was nonsense – he wanted to avoid retirement, not taxes.* Francis had refused to speak to the newspaper ('You know I never talk to the press, what makes you optimistic this time?' was all he would say), so the journalist made something up: 'he has told his laboratory in Cambridge that it was a change in tax laws which made him decide to leave'.[1] This was not true, but it fitted the newspaper owner's hostility to the Labour government and portrayed Crick as one of the mega-rich, like Mick Jagger, who were indeed leaving the country to avoid paying tax.[2] Belief that Crick was leaving for tax reasons became so pervasive that the left-wing magazine the *New Statesman* published a satirical poem about his departure. Francis wrote to correct the misapprehension and received a cheery reply from the poet, Roger Woddis – 'No harm meant!'[3]

The Cricks' apartment in Solana Beach, about seven miles north of the Salk, was a low-rise, modern townhouse, 'a penthouse on top of three bedrooms and two bathrooms', as Francis put it. Their new home had a fine view over the Del Mar racetrack, although as he remarked, 'what are horses to me!'[4] Still, the beach was only half a

---

*Although the tax laws did not drive Crick abroad, for the next few years he had to avoid staying too long on his visits to the UK, to prevent his US income being also taxed in the UK.

Roger Woddis

Howl of Anguish

(After Browning)

Dr Francis Crick is emigrating to the
United States because of taxation.

Nobly, nobly Nobel victor
Doctor Francis slipped away,
Fled from heavy-duty Healey,
Fuming to the USA.

Crippled by the rate of taxes
He was called upon to pay,
Looking round his lab. at Cambridge,
Crick knew where his future lay.

'Here I squinted at the fruitfly,
Here I laboured night and day.
How can I abandon Britain?
How can I afford to stay?'

Anger bubbled in his test-tubes,
Tax-forms overflowed his tray;
Scientists who seek an answer
Cannot turn to God to pray.

What is it that makes him bitter?
Was he robbed, or should we say
Twisted by his double helix,
Governed by his DNA?

mile away. Odile was in charge of decorating and furnishing their home and everything was finished by September when the pair returned from their holiday in Europe.[5] Their social life was much quieter than in Cambridge, Crick explained to a friend, 'though from time to time we find ourselves at quite lively dinner parties', such as those with the geologist Teddy Bullard, his old Cambridge pal, who was now working at the Scripps Institute in La Jolla. And there were brushes with scientific celebrities, for example at a meal at Dick Feynman's, where Francis agreed to the proposal by BBC TV's Philip Daly that he should be filmed in conversation with Feynman and the British physician and polymath Jonathan Miller (nothing came of this).[6] Michael McClure was delighted by the Cricks' move, as it enabled Francis to directly provide his helpful critiques of McClure's work.[7]

Francis's health also improved – on orders from his doctor he lost weight and lowered his blood pressure by cutting out animal fats and by getting more exercise (he swam in the pool and they bought a small trampoline).[8] When Francis went to Denmark in the summer of 1977 while Odile visited her family in France, he reassured her that he was doing as he had been told: 'Yes, I do my exercises every day and am clearly fitter but it will take a few months before I feel I can exercise properly and walk uphill without my pulse going up too much.'[9] He was also visited by one of his lovers during this stay. A year later, he told McClure: 'Odile and I are in good health, by and large, though my hair is now fairly white – I suppose soon I shall have to cultivate a guru image. We try to swim every day but there's been so much to do since we got back that I've still to fit in a walk on the beach.'[10]

The rejuvenated Crick now attended more conferences, gave more lectures and did more travelling, although he was initially hesitant about leaving California and refused to make more than one transatlantic journey per year. The Cricks went to see McClure and his gang of artistic and scientific friends in San Francisco (McClure was keen to take them to Tomasso's Italian restaurant, just down the road from City Lights), they visited Mexico and they toured the Grand Canyon; they even went to Disneyland with the *Nature* staffer and family friend Miranda Robertson.[11]

There was also the possibility of meeting old friends – Kreisel was now based in Stanford, which made it easier for the pair to meet, although they were still nearly five hundred miles apart. Their correspondence also reappears in their archives at around this point (they do not appear to have stopped writing to each other; their letters have simply not been preserved). Kreisel's letters had largely lost their scabrous character (they began prosaically 'Dear Crick'), and were generally devoted to his complex arguments with logicians, physicists and mathematicians, as well as the occasional perceptive critique of some of Crick's ideas. There were flashes of the old Kreisel. He continued to hobnob with the rich and famous, lunching with socialite and palaeoanthropologist Ann Getty; he also got up to his old antics, receiving a registered letter from the husband of a twenty-three-year-old woman with whom he was having an affair, in which the man threatened to beat him up and then kill him.[12] Kreisel was sixty-one years old at the time.

There were new cultural experiences for the Cricks – for

example, Hungarian physicist George Marx sent Francis a recording of Bartók's one-act symbolist opera for two voices, *Bluebeard's Castle*. Francis was unfamiliar with the piece, but was clearly impressed: 'What a remarkable work! (...) Both the singing and the playing come across well although our sitting room is very far from the proper stage setting. A most interesting and unusual experience.'[13]

Francis and Odile also seem to have enjoyed the psychedelic pleasures of southern California – at least, that is one interpretation of a letter from biophysicist Jack Cowan, who studied drug-induced hallucinations. After a visit to the Cricks during which he enjoyed their 'marvellous hospitality', Cowan sent Francis a copy of a book on the effects of mescaline 'which you (and Odile) might find interesting'.[14]

The move to California came at a price, however. Jacqueline and Gabrielle were far away, and although they made regular visits, it was not the same. The move also marked the end of Crick's close collaboration with Sydney Brenner. Permanently separated by thousands of miles, they were on very different paths. Brenner was becoming increasingly involved in the experimental detail of molecular genetics – his research on the nematode was focused on cloning genes, and he was embroiled in debates over the regulation of recombinant DNA in the USA and in Britain.[15] None of this was Crick's cup of tea (he studiously avoided any involvement in the controversies over genetic engineering), while his aim of working on the human brain did not attract Brenner.[16] Two decades of daily mad sessions had come to an end.

Sydney felt this keenly: in January 1978 he wrote to Francis, explaining everything that he had been up to and signing off, rather plaintively, 'we do rather miss you here (especially me).'[17] Less expansive, Crick nevertheless missed Brenner and his insights, and in 1981 he urged Sydney to accept an invitation to become a non-resident Fellow of the Salk, saying it would give him 'great personal pleasure'.[18] Brenner accepted, but although the arrangement gave the pair an annual contact, they never fully recaptured their former closeness.

*

Crick's reintegration into the scientific life of North America was helped by the generosity of Jim Watson – the rift between them over *The Double Helix* was long forgotten. Watson invited Francis and Odile to spend the summer of 1977 at Cold Spring Harbor, which came with a hefty honorarium of $4,000 (around $20,000 today).[19] Watson was also keen for Francis to attend the annual Cold Spring Harbor symposium which that year discussed chromatin, but he recognised that his old friend might need some persuading:

> I realise you are now allergic to such super meetings, but we can insulate you and Odile as long as you like in the more than plush surroundings of a nearby super-large house, soon to be given to the lab by a most benevolent patron. It is on the water, has an immense swimming pool, and can provide you with all the privacy you may want. So I suspect you would have a very good time.[20]

The bribery worked and Francis gradually eased back into the kind of influential role he had played in the 1960s.[21] He was even persuaded to give the symposium opening address, in which he highlighted the twin breakthroughs of DNA sequencing, which promised to reveal the one-dimensional structure of chromosomes, and what he called 'the nucleosome revolution', which was revealing the three-dimensional structure.[22] Crick predicted that, with luck, 'the general solution of the nature of the eukaryotic genome' should be only a few years away.

That was true, but in ways that neither Francis nor virtually anyone else realised. In a series of stunning presentations at the meeting, researchers from MIT and from Cold Spring Harbor showed that in viruses affecting humans, the mRNA for a given gene was much, much shorter than the DNA for that gene. It appeared that a gene was initially transcribed base by base into a long piece of RNA, which was then edited – 'spliced' was the term people used – by the cell to form an mRNA molecule that lacked apparently pointless stretches of sequence.[23] This was completely unlike the situation in bacteria and bacteriophage viruses, where DNA and mRNA were exactly the same length. It also undermined one of the long-standing dogmas of molecular biology: 'anything found to be true of *E. coli* must also be true of elephants', as Jacques Monod had put it in 1961.[24] *Nature* reported that the discovery left the Cold Spring Harbor audience 'amazed, fascinated and not a little bewildered'.[25]

Crick's notebook for the meeting does not reveal quite such a tangle of emotions, but he immediately grasped two major implications. First, gene expression in eukaryotes was much more complicated than anyone imagined – somehow, the cell had to recognise which bits of the sequence to retain and which to snip out, mobilising enzymes that could do this precisely. Second, this discovery might explain the existence of large stretches of repetitive DNA in eukaryotic genomes, and what was known as the C paradox, the inexplicable differences in genome sizes between organisms that do not seem to relate to any degree of biological complexity (for example, the genome of an onion is five times larger than that of a human). Wally Gilbert soon named the two parts of a eukaryotic gene – exons, which are transcribed into mRNA and are expressed, and introns, which interrupt the DNA sequences and are snipped out of an initial version of mRNA by the cell.[26] Francis started thinking hard about all this and its implications for the evolution of genomes, scribbling furiously in the notes he made as colleagues presented their latest surprising results in various meetings.[27]

All this led to another influential Crick think-piece: 'Split Genes and RNA Splicing', which appeared in *Science* in April 1979.[28] The article came about quite fortuitously – Francis had been chatting to the editor of *Science* about how much he had enjoyed a recent Dick Feynman article written for a general audience, and wished the journal published more articles like that. 'Why don't you write one for us?' came the reply, and Francis found himself, as he put it, hoist with his own petard.[29]

The article summarised the discoveries of 1977 using a warm, almost intimate tone, which was evident from the opening sentences: 'In the last two years there has been a mini-revolution in molecular genetics. When I came to California, in September 1976, I had no idea that a typical gene might be split into several pieces and I doubt if anybody else had.'

Having informed the inattentive reader of his move to the USA,

Francis went on to summarise the various hypotheses for how an initial RNA transcription of a eukaryotic gene might be spliced. The most influential part of the article dealt with a question that Crick felt exerted 'an extraordinary fascination for almost everybody concerned' – how this surprising arrangement might have evolved.

After warning that you cannot explain the appearance of a feature in terms of a future use or advantage (Francis called this 'the fallacy of evolutionary foresight'), he explored how the existence of introns might lead to the appearance of new genes coding for new proteins. Even a mutation in a single base pair could make an intron appear or disappear, by removing or introducing whatever signal indicated the division between coding and non-coding sequences, thereby causing an exon to gain or lose nucleotides, altering the protein that was produced. As Francis explained, this was a challenge to the molecular biologists, with their relatively simplistic understanding of what genes were and how they might be selected, and to the population geneticists, who tended to study the transmission of genes in extremely abstract, mathematical ways:

> To grasp what has been happening in evolution we shall have to understand all the mechanisms by which stretches of DNA can be multiplied in the genome or added to or subtracted to it. (…) A molecular biologist who wishes to discuss the evolution of the eukaryotic genome will need not only to know a lot about the way DNA and its transcripts can behave but also something about modern ideas on population genetics.

Crick's article was widely read and discussed; it even garnered some fan mail, with one scientist telling him: 'As usual, you have succeeded in making a difficult problem comprehensible by the lucidity and conciseness not just of your insights but also of your writing style.'[30] Kreisel was equally pleased, telling Crick with typical perception: 'First, molecular biology made a splash because of the apparent astonishing simplicity. Now it continues to be exciting for the opposite reason. It couldn't be better if it had all been planned.'[31]

*

Francis was soon working on a second major article flowing from the 1977 discoveries, focusing on the nature of repetitive or junk DNA and why it is so prevalent in eukaryotic genomes. Together with Leslie Orgel he explored the implications of a throwaway remark he had made in his 'Split Genes' article – 'The theory of the "selfish gene" will have to be extended to any stretch of DNA.' Although Crick later described this work as a sideline, it turned out to be remarkably influential.[32] The idea that genes were replicators that could be considered as 'selfish' because, by increasing the fitness of their carrier, they would increase their copy number in the population, had been popularised by Richard Dawkins in 1976. Crick and Orgel now used this concept to understand the existence of large stretches of DNA that did not seem to code for anything.

The article appeared in April 1980, this time in *Nature*. This was not its intended destination (it was initially written for *PNAS*), but in December 1979 Francis once again found himself using his influence at the journal when he received a letter from Canadian evolutionary biologist W. Ford Doolittle.[33] In May of that year, Doolittle and his colleague Carmen Sapienza had submitted an article to *Science* describing how natural selection would inevitably lead to the spread of sequences of DNA that had no function beyond their ability to be copied – truly selfish genes. After an interminable seven reviews, the article had finally been rejected, and Doolittle now looked to Crick for advice on how to proceed.

Crick sent Doolittle an excited reply, explaining that he had been lecturing about this issue since the beginning of the year and that he and Leslie Orgel were already writing an article on the topic. They had all been thinking along similar lines, he said, and had come up with complementary approaches. Francis encouraged Doolittle to submit his article to *Nature* forthwith and even wrote to the journal to smooth its passage. He told the editor that the 'rather stuffy' *Science* had rejected Doolittle's paper, but that he was sure that *Nature* was 'more adventurous and rather welcomes scientific controversy'.[34]

A few months earlier, Miranda Robertson had reproached Crick for 'faithlessly' sending his split genes article to *Science*; Orgel and Crick therefore decided they would also submit their article on selfish DNA to *Nature*, so that it could appear alongside Doolittle and Sapienza's piece.[35] The journal not only published both papers rapidly, it also considered them to be so important that the bright red cover of that week's issue simply carried the words SELFISH DNA surrounded by a circle of DNA interrupted by the heads of ravenous mythical beasts, drawn by Carmen Sapienza's wife, Linda.[36] Orgel and Crick's article opened with classic Crick clarity:

> The object of this short review is to make widely known the idea of selfish DNA. A piece of selfish DNA, in its purest form, has two distinct properties:
> (1) It arises when a DNA sequence spreads by forming additional copies of itself within the genome.
> (2) It makes no specific contribution to the phenotype.

They then described the evidence that much of the DNA in eukaryotic organisms appears to be junk, explored the potential mechanisms by which this DNA could copy itself and speculated that such sequences might acquire a function through mutation. Although they recognised that there was nothing new in the former idea, they emphasised that thinking of these sequences in terms of selfish DNA was a significant development – 'It could well make sense of many of the puzzles and paradoxes which have arisen over the last 10 or 15 years. The main facts are, at first sight, so odd that only a somewhat unconventional idea is likely to explain them.'

While the views outlined in the two papers are now quite mainstream, at the time the idea was, as *Nature* put it, 'mildly shocking', and provoked what the journal described as a voluminous response, with many scientists feeling uneasy.[37] Crick had expected as much, warning that the idea would arouse strong emotions among those who were firmly wedded to natural selection as the sole explanation of genome evolution.[38] There were so many letters and criticisms that *Nature* soon had to publish four representative replies, with a joint response from Orgel, Crick and Sapienza appearing at the end of the year, accompanied by versions of Linda Sapienza's drawings.[39]

There were two main disagreements expressed in the replies sent to *Nature* and in the many letters Crick received.[40] There was opposition to the use of 'selfish' and 'junk'; Orgel, Crick and Sapienza

Nature Vol. 288 18/25 December 1980   645

Selfish DNA

suggested 'parasitic DNA' as an alternative (this did not catch on). The second issue was the amount of the different kinds of selfish DNA present in eukaryotic genomes, something that Crick and his colleagues said would soon be resolved by the accumulation of sequence data. Which was exactly what happened over subsequent years; the fundamental ideas put forward in the two original *Nature* papers were proved correct. Crick's throwaway remark in his 1979 split genes article turned out to be extraordinarily prescient.

*

As this episode shows, despite Crick's desire to focus on the brain, he was repeatedly drawn into debates about molecular biology. Even the double helix would not leave him alone – neither as a scientific reality, nor as an historical discovery. Arguments over Rosalind Franklin's role in the breakthrough re-emerged in 1979, when Crick published a brief article, 'How to Live with a Golden Helix', in a glossy magazine called *The Sciences*.[41] Crick dismissed Watson's account in *The Double Helix* as a soap opera, and showed how mundane the research involved in the discovery had been, without the drama embroidered by Watson. All this was fine, but his description of Franklin seemed ungenerous and overly critical:

> Rosalind's difficulties and her failures were mainly of her own making. Underneath her brisk manner she was oversensitive and, ironically, too determined to be scientifically sound and to avoid short cuts. She was rather too set on succeeding all by herself and rather too stubborn to accept advice easily from others when it ran counter to her own ideas. She was proffered help but she would not take it.

This shocked some readers, in some cases because they misunderstood 'too determined to be scientifically sound' as meaning Crick felt her stubbornness prevented her from being scientifically sound (in fact he meant that she insisted on being rigorous and this prevented her from taking risks). Professor Charlotte Friend, a cell biologist, was annoyed by what she described as a sly personal assault and wrote a letter of complaint to the editor of the magazine.[42] In a private reply Crick clarified the ambiguous phrase (a correction was soon published) but persisted in his estimation of Franklin's ability:

> You apparently believe Rosalind was a first-rate scientist. I think she was a good experimentalist but certainly not of the first rank. She was simply not in the same class as Eiger or Bragg or Pauling, nor was she as good as Dorothy Hodgkin. (…) First-class scientists take risks. Rosalind, it seems me, was too cautious. She would only take small ones.

Crick asked Klug for his view of the affair; his friend replied in a letter marked NOT FOR PUBLICATION.[43] Klug disagreed with Crick on some points, emphasising Franklin's experimental skills and her crystallographic knowledge, but he accepted that she was 'the cautious type of scientist'. As to why she stuck with her purely crystallographic approach to DNA rather than building models, Klug explained: 'I think it is because she knew very well that she was no Pauling (or, for that matter as it turned out, no Crick). What distinguishes her from the select few was that she was not highly imaginative; but how many well-known scientists are?' That was Francis's point; that was what he meant by 'first rate' – the select few of Pauling, Bragg, Hodgkin … and Crick.

Around this time, the very existence of the double helix came under attack, again, as a series of papers claimed that the DNA molecule was in fact like a ladder, with the two strands lying side by side. Even though Francis had not been involved in structural studies of DNA for decades, researchers sent him their critical views. Initially his replies were good-natured, and he used the arguments to explore what experimental data would be needed to resolve the issue, eventually publishing an article with two colleagues showing why the critics were wrong.[44]

But as strong evidence for the accepted structure of DNA accumulated – including precise measurements of the B form by Crick's collaborator James Wang and the description of the wonky double helix of left-handed or 'Z' DNA by Alex Rich's group at the end of 1979 – Crick gradually became less tolerant.[45] In private letters, he became annoyed when some critics suggested that it did not actually matter which structure was right – one scientist claimed that 'the point of scientific speculation is not whether it is correct, so much, as whether it is "interesting"', while a philosopher who nosed around the problem blithely wrote that he was 'neither concerned nor competent to make scientific judgements'.[46] This provoked an incredulous response from Francis – 'I find it difficult to believe that one can usefully write about scientific work without understanding the science' – and a refusal to respond to subsequent letters.[47] He was slightly more polite to one of the main critics: 'I hope you will forgive me if I don't take much further interest in the SBS problem, since it seems to me that the issue is settled.'[48]

*

Francis also had to field various suggestions about writing popular books, including one on DNA for *Scientific American*, which despite a great deal of work on his part eventually came to nothing.[49] The one proposal that did work out was a book on Directed Panspermia, which had been in the air since Crick and Orgel published their article in 1973. Various publishers and agents had thought that Nobelist co-discoverer of the double helix and aliens would make a best-selling combination, but Orgel did not want to be involved ('Nothing on Earth would persuade me to write a book on Panspermia,' he said) and Crick explained to Kreisel that he was far too busy beginning his work on the nervous system.[50] However, by the end of the decade Francis changed his mind, only to discover that most publishers were wary of his approach, which explored the idea sceptically, as a way of explaining biology. They wanted more aliens.

Eventually, Simon and Schuster nibbled at Crick's proposal

and Francis spent much of his spare time in 1980 writing the book, testing out the chapters on Odile as he wrote. Overall, she was not impressed, telling him that the whole thing reeked of science fiction and that the basic 'theory' was not scientific (Francis addressed these views in the closing chapters; at her request he dedicated the book to her).[51] Kreisel also had difficulties with the manuscript, telling Crick that 'your marshalling of a large body of facts is quite superb. But at least for me, the book is not easy reading.'[52] Kreisel's main critique was that Crick's theory did not make any startling new prediction that did not flow from the accepted course of events.

Published in early 1982, *Life Itself* was short, like all of Crick's books. Most of it was an explanation of the scientific background to his eye-catching theory, rather than speculation about aliens. Taking a cosmic stance resembling that of the aborted 'Scale' book, but focusing on time rather than space, Crick described the origin of the universe and the appearance of life, explained the problems of defining life and emphasised the identical biochemical machinery used by all known life-forms (nucleic acids, genetic code, tRNA, ribosomes and so on). The implication of these similarities is that, at its origin, life was probably restricted to a very small population of cells. The question Crick explored in the final sections of the book was whether that population evolved from non-life, as most scientists thought, or was sent by aliens.

The book's central argument was identical to that of the *Icarus* article written with Orgel nine years earlier – there was no evidence for bacteria having been sent to Earth by aliens, but then again, there was no satisfactory explanation for how life appeared on Earth. He even fleshed out the possible motivations for the aliens sending their only begotten bacteria to Earth, including the idea that they may have lost interest in crewed space travel because they ended up 'cultivating a purely spiritual way of life – possibly supported by specially designed psychedelic drugs'.[53]

The whole thing was expressed in clear, popular language, addressing the adult reader much as Crick had been addressed by the authors of *The Children's Encyclopædia* decades earlier. He repeatedly used simple explanations to emphasise the power of natural selection in a changing environment, for example describing how a rare mutation, if advantageous, can become widespread, all the while keeping the reader's attention on the underlying principle:

> The important thing to notice is that by this simple process *a rare chance event has become common.* (...) When times get tough, true novelty is needed – novelty whose important features cannot be pre-planned and for this we must rely on chance. *Chance is the only source of true novelty.* (...) The important thing at this point is to grasp the broad, general features of the process and to realise clearly how such a simple set of assumptions can lead to such remarkable and unexpected results.[54]

There were also unusual flashes of biblical language, with references to the Psalms and the Gospels. In fact, there was an evangelical urge to Crick's prose – the book was intended not as a book about aliens but as a primer to explain the things about life and evolution which Francis felt everyone should know. In the penultimate chapter, he returned to some of the themes he had explored in the 1960s, such as the disconnect between scientific knowledge and the views of the public:

> The plain fact is that the myths of yesterday, which our forebears regarded not as myths but as the living truth, have collapsed, and while we are uncertain whether we can successfully use any of the remaining fragments, they are too rickety to stand as an organised interlocking body of beliefs. Yet most of the general public seems blissfully unaware of all this, as can be seen by the enthusiastic welcome given to the Pope wherever he travels.[55]

Francis wanted to use cultural obsessions about aliens and interest in the origin of life to explain key parts of scientific knowledge, as a contribution to the replacement of the outdated moral views that perplexed and irritated him. As he explained to Carl Sagan, who had recently published *Cosmos*, 'The real aim of the book, like your own, is to make the layman become aware, despite himself, of the nature of the Universe, and also of natural selection and of molecular biology.'[56]

The book did reasonably well, selling over twenty thousand copies in the US in the first eighteen months, garnering good reviews, and was translated into around a dozen languages, including French, German, Japanese and Spanish.[57] It provoked a huge correspondence, including a complicated letter from Jeremy Prynne, who wondered whether the genetic code itself was some kind of message from aliens.[58] Crick replied that Orgel had already had the same idea, but that it was rather difficult to test.

Inevitably, there were also many cranky letters, including one from Erich von Däniken, the author of *Chariot of the Gods?*, a pseudo-scientific best-seller about ancient alien astronauts intervening in human affairs, who nevertheless described *Life Itself* as brilliant and courageous. Crick replied that von Däniken underestimated the power of natural selection, predicting that future research would reveal the pattern of human evolution, without the need for alien intervention, and would also explain why humans like to believe in gods.[59]

Although much of the science described in *Life Itself* is still valid, including our continued ignorance of what happened all those billions of years ago, history has not been kind to Crick's underlying thesis, nor to his insistence that the aliens must have sent unicellular eukaryotes. Genetic studies now tell us that eukaryotes arose around 2.2 billion years ago, about halfway through the history of life, the product of the extremely unlikely accidental fusion of two kinds of prokaryote – unicellular organisms without a nucleus and with circular chromosomes – that had previously dominated the planet. If there were Senders, they must have sent prokaryotes, and the tiny possibility that those organisms would give rise to multicellular life could not have been part of their plans. Although we still have not created life in a test tube, studies of RNA synthesis and of the strange bacteria to be found in deep-sea ocean vents, together with theoretical explorations of how life might have evolved, have all undermined whatever plausibility Crick's idea might have had. The book has been out of print for decades.

*

Despite all these distractions, Francis was gradually able to think about the brain and how to study it. His aim was to study consciousness, and he began to correspond with a number of scientists, including the British psychologist Richard Gregory, who he had known in Cambridge in the 1950s. Gregory's sophisticated grasp of debates over consciousness and his work on visual illusions led Crick to realise that he needed to start with a simpler question. This was typical of how he approached his scientific interests, as he explained on BBC radio a few years later:

> Well, what I do is, not choose a problem, but to choose a subject, and then try and move around in the subject until I find an idea that yields, something that clicks together. I don't say I am going to try and solve such and such a problem, because it may turn out, especially in biology, that it's insoluble.[60]

On this occasion, the something that clicked together for Crick was the apparently soluble problem of visual perception. Francis was familiar with the pioneering research on the neurophysiology of vision that had been carried out over the previous two decades by David Hubel and Torsten Wiesel, but he was not interested in measuring the activity of single neurons; he was looking for a higher level, more theoretical approach to vision. He found this in the work of David Marr – Francis described him as 'a very brilliant young man'– who he had first met in Cambridge a decade earlier. This nascent collaboration, which produced just one brief research article, could have turned out to be one of the most significant in Crick's career, had it not been cut short by Marr's tragically early death from leukaemia in 1980, aged only thirty-five.[61]

Marr had studied mathematics at Cambridge in the mid-1960s before embarking on a research career that saw him produce some dense theoretical papers about brain structure and function. Following the publication of these papers, Crick and Brenner invited Marr to explain his ideas to them. It took several hours – 'When he left, Sydney and I were exhausted but undeniably impressed,' Crick recalled.[62] They soon gave Marr a job in the development group at the LMB, although he and Crick did not work together. The change in Marr's outlook came in May 1972, at an informal gathering in MIT to discuss his work, which was organised by two of the leading figures of artificial intelligence (AI), Marvin Minsky and Brenner's old friend, Seymour Papert.[63] During this small meeting – also attended by Crick (who was feeling under the weather) and Brenner – Marr grasped the potential of using AI as part of his research; the following year, he began working with Minsky at MIT, aiming to use computer vision to gain an insight into what is happening in our heads. His bold assumption was that whatever the differences in the hardware found in the two systems, similar algorithms would be involved.[64]

   In 1979, as Crick eased into the world of neuroscience, he decided that he would initially explore immediate visual perception, because it involved localised and relatively well-understood areas of the brain. It was also the focus of a great deal of experimental and theoretical work, including by Marr, who was developing algorithmic models of binocular vision, together with a young Italian, Tomaso 'Tommy'

MIT meeting, May 1972. At front, Brenner talks to
Seymour Papert. Above Brenner's head is Horace Barlow.
A pensive, tired-looking Crick is on the left.

Poggio.[65] Excited by Marr and Poggio's work, Francis invited the pair to the Salk for a month. Each morning, the two young men would do their theoretical work, then the three of them would lunch together before spending the whole afternoon doing what Francis excelled at: talking and thinking.

These discussions were staider than the mad sessions Francis had enjoyed with Brenner; the two young men were experts in a field that Francis was just discovering. As he told a friend: 'It's very good for me because they really make me think hard, but it's somewhat exhausting. This weekend they've gone off to the Grand Canyon, leaving me to stew over their equations.'[66] The result was Crick's first neuroscience research paper, co-authored by all three men. Francis was not entirely happy about how it ended up: 'I'm afraid the paper I've been writing with David Marr and Tommy Poggio does get a bit highbrow. What is worse, it doesn't come to any conclusion but talks round the problems ...'[67]

Despite its highfalutin title – 'An Information Processing Approach to Understanding the Visual Cortex' – much of the article dealt with one of the simplest yet mysterious aspects of vision, known as acuity – our ability to distinguish two points that are very close together even though the density of photoreceptors on our retina is apparently too coarse to be able to do this. Using a mixture of mathematics and some relatively crude neuroanatomy of two brain areas, the trio developed a theory of how two static points might be discriminated, treating the visual system as if it were 'a very complex information processing machine'. Although the model made sense – models often do – the insights it provided were quite limited. In real life we can discriminate points that move, something that was excluded from the model, while the lack of detailed experimental evidence meant the article provided only a vague explanation of what might be happening. As the paper warned from the outset, 'To our regret we are not yet able to make detailed and explicit sugges-tions as to what all the neurons in this region are doing.'[68] A few years later, Francis admitted that the article did not deal with the central question – 'how the brain actually does the job'.[69]

*

Crick often described his work as theoretical, but he generally kept his ideas rooted in experimental reality. That did not guarantee he was on the right lines, but it tended to prevent him from getting lost in the stratosphere. It also explains why he was so unimpressed by the vogue for theoretical biology that grew up in the 1970s. For example, the French mathematician René Thom developed something called catastrophe theory, which was supposed to explain many biological phenomena but left many people unconvinced – Kreisel told Crick, 'There is simply no substance to it at all.'[70] Crick's view was equally acerbic; he said the theory was 'pretty useless in biology'.[71] Although Francis recognised Thom's mathematical ability (he had won the Fields Medal, after all), he felt that Thom's biological intuitions had a negative sign – 'any biological idea he might have would probably be wrong.'[72]

Marr's ideas were far more grounded, especially once he began discussing with Crick. Shortly after being diagnosed with leukaemia, Marr had begun work on a book, *Vision*, which would summarise his computational approach to vision and its links with neuroanatomy and psychophysics – studies of human visual perception. When Marr visited Crick in La Jolla in April 1979, he talked in depth with Francis about his approach, which involved dividing the problem of brain function into three parts: first, a logical statement of the problem that has to be solved, then a description of the input and the output of the system, accompanied by an algorithm that could produce the output. Finally, this second level has to be represented physically, in either a brain or a computer.

During their discussions Crick repeatedly questioned Marr, obliging him to defend or discard his ideas, just as he had learned from Kreisel in the 1940s. Marr used these arguments to write a concluding chapter to his book in the form of a dialogue between himself and a sceptic, modelled on Crick. After reading the manuscript of *Vision* twice, Francis felt the book was 'a major achievement' but, as he admitted a few years later, it was only when he went to a series of evening seminars on Marr's book that he became 'a little clearer' on what it all meant.[73]

Some of the reasons for Crick's uncertainty can be seen in a detailed set of criticisms he sent to Marr that provide insights into his scientific method.[74] He began with an explanation of his and Brenner's 'don't worry' method for ignoring certain problems:

> In attacking any scientific problem no progress can be made unless certain difficulties are firmly put to one side. One cannot always justify the choice of what to leave aside and it is a bore to be continually asked to do so. However, from time to time it is wise to stand back from the subject and recognise explicitly what has been ignored.

Crick felt that Marr had not paid sufficient attention to the key part of his theory – the algorithm he believed was used to transform initial sensory information into a more complex representation that could be the basis of vision. As Francis explained: 'if we want to be able to test the theory what is really essential is the algorithm, since without this it is almost impossible to test the idea, either by psychophysics or by neurobiology (electrodes, anatomy, etc).' Crick pursued his point, exploring the general implications and echoing some of the criticisms that had been made of his own ideas in the past:

> I would go so far as to state that the main purpose of a good theory is to suggest new things to measure, the results which will be decisive for the theory and, usually, unexpected from the previous point of view. I notice that your 'predictions' tend to be either things which are really known already or alternatively things which the experimenter totally fails to see how he would test and, moreover, if he could test them would be neither especially surprising nor give decisive support for the theory ...

Although Marr believed his cancer was beaten, he had a series of relapses, the first only two months after he left La Jolla. After another hospital stay, in August 1980, Marr wrote to Francis telling him that he was going home, but that he still had not completed the second half of his book: 'Thank you for your constant concern, and of course for all the fun of working on that article, though my recent contributions have been somewhat subdued ...'[75]

Poggio (*left*), Marr (*centre*) and Crick in 1979.

Marr died in November that year. Crick wrote to Kreisel with the news, describing Marr's death as a tragic loss.[76] Much later, in 1994, Francis explained its impact in his popular science book, *The Astonishing Hypothesis*: 'His incisive mind and his imaginative creativity would surely have helped us through the tangle of difficulties that confront us today. He combined very considerable intellectual powers with the ability to absorb and digest a large amount of experimental evidence of many different kinds.'[77]

Vision was published two years after Marr's death; the publisher sent Francis a beautifully bound copy of the book, which he said he would treasure.[78] Crick later accepted that Marr's work did not fulfil its promise, 'partly because David's type of analysis of a visual problem is not always the correct one, and partly because David undervalued the information that neuroscience provides'.[79] Nevertheless, Marr's approach was hugely influential in terms of laying the foundations of what is now called computational neuroscience.[80]

*

Crick's overall approach to the brain was set out in the kind of perspectival article at which he excelled, published in 1979 as part of a special brain issue of *Scientific American*.[81] The fact that the magazine invited the novice Crick to publish an article alongside some of the leaders in the field shows the high regard in which he was held by the scientific community and the editor's confidence that he would have something interesting to say.[82]

He did not disappoint – in terms of its clarity, insight and power, this article is on a level with his 1957 lecture on the central dogma or his 1961 paper on the triplet code. Unlike those papers, there was no single idea, no overwhelming discovery. Instead, Crick gave an honest description of the failings of current work and the challenges to be faced, accurately summing up the state of the field. He then charted the way to the future. The ideas and insights he outlined still dominate the field, even though most neuroscientists have no idea that Crick was the first to coherently articulate them. Its impact can be seen in the issues that Francis highlighted – how to approach the problem by focusing on one particular aspect of brain function, the importance of theoretical approaches rooted in neuroanatomy, the need for detailed maps of brain areas, the promise of computational approaches to neural networks and the difficulty of detecting the simplicity beneath the complexity. As he put it in what could pass for a description of his whole career, his whole life: 'There are often simple processes underlying the complexities of nature, but evolution has usually overlaid them with baroque modifications and additions. To see through to the underlying simplicity, which in most cases evolved rather early, is often extremely difficult.'

Crick began his article by identifying those areas that seemed likely to make progress using existing approaches – neuroanatomy, neuropharmacology, much of neurophysiology and even brain development. On the other hand, there were issues such as perception, imagination and emotion where it was difficult to even state what had to be explained, which Crick took as a hint that 'our entire way of thinking about such problems may be incorrect'. It was these areas that Francis found most exciting and enticing. He recognised the need to know as much as possible about the basic functioning of the nervous system, but theories were needed that could describe and explain the processing of information in such a complex system. He then focused on visual perception, which he described as 'an astonishing achievement':

> When one reflects on the computations that must have to be carried out before one can recognise even such an everyday scene as another person crossing the street, one is left with a feeling of amazement that such an extraordinary series of detailed operations can be accomplished so effortlessly in such a short space of time.

The problem was that scientists had no idea how sensory stimulation gives rise to conscious perception (we still do not). 'Since this central problem is baffling,' he said, 'we can only turn to more local and detailed problems, hoping that in tackling them we may stumble on the right approach to the more difficult ones.' There was no magic wand here, but an honest description of the challenge. The major difficulty, he wrote, was that 'We are deceived at every level by our introspection.' Our experience of having – being – a brain is rarely a good guide to understanding how it works. A good example of this, he explained, is the widespread idea that perception involves something – a tiny you or homunculus – observing the world through our sense organs. This raises the obvious problem of what is inside the homunculus. Despite its popularity, this idea does not help matters.

The underlying issue that Crick highlighted – one that still haunts us today – was the lack of a broad framework within which experimental studies could be interpreted. He went on to outline three constraints that needed to be considered in developing such a framework. Firstly, the relation between information processing in the brain and the physical stimuli underlying our sensations; secondly, the physical and genetic limits of the nervous system that will affect the kind of computations that are possible; and finally, the kind of mathematics involved in information transmission and storage. He also mused about a fourth set of constraints – the deep evolutionary and developmental history of each species that limits and frames what it can do. However, he reminded his readers that, to paraphrase

Leslie Orgel, evolution is smarter than we are* – nature has sometimes found amazing solutions to specific biological problems.

Much of the remainder of the article was devoted to an issue that would preoccupy Crick for the next two decades – the wiring diagrams of brains, and the need for precise neuroanatomy. He urged neuroanatomists to adopt new molecular methods to accurately describe neuronal cells and their three-dimensional organisation, while theorists needed to highlight the features that would be most useful to measure, as a guide to experimental studies. He was not advocating a focus on structure as the only way of understanding function, but it is evident that nervous system organisation is the basis of activity and will shed light on function. Such neural networks, Crick argued, had many of the properties of the associative nets being studied by Marr and others in their models and computers, in which the strength of certain connections would alter with experience.

As to the best way of tackling the issues that he had identified, Crick suggested that well-studied animals such as flies or rodents were unlikely to provide appropriate answers, so a primate would probably be the place to start, while vision was probably the best system to study. However, that would be only a first step: 'Whatever choices are made about what to tackle first, it seems that we have a long way to go to reach even an outline understanding of brain function that is solidly based on both experiment and theory.'

Although Crick was clear-eyed about the challenges facing neuroscience, he again implicitly framed the importance of this work in terms of how understanding the brain might change humanity's whole outlook, the argument he had been making in public and in private for decades: 'There is no scientific study more vital to man that the study of his own brain. Our entire view of the universe depends on it.' This was the second challenge that Crick had set himself in 1947. After thirty years, and now in his mid-sixties, he was setting out to meet it.

---

*What Crick called Orgel's Second Rule reads 'Natural selection is cleverer than Leslie Orgel'. Orgel to Hodgkin, 11 December 2001, PP/CRI/J/1/8/8.

THE WINDMILLS
OF YOUR MIND

It would be easy to dismiss Crick's switch to studying the brain as the quixotic project of an ageing scientist who did not know his limits. After all, he did not make any decisive breakthrough in understanding the brain – nothing like the double helix, the central dogma or the triplet code. But then again, nobody else did, in Crick's lifetime or since.

Despite the absence of any great discovery, Francis's study of the brain was extremely significant: his work and his outlook helped propel the development of modern neuroscience, which has fused computational models of brain function with precise neuroanatomy, genetic manipulation, neuronal recordings and careful experimentation on memory and perception. Crick's influence was felt virtually as soon as he fully focused his mind on the topic; in the first half of the 1980s, despite being a newcomer, he made influential contributions to neuroanatomy, dream sleep, computer models, attention and visual perception. In 1985 this culminated in an attempt to knit these insights together in what he called a tentative sketch of the neural basis of awareness. All this activity, coupled with his many ideas, contributed to a major scientific shift, shaping our growing understanding of what brains do and how they do it. The approach now shared by neuroscientists all over the world is partly the product of Crick's influence.

Francis was able to play this role because of his reputation, intellect and wide interests – he was, in the words of the historian Christine Aicardi, a 'cross-worlds influencer'.[1] But chance played an equally significant role. Once again, he was in the right place at the right time – southern California, particularly the University of California San Diego (UCSD), was the centre of many of the key developments that in the 1980s led to profound and lasting changes in how we study the brain. This occurred largely through the financial support of the Systems Development Foundation (SDF), which granted around $62 million ($200 million today) in funding for neuroscience and information science.[2] Francis saw that the SDF wanted to make La Jolla a centre for neurobiological research, encouraging collaboration between the Salk and researchers at UCSD. This was something he heartily agreed with – he was already an Adjunct Professor in Biology at UCSD and would soon have a similar honorary post in the Department of Psychology.[3] With the financial situation at the Salk tightening, Francis therefore made his only application for major funding, at the age of sixty-five.[4]

The ambitious five-year project he submitted to the SDF had a budget of over $6 million (around $20 million today) and was intended 'to set up and maintain a small group in theoretical biology, together with funds to carry out related experimental work at The Salk Institute'. In his enthusiastic supporting letter, Salk President de Hoffmann told the SDF that the funding 'would enable Dr. Crick to have a real impact on the "new" neurosciences'.[5]

Although a big chunk of the proposed budget was for the salaries of three theoreticians who would work with Francis, around 10 per cent of the grant was intended to pay for invited visitors to come for extended stays and to fund a monthly seminar series. These interactive, communal elements were essential for realising Crick's vision. As he explained in his application, he wanted to take neuroscience beyond neuroanatomy and neurology, and to enrich the computational ideas pioneered by David Marr, which Crick felt were not sufficiently rooted in biological reality:

I intend to pursue a wide approach, consisting of the one just described plus a lot of evidence from neuroanatomy, neurophysiology, evoked potentials, positron emission tomography (PET) and so on, which *does* concern itself with the detailed wiring and activity inside the brain. This might be called the Integrated Computational approach. To do this I need frequent contact with experimental groups working in this area.

Perhaps the proposal was too ambitious, or maybe Francis was not persuasive enough – his justification for a budget line of $100,000 per annum towards his own salary was certainly overly laconic: 'This needs little comment,' it began. Whatever the case, the SDF refused to pay for those expensive theoreticians and initially awarded 'only' $900,000 over three years, with the possibility of a two-year extension if Crick's contract with the Salk was renewed.[6] Crucially, the budgets for the visitors and the seminars were largely retained, giving Francis the extensive discussions he needed.

Researchers in the UCSD's Institute for Cognitive Science also received generous support from the SDF. Their project, led by Jay McClelland and David Rumelhart, developed a modelling approach to memory and cognition that became known as Parallel Distributed Processing (PDP), which laid the basis for today's artificial intelligence programmes. Crick soon found himself involved in the work of the PDP group, attending their meetings, sometimes twice a week. When he later described his role as that of 'a fringee, or perhaps a gadfly', this was not modesty – McClelland recalled with some irritation how Crick's interventions, made from a sofa at the back of the room, repeatedly pulled the discussion away from the computational aspects to focus on the biological plausibility of a particular neural net.[7]

Despite all this interaction, Crick craved someone he could discuss with, day in and day out, just as he had with Brenner and Watson. In 1979, he urged the Salk to recruit Graeme Mitchison, a brilliant young mathematician and talented pianist who had worked on development at the LMB. Mitchison would be 'the ideal person for me to work with,' Crick said, and funds were found to support him on a two-year sabbatical from Cambridge.[8] When Mitchison arrived in April 1980, Crick wrote excitedly to a colleague: 'Graeme arrived on Thursday and is in splendid form. We hope we've found

Graeme Mitchison

a grand piano for him to practice on. We spent a long time on Sunday sipping champagne in a friend's garden, so much so that my head got tanned.'[9]

The pair soon fell into a routine: Crick would wander into work around midday; he and Mitchison would then discuss in his office at the Salk with its panoramic views of the Pacific and the horizon, the blue sky dotted with hang-gliders. The room, which had once been Bronowski's, was now adorned with a portrait of Bruno, a large plastic model of the brain and a double helix. Next, Crick and Mitchison lunched in the Salk canteen, generally with Orgel, and more chat would follow.[10]

Crick and Mitchison's first project was based on a typically Crickian moment of excitement as he seized on a new experimental finding that many people had overlooked. In 1979, he heard Jennifer Lund of the Medical University of South Carolina describe her work on the tree shrew – a small mammal with an anatomically complex visual cortex and a relatively large brain, which at the time was thought to be closely related to primates.[11] Lund and her postdoctoral researcher, Kathy Rockland, had discovered a stripe-like array of long-range connections across the visual cortex, which they suggested were interspersed with shorter-range connections. This was a compelling demonstration of an unsuspected global organisation in the brain; several years later, Crick recalled his reaction:

> I was agog with excitement but, being a new boy, said nothing, expecting everyone to be as interested and surprised as I was. Nobody said a word. It was only in the bus going home that I quizzed Jenny about them. My conclusion was that people in the vision field couldn't recognise an interesting result when they heard one![12]

Francis subsequently wrote a fan letter to Lund, telling her, 'It will take me a good time to digest your paper fully, as my memory is very poor and only constant reading will get it all into my head. (You have no idea how often I reread your papers.)'[13]

However, Crick and Mitchison thought they had an alternative explanation, and with Lund's encouragement they published it in 1982.[14] Mitchison and Crick proposed that the connections observed by Lund in fact linked parts of the visual cortex that responded to similar features in the visual field. These prolonged axons might form an essential component of feature detection in the brain; by gathering signals from the kind of simple detectors first identified by David Hubel and Torsten Wiesel in the 1950s, they could respond to more complex forms. For example, if the elementary components responded to dots or short lines, these linking neurons might respond to a long line by grouping together signals from the simpler elements. Researchers are still investigating the rules underlying these long-distance connections; for the moment, Crick and Mitchison's hypothesis remains on the table.[15]

*

In 1981, Francis decided to break his self-imposed rule and took two intercontinental trips in the same year. First, in the summer, the Cricks took their usual holiday to England to see family and friends, using Portugal Place as their base once it had been vacated by the student lodgers (Francis and Odile had intended to sell the house in 1978, but changed their minds; Well Cottage was sold in 1980).[16]

Francis visited his London surgeon for his annual oesophagus check-up and they went to the theatre with Gabrielle and Jacqueline. The tickets were arranged by the obliging theatre fiend Peter Lawrence, in what became an annual ritual that continued for over a decade. Each spring, Lawrence would send the Cricks a selection of upcoming London plays that they might be interested in, they would choose the ones they liked the sound of and Lawrence would do the rest.[17] That year, they saw Pinter's *The Caretaker*, *A Month in the Country* by Turgenev, *Measure for Measure*, and Vanbrugh's *The Provoked Wife* (they did not fancy *The Elephant Man*, and had already seen *Amadeus*).

After returning to California, Francis and Odile went on a six-week voyage across the Pacific to Japan, India and Thailand. This was part holiday and part lecture tour – there were talks in Hawaii, Hong Kong, Hyderabad and Kyoto. It was also part business trip; they were accompanied on the opening leg by de Hoffmann, who wanted to set up links between the Salk and various pharmaceutical companies and roped Francis into the meetings.[18] Francis paid greater attention to cultural differences than on his previous journey to the Far East; he told Gunther Stent that visiting Japan had made him realise that he was not such a male chauvinist as he had thought.[19] Much as the Cricks enjoyed themselves, on their return Francis realised it had all taken up far too much time and energy, and he cancelled his European holiday for the following year.[20]

In between these two long trips, the Cricks bought the next-door apartment in their condominium and set about transforming part of it into a studio for Odile.[21] About this time, Francis had yet another big idea, during a symposium in the mountain resort of Aspen, Colorado.[22] One evening, while sitting around a campfire, he heard neuroscientist Christoph von der Malsburg suggest that if the strength, or weight, of a synapse between two neurons could suddenly change, that could be an important component of visual perception.[23] A neuronal network, rather than being fixed, might be able to rapidly alter its dynamics. Looking into the glowing sparks flying up into the dark Colorado night, Crick's mercurial mind linked von der Malsburg's conjecture with the variety of shapes seen on the small projections ('spines') found on the input part of cortical neurons, the dendrites, where synapses are established.[24]

As he wrote immediately after the meeting: 'I had what appears to be a completely novel idea, namely that dendritic spines are mini-muscles, which twitch during neural activation.'[25]

Francis was so excited by his brainwave that he hastily scribbled a seventeen-page document on the topic while still at the meeting; a clean handwritten copy, marked 'Not to be quoted without permission', carried the warning 'some of the detailed facts quoted have not yet been checked'.[26] A few weeks later he submitted the article to the widely read journal *Trends in Neurosciences*, telling a colleague 'it's an amusing idea'.[27]

It was a typical Crick speculative piece – an audacious suggestion based on largely unnoticed experimental data and hypotheses from other researchers. The fundamental idea was that by 'twitching', a dendritic spine could alter the electrical parameters of the synapse. With supporting calculations from Tommy Poggio and MIT post-doctoral researcher Christof Koch, Crick went on to speculate about how this twitching might be produced, hypothesising that spines contained large quantities of contractile proteins such as actin or myosin. This prediction turned out to be basically correct – spines do twitch (but on a much slower timescale than he imagined) and actin is responsible. Technical difficulties still make it impossible to test his fundamental idea that rapid changes in spine shape might temporarily alter synaptic properties and contribute to perception.[28]

*

Crick's interest in spines was fleeting, but he became increasingly focused on the underlying issue – the effect of changing the properties of a neural net, either in a brain or in a computer. A major source of this interest was the work of the PDP group, whose computer models were influenced by the decades-old ideas of psychologists Donald Hebb and Karl Lashley. Hebb had suggested that changing patterns of activity in neural networks underpinned learning, while Lashley argued that objects, concepts and memories were represented in the brain by a distributed network of cells. These concepts appeared contradictory, but PDP programs built upon both of them, allowing large numbers of interconnected components to interact as they sought to identify a stimulus. The idea was that sets of units and their connections would correspond to targets – patterns such as letters or possible outputs of the system. The weights of those connections would change with feedback, depending on how accurately the system had identified the stimulus. By cycling through repeatedly, the system gradually improved its performance, in a process akin to learning. Sometimes the results were unexpected. For example, Rumelhart and McClelland created a program that could work out the rules for the past tenses of English verbs; to everyone's surprise it mistakenly applied those rules to irregular verbs, just as children do – so it output 'go/goed', despite having previously learned the correct form ('go/went').[29] This kind of result strengthened the assumption that similar processes occurred in PDP programs and in human cognition.

Crick was particularly excited by his encounters with two young researchers in the PDP group. Terry Sejnowski was a physicist and mathematician who Crick had first encountered in 1980, while Geoffrey Hinton had a training in psychology and was looking for a post; his first letter to Crick began, inopportunely, 'Dear Sir Francis'.[30] Hinton had a profound grasp of computational approaches – while working at UCSD in 1979, he had organised a workshop that was the predecessor of the PDP group. Two decades later, Sejnowski said that Hinton was 'the seed that led to PDP'.[31] Faced with Mitchison's planned return to Cambridge and impressed by Hinton's ability, Crick urged de Hoffmann to recruit the young man, pleading with the Salk to provide him with someone who could play a similar role to Watson or Brenner:

> I believe it is important that I have a junior colleague whom
> I both like and respect, with interests similar to mine, so that
> I have someone to talk to on a day-to-day basis. (...) I have
> naturally been keeping my eyes open for such a person, but it
> has been hard to discover anyone with all the right qualifica-
> tions and who is also movable. Geoffrey Hinton seems to me
> to meet all these requirements.[32]

Hinton – who knew nothing of this request – eventually moved to Carnegie Mellon University but continued to be involved in the PDP group. Much later, he became a leading figure in artificial intelligence, playing an important role at Google and sharing the Nobel Prize in Physics in 2024.

*

Crick's thinking about the brain became increasingly dominated by the ideas of the PDP group, although he recognised that their views were not sufficiently rooted in biology.[33] His first opportunity to show the importance of the links between theoretical and biological approaches came through what looks like one of his odder interests – a theory of dream sleep, which he developed with Mitchison in 1982.

The initial insight came when Mitchison was modelling a simple associative net with feedback and found that if the weight of the connections was increased beyond a certain point, the system would begin to resonate and became non-functional. This problem could be fixed by making the weight of the connections slightly negative, which Crick described as a kind of unlearning or forgetting.

Crick then drew a bold parallel between the behaviour of Mitchison's program and what happens when we dream. In this phase of sleep, which is accompanied by rapid eye movements (it is called REM sleep), we experience something like everyday events, but when we wake we generally remember little of what was in the dream. Crick hypothesised that the brain might use 'unlearning' to prevent the appearance of dangerous resonances if our synapses became too strong following a day's activity; this was what produced a dream. As he explained with some trepidation to a leading sleep researcher:

> The kernel of our idea, then, is that during REM sleep (...) when the dreamer is really asleep and not waking up, the brain forgets what is then going through the sleeping brain. That is, it has a mechanism akin to the long-term learning mechanism but with the opposite sign. It weakens the appropriate synapses rather than strengthening them.[34]

Unfortunately for Crick, Mitchison's two-year funding for his stay at the Salk came to an end in spring 1982 and he returned to Cambridge. Francis could no longer rely on their daily discussions to develop and test his ideas, so he had to write long letters to Mitchison. These were no substitute for actual conversations, as he complained: 'I very much wish you were still here. Although it's a good discipline to write things down, it's very much easier to be able to talk things over at length.'[35] Furthermore, in Mitchison's absence, Francis had no way of exploring the computational aspects as his programming skills were rudimentary – he had only recently acquired a computer and was struggling to learn BASIC.[36] 'It's a great pity I didn't start on it seriously when you were here,' he lamented to Mitchison.[37]

Progress also slowed because in the summer months Crick became distracted by domestic matters. Although he had decided not to go to England in 1982, Odile needed to visit her ageing aunts in France, leaving Francis 'to do domestic chores, such as watering the flowers', as he put it.[38] He eventually managed to get temporary help, as he explained to a colleague – 'I seem to have acquired a staff of part-time nymphs, to clean, cook, shop and water the flowers, but most of these will fade away when Odile returns.'[39] Nevertheless, a draft article eventually appeared. Crick intended to send it to the *PNAS*, but the newly returned editor of *Nature*, John Maddox, got wind of the project and urged Francis to submit the article to his journal instead. Maddox made a series of criticisms of the draft, which Crick and Mitchison largely accepted (Mitchison came for several weeks to rewrite the article), and it was submitted in November 1982.[40]

However, for the first time in Crick's life, the referees did their job and gave one of his papers a good kicking.[41] Referee #1 was almost Crickian:

1) The same theory was proposed by Jackson in 1932.
2) This theory has lost favour because what meagre experimental evidence there is suggests that REM sleep is important for memory consolidation rather than the reverse.
3) The last thing this field needs is yet another untestable theory.

Crick did not even bother to engage with this, as he told his friend at *Nature*, Miranda Robertson, a few weeks later: 'We don't think much of the comments of Referee No. 1, especially as he hasn't grasped the idea. Referee No. 3 is another matter. Although somewhat peevish, he makes several telling points as well as pointing out actual errors in the paper.'[42] (The referee listed thirty-five faults.)

Even more significant than the referees' comments was Crick's chance encounter with computational scientist John Hopfield of Caltech, a few days after he sent the draft to *Nature*. Crick wrote excitedly to Mitchison: 'GUESS WHAT! I was talking to John Hopfield … He told me that he had been doing simulations on the problem of getting rid of a too dominant component stored in an association net. He actually used the word "unlearning" and described a reverse-Hebbian modification! I told him about our paper.'[43]

Convinced that Hopfield's work gave major theoretical support to the hypothesis about the function of dream sleep, Crick went into overdrive. First, he bombarded Mitchison with detailed summaries of Hopfield's work and the potential parallels with REM sleep, but it eventually became clear that this kind of transatlantic epistolary mad session would not work – 'BUT ENOUGH. Sad you are not here to advise me about all this,' he wrote – so he summoned Mitchison back to the Salk so they could rewrite the article yet again.[44] He also invited French sleep expert Michel Jouvet to visit for three weeks, in the hope of understanding more about REM sleep.[45] And he badgered Hopfield into writing up his discovery and then told *Nature* he would only submit the revised REM sleep article if the journal agreed to it being accompanied by Hopfield's paper.[46]

Crick got his way, partly because he was Crick, and partly because he was right. Whatever the virtues of the REM sleep hypothesis, the link with Hopfield's article was striking, novel and heralded a new cross-disciplinary approach to studies of brain function and computer models (Hopfield shared the 2024 Nobel Prize in Physics with Hinton).

The papers appeared in the same issue of *Nature* in July 1983. Hopfield's was a research letter, but the Crick and Mitchison paper was badged as 'Commentary'.[47] As Francis had expected, the press loved it – there were articles in the *Guardian*, the *Observer*, the *Sunday*

Times and *The New York Times*, he was interviewed on BBC radio, and there was detailed coverage in *Newsweek*, *The Economist*, *New Scientist* and *Psychology Today*.[48] All this attention (Crick called it 'a lot of fa-la-la') produced a slew of letters to both the Salk and *Nature*. Many of the letters from the public were positive, although most were on the content of dreams, which did not interest Francis. In a different register, fringe psychologist and dream obsessive Stan Gooch dismissed Crick's ideas as 'pathetic' and 'both repressive and fascist – that is, psychologically disturbed and politically despicable'.[49]

To Crick's disappointment, the views of the people the article was aimed at – sleep researchers – ranged from mild amusement to outright hostility.[50] As with his ideas about gradients in development, established researchers in the field were dismissive. Michel Jouvet recalled that he found Crick to be 'a very polite man, sometimes charming, sometimes extravagant', but that his hypothesis was simply a rehash of nineteenth-century ideas 'dressed up with computers and neural networks'. Crick's folly, Jouvet felt, was the product of over-reaching ambition – 'no unknown frontiers can resist either molecular biological or British imperialism!' he half-joked.[51] Dutch scientist Dick Swaab was less forgiving, telling Francis that the idea was detrimental to serious sleep research, while, like many others, clinicians Robert Daroff and Ivan Osorio wrote a critical response to *Nature*; when it was not published (no responses were), they claimed the journal 'wanted to protect Crick's image and could not bear to look at the facts'.[52]

Leaving aside the understandable irritation felt by some scientists at Crick muscling in on their territory, these negative responses were provoked by three main factors.

Firstly, Crick and Mitchison's focus on neural nets as an analogy for the human brain was unfamiliar territory for most sleep researchers, who tended to be physiologists not neuroscientists. In fact, at the time, few people grasped the significance of artificial neural nets for understanding behaviour and brain function – one reason why Crick and *Nature* were so keen to drive home the point by simultaneously publishing Hopfield's article.

Second, the use of the term 'unlearning' to describe the change in the activity of the network was unhelpful. It suggested something absolute – a kind of erasure – rather than the subtle phenomenon Mitchison and Hopfield had observed in their artificial neural nets. This was reinforced by the use of the phrase 'We dream in order to forget' in Crick and Mitchison's article. Crick told Kreisel it was intended as a slogan to help people remember the idea, but it misled most readers.*[53]

Finally, as Crick and Mitchison cheerfully admitted, in the absence of evidence for their reverse learning idea, the theory was utterly speculative.[54] Indeed, within a few years, the mechanism they had suggested might produce reverse learning was shown not to occur in REM sleep.[55] All that did not mean the theory was worthless – even if wrong, it might be useful in the development of future parallel processing devices. Crick and Mitchison subsequently returned to dream sleep in a specialist journal, but their article contained nothing new. The tone was downbeat, as they regretted the 'forgetting' claims of the first paper and concluded meekly that researchers could 'usefully remember' that reverse learning, or something similar, 'might be occurring in REM sleep'.[56]

Despite the lack of any test of the theory or any evidence in support of it, the *Nature* article has been cited over five hundred times. Continued interest in the paper is partly because of the Crick halo, partly because of the link with neural nets and partly because the origins and functions of dreaming remain unknown. There might be something in it.

*

Mitchison's return to Cambridge, coupled with the Salk's failure to seduce either Sejnowski or Hinton, left Francis isolated. Despite his discussions with the PDP group and the long visits from colleagues, he was no longer able to enjoy the intense arguments he needed. So he enthusiastically agreed to a suggestion from V. S. Ramachandran

---

*Long before they submitted the article, Crick recognised this problem and suggested a series of alternative words to Mitchison, none of which quite fitted the bill: deleting, erasing, damping, moderating, attenuating, editing, suppressing, quenching and squelching. Crick to Mitchison, 8 July 1982, PP/CRI/J/2/2/4.

and Gordon Shaw, two vision researchers at the University of California, Irvine (UCI), that they should set up an informal discussion group to encourage progress in the field, like the RNA Tie Club. What became known as the Helmholtz Club* was, as Christine Aicardi has pointed out, much more like the small Cambridge scientific clubs that Crick had been a member of in the 1950s, such as the Hardy Club or the $\nabla^2 v$.[57]

The Helmholtz Club met around eight times a year at UCI; the meetings would go on all afternoon, bookended by lunch at UCI and dinner at a restaurant in nearby Costa Mesa. The club, which was initially bankrolled by Crick's SDF grant (later, the Salk picked up the tab), acted as a forum for intensive informal discussion of recent developments in visual neuroscience, often involving the fusion of cognitive psychology and computational approaches.[58] The participants were few in number, but they were extremely high-powered – in 1985, Nobel Prize winner David Hubel began his talk by saying that this was perhaps his most distinguished audience.[59] The discussions could be boisterous, but interruption and criticism was generally taken in good part. For example, although the British psychologist Richard Gregory was given what Francis called a rough time, he readily accepted a second invitation and recalled the club as a wonderful institution.[60]

Gregory was one of two British vision scientists in whom Crick was particularly interested; the other was electrophysiologist Horace Barlow – Francis used his first tranche of SDF funding to invite each of them to the Salk.[61] Like his friendship with Gregory, Crick's acquaintance with Barlow went back to Cambridge in the 1950s (inevitably, it was Kreisel who introduced them).[62] Francis was fascinated by the contrasting approaches of his two old friends: Barlow focused on the responses of single cells, while Gregory specialised in illusions, using simple psychological tests to reveal how the visual system could be tricked into perceiving something that was not there.

In 1972, Barlow proposed an influential theory about how the

---

*Hermann von Helmholtz (1821–1894) was a German physicist who pioneered the electrophysiological study of the nervous system and changed our understanding of visual perception.

activity of single cells in a hierarchical system could produce visual perception, based on what he called five dogmas – hypotheses about how the nervous system might work and a deliberate riff on Crick's central dogma.[63] Francis was attracted by Barlow's confident assertion that conscious experience is nothing more than the activity of neurons but recognised that the challenge was to integrate this reductionist approach with Gregory's equally valid focus on visual experience. This was increasingly at the centre of his thinking over the next two decades.[64]

This problem, which remains unresolved, had both scientific and philosophical aspects. As Crick confessed to Gregory, he was hopelessly prejudiced against philosophers, but he felt he ought to make an attempt to learn something of what they were trying to say, so he accepted an invitation to a symposium on 'The Brain and the Mind' at Johns Hopkins University, Baltimore, in November 1983.[65] Francis was rather wary of what the meeting might hold – 'I am not accustomed to consorting with philosophers,' he told a colleague – but it turned into another decisive moment.[66]

There were several big beasts at the meeting, including the US philosopher Dan Dennett, but it was Canadian philosopher Patricia Churchland who grabbed Crick's attention. Her theme was the mind–brain problem, a topic that Crick found uninspiring, but as Churchland spoke, he was delighted to discover that he agreed with virtually everything she said. He wrote an excited letter to Mitchison about Churchland and her husband and academic partner, Paul, enclosing copies of their papers and telling him, 'You will never believe it, but they say just the sort of things we say! Isn't this incredible?'[67]

Sensing an opportunity, Crick immediately invited the Churchlands to visit the Salk. Three months later, the Cricks took them on a trip to Borrego Springs, on the edge of the Sonoran Desert (Francis advised sensible shoes for walking, but apart from that, 'anything easy to wear and informal will do'). Things moved swiftly, and by August the Churchlands had been hired by UCSD and had bought a house.[68] Much later, Pat Churchland recalled how Francis worked:

He became a close friend, and I learned from him so much about how to think about and through and around a complex problem, such as the neurobiological basis of consciousness or self-control. Once his attention was focused on a particular problem, he was relentless, chewing away at it, reading everything relevant. Francis was fearless in trying out all kinds of theories on anyone available, and he was, if not happy to be wrong, at least not upset by it. This was all terrifically inspiring, of course, but in truth it was also tremendous fun.[69]

The admiration was mutual – Crick told a friend that he could no longer read philosophers ('what they say seems to me a complete waste of time and only makes me irritated'), but he made an exception of the Churchlands, who he considered 'very sound'.[70] Over the decades, Crick found that Pat Churchland was instrumental in further honing his way of thinking. For example, those who imagine that Crick was a simple empiricist, will be surprised to read his rich view of the nature of reality and perception:

> I believe that our picture of parts of the world corresponds very closely with the real world. This is especially true when many apparently distinct lines of evidence (such as those for atoms) lead to the same concept. Yet I am not a 100% realist in that I believe that *all* our knowledge of the real world (including its mere existence) is an inference on our part.[71]

This nuanced materialist view also applied to the question of how best to understand a particular phenomenon, as he explained to the developmental biologist Antonio García-Bellido: 'To prove a theory at any level usually requires data from a lower level. Naturally such mechanisms are based on structure and they necessarily must have a function, ultimately defined in relation to evolution. Mechanisms are not isolated from one another but often interact in complicated ways.'[72]

*

Crick recognised that any account of consciousness and perception had to be rooted in the structures and activities of the cells and regions that make up the brain, but to his surprise he found that there was no good description of the detailed anatomy of the human cortex, and there was not even an answer to the apparently simple question of the number of types of cortical neuron.

Resolving both these issues was essential if PDP models were to be useful for understanding the brain; if it turned out that they were based on anatomically impossible connections, their significance for neuroscience would have to be downgraded. To emphasise this point, when the PDP group summarised its work in two books, Crick's contribution was a chapter on the neuroanatomy of the cortex. 'This sort of work may at first seem rather pedestrian,' Crick explained to the SDF in his annual report for 1982–1983, 'but it should be useful in suggesting ideas as to how the present theoretical neural nets, which are very idealised, can be made more realistic.'[73] Crick's friend, the British psychologist Stuart Sutherland, warned Francis that this was a tricky project: 'I admire your courage in attempting to make sense of anatomical structure in the cortex and I wish you luck – as far as I can see, nobody has had much success in this direction so far, but perhaps nobody has tried hard enough.'[74]

To digest the anatomical literature, Crick enlisted the help of a young anatomist, Chisato Asanuma.[75] Their chapter, 'Certain Aspects of the Anatomy and Physiology of the Cerebral Cortex', appeared in volume 2 of the PDP book *Parallel Distributed Processing: Psychological and Biological Models*, in 1986.[76] The PDP volumes were extremely influential, selling ten thousand copies in the first year, and fifty thousand overall – far more than most academic books.[77] That two volumes of fairly abstruse computational neuroscience could sell so well gives some indication of both the appetite within the scientific community to understand this new approach and the power of the novel insights it provided.

Unlike all the other PDP contributors, Crick and Asanuma were resolutely focused on biology, highlighting not only the known structures and connections of the human brain but also what was not known. 'We are in the embarrassing position of knowing a lot about the neuroanatomy of the macaque monkey,' they wrote, 'while having only a very limited amount of similar information about the human brain.'

Although their chapter dealt with all the major brain structures that connect to the neocortex, Francis was particularly interested in

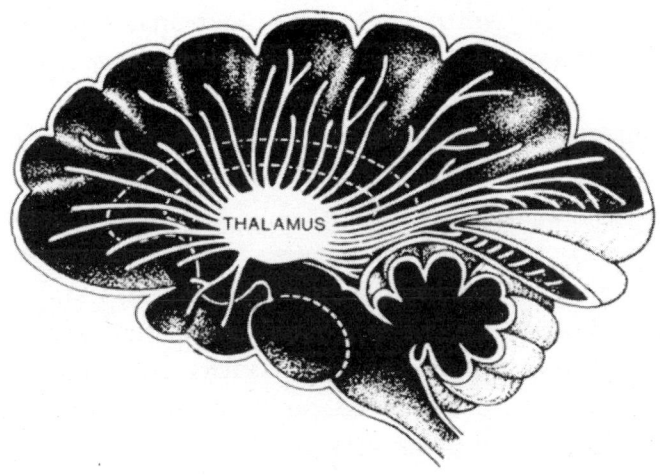

Figure from Crick and Asanuma's book chapter.

the thalamus, a structure deep within the brain. Virtually all information that reaches the neocortex passes through it, and he was struck by some apparent similarities between the links between the thalamus and other brain structures and the way that PDP programs worked. Surrounding the thalamus is a poorly understood structure called the reticular complex – a sheath of tissue a few cells thick, which receives connections from the neurons that pass to the cortex and sends inhibitory signals back into the thalamus. For Crick and Asanuma, this was a remarkable structure occupying a strategic place in the brain; they urged both experimentalists and theoreticians to devote more attention to it.

As the dendritic spines paper had shown, Crick was just as interested in neuroanatomy at the cellular level, and he began to wonder how many different types of neuron there were in the cortex. After a great deal of reading and discussion with neuroanatomists, in June 1983 he completed a draft paper, 'Cell Types in the Neocortex: The Tiling Hypothesis'.[78] Studies of a handful of readily identifiable neuron types in the retina had shown that the dendrites of cells of each type overlapped, but only by a small amount; these groups of tiled, connected cells, could be considered 'mini-nets' and presumably had some function. Crick, with his appetite for finding rules underlying biological phenomena, sought to work out what he called the 'tiling formula', which would reveal the number of cells. Using a series of conservative guestimates he suggested there were around one thousand different cell types in the neocortex. The neuroanatomical uncertainty of the early 1980s can be seen in a statement by Crick that now seems obvious, but was not so at the time:

> The picture of the cortex that emerges from this point of view is that the cortex, far from being rather a mess, is a highly evolved, precise and complex mechanism for handling information. Barlow has already stressed such a point of view. If the retina, he says, can now be seen to be a beautiful piece of 'design', why should we expect less of the cortex?

Although Francis chose not to publish his article, the approach and the execution show him at his boldest, using the power of his mind and extensive reading to answer a fundamental question. Over four decades later, the argument over how to identify cell types continues, but Crick's figure appears to be correct, for the mouse at least.[79]

Francis next became fascinated by the work of psychologist Anne Treisman, of the University of British Columbia, which seemed to provide a link between Marr's ideas and those of the PDP group.[80] In 1980, Treisman had published a paper with Garry Gelade outlining her idea: 'In our model, which we call the feature-integration theory of attention, features are registered early, automatically, and in parallel across the visual field, while objects are identified separately and only at a later stage, which requires focused attention.'

According to Treisman, when we see, certain aspects of an object such as colour, brightness and orientation are all immediately identified in parallel processes; they are then serially combined by attention to form a single perceptual representation in the brain. This theory could be tested by showing people patterned visual stimuli and observing how rapidly they could identify the different components. Crick said that he was electrified when he learned of Treisman's work in 1981, and he immediately began corresponding with her, inviting her to the Salk several times.[81]

Francis decided to focus on identifying the neural bases of

what Treisman called the internal attentional searchlight, which she argued acted to 'bind together' the various elements of a visual scene into a single perception. In late 1983 he began to speculate that the reticular complex played this role, rapidly writing an article which he submitted to the *PNAS* in April 1984; it appeared three months later and became his most influential paper in neuroscience.[82] The article presented a detailed survey of anatomical and psychophysiological evidence and contained two speculative hypotheses:

i) The searchlight is controlled by the reticular complex of the thalamus.
ii) The expression of the searchlight is the production of rapid firing in a subset of active thalamic neurons.

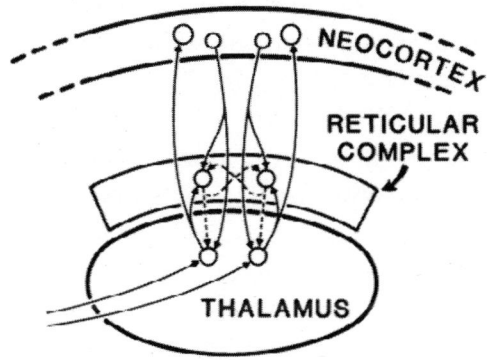

FIG. 1.   The main connections of the reticular complex, highly diagramatic and not at all to scale. Solid lines represent excitatory axons. Dashed lines show GABAergic (inhibitory) axons. Arrows represent synapses.

Crick went on to suggest that rapid changes in synaptic activity could produce briefly connected networks of neurons corresponding to the perception of a particular object. Drawing parallels with the way that artificial intelligence systems processed data, he was making the most of the links between findings from cognitive psychology and from neuroanatomy and neurophysiology. Although he soon realised that his approach was too simple, the article's bold synthetic method explains its influence. As de Hoffmann had predicted, Crick was outlining the shape of the 'new neurosciences'.

*

In 1984, the Cricks went on two trips to the Pacific, first to Tahiti in June, where, on McClure's recommendation, Francis read *The Unspeakable Confessions of Salvador Dali*. Then, over Christmas and the New Year, they visited the Galápagos Islands with the Orgels.[83] A few weeks later, McClure told Crick he wanted to interview him for a journalistic project; sadly, nothing came of the idea.[84] There was lunch with Noam Chomsky and there were social visits – Kirsti Simonsuuri came to stay with her new girlfriend in March.[85] Trivia also distracted him – when he tried to hang a reproduction of a portrait of the young Darwin on his office wall (Darwin, along with Galileo, was Crick's favourite scientist), the jobsworths at the Salk said this was impossible, because of copyright issues. Understandably bemused, Francis obtained a copy of a pencil sketch for the portrait, which he himself hung in his office.[86] Crick's personal archives from this time contain the last clear evidence of a brief affair.[87]

Through all this, Crick's brain kept fizzing, and on his return from the Galápagos he began to draw together the threads of his work in neuroscience thus far. In mid-January he told Mitchison, 'I have been trying to construct a tentative theory of consciousness.'[88] Over subsequent weeks this project gradually took the form of what Crick called a scientific monograph on awareness. It went through many versions and Francis even contacted various academic publishers. Although he gave a brief talk to the PDP group about his work and sheepishly told many of his correspondents what he was up to – 'I have, so help me, written a very rough draft of a monograph on "The Neural Basis of Awareness" (Awareness = consciousness)', he confessed to the Oxford psychologist Colin Blakemore – he was reluctant to show it to anybody. One of the few people who did see a copy was Pat Churchland; Francis sent it to her with the warning 'it's all too tentative to quote' and insisted *'Please don't make copies of it.'*

At around thirty thousand words, the monograph was subtitled 'A Tentative Sketch' and carried a salutary epigraph from Stuart Sutherland: 'The problem of consciousness continues to defeat the human mind.'[89] Divided into twelve brief chapters, the document summarised Crick's views of the pathway from neurons to psychology. He began by outlining his key hypotheses – this was a materialist account, and awareness involved immediate memory, the activity of assemblies of cells and selective attention. Francis emphasised that awareness is associated 'with a small subset of neurons which are *firing very strongly'* – Crick called this the neural correlate of perception, so not necessarily identical to perception, but somehow linked to it. He avoided defining awareness, saying that he would instead guess its main characteristics and develop working hypotheses that followed those features, justifying this by using an historical example:

> If called upon to defend such an approach I would point out that Watson and I did not start our work together by constructing a careful and rigid definition of 'life'. Rather we decided that a key feature was likely to be exact molecular replication. It was this that led us to seek the structure of DNA.

This was not an accurate description of events, but no matter. Francis then went on to explain his fundamental objective: 'My "programme" is to provide such a complete explanation of the mind in neural terms that a dualistic hypothesis will eventually seem unnecessary. Only time can tell whether this programme will be successful.'

Ultimately, however, Crick was not satisfied with this attempt to fulfil the promise he had made nearly forty years earlier. Although his document was a valiant attempt at integrating the neural net approach with neuroanatomical and psychophysiological data, he soon accepted that his ideas needed major revision (he later said that although they were perhaps on the right lines, they were too woolly) and the draft monograph disappeared into his archives.[90]

One lasting contribution to his thinking made by this document came in the conclusion, when he explained that the brain should be approached not with the tools of philosophy, or by the computer metaphor, but 'on its own terms', by deciphering 'the kind of language the brain employs to speak to itself'. Unlike any other researcher at the time, Crick was addressing the most fundamental question of all. He may not have been right, but he was charting the way.

*

This five-year burst of neuroscientific activity might seem haphazard and even frantic, but it was an audacious attack on brain function, using a radically novel approach. He repeatedly published bold hypotheses because that is how his mind worked – he sought to explore the edges of understanding, to provoke new approaches to a problem by imagining an explanation. He was, as he put it in that BBC interview with Lewis Wolpert, trying to move around in the subject until he found 'something that clicks together'.[91] Inevitably, most of his ideas were not correct, but that simply meant that another idea was needed. As he told Pat Churchland, 'You must not fall in love with your theory. If it turns out to look like a dud, drop it and try a different tack.'[92]

Crick's science was moving quickly because he was unsure how much time remained; the threat was not mortality, but imminent retirement and a profound uncertainty about his – and Odile's – future. His initial contract with the Salk had run out in 1981, and although it had twice been extended, the new cut-off date was June 1986, when he would turn seventy. After that, everything was up for grabs: 'We have yet to decide whether to stay here when I do retire or to return to Europe. Alternatively we may travel and visit places for a year or two', he told a friend.[93]

In an expression of this uncertainty, in 1983 they commissioned plans for remodelling Portugal Place, including creating a new studio for Odile.[94] A return to Cambridge was possible, although it was not overwhelmingly attractive. As Francis explained to a colleague, 'I shall have to decide, before too long, where to live in retirement. At the moment, sitting here in the sunshine, Cambridge seems very far away.'[95]

By 1985, things had changed. De Hoffmann gave him an unofficial promise that his contract would be extended until 1988, and Odile had begun to enjoy success on the San Diego art scene, with exhibitions in local galleries ('Mostly nudes, I need hardly say,' Crick remarked).[96] Together with the sale of a Cambridge flat in her name, Odile's income grew such that in 1984 she too had to limit the time she spent in the UK, to avoid paying double taxes.[97] Family matters also seemed more settled – Jacqueline got married to Chris Nichols; they later had two children, Mark and Nicholas.[98] As if to recognise the new reality, after several years of prevarication, Francis finally organised the removal of his piano from Portugal Place, at a cost of £1,000.[99] He also imported a white Mercedes 300E, 'a splendid car', although its rather stately form was very different from the sporty Lotuses and Mustangs he had enjoyed in the past.[100] The licence plate he chose was AT GC.

The Cricks' future was now clearly in California. As he explained to his British lawyer: 'It is our firm intention to remain here indefinitely and, in particular, after my retirement from full-time work. (…) Our centre of interest is clearly in the USA where we have every intention of remaining.'[101] That certainty helped stabilise the Cricks' outlook and enabled Francis to fully focus on the challenge of consciousness. But before he could do that, DNA and Cambridge had one final call to make on his time.

TOWARDS CONSCIOUSNESS

For years, Jim Watson wanted someone to make a movie of *The Double Helix*. 20th Century Fox were keen in the 1970s, but their interest cooled and the project went into limbo.[1] At the end of 1980, film producer Larry Bachmann enquired about buying the rights; Watson was willing to sell, but said that because he had simply played the role of Boswell to Crick's Dr Johnson, Bachmann needed to get Crick on board, too.[2] So Bachmann wrote to 'Sir Francis', inviting the Cricks to Hollywood; Francis took a shine to Bachmann and under pressure from Watson, he signed a contract.[3] For this he received $11,250; Watson, in yet another sign of his affection for Crick, had generously given his friend half the fee.[4]

Bachmann employed a screenwriter, Christopher Wood, who had two James Bond films under his belt (*The Spy Who Loved Me* and *Moonraker*). But he also had a parallel career as 'Timothy Lea', the author of a successful series of smutty books and films (*Confessions of a Window Cleaner*, *Confessions of a Driving Instructor*, etc.). Unfortunately, it was the raucous, vulgar atmosphere of the *Confessions* franchise that Wood brought to his screenplay.

The script, eventually delivered in March 1985, was execrable.[5] Crick was portrayed as a madcap buffoon, wearing frogman's flippers to a May Ball, while a sex-starved Watson was either chasing girls or turning a doodled molecule into a sketch of a large-breasted woman. Franklin was inevitably described as 'a handsome dark-haired woman of 30 who wears heavy spectacles and a white laboratory coat which do nothing to accentuate her femininity,' while in the closing scene Watson and Crick were given honorary degrees the afternoon after completing the structure.

The science was mangled, the history was rubbish and there was no story to speak of. It was not even supposedly funny in a *Confessions* kind of way. Not surprisingly, Bachmann's backers backed out and the project was abandoned. Crick later reminded Watson, 'we were never (officially) shown the screen play and, if we had, I doubt whether we would have liked it'.[6] Officially or not, a copy of the dreadful script made its way into Crick's personal archives. Bachmann repeatedly returned to the idea of a double helix movie over the next two decades, but Crick's consistent advice was that it would be impossible to make a Hollywood film of the story, there being no sex or violence.[7]

Meanwhile, BBC TV had decided to make a drama documentary about the events of 1951–53. With Watson sitting on the film rights to *The Double Helix*, the BBC did its own research, interviewing participants and constructing a detailed timeline of events.[8] The director, Mick Jackson, reassured Francis that they would not be making the same mistakes as Hollywood; Crick remained wary – 'not *too* much drama, please', he implored.[9]

The main consultant on the production was Wilkins, who was interviewed several times and wrote a number of documents exploring his role.[10] He admitted that at the time he barely saw Franklin as a human being, more as a kind of witch, and he attempted to psychoanalyse his relationship with her – fear was the main factor driving their interactions, he claimed.[11] Although Watson declined to be involved, Crick agreed to be a consultant, making suggestions to the production team and renting Portugal Place to the BBC for the duration of the filming.[12] Several scenes were filmed inside the cramped low-ceilinged rooms of the Cricks' home, now decorated with paintings by Odile, while the golden helix above the front door was removed for exterior shots.

Filming lasted nearly two months; the crew lived on site, using

Odile's top-floor studio as the production office. BBC researcher Jane Callander, who spent two years on the project, told Francis how the building's bohemian vibes exerted an effect on the production – as well as organising a memorable party, they held an impromptu large meal for the team in 'the best traditions of the downstairs basement dining room'. They also developed a routine of going up to Odile's studio to work after dinner, 'with a bottle or two of wine to keep us going'.[13]

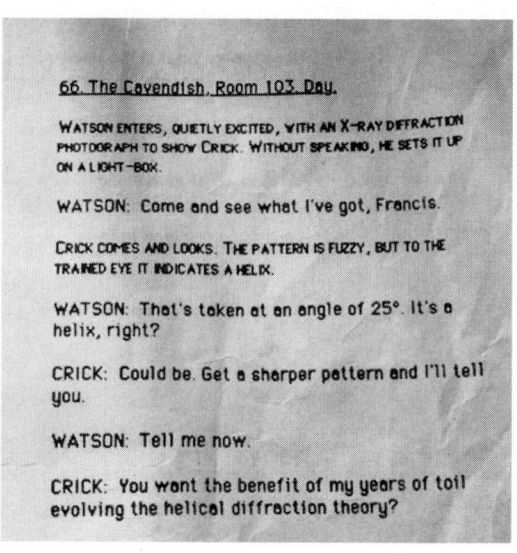

Life Story was broadcast in the UK on 27 April 1987 (in the USA it was titled *The Race for the Double Helix* and was shown five months later) and starred Jeff Goldblum as Watson, Tim Pigott-Smith as Crick, Juliet Stevenson as Franklin and Alan Howard as Wilkins.[14] Perutz told Crick that neither Goldblum nor Pigott-Smith quite got their characters right – Watson was caricatured while Crick's vitality and intellectual force were played down – but Stevenson's performance was 'a great piece of art; she had felt her way into that role with extraordinary perception and sensitivity,' he wrote.[15] Wilkins, said Perutz, was 'so life-like it was hard to believe he did not act himself'. Crick agreed that Stevenson stole the show and although he had some minor criticisms (Watson never chewed gum, the Cambridge party scenes were too manic …) he said the programme 'was probably a much better job that anyone else would have done'.[16] The pace of the production and the level of scientific detail were just right, he said, so people from all walks of life could enjoy it and absorb some of the lessons.[17] However, as he emphasised in his notes for a talk in which he discussed the programme, 'Films are not History'.[18]

Kreisel (not an easy man to please) was irritated by Pigott-Smith's performance because he recalled Crick behaving rather differently, as he explained in typically tortured prose: 'you did not bark out remarks, which Watson liked to do (in my presence), but – made a *few* observations, partly, empirical observations ... partly theoretical observations, also on what *not* to do.' Kreisel recalled this process as being very different to what he described as Franklin's 'IDEA(L) OF REGIMENTED THOUGHT'.*[19] Odile's view of the film was more straightforward – she was happy with how she was portrayed but was disappointed at the paintings chosen by the set designers.[20]

The British critics were extremely positive (the programme later won a BAFTA): the *Sunday Times* said it tore along like a thriller ('the Maltese Falcon with microscopes'), the *Evening Standard* called it 'an alpha-plus boffin drama', while for the *Observer* it was 'quite unforgettable'.[21] The public was equally enthusiastic – the BBC Duty Log, a register of viewers who ring up after a broadcast, included comments such as 'Brilliant', 'Superb', 'Fantastic' and 'It had me in tears at the end'.[22] Larry Bachmann told Crick he was impressed, but admitted that the emphasis on Franklin and Wilkins surprised him: 'That is a good story – a story I never considered doing.'[23]

Three days after *Life Story* aired, BBC Radio 3 broadcast a programme about Franklin's contribution to the discovery. Presented by Lewis Wolpert, *The Dark Lady of DNA* featured members of Franklin's family and all the survivors except Watson, with Franklin represented by Aaron Klug. Opening with an admission by Crick that without Franklin's data they could not have solved the structure, the programme revealed for the first time that Wilkins did not know of Randall's letter to Franklin which gave her the impression that she was solely responsible for DNA research. As Wolpert made

---

*It is not clear how much Kreisel's view of Franklin was based on his brief encounter with her, how much on hearsay at the time, and how much on subsequent presentations of events.

clear, this made the situation impossible for both of them. Highly impressed, Francis wrote a letter of congratulations to Wolpert, saying he thought the programme was excellent.[24]

*

A few weeks before the BBC began filming in Portugal Place, the Cricks had made their usual June visit to England to see family and friends, and to go to the theatre in London – Congreve's *Love for Love* at the National, the RSC's production of *Troilus and Cressida*, David Hare's play about the press, *Pravda*, and a new musical that had recently transferred to the West End, *Les Misérables*.[25] The Cricks stayed at Graeme Mitchison's run-down house in Cambridge, and busied themselves clearing Portugal Place, which they had finally decided to sell. Unusually, Francis agreed to a television interview; this was for a US programme about Freud – since the dream sleep article, he had been obliged to understand Freud's ideas and was now considered an expert. However, his explanation of what he considered to be the real significance of REM sleep was cut from the broadcast and his contribution was limited to 'pontificating' about the cultural impact of Freud's ideas. Nevertheless, he thought the programme was well worth seeing, very balanced and sensible.[26]

After the BBC had finished with Portugal Place, estate agents put the six-bedroom, three-bathroom, four-floor house – 'a property of great fascination and charm' (no mention was made of Odile's erotic decorations in the main bathroom) – on the market for £150,000.[27] To Francis and Odile's delight, it was bought by an LMB colleague and his wife. Although the Cricks no longer owned the house that had been so important in their lives, they were able to stay there on subsequent visits to England.

The sale marked the final step in Francis and Odile's move from Cambridge to California. They had now disposed of virtually all their UK assets and had bought a one-storey hillside house in La Jolla, at the end of Colgate Circle, a rising, curved suburban cul-de-sac. Complete with a small pool, it was still not quite right, so they immediately built an annexe containing a studio for Odile and a study overlooking the garden for Francis, who, ever the amateur architect, sketched out the plans.[28] Once completed, his office was decorated with eight of Odile's nudes.[29]

Gradually the house became a home, but it still needed another tweak, and in 1989 they built what Francis called a folly – a three-metre-square viewing platform in the garden that enabled them to see the hills and, on a clear day, the mountains beyond.[30] Francis never became a US citizen – 'I don't quite feel American yet. But I feel Californian' – he said.[31] In 1988 he explained his attachment to the region around San Diego, using unusually lyrical language:

> Personally, I feel at home in southern California. I like the prosperity and the relaxed way of life. The easy access to the ocean, the mountains, and the desert is also an attraction. There are miles of lovely beaches to walk on – out of season they are usually almost deserted. The mountains are only an hour away ... and often have snow on them in the winter. The highest ones look down on the desert. In spring, if there has been enough winter rain, the desert bursts into flower. Even at other times it has a strange fascination, partly because of the subtle colours and the wide expanse of sky.[32]

Crick's Californian life was not bounded by the Salk, Colgate Circle and the desert – Francis and Odile went to the theatre in San Diego, too. For example, in 1987 they saw *Porgy and Bess* at the Civic Theatre, then, on Odile's birthday, *Antony and Cleopatra* at the Old Globe Theatre in Balboa Park, followed a few weeks later by *The Tempest* at the La Jolla Playhouse.[33] This was the world of the San Diego establishment, with none of the bohemian zest that had some-times characterised their Cambridge lives. But Michael McClure kept them in contact with the earthier aspects of US culture, reporting that he had watched the legendary Marvin Hagler–Sugar Ray Leonard heavyweight boxing match alongside Norman Mailer, or inviting them to a gig where he was reciting his poetry accompanied by Ray Manzarek, The Doors' keyboard player.[34] (Whether the Cricks went is not known.)

Francis also made new scientific friends, including the British neurologist Oliver Sacks, whom he first met at a neuroscience conference in San Diego in May 1986. At dinner one evening, Crick singled out Sacks, grabbed his shoulders and sat him down at the table – 'Tell me stories!' Crick said, wanting to hear about the visual disturbances experienced by Sacks' patients and to discuss what light they might shed on visual processing. The next day, Sacks sent an awed handwritten letter to Crick:

> Dear Dr Crick,
> It was an extraordinary pleasure and privilege meeting you – a little like sitting next to an intellectual nuclear reactor! – I never had a feeling of such incandescence – Wonderful to have such a bright, sharp, laser-like mind illuminate problems and predicaments I see (but whose significance & explanation is quite beyond me).[35]

This meeting led to a friendship that lasted until Crick's death. As well as being enchanted by Sacks' personality, Francis wanted to explore the links between the symptoms of Sacks' patients, their underlying neuroanatomical causes and his own understanding of visual processing. Over the years, each new patient became the object of a series of sharp and perceptive questions from Crick that would mesmerise Sacks and his colleagues. Sacks recalled of one letter: 'It seemed to get deeper and more suggestive every time we read it, and we got the sense that it would need a decade or more of work to follow up on the torrent of suggestions Crick had made.'[36] In a sign of quite how powerful Crick's influence could be, Sacks recalled he began to carry out 'a sort of mental dialogue with him whenever puzzling problems came up … What, I would wonder, would Francis think of this – how would he attempt to explain it? How would he investigate it?'[37]

*

With his eyesight declining slightly, Francis took to wearing pince-nez glasses, mainly at breakfast – 'Odile thinks it gives me a rather old-fashioned look,' he told a friend.[38] Although his tall frame was beginning to stoop, his daily exercise in the pool or along the beach made him feel much better, as he explained to the head of the UCSD Physical Education department, who years earlier had shown Francis how unfit he was: 'I feel much fitter and more alert and am told I look young for my years (I am 71). I cannot thank you too much for initiating this drastic improvement in my way of life.'[39]

Odile again went to see her aunts in 1987, but Francis stayed at home, yearning for her – 'Darling, I'm missing you very much,' he wrote, 'Everything here is quite empty without you. Much much love, Francis.'[40] He stayed behind because they were planning another long trip that October, this time with the Orgels. The itinerary was complex and intensive, including visits to Tokyo, Bangkok, Kathmandu, Hyderabad, Mumbai, Agra and Jaipur, with plenty of talks and media appearances. The couple were interviewed on Indian national television – this was extremely unusual, as Odile generally refused to be interviewed. Crick's host was particularly pleased by the broadcast, describing Odile's small-screen appearance as 'specially glorious'.[41] They also briefly visited Singapore ('too hot and humid,' reported Francis), where they stayed in the Raffles Hotel, which Crick found 'very pleasant in an old-fashioned way'.[42] Overall, the trip was stimulating but strenuous; it was also the last long holiday they ever took.

*

Although Francis was adept at writing letters, memos and scientific articles, he found it remarkably difficult to write his books. This was especially the case for his 1988 memoir, *What Mad Pursuit*, which had a decade-long gestation. In 1978 the Sloan Foundation signed up Crick to write his memoirs, as part of a series of autobiographies they were publishing from scientists and physicians. After a few years, and having made no progress, in 1982 Francis suggested he might instead write a *scientific* memoir, with no reference to his private life.[43] By 1986 he had given up on the idea, telling the Foundation that 'we must face up to the fact that I am not likely to produce a Sloan-type book.'[44] The Foundation persuaded Crick to persist and in August 1987 they received the first draft of what he called 'fragments of my scientific autobiography'.[45] Each brief chapter (at one stage he called it 'A Book of Essays') dealt with the scientific lessons from a different stage of his career – hence the book's subtitle, *A Personal View of Scientific Discovery*. It was only the science that was personal – Francis did not describe how he met Odile, nor mention the birth of his children, nor did he include his own views of events or fellow scientists.

With its focus on science spanning four decades, this was not Crick's version of *The Double Helix*. Nor was it intended to be – as *The New York Times* pointed out with some surprise, the discovery of the structure of DNA was passed over in less than four pages.[46] Nevertheless, most of the scientific lessons Crick presented were drawn from the history of molecular biology. This was true even in the epilogue, which described his new neuroscientific interests:

> The present state of the brain sciences reminds me of the state of molecular biology and embryology in, say, the 1920s and 1930s. Many interesting things have been discovered, each year steady progress is made on many fronts, but the major questions are still largely unanswered and are unlikely to be without new techniques and new ideas.[47]

Francis recognised that – for the moment – the period 1953–1966 represented his greatest contribution to science and contained the richest lessons. His friend Tom Jukes picked up on this elegiac tone in a review for *Science*, 'Halcyon Days'.[48] Crick's reflective mood was not only prompted by advancing age; Frederic de Hoffmann, the president of the Salk, who had consistently supported Crick, was severely ill – he had contracted HIV from contaminated blood and retired for health reasons in November 1988, dying the following year. Crick's SDF money had long since run out, leaving him dependent on Salk funding; while de Hoffmann had always backed him, there was no saying what a new president might do. Retirement, voluntary or imposed, might be just around the corner.

With the future uncertain, Crick used his book to pass on what advice he could. Among the more general lessons that he drew from his career were the 'gossip test', the 'don't worry' approach and a great deal of scepticism about theoretical models in both molecular biology and neuroscience. He also hinted at the importance of having someone to argue with, highlighting the influence of Watson, Brenner and Kreisel in his life, although he acknowledged that his account did not do justice to his long and fruitful association with Brenner, 'an ideal colleague'.[49]

There were novel autobiographical details but Francis the man was largely absent, glimpsed mainly through his ideas and his advice. The writing lacked the bite and sarcasm that he could deploy in meetings or in letters, but Jukes still described Crick's prose as 'vivid, crisp and lively … sparkling with wit and spiced with jokes and anecdotes', while Michael McClure sent Francis an effusive response: 'It's your best book – in assurance, modesty, authority – and vivid immediacy, it is a winner … CONGRATULATIONS on your wonderful book – and thank you! It's a contribution to what is most human in science.'[50] Crick was obviously pleased about it, too – his diary entry for 26 October 1988 read 'My Book Published'.[51]

Some readers found the science hard going ('dauntingly technical' said *The Times*), but for the readers Francis was aiming at – young scientists – the book hit home. For example, a graduate student in molecular biology wrote Crick a fan letter, describing her own search for the right questions and the right approach to answering them: 'Yours was the first account I read which gave a useful description of the necessary mindset, a practical image I can interpret as advice.'[52]

The tone and aim of *What Mad Pursuit* seemed to suggest that Crick was turning into a grand old man of science, dispensing wisdom to the younger generation and recalling past glories from his office overlooking the Pacific Ocean. However, after the frenetic first decade of his late career in neuroscience, he was about to make a significant swerve.

*

In 1988, Francis attended two neuroscience meetings, each in a different Cambridge. Both raised the same fundamental problem in his mind, leading to yet another article in *Nature*.

The first meeting, in Cambridge, England, was a small affair entitled 'The Neuron as a Computational Unit.' Co-organised by Mitchison at King's College, it featured many of the international stars of the new neuroscience – Hinton, Hopfield, Koch, Poggio, Sejnowski – as well as local talent.[53] Preceding the meeting, a two-day workshop introduced experimental neuroscientists to the new world of neural nets, including hands-on experience with PDP software that used back propagation ('backprop' for short). This was the latest advance in using feedback to allow the network to change its behaviour, dependent on how close the output came to a particular target – the feedback flowed back along the same connections that were used to create the output, hence 'back propagation'. By repeated cycles of backprop, the network performed quite complex tasks in a human-like way.

These programs impressed Crick and he pestered Mitchison to tell him what computer he needed to run them.[54] However, there was a snag for anyone interested in networks of real neurons: the dependence on backprop was biologically implausible, because in virtually all cases real neurons work in only one direction.[55] This troubled Francis, who in his PDP book chapter a few years earlier had emphasised the need for anatomical accuracy. The problem persisted, but now at a cellular level.

The second meeting, organised by *Nature*, was held in Cambridge, Massachusetts, in late September and attended by around three hundred people.[56] Although some of the same crowd were involved, leading figures such as Eric Kandel, David Hubel and Antonio Damasio were also there. With a hefty dose of *Nature* hubris, the meeting was entitled 'How the Brain Works'.* Although Francis did not speak, he did chair a session and popped up repeatedly, especially in the discussions of backprop, emphasising its biological implausibility. His mood was irascible, as *Nature* noted in its report: 'A fractious Francis Crick took elaborate pains to point out that a scientifically informative model must be based on structures that actually exist in the nervous system.'[57]

Crick's frustration with this problem had been building over the summer, as he worked on an article about neural networks and their limitations.[58] His friend at *Nature*, Miranda Robertson, had invited him to publish an article on theoretical models and they eventually

---

* We still do not know.

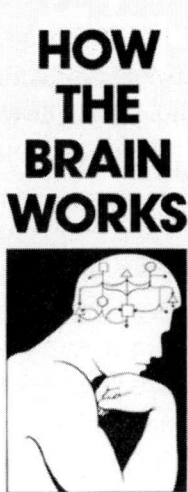

Nature's 11th International Conference

Howard Johnson Hotel, Cambridge, Massachusetts, U.S.A.
28–29 September 1988

agreed he would focus on neural nets.[59] After reviews from two *Nature* staffers, the paper appeared in January 1989, under the rubric 'Commentary'.[60] Entitled with Crickian élan, 'The Recent Excitement About Neural Networks'*, the article summarised how neural nets worked and described their amazing abilities, but Crick's real aim was to emphasise the gap between the structure and function of neural nets and of the nervous system.

No matter how impressive, neural nets could not explain how the brain worked. This was not simply because there was no back-prop in the nervous system (Crick dismissed attempts by Hinton and others to find workarounds). There was a fundamental issue that related to a difference of method, philosophy and objective:

Constructing a machine that works (such as a highly parallel computer) is an engineering problem. Engineering is often

---

* This title was a nod to his 1963 article, 'The Recent Excitement in the Coding Problem'.

based on science, but its aim is different. A successful piece of engineering is a machine which does something useful. Understanding the brain, on the other hand, is a scientific problem. The brain is given to us, the product of a long evolution. We do not want to know how it might work but how it actually does work.*

Crick insisted that the brain had evolved to be adequate, not perfect, and that rather than embodying any deep principles, it might use 'a series of slick tricks to achieve its aim'.† In other words, neuroscientists looking to neural nets for inspiration were probably mistaken. As to the modellers themselves, they were using mathematics 'to give an air of intellectual respectability to an otherwise low-brow enterprise,' Crick said sardonically. Irrespective of the striking behaviour shown by neural nets, the challenge for neuroscience was 'to look inside the brain, both to get new ideas and to test existing ones,' he explained.

This might look like a statement of the obvious, but at the time it was a radical challenge to psychologists and neuroscientists – the structure of the brain was largely the domain of neurologists and anatomists. Crick cannily latched on to recent research about a neurotransmitter receptor that seemed to be involved in synaptic plasticity and memory, and urged researchers to establish the location of such receptors in all types of neurons. 'Learning about neurons, their behaviour and their connections will not by itself solve our problems, but will at least suggest the sort of answers to look for and can be used, often rather decisively, to disprove false theories,' he concluded. As he had explained to Lewis Wolpert a few years earlier, this was the approach he had perfected over the decades – first gain detailed knowledge of a particular question, then look for the idea that yields.[61] It had worked for molecular biology; it should work for the brain, he reasoned.

In his article, Crick was disdainful about neural net theoreticians

---

*This last phrase was nearly a word-for-word quote from his 1963 'recent excitement' article.

†This phrase was taken from his friend V. S. 'Rama' Ramachandran.

('within most modellers a frustrated mathematician is trying to unfold his wings,' he scoffed); this was partly a long-standing prejudice against theoretical approaches that were not rooted in experimental results and partly flowed from his frustration on reading a recent fashionable theoretical study of brain function. The Nobel Prize-winning immunologist Gerald Edelman, like Crick, had switched fields to neuroscience and in 1987 he published *Neural Darwinism: The Theory of Neuronal Group Selection*. This complex book was based on the idea that groups of neurons are selected developmentally and through experience, with the surviving groups recruiting new neurons in the process. Reviewers in *Trends in Neuroscience* and *Nature* reported that Edelman repeatedly changed his definitions and frame of reference, making it hard to know exactly what he meant.[62] Horace Barlow, in *Nature*, said he was unsure 'whether it ushers in a new era in neuroscience, or whether it's just a hopeless muddle' but clearly favoured the latter interpretation.

Early in 1988, Crick decided that he needed to get to grips with Edelman's thinking and, together with Mitchison, began studying Edelman's work in detail. His aim was to set out Edelman's main ideas in an article for neuroscientists – Crick read *Neural Darwinism* so you did not have to. Like other readers, Francis soon became impatient with Edelman's impenetrable style, as he explained in an early draft:

> Reading Edelman, one has the uncomfortable feeling that he has been talking to himself for so long, that he no longer listens to what other people are saying. He seems to have hypnotised both his coworkers and himself into using a grossly inappropriate vocabulary. This gives the appearance of novelty to a lot of already familiar ideas and insulates him from considering in any detail what other workers are doing in this difficult theoretical field.[63]

Mitchison repeatedly urged Crick to maintain a gentlemanly tone, but agreed that there was 'little in the book that had not been said before by others, usually more clearly and with better supporting reasons'.[64]

Crick's article, 'Neural Edelmanism', appeared in *Trends in Neurosciences* in the summer of 1989.[65] As he explained, he wanted to cut through the smokescreen of jargon that clogged up Edelman's writing and highlight what kind of evidence would be needed to prove the existence of neuronal groups in brains. Crick was not persuaded that this supposedly new view of the brain was useful, never mind correct. In private, Crick told Kreisel that Edelman was 'basically a muddled thinker and for this reason conversation with him soon becomes tedious'.[66] A couple of years later, when Edelman was about to move to the Scripps Institute in La Jolla, a journalist from *Scientific American* suggested they might be rivals. 'I don't regard us as rivals,' Crick said, pausing briefly, 'but I think he does.'[67] Relations between the two eventually thawed slightly, and in 2003 Crick even provided a complimentary quote for Edelman's new book.[68]

A far more radical stance about the brain was adopted by the Oxford mathematician and physicist Roger Penrose, who in 1989 published *The Emperor's New Mind*, a best-selling popular science book which claimed to provide completely new insights into consciousness, the brain and the possibility of artificial intelligence. A central point of Penrose's argument was his assertion that because the human brain can compute things that do not follow Turing's computability theory, it cannot work according to the laws of physics. Francis could not follow either Penrose's logic or his mathematics, but he had a friend who could; even before Penrose published his book, Crick's correspondence with Kreisel (who was back in Oxford) became full of discussions of his ideas. Crick began by summarising Penrose's argument and suggesting that Kreisel should talk to him about it:

> His basic idea is that in part of our brain there is some non-computable element present in physical laws which may be being harnessed in the physical basis of thought. As you know, I am not very sympathetic to approaches of this kind. (…) However it occurred to me that you might enjoy talking to Penrose, who is a very clever man. Let me know if anything comes of it.[69]

Kreisel soon reported back that Penrose's primary objective was 'NOT

TO UNDERSTAND THE BRAIN (though this would be a welcome bonus), but to use – preferably, what we already know about – the brain TO UNDERSTAND DEFECTS OF QUANTUM AND RELATIVITY THEORIES.'[70] Crick was not impressed by Penrose's ideas – neither was Kreisel, who understood them a lot better – and concluded that 'whether something is Turing computable has nothing do with how the brain works'.[71] He summed up his opinions to Kreisel:

> As to my own view of the matter, there are some funny things going on in the brain. Almost certainly we shall have to change and expand our ideas, but I would be surprised if it turns out that new laws of physics will be required. … My present reaction is one of deep scepticism that it involves quantum gravity.[72]

*

The appearance of these books showed that Crick, from being a lone and slightly eccentric voice in the world of neuroscience, and one of few who were interested in consciousness, was now one of many. This shift in scientific focus was due to a conjunction of Crick's persistence, the growing dominance of molecular techniques that were revealing unexpected aspects of brain anatomy and function, and the impact of the PDP approach which had led to a revival in philosophical and public interest in consciousness and artificial intelligence. From this point onwards, all of Crick's intellectual power was centred on creating the conditions for the identification of what he called the neural correlates of consciousness.

There were other factors behind Crick's resolute focus. For one, he now knew a lot more – since 1988 he had been attending Pat Churchland's weekly UCSD Philosophy course on 'Consciousness and the Brain' which immersed him in the necessary literature, going back centuries.[73] There were also existential reasons – the uncertainty at the Salk meant that his research career might soon be cut short, and despite his improved health, he was not getting any younger – he and Odile might soon decide that he should stop work completely. There was no reason to wait any longer before directly attacking the problem of consciousness.

There was one final ingredient in Crick's decision to grapple with this most mysterious phenomenon. He thought he had glimpsed the answer.

One of the central issues in the study of visual perception was the 'binding problem' – how the various components of an object (location, size, shape, colour etc.) are assembled together ('bound') to form a perceptual whole. Crick's earlier suggestion that an attentional searchlight, located in the reticular complex of the thalamus, was responsible for binding had been abandoned due to lack of evidence that the neurons in this structure were involved in attention. But in late 1988, Crick heard a talk at the Helmholtz Club that described the discovery of German neuroscientist Wolf Singer that visual stimulation could cause many neurons in the visual cortex to fire at a very fast rate – about forty times a second, or 40 Hz, oscillating in synchrony. What electrified Francis was Singer's demonstration that synchronised cells responded to different but connected aspects of a single visual stimulus. This 40 Hz oscillation looked like it might be part of the solution to the binding problem – by firing together, the cells might be able to indicate the presence of a particular object in the visual field to higher-order cells connected to them.[74]

Crick was astonished to learn that Singer's paper had been rejected without review by *Nature* because 'the subject is of limited interest'.[75] Singer immediately contested the journal's judgement; Crick simultaneously faxed a letter to John Maddox, urging him to reverse the decision and predicting that the paper would come to represent a crucial breakthrough. For whatever reason, *Nature* relented, the paper was published in March 1989 and has since been cited nearly three thousand times.[76]

Francis immediately dug out the draft monograph on consciousness he had abandoned a few years earlier, and in the early months of 1989 began to develop his ideas in various short documents that were circulated to a handful of colleagues.[77] The first draft he worked on, 'Prolegomenon to the Study of Consciousness'*, consisted of

---

* 'Prolegomenon' is both precise and pretentious – many readers, including me and probably you, had to look it up to be sure what it meant, but it is exactly the right word.

nineteen propositions setting out how to develop a neurophysiologi-
cal theory of consciousness. Among the questions he decided to set
aside were those that had bedevilled previous approaches, such as
the definition of consciousness, the function of consciousness, how
to prove a theory of consciousness, the existence of consciousness in
'lower' animals and the implications of unusual states of consciousness, such as hypnotic states or lucid dreams.*

By excluding all these questions, Crick was showing that
he did not intend to develop a theory of everything that would
almost certainly be wrong. His aim was far more focused: to show
how neural correlates of consciousness might be identified. As he
explained:

> If we accept all this we can now frame the basic questions. Our
> assumption is that at any moment consciousness corresponds
> to a special (transient) set of neurons (that are a subset of a
> much larger set of potential candidates) that are firing, prob-
> ably in some special way.
>
> The problem then becomes:
>
> 1) Where are these neurons in the brain?
> 2) What is there special (if anything) about their connections?
> 3) What is there special (if anything) about the way they are
> firing?

If you wanted to understand what was going on at the level of
neurons, then these three questions were – and still are – an excellent
starting point. Francis did not think this approach was the only valid
way of studying consciousness – as he explained to a colleague, 'I do
not myself think that one can solve the problem of the brain solely by

---

*In 1990, Francis wrote a letter to Michael McClure (now lost) about
consciousness in animals and included a gnomic suggestion: 'I suspect that,
lacking language, mystical experiences are easier for them.' McClure was
understandably enthusiastic, but Crick never developed this idea. McClure to
Crick, 9 March 1990, MSS 660, Box 7, Folder 24. I cannot decide if it contains
real insight into what it might be like to be a bat (or whatever), or if it is a kind
of stoner phrase that sounds cool but is in fact empty.

a bottom-up approach. I think it essential to have top-down work as well, but I think that a true understanding can only come by combining both approaches.'[78]

Over the course of 1989, Crick developed these various fragments into an article, now working closely with Christof Koch, who a couple of years earlier had become an Assistant Professor of Biology and Engineering at Caltech. The young Koch (he was less than half Crick's age) soon became an ideal foil and collaborator. He was energetic, smart, not afraid to argue with Francis and he had an excellent grasp of modern neuroscience. He had also been raised a Catholic and retained a spiritual outlook that was in contrast with Crick's views, but that was never an issue between them. Whatever Koch's beliefs, they did not impinge upon his work with Francis.

The pair had met several times over the previous decade, but from 1989 their relationship entered a new phase. As well as exchanging frequent faxes and phone calls, roughly once a month Koch took the two-hour drive from Pasadena to La Jolla, where he would spend the weekend talking with Francis in his study and at the dining table. These discussions were not as intense as Crick's sessions with Brenner, but the more leisurely pace was no doubt more in keeping with Crick's increasingly relaxed approach to life.

Koch initially felt uncomfortable at the way their mealtime talk tended to exclude Odile, so he would try to broaden the conversation, to no avail.* In the end, he accepted that this was the way they lived their lives and had done so for decades.[79] As to Francis, he made an indelible impression on the young Christof, who would be his collaborator until the end:

> He had an unquenchable thirst for details, numbers, and facts.
> He would ceaselessly put hypotheses together to explain
> something, then reject most of them himself. In the morning,
> he usually bombarded me with some bold new hypothesis that

---

*Odile was undoubtedly interested in Crick's scientific work. Not only was she the first reader on many of his popular articles and books, she also read Kreisel's often impenetrable letters on abstruse matters and when they were particularly hard to understand communicated this via Francis. See for example Crick to Kreisel, 15 March 1990, PP/CRI/J/2/10/1.

had come to him in the middle of the night when he couldn't
sleep. … I've encountered brilliance and high achievement,
but rarely true genius. Francis was an intellectual giant, with
the clearest and deepest mind I have ever met.[80]

After nearly a year of discussion, writing and rewriting, Crick's
fragments and notes had become an article, co-authored with Koch,
'Towards a Neurobiological Theory of Consciousness'.[81] Crick told
Kreisel that, as the title implied, the paper did not present a solution
to the problem of consciousness, but rather 'what we feel might be a
fruitful approach to it'.[82] Crick's colleague Antonio Damasio invited
him to submit the article to a new journal he was guest-editing,
Seminars in the Neurosciences; after more substantial re-writing, it
eventually appeared in late 1990.[83]

The article – which has been cited by over one thousand papers
– is remarkable in its boldness and clarity. Taking as its starting point
the striking fact that at the time most research in cognitive science
and the neurosciences did not even mention consciousness, Crick
and Koch clearly stated their position:

> We suggest that the time is now ripe for an attack on the
> neural basis of consciousness. Moreover, we believe that the
> problem of consciousness can, in the long run, be solved only
> by explanations at the neural level. Arguments at the cognitive
> level are undoubtedly important but we doubt whether they
> will, by themselves, ever be sufficiently compelling to explain
> consciousness in a convincing manner.

As well as the 'don't worry' problems that were dismissed in the
various drafts, Crick and Koch now similarly despatched the thorny
problem of what philosophers call qualia – the subjective experience,
of say, seeing red, and knowing whether that is the same experience
in you and me. For Francis, this might or might not be resolvable one
day, but that would depend on first understanding the phenomenon
of experience at a neuronal level.

The paper set out a framework for understanding consciousness that included an attention mechanism that solved the binding

problem – probably through those 40 Hz oscillations – which would activate a short-term memory process. All this would take place in a distributed fashion in the neocortex, although adjacent structures, such as the thalamus and the sheet-like claustrum, might also be involved. 'Incidentally, we see no reason at all why this global unity should require fancy quantum effects,' they quipped. As to the key questions that had to be answered, the article repeated the three points that Crick had articulated over a year before, and added a subsidiary task – determining whether the neurons involved in correlates of consciousness were of any specific type.

The article challenged experimentalists first to confirm the existence and characteristics of the 40 Hz oscillations, then to explore their link with attention and finally to identify the nature and basis of short-term memory. As they emphasised, 'Our tentative theory, most of the elements of which have already been proposed by others, is a programme for research rather than a detailed model.' Therein lay the significance of the paper, and the contrast with approaches like those of Edelman and Penrose. Here was a clear materialist framework for trying to identify neuronal correlates of consciousness, without being bamboozled by philosophical flimflam* or quantum woo and without feeling obliged to explain everything. By focusing scientists' attention on a doable but difficult project, Crick and Koch were bringing consciousness out of the philosophy textbooks and giving it a carefully reasoned place in neuroscience laboratories.

*

Months before the article was published, the scientific community was aware of Crick's thinking. As well as circulating the article as a preprint, Francis also presented his ideas at the annual Cold Spring Harbor symposium, held in June 1990 and devoted to the brain.[84] It was not an easy decision to attend the meeting, as he explained to

---

*The phrase is Pat Churchland's. Churchland, P. (2017), in K. Almqvist and A. Haag (eds.), *The Return of Consciousness: A New Science on Old Questions* (Stockholm: Axel and Margaret Ax:son Johnson Foundation), pp. 39–58, p. 59.

Hugh Huxley: 'I now find travelling and giving talks unreasonably tiring and so I've decided that, as far as possible, I should stay here. I shall be making an exception in the case of this year's big meeting at Cold Spring Harbor but even in that case I hesitated a long time before accepting.'[85]

Francis not only had to speak, and chair a session, he also agreed to Watson's request to give a public lecture as part of Cold Spring Harbor's centennial celebrations (this was sweetened by Watson's offer of a $5,000 honorarium plus first-class return flights, an off-site suite and limousine transport each day to the meeting).[86] In the words of the local organiser, Crick's public lecture, 'How Do We See Things?' was 'nothing short of spectacular ... the single most important event we have had', with a record turnout ('extraordinarily large' according to the *Oyster Bay Chronicle*).[87]

No matter how gratifying, that was not the reason Francis had risked exhausting himself by crossing the continent. The point was the symposium – listening to the other presentations and informally discussing his ideas with colleagues. The article based on Crick's talk that appeared in the symposium proceedings (co-authored with Koch) is much more detailed than he would have been able to present orally; as well as fleshing out some of the ideas in the paper with Koch, it also included some proposed experiments for testing their hypothesis about a searchlight of attention involving synchronised oscillations.[88]

Quite how much the audience grasped is not clear – most of those present worked on very precise neurobiological, genetic or developmental problems in non-primates. Only a handful of researchers gave talks on topics vaguely adjacent to Crick and Koch's proposal, and none had a comparable lucidity and vision. Even the informal chat that scientists value in such meetings was limited, and Crick found it frustrating that in his discussions with Singer, who had first identified the 40 Hz oscillations, they were unable to agree how to prove a link with behaviour.[89] Francis was acutely aware that this remained the weak point of his approach; he was soon dampening Kreisel's enthusiasm for the oscillations because of this uncertainty, and by the beginning of 1991 he was expressing his concern at the absence of any further experimental reports of such synchronisation.[90] Nevertheless,

Crick's approach did not stand or fall with the oscillations – what he and Koch had elaborated was a general approach to finding neural correlates of consciousness. That was of lasting value.

*

Shortly after the end of the Cold Spring Harbor symposium, Francis and Odile flew to England, staying in London for about ten days, going to the theatre and seeing friends.[91] After visits to Cambridge and Oxford, they returned to what was now truly their home, La Jolla. Their stays in England were becoming shorter.

Francis continued to be generous with his time, especially with young people. For example, after bumping into a high school teacher at an airport, he was persuaded to talk to the teacher's ninth-grade science students, a short drive away in east San Diego.[92] Crick's vitality and humour blew them away and their letters of appreciation were charming and heartfelt. For example, Tiffany Blauvelt wrote:

> Before our meeting, I had a warped idea of 'real' scientists. My brain pictured a walking dictionary with thick glasses. Your sense of humour and ability to convey ideas clearly were refreshing to me. It is amazing that one man can know so much about our vast scientific world. You are, in a sense, a vocal biology book … Thankyou for your time and energy.

She added an eagle-eyed PS: 'Great licence plate'.

Crick also invited high school student David Liu of Riverside, California, to come and show him a backprop neural network model of visual processing Liu had developed (he had won second prize in a national competition, attracting the attention of Sejnowski).[93] Liu not only got a nice chat and a cup of tea, when he later sent a card announcing his acceptance at university, Crick replied cheerily, 'So glad to hear that you've been accepted for Harvard. I hope the nets go well. Drop in to see us if you're ever in this part of the world.'*[94]

---

*Liu gave up the nets, came top of his class and is now a Professor at Harvard, where he is pioneering safe and powerful forms of gene editing for application

And there was still the tide of letters from randoms, colleagues and friends that had to be read and replied to. At one point, Kreisel was writing so frequently that Crick responded in exasperation, 'This is in reply to your letters of 15th, 16th, 18th, 22nd and 25th January and of 5th February, together with several enclosures.'*[95] At the same time, Francis became solicitous of those he felt were working too hard (this included Watson), frequently adding a postscript to his letters, 'Never forget, a busy life is a wasted life.'[96] Coming from a man whose busy-ness helped him to do so much, this aphorism – which he appears to have coined – seems odd. Perhaps, as he aged, he was wishing he had not always been so busy.

Nevertheless, Francis was not finished yet. When he sent a copy of his article with Koch to his friend Stuart Sutherland, he noted with a smile that Sutherland had written a terse but accurate entry on Consciousness in the recently published *International Dictionary of Psychology*, which ended as follows: 'Consciousness is a fascinating but elusive phenomenon: it is impossible to specify what it is, what it does, or why it evolved. Nothing worth reading has been written about it.'[97] Crick was amused by Sutherland's sally, but he also took it as a challenge.

---

in medicine. In 2025 he won the prestigious Breakthrough Prize for his work. He was very pleased when I showed him the correspondence on Twitter.
*Virtually all Kreisel's letters from this period are lost. From Crick's replies it appears that as well as complex arguments about logic, Penrose, Edelman, Einstein, the visual system and so on they included discussions about Queen Victoria's supposed disbelief in lesbians.

THE INFLUENCER

There were so many popular books about consciousness in the late 1980s and early 1990s. There were books by physicists, such as Roger Penrose's *The Emperor's New Mind*, which claimed that consciousness was based on unknown quantum effects; there were books by psychologists, such as Bernard Baars' *A Cognitive Theory of Consciousness*, which argued that it was based on what he called a global workspace; and there were books by philosophers, like Daniel Dennett's *Consciousness Explained*, which breezily insisted that many of the problems traditionally associated with understanding consciousness simply did not exist.

Crick's 1994 book, *The Astonishing Hypothesis: The Scientific Search for the Soul*, was part of this publishing wave, but unlike his over-confident contemporaries, he did not present a theory of consciousness. Instead, he outlined a strategy for experimental work on the specific issue of visual awareness.[1] As one reviewer put it, the book was 'fascinating and insightful neuroscience, full of suggestions to keep experimentalists and theoreticians busy for years to come'.[2] This is what Francis wanted to explain, both to the public and his fellow scientists. As he put it, with palpable urgency: 'The message of the book is that now is the time to think scientifically about consciousness (and its relationship, if any, to the hypothetical immortal soul) and, most important of all, the time to start the *experimental* study of consciousness in a serious and deliberate way.'[3]

The 'soul' of the book's subtitle was barely discussed after the opening chapter, in which it was described as a myth. Francis included it partly at the suggestion of the publisher but also because encounters with ordinary believers, as well as his debates with religious scientists such as Sir John Eccles and Christof Koch, had helped him realise that such beliefs could not be ignored or scoffed at.[4] His aim was not to produce a polemic about religion, but rather to show science's ability to address the most difficult of questions.

In a way, the book was not all his own work. The core ideas were the outcome of his intense discussions with Koch, as he made clear in dedicating the book to the young man, 'without whose energy and enthusiasm this book would never have been written', while many of the chapters had been corrected by colleagues whose work he described. Its final form bore the mark of his editor, Barbara Grossman, whose job was to wrench Crick's writing into the kind of popular account he wanted.[5] She scribbled in red pen over virtually every paragraph of his manuscript, killing his darlings and making repeated requests for clarity.[6] After one of her savagings, Francis bristled:

> I hope you will forgive me for saying so, but your comments give the impression that you are overworked and not giving the book the sustained attention it requires. The theme of the book is not an easy topic and it is not possible to present it without giving the reader some difficulties, if only because of the unfamiliar nature of much of the material. ... Please forgive me for writing so frankly.[7]

Grossman took a deep breath and replied politely.

They continued tussling throughout 1992, with Crick repeatedly defending his more complex passages by pointing to the high sales of the complicated popular science books by Stephen Hawking and Penrose. Eventually, he grudgingly accepted her push for simplification and admitted to his agent that the book was much better, 'largely due to Barbara's forceful criticisms'.[8] By the beginning of 1993, the writing was pretty much done, as Grossman showed by returning a lightly edited copy of Crick's latest draft, accompanied by a back-handed compliment: 'It's vastly improved from the earliest stages; I don't think I've ever worked with a manuscript that showed as much change from its first draft to this point in its evolution.'[9]

One early disagreement that rumbled on for months was the book's title.* Crick explained in the opening sentence that his aston-ishing hypothesis was that '"You," your joys and your sorrows, your memories and your ambitions, your sense of personal identity and free will, are in fact no more than the behavior of a vast assembly of nerve cells and their associated molecules.' Grossman objected that this was hardly astonishing or new. Francis cheerfully agreed, but pointed out that nevertheless this position was rejected by vast numbers of people: 'Try talking to any Catholic, Southern Baptist or Mormon,' he fired back.[10] The title remained, although Francis did add an explanatory sentence to the book's opening paragraph: 'This hypothesis is so alien to the ideas of most people alive today that it can truly be called astonishing.'

*

The book opened with Stuart Sutherland's jibe that nothing worth-while had been written on the topic; to avoid the problems that Sutherland was hinting at, Crick explained that he would not deal with free will or qualia.† As he had said several times, faced with two problems that have distracted scientists and excited philosophers for centuries, Francis simply set them to one side. The book was divided into three sections; the first dealt with vision and attention, using striking visual illusions to show that we do not necessarily see what is in front of our eyes and that vision is not a simple process. In the second section, Francis summarised much of the neuroscience he had learned in the previous fifteen years, focusing on neuroanatomy

---

*Sounds familiar.

†Crick did include a brief and chatty appendix on free will, which he jokingly suggested was based 'in or near the anterior cingulate sulcus' – in private he boasted he had been teasing philosophers with this claim for around a decade. Crick to Posner, 4 January 1991, PP/CRI/J/2/11/1.

First rough draft — DO NOT QUOTE.

The Astonishing Hypothesis

An Approach to Visual Awareness

Francis Crick

new page

Consciousness. The having . . . . .   not written on it

Interrelated
both from The Dictionary of Psychology

by Stuart Sutherland

from the Preface : 'It is customary . . . . . worms'

and neural nets. He also explained how neurons work, repeating the assertion from his abandoned monograph from the 1980s, 'The language of the brain is based on neurons.'[11] Consciousness is somehow produced by the activity of networks of neurons; there is nothing else. The final section explained the search for the neural correlates of visual awareness – the elusive awareness neural networks – repeating the questions that had become a mantra over the last five years:

- Where are these neurons in the brain?
- Are they of any particular neuronal type?
- What is special (if anything) about their connections?
- What is special (if anything) about the way they are firing?[12]

Finally, there was a brief, speculative outline of a model, involving connections between the thalamus and the cortex that would allow the appearance of synchronised oscillations and which might be a potential neural correlate of visual awareness. Crick thought it unlikely that all this was correct, but the aim of the book was to create a situation where, as he put it, every laboratory studying vision would have a sign pinned up on the wall that would read:

CONSCIOUSNESS

NOW

The book was finished, but it would be nearly a year before it appeared in print.

*

In the meantime, there was plenty to keep him busy. In 1991 the Cricks had bought two acres of desert on the outskirts of the small town of Borrego Springs, about two hours' drive in a north-easterly direction from La Jolla. They soon began building a bungalow, designed by Francis, with additions from Odile. Progress was slow – the foundations were not laid until the summer of 1992 and the building, at 618 Tilting T Drive, remained sparsely furnished until the end of the following year.[13] Odile oversaw the decor, which was suited to the desert climate and complemented the landscape: white walls and light wood, with furniture in white, black, charcoal and terracotta. The art – the Cricks were always surrounded by art – was mainly Indigenous: wall hangings and masks, together with a large

African sculpture of a humanoid bird-figure in mottled wood, standing guard at the back of the house. Nearby there was a heart outlined on the ground with pebbles, within which the letters F and O were spelled out in small stones – perhaps the work of their grandchildren.

Francis and Odile had long been attracted by the stark beauty of the Californian desert; now they had a second home there, surrounded by creosote bushes, barrel cactuses and palm trees, with the mountains in the distance and a carefully chosen view of the sunset which was often accompanied by huge trains of clouds, tinted purple, pink and gold. The dry, oily scents from the desert plants mingled with the smell of dust and hot rock, changing as night fell and dawn broke. Blasted by the sun in vast deep blue skies, with a landscape that varied from the lunar to the lush, this was a location where Michael McClure's psychedelic visions of the natural world, which so entranced Francis, could find their place.

Francis soon responded to the challenge of planning a garden in such a harsh environment, designing an elaborate watering system and choosing plants that could withstand the arid conditions, with hibiscus cascading over the white walls of the house, a fig tree in the courtyard and a protected area for his beloved roses. In the middle of the central garden was a patch of bare desert, a reminder of what was there before and what would eventually return. Modelled on a Japanese inn or ryokan, each room overlooked the central planted area, with the windows carefully positioned so there was no view into another room. Between the house and the garage there was a breezeway – a covered open area that was always in shadow, where Francis, Odile and their guests could dine, cooled by the funnelled desert zephyrs.

From 1994 the Cricks drove out to their desert house most weeks, leaving La Jolla on Friday and returning on Monday. Francis became known in the community and was even invited to ride in the annual Borrego Springs Desert Festival Parade (he declined).[14] Life in the desert could be challenging, as Crick explained to a colleague: 'I had started to read your article in our desert home, when the electricity went off (due to a wind storm). I was just beginning to continue reading it by candlelight when the lights came on again.'[15] The desert house, its garden and the surrounding landscape played an important role in the Cricks' lives, providing a refuge and a source of stimulation. After a visit, Finnish poet Kirsti Simonsuuri wrote in lyrical terms about their new home: 'Everything about you speaks of beauty and intelligence, quite irresistible! The images of the desert have remained particularly strongly in my mind – the silence and the endurance of the landscape, fine colours and shapes.'[16]

Crick's happiness was captured in a *Scientific American* profile that opened with a striking pen-portrait: 'There is something almost preternaturally jolly about Francis Harry Compton Crick. His eyes and mouth curl up at the corners in a perpetual, wicked grin. His bushy white eyebrows flare out like horns. His ruddy face flushes even darker when he laughs, which he does often and with gusto.'

This relaxed state of mind was reinforced by two pieces of good news from England. Early in 1991 Francis heard that his old college, Gonville and Caius, planned to mark his work by placing a stained-glass window in the college hall – a couple of years earlier the college had installed windows commemorating the population geneticist

R. A. Fisher* and the mathematician John Venn. Francis was 'surprised, flattered and delighted' with the suggestion and approved the double helix design, with two provisos: Watson had to agree (he did) and Crick warned the college that if the window were seen from the outside of the building, the molecule would spiral the wrong way.[17]

A few months later, Crick's impatience with formality and tradition and his hostility to the monarchy was put to the test, as he received a letter from Sir Robert Fellowes, the Private Secretary to the Queen, informing him that 'it would give The Queen much pleasure to appoint you to be a member of the Order of Merit.' The Order of Merit (OM) consists of twenty-four distinguished contributors to a variety of fields, mainly science and culture; membership, Fellowes emphasised, was 'entirely within the Sovereign's gift', with no governmental involvement.[18] Surprisingly, given his previous refusals of all honours, Francis accepted, and in the politest of terms: 'I am both flattered and delighted to learn that the Queen may appoint me to the Order of Merit. Should she do so I would accept with pleasure,' he wrote.[19] His change of mind was partly due to pressure from Odile, who felt that he should not pass up the chance of meeting the Queen.[20] He would be among familiar faces – Fred Sanger had been appointed to the OM in 1986, and Max Perutz two years later. And as Crick enjoyed pointing out to people who continued to address him as Sir Francis, an OM outranked a mere knighthood.[21]

At the beginning of July, the Cricks flew to London for the ceremony, which was noted laconically in Francis's appointment diary: '12:20 Buckingham Palace'.[22] Afterwards there was no big celebration; instead, Francis and Odile went to see Juliet Stevenson in Ariel Dorfman's gripping new revenge drama, *Death and the Maiden*.[23] On his return to California Francis proudly informed a friend: 'I had a cosy chat with the Queen. No bending the knee – only two brief bows going in and two more going out. Odile enjoyed the lunch at the Palace, two days later, with many of the OMs and some of their spouses.'[24]

---

*The Fisher window, showing the 7 x 7 Latin Square from the cover of one of his books, was removed in 2020 when Fisher's lifelong advocacy of eugenics provoked protests in the context of Black Lives Matter.

He later recalled that his conversation with the monarch had mainly been about the weather.[25] Among the OMs at the luncheon were the violinist Yehudi Menuhin, the opera singer Joan Sutherland and the art historian Ernst Gombrich. Odile found Menuhin boorish with his snobby views about the public's taste in music, but enjoyed chatting to Gombrich, while Francis was amused by his conversation with Sutherland, even though he preferred musicals to grand opera.[26]

Crick still maintained his huge correspondence, with thoughtful letters to friends and colleagues mixed in with generous or sometimes sharp replies to unknown correspondents. When a Bavarian radio station requested an interview to mark his seventy-fifth birthday, Francis replied brusquely, 'I never celebrate my birthday and would very much prefer that you don't,' while when a scientist complained that Crick and Koch had not cited his work, Francis provided a savage critique before concluding: 'For all these reasons, I think you should be thankful that no one has published a critical review of your ideas and that they have been allowed to fall into the oblivion that, in my opinion, they deserve.'[27]

However, Crick was courteous to a deeply religious correspondent who sent a present to entice him into an exchange: 'It is exceptionally kind of you to send me a gift of delightful seashells. It is therefore with regret that I must tell you that I feel that further correspondence or discussion would not be fruitful because our points of view are so different. With apologies.'[28] He could also be too nice. In 1993 he received a number of letters from a lonely old German businessman, Rainer Böhlke, offering to leave Francis money in his will. Francis and Odile were concerned for Herr Böhlke, but it turned out that he – or someone using the name – had sent similar letters to many famous people in California, including Isabel Allende, Frank Zappa and Matt Groening.[29] Like the incident with 'Francis Crick Wassmuth', this seems to have been a scam by a deceitful autograph hunter, and Francis fell for it.

His most intense letters involved arguments with some of the heavyweights of the day, such as a decade-long correspondence with the philosopher John Searle, whose views on consciousness sometimes approached his own without ever fully coinciding.[30] Part of the problem was that Searle was a philosopher while Crick was a scientist, and they played by different rules. As Crick explained with regards to Searle's penchant for thought experiments – 'Philosophers, it seems to me, believe they can *establish* something by thought experiments. I don't believe you can establish anything, though you may be able to make a *plausible* case in this way and time may even show, in some instances, you were right.'

All these letters were written in a methodical and rather long-winded way.[31] Francis would first write a draft in long-hand, scoring out mistaken formulations as he went along, before re-reading the whole thing, clarifying his handwriting where it was illegible. The drafts were then typed up on a word processor by his assistant at the Salk; Francis then read over the printed version, editing where necessary, before signing the final corrected letter, which was then sent out by post or, from the beginning of the 1990s, by fax or e-mail.

There were also articles to write. While working on neuroanatomy for his book, Francis had been struck by how little was known about the human brain. Together with neuroanatomist Ted Jones, he vented his irritation in an article entitled 'Backwardness of Human Neuroanatomy', which appeared in *Nature* in January 1993.[32] The core of the article was a howl of frustration at our ignorance: 'It is intolerable that we do not have this information for the human brain. Without it there is little hope of understanding how our brains work except in the crudest way. The object of this paper is to make this need more widely known.'

Although the word did not yet exist, Crick and Jones were arguing for a connectome, a functional map of all the connections between the neurons in the brain.[33] Francis astutely predicted that the recently launched Human Genome Project would eventually reveal new types of neurons that the microscope could not detect, by identifying the specific set of genes that determined each cell type. Pursuing this idea, a year later he suggested that a wealthy foundation should fund a research programme to identify different neuron types and develop techniques for manipulating their activity.[34] In the twenty-first century these approaches have become an essential part of neuroscience, as scientists – often funded by wealthy foundations – have used the kind of molecular markers imagined by Crick to make brain wiring diagrams and explore their function. This wave of research has partly been inspired by Crick's insight and vision.

Although Francis was resolutely focused on the future and on his work on the brain, he was still dogged by DNA. He took a dim view of scientific anniversaries (he told Klug he considered them to be a form of collective madness), but he could not escape the fortieth anniversary of the discovery of the double helix.[35] As he explained crossly to Kreisel in March 1993:

> Last Sunday I had just arrived at Cold Spring Harbour for the first of the '40 years of the Double Helix' meetings. There will be 4 or 5 of them in all. I managed to squash all attempts to celebrate my 70th and 75th birthdays, but it never occurred to me that anyone could be so crazy as to celebrate the 40th anniversary of a molecule. (John Maddox has already started to plan for the 50th anniversary.)[36]

Despite his irritation at all the fuss, Francis was able to use the trips for holidays with Odile. After he had given a double helix anniversary talk at UNESCO in Paris, they drove to southern France and then to Barcelona, before going on to Palma where Francis gave another talk.[37] Then they flew to London, where Peter Lawrence had again arranged their theatre tickets.[38] After a few weeks in Cambridge, they returned to La Jolla, where Francis informed the Salk that from now on, he would be working part time. He was not retiring, not quite, but he recognised that he needed – wanted – to reduce his workload and to enjoy a quieter life.[39]

*

That ambition did not last long. When *The Astonishing Hypothesis* was published in early 1994, it caused a huge stir on both sides of the Atlantic. Unusually, Francis threw himself into the publicity campaign to promote his book, first in the USA and then in England. This involved press, radio and TV interviews, as well as book signings and lectures. There were dozens of reviews and profiles in newspapers and magazines – even editorials in *Nature* and *The Times* – as the media amplified public interest. This went on for months, and so many clippings were sent to the Salk that Francis asked his assistant to start a separate file for the reviews.[40] It is hard to imagine any scientist today enjoying similar international attention.

Although some reviewers found sections of the book hard going, most were enthusiastic. Cultural critic Jonathan Meades lauded the book as the 'highest populism', able to sweep along the ordinary reader, and made a confident prediction: 'Long after he is dead, Crick's successors will irrefutably demonstrate the rightness of his hypothesis.' In *The Times*, Matt Ridley agreed: 'Looking back a century hence, I suspect this book will be seen as prophetic.' *The New York Times* magazine reviewer was impressed, but surprisingly viewed the book as an outspoken attack on religious conceptions of the soul; Crick saw things differently, emphasising that while he felt it unlikely there was an immaterial soul, that could only be demonstrated once science could explain consciousness.[41]

There were also more nuanced reviews from his colleagues, like John Hopfield or Stuart Sutherland, which pleased Francis no end.[42] The review that gave him the greatest satisfaction was in *Nature*, where Richard Gregory called Crick one of the greatest living biologists and said his book was written with clarity and charm, before discussing both the insights and the gaps that characterised Crick's approach, such as his decision not to worry about qualia.[43] Francis was delighted with Gregory's review and wrote excitedly to his friend: 'Thank you so much for a lively and flattering review of my book. The Ramachandrans, the Churchlands and the Damasios were at our house last night and read out passages from it to the assembled company!'[44]

When journalist Daniel Voll cannily asked Crick what his own review of *The Astonishing Hypothesis* would be, Francis replied with typical modesty and accuracy: 'Crick has many interesting ideas and speculations, but no single concrete, plausible proposal.'[45]

The biggest event of the whole tour was a lecture Francis gave at Westminster Central Hall in London, introduced by Lewis Wolpert and co-sponsored by *The Times*. The newspaper also published an article by Crick and an adulatory profile by Wolpert entitled 'Genius of Our Age', which compared Crick to Newton for his ideas and Mozart and Shakespeare for his creativity.[46] The event went amazingly well, with fifteen hundred people crammed into the hall and three hundred and fifty books sold. As a result of all the press coverage and general hoo-ha, the book rocketed to the top of the London non-fiction book chart.[47]

A few days later, Wolpert's suggestion that Crick was up there with Mozart and Shakespeare did not look quite so overblown. When Francis appeared on the flagship BBC radio programme *Start the Week*, his fellow guests were the US poet Maya Angelou, author Salman Rushdie and playwright Tom Stoppard, with biographer Brenda Maddox joining presenter Melvyn Bragg as co-interviewer.[48] All the guests had something to plug, but the discussion kept coming back to Crick's book. Stoppard in particular seemed more interested in talking about *The Astonishing Hypothesis* than in selling tickets for his latest play. Francis emphasised that consciousness was an emergent property of millions of neurons, but Angelou and Stoppard rejected his argument as reductionist, arguing that science could not explain their creative craft. Rushdie was keener to understand how imagination might work and embraced Crick's view. The discussion ranged widely over race relations, history, science and religion; Francis – smart and relaxed, so amused by the whole thing that you could hear the twinkle in his eye – clearly had fun.

One of the most revealing events of the London visit took place behind closed doors, when Francis was interviewed about his book for the recently launched *Journal of Consciousness Studies* (*JCS*). The publication of a new journal generally indicates the gelling of an academic field as researchers become an unofficial community and publishers realise there is money to be made. *Nature* described the appearance of the *JCS* as a defining moment in the study of consciousness; ultimately, the journal's existence was testimony to the influence of Crick and his decades-long focus on the topic – appropriately enough, the interview with Francis became the first article in the first issue.[49]

*

Happy but rather tired, the Cricks left for home the day after Francis's seventy-eighth birthday, returning to their relaxed Californian routine. Francis continued to work part time, wearing his colour-ful shirts, while for amusement they went to concerts (jazz, Mozart, Schubert and Beethoven) and drove out to Borrego Springs most weekends.[50] Unknown folk singer Bob Gramann sent Francis an audio cassette of a song inspired by a phrase from the beginning of *The Astonishing Hypothesis*, 'You're nothing but a pack of neurons'. Tickled by the gift, Francis played the song to some dinner guests, who were delighted.[51]

Crick had lost none of his puckish humour; in August he wrote a satirical advertisement for RENT-A-BRAIN INC., taking the mickey out of neuroscientists' appetites for fashionable but vacuous theor-etical explanations:

> Does your experimental work have an old-fashioned air? Have you had difficulties getting your grant applications approved by study groups? Don't despair! ... Whether you want your interpretation to involve chaos, fractals, complexity theory, artificial intelligence, neural networks (with or without feed-back) or quantum gravity, WE CAN FIND THE MAN TO HELP YOU.
>
> Given your experimental results (or even without them), one of our theorists will provide a suitable interpretation in the form you favour. By a suitable adjustment of parameters, he or she can fit the observations to your preconceived ideas.[52]

Little has changed.

Francis also began work on an article with Christof Koch sum-marising research on visual processing in monkeys and integrating these results with work on humans, in which they concluded that a region known by a confusing variety of names (V1, striate cortex, area 17 or primary visual cortex), was *not* a site of the neural cor-relates of consciousness.[53] They were making progress, of a kind.

Francis was working at a pace that suited him, his book had been a critical and commercial success, Odile was preparing a show of her art for the following spring and the desert was always there to recharge their batteries. Their life had rarely been better.

Then, on 17 October, the staff of the Salk Institute were summoned into the courtyard to hear an announcement. The president, Brian Henderson, had resigned after less than two years in office. Faced with a looming financial crisis and in need of a rapid solution, the Salk trustees decided that Francis Crick, aged seventy-eight and semi-retired, a man with no experience of high-level administration and whose contract specified that he would not play any administrative role, was the best person to be interim president.[54] According to the *Salk Institute Newsletter*, Crick's response was typically sardonic: 'When the Institute's trustees and faculty asked me to become President, I was initially more surprised than pleased.'[55]

On hearing the news, Crick's former assistant Maria Lang wrote Francis a heartfelt note:

> This commitment is an altruistic move on your part and is going to be a sacrifice. I know, since you were trying to figure out how to have more free time. I commend you, Francis, for I know this comes from your love of the Salk. (…)
>
> My concern, though, is that you make sure you have balance in your life – clear your head of Salk frequently by going to the desert, etc.[56]

That did not happen. Instead, Crick's world was turned upside down. His long scientific letters became few and far between and were largely replaced by tedious correspondence with colleagues about health and safety, the quality of seminars and the two things that preoccupy academic administrators – squabbles over space and the frantic search for funding.[57] Crick could find no novel solution to the Salk's financial woes: 'I'm trying to see how we can save money, and postpone expenditure, without stopping anything essential,' he explained. In what seems like a sign of desperation, he even asked film producer Larry Bachmann for Hollywood financial contacts that might help the Salk raise large sums. There were some successes – $2 million here, $350,000 there – but this was peanuts. In a sign that Francis was doing his bit, he now asked autograph hunters for a donation of $10 to the Salk funds (within a few years the sum had gone up to $50).[58] There were also unpleasant matters to deal with – a row with a veterinarian at the Salk who complained about conditions in the animal house supposedly led to a 'screaming match' with Francis; she was sacked and eventually won an expensive court case against the Institute.[59]

Crick tried to remain positive – 'It is indeed not my cup of tea, but as I have to drink it, I've decided I may as well enjoy it!' he told Ramachandran. But it was clearly wearing him down. He discouraged Bernard Baars from coming for an extended visit as he spent most of his time on administration, 'and after I step down, I'm not sure what I will do.' Crick explained his dilemma to Colin Blakemore: 'Parts of the job are novel and interesting, but I regret that my scientific work is being somewhat neglected.'[60] And not only his scientific work. In May, Odile went to Europe to visit family and friends, leaving Francis in La Jolla. After she phoned home one time, Francis told her he had felt a pang of remorse about their situation:

> My Darling,
> I was overjoyed to hear from you – you sounded so lively and cheerful. I'm afraid life here has a certain sameness for you; a change of scene seems to work wonders. We must try to put a little variety into it when you return.[61]

Determined to get back into his scientific groove, Francis invited Koch to visit for the first half of June, taking leave so they could discuss undisturbed. All went well, but shortly afterwards Francis had chest pains while swimming and soon underwent urgent heart surgery. As he convalesced, medication for blood pressure plus daily exercise gradually improving his health and his mood, Odile was able to work wonders with the bland diet he was prescribed and his letters to his friends became more positive. In the middle of August, the future suddenly looked even brighter, as he explained with relief to Bachmann: 'my cardiologist has emphasised the importance of avoiding stress, so I am giving up the job of President at the end of this month.'[62]

The ordeal was over, but he should never have been given the post in the first place.

*

Despite the pressure on his time while he was president, Crick had been able to read a brilliant new academic book by British neuroscientists David Milner and Melvyn Goodale, *The Visual Brain in Action*.[63] Milner and Goodale argued that there were two pathways or streams in the brain that processed visual stimuli: the ventral stream was devoted to rapidly identifying objects, and would be involved in awareness, while the dorsal stream dealt with locating objects in space and organising motor responses – action – and would be largely unconscious. Crick interpreted this link with action as revealing something about the significance or meaning of an object in our visual field – he had already been thinking about how meaning might be represented in the brain, quizzing scientists like Koch and philosophers like Searle about what 'meaning' might mean.[64] Although Francis felt Milner and Goodale's ideas were a little oversimplified, he was convinced they were on the right lines and that the dorsal stream, with its link to action, suggested a broad brain location for meaning. By October 1996, he was integrating these ideas into a working document, 'The Current Crick-Koch Viewpoint on Consciousness'.[65]

Francis had also been able to finish the paper with Koch on the role of primary visual cortex in awareness, in which they claimed that we are not aware of activity in area V1; it was published in *Nature* in May 1995.[66] After the article appeared, a Massachusetts neurologist, Dan Pollen, contacted Crick and criticised their conclusion, arguing in a series of letters and telephone calls that evidence from patients suggested that area V1 might in fact be involved in visual awareness. Crick and Pollen agreed that some kind of publication in *Nature* was necessary to document their agreements and differences, so Francis suggested they adopt an approach that Kreisel had recently employed in their correspondence over Penrose's quantum approach to consciousness. They both agreed Penrose's idea was not worth bothering with, but for different reasons.* To Crick's

---

*Kreisel's argument was logical: 'Penrose overlooks that, BY THEIR logical GENERALITY, LOGICAL RESULTS ARE NOT GOOD ENOUGH FOR SCIENTIFIC CONTRIBUTIONS UNLESS *COMBINED* WITH suitable SPECIFIC scientific KNOWLEDGE.' Crick's critique was empirical, as he explained to Aaron Klug – he considered Penrose's idea that quantum effects

amusement, Kreisel attempted to clarify their views by writing an imaginary dialogue between them.[67] Francis therefore produced a dialogue outlining Pollen's views and his own, telling Pollen, 'I had a lot of fun writing the Dialogue and I think people will enjoy reading it.' But no one did – not Pollen, nor the desk editor at *Nature*, nor even John Maddox. The idea was dropped, and the journal decided it would simply publish Pollen's critique and Crick and Koch's reply.[68] Even then, things did not go smoothly – Crick was unimpressed with Pollen's draft reply and told him so condescendingly: 'I really feel you did not do yourself justice in this draft. I think you've had to write it under pressure, so I suggest you take a deep breath and think it all through carefully. It would do you no good if you published it as it stands and if we wrote an antagonistic reply.'

After some back and forth, the letters, both relatively polite, appeared in September 1995, with each side complaining that the other did not have sufficient evidence to justify their position.*[69]

All this cannot have done Crick's blood pressure any good. In truth, he was not feeling right and at the end of October he had another operation. It was not a success and at the beginning of November he had a sextuple bypass, including the removal of part of his aorta – there was an aneurism that could have killed him at any moment. Although Francis accepted Odile's insistence that he could not travel for some time, he was determined to get back to work as soon as possible; a few days after he left hospital, he was writing internal memos for Koch on visual attention.[70]

*

During his convalescence, Francis was buoyed up by visits from loved ones – first there was Gabrielle together with Jacqueline, accompanied by her family; then Graeme Mitchison visited in May

---

in cellular microtubules produced consciousness was 'pure fantasy', 'extremely flimsy' and 'scientifically irresponsible', but he respected Penrose and wanted to convince him he was wrong. Kreisel to Crick, 22 August 1994, MSS 660, Box 5, Folder 10. Crick to Klug, 25 April 1995, PP/CRI/J/2/15/2.
*This issue remains unresolved, although most evidence supports Crick and Koch's position.

and Kirsti Simonsuuri came in August. Francis reported his progress to Bob Olby: 'A few days ago, Odile and I went for a scramble near Borrego Springs, up one canyon and down another (two hours) and then a slightly uphill walk (one hour) back to the car, so I'm not doing too badly. I'm officially working half-time and trying hard not to work full-time.'[71] By the end of 1996, his recovery was complete, as he cheerfully told a friend: 'I swim about sunset and then pop into the jacuzzi for the twilight.'[72]

One of the first signs that Francis was on the mend had come in the shape of a 'News and Views' article that he sent to *Nature* the previous January, in which he summarised research led by Nikos Logothetis – Francis had been enthusiastically describing the results in letters throughout the year.[73] Logothetis and his PhD student, David Leopold, used a technique called binocular rivalry, which involved projecting different images into a monkey's left and right eyes and then recording from cells in its brain.[74] When each eye is presented with a different stimulus, monkeys – and humans – alternately see one image or the other at irregular intervals. Having previously trained the monkey to press a lever when it saw one of the images, Leopold and Logothetis were able to show that the activity of cells in certain regions of the cortex was correlated with what the monkey was seeing.

This excited Francis for two reasons. Firstly, this activity was not found in area V_1, strengthening his argument with Pollen. Secondly, it seemed this approach might reveal the neural correlates of visual awareness. Although Crick admitted the results were not quite so neat as he would have liked, he told the readers of *Nature* that Logothetis's work represented 'the opening salvoes of a concerted attack on the baffling problem of consciousness'. He concluded with an optimistic prediction that reflected his frustration with the turn that his extensive correspondence on consciousness had taken: 'No longer need one spend time attempting to understand the far-fetched speculations of physicists, nor endure the tedium of philosophers perpetually disagreeing with each other. Consciousness is now largely a scientific problem. It is not impossible that, with a little luck, we may glimpse the outline of the solution before the end of the century.'

That optimism turned out to be misplaced and we are still not really any closer. Nevertheless, writing the article obviously perked Francis up – he soon accepted an invitation to speak at the Society for Neuroscience meeting in Washington DC. He was confident that he would be fit enough to attend and he agreed to give a personal account of the last twenty years of his career. Looking back was not something that interested him, but his recent brush with mortality and his belief that a corner had been turned in the study of consciousness seem to have convinced him that the time was right.

There was also a paradox here. Over the previous two decades, Francis had played a decisive role focusing the attention of both scientists and the public on the problem of consciousness. But now that there was global interest in the question, he was becoming frustrated by the range of theories that were being put forward. He had got what he wanted, but it turned out not to be what he wanted after all. Stuart Sutherland had facetiously suggested that there should be a moratorium on publishing any more books about consciousness and eventually refused to give interviews on the topic; Francis light-heartedly agreed.[75] As he explained in May 1996:

> There is now far too much general interest ... and as far as we are concerned it is going to be a handicap. Unless we are careful, results will trickle out slowly and in a few years time there will be a reaction against consciousness, and it will become unfashionable again. ... Philosophers are not going to solve the problems by themselves whatever they may think. They haven't done it for 2000 years and there is no reason to suppose they will do it now. What they have to do is show us where our ideas are incoherent and they have to point to new types of experiments.[76]

Tetchiness towards philosophers was becoming a feature of his mood. He scolded Dan Dennett for putting too much faith in the power of argument and consistently overstating his case – 'This may be fun for other philosophers, but scientists find it annoying' – while he was aghast to discover that John Searle considered that their disagreements would make no difference to the kinds of experiment that should be done – 'at this point I concluded that trying to under-stand your ideas would be a waste of my time!'[77] Crick emphasised experiments, because that was the only way that reliable knowledge could be obtained. 'I no longer attempt to read philosophical discus-sions,' he told a colleague, '… unless they suggest novel and relevant experiments.' Or, as he put it succinctly to Bob Olby, when it came to philosophers, 'listen to their questions, but don't listen to their answers.'[78]

Crick was becoming equally frustrated with Kreisel. For months – years – Francis had tried to understand his friend's criticisms of Penrose's logical arguments and their link with Penrose's convic-tion about the role of quantum effects in consciousness. Eventually, Francis gave up:

> I have concluded, very reluctantly, that further correspondence with me on this topic would serve no useful purpose. I have read what you have written, carefully, several times, and am quite unable to grasp what you are trying to say. This is partly because of your unfortunate habit of commenting on a point without clearly explaining yourself … but mainly because the topic is above my head.[79]

To Penrose, Crick was even blunter, saying that many of Kreisel's letters were 'both deliberately obscure and abusive'.[80]

As 1996 progressed, Francis's mood and health improved, and in August he wrote a loving card to Odile on her birthday: 'For my wonderful, wonderful Odile, who deserves everything I can give her. Happy Birthday! And all my love, Francis.'[81]

In the autumn, Francis was travelling again. The Cricks had been invited to Tokyo by the Yakult Honsha company; Francis decided to accept what looked like an unattractive proposition – travel halfway round the world to give a thirty-minute talk on 'Brain and Mind' to a non-specialist audience – because it would give them another opportunity to visit Japan and also to have tea with the Emperor and Empress in the Imperial Palace. By chance, Jim and Liz Watson were also visiting Japan; the co-discoverers of the double helix became the star attractions at the 21st Queen Elizabeth II Commemorative Cup horse race in Kyoto, where Crick presented the cup to the winner's owner.[82]

On their return to the US, Francis stopped off in Washington to speak at the Society for Neuroscience meeting.[83] The bulk of his talk was on the 'forbidden word' – consciousness – showing how it had fallen out of favour among scientists in the 1950s, before experiencing a revival in the 1980s and 1990s. He then summarised his most recent ideas before closing on what he still found frustrating – the lack of knowledge about the variety of neuronal types in the brain. Highlighting the way that the Human Genome Project had been launched, Francis called for an equivalent attack on neuroanatomy.

In his conclusion, Crick raised his gaze to a more distant horizon – beyond the neural correlates. The challenge of understanding consciousness would need to be attacked at multiple levels, he argued:

> It will not be enough just to find the neural correlates of consciousness. Not all neurons which appear to follow a percept may be essential for consciousness. Our aim should be to have an accurate theoretical grasp of consciousness in all its aspects. We are highly unlikely to establish such theories as correct without a detailed knowledge of many of the brain's activities, at many levels, from molecules right up to all aspects of our behaviour.

The language of the brain is based in neurons – what else? – but a full explanation of what those networks of neurons are doing would require deep understanding at many different levels.[84]

At the end of his lecture, Francis wondered whether he had contributed anything much to neuroscience. His answer was modest: 'Frankly, rather little, except perhaps as a gadfly,' he responded, repeating the word he had used to describe his involvement in the PDP group over a decade earlier. No doubt he had been irritating and provocative to some, but his fundamental role in neuroscience was far more significant: he shaped the whole field, pointing out the areas that needed more work and encouraging scientists to dare to address the question of consciousness. This was widely recognised at the time – in 1997 Bernard Baars dedicated his book *In the Theater of Consciousness: The Workspace of the Mind* to Francis: 'This book is dedicated to Francis Crick – who knows a fundamental scientific problem when he sees it – for his leadership in bringing scientists back to consciousness.'[85]

The decisive breakthroughs Crick predicted have not yet occurred and we still face most of the challenges he described, but the methods and approach that he advocated remain our best hope of resolving this fundamental problem.

SO WHY WAIT?

After his heart operation, Francis was supposed to take it easy. But although he was working half time, he found it difficult to relax: 'in practise, I am busier than ever,' he explained, 'partly because we have a fairly active social life.'[1] The Cricks went to the theatre – *Uncle Vanya*, Stoppard's *Travesties* – to the opera – *Turandot*, *Madame Butterfly* – and to a recital by Yo-Yo Ma.[2] There were visits from old friends, such as Kirsti Simonsuuri and Clover Southwell, and from Renée Karstens, their au pair forty years earlier and now a successful businesswoman. There were new friends, too – the French artist Niki de Saint Phalle had recently moved to La Jolla and became part of the Cricks' circle; she made Francis a tie showing the double helix and shared Odile's artistic interest in the female form.

To avoid overexertion, and to leave time for both the social whirl and science, Francis now declined virtually all invitations to speak or read articles or books: 'My aim in life at the moment is to read less, not more, so do please excuse me,' he told one colleague. Behind the shield of his assistants, he could be brusque: 'Dr Crick does not want to be interviewed; he wants to lead a quiet life, with his working hours directed to the things that interest him,' read one letter to a journalist, signed by an assistant but written by Crick.[3]

The main thing that interested Francis at this time was a brain

structure called the pulvinar, a poorly understood region of the thalamus that has links to and from the visual regions of the cortex.[4]
In 1992, Crick and Koch had drafted a brief paper on the pulvinar,
suggesting that its different regions might correspond to different
stages of visual processing, with the information travelling back and
forth from the visual cortex through those neuronal connections.
They evidently thought they had found a significant link between
neuroanatomy and function, for they cheekily nodded to Crick's first
Nature paper with Watson: 'It has not escaped our notice that if these
ideas, or something like them, turn out to be correct they might well
apply, mutatis mutandis, to many other thalamic areas.' Nothing
came of the draft, a half-formed thing stamped DO NOT QUOTE,
but the idea that regions of the pulvinar might correspond to stages
in visual processing appeared in *The Astonishing Hypothesis* as 'The
Processing Postulate'.

A couple of years later, Francis contacted the neuroanatomist
Kathleen Rockland, whose work with Jenny Lund on long-range cortical connections had so excited him in 1979. Rockland was studying
neurons that projected from the pulvinar to the cortex, leading Crick
to revive his interest in this structure.[5] Crick encouraged Rockland
to quantify the different kinds of connection between the pulvinar
and the visual cortex; this was more complicated than he realised –
Rockland had to dig out decades-old data and break with the mainly
descriptive traditions of neuroanatomy.[6] Nevertheless, she recognised the importance of this approach – 'You are teaching me the
seduction of numbers!' she told him.[7]

Crick's letters to Rockland showed a degree of neuroanatomical
sophistication that encouraged her to continue this line of research,
despite reduced funding for neuroanatomy. This episode reveals
how Francis could be accepted by people who had spent their careers
studying a topic that he suddenly became interested in. It was not
simply the Crick stardust effect; his sharp mind, informed by assidu-
ous reading and a precise grasp of experimental detail, enabled him
to suggest new approaches and highlight fundamental issues that
the experts had sometimes missed.

By early 1997, Crick and Koch were turning their outline on
the pulvinar into a more detailed paper, enriched by the work of

Rockland and others. They hammered through nearly a dozen drafts and, after some gentle criticism from the reviewers at *Nature*, 'Constraints on Cortical and Thalamic Projections: The No-Strong-Loops Hypothesis' appeared in January 1998.[8]

The paper explored the functional implications of the links between the pulvinar and the visual cortex, focusing on why reciprocal connections from the visual cortex to a given layer of the pulvinar and back again were never found. These were the 'no-strong-loops' of the paper's title (Crick subsequently admitted that 'circuits' would have been better than 'loops').[9] A decade earlier, neuroanatomist Ted Jones noticed that connections between one layer of the thalamus and a given layer of the cortex were not mirrored by a reciprocal connection; instead, the neurons projected to a higher or a lower level of the cortex. Crick and Koch proposed that this multi-layer network reflected a processing hierarchy, mediated by what they called driving connections of neurons. The lack of loops not only enabled the emergence of this functional hierarchy, it also prevented problems; if connections between areas formed a closed circuit, uncontrolled oscillations would emerge as the signal zoomed round the loop, like feedback howling round an audio system.

Although inter-area connections between the thalamus and the visual cortex supported their hypothesis, they needed more information about the extent, location and nature of the synapses involved. Francis used a telling analogy to explain the significance of such precise neuroanatomical data: in determining the structure and function of a molecule, the nature and strength of the bonds is extremely significant; understanding the detail of brain areas would similarly help reveal their structure and function.

Rockland said the paper was delightful, while Graeme Mitchison thought it was very useful; however, although Crick and Koch's hypothesis linked structure and function in a relatively straightforward way, demonstrating its fit to the data had required them to assimilate vast amounts of research carried out by several groups over more than a decade.[10] The paper provided a glimpse into the functional rules underlying one particular brain structure, but the effort involved implicitly highlighted quite how complex the brain is. This in turn suggested that finding the neural correlates of consciousness (NCC) and then explaining how thoughts arise out of neuronal activity might be far away.

*

At the beginning of 1998, Crick and Koch slightly shifted their approach to consciousness, adopting a stance that Francis accepted might be considered to be philosophical.[11] He had consistently argued that qualia should be put aside until progress had been made on identifying the neural correlates of consciousness. But both philosophers and neuroscientists persistently raised the issue – David Chalmers had recently called it 'the hard problem' – and Francis finally felt he had to say something more detailed, in an article with Koch that appeared in the journal *Cerebral Cortex* in March 1998.[12]

After admitting they were now unsure of the significance of the high-frequency oscillations that they once saw as a solution to the binding problem, Crick and Koch repeated some of their vague explanations of why qualia exist and why they cannot be reliably communicated to others. This all came under the heading 'Philosophical Matters', but did not lead to any hypotheses that could be experimentally tested. They seemed to be stuck, and their approach revealed the weakness of philosophy compared to science. There was no way of proving the correctness of their ideas even though they seemed logical; as Crick's decade-long struggle with the genetic code had shown him, just because a hypothesis was elegant, that did not mean it was correct.

Another example of Crick and Koch's more philosophical turn was an article they published in an obscure journal called *Neuropsychoanalysis*, with the ostentatiously arresting title 'The Unconscious Homunculus'.[13] Crick and Koch approvingly quoted an unpublished 1895 manuscript by Freud in which he suggested there were three kinds of neuron in the brain, one of which, called ω, was responsible for mediating consciousness in some unknown way. Freud later dismissed his vague and confused document as 'a kind of madness', but Crick and Koch thought there was method in it. They appear to have been beguiled by Freud's familiar-sounding suggestion that it should be possible to establish 'a coincidence between the characteristics of consciousness that are known to us and processes in the ω neurons which vary in parallel with them'.[14] However, at root Freud was simply arguing that there was a link between brain activity and consciousness – hardly a novel insight.

The bulk of Crick and Koch's article consisted of an exploration of the ideas of cognitive scientist Ray Jackendoff, who a dozen years previously had suggested that we are not actually conscious of our thoughts, only of a sensory representation of them. Crick and Koch then boldly, if not entirely successfully, attempted to link this idea to both Marr's model of visual processing and Freud's idea of the unconscious. Weaving together these disparate threads, Crick and Koch explored the implications of the widespread idea that our brains contain a homunculus – a mini-me representation that controls our behaviour. Many years earlier, Francis had ridiculed this notion; now he thought there might be something in it, with the added twist that this homunculus was not conscious: 'The unconscious homunculus receives information about the world through the senses and thinks, plans, and executes voluntary actions. What becomes conscious then is a representation of some of the activities of the unconscious homunculus in the form of the various kinds of imagery and spoken and unspoken speech.'

Although Crick and Koch suggested a few potential experiments that might explore this tentative working hypothesis, these were not decisive. The paper fizzled out by reiterating that the emergence of qualia from neuronal activity remained a mystery. In 2001, they briefly described some of the ideas in a single-page *Nature* article, 'The Zombie Within', but shed no more light.[15] That was Crick's last paper in *Nature*, a somewhat anti-climactic end to a relationship that had spanned nearly half a century.

Probably the most interesting thing about the *Neuropsychoanalysis* paper was that it was accompanied by commentaries from other scientists, together with a reply by Crick and Koch.[16] Their rather plaintive final paragraph illustrated the gulf between their approach and that of their colleagues, as they pointed out that virtually none of the commentaries on their article proposed any kind of neurobiological experiment: 'If psychoanalysis and neuroscience are to interact effectively there must be more emphasis on possible experiments, especially neuroscientific ones, and less time devoted to describing, ad nauseam, what people thought in the past.'

While this article undoubtedly reflected Koch's philosophical interests, Crick was entirely on board with the ideas presented in it, especially Jackendoff's theory.[17] However, with no clear experimental implications, it was hard to know what to do with their unconscious homunculus and as a result, it had little influence.

*

Far more in keeping with Crick's lifelong scientific outlook were the experimental studies on binocular rivalry being performed by Nikos Logothetis, who had recently moved to the Max Planck Institute at Tübingen. But although Logothetis found neurons that reflected shifting perception in the monkey, and were therefore correlated with consciousness, Crick and Koch were cautious in their interpretation: 'Just because a particular neuron follows the percept, it does not automatically imply that its firing is part of the NCC. The NCC neurons may be mainly elsewhere, such as higher up in the visual hierarchy.'

This hesitancy revealed that what they now meant by 'NCC' was not simply a correlate of consciousness, but, more precisely, those neurons that directly produced consciousness or qualia. As to where these neurons were and how they functioned, Francis was still completely in the dark, as he confessed to Logothetis:

> Is it which type of neuron that matters? Or some manner of firing? Or some special circuit or circuits? (or all of the above!) Does the reproducibility from trial to trial matter? Or the persistence of the firing? Or perhaps as Christof has suggested, some cellular property that can integrate over a limited time, such as a calcium concentration? And how would this activity produce qualia?[18]

Nevertheless, the closest anyone had come to identifying the neural correlates of consciousness was in Logothetis's experimental set-up. To deepen his understanding of what this involved, Francis decided to visit Logothetis in Germany and observe the experiments directly. This was surprising, given his age and his aversion to long-distance travel, but Odile accompanied him for the month of August 1998, and they were able to stop off in England to see family and friends – the last time that Francis would visit the old country.

Once he was back in California, he began to think about how the experimental methods of neuroscience could be improved. The answer, he decided, would come from molecular biology. This insight came partly through his renewed interactions with Sydney Brenner, who had retired from the MRC and was now working at the Scripps Institute, not far from the Salk. While Crick had not paid close attention to the developments in genetic engineering and genomics, Brenner had been in the thick of it and knew what was now possible. Through informal discussions and a Helmholtz Club talk given by Brenner, the old friends explored how the latest developments in molecular genetics could be employed by neuroscientists.

These ideas were given a first public airing in March 1999, when Crick was invited to give three lectures at the University of California San Diego (UCSD) in honour of pioneer neurobiologist Stephen Kuffler. While this accolade showed yet again that Crick was recognised as a leading figure in neuroscience, it turned out to be a lot more work than he anticipated. The lectures, which were given on consecutive days, were each accompanied by a full day of activities including lunches, dinners, banquets and a UCSD television interview.[19] While the second and third lectures, on consciousness, were based on material Francis was used to talking about, the first talk, on the ideas he had been developing with Brenner, was all new, and required a lot of planning.

No sooner were the lectures over than Francis felt unwell and was hospitalised for a couple of days. Suffering from a persistent viral infection, he had been overworking too much and not eating properly. Although he cheerily told his friends he simply had low potassium levels that he was fixing by eating two bananas a day, he was clearly shaken by the incident – a few months later, when Odile returned from a short trip to Europe, the eighty-three-year-old Crick confessed to Colin Blakemore: 'I don't like her to be away for too long'.[20]

*

All that thinking about molecular biology and neuroscience did not go to waste. Francis soon called a meeting of Salk neuroscientists and molecular biologists, urging them to develop new methods in mice and primates that could identify, manipulate and observe neural circuits in action. This initiative rapidly led to new research projects, which encouraged Crick to write an article on the topic for a millennium issue of the *Philosophical Transactions of the Royal Society* – the world's longest-running scientific journal – which appeared on 31 December 1999.*[21] This was not his only encounter with millennium mania: Wedgwood wanted to include his portrait on a twentieth-century commemorative plate (they eventually used the double helix instead), he was invited to the New Year's Eve party at the Millennium Dome in London along with the Queen, Mick Jagger and Tony Blair (he declined), while photographer Carolyn Djanogly persuaded him to sit for her book of Britons who made the century, producing a piercing portrait.[22]

Crick's article, 'The Impact of Molecular Biology on Neuroscience', focused on how the Human Genome Project would provide new tools for characterising the structure and the function of nervous systems.[23] Francis returned to his idea that it would be possible to identify the different types of neuron on the basis of the genes that are expressed in them; now he could precisely outline how the mRNAs expressed in different cells could be compared. He also suggested that the activity of a given neuron might soon be controlled using light – 'This seems rather far-fetched but it is conceivable that molecular biologists could engineer a particular cell type to be sensitive to light in this way,' he wrote. Finally, he proposed that, by using genetic markers from the human genome, the brains of different primate species could be studied.

Each of these techniques – now known respectively as RNA-Seq, optogenetics and transcriptional mapping – have since become commonplace. Confirmation of one of Crick's insights came a few weeks after the article appeared, when a young Austrian researcher, Gero

---

*Everyone except calendar pedants viewed this as the last day of the second millennium.

Miesenböck, sent Francis a letter saying how much he had enjoyed the paper and telling him that one of his predictions was being realised: 'we have been exploring genetic means to sensitise neurons to light, so that distributed activity may be modulated or even synthetically generated in precisely defined sets of neurons,' he wrote.[24] Crick was delighted with the news.

Francis spent much of 2000 reading, taking detailed notes on a huge range of articles, preprints, books and talks, mainly from psychology or cognitive neuroscience, but including more molecular biological studies of how neurons work.[25] He wrote internal memos on qualia, on synapses and consciousness, on attention and on various factors that might be involved in consciousness, such as timing or cortical anatomy.[26] He paid special attention to the mathematical ideas of Giulio Tononi, who would later develop his influential Integrated Information Theory of consciousness. In his notebook, Crick carefully worked through Tononi's equations, returning to them several months later. Like many readers, he was bemused by Tononi's mathematics – 'Not easy to grasp!' he noted in the margin at one point – so decided to express the ideas in words. This clarified Crick's understanding, but left him unconvinced: 'Tononi's argument is that for a neural system to be rich (i.e. have high complexity), it must have a very large number of possible "states" (so be conscious of very many different things) each of which is itself fairly intricate. This is a very valid point, though whether the mathematics helps I'm not clear.'[27]

Michael McClure came to stay with Francis and Odile for a few days in spring 2000, visiting the desert house and giving a poetry reading at D. G. Wills Books in La Jolla, with the Cricks in the audience; he claimed it was 'one of the best readings of my life'.[28] McClure gave Francis three poems that flowed from his recent experience of meditation; after the visit, McClure wrote in his travel notebook, 'Very warm and lovely feeling to be there. They are astonishingly healthy and clear.'[29] There was also a letter from Kirsti Simonsuuri, longing for her friends: 'I do wish you were nearer, for I find travelling such long distances quite strenuous. If only you were in England or in France! But I can think of you and all those lovely times together, in Cambridge, in London, in California.'[30]

Her elegiac tone turned out to be prescient. In 2001, Francis began to feel unwell, and in May, after a series of tests, his physicians removed part of his colon. He had colon cancer. Kreisel, fearful of ill health, did not come to visit, but wrote a long letter expressing shock at the news: 'YOU ARE TAKING A REST, I hope,' he said, before repeating his views about Wittgenstein, at length.[31]

*

Once he was out of hospital, Francis endeavoured to return to normal. Life soon centred once more around discussing with Christof Koch, visiting the desert house and going to the theatre and opera. He even drew on his encounter with surgery and medication in an exchange of views about near-death experiences with English philosopher Antony Flew:

> In the first days after the operation I found that if I shut my eyes I could vividly see the hospital room I was in. It was not just like imagining the room. It was coloured and much more vivid. When I then opened my eyes and saw the real room it was somewhat similar to what I saw with my eyes closed, but very different in detail. In other words, I had an eyes-shut hallucination, based on what I had been seeing with my eyes open.[32]

As his strength returned, Francis gave two talks in San Diego. At the Society for Neuroscience meeting in November, he participated in a round-table discussion with friends and colleagues and even recorded a long interview.[33] At a conference of neurological surgeons, he urged his audience to explore the nature of consciousness while carrying out surgery for conditions such as chronic epilepsy. This lecture led to one of Crick's final papers, which appeared just after his death. After his talk, Crick and Koch discussed their ideas with Los Angeles neurosurgeon Itzhak Fried; the result was a joint article that built on Crick's lecture, Fried's clinical insights and his recent stunning paper with Koch and Gabriel Kreiman.[34] Recording from single cells in awake patients, Fried identified single neurons (in fact, components of networks of neurons) that responded only to surprisingly specific stimuli, such as a photograph of Bill Clinton. These findings appeared to bring the identification of the neural correlates of consciousness in humans that much closer. This powerful article, combining Crick's sharp analytical mind and the technical skills of Fried, Koch and Kreiman, shows the kind of work that Francis might have pursued, had he lived longer.

As well as refusing all invitations to speak outside of southern California, Francis now became determined to avoid new correspondence of any kind and drew up a form letter beginning, 'Dr Francis Crick no longer gives interviews, responds to questionnaires or poses for photographs'.[35] However, some letters from the public still touched him and earned a response. In May 2002, eight-year-old Joshua Rees of Essex sent Francis a charming letter enclosing a copy of his prize-winning school project, in which he described the discovery of the double helix as the major highlight of Queen Elizabeth II's reign.[36] Joshua told Crick he had a particular reason for this choice: 'Well done your discovery has helped to save my mums life.' (The insulin she took for her diabetes was made in genetically engineered microbes.) Francis thanked Joshua for the project and said how pleased he was that the discovery had helped his mother. 'Perhaps you will do science when you grow up, and also make interesting and useful discoveries. I hope so,' Crick wrote.*

Francis continued to pursue his arguments with various colleagues, including John Searle. In December 2002, impatient with not receiving a reply from Searle, he wrote satirically:

> Dear John
> I'm going to sit right down and write myself a letter
> And make believe it came from you.
>
> (Fats Waller)
>
> Happy Newton's Birthday!
> Yours ever,
> Francis[37]

---

*Joshua became a professional footballer. He still recalls Crick's letter and was very grateful to receive a reply.

Despite all these attempts to continue as before, there was no escaping the inevitable, for him or his oldest friends. In February 2002, Francis learned of the death of Leslie Barnett, with whom he had performed the triplet code experiment. A few days earlier, Max Perutz had died. Max had been his friend since 1947 and Francis was bereft: 'I was in touch with Max, by letter and phone, during his last few weeks and feel very sad we can never talk again. He was a most important influence in my scientific life and I've always been very grateful for it.'[38]

Later that year, Crick's cancer returned, and the prognosis was hopeless. Christof Koch was with him in the study at Colgate Circle when the oncologist telephoned with the news. He recalled Crick's stoical reaction: 'He stared off into the distance for a minute or two, and then returned to our reading. This diagnosis was discussed with Odile during lunch, but that was the extent of it for that day ... What mind control! What composure!'[39]

*

Not everything in 2002 was bad. Finally, Sydney Brenner was awarded the Nobel Prize in Physiology or Medicine, together with Robert Horvitz and John Sulston for their work on C. *elegans* and the genetics of development. Francis had nominated his old friend several times and was overjoyed that Sydney's immense contribution had at last been recognised.[40]

Around this time, Francis took various decisions about his intellectual legacy. For decades, librarians from various institutions in the USA and the UK had been pestering him about acquiring his papers; in recent years private collectors had also been after them, which the family viewed with concern.[41] Following many discussions with the Director of the Special Collections and Archives at UCSD, Lynda Claassen, Francis provisionally decided to leave his papers to the university. But in 2001 an agreement was reached with the Wellcome Trust in London, which bought his scientific archive for £1.8 million, half of which was donated by the Heritage Lottery Fund.[42] In a work of invaluable scholarship, these documents were painstakingly catalogued and scanned, and are now available online for anyone to study.[43] His personal papers, much of which consists of letters from others, remained at UCSD along with photocopies of the scientific archive.

During the negotiations with the Wellcome and UCSD, Francis realised that some documents from the 1950s and 1960s had gone missing; others, which he thought were originals, turned out to be high-quality photocopies.[44] He became so agitated about finding some letters from Maurice Wilkins, sent in the early 1950s, that he suggested to his trusted retired assistant, Maria Lang, that she might have retained them, warning her: 'The papers are valueless to you because, since we have Xerox copies, they can easily be identified as mine if anyone tried to sell them (which could be a serious offense).'[45] Most of the documents were eventually located, but important items, including his notebooks for 1952–3, covering the discovery of the double helix, and his notebook for the triplet code experiment of 1961, are still missing.[46]

Later, there were plans to sell part of his extensive personal library. Although a book dealer selected the volumes they wanted to buy, the sale does not appear to have gone through; there is no trace of the catalogue, which would have shed more insight on Crick's tastes and interests.[47]

Most tellingly, Francis dropped his opposition to a series of projects relating to his life and ideas. As far back as 1977, Horace Judson had wanted to publish a collection of Crick's papers on molecular biology, accompanied by a commentary and extracts from his letters. Francis had always refused, but at the beginning of 2003 he finally agreed that Judson should publish *A Mind at Work*, which would be both a book and – very modern – a CD-ROM.[48] Judson died in 2011; nothing came of the project. Francis showed a similar change of mind over proposals to write his biography. Although he had tolerated Olby's 1970 biographical essay, his determination to protect his privacy made him hostile to the idea of a full biography. As he explained in 2000 to one hopeful biographer, 'I do not blow hot and cold, but cold all the time. So I hope that, under the circumstances, you will abandon the idea.'[49] He now allowed both Matt Ridley and Bob Olby to interview him as they assembled material for their very different biographies, which appeared in 2006 and 2009, respectively.

In all these cases, Francis knew the men involved. Olby had followed his work for nearly forty years, Judson for thirty, while Ridley was a personal friend through his wife, the neuroscientist Anya Hurlbert.

Crick trusted them to get it right.

*

Francis had long been exasperated by the media's interest in the discovery of the structure of DNA – 'I really cannot stomach ANOTHER interview about the double helix,' he told one journalist.[50] However, it was evident that the fiftieth anniversary, in spring 2003, would be on a completely different scale from the previous celebrations and that Francis would not be able to avoid it – with the recent completion of a draft of the human genome, the importance of biotechnology in the global economy and DNA having become part of society's DNA, there were plenty of reasons to mark the moment. There was also the unstated recognition that two of those involved – Crick and Wilkins – were frail and would not be around for the next significant anniversary, whenever that might be.

All around the world, the anniversary was a huge cultural event. There were scores of special newspaper articles, TV and radio programmes, there were play readings, dance recitals, exhibitions and artworks galore. There were commemorative postage stamps, and the UK produced a special £2 coin featuring the double helix. There were also scientific meetings at Cold Spring Harbor, at the NIH, at the Royal Society, at King's College London and at the LMB in Cambridge, while in the middle of the celebrations the Human Genome Project announced the latest near-complete version of the genome.

As part of the ballyhoo, both *Science* and *Nature* published special issues. *Science*'s contribution was the more sedate, consisting of a few special commentary pieces that appeared in April.[51] *Nature*, which could claim to have started the whole business, launched the anniversary events at the beginning of the year with a special supplement that reprinted the three original articles from 1953, alongside scene-setting historical pieces by Olby, Brenda Maddox and Maclyn McCarty, who with Avery had shown that genes were made of DNA.

There were also major scientific reviews on DNA repair, replication and recombination, and articles about the double helix as a cultural icon.[52]

All this was more than Francis could take. After the return of his cancer, his health became unpredictable as the chemotherapy often made him ill. By July 2002 he felt that the programme of events being planned by UCSD and the Salk for March 2003, which included a joint appearance with Jim Watson, had got out of hand.[53] The celebrations were downscaled, but even so Francis was unable to attend the anniversary banquet; Brenner stepped into the breach and made a typically excellent speech in Crick's place.[54]

Events in the UK were opulent, with the celebrations spanning a whole week. In London, there was a huge banquet attended by Tony Blair and other bigwigs (David and Victoria Beckham were invited, but did not attend).[55] Peter Lawrence described the atmosphere to Crick's secretary:

> Yesterday I was at this splendid dinner in the Guildhall with trumpet fanfares and security and lots of celebrities and Jim Watson, and I was at the bottom of the hall where all the people are who don't really matter, and the speeches were not very good, and I thought how nice it would have been if Francis could have been there, and how the occasion would have had a completely different feel to it.[56]

Lawrence also recognised that, in fact, Francis would not have enjoyed the junketing, which continued in Cambridge.[57] Watson, on the other hand, revelled in it all, as he received a gold commemorative £2 coin from the Duke of Edinburgh and unveiled a plaque on the wall of the Eagle commemorating the 'we have discovered the secret of life' scene that he had concocted.*

*The plaque has since been amended to include a reference to Franklin, but it still marks Watson's fictitious account.

Safe in La Jolla, Francis managed to avoid official engagements, although he had videotaped brief remarks for some of the events. Nevertheless, his global fame and the significance of his co-discovery were inescapable, but in the most delightful way – the house at Colgate Circle was full of balloons and flowers sent by well-wishers. Gratifyingly, *Nature* marked the close of the celebrations with a page-long editorial praising not the double helix, but Crick's current work on consciousness.[58]

All the articles and speeches around the anniversary prompted Francis to correct a common mistake that was being made about the central dogma. Watson was his first target; in January 2003 he complained to his friend:

> You keep saying that DNA $\rightarrow$ RNA $\rightarrow$ protein is the central dogma. This is quite wrong, and misleads people. The central dogma says that a cell cannot back-translate a nucleic acid sequence to the corresponding protein sequence. Thus the transition RNA $\rightarrow$ DNA is quite compatible with the central dogma, properly defined, but not with your inaccurate version of it.[59]

Soon afterwards, he corrected both Nobel Prize winner Phillip Sharp and the editor of *Science*, both of whom had similarly mischaracterised the central dogma. Francis suggested that the inaccurate version (DNA $\rightarrow$ RNA $\rightarrow$ protein) should be renamed 'Watson's Dogma'.[60]

Despite its brevity, Crick's videotape message to the NIH celebration managed to present a rich view of gene function that was far from the mechanical, DNA-centred approach that some believe him to have had. After explaining that the sequence determination of a protein by DNA is a simple feed-forward process, Francis emphasised that the rate at which these reactions take place is strongly influenced by transcription factors which affect where, when and for how long genes are expressed, in a non-linear fashion. Crick's message ended with a vision of future discoveries which we are still working towards:

> We are confronted not only with a merely feed-forward process but with non-linear dynamic systems, the theory of which is

fragmentary, complex and confused ... There seems to be no limit to the problems that now confront us. I shall not live to see their solutions, but many of you should survive long enough to see many radically new techniques and striking discoveries. Good luck to you.[61]

At the end of May 2003, as the anniversary excitement waned, there was a brief ceremony at the Salk, where the British Consul presented Crick with his gold £2 coin (numbered 0001). Francis was grateful for the gift, although he did grumble to a colleague, 'I expect I shall have to wear a suit'.[62]

*

Crick's final two publications, both on consciousness, marked a return to the approach that had characterised his work with Koch for over a decade. The first, 'A Framework for Consciousness', which appeared as a 'Commentary' in *Nature Neuroscience* at the beginning of 2003, was a summation of their ideas in which they explained that by 'framework' they meant a set of assumptions or a point of view that suggested experimental approaches, rather than a detailed hypothesis: 'A good framework is one that sounds reasonably plausible relative to available scientific data and that turns out to be largely correct. It is unlikely to be correct in all the details.' For example, Crick explained, the double helix structure of DNA suggested a framework for gene action, duplication and so on, that turned out to be largely correct. On the other hand, the precise details of, say, gene structure in eukaryotes or DNA replication were very different to what had been expected.

The article included an idea about motion perception that had intrigued Francis even before he turned to neuroscience. Crick and Koch proposed that activity in sets of neurons captured a brief snapshot of a particular object or aspect of that object, and that motion was represented either by some special activity in those neurons, or by specific sets of motion-detecting neurons. This additional quality would be added to the snapshot, producing the perception of motion. To illustrate the point, Odile drew a picture of movement for the article – a woman in a patterned dress running, her hair streaming behind her, showing how a still image could suggest motion.

In conclusion, Crick and Koch emphasised that the idea of competing coalitions of neurons was the thread linking the various parts of their framework, and repeated Crick's 1999 suggestions for methods that could establish precise neuroanatomical maps of the brain. They took a passing swipe at the obsession with funding 'hypothesis-driven' science at the expense of descriptive research like neuroanatomy – the much-feted Human Genome Project was an entirely descriptive project, they pointed out, and the need to understand brain structure was of a similar significance. The article was an immediate success and with the growing interest in both connectomics and consciousness, it is seen as a foundational contribution.

This article was produced alongside the completion of Koch's academic book *The Quest for Consciousness*, which was published a year later (the title was suggested by Odile over a sun-drenched lunch).[63] Crick told Watson that the article was 'roughly Christof's book without most of the experimental evidence'; conversely, the penultimate chapter of Koch's book was a slightly edited version of the article.[64] Koch had been working on this monograph that summarised their ideas since 1998; the key concepts in the book were the product of their discussions, which he acknowledged by dedicating the book to Francis ('Friend, Mentor, and Scientist'): 'Without his constant guidance, insight, and creativity, this book simply would not have happened. ... I do not know anybody else like him.'

As Koch had drafted chapters over the years, Crick made repeated comments, but the writing was very much Koch's own.[65] Throughout their collaboration, the pair had co-signed their articles, even though Crick generally did most of the writing; this book was different. Crick told Peter Lawrence why he had not co-signed the book with Koch: 'Because, you see, I will not be here.' He wanted to ensure that Koch got all the credit.[66]

Oliver Sacks, who observed Crick and Koch discussing many times, called Koch Crick's 'son in science'; Francis, he said, spoke of *The Quest for Consciousness* 'with great pride, a father's pride'. Sacks recalled that 'it was immensely moving to see how the two men, forty or more years apart in age and so different in temperament and background, had come to respect and love one another so deeply.'[67]

*

Crick's final paper, which he was writing on his death-bed, began life in May 2004 as an internal memo on the function of the claustrum, a poorly understood thin sheet of neurons that lies beneath part of the cortex, receiving inputs from the cortex and projecting back asymmetrically, in the kinds of circuits described in the no-strong-loops paper in *Nature*.[68] By the middle of July, the memo had ballooned into a ten-thousand-word draft review, signed by Crick and Koch, which summarised a huge amount of neuroanatomical literature and homed in on reports of very high-frequency oscillations in a thalamic region adjacent to the claustrum. Although the researchers involved thought these unusual bursts of activity were some kind of freak result, Francis felt they could be decisive elements of the NCC. After outlining a long series of experiments, the conclusion of the draft that Crick took with him into hospital, shortly before he died, ended with a rallying cry to study the loops that characterise the claustrum and those oscillations: 'Do the 1000 Hz oscillations (…) play a key role in consciousness? What could be more important? So why wait?'[69]

After Crick's death, Koch laboured for several months on the manuscript, successfully doing what Francis would have done had he lived – turning the occasionally rambling draft into a more focused article that would honour the ideas and reputation of his friend, colleague and mentor. Koch notably cut all reference to high-frequency oscillations, focusing instead on the functional hints provided by the neuroanatomy of the claustrum, proposing that it plays a global role integrating information on a fast timescale. Neither Crick nor Koch suggested that the claustrum was the seat of consciousness.

The article appeared online in the *Philosophical Transactions of the Royal Society* at the end of June 2005, eleven months after Crick's death, and led to a resurgence of interest in the structure.[70] Koch wisely retained Crick's peremptory final phrases, which expressed the urgency he felt about the issue, even as his life ebbed away: 'What could be more important? So why wait?'

CLOSING TIME

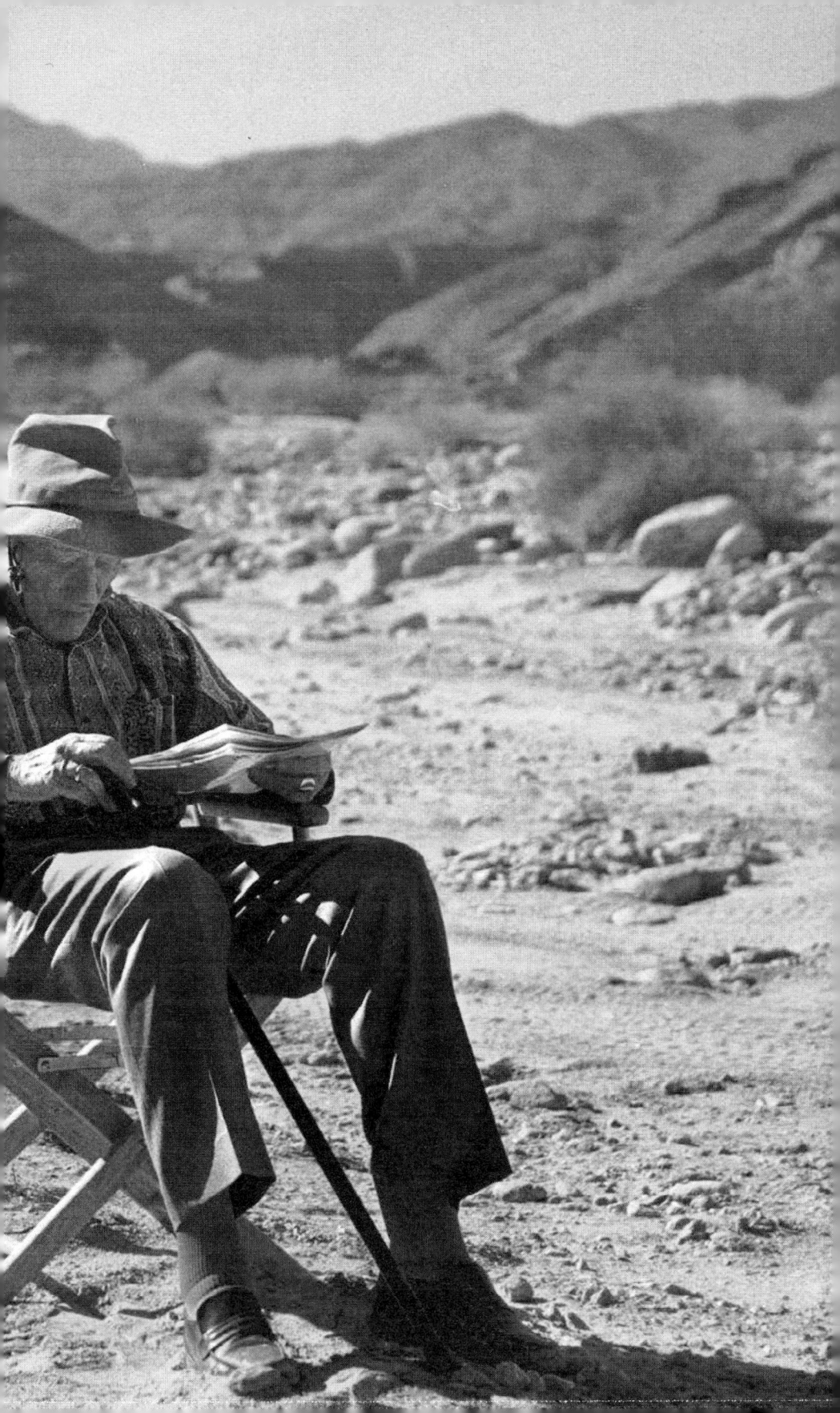

APRIL 2003

Peter and Birgitta Lawrence visit the Cricks at the Borrego Springs desert house. One day, they drive out for a hike; Francis is too ill to walk far, so he stays behind near the car. Sitting on a director's chair in a patch of scrubland, his head protected from the bright spring sun by a hat, he reads a paper on neural networks. When they return two hours later, he is still reading.[1]

Kathleen Rockland gives a talk on her anatomical research at the Helmholtz Club. Francis takes detailed notes.

Antony Barrington Brown, the man who fifty years earlier took *the* photo of Watson and Crick with the double helix, comes to La Jolla to photograph Francis and Odile. They are seated in front of a wooden trellis against a white wall in their garden. The pair beam, Francis smiling the same smile as half a century earlier.

Francis suffers a severe reaction to chemotherapy and spends two days in hospital. On hearing the news, Peter Lawrence remarks: 'when we were with him in Borrego he was not his usual self, but still burning ATP in that wonderful brain. He told me he had chosen a high dose "to test his limits," and I guess he found them.'

MAY 2003

Michael McClure writes to Francis, telling him about a prose piece describing a trip he took to Mexico back in 1962. 'When it's polished I'd like to fly down there and read it to you,' he says.

Pauline Finbow, Francis's Cambridge secretary, comes to visit.

Francis and Odile enjoy a two-week visit from Gabrielle and Jacqueline and her family.

Oliver Sacks writes to Francis: 'I have heard that you have been in poor health lately, but Christof tells me you are undaunted, and still reading mightily. I often think of you with great admiration and affection, and send you my warmest good wishes.'

Kreisel writes to Francis, expressing concern that he has not heard from his old friend. In a gloomy PS attached as a Post-It, Kreisel says he has heart problems and is contemplating suicide.

JUNE 2003

Francis replies to a correspondent who asked about his religious views: 'I am agnostic with a strong inclination to atheism. I think the God hypothesis is bankrupt, and that we have evolved from non-living matter by Natural Selection. Our DNA model only confirmed me in these beliefs.'

US photographer Mariana Cook persuades Francis to pose for a book project. He is seated in a wicker chair, his hands clasped in his lap, his gaze piercing and his eyebrows unruly. To his surprise, the whole process is over in five minutes. Cook is pleased with the result, as are the Cricks. Francis writes: 'Odile and I are delighted with it … and feel it is a wonderful likeness, though it rather clearly shows how old I am now.' Cook asks for some text to accompany the photo; Francis replies that he is too ill to oblige, but suggests these two lines from a poem by James Stephens, which appeared in the 1936 edition of the *Oxford Book of Modern Verse* and had stuck in his mind:

Here in a distant place he holds his tongue
Who once said all his say, when he was young.

JULY 2003

Anand Sarabhai, a PhD student at the LMB in the 1960s, invites Francis to contribute to a modern *Kama Sutra*. Francis declines and suggests he finds someone younger.

Francis tells his old friend Mahlon Hoagland, 'Odile is in fine form and looks after me splendidly.'

AUGUST 2003

Oliver Sacks and neuroscientist Ralph Siegel come for lunch with the Cricks at Colgate Circle; Christof Koch is also there. Siegel writes to Crick: 'For Oliver and I, watching Christof and you was sort of like looking in a mirror. There is the bridge that you two have formed over the years and across the years. The joining of Christof's irrepressible energy and your experience; the way you tease him about the book's completion; the way you two plan for the future is a joy.'

Later, Sacks wrote to Odile: 'I have the most vivid memory of the two of you (and Christof and Ralph), of our lovely lunch in your hill-top home, of the conversation which went in all directions, of Francis's piercing mind, and mischievous imagination and wit, and of the grace and fortitude with which he bore his illness ...'

DECEMBER 2003

Jim Watson takes Francis and Odile out for dinner in La Jolla.

FEBRUARY 2004

Francis proudly sends out signed copies of Christof Koch's book.

MARCH 2004

Jim Watson comes to La Jolla to visit his old friend.

MAY 2004

Francis's granddaughter Kindra sends him a letter, enclosing a photo of her on his shoulders, taken when she was two.

Jim Watson comes to La Jolla to visit his old friend.

JUNE 2004

Francis's son Michael comes to visit, as does Sydney Brenner.

JULY 2004

Francis writes to Pauline Finbow: 'My doctor says I am stable for the time being but that will not last. Meanwhile I am drafting a scientific paper with Christof Koch about a bit of the brain called the claustrum.'

Leslie Orgel visits Francis, finding him 'as excited as a schoolboy about two new ideas that had occurred to him in the past day or two'.

EPILOGUE

On the evening of 28 July 2004, Francis Crick thought his last. He became his admirers.

Mark Bretscher, who had known Crick for over forty years, heard the news on the radio in his Cambridgeshire thatched cottage. Although not surprised – all of Francis's friends knew the cancer was terminal – he was furious that such a brilliant mind could be extinguished. All day he raged, refusing to talk to the journalists who were pestering him for a soundbite.

Letters of condolence from friends and colleagues poured into the Cricks' house at Colgate Circle, all telling Odile of the same terrible sense of loss.[1] As Oliver Sacks wrote:

> I feel, as innumerable people will feel, that a great light, a beacon, has gone from the earth (although its power and prescience will be felt for centuries) – and, in a more personal way, a sense of being orphaned, for he was a father-figure to us all.

Months later, Kirsti Simonsuuri described feelings that are common to the bereaved and were shared by many:

I have been mourning a lot, sometimes it comes with a sharp pang, and sometimes I find myself talking to Francis as if he were quite near. (...) I miss him a lot. We – you, Francis, myself, and occasional friends – had such lovely times, so much joy and life and fun.'[2]

Crick's body was cremated in a private ceremony and his ashes were scattered on the Pacific Ocean. Only his thoughts remain.

Odile survived Francis by a little less than three years, dying on 5 July 2007.

*

Since his death, Crick's reputation has both grown and faded. The decision to name the UK's main biomedical research centre The Francis Crick Institute represented an official recognition of his immense contribution to science. The Crick, as it is known, is a land-mark for London taxi drivers, an architectural behemoth that looms over the area around St Pancras station and plays an equally dom-inant role in biomedical research. On Midland Road, Crick's name is literally written in stone.

At the same time, for both the public and for many scientists, Francis's scientific work has tended to be reduced to those few weeks in 1953 when he and Watson discovered the double helix, and even that collective memory is generally tangled up with misunderstood and mistaken claims about how they supposedly stole Franklin's data.

Although geneticists know of his work on the genetic code, many are unaware of his insights into evolutionary biology, such as his suggestion that protein sequences could be used to compare species, or his writings about the discovery of introns and the significance of junk DNA. Similarly, his influence on modern neuroscience is largely forgotten, even though he first proposed or popularised many of the techniques and approaches that are widely used today. Paradoxi-cally, the importance of Crick's strategy for understanding the brain can be seen in the way that, since his death, studies of consciousness have both blossomed and lost their way. There are currently over two hundred theories of consciousness, which strongly suggests that researchers do not agree what they are studying or how to proceed.[3] Neural correlates of visual perception have been identified but we are no closer to understanding how consciousness emerges from the activity of our brains.

The shift in the public's view of Crick is partly a consequence of changes in our attitudes to scientists as individuals. A lot of research now involves large teams and the contribution of any single scientist is harder to discern. There are also fewer scientific figures who can simultaneously capture the imagination of the public, of the media, and of other scientists; those who now play this role tend to be science communicators, not researchers. No scientist today can excite the kind of international media brouhaha that greeted *The Astonishing Hypothesis* in 1994. Crick, along with Stephen Hawking, was probably the last of his kind – at least for the time being.

Francis would probably have been content with this change. As he told the Wedgwood Company when they decided to use a double helix rather than his portrait on a commemorative plate: 'Discoveries and inventions are more important than the people who make them.'[4] This view applied particularly to himself; his aversion to having his photograph taken, or to being interviewed on television, eventually declined – in 1997 he sat for over thirty hours for a sculptor who was making a bust – but he remained a very private person, ensuring that for over thirty years he had no involvement in public life beyond his science.[5]

Nevertheless, during his lifetime and in the years immediately after his death, Francis was repeatedly compared with great figures of the past. For Kreisel, Francis had the same approach to scientific questions as Newton, the president of the Salk Institute ranked his contribution with those of Darwin and Mendel, while *Nature* simply called him arguably the most influential biologist of the twentieth century.[6]

At a time when many people are wary of singling out individual contributions to scientific discovery, such comparisons can seem overblown. But like the ideas of Darwin, Mendel and Newton, Crick's thinking changed how the rest of us see the world. Furthermore, no matter how collective any enterprise might be, the individuals involved fascinate us and can be a source of inspiration, if we can understand how they were able to do what they did.[7]

Crick's achievements were produced by a combination of luck and his own brilliance. This can be seen most clearly in the aftermath of the key event of his life, the discovery of the double helix, the gold Francis said he and Watson stumbled upon. They made this discovery before anyone else partly by being lucky and ruthless, but what happened next was solely due to Crick's unique ability. After the discovery, none of the other clever people involved – not Watson, nor Franklin, nor Wilkins, nor Randall, nor Pauling, nor Delbrück – sought to draw out the deep implications of the structure. Only Crick did that. In the years that followed, by focusing his knowledge and his intellect, Francis alone was able to glimpse how the flow of information through a cell revealed the deep history of life and the process of evolution. That was not down to luck, it was the product of his mind.

In 1994, Francis described his fundamental activity as 'I read and think'.*[8] He read widely and avidly, seeking to fully understand the field he was studying, even engaging with ideas that might seem eccentric or pointless, because 'there might be something in it'. He was searching for something that could be the starting point for a new idea, concept or hypothesis.[9] And while he was reading, he was thinking, breaking down complex problems to potential simplicity and exploring the broad implications of a finding or interpretation. Sometimes he would conceive of a problem in spatial terms; this was a significant driver of his interest in structures, both molecular and anatomical, as he sought to understand how form and function are intertwined.[10]

His thinking could be so powerful because he was able to totally focus on a problem. As Odile put it, recalling the intense days of February 1953, 'Francis was think think think'; Kreisel told him that an important ingredient of his success was 'the degree of single-mindedness with which you think'.[11] Crick was able to concentrate

---

*In the 1980s, Kindra Crick, then a teenager, visited her grandfather's office overlooking the Pacific Ocean at the Salk Institute and naively asked him what he did all day. 'I think' was his reply.

effectively partly because he was not distracted by other issues. In this respect his lack of interest in politics, which undermined his thinking about science and society, can be seen as an advantage.

Crick's approach was not only think think think; it was also talk talk talk. This enabled him to test his ideas, to drive out the mistaken hunches and to turn half-formed insights into something more productive. In its early days, with Kreisel, Watson or Brenner, this could be raucous, but as he aged the social context became more relaxed, although the intellectual intensity and underlying contradictory approach remained – as Christof Koch described when Francis was in his late seventies: 'He invites people to stay with him a week, a month or sometimes several months. And then there's this very intensive period where you talk with him, all day and evening and then you go out and socialize and talk about science. It's a very unique working style.'[12] This was work, but not as most of us know it. Francis found it fun and hugely productive; he could spend hours thinking and talking.

There were also material factors involved. As well as enjoying Odile's consistent and wholehearted support at home, which freed him from many domestic obligations, Francis worked at a time that seems dream-like to today's scientists. From 1954 he was funded by the MRC and not only had no teaching obligations, he had no research output obligations, either. So long as his boss, Max Perutz, was happy, Francis could do what he wanted. When he moved to the Salk he had an endowed chair with a guaranteed salary, and no requirement to publish articles in leading journals. He wrote only one major grant application in his whole life. He had time and space to think. Able to concentrate solely on his research, for much of his career he did not have to concern himself with the administrative trivia that hampers many modern scientists.

Francis recognised that his career had been charmed and was always extremely grateful for the support he received, particularly from the MRC. The relatively relaxed world in which he worked is one of the reasons why he was able to flourish and produce such extraordinary results. It seems unlikely that he would survive long in today's academia.

He also forced himself to clarify his ideas by writing them down, summarising them in informal documents which went by a variety of titles down the decades – notes, memos, RNA Tie Club documents and so on – but which all served the same purpose. As he developed an idea, a hypothesis, he would distil it in writing, summarise the evidence and the implications, and ask colleagues for their opinions. By repeated cycles he was able to clarify his ideas, to make them shine.

The theories produced by all this thinking and talking and writing had two functions, he said: 'The first is to explain what at first sight are sets of unrelated facts. (...) The second is to suggest new sorts of experiments.'[13] Crick's theories were not explanations of everything, but heuristic devices – approximate solutions that enabled researchers to take the next experimental step, which could then either reveal errors or support a hypothesis. This approach is what gives science its power – its ability to produce increasingly accurate observations and interpretations, based on insights and mistakes.

Being wrong is a key part of the scientific process; insight emerges by pruning away mistaken ideas. That is why Francis was so profligate in his publication of theories and hypotheses – the best way of discovering if an idea is correct is by exposing it to debate and experimental test. If it is wrong, that realisation is itself a step forward. As he said:

> The important thing is that you have lots of ideas and that you learn most are going to be wrong. The trick is to figure out which are the most promising and work on those.[14]

To make that choice, Francis relied on his profound knowledge of the subject and also his intuition, that near-magical quality that is based on unstated, implicit knowledge and a rapid, unconscious exploration of possibilities. This knack was also at the heart of his 'don't worry' approach, as he explained to Kreisel:

> There are at least two reasons for brushing aside. One is that the experimental evidence may be wrong. The other is that it may be misleading because a trivially broader theory may

explain it. It is a test of one's 'biological intuition' (whatever that is) to decide whether to ignore an inconvenient 'fact' or not.[15]

Most scientists would be wary of using their intuition to ignore data points or to set aside a major aspect of their problem – and yet that is what Francis did repeatedly. That this rarely caused any lasting difficulty shows his deep understanding of the problems he was trying to solve.

One of the ways in which Crick's thinking exerted an influence on both scientists and the public was through his ability to explain his ideas in strikingly simple ways, something he learned as he devoured *The Children's Encyclopædia* in the 1920s. As Kreisel told him: 'You don't seem to realise how EXCEPTIONAL your gift is to get TOTAL satisfaction from communicating knowledge.'[16] Crick's gift flowed partly from the clarity of his thinking, and partly from his infectious enjoyment and excitement when talking with others, as Belinda Bullard, a Cambridge student in the mid-1950s, explained to me:

> I found him completely enthralling: constantly asking questions about the origin of everything anyone said, wanting to get to the bottom of even the most trivial things, like why I went to a particular lecture and what I learnt. Then he would launch into whatever he was thinking about at the time.[17]

However, it is striking that this enthusiasm did not extend to more formal tasks – he did not teach undergraduates (as a researcher, he was not required to) and he supervised only a handful of doctoral students and had little to do with their training. With his busy life, full of trips abroad and intense periods of thinking, he would not have made a good supervisor, but even so, he clearly had no appetite for this aspect of science – his most intense and profitable interactions were always with his equals. Furthermore, because his ideas were so wide-ranging, he had no partners who could keep up with all his interests, so he did not create a school of thought. No one else could encompass the wealth of ideas he had in his head.

Interwoven with this lifetime of the most varied scientific activity there was also the life of Crick the man. His many affairs were an expression of his appetite for life, of his belief that, as he put it to Odile, sexual intercourse is a panacea for all kinds of troubles.[18] More unusually, there was also his keen interest in poetry, including his close friendship with Michael McClure and his fascination with McClure's materialist psychedelic poems. This thread ran through the second half of Crick's life, and he did not see it as being in contradiction with his scientific work.

Crick's aesthetic sense can be seen in his frequent use of the word 'beautiful' to describe results or images. He rarely used the term 'elegant', frequently employed by physicists and mathematicians to describe their findings, even though he was trained in these fields. This was not a quirk of vocabulary, but an appreciation of a different aesthetic. Biological results are frequently not elegant; they are often messy and complex. They are nevertheless beautiful, because of their deep evolutionary roots and the contingent factors that have shaped them. In 1953, Francis said that the double helix made him swoon every time he thought of it; this was because of its beauty, not simply its striking chemical elegance. This sense of beauty, of deep relationships underlying complex phenomena, drove Crick's scientific work and also explains his fascination with poetry, in particular with McClure's writings.

McClure's description of the numinous and ecstatic experience of discovery which so impressed Francis – THIS IS THE POWERFUL KNOWLEDGE – came from chewing peyote and the effect of mescaline on his serotonin receptors, but Francis felt the same thing when he perceived the shape of the truth through a fog of data. That open embracing of a poetic appreciation of the world is rare in a scientist, but was an essential part of Crick, part of how he thought and felt, part of what made him the man and the scientist he was.

*

All our lives involve decisive moments as we respond to events and make choices. The outcomes are hard to predict and seem to be caused by a mixture of factors – luck and destiny, genes and environment, chance and necessity. For all his intelligence, Crick's life was no different. Had someone else had Francis's luck, the many turning points in his scientific life might have gone differently, changing the history of science. Similar discoveries would have been made, but not in the same way or with the same élan. We would not know him and this book would never have been written; his renown would be limited to a small circle of friends and family. But even if he had not made those extraordinary discoveries, much of his character would remain and his family and friends would still have known someone remarkable, someone who changed their lives, someone whom they loved and who loved them. Far more than the glittering prizes of scientific glory, that is ultimately what counts, in anyone's life.

On 27 September 2004, the Salk Institute held an open-air celebration of Crick's life, with reminiscences from many of his friends, colleagues and members of his family. The speeches were interspersed with music – English folk songs and airs, including a new arrangement of 'Greensleeves', and some of Francis's favourite tunes by Gershwin and The Beatles. Among the many heartfelt comments, Michael Crick explained that his father's scientific life could be understood as one perpetual argument, with himself, his colleagues and the whole of culture, as he attempted to banish non-materialist explanations of life and consciousness.[19] A lavish memorial brochure was produced, full of memories from a wide range of people who knew, loved and admired Crick. It also included photographs of Francis from throughout his life and images of his office as he had left it.[20] On one wall there were portraits of the young Darwin, of Jacob Bronowski and of Einstein; there were models of the brain and DNA; the chalkboard had 'NO STRONG LOOPS' and 'MEANING' scrawled on it. On his desk there was a framed photograph of Odile.

One of the many friends who attended the ceremony was Michael McClure, who later wrote to Odile about the event:

> It was warming to see you on that day and the spoken remembrances made a cloud of high silvery consciousness from the mingling of so many great biologists and Nobelists. Not only the memories of Francis were wonderful but the sea below and

the sun and handsomeness of the Salk building made it one of the memorable days of my life.[21]

On the day that Francis died, McClure completed a long poem, 'Double Moire', dedicated to his friend, just like his poem 'Moiré' over thirty years earlier.[22] Indeed, the opening two lines of each stanza were taken from the previous poem, a nod to the double helix.[23] In December 2005, McClure finished polishing the poem and sent it to Odile, saying he felt it was the finest he had ever written.

'Double Moire' was full of the muscular sensation and vivid imagery that Francis appreciated in McClure's writing. As is often the case, McClure's meaning is not immediately obvious, but one stanza seems to express the poet's attempt to grapple with his friend's tragically inevitable end:

> PERHAPS WE RETURN TO A POOL
> – STEADY AND SOLID;
> ready and already completed in fireworks
> and lives and non-lives – thin and faint
> as powerful odours stirring
> my moment's soul in the mind of place.

ACKNOWLEDGEMENTS

I never met Francis Crick, so this portrait is based primarily on my interpretation of things he wrote and said, and of how others reacted. I have been lucky enough to receive the help and support of many people who knew Crick well; they have given me advice – and criticism – that has enriched my understanding. Francis's surviving children, Michael and Gabrielle, both kindly talked to me for several hours, giving me context and correcting some of my misunderstandings; they subsequently read the draft manuscript and made extremely useful comments and suggestions. They also gave me permission to quote from the private letters of their parents and to reproduce Odile's drawings. I hope they recognise something of their father here. I first met Kindra Crick, Francis's granddaughter, in 2016 at a Cold Spring Harbor meeting to mark the centenary of Francis's birth. Her interest, advice and memories all helped the book in many ways.

Some of Crick's closest friends and collaborators – Jim Watson, the late Sydney Brenner and Christof Koch – all gave me their time (four days in Sydney's case) and provided me with insights and encouragement. My 2017 trip to Singapore to interview Brenner was part of the pre-history of this biography; focused on his collaboration with Crick, it was generously supported by a Sydney Brenner

Fellowship from Cold Spring Harbor Laboratory and by the BBC Radio Science Unit – I travelled with ace producer Andrew Luck-Baker and together we made a programme about Brenner's life for the BBC World Service focusing on his work with Francis.

In the later stages of the writing, Peter Lawrence and Mark Bretscher, who both worked with Francis in the 1960s and beyond, provided invaluable help. They read the whole book, sent repeated e-mails correcting me or giving me insights, and also provided photos and memories. Peter's impressions of the Cricks' desert house were essential for the passages covering the later years of their lives. Both Peter and Mark were extremely generous with their time, on Zoom and in Cambridge, for which I am very grateful; the book would be much poorer without their contribution.

Other people also provided invaluable assistance: Kathleen Rockland was enthusiastic in helping me deal with the period she and Francis discussed problems of neuroanatomy, Belinda Bullard generously shared her vivid memories of the 1950s, Tim Hunt gave context and confirmation about how Crick was viewed by a younger generation of scientists, while Nancy Hopkins helped me understand her encounter with Crick in 1965 and the difficulties of explaining how and why people had different attitudes in the past. Matt Ridley and Georgina Ferry kindly sent me the interviews they had made with Francis, as well as providing inspiration through their biographical writing. Lucia Vania generously provided me with the photo of her husband, David Marr, with Crick.

Without the help of librarians and archivists in the UK and the USA, none of this would have been possible. An essential prerequisite was the organisation and cataloguing of Crick's papers by the Geisel Library at the University of California San Diego, driven by Lynda Claassen, followed by the Wellcome Trust's decision to buy Crick's academic correspondence and to make it available online, a project overseen by Chris Beckett. Their collective contributions to scholarship and to our understanding of the history of science in the second half of the twentieth century cannot be overstated.

I made two visits to San Diego to study Francis's personal archive; each time, my friend Andrea Fidgett of San Diego Zoo generously showed me the sights (and the zoo!). Both trips were made much easier by Luis Campos's kind invitations for me to speak at Rice University in Houston, which got me across the Atlantic. The staff at the Special Collections in the Geisel Library at UCSD were extremely helpful, in particular Heather Smedberg, Jennifer Donovan and Miriam Camacho Cabrera. I could not have found my way through Crick's personal archives without them. At Cold Spring Harbor, Mila Pollock was kind and welcoming as ever, as were her staff, especially Stephanie Satalino and Katharine Pigliacelli who helped me navigate Bob Olby's largely uncatalogued archive. I also thank Jan Witkowski and Alex Gann of Cold Spring Harbor, who described the 'lost' papers of Francis Crick, discovered among Brenner's archive, and edited an invaluable annotated version of *The Double Helix*, shedding new light on the period 1951–3. Heather Kowalski of the J. Craig Venter Institute in San Diego, Colleen Puterbaugh of the Center for the History of Microbiology/ASM Archives in Baltimore, David Kloepfer of the W.A.C. Bennett Library at Simon Fraser University, Louisiane Ferlier at the Royal Society and Tom Hercock of the BBC Written Archives Centre all squirreled out material for me. Lynsey Darby, the Archivist of St John's College Cambridge, helped solve the mystery of who owns the patch of land in front of 19–20 Portugal Place, while John Wells, Senior Archivist at the Cambridge University Library, found Crick–Prynne correspondence for me.

Adam Rutherford read two of the scene-setting parts of the book – the opening and the chapter on Edwardian ideas – making me sharpen my writing and thinking. Once again, Stephen Curry guided me through the mysteries of X-ray crystallography but is in no way responsible for any errors that remain. Christian Orlic and Luis Campos helped me think more clearly about Crick's work on directed panspermia, sharing their work and insights. Book dealer Jonathan Chiche not only drew my attention to some of Wilkins' eye-popping letters that had recently been auctioned, he also very kindly went to the Jacques Monod archive at the Institut Pasteur for me and dug out various letters that I needed. Kersten Hall was supportive and enthusiastic, tracking down references; he also put me straight on the early history of DNA. Thony Christie (@rmathematicus) has, as always, been generous in his support and his use of social media to help me answer questions.

Writers and broadcasters Roland Pease and Philip Ball were encouraging and insightful at various points in the gestation of the book, while BBC producer Alex Mansfield helped me in ways that only we know. My friend Jerry Coyne revealed the mysteries of the 1954 baseball match Crick attended and was always enthusiastic about the book. Over the years he also gave me space on his blog, whyevolutionistrue.com, to develop ideas that eventually found their way into these pages. Matt Martin, of Birkbeck College, clued me in on McClure's trip to London in 1975, while my friend and colleague, the poet and academic John McAuliffe, discussed McClure and Prynne with me and gave me confidence that I had the right approach. Professor Geoff Ward kindly shared his memories of McClure's visit to Cambridge and his expert insight into American poetry. Amy McClure provided clues to Francis's friendship with her husband and memories of her visits to the Cricks, while Birgitta Lawrence allowed me to quote from her diaries. At the very beginning, discussions with Enrico Coen, Angela Saini and Gaia Vince, during the breaks at a Company of Biologists writing workshop in Sussex, organised by Jenny Rohn, encouraged me to re-examine my ideas and question some of my assumptions.

As the writing neared its end, I retired from the University of Manchester; my colleagues were extremely supportive of this project, in particular Carsten Timmermann of the Centre for the History of Science, Technology and Medicine, and my line manager, Simon Hubbard, who ensured that my sole objective in my final year was finishing the manuscript.

At Profile Books, my then editor, Ed Lake, was very keen about the idea of a Crick biography and, together with my agent, Peter Tallack, did what was needed for the Managing Director of Profile, Andrew Franklin (Rosalind's cousin), to buy the book in 2021. Ed left Profile shortly afterwards, so Nick Humphrey edited the book from the very beginning, discussing and advising at every key point, encouraging me when necessary and showing no signs of concern as the book grew and grew, before finally polishing my prose, killing some (but not all) of my darlings. In the USA, T. J. Kelleher of Basic Books was very supportive from the outset, sending me some very reassuring e-mails about his impressions of the work as it progressed.

TJ has now left publishing for a new beginning, full of green shoots, and I wish him the very best. In its final stages, Penny Daniel of Profile Books yet again smoothly and professionally guided the book home; working with her has been a pleasure, as always. My thanks too to Jonathan Harley for the beautiful layouts, and to Bill Johncocks for another great index.

The most unexpected but essential contributor to the research and writing has been Nathaniel Comfort, who is working on a biography of Jim Watson. When I first started thinking about writing this book, I had no idea he had begun a parallel project. We first met in 2022, at the Cold Spring Harbor meeting to mark the life of Sydney Brenner, and immediately hit it off. Later that year we had our own mad session poring over Rosalind Franklin's archives at Churchill College Cambridge, which led to some significant insights that we crystallised in a 2023 *Nature* article (much improved by our editor, Lucy Odling-Smee) which was accompanied by a BBC radio programme, thanks to Gaia Vince. Nathaniel has been thinking about the role of biography in the history of science for many years, and his insights, as well as his suggestions, criticisms and support, have been invaluable. Having a fellow thinker with whom you can exchange ideas, doubts and discoveries, as well as shoals of e-mails (sometimes several a day), has been extraordinary. Looking at the same events from the different points of view of our two subjects has been endlessly fascinating, and I cannot wait to read his book.

The period of writing was also marked by some sombre events, including the deaths of my brothers-in-law, Tommy Purcell and Clive Boothman. They were two very different men (Tommy would have appreciated the material on consciousness, Clive would have loved reading about McClure), both were funny and great company and they are both much missed.

I have now retired, my children have left home, and my cats are getting old and spend even longer asleep (Ollie sadly died as the book was completed). As ever, Christina Purcell has tolerated my writing habit. I could not have done any of it without her.

LIST OF ARCHIVAL SOURCES

ASMB	Anne Sayre Collection of Rosalind Franklin Materials, Center for the History of Microbiology/American Society of Microbiology Archives, University of Maryland.
AVHL	A. V. Hill Archive, Churchill Archives Centre, Churchill College, Cambridge.
BANC MSS 2003/222 c	Michael McClure Papers: Additions, The Bancroft Library University of California, Berkeley.
BBC Written Archive	BBC Written Archives Centre, Reading.
CAD/1953	Royal Society, London
Delbrück papers	Papers of Max Delbrück, Archives, California Institute of Technology.
Dorn Papers	Edward Dorn Papers, University of Connecticut Library Archives and Special Collections.
EC	Fellows Nomination Archive, Royal Society, London.
FD	National Archives, Kew.
FRKN	Rosalind Franklin Archive, Churchill Archives Centre, Churchill College, Cambridge.
GBR/0014/BRTS	Mark Bretscher Archive, Churchill Archives Centre, Churchill College, Cambridge.
GBR/0014/MISC	Churchill Archives Centre, Churchill College, Cambridge.
GBR/0014/RNDL	John Randall Archive, Churchill Archives Centre, Churchill College, Cambridge.
GBR/0265	Cambridge University Archive.

GBR/0272/NGA	The Papers of Noel Gilroy Annan, King's College, Cambridge.
JDW	James Dewey Watson Archive, Cold Spring Harbor Laboratory.
K/PP178	Maurice Wilkins papers, King's College London.
LAC	Library and Archives Canada, Ottawa.
LP Science	Ava Helen and Linus Pauling Papers, 1873–2013, Special Collections & Archives, Oregon State University.
M2286	Robert Cohn digital collection, 1500s–2016, Stanford University.
MC-0100	Oral History Program on Recombinant DNA, MIT.
MON	Fonds Jacques Monod, Institut Pasteur, Paris.
MsA5	Michael McClure fonds, W.A.C. Bennett Library, Simon Fraser University.
MS. Eng	John Kendrew Archive, Bodleian Library, Oxford.
MSS 176	Leslie Orgel Papers, University of California San Diego Special Collections and Archives.
MSS 660	Francis Crick Personal Papers, 1935–2007, University of California San Diego Special Collections and Archives.
Nirenberg Papers	Marshall W. Nirenberg Papers, Archives and Modern Manuscripts Collection, National Library of Medicine, Bethesda.
OHC-CSHL	Oral History Collection, Cold Spring Harbor Laboratory.
OLBY	Robert Olby Archive, Cold Spring Harbor Laboratory.
PC	Royal Society, London.
PP/CRI	Francis Crick Archive, Wellcome Trust, London.
PP/FGS	Frederick Gordon Spear Papers, Wellcome Trust, London.
PRTZ	The Papers of Max Ferdinand Perutz, Churchill Archives Centre, Churchill College, Cambridge.
RR	Royal Society, London.
SA	British Library Sound Archive.
SB	Sydney Brenner Archive, Cold Spring Harbor Laboratory.
SC 0136	Georg Kreisel Archive, Stanford University.
SC 0222	William Shockley Papers, Stanford University.
SCH	Schrödinger Archive, Dublin Institute for Advanced Studies.
TGA 955	ICA Archive, Tate Gallery Archive, London.

W. L. Bragg   W. L. Bragg papers, Royal Institution, London.
Wellcome   Wellcome Trust Archive, London.
WFAT   Watson Family Asset Trust, Cold Spring Harbor
          Laboratory.

The Wellcome Trust website hosts easily searchable digital versions of the following archives: FRKN, JDW, K/PP178, PP/CRI, SB. Digitised material from Crick, Watson, Nirenberg and others can also be found at https://profiles.nlm.nih.gov.

NOTES

Where intimate letters to Crick are referred to, I have preserved the authors' anonymity and given incomplete shelfmarks. All links given in the notes have been archived at https://archive.org.

PROLOGUE

1   MSS 660, Box 13, Folder 14.
2   Crick to Berg, 15 July 1959, JDW/2/2/402.
3   MSS 660, Oversize MC-006-02. Although this poem was signed 'Mike McClure', McClure later used his full name. The poem has been reprinted in several anthologies, including McClure, M. (2011), *Of Indigo and Saffron: New and Selected Poems* (London: University of California Press), pp. 34–44. Crick to McClure, 18 October 1970, MsA 5.12 MSS 37. Crick, F. (1975), The poetry of Michael McClure: A scientist's view. *Margins* 18, March 1975, pp. 23–4.
4   MSS 660, Oversize MC-006-02. Crick to McClure, undated [1966], MsA 5.12 MSS 37. Crick told McClure that after several years 'I took it down as it was getting a bit dusty, and put it away in a safe place' – Crick to McClure, 18 October 1970, MsA 5.12 MSS 37. McClure told Crick that it was very rare – only 150 were printed, and 'thirty were destroyed in a landslide in Los Angeles' – McClure to Crick, 27 October 1970, MSS 660, Box 7, Folder 14.
5   Crick (1975).
6   Crick to McClure, 9 November 1970, MsA 5.12 MSS 37.
7   Crick (1975).
8   Crick, Application for MRC studentship, undated [July 1947], FD 21/13.
9   Crick, F. (1996), Georg Kreisel: a few personal recollections. In P. Odifreddi (ed.), *Kreiseliana: About and Around Georg Kreisel* (Wellesley, MA: Peters), pp. 25–32, p. 31.
10 Southwell to Crick, 21 October [1970], MSS 660, Box 9, Folder 23.

11 Crick (1996), p. 32.
12 Odile to Kreisel, 10 February 1971, SC 0136, Box 3, Folder 9.
13 May Brenner interview, 14 June 2005, OHC-CSHL.
14 Odile to Francis, 10 and 20 May 1956, MSS 660, Box 2, Folder 25.
15 Odile Crick interview with Olby, undated, OLBY, Box 3.
16 Odile to Kreisel, 10 February 1971, SC 0136, Box 3, Folder 9.
17 Letters to Crick, 7 March and 29 March 1963, MSS 660, Box 4.
18 Letter to Watson, 14 July 1963, JDW/2/2/1558. Letter to Crick, 24
    November 1974, MSS 660, Box 11. Hoopes, L. (2011), Nancy Hopkins
    speech shockers. https://www.nature.com/scitable/forums/women-in-
    science/nancy-hopkins-keynote-speech-shockers-19135206. In 2005 May
    Brenner recalled: 'I'm a woman and Francis reacts rather differently to
    women. (…) I was always much more at ease being with Odile than I was
    with Francis.' May Brenner interview, 14 June 2005, OHC-CSHL.
19 Sisman, A. (2023), *The Secret Life of John le Carré* (London: Profile).
20 Crick's first passport, issued in 1945, described his eyes as grey, as did
    subsequent documents. After 1968, his passports described his eyes as
    blue. MSS 660, Box 13, Folder 2; MSS 660, Box 13, Folder 5.
21 Ridley, M. (2006), *Francis Crick: Discoverer of the Genetic Code* (London:
    Harper). Olby, R. (2009), *Francis Crick: Hunter of Life's Secrets* (Cold Spring
    Harbor, NY: Cold Spring Harbor Laboratory Press).
22 Bretscher, M. S. and Mitchison, G. (2017), Francis Harry Compton Crick
    OM: 8 June 1916 – 28 July 2004. *Biographical Memoirs of Fellows of the Royal
    Society* 63:159–96.
23 In the years before he became established enough to have a secretary who
    typed his letters and retained a carbon copy, his side of these exchanges are
    generally missing. Few of his many hand-written letters have survived or
    are in the public domain.
24 Crick to Clarke, 19 April 1966, PP/CRI/D/1/1/3.
25 PP/CRI/J/1/3/7/1.
26 Crick to Klug, 29 September 1992, PP/CRI/L/1/4/4.
27 Crick to Sonja, undated [1964], SB/11/1/100.
28 In the 1980s Crick repeatedly rebuffed interest from potential biographers,
    saying he was strongly opposed to the idea, before relenting towards the
    end of his life, telling Robert Olby 'As you know, I'm not enthusiastic
    about such projects, but I won't impede it. When it comes to the point I
    might even enjoy it!' Crick to Olby, 18 January 2000, PP/CRI/J/2/20/1.
29 Crick to Rinaldini, 21 January 1991, PP/CRI/J/2/11/1. Koch was staying
    with the Cricks on 11 September 2001: email to the author, May 2025.
30 May Brenner interview, 14 June 2005, OHC-CSHL.
31 Michael Crick interview, May 2022, and Gabrielle Crick interview,
    December 2022.
32 Crick to Annan, 10 October 1997, PP/CRI/J/2/17/4.
33 'Crick for God' was chalked on a Cambridge wall next to 'Keep the lefties
    out' and 'Enoch is right' (amended by another hand to read 'Enoch is a
    right pratt'): PP/CRI/A/1/2/8.

CHAPTER 1

1 Crick, F. (1988), *What Mad Pursuit: A Personal View of Scientific Discovery* (New York: Basic), p. 7. Crick, F. (1994), *The Astonishing Hypothesis: The Scientific Search for the Soul* (New York: Scribner's), p. 85.

2 Crick interview with Christopher Sykes, 1993. https://www.webofstories.com/play/francis.crick/22

3 In November 1946, Francis gave his father a birthday present, a copy of *Leather in Life, Art and Industry*, by J. W. Walter, and inscribed it 'To Poppa, on his birthday, 11th November 1946, from Francis.' An accompanying note read, 'Dear Poppa, I hope you won't chide me for extravagance, but I thought you'd like it – may we make it a Christmas and Birthday present instead? Love, Francis.' In 2024 the book and the note were on sale on eBay.

4 Crick (1988), p. 9.

5 Crick (1988), p. 10.

6 Crick to Kelly, 1 August 2002, PP/CRI/J/1/8/3.

7 Wittet to Crick, 16 September 1996, MSS 660, Box 10, Folder 45.

8 Darwin, C. (1882), On the dispersal of freshwater bivalves. *Nature* 25:529–30.

9 Crick (1988), p. 9.

10 Mee, A. (ed.), (1910), *The Children's Encyclopædia, Volume 3* (London: The Educational Book Company), p. 1584.

11 Crick (1988), p. 9.

12 Crick interview with Christopher Sykes, 1993. https://www.webofstories.com/play/francis.crick/4.

13 Mee (1910), p. 1356.

14 Tracey, M. (2009), *The World of the Edwardian Child – as Seen in Arthur Mee's 'Children's Encyclopaedia' 1908–1910* (n.p.: Hermitage), p. 69. Paulin, R. (2002), Heroes and villains: the case of Arthur Mee's Childrens encyclopedia. *Bulletin of the John Rylands Library* 84:161–70.

15 Olby, R. (2009), *Francis Crick: Hunter of Life's Secrets* (Cold Spring Harbor, NY: Cold Spring Harbor Laboratory Press), p. 18.

16 First to 17 Uphill Road, then to 3 Tretawn Park. MSS 660, Box 12, Folder 17.

17 Olby (2009), plate 7, shows a photograph of Crick and other cast members and suggests this was a production of *H.M.S. Pinafore*. However, there are no Far Eastern characters in this operetta, and it was actually a production of *The Mikado*.

18 Crick (1988). Crick to Sacks, 5 June 2001, PP/CRI/J/1/8/19. Crick's Higher School Certificate was announced, along with hundreds of others, in the *Daily Telegraph*, 6 September 1934.

19 Crick (1988), pp. 12–3.

20 All details from Olby (2009), pp. 54–5. There is a photo of Doreen Dodd in plate 13.

21 Wittet to Crick, 16 September 1996, MSS 660, Box 10, Folder 45.

22 All information on this period taken from Crick's draft of *What Mad Pursuit* – PP/CRI/L/5/5/1/1.

23 Olby (2009), p. 56.

24 Crick, F. (1996), Georg Kreisel: a few personal recollections. In P. Odifreddi

(ed.), *Kreiseliana: About and Around Georg Kreisel* (Wellesley, MA: Peters), pp. 25–32, p. 25.

25 Hawkins, R. A. (2020), The Dudley Refugee Committee and the Kindertransport, 1938–1945. *Jewish Historical Studies* 51:183–201.

26 Isaacson, D. (2020), Georg Kreisel: some biographical facts. In P. Weingartner and H.-P. Leeb (eds.), *Kreisel's Interests: On the Foundations of Logic and Mathematics* (n.p.: College Publications), pp. 87–116.

27 Monk, R. (1990), *Ludwig Wittgenstein: The Duty of Genius* (London: Jonathan Cape), pp. 498–9. Wittgenstein also described the brilliant philosopher Elizabeth Anscombe as not being of Kreisel's calibre. Isaacson (2020), p. 100.

28 Crick (1988), p. 16.

29 Conradi, P. J. (2001), *Iris Murdoch: A Life. The Authorised Biography* (London: Harper Collins). Murdoch and Crick do not seem to have interacted.

30 Crick (1996), p. 27.

31 All material on Crick's Russia trip from Crick's account in PP/ CRI/L/5/5/1/1 and from Dougall, R. (1973), *In and Out of the Box* (London: Collins and Harvill), pp. 144–6. For Crick's route, see Crick notebook, 1945–6, MSS 660, Box 16, Folder 1.

32 Dickson, Broadcast transcript, 1945. https://www.bbc.co.uk/history/ ww2peopleswar/stories/29/a5760029.shtml

33 Crick interview with Ridley, 2003, with the interviewer's permission. Crick to Perutz, 27 May 1987, PP/CRI/J/2/7/1. Crick to Perutz, 1 July 1987, PP/ CRI/J/2/7/2.

34 Crick, Memorandum, undated, MSS 660, Box 20, Folder 12. According to neuroscientist Philip Low, Crick witnessed the debriefing of the German atomic physicist Werner Heisenberg (Olby, 2009, p. 63). This seems unlikely. Heisenberg and nine other captured German physicists were held at Farm Hall, near Cambridge, between 3 July 1945 and 3 January 1946; the key discussion with Heisenberg took place on 8–9 September 1945. Until January 1946 Crick worked for the Department of Torpedoes and Mining in Havant; there is no evidence he was involved in intelligence work at this time or that he ever visited Farm Hall. However, Crick was in Germany for intelligence work in July 1946 (Crick, Diary, 1946, MSS 660, Box 14, Folder 1); it is possible he saw Heisenberg then.

35 Jones, R. V. (1978), *Most Secret War: British Scientific Intelligence, 1949–1945* (London: Hamish Hamilton).

36 Dougall (1973), p. 162.

37 Odile Crick, memoirs, undated [1995?], MSS 660, Box 31, Folder 1.

38 Crick, Diary, 1946, MSS 660, Box 14, Folder 1.

39 Odile Crick, memoirs, undated [1995?], MSS 660, Box 31, Folder 1.

40 Odile to Francis, 3 November 1947, MSS 660, Box 2, Folder 25.

41 Crick, Diary, 1946, MSS 660, Box 14, Folder 1. Only the first eight months of 1946 have this level of detail. There are no diaries for 1947 or 1948.

42 Crick, Diary, 1946, MSS 660, Box 14, Folder 1.

43 Crick to Himsworth, 15 June 1953, PP/CRI/A/2/1.

44 Dougall (1973), p. 162. In 1948 Crick's friend Raoul Colinvaux joked that

Francis needed to find a new atomic bomb before the Russians. Colinvaux to Crick, 1 March 1948, MSS 660, Box 2, Folder 5.

45 Crick (1988), p. 14.

46 Crick (1988), pp. 17–8.

47 Kreisel to Crick, 3 January 1989, MSS 660, Box 5, Folder 5. Dougall (1973), p. 163. Crick to Schrödinger, 12 August 1953, SCH/M/44.

48 Crick, Comments on 'Reservations on Project K', undated [1975], PP/CRI/D/1/2/12.

49 Pauling, L. (1946), Modern structural chemistry. *Chemical and Engineering News* 24:1788–9.

50 Crick (1988), p. 18.

51 Crick (1988), p. 17.

52 Kreisel to Crick, 3 January 1989, MSS 660, Box 5, Folder 5.

53 Dyson, F. (2007), *A Many-Colored Glass: Reflections on the Place of Life in the Universe* (Charlottesville, VA: University of Virginia Press), pp. 58–9.

54 Crick to Hill, 1 May 1947, AVHL II/4/18.

55 Crick to Hill, 2 July [1947], AVHL II/4/18. Crick later recalled that he found the Cambridge physiologist concerned, Hamilton Hartridge, 'a little too bouncy'. Crick (1988), pp. 18–9.

56 Wilkins, M. (2003), *The Third Man of the Double Helix: An Autobiography* (Oxford: Oxford University Press), p. 109.

57 Mellanby, MRC memo, 7 July 1947, FD 21/13. Hill to Crick, 4 July 1947, AVHL II/4/18.

58 Crick, Application for MRC studentship, undated [July 1947], FD 21/13.

59 Crick to Hill, 2 July [1947], AVHL II/4/18.

60 Crick (1988), p. 21.

61 Crick to Hill, 31 July 1947, AVHL II/4/18. MRC to Crick, 3 August 1948, PP/CRI/A/2/1.

62 Fell to Mellanby, 14 August 1947, FD 21/13.

63 Crick kept the tenancy of the St George's flat and sub-let it for a while, producing a small additional income that, together with financial help from his family, enabled him to buy books. Crick (1988), p. 22. Olby (2009), p. 72.

CHAPTER 2

1 Anonymous (n.d.), *History of the Strangeways Research Laboratory (formerly Cambridge Research Hospital) 1912–1962* (n.p.).

2 Collingwood to Crick, 1 September 1947, MSS 660, Box 2, Folder 6.

3 Collingwood to Crick, 9 September 1947, MSS 660, Box 2, Folder 6.

4 Kreisel to Crick, 10 December 1950, MSS 660, Box 5, Folder 3. Crick to Hubel, 2 March 1994, PP/CRI/J/2/14/1.

5 Crick, Interim Note, undated [1949], PP/CRI/A/2/1.

6 Odile to Francis, 3 November 1947, MSS 660, Box 2, Folder 25.

7 Fell to Herrald, 12 July 1948, FD 21/13.

8 Crick interview with Olby, 8 March 1968, PP/CRI/H/4/13.

9 Crick to Hardy Fallding, 22 August 1989, PP/CRI/J/2/9/2.

10 Crick, F. H. C. and Hughes, A. F. W. (1950), The physical properties of

cytoplasm. A study by means of the magnetic particle method. Part I. Experimental. *Experimental Cell Research* 1:37–80, p. 73.

11 Crick, F. H. C. (1950), The physical properties of cytoplasm. A study by means of the magnetic particle method. Part II. Theoretical treatment. *Experimental Cell Research* 1:505–33.

12 PP/CRI/M/1/1.

13 Fell to Mellanby, 14 August 1947, FD 21/13. Crick interview with Olby, 8 March 1968, PP/CRI/H/4/13.

14 Crick interview with Olby, 8 March 1968, PP/CRI/H/4/13.

15 PP/FGS/C/29.

16 Crick interview with Olby, 8 March 1968, PP/CRI/H/4/13. Crick, F. (1988), *What Mad Pursuit: A Personal View of Scientific Discovery* (New York: Basic), p. 22. In his 1968 interview, Crick told Olby, 'I remember pointing out that radiation did reduce the viscosity in a very strange way suggesting the molecules were long or something,' Five years later, he recalled 'I am fairly sure that the whole theme of the lecture was that the central problem of biology was to explain how genes replicated and how they acted and to point out that the main thing they were likely to do was to control the synthesis of proteins, in particular their amino acid sequences. Unfortunately I have no documents to support this recollection.' Crick to Olby, Detailed remarks, undated [April 1973], PP/CRI/H/4/13.

17 André Boivin claimed to have extended Avery's finding to *E. coli*, but this could not be replicated. Cobb, M. (2015), *Life's Greatest Secret: The Race to Crack the Genetic Code* (London: Profile).

18 Crick interview with Olby, 8 March 1968, PP/CRI/H/4/13.

19 Crick interview with Olby, 8 March 1968, PP/CRI/H/4/13.

20 Crick, Interim Note, undated [1949], PP/CRI/A/2/1.

21 When the head of the MRC, Sir Edward Mellanby, interviewed Crick, he asked him about Perutz's proposed unit. As Crick recalled, 'At that point I think he said he had on his desk the application to support a possible MRC unit under Max Perutz. And he slightly horrified me by saying do you think we should support these foreigners? I said of course you should support him. I was surprised he should ask my advice.' Crick interview with Georgina Ferry, 3 June 2004, with the interviewer's permission. See also Ferry, G. (2007), *Max Perutz and the Secret of Life* (London: Chatto & Windus), p. 135. Crick suggests this meeting occurred after he had been working at the Strangeways for some time, but the MRC Unit was created before he joined Strangeways; this incident presumably occurred when Crick met Mellanby in the middle of 1947.

22 Ferry (2007).

23 Gutfreund interview with Georgina Ferry, 25 June 2004, with the interviewer's permission.

24 Crick interview with Georgina Ferry, 3 June 2004, with the interviewer's permission.

25 Holmes, K. C. (2001), Sir John Cowdery Kendrew, 24 March 1917 – 23 August 1997. *Biographical Memoirs of Fellows of the Royal Society of London*

47:311–32. Wassarman, P. M. (2020), *A Place in History: The Biography of John C. Kendrew* (Oxford: Oxford University Press).

26 Odile to Francis, 24 September 1947 and 4 February 1948, MSS 660, Box 2, Folder 25.

27 Odile to Francis, 16 September 1947, MSS 660, Box 2, Folder 25.

28 Odile to Francis, 5 January 1948 and 28 April 1948, MSS 660, Box 2, Folder 25.

29 Odile to Francis, 22 October 1947 and 21 July 1948, MSS 660, Box 2, Folder 25.

30 Crick, Diary, 1949, entry for 27 April, MSS 660, Box 14, Folder 2.

31 Crick interview with Olby, 8 March 1968, PP/CRI/H/4/13. Odile to Francis, 7 April 1948, MSS 660, Box 2, Folder 25.

32 Crick interview with Olby, 8 March 1968, PP/CRI/H/4/13.

33 Odile to Francis, 21 December 1948, MSS 660, Box 2, Folder 25.

34 Odile to Francis, 20 May 1949, MSS 660, Box 2, Folder 25.

35 Odile to Francis, 18 February 1948, MSS 660, Box 2, Folder 25.

36 Crick, Early memories, undated, MSS 660, Box 31, Folder 14. Obituary of Harry Crick, *Northampton Independent*, 8 February 1948.

37 Odile to Francis, 2 February 1948, MSS 660, Box 2, Folder 25. Wilkins to Crick, 3 February 1948, PP/CRI/H/1/42/4.

38 Odile to Francis, 21 December 1948, MSS 660, Box 2, Folder 25.

39 On 12 February 1949, Crick noted in his diary: 'To Kings Lynn. Muddle about trains. Met Mr and Mrs Speed'. Crick, Diary, 1949, entry for 12 February, MSS 660, Box 14, Folder 2. Interview with Gabrielle Crick, December 2022.

40 Annie Crick to Francis Crick, undated, MSS 660, Box 2, Folder 12.

41 All quotes from undated letters to Crick, MSS 660, Box 4.

42 Odile to Francis, 18 February 1948, 5 November [1947] and 2 September 1948, MSS 660, Box 2, Folder 25.

43 Odile to Francis, 11 May 1948, MSS 660, Box 2, Folder 25.

44 For example, Odile to Francis, 9 July 1948, MSS 660, Box 2, Folder 25.

45 Odile to Francis, 24 July 1948, MSS 660, Box 2, Folder 25.

46 Odile to Francis, 11 January 1949, MSS 660, Box 2, Folder 25.

47 The meeting with Perutz and Bragg was on 25 February: Crick, Diary, 1949, entry for 25 February, MSS 660, Box 14, Folder 2. On 22 February Crick wrote to Mellanby requesting a meeting, which took place on 28 February. MRC to Crick, 23 February 1949, PP/CRI/A/2/1.

48 Crick to Hill, 7 March 1949, AVHL II/4/18.

49 Hill to Crick, 11 March 1949, PP/CRI/A/2/1.

50 Crick, Diary, 1949, entry for 25 February, MSS 660, Box 14, Folder 2.

51 Bragg to Mellanby (extract), 21 March 1949, FD 21/13.

52 Perutz to Landsborough Thomson, 22 March 1949, FD 21/13.

53 MRC to Crick, 13 April 1950 and 9 June 1951, PP/CRI/A/2/1. By June 1951, Crick was earning £830 per annum. Even with tax and deductions, this was a substantial increase on his £400 untaxed studentship.

54 Odile to Francis, 15 March 1949, 24 April 1949 and 5 May [1949], MSS 660, Box 2, Folder 25.

55 Odile to Francis, undated [August 1949], MSS 660, Box 2, Folder 25.

56 Odile to Francis, 27 May 1949, MSS 660, Box 2, Folder 25.
57 Odile to Francis, [early June 1949], MSS 660, Box 2, Folder 25.
58 Odile to Francis, Wednesday [July 1949], MSS 660, Box 3, Folder 2.
59 Odile to Francis, Thursday [30 June 1949], MSS 660, Box 2, Folder 25.
60 Odile to Francis, 26 August 1949, MSS 660, Box 2, Folder 25.
61 Odile to Francis, undated [early August 1949], MSS 660, Box 3, Folder 2.
62 Odile to Francis, 26 August 1949 [sic], MSS 660, Box 2, Folder 25. This is misdated as it was clearly written before their wedding.
63 Crick (1988), p. 44.
64 Correspondence with Egon and Eshag, MSS 660, Box 3, Folder 22 and Folder 26.
65 Crick, Interim Note, undated [1949], PP/CRI/A/2/1.
66 Crick notebooks, 1949–1951, PP/CRI/G/1/2, PP/CRI/G/1/3, PP/CRI/G/1/4 and PP/CRI/G/1/5.
67 Crick (1988), p. 45.
68 In July 1949, Peterhouse – Perutz's and Kendrew's college – turned down Crick's application, saying 'we do not see our way to admitting you'. Tutor of Peterhouse to Crick, 30 July 1949, MSS 660, Box 12, Folder 14.
69 Bragg, L., Kendrew, J. and Perutz, M. (1950), Polypeptide chain configurations in crystalline proteins. *Proceedings of the Royal Society A* 203:321–57.
70 Pauling, L., Carey, R. and Branson, H. (1951), The structure of proteins: two hydrogen-bonded helical configurations of the polypeptide chain. *Proceedings of the National Academy of Sciences USA* 37:205–11.
71 Crick (1988), p. 58. Ferry (2007), p. 145.
72 Crick, W. L. Bragg: a few personal recollections, undated [1990], PP/CRI/J/2/10/1.
73 Crick (1988), p. 49.
74 Ferry (2007), p. 148.
75 Olby (2009), pp. 108–11.
76 Crick interview with Georgina Ferry, 3 June 2004, with the interviewer's permission.
77 Crick (1988), p. 50.
78 Francis to Odile, Friday [10 August 1951], MSS 660, Box 22, Folder 21.
79 Interviews with Michael Crick (May 2022) and Gabrielle Crick (December 2022). At the memorial meeting held at the Salk Institute after his death, Jacqueline said that he was 'not a hands-on, bedtime-story, teach-you-to-ride-a-bike kind of Dad'. *Remembering Francis Crick*, undated [September 2004], SB/10/56.
80 Kreisel to Crick, 24 September 1951, MSS 660, Box 5, Folder 3.
81 Bragg to Watson, undated [1967], JDW/2/2/215.

CHAPTER 3

1 Watson, J. (2012), *The Annotated and Illustrated Double Helix*, edited by A. Gann and J. Witkowski (London: Simon and Schuster), pp. 27, 29.
2 Hall, K. (2014), *The Man in the Monkeynut Coat: William Astbury and the Forgotten Road to the Double-Helix* (Oxford: Oxford University Press).

3 Crick, F. (1988), *What Mad Pursuit: A Personal View of Scientific Discovery* (New York: Basic), p. 64.
4 Odile Crick interview with Olby, undated, OLBY, Box 3.
5 Crick (1988), p. 64.
6 Crick to Watson, 31 March 1966, PP/CRI/I/3/8/4. Crick interview with Olby, 8 March 1968, PP/CRI/H/4/13.
7 Gosling, Some recollections of DNA studies in the Biophysics Laboratories of King's College, undated [February 1976], K/PP178/5/24.
8 Astbury, W. and Bell, F. (1938), X-ray study of thymonucleic acid. *Nature* 141:747–8.
9 Olby, R. (1968), Before the double helix. *New Scientist*, 27 June 1968, pp. 679–81. Gosling, Some recollections of DNA studies in the Biophysics Laboratories of King's College, undated [February 1976], K/PP178/5/24. Stokes, A note on the history of the determination of the structure of DNA, undated [April 1976], K/PP178/5/24.
10 Jim Watson to Elizabeth Watson, 9 October 1951, JDW/2/2/1934.
11 Crick, notebook, 1951–1952, PP/CRI/G/1/5.
12 Wilkins to Olby, May 1986, K/PP178/5/8.
13 Jim Watson to Elizabeth Watson, 9 October 1951, JDW/2/2/1934.
14 Crick interview with Olby, 8 March 1968, PP/CRI/H/4/13.
15 Bragg to Watson, undated [1967], JDW/2/2/215. In *The Double Helix* Watson describes Crick as furious, accusing Bragg of plagiarising his work. Following protests by both Crick and Bragg on reading early drafts of the book, Watson altered his account, but only to include the version given here as well as his previous description, thereby making two events out of one.
16 Solcova, A. and Krizek, M. (2011), Vladimír Vand (1911–1968): Pioneer of computational methods in crystallography. *IEEE Annals of the History of Computing* 33:38–44.
17 Crick interview with Olby, 8 March 1968, PP/CRI/H/4/13. Cochran, W. (1987), Citation classic. *Current Contents* 18 May 1987, p. 16. Olby, R. (2009), *Francis Crick: Hunter of Life's Secrets* (Cold Spring Harbor, NY: Cold Spring Harbor Laboratory Press), p. 116.
18 Crick to Watson, 31 March 1966, PP/CRI/I/3/8.
19 Crick to Olby, 20 August 1968, PP/CRI/D/2/29. Crick, Tasting notes, 31 October 1951, PP/CRI/D/2/29.
20 Crick interview with Olby, 8 March 1968, PP/CRI/H/4/13.
21 Crick to Galloway, 9 October 1985, PP/CRI/J/2/5/3.
22 Bragg to Watson, undated [1967?], JDW/2/2/215.
23 According to Cochran (1987) he had already taken these photographs and put them to one side. The text of Cochran and Crick (1952) (see next note) and the acknowledgements suggests that the version given here, which follows that of Olby (2009), is correct.
24 Cochran, W. and Crick, F. (1952), Evidence for the Pauling-Corey α-helix in synthetic polypeptides. *Nature* 169:234–5.
25 Cochran (1987).
26 Olby (2009), pp. 118–9. Olby gives no source for this diary entry.

27   Crick, The height of the intermolecular vector peaks in protein Pattersons, October 1951, PP/CRI/H/1/6.
28   Stokes, A note on the history of the determination of the structure of DNA, undated [April 1976], K/PP178/5/24.
29   Crick to Watson, 31 March 1966, PP/CRI/I/3/8/4.
30   Maddox, B. (2002), *Rosalind Franklin: The Dark Lady of DNA* (London: Harper Collins).
31   Franklin to Randall, 19 December 1950, OLBY, Box 17. This is a photocopy of the original, the location of which is unknown. This letter has never been quoted or reproduced. This copy was sent to Olby by Randall on 27 August 1968 (GBR/0014/RNDL 3/1/6), but neither the original nor a copy is to be found in Randall's archives, which contain a frustrated note by Randall from December 1983, recording the absence of the originals: 'IMPORTANT PAPERS – COPIES ONLY. (…) I do not know who has the originals. Possibly Dr. Olby.'
32   Franklin to Sayre, 1 March 1952, ASMB.
33   Watson (2012), pp. 63–4.
34   Olby (2009), p. 131. Crick's appointments diary for 1951 is missing.
35   This account is based on Watson's version in *The Double Helix*. See also Markel, H. (2021), *The Secret of Life: Rosalind Franklin, James Watson, Francis Crick, and the Discovery of DNA's Double Helix* (London: Norton), pp. 208–9.
36   Crick mentioned this in his notes for a 1961 lecture, 'The Gene: History of the DNA Model', given in Cambridge (January), then in Oxford (May). Crick, Diary, 1960–61, MSS 660, Box 14, Folder 12. Crick, The discovery of the structure of DNA – lecture notes, undated [1961], PP/CRI/H/1/42/2. These notes are written on Harvard University notepaper, but there is no record of such a lecture during his time at Harvard, suggesting he simply used some headed notepaper he had brought back with him (many of his lecture notes at this time were written on odd bits of headed notepaper, or even shop receipts – see PP/CRI/H/2/25). Details of the series of Oxford lectures on Case Studies in Biological Discovery organised by A. C. Crombie can be found in PP/CRI/E/1/9/4. When he agreed to do the talk, Crick wrote: 'I detect in the end of your letter that a manuscript might be required. This I cannot agree to do.' Crick to Crombie, 11 February 1961, PP/CRI/E/1/9/4. In summer 1962, Watson established a detailed timeline of the events leading to the discovery of the double helix, but the MRC Report was not mentioned; it is passed over in half a sentence in *The Double Helix*. Watson, Summary of events leading to solution of DNA structure, August 1962, WFAT, Folder 14.
37   Watson (2012), p. 77.
38   Crick, notebook, 1951–1952, PP/CRI/G/1/5.
39   Crick, The discovery of the structure of DNA – lecture notes, undated [1961], PP/CRI/H/1/42/2.
40   Crick and Watson, The structure of sodium thymonucleate (draft), undated [December 1951], PP/CRI/H/1/42/1. Note the author order.
41   Crick interview with Olby, 8 March 1968, PP/CRI/H/4/13.
42   No date is given for this visit in *The Double Helix*. According to Wilkins, M. (2003), *The Third Man of the Double Helix: An Autobiography* (Oxford:

Oxford University Press), p. 171, it took place two weeks after Franklin's talk. On Tuesday 11 December, Wilkins wrote to Crick apologising for dashing off 'the previous Saturday', implying that the King's group went to Cambridge on Saturday 8 December, a little over two weeks after Franklin's talk, which is the timing I have adopted here.

43 Crick interview with Olby, 8 March 1968, PP/CRI/H/4/13.
44 Wilkins to Crick, 11 December 1951, SB/11/1/177.
45 Crick and Watson to Wilkins (draft), 13 December 1951, SB/11/1/177.
46 Watson (2012), p. 101.
47 Crick, notebook, 1951–4, PP/CRI/G/1/6.
48 Olby, Dating the DNA story, undated [April 1968], K/PP178/5/8.
49 Bragg to Hill, 18 January 1952, AVHL II/4/18.
50 All material from Olby (2009), p. 136.
51 Kreisel to Crick, 27 December 1951, MSS 660, Box 5, Folder 3.
52 Crick, notebook, 1951–1952, PP/CRI/G/1/5. Crick's 1952–1953 notebook is missing; there is a vacant shelfmark in the Wellcome collection – PP/CRI/G/1/7.
53 Wilkins to Crick, undated [early 1952], PP/CRI/H/1/42/4. Wilkins in fact wrote 'Sperm Squid'. The photograph was published a year later in Wilkins, M. and Randall, J. (1953), Crystallinity in sperm heads: Molecular structure of nucleoprotein in vivo. *Biochimica et Biophysica Acta* 10:192–3.
54 Wilkins to Olby, 28 May 1968, K/PP178/5/8.
55 Kreisel to Crick, 18 April 1951, PP/CRI/A/2/5.
56 Kreisel to Crick, 22 March 1952 and 2 April 1952, MSS 660, Box 5, Folder 3.
57 Crick to Olby, undated [1970?], PP/CRI/H/4/13.
58 The talk was intriguingly entitled 'What Happened to the Moon?' Del Squared V Club Minute book, 1951–1956, GBR/0265/UA/SOC.XXIX.1/5.
59 Crick interview with Olby, 18 March 1968, PP/CRI/H/4/13.
60 Olby, R. (1970), Francis Crick, DNA, and the central dogma. *Daedalus* 99:938–87.
61 The two men were slightly in awe of each other's intellectual ability, but this became evident only in 1970, when they were interviewed separately by Olby. Crick to Olby, 5 August 1970, PP/CRI/D/2/29.
62 Griffith to Crick, 11 November 1952, PP/CRI/H/1/42/8. Griffith to Crick, 2 March 1953, SB/11/1/49. Crick to Bates, 8 September 1997, PP/CRI/J/2/17/3.
63 Chargaff, E. (1978), *Heraclitean Fire: Sketches from a Life Before Nature* (New York: Rockefeller University Press), p. 100, gives the dates as 24–27 May 1952.
64 Judson, H. (1996), *The Eighth Day of Creation: Makers of the Revolution in Biology* (Plainview, NY: Cold Spring Harbor Laboratory Press), p. 119. Crick to Watson, 31 March 1966, PP/CRI/I/3/8/4.
65 Chargaff (1978), p. 101.
66 Chargaff (1978), p. 102.
67 Crick interview with Olby, 8 March 1968, PP/CRI/H/4/13. Crick's recollection was that Chargaff said '"Well of course there is the 1:1 ratios". So I said "What is that?", so he said, "Well it is all published!" Of course, I had never read the literature, so I would not know.'

68 Crick told Olby in 1970: 'I used to think that he [Chargaff] had bad luck in not realising that his rule suggested how DNA was replicated, but I have since come to believe that it was not bad luck but simply obtuseness on his part (not for publication!).' Crick to Olby, 21 December 1970, PP/CRI/D/2/29.

69 Crick interview with Olby, 8 March 1968, PP/CRI/H/4/13.

70 Crick to Watson, 31 March 1966, PP/CRI/I/3/8/4. Crick's notebook for this period is missing.

71 Wilkins to Crick, 21 August 1952, PP/CRI/D/2/29.

72 Maxwell to Randall, 1 July 1953; Randall to Maxwell, 3 July 1953; Maxwell to Randall, 21 July 1953, GBR/0014/RNDL 3/1/6. These are photocopies; the whereabouts of the originals are unknown.

73 Anonymous (1953), *Discussions of the Faraday Society 13: The Physical Chemistry of Proteins* (London: Faraday Society).

74 Judson (1996), p. 118.

75 Wilkins, M., Gosling, R. and Seeds, W. (1951), Nucleic acid: an extensible molecule? *Nature* 167:759–60.

76 Franklin, Notes for colloquium on molecular structure, undated [1951], FRKN/3/2.

77 K/PP178/5/24.

78 Stokes, A note on the history of the determination of the structure of DNA, undated [1976], K/PP178/5/24.

79 Judson (1996), p. 119.

80 Judson (1996), p. 118.

81 Judson (1996), p. 123.

82 Crick, F. (1952), Is α-keratin a coiled coil? *Nature* 170:882–3.

83 Pauling, L. and Corey, R. (1953), Compound helical configurations of polypeptide chains: structure of proteins of the α-keratin type. *Nature* 171:59–61. Hager, T. (1995), *Force of Nature: The Life of Linus Pauling* (New York: Simon and Schuster), pp. 413–6.

84 Crick interview with Olby, 8 March 1968, PP/CRI/H/4/13.

85 Crick, F. (1953), The unit cells of four proteins. *Acta Crystallographica* 6:221–2.

86 Interview with Michael Crick, May 2022. Crick to Boys Smith, draft letter, undated [May 1952], MSS 660, Box 12, Folder 14.

87 January to Crick, 2 July 1952, MSS 660, Box 3, Folder 16. MRC to Crick, 17 March 1952, PP/CRI/A/2/1. Crick to Miller, 21 February 1985, PP/CRI/J/2/5/1.

88 Crick to Harker, 21 January 1953, PP/CRI/D/1/1/8. Harker's letter confirming the arrangement was sent on 7 January 1953, putting Crick's acceptance at the end of 1952.

89 Crick to Wyckoff, 15 January 1953, PP/CRI/C/1/1.

90 Olby (2009), p. 202.

91 Kreisel to Crick, undated [1953], MSS 660, Box 6, Folder 7.

92 Watson (2012), p. 162.

CHAPTER 4

1   Interview with Michael Crick, May 2022. The letter has been widely
    reproduced, including on the internet, and in Olby, R. (2009), *Francis
    Crick: Hunter of Life's Secrets* (Cold Spring Harbor, NY: Cold Spring Harbor
    Laboratory Press).

2   This idea was first put forward in the late 1940s by the British chemist
    Masson Gulland, and by the French geneticist André Boivin (both of whom
    were dead by 1949, Gulland in a train accident, Boivin from cancer). Cobb,
    M. (2015), *Life's Greatest Secret: The Race to Crack the Genetic Code* (London:
    Profile).

3   Watson, J. (2012), *The Annotated and Illustrated Double Helix*, edited by A.
    Gann and J. Witkowski (London: Simon and Schuster).

4   Maddox, B. (2002), *Rosalind Franklin: The Dark Lady of DNA* (London:
    Harper Collins), p. 191.

5   Wilkins to Crick, 'Fri' [23 January 1953], SB/11/1/177. The identification of
    this date is by Gann, A. and Witkowski, J. (2010), The lost correspondence
    of Francis Crick. *Nature* 467:519–24.

6   Randall to Franklin, 17 April 1953; Franklin to Randall, 23 April 1953,
    GBR/0014/RNDL/3/1/6.

7   Pauling, L. and Corey, R. (1953), A proposed structure for the nucleic
    acids. *Proceedings of the National Academy of Sciences USA* 39:84–97. Crick
    to Watson, 31 March 1966, PP/CRI/I/3/8/4. Crick's 1961 lecture notes on
    the history of the discovery include the words 'Bragg upstairs'. Crick, The
    discovery of the structure of DNA, undated [1961], PP/CRI/H/1/42/2.

8   Watson (2012), p. 173, n. 4.

9   This MRC Biophysics Committee was set up in 1947, 'to establish contact
    between the different groups of people working for the Council in
    this field' – Letter from the Committee Secretary to Perutz, April 1954,
    reproduced in Perutz, M., Wilkins, M. H. F. and Watson, J. D. (1969), DNA
    helix. *Science* 164:1537–9, p. 1538.

10 Perutz et al. (1969).

11 Cowan to Crick, Mon 19 [January 1953], MSS 660, Box 2, Folder 11.

12 Crick to Klug, 6 May 2003, PP/CRI/J/1/8/11.

13 Fuller, W. (2003), Who said 'helix'? *Nature* 424:876–8. Gosling interview,
    Nature podcast, 20 April 2013. https://www.nature.com/articles/
    d41586-019-01347-8/

14 Maddox (2002), pp. 177–8.

15 Wilkins made clear to Watson when he showed him the photograph that
    he did not consider the helical nature of the B form to be an issue of major
    significance. Watson (2012), p. 183.

16 Kreisel to Crick, undated [14 June 1995], MSS 660, Box 6, Folder 1.

17 In 2013 Photograph 51 was the focus of a brilliant rap battle by seventh
    graders from Oakland, California. https://www.youtube.com/
    watch?v=35FwmiPE9tI

18 Crick to Hamilton, 6 December 1955. This was sold by Christie's in
    February 2023. Crick explained: 'I think you should realise that the
    X-ray data which Jim and I used was almost entirely Rosalind Franklin's
    measurements of the dimensions of the two forms, A and B and a very

rough idea of their intensity distributions.' Crick never referred to
Watson's description of the image. Crick, The discovery of the structure
of DNA – lecture notes, undated [1961], PP/CRI/H/1/42/2. Crick, Diary,
1960–1961, MSS 660, Box 14, Folder 12. In *The Double Helix*, Watson records
that as he returned to Cambridge that night he made a sketch of what he
could recall of the photograph on a newspaper, noting the key fact that the
height of each turn of the molecule was 34Å – he later claimed that Wilkins
had told him that each turn of the helix contained 10 bases. Whether any of
this is true is hard to know.

19 Wilkins to Crick, Thurs [5 February 1953], PP/CRI/H/1/42/4.
20 Wilkins, M. (2003), *The Third Man of the Double Helix: An Autobiography*
(Oxford: Oxford University Press), p. 203.
21 I stole this joke from Nathaniel Comfort, who used it in an early draft of
his account of this meal.
22 Randall to Franklin, 17 April 1953; Franklin to Randall, 23 April 1953,
GBR/0014/RNDL/3/1/6.
23 Crick interview with Olby, 8 March 1968, PP/CRI/H/4/13.
24 Crick, F. (1953a), The Fourier transform of a coiled-coil. *Acta
Crystallographica* 6:685–9. Crick, F. (1953b), The packing of α-helices: simple
coiled-coils. *Acta Crystallographica* 6:689–97. The first paper thanked Kreisel
'for a number of interesting discussions and in particular for suggesting
the use of Parseval's theorem at a crucial point' (p. 689).
25 Odile Crick interview with Olby, undated, OLBY, Box 28. In *The Double
Helix*, Watson describes going to see *Ecstasy*, a censored version of a racy
1933 film starring Hedy Lamarr, during this period. Olby discovered
when the film was shown in Cambridge and tried to calibrate this with
Watson's account but was unable to do so. As he wrote to Crick: 'All this,
I know, seems trivial, but it does give me grounds for treating Watson's
account with considerable caution.' Olby to Crick, 21 October 1969, PP/
CRI/D/2/29.
26 Kreisel to Crick, 4 March 1953, MSS 660, Box 5, Folder 3.
27 Crick, F. and Watson, J. (1954), The complementary structure of
deoxyribonucleic acid. *Proceedings of the Royal Society of London A* 223:80–96.
28 Crick to Watson, 13 April 1967, PP/CRI/I/3/8/4.
29 It became public knowledge shortly after the Nobel Prize, when the
Cambridge News headlined 'Nobel theory was discussed in "pub"'.
Cambridge News, 19 October 1962, SB/9/1/18.
30 Bains to Crick, 19 April 1965; Crick to Bains, 14 May 1965, SB/11/7.
31 Astbury, W. and Bell, F. (1938), X-ray study of thymonucleic acid. *Nature*
141:747–8.
32 Judson, H. F. (1996), *The Eighth Day of Creation: Makers of the Revolution in
Biology. Expanded Edition* (Plainview, NY: Cold Spring Harbor Laboratory
Press), p. 137.
33 Crick interview with Olby, 8 March 1968, PP/CRI/H/4/13.
34 Crick interview with Olby, 8 March 1968, PP/CRI/H/4/13. Crick to
Casement, 23 January 1981, PP/CRI/D/1/4/3.
35 Crick to Bretscher, 13 May 2003, GBR/0014/BRTS 42/73. Bretscher, M. and

Mitchison, G. (2017), Francis Harry Compton Crick OM: 8 June 1918 – 28 July 2004. *Biographical Memoirs of Fellows of the Royal Society* 63:159–96.

36 Crick interview with Olby, 8 March 1968, PP/CRI/H/4/13.

37 Judson, H. (1996), p. 143.

38 As Crick said, 'The reason for that, there is no doubt in my mind at all, was the failure of Bragg, Kendrew and Perutz on the alpha helix.' Crick interview with Olby, 8 March 1968, PP/CRI/H/4/13.

39 Crick to Olby, undated [1973], PP/CRI/H/4/13.

40 Crick interview with Olby, 8 March 1968, PP/CRI/H/4/13.

41 Olby (2009), p. 165.

42 Watson (2012), p. 207.

43 Notes on Current Research prepared for the visit of the Biophysics Research Committee, 15 December 1952, K/PP178/2/22.

44 Crick to Elkin, 22 December 1999, PP/CRI/J/2/19/2. Crick to Maddox, 3 March 2000, PP/CRI/J/2/20/1. Crick interview with Olby, 8 March 1968, PP/CRI/H/4/13.

45 Crick interview with Olby, 8 March 1968, PP/CRI/H/4/13. Aaron Klug pointed out to Watson: 'Only Francis would have known the meaning of the space group C2 at the time. I think this is of genuine scientific interest.' Klug to Watson, 9 December 1966, PP/CRI/I/3/8/4.

46 Franklin, Notes for Colloquium on Molecular Structure, undated [1951], FRKN/3/2. Klug, A. (2004), The discovery of the DNA double helix. *Journal of Molecular Biology* 335:3–26. In 1969 Watson argued: 'The relevant fact is not that I *could have* copied down Rosalind's seminar data on the unit cell dimensions and symmetry, but that I *did not.*' Perutz et al. (1969), p. 1539.

47 When Crick saw a draft of Franklin's second *Nature* paper at the end of May (she had sent it to Watson), he wrote to her raising the issue of the space group, questioning whether her evidence actually justified the description and highlighting the significance of her claim – 'The point is important because if the unit cell is strictly C2 one must have the DNA chains in pairs, running in opposite directions.' Crick to Franklin, 5 June 1953, PP/CRI/I/3/5. There is no record of any reply, but a similar formulation appears in her article: Franklin, R. and Gosling, R. (1953b), Evidence for 2-chain helix in crystalline structure of sodium deoxyribonucleate. *Nature* 172:156–7.

48 Judson (1996), p. 95.

49 Crick, F. (1988), *What Mad Pursuit: A Personal View of Scientific Discovery* (New York: Basic), p. 65.

50 Watson (2012), p. 209.

51 https://whyevolutionistrue.com/2016/06/08/happy-100th-birthday-francis-crick-1916–2004. Kindra Crick recalled a conversation with Watson in 2013: 'Memorable scenes such as them winging it into the Eagle pub and Crick announcing, "We have discovered the secret of life!" are fiction. But, as I was later told by Watson, this narrative captured the spirit of the moment in the pub that day. If you truly understand what they saw in those paired bases, you can understand the sense of awe they must

have felt – that is, if they were right.' http://www.kindracrick.com/
my-grandad-francis-crick.html

52 Watson to Delbrück, 12 March 1953, Delbrück papers, Box 23, Folder 22.
Crick interview with Olby, 8 March 1968, PP/CRI/H/4/13.

53 Olby (2009), p. 169. 'I did in fact check all the distances and alter the
coordinates a little if there was one distance a bit too short or too long. But
being a bit lazy and not having at my fingertips the formula for an angle
between three points, I never checked the angles. So you will find that the
distances are pretty good, but some of the angles are really a bit off. This
was simply laziness on my part in not checking them.' Crick interview
with Olby, 8 March 1968, PP/CRI/H/4/13.

54 Crick to Watson, 31 March 1966, PP/CRI/I/3/8/4.

55 Crick interview with Olby, 8 March 1968, PP/CRI/H/4/13. 'I worked
out a theorem which now escapes me which expressed the geometrical
restraint of the other base on this one. I knew that as long as I obeyed this
geometrical rule – some projection of something on something else – one
could do it. So all the model building was done on a sugar, a phosphate
and a base and just the first atom of the next sugar, which you had to place
in the right position.'

56 Crick interview with Olby, 8 March 1968, PP/CRI/H/4/13. Todd later
wrote that he instantly recognised that the model was essentially correct
– his own research had suggested that hydrogen bonds existed in the
DNA molecule, and that the bases were flat, perpendicular to the sugar-
phosphate chains. Todd, A. (1983), *A Time to Remember: The Autobiography of
a Chemist* (Cambridge: Cambridge University Press), p. 89. After Pauling's
publication of the α-helix, Todd recalled he told Bragg that 'any competent
organic chemist' would have come up with the correct structure, given
the crystallographic evidence. Mortified, Bragg insisted that all structures
coming from the Cavendish henceforth had to meet with Todd's approval
before being submitted for publication. A more obvious solution to solving
the structure of DNA would have been to collaborate with Todd, whose
research focused on the chemistry of nucleic acids and for which he would
be awarded the Nobel Prize in 1957. That does not appear to have been an
option, for reasons that seem to have their root in the arcane departmental
politics of Cambridge at the time. Todd, like Bragg, established his career
while at the University of Manchester.

57 Wilkins to Crick, 'Sat' [7 March], PP/CRI/H/1/42/4.

58 Judson (1996), p. 151.

59 Crick, F. (1979), How to live with a golden helix. *The Sciences*, September
1979, pp. 6–9, p. 9.

60 Crick (1988).

61 Klug (1968), Rosalind Franklin and the discovery of the structure of DNA.
Nature 219:808–10. Klug (2004). Maddox (2002).

62 Maddox (2002), pp. 201–2. Klug (1968, 2004).

63 Ferry G. (1998), *Dorothy Hodgkin: A Life* (London: Granta), pp. 275–6.

64 Klug (2004).

65 Watson (2012). In a 1979 letter to Crick marked 'NOT FOR
PUBLICATION', Aaron Klug wrote that Franklin 'lacked the imagination

to recognise the truth of what you had been telling her, and, moreover, stuck to the safer, analytical approach'. Klug to Crick, 9 October 1979, PP/CRI/D/2/19.

66 Crick (1979).

67 Maddox (2002), p. 202.

68 'She had no collaborator to help pull her out of the groove she had dug, but it is clear that by early 1953 she had already begun to do so by her own efforts'. Klug to Crick, 9 October 1979, PP/CRI/D/2/19.

69 Crick, Diary, 1960–61, entries for 24 January and 25 May 1961, MSS 660, Box 14, Folder 12.

70 Crick, The discovery of the structure of DNA – lecture notes, undated [1961], PP/CRI/H/1/42/2.

CHAPTER 5

1 Crick, A structure for D.N.A., undated [March 1953], MSS 660, Box 26, Folder 5. This is the earliest version of the article. There are six subsequent undated typescripts, many with corrections by Crick, at PP/CRI/H/1/11.

2 'In point of fact we agreed that his name should go first on the first Nature letter (as I was working on haemoglobin at the time the work was done), and my name first on the fuller paper, which is yet to come. We tossed for the second Nature letter – which he won. The Cold Spring Harbor paper he was asked to give, so we put him first.' Crick to Hamilton, 20 June 1953; archived at: http://tinyurl.com/FC-LH-20-Jun-1953. This was sold by Christie's in February 2023.

3 Watson, Summary of events leading to solution of DNA structure, August 1962, WFAT, Folder 14. Kendrew's involvement is described in Wilkins, M. (2003), *The Third Man of the Double Helix: An Autobiography* (Oxford: Oxford University Press). Crick noted in his appointment diary for 17 April 1953 'Rosy and Raymond' and for 20 April 1953 'p.m. Randall', MSS 660, Box 14, Folder 3. I assume this latter date referred to Randall's visit to see the structure, but it could have been a meeting in London.

4 Wilkins (2003), p. 214.

5 Wilkins, DNA history, 21 January 1985, K/PP178/5/27/1.

6 Watson was working with Boris and Harriet Ephrussi on a bacterial project.

7 Crick, Diary, 1953, entry for 14 March, MSS 660, Box 14, Folder 3. This looks like a later addition and Crick suggested as much forty-five years later – Crick to de Chadarevian, 5 January 1998, PP/CRI/J/2/18/1.

8 Crick to Watson, 31 March 1966, PP/CRI/I/3/8/4.

9 Crick to Trotter, 18 March 1953, M2286_3627.

10 Wilkins to Crick, 13 March 1953, PP/CRI/H/1/42/4. This draft was apparently the second typescript version in the Wellcome archive – PP/CRI/H/1/11/2. On the verso of the final page are a series of pencilled comments, dated 18 March, apparently from a member of Wilkins' group: 'We should easily beat the Cambridge boys to the press with the cooperation of the Professor!' 'Professor' referred to Randall.

11 Maddox, B. (2002), *Rosalind Franklin: The Dark Lady of DNA* (London: Harper Collins), p. 209.

12 Wilkins to Crick, 13 March 1953, PP/CRI/D/2/29. Wilkins to Crick, Mon [March 1953], SB/11/1/177.
13 Crick, DNA, undated [1953], PP/CRI/H/1/16.
14 Wilkins to Crick, Mon [March 1953], SB/11/1/177. Wilkins to Crick, Thurs [March 1953], PP/CRI/D/2/29. According to this card 'there was a frantic chaos at the last moment – no typists for typing (Pauline helped us out) & two missing figures which after a long search turned up in Randall's bag & in Rosie's room.' 'Pauline' was Pauline Cowan. Remaining material in this paragraph from Gann, A. and Witkowski, J. (2010), The lost correspondence of Francis Crick. *Nature* 467:519–24.
15 Wilkins to Crick, undated [March 1953], PP/CRI/H/1/42/4.
16 Crick, draft letter to Wilkins, undated [March 1953], OLBY, Box 3. This letter is a photocopy of a draft, with no indication of where Olby obtained it or where the original is. Olby quoted extensively from this letter – Olby, R. (2009), *Francis Crick: Hunter of Life's Secrets* (Cold Spring Harbor, NY: Cold Spring Harbor Laboratory Press), pp. 190–1. The letter was clearly sent, for Wilkins replied to the points within it: Wilkins to Crick, 'Mon' [23 March 1953], SB/11/1/177. The date is supplied by Gann and Witkowski (2010), who also quote large extracts from this letter.
17 There is no mention of such a meeting in Crick's appointment diary, in any contemporary account or in any of the memoirs of those involved. Nevertheless, Olby assumes that it did take place, although Franklin may not have been there. Olby (2009), p. 191. In 1999, following questioning by Franklin's biographer, Brenda Maddox, Crick wrote, surprisingly, 'until now it had never occurred to me to ask myself whether Randall was very upset that Jim and I put forward the double helix.' Crick to Brenda Maddox, 11 May 1999, PP/CRI/J/1/6/12/1.
18 Wilkins to Crick, 'Mon' [23 March 1953], SB/11/1/177. The date is supplied by Gann and Witkowski (2010).
19 Wilkins to Hamilton, 19–20 March 1953, K/PP178/3/14/1.
20 Randall, J. T. and Jackson, S. F. (eds.), (1953), *Nature and Structure of Collagen* (London: Butterworths Scientific Publications), p. 249.
21 Holmes, K. C. (2004), Driven to diffraction. *Nature* 431:1037–8.
22 Crick to Wilkins, undated [late March 1953], SB/11/1/177.
23 The submission date of 2 April is given on each paper. There is no letter from Bragg in his archive referring to the submission of this first paper. However, there is a letter referring to the second *Nature* paper: Bragg to Gale, 8 May 1953, W.L. BRAGG/42A/68. The *Nature* archive for this period was destroyed during an over-enthusiastic office clear-out in the 1960s.
24 Watson, J. D. and Crick, F. H. C. (1953a), A structure for deoxyribose nucleic acid. *Nature* 171:737–8. Wilkins, M. H. F., Stokes, A. R. and Wilson, H. R. (1953), Molecular structure of deoxypentose nucleic acids. *Nature* 171:738–40. Franklin, R. E. and Gosling, R. (1953a), Molecular configuration in sodium thymonucleate. *Nature* 171:740–1. The collective heading is often mistakenly included as part of the title of Watson and Crick's paper (including on the Nature website!). Note that each article referred to DNA in a different way. The four to five month publication delay for

Nature papers at this time is given in Gale to Bragg, 4 April 1952, W.L. BRAGG/42A/29.

25 Crick, F. (1974), The double helix: a personal view. *Nature* 248:766–9.

26 Crick, The double helix: a personal view [draft], [January 1974], PP/CRI/H/5/10.

27 Crick (1974). The opening sentence of the Wilkins paper pointed out that 'the biological properties of deoxypentose nucleic acid suggest a molecular structure of great complexity' but went no further – the uninitiated reader would have no idea what those properties might be. There was no mention of function in Franklin and Gosling's paper.

28 Kreisel to Crick, 23 April 1954 and 15 May 1954, MSS 660, Box 5, Folder 3.

29 Kreisel to Crick, 30 April 1953, MSS 660, Box 5, Folder 3.

30 Watson, J. D. (2001), *Genes, Girls and Gamow* (Oxford: Oxford University Press). Olby (2009), p. 181.

31 Hager, T. (1995), *Force of Nature: The Life of Linus Pauling* (New York: Simon and Schuster), p. 428.

32 Watson and Crick, The stereochemical structure of DNA, undated [April 1953], WFAT, Folder 17.

33 Delbrück to Weaver [with note to Pauling], 17 April 1953, LP Science, Box 9.001, Folder 1.39.

34 Pauling to Delbrück, 20 April 1953, LP Science, Box 9.001, Folder 1.39.

35 Watson (2001).

36 Watson to Delbrück, 21 May 1953, Delbrück papers, Box 23, Folder 22. Olby, R. (1994), *The Path to the Double Helix* (New York: Dover), p. 421.

37 Bragg to Gale, 8 May 1953, W.L. BRAGG/42A/68. Crick, Diary, 1953, entry for 8 May, MSS 660, Box 14, Folder 3. This looks like a later addition and Crick suggested as much forty-five years later: Crick to de Chadarevian, 5 January 1998, PP/CRI/J/2/18/1. According to Watson, Bragg was frightfully keen about the structure and its implications 'and insists on talking about it everywhere'. Watson to Delbrück, 21 May 1953, Delbrück papers, Box 23, Folder 22. The co-editor of *Nature* thanked Bragg for indicating on his submission letters when he thought a paper required rapid publication. Gale to Bragg, 4 April 1952, W.L. BRAGG/42A/29.

38 Crick to Hamilton, 20 June 1953; this was sold by Christie's in February 2023. Olby, R. (1970), Francis Crick, DNA, and the central dogma. *Daedalus* 99:938–87.

39 Watson, J. D. and Crick, F. H. C. (1953b), Genetical implications of the structure of deoxyribonucleic acid. *Nature* 171:964–7, p. 965. This article used a fourth term for DNA, the one we are now familiar with.

40 Cobb, M. (2013), 1953: When genes became 'information'. *Cell* 153:503–6.

41 For more on 'information', see Cobb (2013) and Cobb, M. (2015), *Life's Greatest Secret: The Race to Crack the Genetic Code* (London: Profile).

42 The lectures, by zoologist J. Z. Young, were published in *The Listener* each week, beginning on 2 November 1950.

43 Jacob, F. (1988), *The Statue Within: An Autobiography* (London: Unwin Hyman), p. 269. Watson to Delbrück, 21 May 1953, Delbrück papers, Box 23, Folder 22.

44 Wilkins (2003), p. 224.

45 The pair initially considered including Wilkins' photographs of bacteriophage DNA and making him a co-author. Watson to Delbrück, 21 May 1953, Delbrück papers, Box 23, Folder 22.

46 Watson, J. D. and Crick, F. H. C. (1953c), The structure of DNA. *Cold Spring Harbor Symposia on Quantitative Biology* 18:123–31.

47 Watson (2001), p. 19.

48 Jacob (1988), p. 271.

49 Bragg to Martin, 21 August 1953, W.L. BRAGG/42A/72. Within a month of submission, the article was subject to the lightest of light touch reviews by Dorothy Hodgkin. Hodgkin, Referee's report, 14 September 1953, RR/79/230.

50 Franklin, R. E. F. and Gosling, R. G. (1953b), Evidence for 2-chain helix in crystalline structure of sodium deoxyribonucleate. *Nature* 172:156–7. According to Klug, C2 symmetry is not mentioned in the Crick and Watson 1954 article because 'there would have been some embarrassment about mentioning the source of their knowledge of the C2 symmetry' – Klug, A. (2004), The discovery of the DNA double helix. *Journal of Molecular Biology* 335:3–26, p. 19. However, Klug (like all subsequent historians) did not notice that the 1954 Crick and Watson article contains a clear reference to their use of the data from Franklin and Wilkins in the MRC report. 'Embarrassment' was not the reason Watson did not refer to C2 symmetry in the article.

51 Watson to Bretscher, 16 September 2016, courtesy of Mark Bretscher. Crick to Elkin, 22 December 1999, PP/CRI/J/2/19/2. Crick to Maddox, 25 July 2002, PP/CRI/J/2/22/1.

52 Watson to Crick, 9 October 1953, PP/CRI/H/1/42/3. Watson suggested that some of this came from 'minor Cambridge biochemists' but named no names – Watson (2001), p. 21.

53 Cobb, M. and Comfort, N. (2023), What Watson and Crick really took from Franklin. *Nature* 616:657–60.

54 Crick, F. and Watson, J. (1954), The complementary structure of deoxyribonucleic acid. *Proceedings of the Royal Society of London A* 223:80–96, pp. 94–5.

55 As Crick put it in January 2000: 'I'm sure there are people who think we didn't give Rosalind enough credit, although we tried to. Did Rosalind herself ever complain to anyone that we didn't credit her sufficiently?' Crick to Elkin, 11 January 2000, PP/CRI/J/1/8/5/2. Elkin, who was preparing a biography of Franklin which she did not complete before she died, sent Crick copies of Franklin's notebooks and asked him to comment on them. Elkin published an article on Franklin – Elkin, L. O. (2003), Rosalind Franklin and the double helix. *Physics Today* 56(3):42–8.

56 Crick, F. H. C. (1995), DNA: A cooperative discovery. *Annals of the New York Academy of Sciences* 758:198–9.

57 Wilkins to Crick, 5 October 1998; Crick to Wilkins, 11 October 1999, K/PP178/3/5/17.

58 Franklin to Crick, 10 April 1953, PP/CRI/D/2/29. Crick, Diary, 1953, entry for 17 April, reads 'Rosy and Raymond'. MSS 660, Box 14, Folder 3.

59 Watson (2012). Crick to Franklin, 5 June 1953, PP/CRI/I/3/5.

60 Ferry, G. (1998), *Dorothy Hodgkin: A Life* (London: Granta).

61 Friedberg, E. C. (2010), *Sydney Brenner: A Biography* (Cold Spring Harbor, NY: Cold Spring Harbor Laboratory Press), p. 68.
62 Witkowski, J. A. (2002), Mad hatters at the DNA tea party. *Nature* 415:473–4. This includes a facsimile of the full diary entry.
63 Friedberg (2010), p. 69.
64 Olby (2009), p. 199. The hoax letter is not in the public domain.
65 Peter Pauling to Watson, October and November 1953, JDW/2/2/1385. Linus Pauling explained that when he saw the hoax letter he initially thought that he had indeed written it and spent an hour or so working out that he had not. LP Science, Box 9.001, 1.40 and 1.42.
66 Wilkins to Hamilton, 28 May 1953, K/PP178/3/14/1.
67 *News Chronicle*, 15 May 1953, FRKN/6/4.
68 *The New York Times*, 17 May 1953, JDW/2/4/2/3. It does not appear in *The New York Times* online archive and presumably only appeared in certain editions.
69 *The New York Times*, 13 June 1953.
70 Crick, Passport, MSS 660, Box 13, Folder 2.
71 *Sunday Times*, 21 June 1953. *Birmingham Post*, 20 June 1953. *News Chronicle*, 9 July 1953. *South China Sunday Post*, 19 July 1953. Watson (2001), p. 3, refers to an article in the *Sunday Telegraph*, which did not exist at the time; this is probably a confusion with the *Sunday Times*.
72 Crick, F. H. C. (1953), The structure of life. *Sunday Times*, 28 June 1953. Watson, J. D. W. (1953), Structure of life. *Sunday Times*, 12 July 1953.
73 Bruce to Franklin, Friday [22 May 1953], FRKN/6/4. Cobb and Comfort (2023). Watson heard that Bruce had also approached Bragg and wearily told Max Delbrück about it. Watson to Delbrück, 21 May 1953, Delbrück papers, Box 23, Folder 22. Watson alerted one of his correspondents to the impending appearance of the article at the beginning of June. This letter has been lost, but is referred to in Fourcade to Watson, 30 May 1953, JDW/2/2/614.
74 PP/CRI/M/1/1 includes all three *Nature* articles from April 1953, bound together. For a precise bibliographic description of the single preprints and of the three articles bound together, see JDW/2/7/5/20.
75 PC/3/8/6. I bought a copy of the programme on eBay for a paltry sum. See also Anonymous (1954), Conversaziones 1953. *Notes and Records of the Royal Society of London* 11:1–5. The DNA exhibit was added to the Conversazione late on – it was decided at a meeting of the Royal Society Soirée Committee (chaired by Bragg), on 22 May 1953. CAD/1953.
76 PP/CRI/H/1/16. Crick's entry for the evening of the Conversazione reads 'RS soirée?' Crick, Diary, 1953, entry for 26 June, MSS 660, Box 14, Folder 3. Crick, Diary, 1953, entry for 15 July, MSS 660, Box 14, Folder 3.
77 de Chadarevian, S. (2003), Portrait of a discovery: Watson, Crick, and the double helix. *Isis* 94:90–105.
78 Bragg to Martin, 21 August 1953, W. L. BRAGG/42A/72.
79 Wilkins to Hamilton, 28 May 1953, K/PP178/3/14/1.
80 W. L. BRAGG/40B/123–8. Crick to Newby, 23 July 1953, BBC Written Archive. Newby to Crick, 22 July 1953 and 4 August 1953, MSS 660, Box 1,

Folder 24. Crick later claimed he made two separate broadcasts: Crick to Bragg, 31 October 1966, PP/CRI/D/1/1/2.

81 Boltz, Talks Booking Requisition, July 1953, BBC Written Archive. Crick interview with Olby, 8 March 1968, PP/CRI/H/4/13.

82 Crick interview with Olby, 8 March 1968, PP/CRI/H/4/13. Crick to Bragg, 31 October 1966, PP/CRI/D/1/1/2. Talks Booking Requisition, 24 July 1953; Newby, Talks Proposals Form, 22 July 1953; Crick to BBC, 1 August 1953; Crick to Newby, 3 August 1953, BBC Written Archive. BBC producer P. H. Newby was 'deeply disappointed that you are prevented from speaking about your research on the 3rd programme.' Newby to Crick, 4 August 1953, MSS 660, Box 1, Folder 24. Arrangements were made to ensure that the rebroadcast did not go ahead: Newby to Holme, 4 August 1953; Provan to AHCP Ops. (Rec) BH, 4 August 1953; Miles Coventry to Provan, 7 August 1953, BBC Written Archive.

83 Watson to Crick, 9 October 1953, PP/CRI/H/1/42/3.

84 Watson to Crick, 16 December 1953, PP/CRI/H/1/42/3.

85 Watson travelled to Edinburgh and on to Glasgow at the same time but made no mention of accompanying Crick. Watson (2001), pp. 12–14.

86 Swann to Crick, 23 January 1953, PP/CRI/E/1/1/1.

87 MSS 660, Box 12, Folder 12. Crick noted 'Edinburgh' in his diary. Crick, Diary, 1953, entry for 13 May, MSS 660, Box 14, Folder 3.

88 Crick to Watson, 21 February 1954, PP/CRI/D/4/4.

89 Crick to Morrison-Low, 18 April 1985, PP/CRI/J/2/5/1. Dr Rebekah Higgitt, Principal Curator of Science at the National Museum of Scotland, kindly sent me a photo of the model. Towards the end of his life, Crick forgot this incident, asking historian Soraya de Chadarevian, 'Exactly what is the model that ended up in Edinburgh?' Crick to de Chadarevian, 5 January 1998, PP/CRI/J/2/18/1.

90 Crick to MRC, 10 May 1953, FD 21/13.

91 Crick to Himsworth, 15 June 1953, PP/CRI/A/2/1.

92 Perutz to Duncan, 13 July 1953, FD 21/13.

93 FD 21/13.

94 Francis Crick to Michael Crick, 9 June 1953, MSS 660, Box 2, Folder 24.

95 Ratcliffe to Crick, 28 July 1953, MSS 660, Box 10, Folder 20.

96 Crick interview with Olby, 8 March 1968, PP/CRI/H/4/13.

97 Olby (2009), p. 198.

98 Olby (2009), p. 196.

99 Crick to Schrödinger, 12 August 1953, SCH/M/44.

100 Crick to Crow, 28 June 1991, PP/CRI/J/2/11/1.

CHAPTER 6

1 Cunard, *Programme of Events for the Mauretania*, 27 August 1953.

2 Odile Crick interview with Olby, undated, OLBY, Box 3.

3 Olby, R. (2009), *Francis Crick: Hunter of Life's Secrets* (Cold Spring Harbor, NY: Cold Spring Harbor Laboratory Press), p. 204.

4 Crick to Watson, undated [December 1953], JDW/2/2/403.

5 Cricks to Watson, undated [December 1953], JDW/2/2/400.

6 Kendrew, J. (1954), Structure of proteins. *Nature* 173:57–9.

7   Crick to Kendrew, 8 February 1954, MS. Eng.C.2601 o.7.
8   Olby (2009), p. 211.
9   Of twenty references cited by Kendrew in his article on the meeting, five were to Crick's work.
10 Tulinsky, A. (1996), The protein structure project, 1950–1959: first concerted effort of a protein structure determination in the US. *Annual Reports in Medical Chemistry* 31:357–66.
11 Kartha, G., Bello, J. and Harker, D. (1967), Tertiary structure of ribonuclease. *Nature* 213:862–5.
12 Crick to Watson, 7 March 1954, PP/CRI/D/4/4.
13 Magdoff, B. S. and Crick, F. H. C. (1955a), Ribonuclease 2. Accuracy of measurement and shrinkage. *Acta Crystallographica*, 8:461–8. Magdoff, B. S. and Crick, F. H. C. (1955b), A new crystal form of ribonuclease. *Acta Crystallographica*, 8:468–72. Crick, F. H. C. and Magdoff, B. S. (1956), The theory of the method of isomorphous replacement for protein crystals. I. *Acta Crystallographica*, 9:901–8. Magdoff, B. S., Crick, F. H. C. and Luzatti, V. (1956), The 3-dimensional Patterson function of ribonuclease-II. *Acta Crystallographica*, 9:156–62.
14 Olby (2009), pp. 211–2.
15 See MS. Eng.C.2601 o.7. and MS. Eng.d.2130 C.36.
16 Chargaff could not resist saying that he thought the second Watson and Crick *Nature* article 'stinks'. Crick to Kendrew, 8 February 1954, MS. Eng.C.2601 o.7.
17 Olby (2009), p. 196.
18 Crick to Watson, 7 March 1954, PP/CRI/D/4/4.
19 Crick to Kendrew, undated [December 1953], MS. Eng.C.2601 o.7.
20 Kendrew to Watson, 23 January 1954, JDW/2/2/978.
21 Kendrew to Watson, 23 January 1954, JDW/2/2/978.
22 Crick to Watson, 3 February 1954, PP/CRI/D/4/4. Randall's very rude letter and the secretary's nasty little note have been lost.
23 Crick to Watson, undated [early 1954], JDW/2/2/403.
24 Wilkins to Crick, 12 March 1954, MSS 660, Box 10, Folder 38. Although Wilkins moderated some of his irritation in a covering note dated two days later – 'I want to emphasise that in spite of the hard things I say that in other respects, believe it or not, I still have friendly feelings left towards you. You do have very good qualities & I like you for them' – he insisted that 'the views I have expressed in the rude letter are shared by many. It probably seems most unjust to you but there it is.' Crick told Watson, 'I've had a striking letter from Maurice, who is very upset about the collagen business, but have written a very friendly reply.' Crick to Watson, 21 March 1954, PP/CRI/D/4/4.
25 Crick to Watson, 21 February 1954, PP/CRI/D/4/4.
26 Crick to Watson, 21 March 1954 and 21 February 1954, PP/CRI/D/4/4.
27 Watson to Crick, 13 February 1954, PP/CRI/H/1/42/3.
28 Watson to Crick, 12 November 1953, PP/CRI/H/1/42/3.
29 Crick to Kendrew, undated [December 1953], MS. Eng.C.2601 o.7.
30 Crick, F. (1954a), Structure and function of DNA. *Discovery*, January 1954, pp. 12–7.

31 Crick to Watson, 3 February 1954, PP/CRI/D/4/4. Wilkins' friend Leonard Hamilton told Crick it was unlikely that Wilkins would accept co-authorship, and that Crick should get Hamilton to write the article, as he could provide 'an objective account'. Crick refused, pointing to the prestige of an article in *Scientific American* and the fee of $200. Hamilton to Wilkins, 13 March 1954, K/PP178/3/14/1.

32 Crick to Watson, undated [December 1953], PP/CRI/D/4/4.

33 Crick, F. (1954b), The structure of the hereditary material. *Scientific American* 191, October 1954, pp. 54–61, p. 54.

34 Crick (1954b).

35 Judson (1996), p. 264.

36 Gamow to Watson and Crick, 8 July 1953, JDW/2/3/14/11.

37 Gamow to Crick, 7 November 1953, SB/11/1/50. In early October, Crick elliptically wrote to Watson 'to remind you about Gamow!' Crick to Watson, 7 October 1953, PP/CRI/D/4/4.

38 After reading Gamow's letter, Crick wrote to Watson: 'On 4th Dec. Gamow is paying us a visit. He is trying to see how DNA can synthesise protein, but I shall know better after he's been. I don't think he really has a good grasp of the problem – yet.' Crick to Watson, 22 November 1953, PP/CRI/D/4/4.

39 Watson (2001), p. xxiv.

40 Olby (2009), p. 221.

41 Gamow and Tompkins, draft article, JDW/2/7/2/1. Gamow to Crick, 8 March 1954, PP/CRI/H/1/42/5.

42 Gamow, G. (1954a), Possible mathematical relation between deoxyribonucleic acid and proteins. *Det Kongelige Danske Videnskabernes Selskab, Biologiske Meddelelser* 22:3–13.

43 Gamow, G. (1954b), Possible relation between deoxyribonucleic acid and protein structures. *Nature* 173:318.

44 Crick to Watson, undated [December 1953], PP/CRI/D/4/4.

45 Gamow to Crick, 10 January 1954, PP/CRI/H/1/42/5.

46 Francis to Odile, 27 January 1954, MSS 660, Box 22, Folder 21.

47 Francis to Odile, 14 February 1954, MSS 660, Box 22, Folder 21.

48 Francis to Odile, 1 March and 7 March 1954, MSS 660, Box 22, Folder 21.

49 Crick to Watson, 7 March 1954, PP/CRI/D/4/4.

50 Odile to Francis, 19 March 1954, MSS 660, Box 2, Folder 25.

51 Francis to Odile, 14 March 1954, MSS 660, Box 22, Folder 21.

52 Francis to Odile, 14 March 1954, MSS 660, Box 22, Folder 21.

53 Francis to Odile, 14 June 1954, MSS 660, Box 22, Folder 21.

54 Francis to Odile, 13 April 1954, MSS 660, Box 22, Folder 21.

55 Francis to Odile, 20 May 1954, MSS 660, Box 22, Folder 21.

56 Kreisel to Crick, 23 April and 15 May 1954, MSS 660, Box 5, Folder 3.

57 A new repayment schedule was set out by Kreisel: Kreisel to Crick, 4 June 1954, MSS 660, Box 5, Folder 3.

58 Francis to Odile, 21 June 1954, MSS 660, Box 22, Folder 21.

59 Letter to Crick, 18 June 1954, MSS 660, Box 11.

60 Crick to Watson, 1 July 1954, JDW/2/2/403. My baseball correspondent, Jerry Coyne, writes: 'Playing at their home field, the Polo Grounds, the

New York Giants beat their great rivals Brooklyn 4–3. At the end of the regulation nine innings, the game was tied 2–2 after the Dodgers scored two runs at the top of the ninth. The game then went into four extra innings, with Brooklyn scoring another run at the top of the thirteenth on a home run by catcher Roy Campanella. But New York then put the game to bed after scoring two runs in their half of the inning. The game lasted nearly four hours and must have been exciting!'

61 Francis to Odile, 14 June 1954, MSS 660, Box 22, Folder 21.
62 Kreisel to Crick, 4 June 1954, MSS 660, Box 5, Folder 3.
63 Crick to Watson, 1 July 1954, JDW/2/2/403.
64 Judson, H. F. (1996), *The Eighth Day of Creation: Makers of the Revolution in Biology, Expanded Edition* (Plainview, NY: Cold Spring Harbor Laboratory Press), p. 280.
65 Judson (1996), p. 281.
66 Judson (1996), p. 282.
67 Brenner, S. (2001), *My Life in Science* (as told to Lewis Wolpert). E. F. Friedberg and E. Lawrence (eds.), (London: BioMed Central), p. 62.
68 de Chadarevian, S. (2002), *Designs for Life: Molecular Biology after World War II* (Cambridge: Cambridge University Press), p. 190.
69 Crick (1988), p. 95. Watson (2001), Chapters 12 and 13.
70 Watson (2001), p. 88.
71 Odile to Francis, 3 September 1953, MSS 660, Box 2, Folder 25.
72 Green to Crick, undated [April-May 1980], PP/CRI/D/1/4/7.
73 Crick to Watson, 22 September 1954, JDW/2/2/403.
74 Kendrew to Watson, 2 October 1954, JDW/2/2/978.
75 Newby to Crick, 22 July 1953, MSS 660, Box 1, Folder 24. The fruitless correspondence between Crick and Academic Press stretched from 1954–1960: SB/11/1/2.
76 Crick interview with Olby, undated, OLBY, Box 12.

CHAPTER 7

1   Crick to Brenner, 3 January 1955, SB/1/1/131. Crick to Watson, undated [May 1955], JDW/2/2/403.
2   MSS 660, Box 2, Folder 19.
3   Crick to Brenner, 21 August 1956, SB/1/1/131.
4   Crick to Watson, 21 October 1954, JDW/2/2/403. Creager, A. N. H. (2022), Tobacco Mosaic Virus and the history of molecular biology. *Annual Review of Virology* 9:39–55.
5   Kendrew to Watson, 2 October 1954, JDW/2/2/978.
6   Crick to Franklin, 12 November 1954 and 8 December 1954, FRKN/2/33.
7   Maddox, B. (2002), *Rosalind Franklin: The Dark Lady of DNA* (London: Harper Collins), p. 254.
8   Cohen, B. (ed.), (2007), *Odile Crick: Memorial Exhibition* (n.p.: Leucadia Art Press), p. 18.
9   Crick to Brenner, Friday [September 1954] and 27 September 1954, SB/1/1/131.
10 Crick to Franklin, 8 December 1954, FRKN/2/33.
11 Crick to Hargittai, 13 April 2001, PP/CRI/J/2/21/1.

12 Watson (2001), p. 53. There is no scholarly study, not even a single article, on the RNA Tie Club. Watson, Orgel and Rich planned a book of the publications, letters and preprints connected to the Club, but it was never published. See JDW/2/7/2/6 and JDW/2/7/2/1.

13 Organization Charter of the RNA Tie Club, undated, JDW/2/7/2/6.

14 Watson to Crick, 10 February 1955, PP/CRI/D/2/45.

15 Hoagland, M. (1990), *Toward the Habit of Truth: A Life in Science* (London: Norton). Hoagland, M. B. (2003), Celebrating complementarity. *Annals of Internal Medicine* 148:583–6.

16 Iskandar's book *Qābūs Nāma* had recently been translated into English.

17 Crick to Brenner, 6 July 1955, SB/1/1/131.

18 See for example his notebook for January 1955, PP/CRI/G/1/11.

19 Ingram, V. (2004), Sickle-cell anemia hemoglobin: the molecular biology of the first 'molecular disease' – the crucial importance of serendipity. *Genetics* 167:1–7.

20 Crick to Brenner, 6 July 1955, SB/1/1/131.

21 Crick, F. (1988), *What Mad Pursuit: A Personal View of Scientific Discovery* (New York: Basic Books), p. 104.

22 Kreisel to Crick, undated [early 1955], MSS 660, Box 5, Folder 3. Kreisel to Crick, 7 September 1956, MSS 660, Box 5, Folder 4.

23 Crick to Watson, undated [May 1955], JDW/2/2/403.

24 Crick to Brenner, 6 July 1955, SB/1/1/131. Watson, J. D. (2001), *Genes, Girls and Gamow* (Oxford: Oxford University Press), pp. 178–9. Odile to Francis, undated [1955], MSS 660, Box 3, Folder 2. Crick to Bachmann, 19 August 1982, PP/CRI/J/13.

25 Crick to Raper, 11 March 1955, PP/CRI/D/2/45.

26 Watson (2001), p. 174.

27 Crick to Rich, 12 January 1955, SB/11/1/113. Odile Crick, Memoir, undated, MSS 660, Box 22, Folder 21.

28 Rich to Crick, 27 May 1955, SB/11/1/113.

29 During their holiday, Kreisel's piles were so bad he had to carry a rubber ring to sit on to relieve the pain. Crick, F. (1996), Georg Kreisel: a few personal recollections. In P. Odifreddi (ed.), *Kreiseliana: About and Around Georg Kreisel* (Wellesley, MA: Peters), pp. 25–32. Odile to Francis, 23 July 1955, MSS 660, Box 2, Folder 25. In her letter, Odile wrote 'Syd', but was clearly referring to Sid Bernhard.

30 Crick to Rich, 6 April 1998, PP/CRI/J/2/19/1. Interview with Alex Rich, 20 August 2006, OHC-CSHL.

31 Bamford, C., et al. (1955), Structure of polyglycine. *Nature* 176:396–7.

32 Crick to Brenner, 30 August 1955, SB/1/1/131. Crick, F. and Rich, A. (1955), Structure of polyglycine II. *Nature* 176:780–1.

33 Crick and Rich (1955).

34 Dunitz, J. D. and Joyce, G. F. (2013), Leslie Eleazer Orgel: 12 January 1927 – 27 October 2007. *Biographical Memoirs of the Fellows of the Royal Society* 59:277–89. Zhang, S. and Wittig, B. (2015), Alex Rich: 1924–2015. *Nature Biotechnology* 33:593–8.

35 Subramanian, E. (2001), G. N. Ramachandran. *Nature Structural Biology* 8:489–91.

36 Cowan, P. M., McGavin, S. and North, A. C. T. (1955), The polypeptide chain configuration of collagen. *Nature* 176:1062–4.

37 Crick to Brenner, 4 November 1955, SB/1/1/131.

38 Ramachandran to Rich, 20 November 1955, SB/11/1/109.

39 Crick (1988), p. 67.

40 Harrison to Randall, 24 July 1972, GBR/0014/RNDL/3/1/6. Harrison was Pauline Cowan's married name.

41 Ridley, M. (2006), *Francis Crick: Discoverer of the Genetic Code* (London: Harper), p. 90.

42 Kreisel to Crick, 23 November 1955, MSS 660, Box 5, Folder 3.

43 PP/CRI/H/1/40. *London Calling Europe* 406, 27 November – 3 December 1955; 407, 4–10 December 1955; 424, 1–7 April 1956. 'What is a gene' (PP/CRI/H/2/7) is the same length and style as the other talks. It refers to Benzer coming to the Cavendish 'next year', which would situate it after October 1956, when Benzer's fellowship was approved (Crick to Brenner, 25 October 1956, SB/1/1/131). There are no listings corresponding to 'What is a gene' in the *Radio Times* or *London Calling Europe,* but between 2 and 30 December 1956 *London Calling Europe* did not carry talk titles for the 'Frontiers of Knowledge' slot where Crick broadcast the other three talks. This fourth talk was probably given in this slot during this period in December 1956.

44 PP/CRI/H/1/40. Elsewhere Crick was more downbeat, saying that the result had caused 'no great surprise though the development was of great interest.' *Daily Telegraph,* 29 October 1955.

45 Maddox, J. (1980), Crick's 'selfish DNA'. *The Listener,* 10 July 1980, p. 43.

46 Crick to Brenner, 6 July 1955, SB/1/1/131.

47 Crick to Brenner, 20 October 1955, SB/1/1/131.

48 Crick to Brenner, 25 October 1955, SB/1/1/131.

49 Crick to Perutz, 7 June 1956, PP/CRI/D/1/1/16.

50 Rich, A., et al. (1961), The molecular structure of polyadenylic acid. *Journal of Molecular Biology* 3:71–86. Watson (2001), p. 128.

51 Watson (2001), p. 224.

52 Crick to Brenner, 31 December 1955, SB/1/1/131.

53 Odile to Francis, 21 December 1955, MSS 660, Box 2, Folder 25.

54 Letters to Crick, 1956–8, MSS 660, Box 4.

55 Crick to Rich, 27 January 1956 and 11 February 1956, SB/11/1/113. It is not clear what this broadcast was. *Questions in the Air* was recorded on 7 March 1956, and broadcast on 11 March. Programme for recording, MSS 660, Box 13, Folder 9. Crick diary entries for 7 March 1956, MSS 660, Box 14, Folder 6. Lang to Crick, 30 August 1960, PP/CRI/H/2/39.

56 Wolstenholme, G. E. W. and Millar, E. C. P. (eds.), (1957), *Ciba Foundation Symposium on the Nature of Viruses* (London: Churchill). Full details of the meeting can be found in FRKN/2/34.

57 Crick, F. H. C. and Watson, J. D. (1956), Structure of small viruses. *Nature* 177:473–5.

58 Crick, F. H. C. and Watson, J. D. (1957), Virus structure: general principles. In G. E. W. Wolstenholme and E. C. P. Millar (eds.), *Ciba Foundation Symposium on the Nature of Viruses* (London: Churchill), pp. 5–18.

59 Franklin, R. E., Klug, A. and Holmes, K. C. (1957), X-ray diffraction studies of the structure and morphology of Tobacco Mosaic Virus. In G. E. W. Wolstenholme and E. C. P. Millar (eds.), *Ciba Foundation Symposium on the Nature of Viruses* (London: Churchill), pp. 39–55.

60 Gierer, A. and Schramm, G. (1956), Infectivity of ribonucleic acid from tobacco mosaic virus. *Nature* 177:702–3.

61 FRKN/2/34.

62 Maddox (2002), p. 268. Crick to McClain, 10 February 1998, PP/ CRI/J/2/18/1. Kindra Crick has a crumpled photo of Odile, Francis and an unidentified man in the Spanish countryside. On a rock in the photo is a woman's handbag resembling that carried by Franklin in the photo of the Madrid conference, suggesting the photo was taken by Franklin.

63 Rich to Franklin, 14 May 1956, FRKN/3/6. 'My how I envy you both!' added Rich.

64 Crick, Griffith and Orgel, Comma-less codes, May 1956, PP/CRI/H/2/3.

65 Crick, F. H. C., Griffith, J. S. and Orgel, L. E. (1957), Codes without commas. *Proceedings of the National Academy of Sciences USA* 43:416–21.

66 Watson (2001), p. 50.

67 Crick to Watson, 15 July 1956, JDW/2/2/402.

68 Crick to Brenner, 17 July 1956, SB/1/1/131.

69 Odile to Francis, 20 May 1956, MSS 660, Box 2, Folder 25. Belinda Bullard was a Natural Sciences student at Girton College and was friends with Watson and Crick. Her letters to Watson from this period (JDW/2/2/250) are charming and full of 1950s atmosphere. She went on to have a distinguished career in the study of muscle physiology. Her father, the geophysicist Sir Edward Bullard (knighted in 1963), was a fellow at Gonville and Caius and then at Clare, while her mother Margaret was the author of a gossipy and mildly salacious roman à clef about Cambridge in the 1930s, *A Perch in Paradise*, which Francis read in 1952. After helping found Churchill College, Sir Edward left Cambridge for the University of California San Diego in 1974 and continued his interactions with Crick, in particular on the origins of life.

70 Odile to Francis, 6 June 1956, MSS 660, Box 2, Folder 25.

71 Letters to Crick, 1956–8, MSS 660, Box 9.

72 Odile to Francis, 1–9 July 1956, MSS 660, Box 2, Folder 25.

73 Francis to Odile, 29 July 1956, MSS 660, Box 22, Folder 21.

74 Odile to Francis, 25 July 1956, MSS 660, Box 2, Folder 25.

75 Odile to Francis, 1 August 1956 and 4 August 1956, MSS 660, Box 2, Folder 25.

76 Kreisel to Crick, 17 July 1956, MSS 660, Box 5, Folder 4.

77 Letter to Crick, 5 September 1956, MSS 660, Box 4.

78 Letter to Crick, Weds [December 1956], MSS 660, Box 9.

79 Bragg to Crick, 26 June 1956, W.L. BRAGG/83P/1. Crick to Bragg, 16 August 1956, W.L. BRAGG/83P/4. Bragg to Crick, 23 November 1956, W.L. BRAGG/83P/20. Crick to Bragg, 8 December 1956, W.L. BRAGG/83P/37.

80 Crick, F. H. C. and Kendrew, J. C. (1957), X-ray analysis and protein

structure. *Advances in Protein Chemistry* 12:133–214. Quotes are from pp. 135, 139, 142, 205.

81 Crick to Brenner, 30 August 1956, SB/1/1/131.

82 Crick to Spiegelman, 9 October 1956, SB/11/1/136. The typed letter mistakenly has 'charge' not 'change'.

83 Bullard to Watson, 8 February 1957, JDW/2/2/250. Lorna Martin married zoologist Avrion Mitchison – Watson (2001), pl. XIV.

84 These letters cover much of 1957. MSS 660, Box 5, Folder 4.

85 Franklin to Sayre, 25 October 1956, ASMB.

86 Crick to Watson, 19 November 1956, PP/CRI/D/2/45. On 14 November, Franklin told Watson that since returning from the USA 'I've spent all my time being ill'. Franklin to Watson, 14 November [1956], JDW/2/2/618.

87 Crick to Brenner, 22 October 1956, SB/1/1/131. D [Dorothea Raacke] to Crick, 19 November 1974, MSS 660, Box 11, Folder 7.

88 Maddox (2002), p. 288.

89 Franklin to Watson, 14 November [1956], JDW/2/2/618. Maddox (2002), p. 288.

90 Bullard to Watson, 17 February 1957, JDW/2/2/250. Maddox (2002), p. 291.

91 Maddox (2002), pp. 288–9.

92 Maddox (2002), p. 293.

93 Maddox (2002), p. 254. In 1954 Crick said it would be 'rash' to publish a particular figure – Crick to Franklin, 8 December 1954, FRKN/2/33. Bea Magdoff commented 'he's been known to be much more brazen with his intuitive notions' – Magdoff to Franklin, 16 June 1955, FRKN/2/33. The figure in question appeared as Figure 3 in Franklin, R. (1955), Structure of tobacco mosaic virus. *Nature* 175:379–81.

94 Crick to Franklin, 23 May 1957, FRKN/2/34. Even kind, mild-mannered Max Perutz described one part of Franklin's draft as 'far-fetched' and complained that that whole article was written 'in an aggressively dogmatic style which conveys the impression to the reader that the writer is trying to quash her critics.' Perutz to Franklin, 6 June 1957, FRKN/2/34. No article was published, and no completed manuscript corresponding to this paper is in her archives.

95 Crick to Maddox, 26 November 2001, OLBY, Box 4.

96 Maddox (2002), pp. 292–8.

97 After her death, Alex Rich wrote: 'I had known of her illness and as recently as last February had speculated with Hugh Huxley about the probable cause of it, but nonetheless felt a considerable shock when it developed so rapidly.' Rich to Crick, 2 May 1958, PP/CRI/D/1/1/17.

98 de Chadarevian, S. (2002), *Designs for Life: Molecular Biology After World War II* (Cambridge: Cambridge University Press), p. 224.

99 Sayre, A. (1975), *Rosalind Franklin and DNA* (London: Norton), pp. 186–7.

100 Rich to Crick, 2 May 1958, PP/CRI/D/1/1/17. *The New York Times*, 20 April 1958. *The Times*, 19 April 1958. Bernal, J. D. (1958), Dr. Rosalind E. Franklin, *Nature* 182:154.

101 Blow to Crick, 29 April 1958, GBR/0014/MISC 90/1. In what appears to

be a reply to Rich's letter, Crick made no mention of Franklin's death, or of Rich's aghast reaction: Crick to Rich, 14 May 1958, SB/11/1/113.

102 Wilkins to Hamilton, 28 April 1958, K/PP178/3/14/2.

103 Maddox (2002), p. 307. Crick notebook, 1957–1958, PP/CRI/G/1/14. There are however entries for 15, 18 and 19 April 1958, and for every day of the subsequent week.

104 *Manchester Guardian*, 18 April 1958. The funeral had already taken place.

CHAPTER 8

1 Interview with Brenner, April 2017, Cold Spring Harbor Laboratory Archives. Cobb, M. (2018), The mad sessions of Francis Crick and Sydney Brenner. *Research Culture: Collaboration Collections* (London: Royal Society), pp. 57–64.

2 *Sydney Brenner: A Revolutionary Biologist*, BBC World Service programme, 2017. https://www.bbc.co.uk/sounds/play/w3cstxnk

3 *Sydney Brenner: A Revolutionary Biologist*.

4 Brenner, S. (2001), *My Life in Science* (as told to Lewis Wolpert). E. F. Friedberg and E. Lawrence (eds.), (London: BioMed Central), p. 63.

5 Crick, F. (2002), Cambridge and the code. *The Scientist* (Supplement), 5 March 2002, p. 4.

6 *Sydney Brenner: A Revolutionary Biologist*.

7 Judson, H. F. (1996), *The Eighth Day of Creation: Makers of the Revolution in Biology, Expanded Edition* (Plainview, NY: Cold Spring Harbor Laboratory Press), p. 330.

8 Although the published title was 'On protein synthesis', the meeting programme gave the title as simply 'Protein synthesis' – PP/CRI/E/1/5/4.

9 Crick, F. H. C. (1958), On protein synthesis. *Symposia of the Society for Experimental Biology* 12:138–63. There is no known manuscript, but Mark Bretscher rescued a late typescript from the skips outside the Hut, including annotations and edits by Crick and the plea 'Please correct my spelling!' GBR/0014/MISC 90/1. A digital copy can be found on the Cambridge LMB website https://www2.mrc-lmb.cam.ac.uk/wordpress/wp-content/uploads/6-Crick_On_Protein_Synthesis-rd.pdf. Brenner's copy of the final typescript is at SB/11/5/4.

10 Judson (1996), p. 335.

11 Jacob, F. (1988), *The Statue Within* (London: Unwin Hyman), pp. 287–8.

12 Crick, Ideas on protein synthesis, October 1956, PP/CRI/H/2/6.

13 Spiegelman, S. (1957), Nucleic acids and the synthesis of proteins. In W. D. McElroy and B. Glass (eds.), *A Symposium on the Chemical Basis of Heredity* (Baltimore: Johns Hopkins Press), pp. 232–67, p. 232.

14 Crick, F. H. C. (1957), Discussion. In E. M. Crook (ed.), *The Structure of Nucleic Acids and Their Role in Protein Synthesis. Biochemical Society Symposium 14* (Cambridge: Cambridge University Press), p. 12.

15 It was probably easier for Crick to suggest the sequence hypothesis before many protein structures had been determined, than when the bewildering variety of protein structures began to be revealed. Morange, M. (2006), The

protein side of the central dogma: permanence and change. *History and Philosophy of the Life Sciences* 28:513–24.

16 Crick (1958), p. 142.

17 Sibley to Crick, 11 November 1958; Crick to Sibley, 24 November 1958; Sibley to Crick, 1 December 1958; Crick to Sibley 10 December 1958; Sibley to Crick, 19 December 1958, SB/11/1/128. Sibley, C. G. and Johnsgard, P. A. (1959), An electrophoretic study of egg-white proteins in twenty-three breeds of the domestic fowl. *The American Naturalist* 93:107–15. Sibley, C. G. (1962), The comparative morphology of protein molecules as data for classification. *Systematic Zoology* 11:108–18.

18 Crick interview with Olby, undated, OLBY, Box 27.

19 Ingram, V. M. (1956), A specific chemical difference between the globins of normal human and sickle-cell anaemia haemoglobin. *Nature* 178:792–4.

20 Ingram, V. M. (1957), Gene mutations in human haemoglobin: the chemical difference between normal and sickle cell haemoglobin. *Nature* 180:326–8.

21 *The Times*, 23 August 1957.

22 Crick (1958), p. 143.

23 Crick to Watson, 14 November 1957, PP/CRI/D/2/45.

24 Watson to Crick, 24 November 1957, PP/CRI/D/2/45. Meselson, M. and Stahl, F. W. (1958), The replication of DNA in *Escherichia coli*. *Proceedings of the National Academy of Sciences USA* 44:671–82. Letters to Crick, 27 November 1957 and 8 January 1958, MSS 660, Box 9.

25 Crick to Watson, 5 March 1958, PP/CRI/D/2/45.

26 Hoagland, M. B. (1990), *Toward the Habit of Truth: A Life in Science* (London: Norton), p. 116.

27 de Chadarevian, S. (2002), *Designs for Life: Molecular Biology after World War II* (Cambridge: Cambridge University Press).

28 Benzer, S. (1991), Interview by Heidi Aspaturian. Pasadena, California, September 11–February 1991. Oral History Project, California Institute of Technology Archives.

29 de Chadarevian (2002).

30 Pontecorvo to Crick, 8 October 1958, MSS 660, Box 8, Folder 33.

31 Pontecorvo sounded Crick out about moving to Glasgow, together with Brenner. Pontecorvo to Crick, 1 September 1957, MSS 660, Box 8, Folder 33.

32 Cantoni to Crick, 8 November 1957, SB/11/1/20. Evans to Crick, 31 October 1958, SB/11/1/42. Lingane to Crick, 1 June 1959, SB/11/1/74. Brenner to Crick, 24 March 1959, PP/CRI/D/1/1/2.

33 Crick to MRC, 19 April 1958; MRC to Crick, 13 March 1959, FD 21/13.

34 Rothschild to Himsworth, 18 November 1958, FD 21/13. Brenner to Crick, 24 March 1959, PP/CRI/D/1/1/2. Klug to Crick, 28 May 1959, PP/CRI/D/1/1/11.

35 Crick interview with Georgina Ferry, 3 June 2004, with the interviewer's permission.

36 Crick to Crook, 7 August 1963, SB/11/1/20.

37 This trip was arranged in 1958. Crick to Watson, 5 March 1958, PP/CRI/D/2/45.

38 Crick to Doty, 2 December 1958, SB/11/1/59. Rich to Crick, 12 December 1958, SB/11/1/113.

39 Crick to Bloch, 18 December 1958, SB/11/1/59. The three exam papers
    (the last was in May), together with the course reading list, are at PP/
    CRI/E/1/7/3/3; Crick's lecture outlines are at PP/CRI/E/1/7/3/2; his
    background notes are at PP/CRI/E/1/7/3/4.
40 Crick to Strominger, 10 March 1959, SB/11/1/119.
41 Crick to Brenner, 7 February 1959, SB/1/1/131.
42 Crick to Brenner, 17 March 1959, SB/1/1/131.
43 Crick to Brenner, 11 April 1959, SB/1/1/131.
44 EC/1959/08.
45 PP/CRI/A/3/2/1.
46 Crick to Brenner, 17 March 1959, SB/1/1/131.
47 Perutz to Crick, 11 March 1959, PP/CRI/D/1/1/16. Crick to Brenner, 11
    April 1959, SB/1/1/131.
48 Crick to Brenner, 27 July 1959, SB/1/1/131.
49 Crick to Lingane, 11 June 1959, SB/11/1/74.
50 Crick, F. H. C. (1959), The present position of the coding problem. *Structure
    and Function of Genetic Elements, Brookhaven Symposium in Biology* 12:35–9.
51 Crick to Brenner, 27 July 1959, SB/1/1/131.
52 Crick to Brenner, 17 August 1959, SB/1/1/131.

CHAPTER 9
1   Jacob, F. (1988), *The Statue Within: An Autobiography* (London: Basic Books),
    p. 311.
2   Brenner and Crick, Some footnotes on protein synthesis – Note for the
    RNA Tie Club, December 1959, PP/CRI/H/2/34.
3   Jacob (1988), p. 312.
4   Crick, F. (1979), Sailing with Jacques. In A. Lwoff and A. Ullmann (eds.),
    Origins of Molecular Biology: A Tribute to Jacques Monod 1910–1976 (London:
    Academic Press), pp. 225–9.
5   Jacob (1988), p. 313.
6   Brenner and Crick, What are the properties of genetic RNA?, May 1960,
    PP/CRI/H/2/41.
7   Brenner, S., Jacob, F. and Meselson, M. (1961), An unstable intermediate for
    carrying information from genes to ribosomes for protein synthesis. *Nature*
    190:576–81. Gros, F., et al. (1961), Unstable ribonucleic acid revealed by
    pulse labelling of Escherichia coli. *Nature* 190:581–5. Cobb, M. (2015a), Who
    discovered messenger RNA? *Current Biology* 25:R526–32. Meselson, M.
    (2014), François and 'X'. *Research in Microbiology* 165:313–5.
8   Crick to Handler, 19 July 1960, PP/CRI/E/1/8/6.
9   Crick, Genes and atoms – radio talk, 20 July 1960, PP/CRI/H/2/38. The
    talk was published in *The Listener*, 4 August 1960.
10 Taylor to Crick, 1 August 1960; Crick to Taylor, 11 August 1960,
    SB/11/1/153.
11 Crick, Living matter – radio talk, 14 September 1960, PP/CRI/H/2/39.
12 Crick, Lecture notes – Korkes Memorial Lecture, undated [1960], PP/
    CRI/E/1/8/6.
13 Crick and Orgel, On loopy codes, undated [1961], PP/CRI/H/3/2.
14 Crick to Rich, 28 April 1961, SB/11/1/113.

15 Kreisel to Crick, undated; February 1961; 1 May 1961; 7 May 1961, MSS 660, Box 5, Folder 4.

16 Crick to Delbrück, 19 June 1961, SB/11/1/37. Crick, Diary, 1959–1960, MSS 660, Box 14, Folder 10.

17 Albritton to Crick, 20 February 1961, SB/11/1/1. Cobb, M. (2017), The prehistory of biology preprints: A forgotten experiment from the 1960s. *PLoS Biology* 15:e2003995.

18 Mark Bretscher pointed out this essential difference.

19 Brenner, S., et al. (1961), The theory of mutagenesis. *Journal of Molecular Biology* 3:121–4.

20 Crick needed to give the mutant strain an identifier but could not remember what letters had already been used in the lab's labelling system, so he used his initials because he was sure that no one else would have used them. Judson, H. (1996), *The Eighth Day of Creation: Makers of the Revolution in Biology* (Plainview, NY: Cold Spring Harbor Laboratory Press), p. 442. Crick, F. (1988), *What Mad Pursuit: A Personal View of Scientific Discovery* (New York: Basic), p. 128.

21 Crick, General nature of the genetic code, Verbatim transcript, November 1964, PP/CRI/H/3/13.

22 Crick to Lechevallier, 12 April 1961; Crick to Latarjet, 16 November 1961, PP/CRI/E/1/9/5.

23 Streisinger, G., et al. (1961), Genetic studies concerning the lysozyme of phage T4. In *Deoxyribonucleic Acid: Structure, Synthesis and Function: Proceedings of the 11th Annual Reunion of the Société de Chimie Physique, June 1961* (Oxford: Pergamon Press), pp. 186–9, p. 188.

24 MSS 660, Box 17, Folder 12.

25 Crick (1988), p. 129. Perutz to Crick, 21 July 1961, SB/11/1/97. Brenner to Crick, 27 July 1961, PP/CRI/D/1/1/2.

26 Moscow photographs in SB/11/4/7. Watson's Moscow snaps, including images of the Titov parade on Red Square seen from Maxwell's balcony in JDW/1/15/10.

27 Watson, J. D. (2001), *Genes, Girls and Gamow* (Oxford: Oxford University Press), pp. 264–5.

28 Meselson recalled: 'there is a terrible snobbery that either a person who's speaking is someone who's in the club and you know him, or else his results are unlikely to be correct. And here was some guy named Marshall Nirenberg; his results were unlikely to be correct, because he wasn't in the club. And nobody bothered to be there to hear him.' Judson (1996), p. 464. Cobb, M. (2015b), *Life's Greatest Secret: The Race to Crack the Genetic Code* (London: Profile). Portugal, F. H. (2015), *The Least Likely Man: Marshall Nirenberg and the Discovery of the Genetic Code* (London: MIT Press). According to Watson, Alfred Tissières and Wally Gilbert also heard Nirenberg speak – Watson (2001), p. 265.

29 Judson (1996), p. 464.

30 Perutz to Crick, 21 July 1961, SB/11/1/97. Cobb (2015b).

31 Judson (1996), p. 464. Nirenberg interview with Ruth Harris, 1995–1996, NIH archives, archived at https://tinyurl.com/Harris-Nirenberg-Interview.

32 Crick, F. H. C., et al. (1961), General nature of the genetic code for proteins. *Nature* 192:1227–32, p. 1229. Yanofsky, C. (2007), Establishing the triplet nature of the genetic code. *Cell* 128:815–8. Cobb, M. (2021), A breakthrough from 60 years ago: 'General nature of the genetic code for proteins' (1961). *Natural Sciences* 2021:e10018.

33 Crick et al. (1961), p. 1228.

34 Crick to Benzer, 28 October 1961, SB/11/1/10.

35 Crick (1988), p. 133.

36 Crick to Sinnsheimer, 9 October 1961, PP/CRI/E/1/10/4/3.

37 Crick (1988), p. 134.

38 Crick's notebook for this period is missing, but many years later Mark Bretscher found a battered file in the LMB which he immediately recognised as containing some of Francis's notes on the acridine mutant experiment. A PDF of the key page can be found on the LMB website (archived at https://tinyurl.com/Crick-acridine); the original is in the Churchill College Archives: GBR/0014/MISC 90/2.

39 Crick to Judson, 21 March 1978, PP/CRI/D/3/10.

40 Crick (1988), p. 134.

41 SB/2/1/54.

42 Benzer to Crick, 29 November 1961, SB/11/1/10.

43 Crick to Benzer, 7 December 1961, SB/11/1/10.

44 Brenner, S. (2001), *My Life in Science* (as told to Lewis Wolpert). E. F. Friedberg and E. Lawrence (eds.), (London: BioMed Central), pp. 96–7.

45 Barnett, L., et al. (1967), Phase-shift and other mutants in the first part of the rII B cistron of bacteriophage T4. *Philosophical Transactions of the Royal Society of London B* 252:487–560.

46 Crick to Shulman, 7 April 1966, PP/CRI/D/1/1/18. Crick (1988), p. 135. The manuscript spans five files: SB/2/1/115–119; the Leonardo joke can be seen at http://libgallery.cshl.edu/archive/files/f12db6aad7ba23e3a72255ce8d2c3bfb.jpg

47 Benzer to Crick, Detailed comments, 29 November 1961; Crick to Benzer, 7 December 1961, SB/11/1/10.

48 Crick et al. (1961), p. 1232.

49 Crick to Latarjet, 16 November 1961, PP/CRI/E/1/9/5. Crick to Nirenberg, 16 November 1961, PP/CRI/D/1/1/14.

50 Mark Bretscher, e-mail to the author, 16 May 2024.

51 Crick et al. (1961), p. 1227.

52 Judson (1996), p. 468.

53 Brenner (2001), p. 97.

54 Brenner (2001), p. 96.

55 Crick et al. (1961), p. 1232.

56 Nirenberg to Crick, 15 January 1962, Nirenberg Papers, Box 4, Folder 31.

57 Jacob to Brenner, 13 December 1961, SB/1/1/300.

58 Stent to Crick, 10 January 1962, SB/11/1/139.

59 John [Kendrew] to Crick and Brenner, 15 December 1961, SB/11/1/99. Benzer to Crick, 30 December 1961, SB/11/1/10.

60 Crick to Benzer, 15 January 1962, SB/11/1/10. Crick pointedly remarked,

'We have had a busy time impressing [the media] with the importance of Nirenberg's story. It was lucky we left in that bit of our Nature paper.'

61 *Sunday Times*, 31 December 1961.

62 Crick told Nirenberg he had tried to set the record straight with journalists: 'I have stressed that it is your discovery which was the real breakthrough'. Crick to Nirenberg, 4 January 1962, Nirenberg Papers, Box 4, Folder 31. Nirenberg responded: 'I haven't seen the English newspapers but the American press has been saying that this type of work may result in (1) the cure of cancer and allied diseases (2) the cause of cancer and the end of mankind, and (3) a better knowledge of the molecular structure of God. Well, it's all in a day's work.' Nirenberg to Crick, 15 January 1962, Nirenberg Papers, Box 4, Folder 31.

63 *The Listener*, 11 January 1962.

64 Crick, Cracking the genetic code, 22 January 1962, PP/CRI/H/3/7.

65 *The New York Times*, 2 February 1962.

66 Crick to Stein, 9 February 1962, PP/CRI/E/1/10/4/1.

67 Crick to Fisher, Knight & Co. Ltd., 25 April 1962, SB/11/1/46. All awards letters can be found in PP/CRI/A/3/6. Crick to Stent, 23 March 1962. Crick put an exclamation mark after 'press conference' in Yang's letter explaining the arrangements for his visit: Yang to Crick, 12 March 1962, PP/CRI/E/1/10/4/1.

68 Crick to Sinnsheimer, 23 March 1962, PP/CRI/E/1/10/4/1.

69 Crick to Benzer, 9 January 1962, SB/11/1/10.

70 Itinerary for F. H. C. Crick, April 1 – April 20, 1962, PP/CRI/E/1/10/4/1. Bernhard to Crick, 31 January 1962, PP/CRI/E/1/10/4/1. Crick to Novick, 4 December 1961, PP/CRI/E/1/10/4/1. Novick to Crick, 4 April 1962, PP/CRI/E/1/10/4/1.

71 Odile to Francis, 22 March 1962, MSS 660, Box 3, Folder 1. Crick's itinerary was incredibly hectic: PP/CRI/E/1/10/4/1.

72 Crick to President of the Research Corporation, 11 March 1963, PP/CRI/A/3/6.

73 Watson, Introduction to the Easton Press edition of *The Double Helix*, 1 August 2009, JDW/2/3/7/47.

74 Monod to Crick, 29 December 1961, PP/CRI/D/2/26.

75 Crick to Monod, 31 December 1961, PP/CRI/H/3/5/1.

76 Crick's diary entry for 24 January 1961 reads: 'The gene: history of the DNA model. 8.30 pm (Old School) History and Philosophy of Science': MSS 660, Box 14, Folder 12. The following day, Crick wrote to Watson, saying he had given the talk, adding 'but don't worry. In your phrase "nobody heard it". How's your version of the history going,' suggesting Watson was already thinking of writing about the discovery. Crick to Watson, 25 January 1961, JDW/2/2/404.

77 *Guardian*, 30 December 1961.

CHAPTER 10

1 Crick to Stent, 26 January 1962, PP/CRI/E/1/10/4/1.

2 Crick's diary entry for 27 August 1962 reads 'Mr Hyam Hi Fi' – MSS 660,

Box 14, Folder 13. Odile to Francis, 26 January 1966, MSS 660, Box 3, Folder 1.

3   de Chadarevian, S. (2002), *Designs for Life: Molecular Biology after World War II* (Cambridge: Cambridge University Press). Ferry, G. (2007), *Max Perutz and the Secret of Life* (London: Pimlico).

4   Alison [Auld] to Crick, 5 March 1962, PP/CRI/E/1/10/4/1.

5   Crick's diary reads: '28 May – Queen's visit. 2:30 Jim lecture. Lab Party.' Crick, Diary, 1962, 28 May entry, MSS 660, Box 14, Folder 13.

6   Correspondence between Crick and 10 Downing Street, 7 and 14 May 1963, MSS 660, Box 12, Folder 16. Kendrew sent a telegram to Crick explaining that the government wanted an immediate response. Crick replied 'DECLINE CBE FOR ME. CRICK'. PP/CRI/A/3/6.

7   de Chadarevian (2002).

8   The photo can be found on the Cambridge LMB website at http://www2. mrc-lmb.cam.ac.uk/photo-archive/crick-brenners-blackboard/

9   PP/CRI/A/3/1/1.

10 Bretscher to Olby, e-mail, 26 January 2006, OLBY, Box 30.

11 Olby, R. (2009), *Francis Crick: Hunter of Life's Secrets* (Cold Spring Harbor, NY: Cold Spring Harbor Laboratory Press), pp. 1–3. Crick to Watson, 30 October 1962, PP/CRI/A/3/1/2.

12 Crick to Engelhardt, 30 October 1962, PP/CRI/A/3/1/2.

13 Hans Boye filmed the party at the LMB to celebrate Perutz and Kendrew's Nobel: https://www.youtube.com/watch?v=goeFVYJ_6EM

14 Crick to Coulson, 14 November 1962, PP/CRI/A/3/1/2.

15 A brief video of the ceremony can be seen at the Nobel Prize website https://www.nobelprize.org/prizes/medicine/1962/award-video/

16 https://www.christies.com/en/lot/lot-5857954. The five handwritten pages of Watson's speech, together with Crick's note, were auctioned in 2014 for $365,000.

17 Crick to Wilkins, 30 October 1962; Crick to Watson, 30 October 1962, PP/CRI/A/3/1/2.

18 In the written version of his lecture, Wilkins referred to 'my late colleague Rosalind Franklin who, with great ability and experience of X-ray diffraction, so much helped the initial investigations on DNA'. Wilkins, M. F. H. (1962), The molecular configuration of nucleic acids. Nobel Lecture, December 11, 1962. Archived at https://tinyurl.com/Wilkins-Nobel-Lecture. Randall later wrote to Gosling about the significance of the King's MRC unit for the work on DNA: 'I have always felt that Maurice's Nobel Lecture did rather less than justice to this setting and particularly to the contribution of yourself and Rosalind.' Randall to Gosling, 29 August 1972, RNDL/3/1/6.

19 Crick to Kreisel, 28 December 1962, SC 136, Box 3, Folder 9. Undated newspaper cutting, PP/CRI/A/1/4.

20 Crick to Kreisel, 28 December 1962, SC 136, Box 3, Folder 9.

21 Gouyon, J.-B. (2018), From engaged citizen to lone hero: Nobel Prize laureates on British television, 1962–2004. *Public Understanding of Science* 27:446–57. Boon, T. (2019), 1962: 'What manner of men?': Meeting scientists through television. *Public Understanding of Science* 28:372–8.

22 Gouyon (2018), p. 449.
23 All quotes from *The Prizewinners*, BBC TV, Wellcome, 3614D and 3615D.
24 *Observer*, 9 December 1962.
25 *Sunday Times*, 23 December 1962.
26 PP/CRI/I/2/4.
27 *Newcastle Journal*, 15 December 1962. *Guardian*, 2 January 1963.
28 *Belfast Telegraph*, 12 December 1962.
29 *Daily Herald*, 12 December 1962. *Newcastle Journal*, 15 December 1962.
30 Cockroft to Himsworth, 4 March 1960, FD 21/13.
31 Crick's correspondence with Winston Churchill – including the crumpled returned cheque – can be found in MSS 660, Box 2, Folder 1. Crick also sent a slightly priggish letter to the secretary of the MRC, informing him of his resignation from the college and the reasons for it, concluding, 'It is a comfort to me that the Medical Research Council is never likely to be as foolish as the Trustees in this respect.' Crick to Himsworth, 8 September 1961, FD 21/13.
32 Crick to Churchill, 12 October 1961, MSS 660, Box 2, Folder 1. The letter is quoted in full in Olby (2009), p. 312. Ridley (2006).
33 *Sunday Times*, 19 December 1965. For Crick's later change of mind, see draft article attached to Crick to Kelly, 14 June 2000, PP/CRI/J/2/20/1.
34 *Observer*, 9 December 1962.
35 Anonymous (1960), Research institute to be established in California. *Science* 131:1088.
36 Bourgeois, S. (2013), *Genesis of the Salk Institute: The Epic of Its Founders* (London: University of California Press).
37 Salk to Crick, 17 October 1961 and 31 October 1961, PP/CRI/C/1/3.
38 Ryan, Declaration, 18 March 1963, PP/CRI/C/1/2. Photographs of the construction of the building can be seen at PP/CRI/C/1/8.
39 Bourgeois (2013), p. 117.
40 DR to DCMO, 23 October 1961, FD 21/13.
41 Various letters, October 1961 – March 1962, FD 21/13.
42 MRC to Crick, 8 February 1962, FD 21/13.
43 Crick's diary entry for 19 January 1963 reads 'Well Cottage'. Crick, Diary, 1962–1963, MSS 660, Box 14, Folder 14.
44 Monod to Crick, 26 June 1963; Crick to Monod, 16 September 1963, MSS 660, Box 17, Folder 4. Crick to Monod, 25 May 1963, MON. Cor. 04.
45 Monod to Crick, 23 September 1963, MSS 660, Box 17, Folder 4.
46 Crick, F. (1979), Sailing with Jacques. In A. Lwoff and A. Ullmann (eds.), *Origins of Molecular Biology: A Tribute to Jacques Monod 1910–1976* (London: Academic Press), p. 227. A garbled account of this trip appeared in *Le Figaro*, 20 August 1969, much to Monod's amusement – Monod to Crick, 26 August 1969, PP/CRI/D/2/26.
47 Crick (1979). Correspondence over the purchase and sale of *Kiwi II* can be found in MSS 660, Box 17, Folder 4.
48 Crick (1979), p. 227.
49 OLBY, Box 29.
50 Interview with Michael Ashburner, 14 June 2005, OHC-CSHL. The

transcript states the films were 'B-movies' rather than the clearly audible 'blue movies'. Ridley (2006), p. 136.

51 Interview with Michael Ashburner, 14 June 2005, OHC–CSHL.
52 *The Code of Life*, BBC TV, 2011.
53 Playlist provided by Henry Selby-Lowndes, the son of the photographer, Guy Selby-Lowndes.
54 Interview with Gabrielle Crick, December 2022.
55 Crick, Diary, 1962–1963, MSS 660, Box 14, Folder 14. Cricks, House diary, 1966, MSS 660, Box 26, Folder 8.
56 MSS 660, Box 26, Folder 6. The Lending Book contains around fifty entries spanning a decade or so, most relating to 1962–3.
57 PP/CRI/E/1/11–14.
58 Crick to Herndon, 6 January 1964, PP/CRI/E/1/12/4. Haselkorn to Crick, 10 December 1964; Crick to Haselkorn, 10 December 1964, PP/CRI/E/1/13/5.
59 Ford to Crick, 30 December 1963, PP/CRI/E/2/3.
60 Crick to Ford, 2 January 1964, PP/CRI/E/2/3.
61 Crick to Bragg, 25 March 1963; Crick to Nirenberg, 24 April 1963; Oppenheimer to Crick, 19 April 1963, PP/CRI/E/2/2. Crick to Berg, 7 February 1966; Yon to Crick, 31 March 1966, PP/CRI/E/2/5.
62 PP/CRI/E/2/2, PP/CRI/E/2/3, PP/CRI/E/2/4 and PP/CRI/E/2/5.
63 Frutkin to Crick, 21 January 1965, PP/CRI/E/2/4. Goode to Crick, 3 August 1966; Crick to Goode, 25 August 1966, PP/CRI/E/2/5.
64 Lumry to Crick, 29 April 1966, PP/CRI/E/2/5.
65 SB/11/1/98.
66 Khorana to Crick, 17 November 1965, PP/CRI/E/1/13/19.
67 Crick to Kamen, 8 September 1986, PP/CRI/J/1/1/9/2.
68 PP/CRI/E/2/1.
69 Crick to Kamen, 12 November 1986, PP/CRI/J/1/1/9/2.
70 Garnett to Crick, 18 November 1963, PP/CRI/E/2/3. Ancell to Crick, 11 December 1970, PP/CRI/D/1/1/1.

CHAPTER 11

1 Crick, F. H. C. (1963), The recent excitement in the coding problem. *Progress in Nucleic Acid Research and Molecular Biology* 1:163–217.
2 Mark Bretscher, e-mail to the author, 16 May 2024.
3 PP/CRI/E/1/12/1.
4 Crick to Brenner, 23 January 1964, SB/1/1/132.
5 Crick to Brenner, Sunday [February 1964], SB/1/1/132.
6 Mark Bretscher explained Khorana's technique to me in more detail, but I decided to keep it simple.
7 Odile to Francis, 19 June 1963, MSS 660, Box 3, Folder 1.
8 Crick to Brenner, 25 February 1965, SB/1/1/132.
9 Crick to Watson, 5 April 1965, SB/11/1/17. Odile Crick to Watson, 15 March 1965, JDW/2/2/404.
10 It is not known who first drew up the table this way. It can also be seen in Watson's letters at the time – Watson to Crick, 31 March 1965, PP/CRI/D/2/45 – but it seems probable that it was Crick, although his precise

way of doing things was not followed. For example, Crick asked Nirenberg to consistently use the 'standard order CUAG' in his table, but the order that was soon adopted was UCAG. Crick to Nirenberg, 6 April 1965, PP/CRI/D/1/1/14. Crick's file on the 1965 Gordon Conference includes twenty duplicated tables, with the order UCAG, each carrying a different genetic code in Crick's hand. All the codes are incorrect, and it is unclear what they refer to. PP/CRI/E/1/13/10.

11 Crick, F. H. C. (1966), The genetic code – yesterday, today, and tomorrow. *Cold Spring Harbor Symposia on Quantitative Biology* 31:3–9.

12 Crick to Nirenberg, 6 April 1965, PP/CRI/D/1/1/14.

13 Crick to Khorana, 29 April 1965, PP/CRI/D/1/1/11.

14 Cobb, M. (2017), The prehistory of biology preprints: a forgotten experiment from the 1960s. *PLoS Biology* 15:e2003995.

15 Crick, F. H. C. (1965), Codon–anticodon pairing: the wobble hypothesis, NIH Information Exchange Group No. 7 Memo 14, PP/CRI/H/3/16. The circulation of IEG memos does not appear to have been particularly rapid, if this is typical – it was received by the NIH on 2 June 1965 and circulated on 21 July. Nevertheless, this was a substantial improvement on the pace of traditional publishing.

16 Crick, F. H. C. (1966), Codon–anticodon pairing: the wobble hypothesis. *Journal of Molecular Biology* 19:548–55. At least one correspondent noticed the differences in tone between the IEG pre-print and the published version: Dunnill to Crick, 23 January 1967, PP/CRI/D/1/1/4.

17 Osgood, E. E. (1965), An ordered triplet code for messenger ribonucleic acid with no two triplets coding for the same amino-acid. *Nature* 206:471–3.

18 Crick to Osgood, 8 June 1965, PP/CRI/D/1/1/15.

19 Crick to Watson and Nirenberg, 28 April 1965, PP/CRI/D/2/45.

20 Watson to Crick, 10 May 1965, PP/CRI/D/2/45. Nirenberg to Crick, 1 June 1965, PP/CRI/E/1/13/10. Portugal, F. (2015), *The Least Likely Man: Marshall Nirenberg and the Discovery of the Genetic Code* (London: MIT Press), pp. 119–20.

21 Crick to Nirenberg, 8 June 1965, PP/CRI/E/1/13/10.

22 PP/CRI/E/1/14/13 contains all information regarding the lecture, including details of the six vinyl ('wax') discs of the speech sent to Crick in 1969. The archived version of the talk is at LAC 497678.

23 Crick, The general nature of the genetic code, November 1964, PP/CRI/H/3/13. Crick, F. H. C. (1965), General nature of the genetic code. In *Proceedings of the Robert A. Welch Foundation Conferences on Chemical Research. VIII. Selected Topics in Modern Biochemistry* (Houston: n.p.), pp. 43–65. At many points Crick had to completely rewrite the text. Crick to Doherty, 18 January 1965, PP/CRI/E/1/12/15.

24 PP/CRI/E/1/11/10.

25 Cobb (2017).

26 Odile to Francis, 2 March 1966, MSS 660, Box 3, Folder 1.

27 Odile to Francis, 26 January and 7 February 1966, MSS 660, Box 3, Folder 1.

28 For details of these and subsequent tests, see Gospe to Crick, 3 November 1967, MSS 660, Box 9, Folder 6. Holter to Crick, 24 November 1967; Crick to Holter, 6 December 1967, PP/CRI/D/1/1/8.

29 Thomas, T. F. (1966), Anthony Foster Crick: an appreciation. *Australasian Radiology* 10:168–9.
30 EC/1966/18.
31 Cricks, House diary, 1966, MSS 660, Box 26, Folder 8.
32 Crick's notes and various drafts of the manuscript can be found at PP/CRI/H/4/7. The lecture was published as Crick, F. H. C. (1967), The Croonian Lecture, 1966 – The genetic code. *Proceedings of the Royal Society of London B* 167:331–47.
33 Friedberg, E. C. (2010), *Sydney Brenner: A Biography* (Cold Spring Harbor, NY: Cold Spring Harbor Laboratory Press), p. 150. Brenner, S., et al. (1967), UGA: A third nonsense triplet in the genetic code. *Nature* 213:449–50.
34 Crick to Cairns, 3 November 1965; Cairns to Crick, 17 March 1966, PP/CRI/E/1/14/10. Crick noted his suggested title on the letter from Cairns.
35 According to Mark Bretscher, who was there, Francis was intensely embarrassed. Interview with Mark Bretscher, January 2024. *The New York Times*, 25 March 2003. Ridley (2006). In 1995 Rollin Hotchkiss coyly recalled that Crick had been 'challenged with an alternative model. After graciously and enthusiastically welcoming it, he signalled that he did not feel obliged in the least to alter his basic philosophy' – Hotchkiss, R. D. (1995), 'The Night Before Crickmas': A poem and deliverance. *Annals of the New York Academy of Sciences* 758:205–7. John Cairns recalled that Watson 'devised a Bacchanalian interlude' but 'he preferred to cast a veil over the details'– Cairns, J. (1999), Last days in Arcadia. *Nature* 401:19. Cairns warned Crick he was going to write about the event; Crick replied: 'By all means write about the party in 1966, though I would like to see it before you submit it'. Cairns to Crick, 13 November 1998 and 2 June 1999; Crick to Cairns, 23 November 1998 and 2 June 1999, PP/CRI/J/1/6/3. For Watson's account of the day's events, see Watson, J. D. (2001), *Genes, Girls and Gamow* (Oxford: Oxford University Press).
36 Hotchkiss (1995). Cairns (1999).
37 Crick to Cairns, 17 June 1966, PP/CRI/E/1/14/10.
38 Witkowski to Crick, 11 May 2003, PP/CRI/J/1/8/3. Watson intended to print a photograph of Crick and 'Fifi' in *Genes, Girls and Gamow* – 'it seems too jolly not to reproduce' he told Crick. Crick was prepared to go along with publication 'but Odile is very much against including it so I suggest you leave it out.' Watson to Crick, 4 December 2000; Crick to Watson, 12 December 2000, PP/CRI/J/1/7/23. Mark Bretscher kindly sent me scans of his photographs.
39 Crick, F. (1988), *What Mad Pursuit: A Personal View of Scientific Discovery* (New York: Basic), p. 80. This first title for Watson's book is explained in *The Double Helix*. In 1955, Watson was on a walking holiday in Italy and bumped into Bill Seeds from King's College, who hailed him with the apparently sarcastic greeting 'How's Honest Jim?' In his book, Watson referred to Seeds as 'Willy', but this was Watson's own childish nickname for Seeds, who was universally referred to as Bill. Seeds may have been riffing on *Lucky Jim*; Watson hoped to echo this reference and Joseph Conrad's novel *Lord Jim*. Two drafts of *Honest Jim* that were sent to Crick can be found at PP/CRI/I/3/8/2 (1966) and PP/CRI/I/3/8/3 (1967). For

Watson's account of the writing of *The Double Helix*, Crick's reaction and the book's reception, see Watson, J. D. (2007), *Avoid Boring People and Other Lessons from A Life in Science* (Oxford: Oxford University Press).

40 PP/CRI/I/3/8/2.

41 Watson (2007).

42 Reeder to Watson, Monday [Summer 1965], JDW/2/2/1506.

43 Reeder to Watson, 20 August 1965 and 15 November 1965, JDW/2/2/1506.

44 Watson, Introduction to the Easton Press edition of *The Double Helix*, 1 August 2009, JDW/2/3/7/47. Watson (2007). de Santillana to Watson, 24 April 1964, JDW/2/2/1600.

45 Crick to Watson, 31 March 1966, PP/CRI/I/3/8/4. Crick's pencil notes on the text can be found at the end of the manuscript, PP/CRI/I/3/8/2.

46 Watson to Crick, 10 May 1966, PP/CRI/I/3/8/4.

47 Crick to Gros, 17 April 1969, PP/CRI/D/1/1/7. Crick to Magdoff-Fairchild, 27 June 1966, PP/CRI/D/1/1/13. The voyage to Spetsai did not go entirely smoothly, with engine repairs necessary at Xanthe. A fragment of Crick's log of this trip, from 7 July 1966, can be seen at https://auction. universityarchives.com/auction-lot/francis-crick-virtually-unobtainable-handwritten_361442 EBAE

48 Doty to Crick, 16 March 1967, PP/CRI/I/3/8/4.

49 Crick to Watson, 27 September 1966, JDW/2/3/7/2.

50 Crick to Watson, 10 October 1966; Crick to Wilson, 10 October 1966, PP/CRI/I/3/8/4.

51 Wilkins to Watson, 8 October 1966, PP/CRI/I/3/8/4.

52 Watson to Crick. 19 October 1966, PP/CRI/I/3/8/4.

53 Baker to Crick, 18 October 1966, PP/CRI/I/3/8/4.

54 Watson to Wilkins, 26 November 1966, PP/CRI/I/3/8/4.

55 Crick to Wilson, 21 October 1966; Crick to Watson, 1 November 1966, PP/CRI/I/3/8/4.

56 Watson to Crick, 23 November 1966, PP/CRI/I/3/8/4.

57 Pauling to Watson, 20 October 1966, JDW/2/2/1384.

58 Watson told Bragg that Crick had raised no objection to publication. Bragg to Himsworth, 22 November 1966, FD 9/1391. In all correspondence, Bragg's contribution was referred to as a Preface; in the published book it is called a Foreword.

59 Crick to Pusey, 23 December 1966, PP/CRI/I/3/8/4.

60 Crick to Watson, 1 December 1966, PP/CRI/I/3/8/4.

61 Crick to Wilkins, 19 January 1967, PP/CRI/I/3/8/4.

62 Watson to Crick, 24 March 1967, PP/CRI/I/3/8/4.

63 Crick to Watson, 13 April 1967, PP/CRI/I/3/8/4.

64 Pusey, Bragg, Wilkins, Pauling, Wilson, Edsall, Doty, Kendrew, Perutz and Klug. Edsall and Doty were Harvard professors whom Crick tried to persuade of his cause, with little success.

65 Mark Bretscher, e-mail to the author, 21 May 2024.

66 Bragg to Crick, 19 April 1967, PP/CRI/I/3/8/4. Two days earlier, Crick had claimed 'Bragg is beginning to wobble': Crick to Doty, 17 April 1967, PP/CRI/D/1/1/4. Crick to Bragg, 28 April 1967, PP/CRI/I/3/8/4. A

final-ish version of the manuscript from around this time, still called *Base Pairs*, can be found at PP/CRI/I/3/8/1.

67 Wilson to Montgomery, 24 May 1967 and 1 June 1967, PP/CRI/I/3/8/4. The lawyer's fee was $25. Hamilton to Crick, 25 May 1967, PP/CRI/D/1/1/8. Montgomery to Hamilton, 29 May 1967, PP/CRI/I/3/8/4.

68 Crick to Hamilton, 30 May 1967, PP/CRI/D/1/1/8.

69 Watson to Kendrew, 19 June 1967, JDW/2/2/978.

70 Hamilton to Crick, 19 September 1967; Hamilton to Wilkins, 11 October 1967, PP/CRI/I/3/8/4. Watson to Kendrew, 19 June 1967, JDW/2/2/978. Watson to Donohue, 19 September 1967, JDW/2/3/7/5.

71 Crick to Hamilton, 25 September 1967, PP/CRI/I/3/8/4.

72 Montgomery to Hamilton, 9 October 1967, PP/CRI/I/3/8/4.

73 Hamilton to Crick, 15 February 1968, PP/CRI/D/1/1/8.

74 Crick to Hamilton, 23 February 1968, PP/CRI/D/1/1/8.

75 Thompson to Watson, 30 May 1967 and 28 September 1967, JDW/2/3/7/5.

76 JDW/2/3/7/5. Watson retained six copies of the offending jackets.

77 Watson to Thompson, 8 April 1968, JDW/2/3/7/5.

78 Watson to Thompson, 16 April 1968; Wilson to Watson, 11 April 1968, JDW/2/3/7/5. The publishers had been warned that their publicity material was 'too strong' the previous year. Watson to Thompson, 25 October 1967, JDW/2/3/7/7.

79 *Evening Standard*, 10 January 1968.

80 McClure to Brakhage, 7 September 1968, in C. Luna (ed.), (2011), *The Flame is Ours: The Letters of Stan Brakhage and Michael McClure 1961–1978* (n.p. Big Bridge), pp. 136–7.

81 *Scientific Research*, 16 September 1968, JDW/2/4/3/27. Watson to Stent, 13 March 1978, JDW/2/2/1737.

82 Perutz, M., Wilkins, M. and Watson, J. (1969), DNA helix. *Science* 164:1537–9, p. 1539.

83 Crick (1988), p. 81.

84 Watson to Crick, 15 December 1969, PP/CRI/D/2/45.

85 Nirenberg to Crick, 14 January 1966; Nirenberg to Khorana, 14 January 1966, PP/CRI/D/1/1/11.

86 Khorana to Crick, 18 April 1966, PP/CRI/D/1/1/11.

87 Crick to Nirenberg, 21 April 1966, PP/CRI/D/1/1/11.

88 Nirenberg to Crick, 7 May 1966, PP/CRI/D/1/1/14.

89 Crick to Nirenberg, 10 May 1966, PP/CRI/D/1/1/14.

90 Pelc, S. R. and Welton, M. G. E. (1966), Stereochemical relationship between coding triplets and amino-acids. *Nature* 209:868–70. Welton, M. G. E. and Pelc, S. R. (1966), Specificity of the stereochemical relationship between ribonucleic acid-triplets and amino-acids. *Nature* 209:870–2. Crick to Pelc, 25 October 1966, PP/CRI/D/1/1/16.

91 Crick, F. (1967), An error in model building. *Nature* 213:798. Anonymous (1966), Origin of genetic code. *Nature* 212:1397. Crick to Maddox, 5 January 1967, K/PP178/3/5/15.

92 Crick to Wilkins, 15 January and 18 January 1967, PP/CRI/H/4/8.

CHAPTER 12

1 Brenner, S. (1988), Introduction, in W. B. Wood and the community of C. *elegans* researchers (eds.), *The Nematode Caenorhabditis elegans* (Cold Spring Harbor, NY: Cold Spring Harbor Laboratory Press), pp. ix-xiv.

2 Perutz to Himsworth, 13 November 1964, FD 21/14.

3 Brenner to Cornforth, 21 November 1968, SB/1/1/125.

4 Brenner, S. (1974), The genetics of *Caenorhabditis elegans. Genetics* 77:71–94.

5 PP/CRI/H/4/12.

6 Brenner, undated and untitled note, SB/2/3/45. Crick, F. H. C. (1973), Project K: 'The complete solution of *E. coli'. Perspectives in Biology and Medicine* 17:67–70.

7 Crick to Penrose, 11 April 1968; Penrose to Crick, 16 April 1968, PP/ CRI/D/1/1/16.

8 Brett to Crick, 21 August 1968, PP/CRI/D/1/1/16.

9 Crick to Brenner, 30 July 1968, SB/1/1/132.

10 Lawrence, P. A. (1966), Gradients in the insect segment: The orientation of hairs in the milkweed bug *Oncopeltus fasciatus. Journal of Experimental Biology* 44:607–20. Crick to Lawrence, 27 September 1968, courtesy of Peter Lawrence.

11 Turing, A. M. (1952), The chemical basis of morphogenesis. *Philosophical Transactions of the Royal Society of London B* 237:37–72. Crick's impression of Turing was that he 'was obviously exceptional, even on such a short acquaintance' – Crick to Braddick, 9 November 1984, PP/CRI/J/2/4/4.

12 Stumpf, H. F. (1966), Mechanism by which cells estimate their location within the body. *Nature* 212:430–1. Stumpf was killed in a car accident a few months later. Locke, M. (1966), Hypotheses for gradient mechanisms in insect epidermis. *Naturwissenschaften* 53:510.

13 Wolpert, L. (1968), The French flag problem: A contribution to the discussion on pattern development and regulation. In C. H. Waddington (ed.), *Towards a Theoretical Biology* (Edinburgh: Edinburgh University Press), pp. 125–33. Wolpert, L. (1969), Positional information and the spatial pattern of cellular differentiation. *Journal of Theoretical Biology* 25:1–47.

14 Lewis Wolpert, Web of Stories, https://www.youtube.com/ watch?v=fB7rIavXFbw. Sydney Brenner, Web of Stories, https://www. youtube.com/watch?v= L1qj8rKFG8E.

15 Crick to Locke, undated [January 1970], PP/CRI/H/4/22.

16 Perutz to Himsworth, 13 November 1964, FD 21/14. de Chadarevian, S. (2002), *Designs for Life: Molecular Biology after World War II* (Cambridge: Cambridge University Press).

17 Bretscher, Francis, undated, courtesy of Mark Bretscher.

18 Kauffman to Crick, 16 October 1974, PP/CRI/D/1/2/6.

19 Crick to Sachs, 17 September 1970, PP/CRI/D/1/1/18.

20 Perutz to Lush, 13 March 1967 and Perutz to Whittaker, 4 May 1967, FD 21/14.

21 Crick, untitled table, undated [1972], SB/2/3/45.

22 Crick to McConnell, 6 May 1969, PP/CRI/D/1/1/13. Crick to Pratt, 5 March 1968; Pratt to Crick, 27 March [1968], PP/CRI/D/1/1/16.

23 Carter to Crick, 23 September 1970; Crick to Carter, 2 October 1970, PP/
    CRI/D/1/1/3.
24 Crick to Bernal, 20 January 1969, PP/CRI/D/1/1/2.
25 Crick, Morphogenesis of nervous system, August 1968, PP/
    CRI/E/1/16/8.
26 Crick, F. (1970), Diffusion in embryogenesis. *Nature* 225:420–2. PP/
    CRI/H/4/22.
27 Crick to Wolpert, 18 December 1969; Maloney to Crick, 19 December 1969;
    PP/CRI/D/2/50. Crick to Maddox, 1 January 1970, PP/CRI/D/2/27.
28 Anonymous to Crick, 2 January 1970, PP/CRI/H/4/22.
29 Maddox to Crick, 14 May 1970; Crick to Maddox, 10 June 1970, PP/
    CRI/D/2/27.
30 Brachet to Crick, 12 February 1970, PP/CRI/D/1/1/2. Runnström to
    Crick, 1 March 1970, PP/CRI/D/1/1/17. Rutherford to Crick, 9 March
    1970, PP/CRI/D/1/1/17.
31 Wolpert to Crick, 31 December 1969, PP/CRI/D/2/50.
32 Deuchar, E. M. (1970), Diffusion in embryogenesis. *Nature* 225:671.
33 Crick to Deuchar, 13 February 1970; Deuchar to Crick, 16 February 1970;
    Crick to Deuchar, 23 February 1970, PP/CRI/D/1/1/4.
34 Lawrence, P. A., Crick, F. H. C. and Munro, M. (1972), A gradient of
    positional information in an insect, *Rhodnius*. *Journal of Cell Science* 11:815–
    53. The manuscript, with extensive edits by Crick and Lawrence, can be
    found at PP/CRI/H/5/3.
35 Lawrence, P. A. (1973), A clonal analysis of segment development in
    Oncopeltus (Hemiptera). *Journal of Embryology and Experimental Morphology*
    30:681–99.
36 Garcia-Bellido, A., Ripoll, P. and Morata, G. (1973), Developmental
    compartmentalisation of the wing disk of *Drosophila*. *Nature New Biology*
    245:251–3. Lawrence interview with Deichmann, 4 October 2015, Jacques
    Loeb Centre, archived at https://tinyurl.com/Lawrence-Interview.
37 Crick to Phillips, 24 February 1978, PP/CRI/D/1/3/14. Crick, F. H.
    C. and Lawrence, P. A. (1975), Compartments and polyclones in insect
    development. *Science* 189:340–7. There was some discussion about sending
    the article to *Nature*: Miranda Robertson, an Associate Editor of *Nature* and
    a friend of the Cricks, wrote: 'don't forget to bear us in mind when you've
    finished the compartments article (...) love, Miranda.' Robertson to Crick,
    15 November 1974, PP/CRI/D/2/27.
38 Crick and Lawrence (1975). Late in the process of writing the article, Crick
    passed Lawrence on the stairs at the LMB and asked him to choose the
    order in which their names would appear on the paper. For Lawrence,
    this was another sign of Crick's open attitude when working with a junior
    member of staff, treating him as an equal. E-mails from Peter Lawrence to
    the author, March 2024.
39 Lawrence, P. A. (2016), Francis Crick: A singular approach to scientific
    discovery. *Cell* 167:1436–9.
40 Crick and Lawrence (1975), p. 347. Various versions of the manuscript can
    be found at PP/CRI/H/5/11. In a draft Crick explored the idea of the
    'epigenetic landscape', which he had discussed with C. H. Waddington,

who had developed this concept. Crick to Waddington; Waddington to Crick, June-July 1974, PP/CRI/D/1/2/17. Lawrence and Crick deleted all reference to potential parallels with vertebrate development, while the *Science* editorial team churlishly cut a generous reference to 'the genius of Garcia-Bellido'.

41 Ridley (2006), pp. 156–7.

42 Lewis to Francis and Odile, a Monday with Christmas approaching [1968], MSS 660, Box 6, Folder 16.

43 *The Times*, 24 July 1967. The list of signatories was accompanied by an extensive text supposedly written while its author, American student Stephen Abrams, was stoned. Seddon, T. (2020), Immoral in principle, unworkable in practice: Cannabis law reform, the Beatles and the Wootton Report. *British Journal of Criminology* 60:1567–84.

44 Crick to Lwoff, 3 December 1975, PP/CRI/D/1/2/7.

45 Crick to Genovés, 27 March 1968, PP/CRI/D/1/1/7.

46 Edholm, O. (1969), Professor Samueloff and Mr. Muallem. *Nature* 224:1137–8. Edholm to Crick, 20 November 1969; Crick to Edholm, 24 November 1969, PP/CRI/D/1/1/5. Samueloff to Crick, 5 February 1970, PP/CRI/D/1/1/18.

47 *The Times*, 30 September 1969.

48 Anonymous (1967), Biologists postpone Greek meeting. *Science* 156:1348.

49 Crick to Grunberg-Manago, 30 August 1967; Grunberg-Manago to Crick, 11 September 1967; Crick to Evangelopoulos, 29 November 1967, PP/CRI/E/1/17/7/1.

50 Crick to Berg, 22 December 1967, PP/CRI/E/1/17/7/2. Crick to Evangelopoulos, 14 March 1968, PP/CRI/E/1/17/7/1.

51 Crick. F. (1968), On running a summer school. *Nature* 220:1275–6.

52 PP/CRI/E/1/17/7/3. Crick translated the French appeal himself.

53 The letters to and from the Ambassador have been lost. Summaries can be found in Crick to Evangelopoulos, 10 April 1969, PP/CRI/E/1/17/7/1 and in Crick to Sorokos, 24 January 1972, PP/CRI/D/1/2/2. Mark Bretscher, e-mail to the author, 2 November 2023.

54 Crick to Gros, 19 March 1969, PP/CRI/D/1/1/7. One over-excited British scientist claimed in a circular that the Spetsai meeting was 'organised by the "junta" in the main to provide "window dressing" for their abominable regime'. Crick objected that he did not support the junta and immediately obtained an apology. Crick to Pollack, 14 March 1969; Pollack to Crick, 19 March 1968, PP/CRI/D/1/1/16.

55 Gros admitted that few of the signatories were prepared to do anything, and that after producing a pamphlet on freedom in Greece, the committee would dissolve. Gros to Crick, 21 May 1969, PP/CRI/D/1/1/7. Tissières to Crick, 29 April 1969, PP/CRI/E/1/17/7/2. Bretscher and Clark, Circular letter, 23 April 1969, PP/CRI/E/1/17/7/1.

56 A page of Crick's notes from the 1969 meeting, headed '1. Evening discussions – Today. 8.30 pm' has been misfiled as part of a folder on 'Lab Lectures' dated 1968, PP/CRI/E/1/16/8.

57 These were a trip to the ancient theatre at Epidavros and a boat cruise. Crick, Notes for 'Welcome to Spetsai' [July 1969], PP/CRI/E/1/17/7/4.

These notes are on the verso of page 5 of the notes for his lecture on embryonic development and are crossed out, presumably indicating that this passage was not to be confused with the lecture notes.

58 Crick to Arnstein, 14 November 1969, PP/CRI/D/1/1/1. Bretscher, M. S. and Mitchison, G. (2017), Francis Harry Compton Crick OM: 8 June 1916 – 28 July 2004. *Biographical Memoirs of Fellows of the Royal Society* 63:159–96, p. 190.

59 Singer to Crick, 2 September 1969, PP/CRI/D/1/1/18.

60 Crick to Arnstein, 14 November 1969, PP/CRI/D/1/1/1. *The Times*, 8 March 1969. Grunberg-Manago, M. (1989), Preface. In M. Grunberg-Manago, B. F. C. Clark and H. G. Zachau (eds.), *Evolutionary Tinkering in Gene Expression* (London: Plenum), pp. v-vi.

61 Crick, F. H. C., et al. (1969), International conferences *Nature* 224:93–4.

62 Crick to Arnstein, 14 November 1969. PP/CRI/D/1/1/1. *The Times*, 8 March 1969.

CHAPTER 13

1 Elsasser, W. (1958), *The Physical Foundations of Biology: An Analytical Study* (London: Pergamon). Crick responded in a letter of 16 December 1958, which Elsasser described as 'a very lengthy and extremely kind letter going through a detailed criticism of my book', but which has been lost. All that survives of the correspondence is Elsasser to Crick, 2 November 1959 and Crick to Elsasser, 19 November 1959, SB/11/1/43. Crick said of this exchange 'I didn't seem to be making any headway with him' – Crick to Waddington, 9 November 1967, PP/CRI/I/2/6/5. Crick and Elsasser renewed their correspondence in 1969–70, to no great consequence – PP/CRI/D/1/1/5.

2 Mora, P. (1963), Urge and molecular biology. *Nature* 199:212–9. Crick's copy, with Mora's dedication and some underlining in red ink, can be found at PP/CRI/H/4/1/2.

3 Weaver to Resident and Non-Resident Fellows, 18 March 1964 and Crick to Weaver, 8 May 1964, PP/CRI/C/1/2. Crick to Weaver, 6 July 1964, PP/CRI/C/1/2.

4 Crick, F. (1966), *Of Molecules and Men* (Seattle: University of Washington Press).

5 Crick (1966), p. 57.

6 For a collection of reviews, see PP/CRI/I/2/6/6.

7 Wigner, E. P. (1967), Explaining consciousness. *Science* 156:798–9. Waddington, C. H. (1967), No vitalism for Crick. *Nature* 216:202–3.

8 PP/CRI/E/1/15/12. MSS 660, Box 1, Folder 35, including Sacks to Crick, 4 December 1967.

9 Annan to Crick, 14 December 1967, PP/CRI/D/1/1/1. Crick, Notes: The social impact of biology, undated [1968], PP/CRI/E/1/16/13/1. The lecture was recorded by the BBC and broadcast on Radio 3 on 19 February 1969. *Radio Times*, 15 February 1969. The BBC holds a copy of the recording and I have been able to listen to it. The editor of *The Listener* sent Crick a transcript (now lost) but said it was 'fairly blurred' and needed 'recasting and cutting' before it could be published. Crick's secretary replied that

he had 'reluctantly decided that he needs more time to think about a number of the topics before he commits himself to print'. Miller to Crick, 24 January 1969; Crick secretary to Miller, 23 January 1969; Crick to Miller, 6 February 1969, PP/CRI/D/1/1/13.

10 Crick to Annan, 1 October 1968; Gue to Crick, 28 October 1968, PP/CRI/D/1/1/1.

11 He actually said (and wrote in his notes) 'between consulting adults in private', which makes no sense. Crick, Notes: The social impact of biology, undated [1968], PP/CRI/E/1/16/13/1.

12 Anonymous (1968), Sociology: Logic of biology. *Nature* 220:429–30. *Sunday Telegraph*, 23 February 1969. Maurice Wilkins told Crick that he approved of his opposition to war and militarism and 'to a lesser extent' his call for the legalisation of cannabis, but said nothing about his more outlandish proposals. Wilkins to Crick, 8 November 1968, PP/CRI/D/1/1/1.

13 Annan to Crick, 4 November 1968, PP/CRI/D/1/1/1.

14 Crick to Annan, 8 November 1968, NGA/5/1/203/1. This letter is missing from Crick's Wellcome archive.

15 Crick, F. (1979), Sailing with Jacques. In A. Lwoff and A. Ullmann (eds.), *Origins of Molecular Biology: A Tribute to Jacques Monod 1910–1976* (London: Academic Press), pp. 225–9. Monod, J. (1971), *Chance and Necessity: An Essay on the Natural Philosophy of Modern Biology* (New York: Knopf).

16 Kermode to Crick, 20 March 1977, PP/CRI/D/1/2/6. This letter begins 'How are your thoughts on *Monod*? Or indeed on *Crick*?' perhaps suggesting that they had discussed the matter earlier. There was no further reference in their correspondence to a 'Crick' book, which appears to have been a throwaway remark.

17 Crick, Chance and Necessity, 25 October 1972, PP/CRI/E/1/20/15.

18 Crick to Kermode, 10 March 1978, PP/CRI/D/1/2/6. Crick explained: 'Had he lived I think I would have had a go at it. It would have been fun to discuss it all with him, Now he has gone I find I no longer have the stomach for it.' See also Crick (1979). Kermode reminded Crick about the Monod project several times, but Crick was too busy. Crick to Kermode, 10 January 1980, PP/CRI/D/1/4/11.

19 Crick to Wolstenholme, 4 January 1962, PP/CRI/E/1/10/16.

20 Wolstenholme, G. (ed.), (1963), *Man and His Future* (Boston: Little, Brown).

21 Wolstenholme (1963), pp. 17, 21.

22 Wolstenholme (1963), pp. 275–6.

23 Wolstenholme (1963), pp. 284–5.

24 Wolstenholme (1963), p. 275.

25 Greer, G. (1984), *Sex and Destiny* (London: Secker and Warburg), p. 289.

26 Weindling, P. (2012), Julian Huxley and the continuity of eugenics in twentieth-century Britain. *Journal of Modern European History* 10:480–99. Bashford, A. (2022), *An Intimate History of Evolution: The Story of the Huxley Family* (London: Allen Lane).

27 Wolstenholme (1963), p. 101.

28 Kay, L. E. (1992), *The Molecular Vision of Life: Caltech, the Rockefeller Foundation, and the Rise of the New Biology* (Oxford: Oxford University

Press). Paul, D. B. and Brosco, J. B. (2013), *The PKU Paradox: A Short History of a Genetic Disease* (Baltimore: Johns Hopkins University Press).

29 Paul, D. B. (2017), Norm change in genetic services: how the discourse of choice replaced the discourse of prevention. *Varia Historia* 33:21–47. Donohue, C. R. (2023), 'The bare replacement': Geneticists' and bioethicists' support of eugenics, from after the Second World War to the Human Genome Project. *Revista Brasileira de História* 43:225–52.

30 Reece, R. L. (1966), Man and his future. *Journal of the American Medical Association* 195:141. Berrill, N. J. (1964), Man and his future. *Perspectives in Biology and Medicine* 7:368–9, p. 368. Crow, J. F. (1965), Modifying Man: Muller's eugenics and Lederberg's euphenics. *Science* 148:1578–80, p. 1580.

31 Lasagna, L. (1965), Man and his future. *Quarterly Review of Biology* 40:229.

32 Wagner, F. (1965), Manipulation of human germ-plasm – a way to solve the problem of civilization? *Universitas* 8:159–69, p. 165.

33 Crick to Davis, 22 April 1970, PP/CRI/D/1/1/4. In his lecture, Crick defended his idea, saying it was no worse for the child than taking a fully grown eighteen-year-old and conscripting them into the army where they might be killed.

34 Crick to Davis, 22 April 1970, PP/CRI/D/1/1/4.

35 Crick to Snow, 17 April 1969, PP/CRI/D/1/1/18.

36 *Riverside Daily*, 6 March 1969, PP/CRI/D/2/39.

37 Shockley to Crick, 17 March 1969, PP/CRI/D/2/39.

38 Crick to Shockley, 2 April 1969, PP/CRI/D/2/39.

39 Crick to Shockley, 18 April 1969, PP/CRI/D/2/39. Jensen, A. (1969), How much can we boost IQ and scholastic achievement? *Harvard Educational Review* 39:1–123. For a contemporary critique, see for example, Lewontin, R. (1970), 2. Further remarks on race and the genetics of intelligence. *Bulletin of the Atomic Scientists*, May 1970, pp. 23–5.

40 Shockley to Crick, 18 February 1970; Crick to Shockley, 23 February 1970, PP/CRI/D/2/39. Crick telephone conversation with Shockley, 4 February 1971, SC0222, Box 29. https://purl.stanford.edu/jm718fv8848

41 Crick to Jensen, 30 July 1975, PP/CRI/D/1/2/5.

42 Page, Open letter and resolution, January 1972, PP/CRI/D/2/14. Crick was not cancelled for signing this. For example, in 1973, the left-wing scientist Steven Rose invited Crick to present the kind of views he had expressed in signing the Page petition at a conference on the social implications of brain research. Crick declined. Rose to Crick, 4 May 1973, PP/CRI/E/2/12.

43 Crick to Jensen, 21 February 1972, PP/CRI/D/1/2/5.

44 Perutz to Crick, undated, PP/CRI/D/2/14.

45 PP/CRI/D/2/34, PP/CRI/D/2/14. One of the few documents with marginal marks (not necessarily by Crick) is a brochure published by The Party for Workers Power, *Racism, Intelligence and the Working Class*. Crick does not seem to have noticed that the brochure quoted Jensen from *The New York Times*, 31 August 1969, revealing his complete ignorance of genetics: 'There are intelligence genes, which are found in populations in different proportions, somewhat like the distribution of blood types. The

number of intelligence genes seems lower, overall, in the black population than in the white.'

46 PP/CRI/D/2/34.
47 Crick to Caldecote, 19 September 1972, PP/CRI/E/2/11.
48 Maddox to Crick, 20 October 1971; Crick to Maddox, 25 October 1971, PP/CRI/E/2/10.
49 Ridley (2006), p. 161.
50 Mayr to Crick, 14 April 1971, PP/CRI/D/1/2/8.
51 Edsall to Crick, 30 April 1971, PP/CRI/D/2/14.
52 Crick to Edsall, 10 June 1971, PP/CRI/D/2/14.
53 Pauling, L. (1968), Reflections on the new biology: Foreword. *UCLA Law Review* 15:267–72, p. 269: 'I have suggested that there should be tattooed on the forehead of every young person a symbol showing possession of the sickle-cell gene or whatever other similar gene, such as the gene for phenylketonuria, that he has been found to possess in single dose. If this were done, two young people carrying the same deleterious defective gene in single dose would recognise this situation at first sight, and would refrain from falling in love with one another. It is my opinion that legislation along this line, compulsory testing for defective genes before marriage, and some form of public or semi-public display of this possession, should be adopted.'
54 The unsourced quotation read: 'Races differ, not only in the colour of their skins, but in other physical ways and especially in temperament and innate intelligence. Scientists tell us that these differences are not the result of environment only, but mainly of heredity. Men are not born equal. That is something which has not got through to the politicians.' *East Kent Times and Mail*, 3 December 1976. This could easily have been said by Crick.
55 Crick to Edsall, 22 February 1971; Edsall to Crick, 5 March 1971; Crick to Edsall, 29 March 1971, PP/CRI/D/2/14.
56 Medawar, P. B. (1977), Unnatural science. *New York Review of Books*, 3 February 1977. Crick to Medawar, 31 January 1977, PP/CRI/D/2/25.
57 Crick to Mayr, 21 April 1971, PP/CRI/D/1/2/8.
58 Medawar to Crick, 4 February 1977, PP/CRI/D/2/25. This is clearly a joke.
59 Crick, interview with Jones [uncorrected transcript], 18 February 1981, PP/CRI/D/1/4/10. Crick opposed publication of the interview partly because he had mistakenly identified Shockley as the man behind the La Jolla Nobelist sperm bank that he had been invited to join (he repeatedly refused). Crick to Jones, 8 July 1981, PP/CRI/D/1/4/10. For the invitation to donate his 'germinal substance' and his reply, see Graham to Crick, 22 May 1980; Crick to Graham, 27 May 1980, PP/CRI/D/1/4/7.
60 MSS 660, Box 36, Folder 8. The LMB in Cambridge also holds a copy of the programme. My thanks to Professor Catherina Becker for sharing her memories of this programme, which I have not been able to watch.
61 Raab to Crick, undated [August 1994], PP/CRI/J/1/4/16. Crick to Raab, 2 September 1994, PP/CRI/J/2/14/3. I posted Crick's letter on Twitter; journalist Antonio Regalado hunted out the recipient, Nathan Raab, and posted his letter to Crick. Raab – who still has Crick's letter – was amazed

to discover the correspondence. The thread can be found here: https://x. com/matthewcobb/status/1796529892475203820

CHAPTER 14

1   Commoner, B. (1959), Replication of Tobacco Mosaic Virus: A re-examination of theories. *Nature* 184:1998–2001.
2   Commoner, B. (1964a), Roles of deoxyribonucleic acid in inheritance. *Nature* 202:960–8; Commoner, B. (1964b), Deoxyribonucleic acid and the molecular basis of self-replication. *Nature* 203:486–91.
3   Anonymous (1968), Central dogma, right or wrong? *Nature* 218:317.
4   Commoner, B. (1968), Failure of the Watson-Crick theory as a chemical explanation of inheritance. *Nature* 220:334–40.
5   Fleischman, P. (1970), The chemical basis of inheritance. *Nature* 225:30–2. Hershey, A. D. (1970), Genes and hereditary characteristics. *Nature* 226:697–700. Crick to Potter, 17 April 1969, PP/CRI/D/1/1/16. Crick to Thorpe, 9 January 1969, PP/CRI/D/1/1/19.
6   Wu, T. T. (1969), Secondary structures of DNA. *Proceedings of the National Academy of Sciences USA* 63:400–5.
7   Crick to Wilkins, 3 September 1969, PP/CRI/D/2/48.
8   Wilkins, M. H. F., Wilson, H. R. and Hamilton, L. D. (1970), Secondary structures of DNA. *Proceedings of the National Academy of Sciences USA* 65:761–2.
9   Crick to Edsall, 23 January 1970 and 15 January 1970, PP/CRI/D/2/48.
10 Donohue, J. (1969), Fourier analysis and the structure of DNA. *Science* 165:1091–6.
11 Wilkins, M. H. F., et al. (1970), Some misconceptions on Fourier analysis and Watson-Crick base pairing. *Science* 167:1693–4. Crick, F. H. C. (1970), DNA: Test of structure? *Science* 167:1694. Arnott, S. (1970), Crystallography of DNA: Difference synthesis supports Watson-Crick base pairing. *Science* 167:1694–70. Donohue, J. (1970), Fourier series and difference maps as lack of structure proof: DNA as an example. *Science* 167:1700–2.
12 Donohue sent Crick a light-hearted letter enclosing a newspaper cutting reporting the result of a recent horse race in which the initial front-runner, 'Double Helix', had 'tired badly in late stages, couldn't hold winner' and came in second. Donohue to Crick, 27 April 1970, PP/CRI/D/2/11/1. The file includes the newspaper cutting.
13 Anonymous (1970), The fly in the Fourier. *Nature* 226:404–5.
14 Crick to Donohue, 6 July 1970, PP/CRI/D/2/11/1.
15 Donohue, J. (1970), The fly in the Fourier. *Nature* 227:317. There was talk of Crick producing an article for *Nature* on the dispute, but Donohue insisted there would have to be a reply from himself and a summary of the affair from an 'unprejudiced titan' of crystallography – Donohue to Maddox, 10 August 1970, PP/CRI/D/2/11/1.
16 Wu remained convinced he was correct. Wu, T. T. (2019), 'Politics dictates scientific truth', unpublished note. https://archive.org/details/view1_202107
17 Anonymous (1970), Central dogma reversed. *Nature* 226:1198–9. Both articles were almost certainly written by John Tooze. Coffin, J. (2021), 50th

anniversary of the discovery of reverse transcriptase. *Molecular Biology of the Cell* 32:91–7.

18 Crick to Maddox, 7 July 1970, PP/CRI/D/2/27.

19 Crick, F. H. C. (1970), Central dogma of molecular biology. *Nature* 227:561–3.

20 Crick, The general nature of the genetic code, Verbatim transcript, November 1964, PP/CRI/H/3/13.

21 Crick to Temin, 17 September 1970, PP/CRI/D/1/1/19.

22 Crick, F. H. C. (1968), The origin of the genetic code. *Journal of Molecular Biology* 38:367–79. Orgel, L. (1968), Evolution of the genetic apparatus. *Journal of Molecular Biology* 38:381–93.

23 *Nature* invitation card to 31 October 1969 conference, PP/CRI/E/1/17/1. Anonymous (1970), The *Nature* centenary dinner. *Notes and Records of the Royal Society* 25:9–15. Crick's notes for his talk, an attendance list and correspondence with *Nature* can be found at PP/CRI/E/1/17/11. A page of early outline notes for the talk can be found at MSS 660, Box 20, Folder 9. Maddox to Crick, 12 May 1969, PP/CRI/E/1/17/11. Despite dozens of journalists being invited, I have found no media report of the event.

24 Maddox to Crick, 3 November 1969, PP/CRI/E/1/17/11. Crick agreed to be filmed for a BBC TV programme to mark the centenary; this never materialised. Crick to Maddox, 29 May 1969; Maddox to Crick, 4 June 1969; Sheehan to Crick, 18 August 1969; Crick to Sheehan, 3 September 1969, PP/CRI/E/1/17/11.

25 Crick to Maddox, 1 May 1970, PP/CRI/D/2/27. The various versions of the article can be found at PP/CRI/H/4/17.

26 Crick, F. H. C. (1970), Molecular biology in the year 2000. *Nature* 228:689–91.

27 Sverdlow, E. D. (2000), Francis Crick in his prognoses for 2000 was almost absolutely correct. *Russian Journal of Bioorganic Chemistry* 26:686–91.

28 Crick, How molecular is biology?, undated [1969], PP/CRI/E/1/17/11.

29 For example, Britten. R. J. and Kohne, D. E. (1968), Repeated sequences in DNA. *Science* 161:529–40.

30 The papers associated with the meeting can be found at PP/CRI/E/1/19/6.

31 Anonymous (1971), Circles, spacers and satellites on the Riviera. *Nature New Biology* 231:68.

32 PP/CRI/E/1/19/7, PP/CRI/E/1/19/8.

33 Hershko, A., et al. (1971), 'Pleiotypic response'. *Nature New Biology* 232:206–11.

34 Crick, F. H. C. (1971), General model for the chromosomes of higher organisms. *Nature* 234:25–7.

35 Crick to Brenner, 5 August 1971, SB/1/1/133.

36 Crick to Maddox, 3 September 1971, PP/CRI/D/2/27.

37 This meeting is implied in Crick, Notes for lab talk, 3 Sept [1971], PP/CRI/H/5/1/2. There were generally six postulates, but in one draft there were seven. PP/CRI/H/5/1/1.

38 PP/CRI/H/5/1/1, PP/CRI/H/5/1/2.

39 Brenner, On the paucity of 'mutable' genes in higher organisms, undated [August 1971], PP/CRI/H/5/1/2.

40 Kearsley Travel, Itinerary, undated [August-September 1971], PP/CRI/E/1/19/9. Crick to Lawrence, 11 September 1971, courtesy of Peter Lawrence.

41 Crick, Notes for lab talk, 3 Sept [1971], PP/CRI/H/5/1/2. Judson to Crick, 9 September 1971, PP/CRI/D/1/2/5.

42 Crick to Maddox, 3 September 1971, PP/CRI/D/2/27. In a manuscript version of the letter, Crick crossed out the following phrase: 'There is one joke but I don't see why your editorial writers should be the only people allowed to make them.' Crick to Maddox, rough draft, undated [September 1971], PP/CRI/H/5/1/2. I have not been able to work out what the joke was.

43 Sagan, C. (ed.), (1973), *Communication with Extraterrestrial Intelligence (CETI)* (London: MIT Press), p. 53.

44 Crick, Author's questionnaire, 2 April 1981, PP/CRI/J/7/1/2.

45 Gold, T. (1960), 'Cosmic garbage'. *Air Force and Space Digest,* May 1960, p. 65. Sagan (1973), p. 67.

46 Crick to Lawrence, 11 September 1971, courtesy of Peter Lawrence.

47 Crick to Lawrence, 11 September 1971, courtesy of Peter Lawrence.

48 Ohta, T. and Kimura, M. (1971), Functional organization of genetic material as a product of molecular evolution. *Nature* 233:118–9. Crick to Kimura, 22 September 1971, PP/CRI/D/1/2/6.

49 Anonymous (1971), Models or molecules? *Nature New Biology* 233:160.

50 Crick, A general model for the chromosomes of higher organisms – Nice, September 1971, PP/CRI/E/1/19/10. A few weeks later, he gave a version of this talk to the LMB but did not include this claim. Crick, Chromosome model – Lab lecture talk, 19 October 1971, PP/CRI/E/1/19/11.

51 Crick to Maddox, 15 October 1971; Maddox to Crick, 18 October 1971, PP/CRI/D/2/27.

52 Crick to Medawar, 21 April 1977, PP/CRI/D/3/4.

53 Kreisel to Crick, 12 February 1980, MSS 660, Box 5, Folder 4. Crick to Winter, 30 September 1974, PP/CRI/D/1/2/17. Jukes to Crick, 18 January 1973, PP/CRI/D/1/2/5. Why Crick and Orgel persisted with their emphasis on molybdenum in the light of Jukes' explanation is not clear.

54 Anonymous (1971), Unravelling the chromosome. *Nature* 234:10.

55 Crick to Lewin, 26 November 1971, PP/CRI/D/2/27.

56 Paul, J. (1972), General theory of chromosome structure and gene activation in eukaryotes. *Nature* 238:444–6.

57 Crick to Silvestri, 24 November 1971, PP/CRI/E/1/19/13.

58 Crick to Hastings, 6 October 1971, PP/CRI/E/2/10. See the photos in Mukhin to Crick, undated [November-December 1972], PP/CRI/D/1/2/8 and in Sagan (1973), p. xxvii. Crick's view of the photos was that 'it is obvious we were all enjoying ourselves' – Crick to Mukhin, 13 December 1972, PP/CRI/D/1/2/8.

59 Crick to Monsieur le Maire, 22 September 1971, PP/CRI/D/1/2/8. Crick to Beermann, 3 November 1971, PP/CRI/E/1/19/12.

60 Crick to Maddox, 25 October 1971, PP/CRI/E/2/10.

61 Crick to Rich, 24 November 1971, PP/CRI/E/1/20/5. Crick to Sonneborn, 10 January 1972, PP/CRI/E/2/11.
62 Crick to Chorąży, 20 March 1972, PP/CRI/E/2/11.
63 Letters to Crick, undated, MSS 660, Box 10.
64 Crick to Thomas, 24 November 1971, PP/CRI/D/1/2/14.
65 Crick to Soderberg, 29 November 1971, PP/CRI/D/1/2/13.
66 Crick to Rich, 21 January 1972 and 10 February 1972, PP/CRI/E/1/20/5. Crick to Subak-Sharpe, 12 February 1972, PP/CRI/E/2/11. Crick to Olby, 22 February 1972, PP/CRI/D/2/29.
67 Bretscher, Francis, undated, courtesy of Mark Bretscher. Bretscher, M. S. and Mitchison, G. (2017), Francis Harry Compton Crick OM: 8 June 1916 – 28 July 2004. *Biographical Memoirs of Fellows of the Royal Society* 63:159–96, p. 182.
68 GBR/0014/BRTS 40.
69 Foakes, Diary entries from 1.6.71 to 27.7.72, OLBY, Box 3. Foakes was Sue Barnes' married name.
70 Crick to Rich, 29 February 1972, 9 March 1972 and 20 March 1972, PP/CRI/E/1/20/5. Crick to Orgel, 25 February 1972, MSS 176, Box 40, Folder 16.
71 See for example Crick to Orgel, 16 October 1972, MSS 176, Box 40, Folder 16.
72 Crick to Määløe, 16 June 1972, PP/CRI/D/1/2/8.
73 Royal Society, Press statement, 21 November 1972, FD 21/14.
74 Crick to Kumar, 10 February 1972, PP/CRI/E/2/11. Crick to Noll, 10 May 1972, PP/CRI/D/1/2/9. Paul to Crick, 19 October 1972; Crick to Paul, 3 November 1972, PP/CRI/D/1/2/11.
75 Crick, MIT Lecture notes, April 1972, PP/CRI/E/1/20/5.
76 Crick to Latner, 14 November 1972, PP/CRI/D/1/2/7.
77 Olby, R. (2009), *Francis Crick: Hunter of Life's Secrets* (Cold Spring Harbor, NY: Cold Spring Harbor Laboratory Press), p. 354.
78 Kornberg, R. D. (1974), Chromatin structure: a repeating unit of histones and DNA. *Science* 184:868–71.
79 Crick and Orgel, drafts, undated, PP/CRI/H/5/7/1.
80 Barnes to Crick, 21 September 1972, MSS 176, Box 40, Folder 16. Crick, F. H. C. and Orgel, L. E. (1973), Directed panspermia. *Icarus* 19:341–6.
81 Crick to Weldon, 30 May 1974, PP/CRI/D/1/2/16. Crick to Kreisel, 2 December 1977, PP/CRI/D/3/8.
82 Crick and Orgel, On loopy codes, undated [1961], PP/CRI/H/3/2.
83 Crick, F. H. C., Griffith, J. S. and Orgel, S. E. (1957), Codes without commas. *Proceedings of the National Academy of Sciences USA* 43:416–21.
84 Crick, Griffith and Orgel, Comma-less codes, May 1956, PP/CRI/H/2/3.

CHAPTER 15

1 Mor to Crick, 8 September 1949, MSS 660, Box 7, Folder 37.
2 Crick to Snow, 23 September 1963, MSS 660, Box 9, Folder 20.
3 Snow, C. P. (1959), *The Two Cultures and the Scientific Revolution* (Cambridge: Cambridge University Press). Leavis, F. R. (1962), *Two Cultures? The Significance of C. P. Snow* (London: Chatto & Windus). Ortolano, G. (2004),

Human science or a human face? Social history and the 'two cultures' controversy. *Journal of British Studies* 43:482–505. Hall, A. R. (1963), Review. *Scientific American* 208, August 1963, p. 129–30.

4 Snow, C. P. (1963), The two cultures: a second look. *Times Literary Supplement*, 25 October 1963. Bronowski, J. (1964), The abacus and the rose: a dialogue after Galileo. *The Nation*, 4 January 1964, PP/CRI/I/3/7.

5 Crick, F. (1975), The poetry of Michael McClure: A scientist's view. *Margins* 18, March 1975, pp. 23–4. Crick's article is widely available on the internet. The magazine can be found at MSS 660, Box 7, Folder 15.

6 Pascal to Crick, 31 March 1966; Crick to Pascal, 19 April 1966, PP/CRI/H/3/20. Pascal to McClure, 31 March 1966, MsA 5.12 MSS 37.

7 McClure to Crick, 7 September 1970, MSS 660, Box 7, Folder 14. Crick's copy of *The Surge* is at MSS 660, Box 7, Folder 13.

8 Crick to McClure, 18 October 1970, MsA 5.12 MSS 37.

9 McClure to Crick, 27 October 1970, MSS 660, Box 7, Folder 14.

10 McClure, M. (1971), 'Moiré'. *The Paris Review* 51:12–17.

11 Geoff Ward, e-mail to the author, 22 January 2025.

12 Crick to McClure, 9 November 1970, MsA 5.12 MSS 37.

13 Crick to McClure, 20 January 1971, MsA 5.12 MSS 37.

14 Crick to Snow, 23 September 1963, MSS 660, Box 9, Folder 20.

15 Miles, B. (2017), *In the Sixties* (London: Rocket 88), p. 330.

16 Dobran, R. (ed.), (2017), *The Collected Letters of Charles Olson and J. H. Prynne* (Albuquerque: University of New Mexico Press). Mellors, A. (2016), wynsum wong: J. H. Prynne inside and outside The English Intelligencer. In I. Brinton (ed.), *For the Future: Poems and Essays in Honour of J. H. Prynne on the Occasion of his 80th Birthday* (Bristol: Shearsman), pp. 141–53, p. 145. Ford, M. (2010), Hide and be found. *New York Review of Books*, 19 August 2010.

17 Prynne to Dorn, 22 January 1963, Dorn Papers, Box 13, Folder 329.

18 Thanks to Geoff Ward for this clarification.

19 Bretscher, Francis, undated, courtesy of Mark Bretscher. 'Jeremy Prynne did show me a copy a few months ago but I am delighted to have one for myself, direct from you' – Crick to McClure, 18 October 1970, MsA 5.12 MSS 37.

20 Crick to McClure, 3 February 1971 and 16 February 1971, MsA 5.12 MSS 37.

21 Crick to McClure, 3 February 1971, MsA 5.12 MSS 37.

22 https://www.emptymirrorbooks.com/keenan/b1965-10.html

23 Crick to McClure, 16 February 1971 and 3 May 1971, MsA 5.12 MSS 37.

24 McClure to Crick, 31 January 1971, MSS 660, Box 7, Folder 14.

25 McClure to Crick, undated [1975], MSS 660, Box 7, Folder 15.

26 'Just spoke on the phone with Herbert Marcuse. He said he had not met you – and he would enjoy doing so very much.' McClure to Crick, 16 and 18 November 1970, MSS 660, Box 7, Folder 14.

27 Brenner borrowed it; it was probably more up his street than Crick's. Cricks, Lending Book, MSS 660, Box 26, Folder 6.

28 Crick to McClure, 5 October 1974, MsA 5.12 MSS 37. Jacob to Crick, 28 October 1974, MSS 660, Box 7, Folder 15. Crick (1975).

29 Crick to McClure, 1 January 1975, MsA 5.12 MSS 37.

30 McClure to Crick, undated [1975], MSS 660, Box 7, Folder 15.
31 Crick to McClure, 1 January 1975, MsA 5.12 MSS 37.
32 McClure, notebook: 1975 Apr 30 to 1975 Dec 10, BANC MSS 2003/222 c, Box 8, Folder 4. Crick's diary entry for 20 October 1975 reads: 'Mike McClure 8.30'. Crick, Diary, 1975–76, MSS 660, Box 14, Folder 22. It is not clear what this refers to – McClure arrived in the UK on 26 October (McClure, Travel notebook: 1975 Apr 30 to 1975 Dec 10, BANC MSS 2003/222 c, Box 8, Folder 4). The Poetry of the Americas Conference lasted from 27 October to 1 November (McClure's reading can be heard at SA 1CA0017786). McClure was in Cambridge on 30 October 1975 and wrote a couple of poems in a copy of Tom Stoppard's play *Travesties* which he inscribed on that date (McClure and Stoppard had struck up a friendship in San Francisco the previous year).
33 Ward, G. (2014), Underground rivers, new bridges. *Homertonian* 18, July 2014, pp. 3–5, p. 4.
34 Geoff Ward, e-mail to the author, 20 January 2025.
35 McClure to Crick, undated [1975] and 5 December 1975, MSS 660, Box 7, Folder 15.
36 Hollander, A Shape of Life, September 1968, MSS 660, Box 4, Folder 19.
37 Duncan to Crick, 6 August 1968, PP/CRI/D/1/1/4. Crick kept the canto: MSS 660, Box 3, Folder 18.
38 Holmes, J. (2023), A poetics of enquiry in Ronald Duncan's Man. *Interdisciplinary Science Reviews* 48:511–23.
39 Crick to Duncan, 19 August 1968, PP/CRI/D/1/1/4.
40 Duncan to Crick, 21 August 1968, MSS 660, Box 3, Folder 18.
41 Holmes (2023), p. 520.
42 Duncan, R. (1971), *Man: Part Two* (London: Rebel Press). Crick (1975).
43 Flyer for *For the Few* by Ronald Duncan, undated, MSS 660, Box 3, Folder 18. The price was £10; Crick wrote on the leaflet: 'Sent cheque. 5 Oct 77'.
44 Bax to Crick, 2 April 1969; Crick to Bax, 3 April 1969; Bax to Crick, 15 April 1969, PP/CRI/D/1/1/1. *International Times* 54, 11 April 1969. ICA *Eventsheet*, April [1969], TGA 955/14/20. More details of the event, which was one of three (the first, a week earlier, was 'Prose Poetry Jazz' and included a reading of J. G. Ballard's 'Plan for the Assassination of Jacqueline Kennedy') can be found in ICA Press Release, undated [April 1969], TGA 955/13/6/18.
45 Westminster Poetry Festival flyer, 1970, MSS 660, Box 18, Folder 7. Crick's appointment diary for 1970 is missing; it is not known if he attended.
46 Guppy to Crick, 17 September 1969, MSS 660, Box 4, Folder 7.
47 McClure to Crick, 23 February 1971, MSS 660, Box 7, Folder 14.
48 Crick, The Story of A, undated, MSS 660, Box 20, Folder 11.
49 McClure, M. (1978), Editors' statements. *Coevolution Quarterly*, Fall 1978, p. 4.
50 McClure to Francis and Odile, 12 April 1978; Crick to McClure, 1 May 1978, PP/CRI/D/1/3/12.
51 Kindersley to Crick, 20 February 1975, PP/CRI/D/2/17A.
52 The galley proof of the Introduction/Preface – now called a Foreword – is

at PP/CRI/D/2/17A. Ross MacDonald, M. (1975), *The Origin of Johnny* (New York: Knopf).

53 Crick to Kindersley, 26 February 1976, PP/CRI/D/2/17A. Alongside the poem is the handwritten comment 'Whistles from the gallery!' – PP/CRI/H/6/3/2. Another set of drafts can be found at PP/CRI/H/6/3/1.

54 Kindersley to Crick, 4 September 1976, PP/CRI/H/6/3/2.

55 Cox to Kindersley, 1 September 1976, PP/CRI/H/6/3/2.

56 MSS 660, Box 1, Folder 36.

57 PP/CRI/H/6/3/3.

58 Crick to Bryan, 27 September 1976, PP/CRI/D/3/1.

59 Kindersley to Crick, 4 January 1977, PP/CRI/H/6/3/2.

60 Crick to Bryan, 18 and 19 January 1977, PP/CRI/D/3/3. Crick to Bryan, 4 April 1977, PP/CRI/D/3/4. Crick to Bryan, 13 July 1977, PP/CRI/D/3/6.

61 Crick to Bryan, 24 February 1977, PP/CRI/D/3/3.

62 Wassmuth to Crick, 5 September 1977, MSS 660, Box 10, Folder 31. Crick replied positively on 26 September (also in PP/CRI/D/3/7); the draft of his final response is dated 1 November 1977.

63 Anderson, R. (1982), Hey Mister, can we have your autograph? *Sports Illustrated*, 12 April 1982. Crick's handwritten covering letter to 'Mr Wassmuth' was sold at auction in November 2011.

CHAPTER 16

1 Crick to Orgel, 1 November 1972, MSS 176, Box 40, Folder 16.

2 Crick to Fouracre, 15 December 1970, MSS 660, Box 19, Folder 9.

3 The public version can be seen at https://archive.org/details/thednastory_201611. The initial scripts were written by Francis. MSS 660, Box 19, Folders 9 and 10. See also Shaw to Crick, 18 November 1971, MSS 660, Box 19, Folder 9. Crick to Watson, 10 October 1972, PP/CRI/D/2/45.

4 *Guardian*, 9 August 1972.

5 The university version of the film is not currently available online.

6 McQuillen to Crick, 30 May 1973; Crick to McQuillen, 13 June 1973, PP/CRI/D/1/2/8. Scientist Tracey Sonneborn sent Francis a fan letter, saying he was delighted with the film. Sonneborn to Crick, 24 February 1974, PP/CRI/D/1/2/13.

7 Crick to Swann, 3 May 1974, PP/CRI/D/1/2/13. *Radio Times*, 6 July 1974. Crick's diary for 8 May 1974 – two months before the broadcast – reads '9:35 BBC II TV DNA' (MSS 660, Box 14, Folder 20). There was no DNA programme that day, suggesting the initial broadcast date was subsequently changed. *The Listener* published a transcript of the programme; Crick kept a copy of the magazine and also sent one to Watson (PP/CRI/I/2/14). Crick to Watson, 24 July 1974, PP/CRI/D/2/45. *Observer*, 14 July 1974. *Guardian*, 9 July 1974. Over two years later, a US version was broadcast in the PBS 'Nova' slot, with a new commentary by Isaac Asimov.

8 Newmark, P. (1974), Human face of Watson and Crick. *Nature* 250:361.

9 Crick to Watson, 24 July 1974, PP/CRI/D/2/45.

10 Daly to Crick, MSS 660, Box 1, Folder 24.

11 Crick to Bronowski, 4 March 1974; Bronowski to Crick, 16 March 1974, MSS 660, Box 1, Folder 26.

12 Jones to Crick, 4 November 1975, MSS 660, Box 1, Folder 24. Crick's script for the programme is in this folder.

13 Davies to Crick, 6 December 1973 and 10 January 1974, PP/CRI/D/2/27. Crick, F. (1974), The double helix: a personal view. *Nature* 248:766–9.

14 Watson said he 'enjoyed much' the article (Watson to Crick, 20 May 1974, PP/CRI/D/2/45) while another colleague described it as 'a serious note written with poise as well as uncommon good sense and humour'. Kurland to Crick, 9 May 1974, PP/CRI/D/1/2/6.

15 Klug, A. (1974), Rosalind Franklin and the double helix. *Nature* 248:787–8. Chargaff, E. (1974), Building the Tower of Babble. *Nature* 248:776–9. Stent, G. S. (1974), Molecular biology and metaphysics. *Nature* 248:779–81. Windsor, D. A. (1974), Molecular biologists come of age in Aries. *Nature* 248:788. Crick to Stent, 22 February 1974, PP/CRI/D/1/2/13. Stent admitted to Crick that his article was 'a bit far out' – Stent to Crick, 19 April 1974, PP/CRI/D/1/2/13.

16 Suddath, F. L., et al. (1974), Three-dimensional structure of yeast phenylalanine transfer RNA at 3.0Å resolution. *Nature* 248:20–4. Robertus, J. D., et al. (1974), Structure of yeast phenylalanine tRNA at 3Å resolution. *Nature* 250:546–51.

17 Kim, S. H., et al. (1974), Three-dimensional tertiary structure of yeast phenylalanine transfer RNA. *Science* 185:435–40.

18 Blow to Editor, 31 July 1974, PP/CRI/D/2/35.

19 Crick to Rich, 31 July 1974, PP/CRI/D/2/35.

20 Rich to Crick, 9 August 1974, PP/CRI/D/2/35.

21 Lewin, R. (1974), Transfer RNA researchers argue about 'borrowed' data. *New Scientist*, 19 September 1974, pp. 708–9. PP/CRI/D/2/35.

22 Crick to Rich, 4 September 1974 and 5 December 1974, PP/CRI/D/2/35.

23 Rich to Crick, 27 November 1974, PP/CRI/D/2/35.

24 Crick to Rich, 4 September 1974, PP/CRI/D/2/35.

25 Crick to Fuller, 15 May 1975, PP/CRI/D/1/2/1. Various drafts and correspondence with Fuller can be found in PP/CRI/H/6/12. The article was initially known as 'Writhing Numbers for Bird Watchers' or 'The Writhing Number Made Easy'. The 'bird watchers' business was a nod to a document Crick wrote for Watson the bird watcher in 1951, 'X-ray Crystallography for Bird Watchers'. It turned out that the Writhing Number was not what Crick was interested in. Crick, F. H. C. (1976), Linking numbers and nucleosomes. *Proceedings of the National Academy of Sciences USA* 73:2639–43.

26 Kornberg, R. D. and Thomas, J. O. (1974), Chromatin structure: oligomers of the histones. *Science* 184:865–9. Kornberg, R. D. (1974), Chromatin structure: a repeating unit of histones and DNA. *Science* 184:868–71. Noll, M. (1974), Subunit structure of chromatin. *Nature* 251:249–51.

27 Crick, F. H. C. and Klug, A. (1975), Kinky helix. *Nature* 255:530–3. Crick to Felsenfeld, 6 October 1975, PP/CRI/D/1/3/6. Crick to Bower, 29 April 2002, PP/CRI/J/2/22/1.

28 Davies to Crick, 16 April 1975, PP/CRI/H/5/20.

29 Leth Bak, A. and Zeuthen, J. (1976), Evidence for a folded structure of human chromosomes. *Hereditas* 82:1–6.

30 Crick to Klug, 7 October 1976, PP/CRI/D/3/1.

31 Crick to Callan, 12 October 1976, PP/CRI/D/3/1.

32 Rudkin to Crick, 5 January 1977, PP/CRI/D/1/3/15.

33 Callan to Crick, 12 January 1977, PP/CRI/D/1/3/3.

34 Crick to Leth Bak, 12 November 1976, PP/CRI/D/3/2.

35 Crick to Leth Bak, 13 December 1976 and 22 December 1976, PP/CRI/D/3/2. Leth Bak, A., Zeuthen, J. and Crick, F. H. (1977), Higher-order structure of human mitotic chromosomes. *Proceedings of the National Academy of Sciences USA* 74:1595–9. Crick to Watson, 17 January 1977; Crick to Klug, 17 January 1977; Crick to Callan, 18 January 1977, PP/CRI/D/3/3.

36 Crick to Klug, 30 March 1977, PP/CRI/D/3/4. Crick to Ris, 19 May 1977, PP/CRI/D/3/5.

37 Crick to Klug, 4 October 1977, PP/CRI/D/3/7.

38 MSS 660, Box 17, Folder 10. MSS 660, Box 12, Folder 18. When I announced on Twitter that Crick had this type of car, Dr Tori Herridge quipped 'Of course he did'.

39 Crick to Kendall, 15 January 1975, PP/CRI/D/1/2/6.

40 MSS 660, Box 17, Folder 13.

41 Perutz to Gray, 22 June 1975, FD 21/14.

42 Crick to Gray, undated [June 1975], FD 21/14. Klug to Kavenoff, 4 July 1975, PP/CRI/D/1/2/6. Crick to Jukes, 12 July 1976 and 2 August 1976, PP/CRI/D/1/2/5. Crick, Diary, 1975–1976, MSS 660, Box 14, Folder 22.

43 Crick to Fairchild, 10 March 1972, PP/CRI/D/1/2/1.

44 MSS 660, Box 9, Folder 17.

45 Simonsuuri to Francis and Odile, 21 May 1981, MSS 660, Box 9, Folder 17.

46 Vickers to Perutz, 25 June 1973, FD 21/14.

47 Perutz to Vickers, 20 July 1973, FD 21/14.

48 Mollon, J. (2013), Caius remembers Crick. *Once a Caian…* 13:2–5.

49 de Hoffmann to Crick, 11 August 1975, MSS 660, Box 13, Folder 10.

50 de Hoffmann to Crick, 2 September 1975, MSS 660, Box 13, Folder 10.

51 de Hoffmann to Crick, 15 June 1976, MSS 660, Box 13, Folder 10.

52 Olby, R. (2009), *Francis Crick: Hunter of Life's Secrets* (Cold Spring Harbor, NY: Cold Spring Harbor Laboratory Press), p. 368. de Hoffmann to Crick, 6 April 1976; Crick to de Hoffmann, 18 April 1976, MSS 660, Box 13, Folder 10.

53 Crick to de Hoffmann, 18 April 1976, MSS 660, Box 13, Folder 10.

54 de Hoffmann to Crick, 9 May 1976, MSS 660, Box 13, Folder 10.

55 Crick to de Hoffmann, 8 and 13 June 1976, MSS 660, Box 13, Folder 10.

56 Crick to de Hoffmann, 8 June 1976, MSS 660, Box 13, Folder 10.

57 Crick to de Hoffmann, 6 January 1976, MSS 660, Box 13, Folder 10.

58 Crick to Bryan, 27 September 1976, PP/CRI/D/3/1.

59 Crick to Klug, 30 September 1976, PP/CRI/D/3/1.

60 Crick to Kornberg, 26 October 1976, PP/CRI/D/1/2/6.

61 Crick to Fouracre, 5 April 1977, PP/CRI/D/1/3/6.

62 Simonsuuri to Odile Crick, 13 November 1976, MSS 660, Box 24, Folder 4.

63 Crick to Brenner, 10 and 16 November 1976, SB/1/1/133.

64 Crick to Perutz, 14 December 1976, PP/CRI/D/3/2.
65 Crick to Perutz, 13 January 1977, PRTZ 3/2/4.
66 Brenner, draft memo [to Perutz], undated [early 1977], SB/1/1/133.
67 Crick to Perutz, 17 February 1977, MSS 660, Box 13, Folder 10.
68 Perutz to Gray, 22 February 1977, FD 21/14.
69 Salk Institute, Press release, 31 March 1977, PP/CRI/D/1/2/6. de Hoffmann to Crick, 3 January 1977, MSS 660, Box 13, Folder 10.
70 Crick to Cleary, 2 February 1976, FD 21/14. Ridley, M. (2006), *Francis Crick: Discoverer of the Genetic Code* (London: Harper), p. 178.

CHAPTER 17

1 *Sunday Times*, 27 March 1977.
2 *The Times*, 29 March 1977.
3 *New Statesman*, 1 April 1977. Woddis to Crick, 16 May 1977, PP/CRI/D/1/3/19. Crick kept a copy of Woddis's poem – MSS 660, Box 21, Folder 9.
4 Crick to Lwoff, 1 August 1977, PP/CRI/D/3/6.
5 Crick to Hill, 25 July 1977, PP/CRI/D/1/3/8.
6 Mead to Crick, 1 March 1977, PP/CRI/D/1/3/12. Daly to Crick, 28 March 1977 and 2 May 1977, PP/CRI/D/1/3/4.
7 McClure to Crick, 7 January 1977, MSS 660, Box 7, Folder 19. Crick's letter has been lost.
8 Crick to Klug, 4 October 1977, PP/CRI/D/3/7.
9 Francis to Odile, 6 September 1977, MSS 660, Box 22, Folder 21.
10 Crick to McClure, 15 October 1978, MsA 5e.1.
11 McClure to Francis and Odile, 20 February 1979, MSS 660, Box 7, Folder 21. Crick to McClure, 20 March 1979, PP/CRI/D/1/4/13. Trivers to Crick, 24 April 1979, PP/CRI/D/1/4/19. Crick to Orgel, 9 August 1979, PP/CRI/D/1/4/15. Crick to Brenner, 5 February 1979, SB/1/1/133. Crick to Petitto, 6 March 1986, PP/CRI/J/2/6/1. Robertson to Crick, 22 February 1979, PP/CRI/D/1/4/17.
12 Kreisel to Crick, 17 January 1983 and 15 May 1985, MSS 660, Box 5, Folder 5.
13 Crick to Marx, 15 May 1978, PP/CRI/D/1/3/12.
14 Cowan to Crick, 20 April 1981, PP/CRI/D/1/4/3. The book was Klüver, H. (1967), *Mescal and the Mechanisms of Hallucination* (Chicago: Chicago University Press).
15 For more on Brenner's activity, see Cobb, M. (2022), *The Genetic Age: Our Perilous Quest to Edit Life* (London: Profile), published in the USA as *As Gods: A Moral History of the Genetic Age* (New York: Basic).
16 Cobb, M. (2025), The curious incident of Crick in the night-time and other Asilomar enigmas. *Journal of the History of Biology* 58:49–66.
17 Brenner to Crick, 5 January 1978, PP/CRI/D/2/6.
18 Crick to Brenner, 22 January 1981, SB/1/1/134.
19 Keen to Crick, 14 July 1977, PP/CRI/E/1/25/18.
20 Watson to Crick, 15 August 1975, JDW/2/2/405.
21 Watson to Crick, 27 June 1976 and 14 October 1976, JDW/2/2/405.
22 Crick, Opening comments, 1 June 1977, PP/CRI/E/1/25/18.

23 Witkowski, J. A. (1988), The discovery of 'split' genes: a scientific revolution. *Trends in Biochemical Sciences* 13:110–13. Cobb, M. (2015), *Life's Greatest Secret: The Race to Crack the Genetic Code* (London: Profile).

24 Monod, J. and Jacob, F. (1961), Teleonomic mechanism in cellular metabolism, growth and differentiation. *Cold Spring Harbor Symposia on Quantitative Biology* 26:389–401, p. 393.

25 Sambrook, J. (1977), Adenovirus amazes at Cold Spring Harbor. *Nature* 268:101–4.

26 Gilbert, W. (1978), Why genes in pieces? *Nature* 271:501. Crick, F. (1979), Split genes and RNA splicing. *Science* 204:264–71.

27 PP/CRI/E/1/26/11.

28 Crick (1979).

29 Crick to Olby, 7 March 2001, PP/CRI/J/2/21/1.

30 Mahler to Crick, 19 April 1979, PP/CRI/D/1/4/13.

31 Kreisel to Crick, 26 December 1978, PP/CRI/D/2/20.

32 Crick to Ohno, 22 January 1981, PP/CRI/J/2/1/1.

33 Doolittle to Crick, 10 December 1979, PP/CRI/D/1/4/4.

34 Crick to Doolittle, 2 January 1980, PP/CRI/D/1/4/4. Crick to Newmark, 9 January 1980, PP/CRI/D/1/4/14.

35 Robertson to Crick, 22 February 1979, PP/CRI/D/1/4/17. Doolittle, W. F. and Sapienza, C. (1980), Selfish genes, the phenotype paradigm and genome evolution. *Nature* 284:601–3. Orgel, L. E. and Crick, F. H. C. (1980), Selfish DNA: the ultimate parasite. *Nature* 284:604–7. Drafts of the Orgel and Crick article and correspondence with *Nature* are at MSS 176, Box 16, Folders 1–3.

36 Doolittle to Crick, 17 April 1980, PP/CRI/D/1/4/4. For a poor photocopy of the cover (not available on the *Nature* website and sadly removed from bound volumes in most libraries) see PP/CRI/H/6/13/1.

37 Anonymous (1980), Can DNA properly be called selfish? *Nature* 285:604.

38 Crick to Newmark, 9 January 1980, P/CRI/D/1/4/14.

39 Cavalier-Smith, T. (1980), How selfish is DNA? *Nature* 285:617–18. Dover, G. (1980), Ignorant DNA? *Nature* 285:618–19. Smith, T. F. (1980), Occam's razor. *Nature* 285:620. Reid, R. A. (1980), Selfish DNA in 'Petite' mutants. *Nature* 285:620. Orgel, L. E., Crick, F. H. C. and Sapienza, C. (1980), Selfish DNA. *Nature* 288:645–6.

40 PP/CRI/H/6/13/4, PP/CRI/H/6/13/7, PP/CRI/H/6/13/8.

41 Crick, F. (1979), How to live with a golden helix. *The Sciences*, September 1979. For all material relating to the publication of the article see PP/CRI/D/1/4/18.

42 Friend to Smith, 24 August 1979; Friend to Crick, 11 September 1979; Crick to Friend, 18 September 1979, PP/CRI/D/1/4/6. In a similar vein, see: Markham to Crick, 12 September 1979; Crick to Markham, 18 September 1979, PP/CRI/D/1/4/13.

43 Klug to Crick, 18 September 1979 and 9 October 1979, PP/CRI/D/2/19.

44 See for example the correspondence with Pohl, MSS 660, Box 8, Folder 31. Crick, F. H. C., Wang, J. C. and Bauer, W. R. (1979), Is DNA really a double helix? *Journal of Molecular Biology* 129:449–61. The title of this article is a notable exception to Betteridge's law of headlines.

45 Wang, J. C. (1979), Helical repeat of DNA in solution. *Proceedings of the National Academy of Sciences USA*, 76:200–3. Wang, A. H.-J., et al. (1979), Molecular structure of a left-handed double helical DNA fragment at atomic resolution. *Nature* 282:680–6.

46 Stokes to Crick, 1 May 1980, PP/CRI/D/1/4/18.

47 Crick to Stokes, 8 May 1980, PP/CRI/D/1/4/18. Stokes, T. D. (1982), The double helix and the warped zipper – an exemplary tale. *Social Studies of Science* 12:207–40.

48 Crick to Sasisekharan, 24 January 1979, PP/CRI/D/1/4/18.

49 PP/CRI/H/6/10.

50 Raines to Crick, 10 September 1973; Crick to Raines, 18 September 1973, MSS 176, Box 40, Folder 16. Orgel to Crick, 24 September 1973, MSS 176, Box 40, Folder 16. Crick to Kreisel, 17 March 1978, PP/CRI/D/3/10.

51 Crick to Mayhew, 15 April 1981, PP/CRI/J/2/1/2.

52 Kreisel to Crick, 23 November 1981, MSS 660, Box 5, Folder 5.

53 Crick, F. (1981), *Life Itself: Its Origin and Nature* (New York: Simon & Schuster), p. 156.

54 Crick (1981), pp. 57–8.

55 Crick (1981), p. 164

56 Crick to Sagan, 21 December 1981, PP/CRI/D/1/4/18.

57 Mayhew to Crick, 7 September 1983, PP/CRI/J/1/1/11/2. Reviews – PP/CRI/J/7/1/4. Translations – PP/CRI/J/7/1/3.

58 Prynne to Crick, 22 March 1982; Crick to Prynne, 29 March 1982, PP/CRI/J/7/1/5. Crick had a sharp exchange with Bishop Hugh Montefiore, who had been a Cambridge sparring-partner and had reviewed the book critically in *Nature*: Montefiore, H. (1982), Heavenly insemination. *Nature* 296:496–7. Crick to Montefiori, 22 April 1982 and 4 May 1982; Montefiore to Crick, 28 April 1982, PP/CRI/J/7/1/5.

59 von Däniken to Crick, 8 June 1972; Crick to von Däniken, 19 June 1982, PP/CRI/J/7/1/5.

60 Wolpert, L. and Richards, A. (1988), *A Passion for Science* (Oxford: Oxford University Press), p. 93.

61 Crick, F. H. C., Marr, D. C. and Poggio, T. (1980), An information processing approach to understanding the visual cortex. In F. O. Schmitt (ed.), *The Cortex*, (Cambridge, MA: MIT Press), pp. 503–5.

62 Crick, F. H. (1991), untitled. In L. Vaina (ed.), *From the Retina to the Neocortex: Selected Papers of David Marr* (Boston: Birkhauser), pp. 313–4, p. 313.

63 Crick, Why I study biology, uncorrected transcript, 24 February 1971, PP/CRI/E/1/19/3. For the MIT meeting: PP/CRI/E/1/20/6.

64 For a brief non-technical summary of Marr's work and its impact, see Cobb, M. (2020), *The Idea of the Brain: A History* (London: Profile).

65 Marr, D. and Poggio, T. (1976), Cooperative computation of stereo disparity. *Science* 194:283–7.

66 Crick to Kornberg, 23 April 1979, PP/CRI/D/1/4/11.

67 Crick to Marr and Poggio, 7 May 1979, MSS 660, Box 7, Folder 6. Crick to Powell, 14 August 1979, PP/CRI/D/1/4/16.

68 Crick, Marr and Poggio (1980), p. 503.

69 Crick to Churchland, 9 February 1984, PP/CRI/J/2/4/1.
70 Kreisel to Crick, 11 November 1979, MSS 660, Box 5, Folder 4.
71 Crick to Voevodsky, 25 March 1977, PP/CRI/D/3/7.
72 Crick, F. (1988), *What Mad Pursuit: A Personal View of Scientific Discovery* (New York: Basic), p. 136.
73 Crick to Mitchison, 10 June 1983, PP/CRI/J/2/3/3.
74 Crick to Marr, 13 December 1979, PP/CRI/H/6/18. All subsequent quotes from Crick's critique are taken from this letter and the seven-page enclosure that accompanied it.
75 Marr to Crick, 16 August [1980], MSS 660, Box 7, Folder 6.
76 Crick to Kreisel, 30 November 1980, SC0136, Box 35, Folder 46.
77 Crick, F. (1994), *The Astonishing Hypothesis: The Scientific Search for the Soul* (New York: Charles Scribner's Sons), p. 77.
78 Marr, D. (1982), *Vision: A Computational Investigation into the Human Representation and Processing of Visual Information* (London: MIT Press). Crick to Allen, 12 May 1982, PP/CRI/J/2/2/3.
79 Crick to Roth, 30 August 1993, PP/CRI/J/2/13/2.
80 Cobb (2020).
81 Crick, F. H. C. (1979), Thinking about the brain. *Scientific American* 241, September 1979, pp. 219–33. All subsequent quotes are from this article.
82 The correspondence relating to this article has been lost.

CHAPTER 18

1 Aicardi, C. (2016), Francis Crick, cross-worlds influencer: A narrative model to historicize big bioscience. *Studies in the History and Philosophy of Biological and Biomedical Sciences* 55:83–95.
2 Aicardi, C. (2014), Of the Helmholtz Club, South-California seedbed for visual and cognitive neuroscience, and its patron Francis Crick. *Studies in the History and Philosophy of Biological and Biomedical Sciences* 45:1–11. See also PP/CRI/C/3/1 and PP/CRI/C/3/2. The SDF was a spin-off of the Systems Development Corporation, which originated in the RAND Corporation, a postwar creation of the US Air Force and the Douglas Aircraft Company. The SDF closed in June 1988, having given away all its money; Ishihara to Crick, 22 June 1988, PP/CRI/C/3/2.
3 Crick to de Hoffmann, 16 December 1981, PP/CRI/J/1/1/5. Crick to Reynolds, 19 May 1983, PP/CRI/J/2/3/3.
4 Bourgeois, S. (2013), *Genesis of the Salk Institute: The Epic of Its Founders* (London: University of California Press). In 1981 Crick obtained $30,000 from the Air Force Office of Scientific Research. Crick to Irving, 20 May 1981, PP/CRI/J/2/1/3. The $30,000 grant was approved in October; Crick to Klopf, 23 October 1981, PP/CRI/J/2/1/4.
5 Crick, Application to SDF, January 1982, PP/CRI/C/3/1. de Hoffmann to Smith, draft letter, 15 January 1982, PP/CRI/C/3/1.
6 Crick to de Hoffmann, 15 July 1982, PP/CRI/C/3/2.
7 Rumelhart, D. (1995), From searching to seeing. In P. Baumgartner and S. Payr (eds.), *Speaking Minds: Interviews with Twenty Eminent Cognitive Scientists* (Princeton: Princeton University Press), pp. 189–201. Crick, F. (1994), *The Astonishing Hypothesis: The Scientific Search for the Soul* (New

York: Charles Scribner's Sons), p. 186. Olby, R. (2009), *Francis Crick: Hunter of Life's Secrets* (Cold Spring Harbor, NY: Cold Spring Harbor Laboratory Press), pp. 390–1. Crick, Diaries, 1982 and 1983, MSS 660, Box 14, Folders 26 and 27. Crick's notes from some of these meetings can be found at PP/CRI/L/1/1/7B.

8 Crick to de Hoffmann, 21 June 1979, PP/CRI/D/1/4/4.

9 Crick to Kornberg, 8 April 1980, PP/CRI/D/1/4/11.

10 Crick to Churchland, 9 February 1984, PP/CRI/J/2/4/1. Crick to Lockhart, 14 January 1982, PP/CRI/J/2/2/1. Crick to Totsumoto, 28 January 1982, PP/CRI/J/2/2/1. Ridley, M. (2006), *Francis Crick: Discoverer of the Genetic Code* (London: Harper Press), p. 188. Crick to Mitchison, 30 March 1983 and 7 April 1983, PP/CRI/J/2/3/2.

11 PP/CRI/E/1/27/4. Rockland, K. S. and Lund, J. (1982), Widespread periodic intrinsic connections in the tree shrew visual cortex. *Science* 215:1532–4.

12 Crick to Schiller, 2 January 1986, PP/CRI/J/2/6/1.

13 Crick to Lund, 12 November 1980, PP/CRI/D/1/4/12.

14 Mitchison, G. and Crick, F. (1982), Long axons within the striate cortex: their distribution, orientation, and patterns of connection. *Proceedings of the National Academy of Sciences USA* 79:3661–5. Crick to Lund, 5 February 1982, PP/CRI/J/2/2/1. Crick to PNAS, 5 March 1982, PP/CRI/J/2/2/2.

15 Rockland, K. S. (2022), Clustered intrinsic connections: not a single system. *Frontiers in Systems Neuroscience* 16:910845. Chavane, F., Perrinet, L. U. and Rankin, J. (2022), Revisiting horizontal connectivity rules in V1: from like-to-like towards like-to-all. *Brain Structure and Function* 227:1279–95.

16 Crick to January, 6 February 1978, PP/CRI/D/3/9. Surridge, Biographical notes, 7 October 1999, PP/CRI/J/1/7/19/1.

17 Crick to Lawrence, 6 February 1981, PP/CRI/J/2/1/1. Crick to Lawrence, 2 March 1981, PP/CRI/J/2/1/2.

18 Lectures during trip, undated [1981], PP/CRI/E/1/29/19.

19 Crick to Stent, 15 December 1981, PP/CRI/D/1/4/18.

20 Crick to Bhargava, 14 October 1981, PP/CRI/E/1/29/20. Crick to Blakemore, 18 December 1981, PP/CRI/D/1/4/2.

21 Crick to Levitt, 23 October 1981, PP/CRI/J/2/1/4. Crick to Bates, 12 May 1982, PP/CRI/J/2/2/3.

22 The altitude in Aspen did not agree with Francis; he reported that 'any intellectual work was most burdensome, as was carrying things upstairs.' Crick to Mayerson, 7 February 1983, PP/CRI/J/2/3/1. It may also have affected his mood – after the meeting he apologised profusely for having criticised a colleague's talk 'in such an aggressive manner' (his victim took it in good part and said he was touched by Crick's letter). Crick to Harth, 9 September 1981; Harth to Crick, 22 September 1981, PP/CRI/D/1/4/8.

23 Crick, F. (1982), Do dendritic spines twitch? *Trends in Neurosciences* 5:44–6.

24 Crick to Lund, 23 September 1980, PP/CRI/D/1/4/12.

25 Crick to Mountcastle, 14 September 1981, P/CRI/D/1/4/13. Crick, Report, 5 September 1981, PP/CRI/E/1/29/16.

26 PP/CRI/H/7/3.

27 PP/CRI/L/1/1/1. Crick to Swindale, 21 October 1981, PP/CRI/D/1/4/ 18. Crick (1982).

28 Fischer, M., et al. (1998), Rapid actin-based plasticity in dendritic spines. *Neuron* 20:847–54. Runge, K., Cardoso, C. and de Chevigny, A. (2020), Dendritic spine plasticity: function and mechanisms. *Frontiers in Synaptic Neuroscience* 12:36.

29 Rumelhart, D. and McClelland, J. (1986), On learning the past tenses of English verbs. In D. E. Rumelhart, J. L. McClelland and the PDP Research Group (eds.), *Parallel Distributed Processing: Explorations in the Microstructure of Cognition*, vol. 2: *Psychological and Biological Models* (Cambridge, MA: MIT Press), pp. 216–71.

30 Mandell to Crick, 8 January 1980, PP/CRI/D/1/4/13. Crick, Diary, 1980, entry for 24–25 January, MSS 660, Box 14, Folder 24. Hinton to Crick, 17 June 1981, PP/CRI/D/1/4/8.

31 Anderson, J. A. and Rosenfeld, E. (eds.), (1998), *Talking Nets: An Oral History of Neural Networks* (Cambridge, MA: MIT Press), p. 323.

32 Crick to de Hoffmann, 2 October 1981, PP/CRI/J/2/1/4.

33 Crick to Poggio, 11 February 1982, PP/CRI/J/2/2/1. These notes would appear to be at PP/CRI/L/1/1/7B/3.

34 Crick to Dement, 17 May 1982, PP/CRI/J/2/2/3.

35 Crick to Mitchison, 7 June 1982, PP/CRI/J/2/2/3.

36 Crick to Robertson, 4 March 1983, PP/CRI/J/2/3/2.

37 Crick to Mitchison, 29 March 1982, PP/CRI/J/2/2/2.

38 Crick to Mitchison, 21 July 1982, PP/CRI/J/2/2/4.

39 Crick to Blumenfield, 16 August 1982, PP/CRI/J/2/2/4.

40 Crick to Mitchison, 16 August 1982, PP/CRI/J/2/2/4. Crick to Robertson, 4 November 1982, PP/CRI/J/2/2/6. Maddox to Crick, 15 October 1982, MSS 660 Box 20, Folder 14. Crick's friend at *Nature*, Miranda Robertson, explained that as long as he responded to Maddox's suggestions, then even if one reviewer hated the article, they would still publish it, perhaps accompanied by a comment from the reviewer. Robertson to Crick, 12 October 1982, MSS 660 Box 20, Folder 14.

41 MSS 660, Box 20, Folder 14.

42 Crick to Robertson, 1 February 1983, PP/CRI/J/2/3/1.

43 Crick to Mitchison, 30 November 1982, PP/CRI/J/2/2/6.

44 Crick to Mitchison, 17 January 1983, PP/CRI/J/2/3/1.

45 Crick to Jouvet, 13 January 1983, PP/CRI/J/2/3/1. Crick to Jouvet, 13 May 1983, PP/CRI/J/2/3/3.

46 Crick to Mitchison, 15 December 1982, PP/CRI/J/2/2/6. Crick to Poggio, 7 March 1983, PP/CRI/J/2/3/1. Crick to Robertson, 4 March 1983, PP/ CRI/J/2/3/2.

47 Crick, F. and Mitchison, G. (1983), The function of dream sleep. *Nature* 304:111–4. Hopfield, J. J., Feinstein, D. I. and Palmer, R. G. (1983), 'Unlearning' has a stabilizing effect in collective memories. *Nature* 304:158–9.

48 Material relating to the article is in three files at PP/CRI/J/7/6. Crick to Jouvet, 13 May 1983, PP/CRI/J/2/3/3. Deehan to Crick, 26 July 1986, PP/ CRI/J/7/6/3. *Guardian*, 15 July 1983. *The Economist*, 23 July 1983. *New*

York Times, 25 July 1983. *New Scientist*, 28 July 1983. *Observer*, 31 July 1983. *Sunday Times*, 21 August 1983. *Newsweek*, 8 August 1983. Melnechuk, T. (1983), The dream machine. *Psychology Today*, November 1983, pp. 22–34. Crick wrote a response to the author of the *Sunday Times* article, criticising various points: Crick to Gillie, 29 August 1983, PP/CRI/J/7/6/1.

49 Gooch to Crick, 7 August 1983, PP/CRI/J/7/6/3. Gooch, S. (1984), *Creatures from Inner Space* (London: Rider), p. 209.

50 Crick to Hobson, 9 August 1983, PP/CRI/J/2/3/4.

51 Jouvet, M. (1992), *The Paradox of Sleep: The Story of Dreaming.* (Cambridge, MA: MIT Press), pp. 19 and 126.

52 Olby (2009), pp. 396–7. Daroff to Crick, 29 September 1985; Daroff and Osorio, Matters arising, undated [September 1985], PP/CRI/J/7/6/3. Olby's references for the letters from Swaab and from Daroff are confused and I have been unable to locate the originals.

53 '"We dream in order to forget" is really a slogan, to help people remember the idea rather than to put it over precisely. It's put in quotation marks because it's supposed to be a quotation, but exactly who said it is uncertain.' – Crick to Kreisel, 7 January 1983, PP/CRI/J/2/3/1.

54 Crick and Mitchison tried to find supporting evidence for their theory by explaining the relatively large cortex in the echidna (an egg-laying mammal) in terms of the absence of REM sleep in this species. However, it was subsequently shown that echidnas do indeed have REM sleep. Nicol, S. C., et al. (2000), The echidna manifests typical characteristics of rapid eye movement sleep. *Neuroscience Letters* 283:49–52.

55 Crick to Anderson, 10 November 1990, PP/CRI/J/2/10/2.

56 Crick, F. and Mitchison, G. (1986), REM sleep and neural nets. *The Journal of Mind and Behavior* 7:229–49. An abridged version of this article was re-published in 1995 in *Behavioural Brain Research* 69:147–55.

57 The significance of the Helmholtz Club was first explored by Christine Aicardi in her pioneering article on this period in Crick's life (Aicardi, 2014), from which many of the details of the Club are taken.

58 Crick to Beckman, 20 July 1990, PP/CRI/J/2/10/2. Crick asked Beckman for $60,000 to support the Club over the next five years.

59 Aicardi (2014), p. 8.

60 Crick to Gregory, 13 November 1985, PP/CRI/J/2/5/3. Gregory to Packer, e-mail, 1 March 2005, OLBY, Box 4.

61 Crick, Report for SDF, [July 1983], PP/CRI/C/3/2.

62 Crick, F. (1988), *What Mad Pursuit: A Personal View of Scientific Discovery* (New York: Basic), p. 148.

63 Barlow, H. B. (1972), Single units and sensation: a neuron doctrine for perceptual psychology. *Perception* 1:371–94. Barlow, H. B. (2009), Barlow's 1972 paper. *Perception* 38:795–807. For more on Barlow, see Cobb, M. (2020), *The Idea of the Brain: A History* (London: Profile).

64 Barlow (1972), p. 381.

65 Crick to Gregory, 13 May 1983, PP/CRI/J/2/3/3. For the Johns Hopkins meeting, see PP/CRI/K/2/18.

66 Crick to McKusick, 10 March 1983, PP/CRI/J/2/3/2.

67 Crick to Mitchison, 14 December 1983, PP/CRI/J/2/3/5.

68 Crick to Churchland, 29 November 1983, PP/CRI/J/2/3/5. Crick to Glaser, 1 August 1984, PP/CRI/J/2/4/3.

69 Churchland, A story from Pat, https://patriciachurchland.com/story-2/

70 Crick to Longuet-Higgins, 17 January 1984, PP/CRI/J/2/4/1.

71 Crick to Paul Churchland, 28 October 1985, PP/CRI/J/2/5/3.

72 Crick to Garcia-Bellido, 11 November 1985, PP/CRI/J/2/5/3.

73 Crick, Report for SDF, [July 1983], PP/CRI/C/3/2.

74 Sutherland to Crick, 8 May 1981, PP/CRI/D/1/4/18.

75 Crick to Mitchison, 17 January 1983, PP/CRI/J/2/3/1.

76 Crick, F. and Asanuma, C. (1986), Certain aspects of the anatomy and physiology of the cerebral cortex. In D. E. Rumelhart, J. L. McClelland and the PDP Research Group (eds.), *Parallel Distributed Processing: Explorations in the Microstructure of Cognition*, vol. 2: *Psychological and Biological Models* (Cambridge, MA: MIT Press), pp. 333–71.

77 Rumelhart, D. E., McClelland, J. L. and the PDP Research Group (eds.), (1986), *Parallel Distributed Processing: Explorations in the Microstructure of Cognition*. vol. 1: *Foundations*; vol. 2: *Psychological and Biological Models* (Cambridge, MA: MIT Press). In 1987, Crick told John Maddox that 'incredible as it may seem', the PDP books had 'already sold 10,000 copies'. Crick to Maddox, 8 January 1987, PP/CRI/J/1/1/11/2. The overall figure of 50,000 is from Sejnowski, T. (2018), *The Deep Learning Revolution* (London: MIT Press), p. 118.

78 Crick, Cell types in the neocortex – the tiling hypothesis, 6 June 1983, PP/CRI/L/1/1/3. Crick planned to submit the article to the *PNAS* and gave two talks on the topic in the summer of 1983, one in Alabama, the other in Oxford. Crick to Gilbert, 12 May 1983, PP/CRI/L/1/1/3. PP/ CRI/K/2/10. Blakemore to Crick, 29 June 1983, PP/CRI/K/2/11.

79 Wei, J.-R., et al. (2022), Identification of visual cortex cell types and species differences using single-cell RNA sequencing. *Nature Communications* 13:6902. Yao, Z., et al. (2023), A high-resolution transcriptomic and spatial atlas of cell types in the whole mouse brain. *Nature* 624:317–32.

80 Crick to Sutherland, 19 May 1981, PP/CRI/D/1/4/18.

81 Crick to Treisman, 28 April 1981 and 11 September 1981, PP/ CRI/D/1/4/19.

82 Crick produced a series of internal notes on this issue, beginning on 16 December 1983: PP/CRI/L/1/1/5A. Crick, F. (1984), Function of the thalamic reticular complex: the searchlight hypothesis. *Proceedings of the National Academy of Sciences USA* 81:4586–90. This paper has over one thousand citations.

83 McClure to Crick, 20 January 1984 and 31 July 1984, MSS 660, Box 7, Folder 24. Crick to Mitchison, 20 December 1984, PP/CRI/J/2/4/4.

84 McClure to Crick, 2 February 1985, MSS 660, Box 7, Folder 24. Crick's pencilled 'Yes' and a suggestion of a September date can be seen on the letter.

85 Crick, Diary, 1985, entry for 24 January, MSS 660, Box 14, Folder 28. Crick to Petitto, 23 January 1985, PP/CRI/J/2/5/1.

86 Crick to Keynes, 30 January 1986, PP/CRI/J/2/6/1. Crick to Deaton, 12

August 1986, PP/CRI/J/2/6/2. Keynes to Crick, 6 February 1986, PP/CRI/J/1/1/9/2. Crick to Keynes, 14 February 1986, PP/CRI/J/1/1/9/2.

87 Letter to Crick, 2 July 1985, MSS 660, Box 11.
88 Crick to Mitchison, 16 January 1985, PP/CRI/J/2/5/1. Crick to Mayhew, 12 February 1985, PP/CRI/J/2/5/1. PP/CRI/L/1/1/7D. Crick to MacLeod, 1 March 1985, PP/CRI/J/2/5/1. Crick to Blakemore, 25 February 1985, PP/CRI/J/2/5/1. Crick to Churchland, 1 March 1985, PP/CRI/J/2/5/1.
89 PP/CRI/L/5/4.
90 Crick, Report for SDF, undated [July 1985], PP/CRI/C/3/2. Crick to Desimone, 25 January 1990, PP/CRI/J/2/10/1.
91 Wolpert, L. and Richards, A. (1988), *A Passion for Science* (Oxford: Oxford University Press), p. 93.
92 Churchland, A story from Pat, https://patriciachurchland.com/story-2/
93 Crick to Bates, 12 May 1982, PP/CRI/J/2/2/3.
94 Crick to Boston, 27 September 1983, PP/CRI/J/2/3/4.
95 Crick to Longuet-Huggins, 15 February 1983, PP/CRI/J/2/3/1.
96 Crick to Petitto, 23 January 1985, PP/CRI/J/2/5/1.
97 Crick to Prynne, 21 May 1984, PP/CRI/J/2/4/2. Crick to Cook, 3 November 1983, PP/CRI/J/2/3/5.
98 Crick to Lander, 17 September 1985, PP/CRI/J/2/5/2.
99 Crick to Mitchison, 10 October 1986, PP/CRI/J/2/6/2.
100 Crick to Eigen, 10 February 1986, PP/CRI/J/2/6/1. To pimp his ride, Crick got the radio-stereo player removed, a high-level brake light installed inside the rear window and a band of tint added to the top of the windscreen. Crick to Ero-Cal, 24 January 1986, PP/CRI/J/2/6/1.
101 Crick to Cook, 11 November 1985, PP/CRI/J/2/5/3.

CHAPTER 19

1 Crick to Brenner, 22 March 1977, SB/1/1/133.
2 Bachmann to Crick, 22 December 1980, PP/CRI/J/13.
3 Crick to Bachmann, 19 February 1981, PP/CRI/J/2/1/1. Photographs of the Cricks on set, together with three unidentified people, one of whom is presumably Bachmann, can be found at PP/CRI/J/13.
4 Crick to Watson, 1 April 1982, PP/CRI/J/2/2/2.
5 Wood, The Double Helix – From the book by James D. Watson, MSS 660, Box 20, Folder 1.
6 Crick to Watson, 11 March 1985, PP/CRI/J/2/5/1.
7 In 1999, Bachmann was still keen and persuaded Oscar-winning screenwriter John Briley to start work on a script; Crick's response was the same. Nothing ever came of Bachmann's project. Bachmann to Crick, 15 May 1998 and 21 April 1999; Crick to Bachmann, 11 June 1998 and 15 July 1999, PP/CRI/J/1/6/2.
8 *Guardian*, 27 April 1987. Callander, Chronology of the double helix (Revised), undated [1986], K/PP178/5/27/1. This invaluable twenty-page timeline has columns detailing events in Cambridge, London and Elsewhere, together with sources.
9 Crick to Jackson, 24 April 1986, PP/CRI/J/2/6/1.

10　K/PP178/5/27/1 and K/PP178/5/27/2 contain Wilkins' papers relating to the production.

11　Wilkins, Extra notes on double helix history for Horizon, 14 June 1985, K/PP178/5/27/1.

12　Crick received £3,000 for his consultancy, two-thirds of which was shared equally by Gonville and Caius and Churchill College. van Beuren to Crick, 28 August 1984, MSS 660, Box 20 Folder 2. Correspondence relating to the production can be found at PP/CRI/J/2/5/2.

13　Callander to Crick, 29 October 1986, PP/CRI/J/1/1/2/2.

14　The *Radio Times* showed Goldblum and Pigott-Smith on the cover, with the title 'Gene geniuses'. *Radio Times*, 25 April 1987. Peter Lawrence found a copy of the script in Portugal Place after the crew had departed; over the years, it got used for scrap paper. Only two sheets remain. The film can be seen, in two parts, at https://www.dailymotion.com/video/xitlyu and https://www.dailymotion.com/video/xitmu3 and in 2025 was available on BBC iPlayer.

15　Perutz to Francis and Odile, 25 December 1987, MSS 660, Box 20, Folder 2.

16　Crick to Bachmann, 26 May 1987, PP/CRI/J/1/1/2/2. Crick to Blakemore, 15 June 1987, PP/CRI/J/2/7/1.

17　Crick, F. (1988), *What Mad Pursuit: A Personal View of Scientific Discovery* (New York: Basic), p. 88.

18　PP/CRI/L/1/3/3.

19　Kreisel to Crick, 27 August 1993, MSS 660, Box 5, Folder 9.

20　Crick to Bachmann, 26 May 1987, PP/CRI/J/1/1/2/2.

21　*Sunday Times*, 3 May 1987. *Evening Standard*, 27 April 1987. *Observer*, 3 May 1987.

22　MSS 660, Box 20, Folder 2.

23　Bachmann to Crick, 30 April 1987, PP/CRI/J/1/1/2/2.

24　Crick learned that Wilkins had not seen Randall's letter on hearing the programme. Crick to Wolpert, 2 March 1988, PP/CRI/J/2/8/1.

25　Crick, Diary, 1986, MSS 660, Box 14, Folder 30.

26　Crick to Mitchison, 20 February 1987, PP/CRI/J/2/7/1. The programme, *Freud Under Analysis*, can be seen at https://archive.org/details/FreudUnderAnalysis

27　MSS 660, Box 18, Folder 14.

28　Crick to Rinaldini, 9 September 1986, PP/CRI/J/2/6/2. Crick to Naegle, 9 September 1986, PP/CRI/J/2/6/2. Crick to Mitchison, 20 August 1987, PP/CRI/J/2/7/2. Crick to Asanuma, 7 January 1988, PP/CRI/J/2/8/1.

29　Voll, D. (1994), Soul searching with Francis Crick. *Omni*, February 1994, pp. 46–53.

30　Crick to Rinaldini, 15 September 1989, PP/CRI/J/2/9/2.

31　*Los Angeles Times*, 28 February 1994.

32　Crick (1988), p. 145.

33　Crick, Diary, 1987, MSS 660, Box 14, Folder 31.

34　McClure to Crick, 11 April 1987 and 21 May 1987, MSS 660, Box 7, Folder 24. The flyer is in MSS 660, Box 7, Folder 26.

35　Sacks to Crick, 30 May 1986, PP/CRI/J/1/1/15/2.

36　Sacks, O. (2015), *On the Move: A Life* (London: Picador), p. 347.

37　Sacks (2015), p. 350.

NOTES TO PP. 400–408

38 Crick to Braitenberg, 27 July 1987, PP/CRI/J/2/7/2.
39 Crick to Hunt, 19 January 1988, PP/CRI/J/2/8/1.
40 Francis to Odile, 14 June 1987, MSS 660, Box 32, Folder 7.
41 Bhargava to Crick, 30 November 1987, PP/CRI/J/1/1/2/2. Crick to Bhargava, 22 December 1987, PP/CRI/J/2/7/2. For a typical response from Odile to a television invitation, see Crick to von Troschke, 14 February 1994, PP/CRI/J/2/14/1. Francis agreed that she came over very well – Crick to Chakrabarti, 7 January 1987, PP/CRI/J/2/8/1.
42 Crick to Chakrabarti, 20 August 1987, PP/CRI/J/2/7/2.
43 Crick to White, 3 May 1982, PP/CRI/J/2/2/3. See also MSS 660, Box 33, Folder 12.
44 Crick to Wanner, 13 May 1986, PP/CRI/J/2/6/1.
45 Crick to Panem, 2 February 1987, PP/CRI/J/2/7/1. PP/CRI/L/5/5/1/1. Notes and drafts can be found at PP/CRI/L/5/5.
46 *New York Times*, 9 April 1989.
47 Crick (1988), pp. 162–3.
48 Jukes, T. H. (1989), Halcyon days. *Science* 243:219–20.
49 Crick (1988), pp. xi-xii.
50 McClure to Crick, 31 March 1989, MSS 660, Box 7, Folder 25.
51 Crick, Diary, 1988, MSS 660, Box 14, Folder 32.
52 Herschbach to Crick, 14 March 1991, PP/CRI/J/1/3/7/1.
53 PP/CRI/K/7/5.
54 Crick to Mitchison, 21 July 1988, PP/CRI/K/7/5.
55 The creators of these neural nets recognised this problem – see for example the handout for use with two of the algorithms used in these programs. PP/CRI/K/7/5.
56 PP/CRI/K/7/9.
57 Anderson, A. and Palca, J. (1988), Who knows how the brain works? *Nature* 335:489–91.
58 PP/CRI/L/1/2/2.
59 Crick to Robertson, 11 and 28 April 1988, PP/CRI/J/2/8/1.
60 Crick, F. (1989), The recent excitement about neural networks. *Nature* 337:129–32.
61 Wolpert, L. and Richards, A. (1988), *A Passion for Science* (Oxford: Oxford University Press), p. 93.
62 Edelman, G. (1987), *Neural Darwinism: the Theory of Neuronal Group Selection* (New York: Oxford University Press). Willshaw, D. (1989), Neural Darwinism. *Trends in Neurosciences* 11:511–2. Barlow, H. B. (1988), Neuroscience: a new era? *Nature* 331:571.
63 Crick, Neural Edelmanism, 21 October 1988, PP/CRI/L/1/2/6/2.
64 Mitchison, Notes on Neural Edelmanism, undated [1988], PP/CRI/L/1/2/6/2.
65 For all material relating to the article see PP/CRI/L/1/2/6. Crick, F. (1989), Neural Edelmanism. *Trends in Neurosciences* 12:240–8
66 Crick to Kreisel, 13 August 1990, PP/CRI/J/2/10/2.
67 Horgan, J. (1992), The Mephistopheles of neurobiology. *Scientific American* 266, February 1992, pp. 32–3, p. 33.

68 Crick to Black, 17 November 2003, PP/CRI/J/1/8/5/1. See also correspondence with Edelman in this file.
69 Crick to Kreisel, 7 April 1989, PP/CRI/J/2/9/1.
70 Kreisel to Crick, 12 April 1989, PP/CRI/J/2/9/1.
71 Crick to Mitchison, 23 February 1990, PP/CRI/J/2/10/1. Crick wrote: 'Penrose's main case appears to be that there is something funny about quantum mechanics (that might be put right by a theory for quantum gravity) and that since he thinks there is something funny about consciousness, wouldn't it be wonderful if the first would explain the second.' This view is still popular in certain quarters.
72 Crick to Kreisel, 3 May 1989, PP/CRI/J/2/9/1. Crick to Kreisel, 8 January 1990, PP/CRI/J/2/10/1.
73 Crick to Mitchison, 23 February 1990, PP/CRI/J/2/10/1. Crick was nominally the co-organiser, but repeatedly expressed his surprise about this. Course materials can be found at PP/CRI/L/1/3/4A.
74 This phenomenon had been predicted a few years earlier by Christoph von der Malsburg. von der Malsburg, C. and Schneider, W. (1986), A neural cocktail-party processor. *Biological Cybernetics* 54:29–40.
75 Crick to Maddox, 4 January 1989, PP/CRI/J/2/9/1.
76 Gray, C. M., et al. (1989), Oscillatory responses in cat visual cortex exhibit inter-columnar synchronisation which reflects global stimulus properties. *Nature* 338:334–7. See also Stryker, M. P. (1989), Is grandmother an oscillation? *Nature* 338:297–8.
77 Crick to Desimone, 25 January 1990, PP/CRI/J/2/10/1.
78 Crick to Staddon, 1 March 1989, PP/CRI/J/2/9/1.
79 Interview with Christof Koch, 28 February 2024.
80 Koch, C. (2012), *Consciousness: Confessions of a Romantic Reductionist* (London: MIT Press), p. 20.
81 Crick, F. and Koch, C. (1990a), Towards a neurobiological theory of consciousness. *Seminars in the Neurosciences* 2:263–75. Drafts of this article can be found at PP/CRI/L/1/3/1.
82 Crick to Kreisel, 8 January 1990, PP/CRI/J/2/10/1.
83 Crick to Damasio, 12 March 1990, PP/CRI/J/2/10/1.
84 All material relating to the meeting is at PP/CRI/K/9/5.
85 Crick to Huxley, 9 February 1990, PP/CRI/J/2/10/1.
86 Watson to Crick, 28 January 1990, PP/CRI/K/9/5.
87 Cutting to Crick, 4 June 1990, PP/CRI/K/9/5.
88 Crick, F. and Koch C. (1990b), Some reflections on visual awareness. *Cold Spring Harbor Symposia on Quantitative Biology* 55:953–62. There are no notes for Crick's talk. PP/CRI/L/1/3/1/4.
89 Crick to Singer, 9 July 1990, PP/CRI/J/2/10/2.
90 Crick to Posner, 4 January 1991, PP/CRI/J/2/11/1. Crick to Kreisel, 24 August 1990, PP/CRI/J/2/10/2.
91 Crick to Lawrence, 30 March 1990, PP/CRI/J/2/10/1.
92 Crick to Miller, 25 May 1990, PP/CRI/J/2/10/1. Material relating to Crick's visit to the school can be found at PP/CRI/J/1/3/7/1.
93 Crick to Liu, 21 July 1989, PP/CRI/J/2/9/2.

94 Crick to Liu, 17 January 1990, PP/CRI/J/2/10/1. For my Twitter exchange with Liu, see https://x.com/matthewcobb/status/1784301663169241439
95 Crick to Kreisel, 20 February 1990, PP/CRI/J/2/10/1.
96 For example, Crick to Luskin, 31 March 1989, PP/CRI/J/2/9/1.
97 Crick to Sutherland, 5 April 1990, PP/CRI/J/2/10/1.

CHAPTER 20
1 Crick, F. (1994), *The Astonishing Hypothesis: The Scientific Search for the Soul* (New York: Charles Scribner's Sons.
2 Patel, K. (1996), Big shot in the mind field. *Times Higher Education Supplement*, 24 May 1996.
3 Crick (1994), p. xii.
4 Crick told Koch that the publisher had suggested the inclusion of 'soul' in the title – Christof Koch, e-mail to the author, May 2025. On *Start the Week*, BBC Radio 4, 23 May 1994, Crick described the title as provocative. Brenda Maddox, the co-interviewer, suggested the title was 'sellable'; Francis giggled. In October 1981, Colin Blakemore recorded a brief debate between Crick and Eccles at the Society for Neuroscience meeting. Olby made a partial transcript: Crick/Eccles debate on soul/brain, OLBY, Box 5.
5 Grossman to Crick, 18 November 1991, PP/CRI/L/1/4/4.
6 PP/CRI/J/7/8/1/1/2.
7 Crick to Grossman, 15 January 1992, PP/CRI/J/2/12/1.
8 Crick to Bryan, 27 July 1992, PP/CRI/J/2/12/2. Once Crick and Grossman met, their relations became much more relaxed – 'No trouble in New York with my Editor …' he told a friend in summer 1992, 'All that remains is the labour of perfecting the entire book.' Crick to Voll, 27 July 1992, PP/CRI/J/2/12/2. Crick told Grossman: 'I really enjoyed meeting you in the flesh, after all our other communications, and feel encouraged about the progress of the book.' Crick to Grossman, 23 July 1992, PP/CRI/J/2/12/2.
9 Grossman to Crick, 4 January 1993, PP/CRI/J/7/8/1/1/1.
10 Crick to Grossman, 3 March 1992, PP/CRI/J/2/12/1.
11 Crick (1994), p. 256.
12 Crick (1994), p. 207.
13 Crick to Kreisel, 7 October 1991, PP/CRI/J/2/11/2. Crick to Kreisel, 10 August 1992, PP/CRI/J/2/12/2. Crick to Rinaldini, 1 April 1993, PP/CRI/J/2/13/1. Peter Lawrence, e-mail to the author, April 2024. Birgitta Lawrence, Diary, courtesy of Birgitta Lawrence. Lawrence, P. (2016), Francis Crick: A singular approach to scientific discovery. *Cell* 167:1436–9. Ridley, M. (2006), *Francis Crick: Discoverer of the Genetic Code* (London: Harper), p. 199. Francis and Odile to Olby, New year's greeting card, undated, OLBY, Box 3.
14 Geist to Cassidy, 21 September 1994, PP/CRI/J/2/14/3.
15 Crick to Karten, 30 November 1994, PP/CRI/J/2/14/4.
16 Simonsuuri to Odile and Francis, 5 September 1993, MSS 660, Box 9, Folder 18.
17 Edwards, A. (2005), Caius stained glass. *Once a Caian…* 2:12–13. See also MSS 660, Box 32, Folder 14. The window was eventually installed in 1992, along with windows celebrating the mathematician George Green,

the discoverer of the neutron Sir James Chadwick and the physiologist Sir Charles Sherrington. Crick to Edwards, 27 February 1991, PP/CRI/L/1/4/4.

18 Fellowes to Crick, 29 October 1991, PP/CRI/L/1/4/4. See also MSS 660, Box 13, Folder 1 and Ford to Crick, 28 November 1991, PP/CRI/L/1/4/4.

19 Crick to Fellowes, 4 November 1991, PP/CRI/L/1/4/4.

20 *Los Angeles Times*, 28 February 1994.

21 See for example, Crick to Williams, 28 April 1994, MSS 660, Box 10, Folder 43.

22 MSS 660, Box 13, Folder 1. Crick, Diary entry for 7 July, Diary, 1992, MSS 660, Box 15, Folder 4.

23 Diary entry for 7 July, Crick, Diary, 1992, MSS 660, Box 15, Folder 4.

24 Crick to Voll, 27 July 1992, PP/CRI/J/2/12/2.

25 Crick to Matt and Anya Ridley, 16 February 2001, PP/CRI/J/2/21/1.

26 Olby, R. (2009), *Francis Crick: Hunter of Life's Secrets* (Cold Spring Harbor, NY: Cold Spring Harbor Laboratory Press), p. 435.

27 Koelle to Crick, 23 March 1991; Crick to Koelle, 26 March 1991, PP/CRI/L/1/4/4. Crick to Walker, 25 August 1994, PP/CRI/J/2/14/3.

28 Crick to Hahn, 3 August 1993, PP/CRI/J/2/13/2.

29 Crick to Böhlke, 8 November 1993, PP/CRI/J/2/13/2. *Los Angeles Times*, 27 September 1993. There is no evidence that Crick ever realised that Böhlke was a fraud, but none of Böhlke's letters are in his archive. Whoever was behind the Böhlke letters seems to have been active at least until 2019, as described by cartoonist Ulli Lust: https://popula.com/2019/02/17/the-autograph-collector/

30 Crick, Some comments on The Rediscovery of Mind for John Searle, 1 September 1992, PP/CRI/J/2/12/2.

31 Uniquely, much of Crick's correspondence for 1992 has been preserved in all its stages: PP/CRI/L/1/4/4. Crick to Poggio, 29 August 1994, PP/CRI/J/2/14/3.

32 PP/CRI/L/1/4/3. Crick, F. and Jones, E. (1993), Backwardness of human neuroanatomy. *Nature* 361:109–10.

33 Cobb, M. (2020), *The Idea of the Brain: A History* (London: Profile Books).

34 Crick to Chuck [Stevens], 24 February 1994, PP/CRI/J/2/14/1.

35 Crick to Klug, 29 September 1992, PP/CRI/L/1/4/4.

36 Crick to Kreisel, 9 March 1993, PP/CRI/J/2/13/1.

37 Crick to Bernard, 14 January 1993, PP/CRI/J/2/13/1.

38 Crick to Lawrence, 11 March 1993, PP/CRI/J/2/13/1. Crick, Diary, 1993, MSS 660, Box 15, Folder 5.

39 See for example Crick to Landau, 16 December 1993, PP/CRI/J/2/13/2.

40 Lang to Marshall, 10 November 1993, PP/CRI/J/2/13/2. PP/CRI/J/7/8/4/2. *Los Angeles Times*, 28 February 1994. *The Times*, 9 May 1994. Anonymous (1994), Crick on consciousness. *Nature* 369:86.

41 Reviews can be found in PP/CRI/J/7/8/4. *The Times*, 16 May 1994. *New York Times Magazine*, 27 February 1994. For a particularly irate review from a Christian perspective see *The Southern Cross*, 10 February 1994, PP/CRI/K/13/1.

42 Hopfield, J. (1994), An envisioning of consciousness. *Science* 263:696.

For Crick's response, see Crick to Hopfield, 15 February 1994, PP/ CRI/J/2/14/1. *Daily Telegraph*, 28 May 1994.

43 Gregory, R. (1994), DNA in the mind's eye. *Nature* 368:359–60.

44 Crick to Gregory, 6 April 1994, PP/CRI/J/2/14/2.

45 Voll, D. (1994), Soul searching with Francis Crick. *Omni*, February 1994, pp. 46–53.

46 *The Times*, 2 May and 3 May 1994.

47 Huxley to Geist, 26 May 1994, PP/CRI/J/7/8/4/1. *The Times*, 26 May 1994. *Evening Standard*, 6 June 1994.

48 *Start the Week*, BBC Radio 4, 23 May 1994.

49 Gray, J. (1995), The Emperor's new rag. *Nature* 377:265. PP/ CRI/J/7/8/4/1. Clark, J. and Crick, F. (1994), Interviews. *Journal of Consciousness Studies* 1:10–24.

50 Thompson, L. (1994), Dark knight of the soul. *Helix*, June 1994, pp. 44–8, p. 48. Crick, Diary, 1994, MSS 660, Box 15, Folder 6.

51 Gramann to Crick, 21 August 1993, PP/CRI/J/1/4/7. Crick to Gramann, 29 August 1994, PP/CRI/J/2/14/3. The song later featured on Gramann's CD *Mostly Live*, which is available online.

52 Crick to Koch, 9 August 1994, PP/CRI/J/2/14/3.

53 Crick to Koch, 12 October 1994, PP/CRI/J/2/14/4.

54 'Semi-retired' was a term Crick used; Crick to Uzielli, 8 March 1994, PP/ CRI/J/2/14/1. Crick, Notes on visits, 4 May 1994, MSS 176, Box 40, Folder 17. MacIlwain, C. (1994), Salk Institute president is replaced. *Nature* 372:396.

55 *Salk Institute Newsletter* 49, Winter 1995, MSS 660, Box 21, Folder 7.

56 Lang to Crick, 14 October 1994, PP/CRI/J/1/4/11/1.

57 Crick to all members of the Salk Institute, 17 November 1994, PP/ CRI/J/2/14/4. Crick to O'Leary, 25 May 1995, PP/CRI/J/2/15/3. Crick to Albright, Heinemann, O'Leary, Sejnowski and Stevens, 28 October 1994, PP/CRI/J/2/14/4.

58 Crick to Stern, 21 December 1994, PP/CRI/J/2/14/4. Crick to Ramachandran, 27 October 1994, PP/CRI/J/2/14/4. Crick to Johnson, 9 February 1995, PP/CRI/J/2/15/1. Hubbs to Crick, 1 March 1995, PP/ CRI/J/2/15/2. Crick to Abercrombie, Pitman and Dickman, 15 February 1995, PP/CRI/J/2/15/1. $10 – e.g. Crick to Lee, 17 February 1995, PP/ CRI/J/2/15/1. $50 – e.g. Murray to Shaw, 19 July 2002, PP/CRI/J/2/22/1.

59 Dalton, R. (1998), Salk Institute investigated after claims of inhumane research. *Nature* 394:709. The jury awarded the vet $4.7 million in damages.

60 Crick to Ramachandran, 27 October 1994; Crick to Baars, 20 December 1994, PP/CRI/J/2/14/4. Crick to Blakemore, 6 March 1995, PP/ CRI/J/2/15/2.

61 Francis to Odile, 14 May 1995, MSS 660, Box 22, Folder 21.

62 Crick to Bachmann, 18 August 1995, PP/CRI/J/2/15/4.

63 Milner, D. and Goodale, M. (1995), *The Visual Brain in Action* (Oxford: Oxford University Press). See for example Crick to Hubel, 26 September 1995, PP/CRI/J/2/15/5.

64 Crick to Koch and Crick to Searle, 12 August 1994, PP/CRI/J/2/14/3. *Remembering Francis Crick*, undated [September 2004], SB/10/56.

65 Crick to Koch, 4 October 1996, PP/CRI/J/2/16/4.

66 Crick, F. and Koch, C. (1995a), Are we aware of neural activity in primary visual cortex? *Nature* 375:121-3.

67 Kreisel, untitled, undated [1994], PP/CRI/J/1/4/10. Crick to Kreisel, 21 December 1994, PP/CRI/J/2/14/4.

68 PP/CRI/J/2/15/4.

69 Pollen, D. A. (1995), Cortical areas in visual awareness. *Nature* 377:293-4. Crick, F. and Koch, C. (1995b), Cortical areas in visual awareness. *Nature* 377:294-5.

70 Geist to Patricia Churchland and Ramachandran, 10 November 1995, PP/CRI/J/2/15/6. Geist to Kreisel, 20 November 1995, MSS 660, Box 31, Folder 11. Crick, Internal Memo I and II, 20 December 1995, PP/CRI/J/2/15/6. Crick to Bazan, 21 December 1995, PP/CRI/J/2/15/6.

71 Crick to Olby, 24 April 1996, PP/CRI/J/2/16/2.

72 Crick to Siegelmann, 20 December 1996, PP/CRI/J/2/16/4.

73 Crick, F. (1996), Visual perception: rivalry and consciousness. *Nature* 379:485-6.

74 Leopold, D. A. and Logothetis, N. K. (1996), Activity changes in early visual cortex reflect monkeys' percepts during binocular rivalry. *Nature* 379:549-53.

75 Crick to Sutherland, 3 December 1996, PP/CRI/J/2/16/4. Geist to Mechsner, 12 November 1996, PP/CRI/J/2/16/4.

76 Patel (1996).

77 Crick to Dennett, 13 June 1996; Crick to Searle, 8 April 1996, PP/CRI/J/2/16/2.

78 Crick to Velmans, 23 August 1996, PP/CRI/J/2/16/3. Olby (2009), p. 418. Crick expressed this idea, less succinctly, to Searle: 'I think it is useful for philosophers to pose questions, but I wish they were a little more modest in suggesting answers to them.' Crick to Searle,1 May 1996, PP/CRI/J/2/16/2.

79 Crick to Kreisel, 17 September 1996, PP/CRI/J/2/16/3. This seemed to do the trick; Kreisel explained his criticisms to Penrose, although there was no sign of any real movement on the physicist's part. Crick to Kreisel and Crick to Penrose, 20 December 1996, PP/CRI/J/2/16/4.

80 Crick to Penrose, 4 April 1997, PP/CRI/J/2/17/2.

81 Francis to Odile, 11 August 1996, MSS 660, Box 22, Folder 21.

82 Crick to Watanabe, 13 November 1996; Crick to Serizawa, 16 October 1996, PP/CRI/J/2/16/4. Crick to Watanabe, 12 September 1996, PP/CRI/J/2/16/3. Geist, Faculty news item for *Signals*, 4 December 1996, PP/CRI/J/2/16/4.

83 PP/CRI/K/15/4/2. This was also the first time he had met Dan Pollen.

84 See for example. Rose, S. (1994), Representing Grandma. *London Review of Books*, 7 July 1994.

85 Baars, B. (1997), *In the Theatre of Consciousness: The Workspace of the Mind* (Oxford: Oxford University Press). Crick thanked Baars for his 'very generous dedication'. Crick to Baars, 6 February 1997, PP/CRI/J/2/17/1.

CHAPTER 21

1   Crick to Stent, 25 June 1998, PP/CRI/J/2/18/2.

2   Crick, Diary, 1997, MSS 660, Box 15, Folder 9. Crick, Diary, 1998, MSS 660, Box 15, Folder 10.

3   Crick to Friednan, 28 January 1997, PP/CRI/J/2/17/1. Geist to Weld, 23 January 1997, PP/CRI/J/2/17/1.

4   Crick and Koch, Visual awareness and the pulvinar: some neuroanatomical questions, 24 November 1992, PP/CRI/L/1/5/16.

5   Crick to Rockland, 8 September 1994; Rockland to Crick, 20 September 1994 and 12 January 1995, PP/CRI/J/1/4/16.

6   Crick to Rockland, 27 July 1995, PP/CRI/L/1/5/8B. Crick to Rockland, 18 December 1996; Rockland to Crick, 18 December 1996, PP/CRI/J/1/5/17.

7   Rockland to Crick, 14 August 1995, PP/CRI/L/1/5/8B.

8   Crick, F. and Koch, C. (1998a), Constraints on cortical and thalamic projections: the no-strong-loops hypothesis. *Nature* 391:245–50.

9   Crick to Thomas, 23 April 1998, PP/CRI/J/2/18/1.

10   Rockland to Crick, 9 June 1997, PP/CRI/J/1/5/17. Mitchison to Crick, 21 June 1998, PP/CRI/L/1/7/4/1.

11   Crick to Jokic, 7 January 1998, PP/CRI/J/2/18/1.

12   Crick, F. and Koch, C. (1998b), Consciousness and neuroscience. *Cerebral Cortex* 8:97–107.

13   Crick F. and Koch, C. (2000a), The unconscious homunculus. *Neuropsychoanalysis* 2:3–11. Crick and Koch's article was a slightly amended version of a book chapter with the same title, published in Metzinger, T. (ed.), (2000), *The Neuronal Correlate of Consciousness: Empirical and Conceptual Questions* (Cambridge, MA: MIT Press), pp. 103–110.

14   For a discussion of Freud's document in the context of contemporaneous work on the brain, see Cobb, M. (2020), *The Idea of the Brain: A History* (London: Profile).

15   Koch, C. and Crick, F. (2001), The zombie within. *Nature* 411:893. Note the order of authors.

16   Crick, F. and Koch, C. (2000b), The unconscious homunculus: response to the commentaries. *Neuropsychoanalysis* 2:48–59. Correspondence relating to the article and drafts of Crick and Koch's original article, the commentaries and Crick and Koch's reply can be found at PP/CRI/L/1/7/4.

17   Crick, lecture at UCSD, https://www.youtube.com/watch?v=1Kvv7fKadyc

18   Crick to Logothetis, 18 February 1998, PP/CRI/J/2/18/1.

19   PP/CRI/L/1/6/13.

20   Crick to Rich, 6 April 1999, PP/CRI/J/1/6/19/1. Crick to Blakemore, 2 August 1999, PP/CRI/J/2/19/2.

21   Siegel, R. M. and Callaway, E. M. (2004), Francis Crick's legacy for neuroscience: between the α and the Ω. *PLoS Biology* 2:e419. Crick to Zeki, 2 February 1999, PP/CRI/L/1/6/8. This folder also contains multiple drafts of Crick's article.

22   Crick to Michell, 11 May 1999, PP/CRI/J/1/6/19/1. Crick to Frost, 13 July 2000, PP/CRI/J/2/20/1. Crick to Gregory, 9 August 1999, PP/CRI/J/1/6/19/2. Crick to Djanogly, 4 September 1998, PP/CRI/J/2/18/2.

See also Crick to Djanogly, 22 October 1999, PP/CRI/J/2/19/2. Djanogly, C. (1999), *Centurions: A Photographic Tribute to 100 Men & Women Who Have Changed the Face of 20th Century Britain* (London: André Deutsch).

23 Crick, F. (1999), The impact of molecular biology on neuroscience. *Philosophical Transactions of the Royal Society of London B* 354:2021–5.

24 Miesenböck to Crick, 9 February 2000, PP/CRI/J/1/7/14/1.

25 PP/CRI/L/1/8/3/1 and PP/CRI/L/1/8/3/2.

26 PP/CRI/L/1/7.

27 PP/CRI/L/1/8/4/2.

28 McClure to Francis and Odile, 30 April 2000, MSS 660, Box 7, Folder 28. The reading was recorded and can be seen at https://www.youtube.com/watch?v=ihovCt9w8Mw and https://www.youtube.com/watch?v=e-UhaPUOvaA (Crick can be seen in the final seconds, and in the opening titles).

29 McClure, Travel notebook, 1999 Oct 25 to 2000 July 10, BANC MSS 2003/222 c, Box 31, Folder 4.

30 Simonsuuri to Crick, 11 May 2000, MSS 660, Box 9, Folder 18.

31 Kreisel to Crick, 25 June 2001, MSS 660, Box 6, Folder 6.

32 Crick to Flew, 5 June 2001, PP/CRI/J/2/21/1.

33 PP/CRI/K/20/8/2. https://www.youtube.com/watch?v=mXGZ3euhq4g

34 Crick, F., et al. (2004), Consciousness and neurosurgery. *Neurosurgery* 55:273–82. For some brief correspondence on this article, see Fried to Crick, 30 December 2003, PP/CRI/J/1/8/8.

35 Crick, untitled draft, undated [2002–3], PP/CRI/J/2/23/1.

36 Rees to Crick, undated [May 2002] and Crick to Rees, 29 May 2002, PP/CRI/J/1/8/18.

37 Crick to Searle, 23 December 2002, PP/CRI/J/2/22/2.

38 Crick to Thomas, 1 March 2002, PP/CRI/J/2/22/1.

39 Koch, C. (2012), *Consciousness: Confessions of a Romantic Reductionist* (London: MIT Press), pp. 162–3.

40 Crick, untitled, 7 October 2002, PP/CRI/J/1/8/2.

41 Rinaldi, A. (2006), Private ownership of public heritage. *EMBO Reports* 7:571–5. For correspondence with Crick about his archive, from various potential buyers, see PP/CRI/J/12/1.

42 Crick to Olby, 22 July 1998, PP/CRI/J/2/18/2. Dalton, R. (2001), The history man. *Nature* 411:732–3. Abbott, A. and Dalton, R. (2001), Wellcome bid sees Crick archive return home. *Nature* 414:678.

43 Beckett, C. (2003), For the record: the Francis Crick Archive at the Wellcome Library. *Medical History*, 48:245–60. For Crick's brief comments on Beckett's manuscript, see Crick to Pearson, 15 December 2003, PP/CRI/J/1/8/22.

44 Crick to Olby, 27 August 2001, PP/CRI/J/2/21/2. Crick to Judson, 6 July 2001, PP/CRI/J/1/7/11. For all details regarding the missing documents, see PP/CRI/J/12/2. Beckett, C. (2006), The scientific papers of Francis Crick. A footnote on custodial history. *The Mendel Newsletter* 15:3–8.

45 Crick to Lang, 4 September 2001, PP/CRI/J/2/21/2.

46 The Wellcome Collection has optimistically retained shelfmarks for these

missing notebooks, should they eventually turn up: PP/CRI/G/1/7, PP/CRI/G/1/15.

47 MSS 660, Box 10, Folder 3.
48 Crick to Judson, 12 July 2002; Judson to Crick, 3 January 2003, PP/CRI/J/1/8/10.
49 Johnson to Crick, 4 February 2000; Crick to Johnson, 11 February 2000, PP/CRI/J/1/7/11.
50 Crick to Jacobs, undated, PP/CRI/J/2/23/1.
51 *Science*, 11 April 2003.
52 *Nature*, 23 January 2003.
53 Watson to Crick, 16 July 2002, PP/CRI/J/1/8/22.
54 Klug to Crick, 14 March 2003, PP/CRI/J/1/8/11.
55 *Sunday Times*, 2 February 2003.
56 Lawrence to Murray, 23 and 4 April 2003, PP/CRI/J/1/8/12/1. Lawrence told me that the paparazzi outside the Guildhall were disappointed that the Beckhams did not show up.
57 SB/4/1/158.
58 Finbow to Olby, undated [early 2013], OLBY, Box 20. Anonymous (2003), Crick's immodest ambitions. *Nature* 422:455.
59 Crick to Watson, 27 January 2003, PP/CRI/J/1/8/22. The typed letter has 'comparable' not 'compatible'. Six weeks earlier, Crick had written to Watson: 'The Central Dogma is not just DNA → RNA → protein (this is your version of it). The Central Dogma says, in effect, you can't back-translate from protein to nucleic acid. Thus it is perfectly compatible with reverse transcriptase.' Watson appears to have paid no attention. Crick to Watson, 10 December 2002, PP/CRI/J/1/8/22.
60 Crick to Sharp, draft, undated [February 2003], PP/CRI/J/2/23/1. Sharp to Crick, 24 February 2003, PP/CRI/J/1/8/19. Crick to Kennedy, 22 April 2003, PP/CRI/J/1/8/11.
61 Crick, Videotape for NIH Scientific Symposium, 14 April 2003, PP/CRI/J/1/8/22.
62 PP/CRI/K/22/12. Crick to Henderson, 20 May 2003, PP/CRI/J/1/8/8.
63 Crick, F. and Koch, C. (2003), A framework for consciousness. *Nature Neuroscience* 6:119–26. Koch, C. (2004), *The Quest for Consciousness: A Neurobiological Approach* (Englewood, CO: Roberts), p. xvii.
64 Crick to Watson, 15 December 2003, PP/CRI/J/1/8/22.
65 See PP/CRI/L/1/8/13.
66 Lawrence, P. A. (2016), Francis Crick: A singular approach to scientific discovery. *Cell* 167:1436–9.
67 Sacks, O. (2015), *On the Move: A Life* (London: Picador), p. 355.
68 Crick, What is the function of the claustrum?, Internal Memo, 7 May 2004, PP/CRI/L/1/8/27/2/2/4.
69 Crick and Koch, What is the function of the claustrum?, 28 July 2004, PP/CRI/L/1/8/27/2/2/4.
70 Crick. F. C. and Koch, C. (2005), What is the function of the claustrum? *Philosophical Transactions of the Royal Society B* 360:1271–9. For a review of more recent ideas and the impact of the Crick and Koch paper, see Smith,

J. B., Lee, A. K. and Jackson, J. (2020), The claustrum. *Current Biology* 30:R1401–6.

CLOSING TIME

1 References for this and subsequent paragraphs: Crick, Appointment diary, 2003, MSS 660, Box 15, Folder 15. Lawrence, P. (2009), A scientist unparalleled. *Current Biology* 19:R1015–8. Crick, Notes on Kathleen Rockland's Helmholtz Club paper on honeycomb-like mosaic at the border of layers 1 and 2 in cerebral cortex, April 2003, PP/CRI/L/1/8/9/1. Lawrence to Murray, 24 April 2003, PP/CRI/J/1/8/12/1. McClure to Crick, 7 May 2003, MSS 660, Box 7, Folder 29. Crick to Sejnowski, 7 May 2003, PP/CRI/J/1/8/19. Kreisel to Crick, 26 May 2003, MSS 660, Box 6, Folder 6. Crick to Hsu, 17 June 2003, PP/CRI/J/1/8/8. Crick to Cook, 23 June 2003, PP/CRI/J/1/8/3. MSS 660, Box 33, Folder 15. Shortly before he died, Crick gave the portrait by Mariana Cook to Christof Koch, inscribed 'For Christof – Francis – keeping an eye on you!' It now hangs in Koch's office. Sarabhai to Crick, 14 July 2003; Crick to Sarabhai, 16 July 2003, PP/CRI/J/1/8/19. Crick to Hoagland, 14 July 2003, PP/CRI/J/1/8/8. Siegel to Odile and Francis, 10 August 2003, PP/CRI/J/1/8/19. Sacks to Odile Crick, 28 July 2004, MSS 660, Box 12, Folder 6. Crick to Watson, 15 December 2003, PP/CRI/J/1/8/22. Kindra Crick to Francis Crick, May 2004, MSS 660, Box 2, Folder 23. Crick, Appointment diary, 2004, MSS 660, Box 15, Folder 16. Crick to Finbow, 12 July 2004, OLBY, Box 11. Orgel, L. E. (2004), Francis Crick (1916–2004). *Science* 305:1118.

EPILOGUE

1 MSS 660, Box 24, Folder 30.
2 Simonsuuri to Odile Crick, 19 October 2004, MSS 660, Box 24, Folder 1.
3 Kuhn, R. L. (2024), A landscape of consciousness: Toward a taxonomy of explanations and implications. *Progress in Biophysics and Molecular Biology* 190:28–169.
4 Crick to Frost, 13 July 2000, PP/CRI/J/2/20/2.
5 Crick to Klug, 16 September 1997, PP/CRI/J/2/17/3. The bust was by John Houser. It incorporates a single helix, as in the sculpture outside Portugal Place, and was cast in bronze. In 2013 it was bought by Mill Hill School, where it is now on display.
6 Kreisel to Crick, 18 June 1996, MSS 660, Box 6, Folder 2. *Remembering Francis Crick*, undated [September 2004], SB/10/56. Rich, A. (2004), Francis Crick (1916–2004). *Nature* 430:845–7.
7 Peter Lawrence and Mark Bretscher encouraged me to write the following summation of Crick's approach to science, to complement their own views. Lawrence, P. A. (2016), Francis Crick: A singular approach to scientific discovery. *Cell* 167:1436–9. Bretscher, M. S. and Mitchison, G. (2017), Francis Harry Compton Crick OM: 8 June 1916 – 28 July 2004. *Biographical Memoirs of Fellows of the Royal Society* 63:159–96.
8 Daily Transcript, 7 September 1994, PP/CRI/J/7/8/4/2.
9 Wolpert, L. and Richards, A. (1988), *A Passion for Science* (Oxford: Oxford University Press), p. 93.

10　Kreisel to Crick, 20 December 1992, MSS 660, Box 5, Folder 8.

11　Odile Crick interview with Olby, undated, OLBY, Box 28. Kreisel to Crick, 4 March 1997, MSS 660, Box 6, Folder 4.

12　*Los Angeles Times*, 28 February 1994.

13　Crick to Kreisel, 7 October 1991, PP/CRI/J/2/11/2.

14　*Remembering Francis Crick*, undated [September 2004], SB/10/56.

15　Crick to Kreisel, 7 October 1991, PP/CRI/J/2/11/2.

16　Crick to Kreisel, 13 January 1998, MSS 660, Box 6, Folder 4.

17　Bullard, e-mail to the author, May 2024.

18　Odile to Francis, 1–9 July 1956, MSS 660, Box 2, Folder 25.

19　Michael Crick, e-mail to the author, September 2024.

20　*Remembering Francis Crick*, undated [September 2004], SB/10/56. https://libgallery.cshl.edu/items/show/75988

21　McClure to Odile Crick, 9 December 2005, MSS 660, Box 7, Folder 29.

22　McClure, M. (2007) Double Moire. *The American Poetry Review* 36(3):50–4. Although the first poem was called 'Moiré', the title of 'Double Moire' contained no é. For an exploration of the poem, see Benz, S. (2018), 'Sing[ing] of the middle way': Michael McClure's venture for a new mode of thought between science and mysticism. *Current Objectives of Postgraduate American Studies* 19:1–24.

23　McClure to Odile Crick, 9 December 2005, MSS 660, Box 7, Folder 29. McClure explained the structure of the poem: 'In this way, Moire is doubled – honoring Francis' elucidation of the molecule. There is a zen or chan glow to the poem but those practices are not religion and are, in formal sense, aesthetic. I think Francis would approve and I truly hope the poem pleases you.'

LIST OF
ILLUSTRATIONS

Black and white

pp. x–xi Composite image of Crick lecturing, by Bradley Smith (Wellcome Collection PP/CRI/A/1/2/7)

p. 10 Francis and Odile, Portugal Place, 1950s (Crick family collection)

pp. 18–19 Watson, Crick and the double helix, 1953 (Antony Barrington Brown)

p. 22 Francis as a young boy (Crick family collection)

p. 42 Cartoon of Crick, 1949, by Frederick Spear (Wellcome Collection PP/FGS/C/29)

p. 48 Telegram from Odile to Francis, May 1949 (UCSD Library, MSS 660, Box 2, Folder 25)

p. 71 Sketch by Wilkins of X-ray image of DNA, 1952 (Wellcome Collection PP/CRI/D/2/29)

p. 75 Watson and Crick, June 1952 (Wellcome Collection PP/CRI/A/1/2/1)

p. 84 Note from Pauline Cowan to Crick, January 1953 (UCSD Library, MSS 660, Box 2, Folder 11)

p. 91 Structure of base pairs, Watson and Crick, 1954 (Proceedings of the Royal Society A 223:80–96)

p. 100 Drawings of DNA by Francis and Odile, 1953 (Wellcome Collection, PP/CRI/H/1/16, *Nature*, 25 April 1953)

p. 103 Cover of *Nature*, 25 April 1953

p. 115 Programme, Royal Society Conversazione, 1953 (Author's collection)

p. 118 Graph of A:T, G:C and A:G ratios, 1953 (Wellcome Collection)

p. 119 University of Edinburgh poster for Crick talk, 1953 (UCSD Library, MSS 660, Box 12, Folder 12)

pp. 122–3 Crick lecturing, Cold Spring Harbor, 1963 (CSHL Archive)

p. 126 Odile, Christmas card from the Cricks to Watson, 1953 (Odile Crick, gouache on paper/Crick family collection)

p. 134 Gamow to Crick, May 1954 (Wellcome Collection PP/CRI/H/1/42/5)

p. 318 Portrait of Michael McClure, 1970 (Underwood Archives, Inc/Alamy)

p. 320 Crick to McClure, 3 February 1971 (Simon Fraser University, MsA 5.12 MSS 37)

pp. 330–31 Crick portrait, 1978 (Arnold Newman/Getty Images)

p. 347 'Howl of Anguish', by Roger Woddis, 1976 (UCSD/MSS 660. Box 21, Folder 9)

p. 355 Drawing of Selfish DNA (Linda Sapienza/*Nature* 288:645)

p. 362 MIT Marr Meeting, May 1972 (CSHL/SB/8/3/9)

p. 366 Poggio, Marr and Crick, 1976 (Lucia Vaina)

p. 373 Photograph of Graeme Mitchison (Obituary, *Telegraph*, 12 July 2018)

p. 387 Crick and Asanuma, drawing of brain, 1986 (*Parallel Distributed Processing* Vol 2/Crick family collection)

p. 389 Crick, drawing of thalamus, 1984 (*PNAS* 81:4586–90/Crick family collection)

p. 396 Script for *Life Story* (Peter Lawrence/BBC)

p. 405 Poster for Nature meeting on the brain (Wellcome Collection PP/CRI/K/7/9)

p. 421 Draft of *The Astonishing Hypothesis*

p. 422 Page of *The Astonishing Hypothesis*

p. 423 Cricks, New Year Greetings Card, 1990s (CSHL, OLBY, Box 3)

p. 455 £2 double helix coin

p. 456 Odile and Crick outside La Jolla, 2003 (Peter Lawrence)

p. 459 Odile, drawing for Crick and Koch, 2003 (Crick family collection/ *Nature Neuroscience*, 6:119–26)

pp. 462–3 Crick sitting reading in the desert, 2003 (Peter Lawrence)

Colour plates

1. Crick on the beach at Cold Spring Harbor, 1954 (UCSD, MSS 660, Box 16, Folder 7/Crick family collection)

2. The first draft of the Watson and Crick paper on the structure of DNA, 1953 (UCSD, MSS 660, Box 26, Folder 5/Crick family collection)

3. Model of the double helix (National Museum of Scotland, IL.2010.2)

4. Fiftieth birthday celebrations, Cold Spring Harbor Laboratory, 1966 (Photo: Mark Bretscher)

5. LMB Governing Board, 1967 (MRC Laboratory of Molecular Biology)

6. Francis Crick and Christof Koch (Crick family collection)

7. Crick and Watson, 1993 (Pierre Perrin/Getty Images)

8. Sketch of Kreisel by Odile, late 1940s (Odile Crick, ink on paper/Crick family collection)

9. Crick at the helm of his boat, mid 1960s (Crick family collection)

10. Sketch of Crick in the Green Door by Odile, late 1940s (UCSD, MSS 660, Oversize FB-473/Odile Crick, ink on paper/Crick family collection)

11. The Crick family punting in Cambridge, mid-1950s (Maurice S. Fox/Crick family collection)

While every effort has been made to contact copyright-holders of illustrations, the author and publishers would be grateful for information about any illustrations where they have been unable to trace them, and would be glad to make amendments in further editions.

INDEX

Note: The index covers the main text but not the endnotes. Page references in *italic* denote relevant illustrations, while the suffix 'n' indicates useful material in a footnote.

nash

T ... A
A ... T
T - A

Ycas
Year

st ... sApA — P C p CpA

1962   1965

pU U U U pU pC

NA

poly UC
AU